WOOD

TECHNOLOGY
AND PROCESSES

WOOD

TECHNOLOGY AND PROCESSES

Fourth Edition

JOHN L. FEIRER
Distinguished Faculty Scholar
Western Michigan University

GLENCOE
McGraw-Hill

New York, New York   Columbus, Ohio   Mission Hills, California   Peoria, Illinois

Reviewers:

Bill Schaaf
Wood Technology Instructor
Jefferson County Schools
Arvada, Colorado

Charles A. Park
Woodworking Instructor
Metamora Township High School
Metamora, Illinois

Steven A. Ramsey
Industrial Education Teacher
Tremont High School
Tremont, Illinois

Glencoe/McGraw-Hill
A Division of The **McGraw·Hill** Companies

Send all inquires to:
Glencoe/McGraw-Hill
3008 W. Willow Knolls Drive
Peoria, IL   61614-1083

ISBN 0-02-677610-3 (Text)
ISBN 0-02-677611-1 (Instructor's Resource Guide)
ISBN 0-02-677612-X (Student Workbook)

Printed in the United States of America
   5 6 7 8 9 10 11 12   QPH   01 00 99 98 97

Table of Contents

Preface

Woodworking has always been one of the most popular of all industrial technology subjects. It is also one of our most popular leisure-time activities. In spite of the many new materials and courses developed in recent years, woodworking has increased rather than decreased in favor. The reasons are clear. Wood is one of our most abundant materials. It is also one of the easiest to work with. Products made of wood have general usefulness. The tools and machines especially suited to school laboratories and home workshops are readily available.

This edition includes much new information on wood products and woodworking processes. Major features of this new edition include:

● *Information on the use of high technology in the wood industry.* Chapter 1 introduces the subject of high technology and outlines the focus the new developments will bring to the wood products industry. Illustrated in full color, this high-tech essay offers a broad overview of technical change in the industry.

● *Features on various aspects of wood and the wood industry.* These short features focus on a single theme. Interesting and appropriate, they provide information that supplements the main text discussions.

● *Expanded information on careers.* Career information in Chapter 8 of the text is supplemented by a series of seven career vignettes. There is one vignette at the end of each of the book's sections. Each of these vignettes, entitled "Thinking about a Career," profiles an individual in a wood-industry career. A wide cross section of careers is discussed.

● *Math quizzes and basic skills activities.* Correct and precise measuring is encouraged through the inclusion of several short math quizzes. Activities to strengthen science, math, and reading skills are at the end of each section.

● *Customary/metric measurement.* An introduction to the two basic systems of measurement, customary and metric, is provided. Throughout the text, customary measurements are given in metric whenever that is practical.

● *A strong emphasis on good design.* The principles of good design are explored in the text and given practical application in the Project Section.

● *Project section.* Selected for use and appeal, the projects are designed to test and develop manual skills at a variety of ability levels.

● *Information on wood science.* The relationship of trees to our general environment is detailed. Forest conservation is discussed, as are problems of pollution and erosion. The use of trees to reduce both of these problems is discussed.

● *Information on industry and technology.* The use of wood in manufacturing and construction is covered as well as the systems approach to the industrial technologies. The general techniques of upholstery and patternmaking are discussed.

● *Problem solving and critical thinking.* Throughout the text, both problem solving and critical thinking are included. Some review questions are designed to elicit critical thinking by asking students to explain choices they might make. Problem solving is stressed by means of some math quizzes and the science experiments included at the ends of sections. Since much of the book is devoted to how-to material, problem solving occurs naturally as students attempt to master the processes.

The book is divided into eight sections, each heavily illustrated.

Sections I-IV give instruction on the fundamental processes in hand woodworking. Particular stress is placed on student participation in laboratory activities. Written in informal style, the chapters are well illustrated. They provide extensive information about tools, materials, and the ways to use them. The chapters are organized in the approximate order in which their information will be needed to make larger projects. Tools, materials, and processes have been carefully evaluated.

Section V describes the use of fundamental machine tools in woodworking. Each tool has been discussed in detail. This is done so that the instructor may conveniently determine what machines are desirable and in what order the students should be allowed to use them. Small woodworking machines have been used to illustrate instruction since these are best for most school laboratories and home workshops.

Section VI discusses wood science. It provides information on the effect of trees on our environment. Lumbering and forestry are explored in some detail.

Section VII deals with the four industrial technologies—manufacturing, construction, communication, and transportation—as they relate to the woodworking industries. The importance of woodworking to our economic system is covered. Chapter 68, Upholstery, which is part of wood manufacturing, and Chapter 69, Patternmaking and Model Making, which is part of metal manufacturing, are also included in this section.

Section VIII consists of projects that can be constructed using the processes and materials discussed in the book. These projects provide an opportunity to develop manual skills. They also offer an opportunity to evaluate design.

Section I.

Woodworking Technology

Chapter 1

High Technology in Woodworking

After studying this chapter, you will be able to:
- Define *technology*.
- List the three major characteristics of technology.
- List the five basic units of a computer.
- Give two examples of computer software programs useful to builders.
- Name the four basic parts of a numerical-control (N/C) machine.
- Name three types of work for which robots are well-suited.
- List five benefits offered by a woodworking class.

LOOK FOR THESE TERMS

binary code	computer program	program
bit	computer software	programmer
CAD (computer-aided design)	CPU (central processing unit)	RAM (random access memory)
	disk drive	robot
CAM (computer-aided manufacturing)	input device	ROM (read-only memory)
	laser	science
chip	monitor	technology
computer	numerical control (N/C)	
computer hardware	printer	

Technology helps people meet their daily needs. *Technology* is the use of science to achieve a practical purpose. Thousands of years ago, in the Stone Age, people used primitive tools such as the axe and the hammer. These tools were made first from stone. Later, early humans developed ways of making tools from bronze and iron.

Early woodworking tools were primitive. It was not until the early 1700s that many different kinds of woodworking tools were developed for various specialized trades. Those tools included some still familiar to carpenters and cabinetmakers. Tools also were developed for coachmakers, organ builders, violin makers, and shipwrights. The Industrial

Revolution signaled the beginning of manufacturing on a large scale. The discovery of the steam engine added power to tools. Fig. 1-1. Contrast this method with that now used. Figure 1-2 shows one station in a computer-operated sawmill.

Science and technology, though closely related, are very different. *Science* is knowledge learned from experiments. Scientists make new discoveries. Technologists put these discoveries to use. Technology has three major characteristics:

- It is based on discoveries in science.
- It deals with the uses of tools and machines.
- It depends on various forms of energy as a source of power.

Some of the recent developments in wood technology include more efficient machines, the use of manufactured wood panels, and improved wood preservatives. Stronger adhesives and better finishes are now made from plastics. Four high-tech developments that are changing the way wood products are produced are numerical-controlled machines, computers, robots, and lasers.

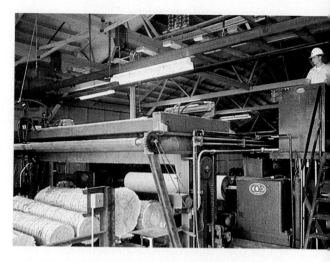

1-2. Many sawmill operations are controlled by computer. Here a log is being cut into short lengths.

1-1. This is the way logs were cut before the development of the steam engine. The log was not always placed on trestles. It was sometimes placed over a pit. The two people doing the work were known as sawyers. This term is still used to describe certain sawmill workers.

COMPUTERS

A *computer* is an electronic device that receives and stores information. It uses this information to solve problems. Computers are widely used in woodworking construction and manufacturing. Computers control the cutting of logs into lumber. Computers are used to design and build energy-efficient houses. They are used to control the inventory of materials in a furniture factory. Computers are also used in ways that are not so easy to see. For example, the computer designs floor and roof trusses. This speeds up house design and construction. Without the computer, it would take a designer and drafter up to a week or more to design the kitchen cabinets for a custom-built home. With a computer, the same job can be done in less than one hour.

Like any other tool, the computer increases your ability to do intelligent work. It enables you to work problems quickly—with greater accuracy. The computer extends human brainpower just as a table saw extends human muscle power.

1-3. The monitor, central processing unit, hard drive, and floppy disk drive are all in one unit in this computer system. The keyboard, mouse, and CD-ROM drive are separate. A CD-ROM drive accepts optical disks which are read by means of a laser. Enormous amounts of information can be stored on optical disks. One five-inch disk can hold an entire encyclopedia.

HARDWARE

Equipment that makes up a computer system is called *hardware*. The personal computer usually consists of five basic units. Fig. 1-3.

1. An *input device*. On most personal computers, this appears to be a typewriter keyboard. The input device is used to send information into the computer.
2. The *central processing unit (CPU)*, plus the memory chips containing memory, control, and operating units. These units are often in the same cabinet as the keyboard or the disk drive. In some computer systems, the keyboard and/or the disk drive is a separate unit.
3. A *monitor*, or *display device*. This looks like the picture tube on a television set. The computer prints out words or pictures on the screen of the display device. A home television set can be connected to the computer. Some computers have a monitor on top of the central processing unit.
4. A *disk drive*. This holds the magnetic disk tape that stores the software (program)

used with the comptuer. The disk tape is the external memory that can feed information into the central processing unit as needed.
5. The *printer*. This is a high-speed typewriterlike device that prints the hard copy of the output from the computer. A *plotter* is a type of printer that produces drawings.

THE CHIP

The chip is the all-important electronic building block used in computers. It is a microelectronic device less than one-eighth the size of a postage stamp. The *chip* is complicated electronic circuitry on a silicon base, with tiny switches joined by "wires." These wires are etched on a thin film of metal. The chip can hold thousands of electronic "parts."

The chip, with its many "switches," allows electricity to flow or not to flow. In a computer, when the switch is "on," it represents a "1." When the switch is "off," it represents a "0."

COMPUTER MATH

Any numeral can be written using either ten digits (the *decimal system*) or two digits (the *binary code*). Table 1-A. The computer's language is written in binary code.

It is not hard to understand the binary code. Really, there are just two new ideas that must be grasped. First, decimal numbers—the kind of numbers we ordinarily use for our money and for metric measurement—are built on a base of 10. Binary numbers, though, are built on a base of 2. The second thing to learn about the binary code is that the system uses only two numbers: 1 and 0. In other words, the numbers 2, 3, 4, 5, 6, 7, 8, and 9 are not used in the binary system.

The question arises—how do you count to two, without a 2? It is simple. The value of the binary number increases by two times as you move it one space to the left. Fig. 1-4. To get two in binary then, simply move the 1 one space to the left and add zero. Thus, 10 in binary is the same as 2 in decimal.

Each digit—either 1 or 0—in a binary numeral is called a *bit* (short for "binary digit"). This is important to remember because information moves through a computer a bit at a time. While the binary code may seem awkward to those who are used to the decimal system, it is simplicity itself to the computer. This is because the basic electronic unit inside the computer (the chip) can exist in only two possible states: current on or current off.

HOW A COMPUTER OPERATES

To communicate, computers convert. Computers change the numbers, letters, and symbols in the binary code (two digits) of computer math. The digit "1" is like an electrical switch that is "on." The digit "0" represents the switch when it is "off."

Most personal computers digest information in chains of eight electrical pulses called a *byte*. Think of these eight pulses as a bank of eight light bulbs. When a bulb is "on" in the series of eight bulbs, it represents a "1." When the bulb is "off," it represents a "0." These eight bulbs can be arranged in 256 different combinations. This is much more capacity than is needed to cover the 26 letters of the alphabet (capitals and lower case), 10 numbers, 13 punctuation marks, symbols,

Table 1-A. Decimal Numerals and Binary Numerals

Number	Decimal Numeral	Binary Numeral
None	0	0
One	1	1
Two	2	1 0
Three	3	1 1
Four	4	1 0 0
Five	5	1 0 1
Six	6	1 1 0
Seven	7	1 1 1
Eight	8	1 0 0 0
Nine	9	1 0 0 1
Ten	1 0	1 0 1 0
Eleven	1 1	1 0 1 1
Twelve	1 2	1 1 0 0
Thirteen	1 3	1 1 0 1
Fourteen	1 4	1 1 1 0
Fifteen	1 5	1 1 1 1
Sixteen	1 6	1 0 0 0 0

1-4. The way in which binary numerals are added to equal decimal numerals. Note how 2, 3, and 5 are written in binary code.

Binary Numerals

10 . . . . (2+0)

11 . . . . (2+1)

101 . . . . . . (4+0+1)

Decimal Numerals

2

3

5

musical scales, and other input items that might be needed. The input instructions are processed by a CPU (central processing unit). For most personal computers, this is often only a single chip. To store excess information, *memory* chips are needed. The CPU is the "brain" of a computer.

There are two types of memory chips. The *RAM (random access memory) chip* can be thought of as pages in a notebook. On these pages, you write the information you would like to use later when performing an operation or figuring out a problem. The information in the RAM chip is there only temporarily. When you have finished with the information, it is erased.

The *ROM (read-only memory) chip* is like a reference book. It contains information that you will refer to again and again when using the computer. This information is on the chip permanently. The ROM information memory chip is put there by the manufacturer of the computer. The CPU uses the ROM memory chip to find out how to do certain things. For example, it uses the chip to show a character on the screen or to send output information.

1-5. The computer can be used as a drafting and design tool. Here, it is being used for designing.

SOFTWARE

Software is the program that tells the computer what to do and how to do it. Software is written by *programmers*. To solve a problem, a computer must have instructions. Without instructions, the computer cannot solve the problem. With instructions, it can follow the directions step-by-step until the job is completed. This is true for any problem solved with a computer. The job may be adding a column of numbers or designing a roof truss. These detailed instructions are called the *computer program*.

CAD/CAM

CAD/CAM systems are changing the way in which homes and furniture are designed, drawn, and built. CAD is the abbreviation for *computer-aided design*. (CAM is the abbreviation for "computer-aided manufacturing.") CAD is a means of using a computer to produce a design. The cutting and pasting is done electronically. The main advantage of

CAD is that it eliminates repetition. Once a design is created, it rarely has to be completely redrawn. The computer stores all the information. Every design can be kept on file and is always accessible. New designs are created by selecting elements from existing designs and putting them together. The computer lets you set up a file of frequently needed design elements, parts, and symbols. You simply call these up and "plug" them into your drawing. Fig. 1-5. Line weight and lettering are standardized. These essentials are part of the program. As you change the design, there is never a loss of quality. This could occur if you were making the drawings by hand.

Using CAD, a drafter can create a drawing using elements in the computer's storage unit. The efficient use of CAD systems depends on the programs (software) that are available. For example, an architect will use programs dealing with designing homes, rooms, floor plans, and cabinets. A building contractor will use programs involving bidding and scheduling. He or she may also use programs for office functions such as payroll.

CAM (*computer-aided manufacturing*) is the other part of the CAD/CAM system. CAM systems take the design from the CAD system. Using computers, numerical control machines, and robots, they produce the product in the factory.

COMPUTER PROGRAMS (SOFTWARE)

Computers are used in every step of building houses and furniture. Here are a few examples of available programs. These programs are very useful to the architect and builder.

A program entitled *Energy Performance Design System (EPDS)* allows the architect and builder to check energy saving. He or she can check various ideas for walls, floors, ceilings, windows, doors, siding, and roofing. The program helps the user identify those kinds that save the most energy. The builder can tell the home buyer exactly how much the heating and cooling bill will be at current energy costs.

A program on *truss design* can be used by manufacturers of truss systems for floors and roofs. This program develops various truss designs. It makes cutting lists for the design.

It does structural analysis. With a plotter attachment, it produces drawings and stock-cutting lists. Fig. 1-6.

A program on *cabinet designs* can be used to build kitchen cabinets and fixtures for stores. This program is useful for custom woodworking shops. Information (called *input*) must be fed into the computer. This information includes the size of the area and the woods to be used. It also includes the kinds of doors and drawers. In less than one hour, drawings and stock-cutting lists are produced. Fig. 1-7.

Many different programs in *business management* are available. These include bidding, scheduling, and payroll. Fig. 1-8.

Computer programs for furniture manufacturers are available. These programs include furniture design. Programs for numerically controlled machines are also available.

1-7. Computer-aided design assures consistency of detail on a variety of furniture styles.

Fig. 1-6. These technicians are using a computer to help them work out a design problem.

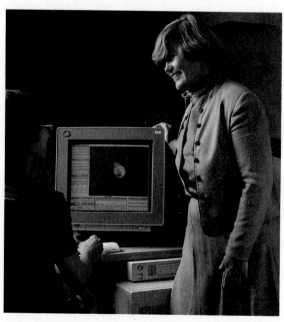

1-8. Construction and manufacturing industries use computers for several office practices.

1-9. A numerically controlled router.

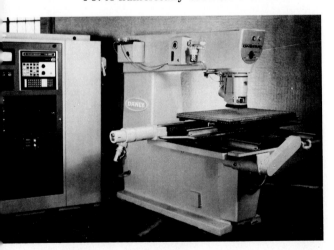

NUMERICAL CONTROL
(N/C and CNC)

If you make a mistake in setting up a machine or adjusting the cutting tool, the part will probably be ruined and end up as scrap. To prevent this, many woodworking and furniture factories have installed numerically controlled machines. Fig. 1-9. *Numerical control (N/C)* is a system for directing the work of the machine by means of numerical instructions coded on a tape. The tape stores instructions that it feeds to the machine at the proper time. The N/C machine then performs a series of operations automatically. Fig. 1-10. N/C machines are still found in most school laboratories. Most modern factories, however, use *computer numerical control (CNC)*. The tape is omitted, and a computer supplies the code to the machine.

An N/C machine consists of the following four basic parts:
1. The *control unit*. This is an electronic device that holds the tape.
2. The *tape*. This tape is punched with a series of holes. Each hole provides an electronic impulse to the machine's motors.
3. The *woodworking machine* itself (such as a router). This machine's motors follow the directions from the tape.

1-10. The decorations on the backs of these chairs were cut partly to shape by a numerically controlled router.

4. *Electronic feedback devices*. These control how much tool movement has taken place. They relay this information to the control unit.

Before an N/C machine can operate, a programmer must study the working drawing of the part. The *programmer* prepares the written steps for the full machining cycle. These instructions are written in correct order, just as you did when you prepared a plan of procedure. The instructions are punched on a 1-inch wide tape as a series of holes by a tape punching machine. (This machine is similar to a typewriter.) The tape must be checked for accuracy. The programmer then compares the tape to the written instruction.

The tape is approved for production. It is then sent to the machine operator along with the drawing and the written program. The endless tape for the part is placed in the control unit. The proper cutting tool is installed on the machine. The wood or other material is clamped to the table. The operator rechecks the control unit and the machine. Often, a "dry run" of the program is made without the workpiece in place. This is done to make sure the tape is correct. Once everything is in order, the operator punches the correct buttons to begin the machining. From then on, all the machining is done automatically. A great advantage of N/C is that the tape for each part of a product can be stored. Then, whenever more parts of the design are needed, the tape can be put back in the control unit for additional production.

ROBOTS

A *robot* is a machine that does a job normally done by a human being. The term *robot* comes from the Czech word *robota*, which means "forced labor." Robots can be programmed by a computer. They can move parts or tools through specific sequences of movements. A robot can be "taught" to do new jobs. Accessories can extend the capabilities of a robot. Robots also can do automatic drilling, milling, cutting, and paint spraying.

Robots differ from other automated machinery. A typical robot has one or more arms (called "manipulators"), hands (called "end effectors"), a controller, and a power supply. It might also have an array of sensors. These provide feedback information.

Robots are produced in many sizes and designs. Robots are made primarily of metal and plastics. They have electronic circuitry, a memory system, a control system, and power drive. This drive is needed to operate the hands and arms. The control system can be an electronic control that is manually programmed. It might also be a computer (microprocessor) control. Fig. 1-11. The power drive can be hydraulic, electric, or pneumatic.

In the woodworking industry, robots are used primarily for material handling. For example, they are used to move large sheets of panel stock. They are used also for finishing.

The industrial finishing robot is used in furniture factories and other woodworking factories. This robot is a mechanical painter with a "brain." Fig. 1-12. The robot can duplicate the motions of a skilled wood finisher. The finisher can be programmed for different kinds, styles, and sizes of furniture. The program can be recalled as needed whenever the same kind of furniture is produced.

1-11. This manually controlled robot can store eight program sequences to do a variety of tasks.

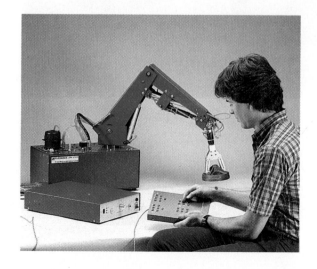

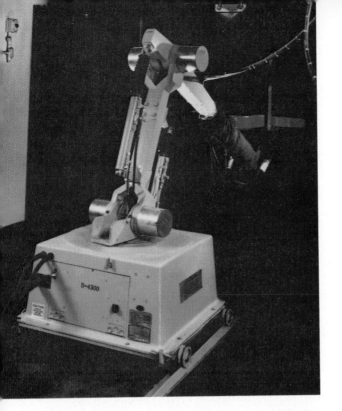

1-12. This robot is used for spraying on a finish as parts or products move along the assembly line.

In industry, robots have several advantages. They are often used for the following types of work:

● *Hazardous work*. The robot can spray materials that might harm the health of humans. The robot does not have to wear a face mask.

● *Monotonous work*. Workers find wood finishing so repetitive that it becomes a dull and tedious job. The robot will produce the same quality finish all day long. A robot can work 24 hours a day, if needed.

● *Precision work*. The robot repeats each operation in precisely the same way. Thus, identical finishes can be applied to all units passing by it. The finish will always be of uniform thickness and coverage.

LASERS

The laser is one of our greatest scientific discoveries. It has changed many of the processes used in wood technology. The term *laser* is an acronym. (An *acronym* is a word made up of the first letter of several words.) *Laser* stands for Light Amplification by Stim-

ulated Emission of Radiation. A laser is a machine that strengthens a beam of light. Very simply, the laser produces narrow beams of intense light. The light can be focused on a spot that is very small. Fig. 1-13. The laser can produce heat of over 7,500 degrees F. This concentrated energy will penetrate a variety of materials. The laser beam can be compared to a magnifying glass. It concentrates a beam of light.

Because a laser can be focused on a small spot, it can be used for various manufacturing processes. It can be used for cutting, drilling, and etching. All types of materials can be cut with the laser. These materials include wood, plastic, and cork. They can be cut to very precise designs. In fact, the cutting is so sharp that the edges do not have to be worked in any other way. For example, they do not need to be filed or sanded.

A laser is also used for drilling. Some materials drilled by a laser are difficult to drill by any other method. For example, the laser can drill a hole in a diamond. The laser is also widely used to cut and etch wood materials. Fig. 1-14. Next time you visit a fine gift shop, inspect desk sets made from hardwood such as walnut or mahogany. Some may have very finely etched pictures on the surfaces. This etching was done with a laser.

Lasers also are used to measure electronically. Lasers are very useful in surveying. For example, the U.S. Forest Service and large lumber companies laser-survey the boundaries of forest lands. This can be done even in difficult terrain. The laser measuring system is called the "laser range pole." It consists of

1-13. A typical laser unit. The pumping source helps generate light in the laser crystal.

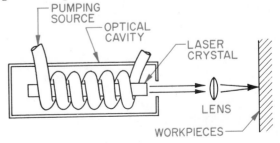

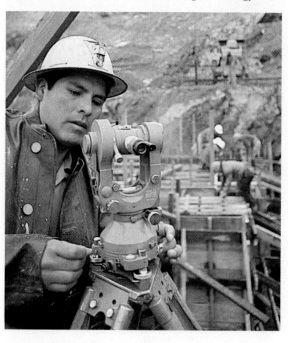

1-15. This surveyor is adjusting the laser transmitter. Laser surveying is more accurate than that done by conventional methods.

1-14. A laser beam can be used to cut decorative designs in wood.

1-16. This diagram shows how a laser range pole is used. A beam of invisible light from the laser intersects the beam of light from the receiver.

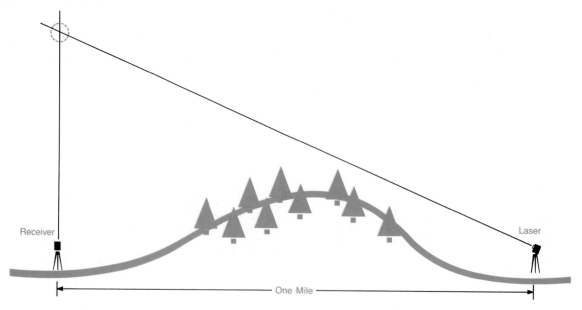

a laser transmitter and receiver. Both units are lightweight. They can be easily carried in rugged mountain country. Fig. 1-15. The transmitter sends a thin column of laser light up from a corner marker. This laser beam is invisible to the human eye. However, it can be picked up by electronic eyes in a receiver placed at another corner marker a mile or more away. This receiver can be adjusted until the indicator light shows that it is correctly aligned with the laser beam. Fig. 1-16. This tells the foresters where to place survey stakes that are exactly a certain distance apart. This laser-survey system is effective up to two and one-half miles in daylight and five miles at night.

WOODWORKING AND THE NEW TECHNOLOGIES

Devices such as lasers and robots are not used for every job in woodworking. Even in factories, many jobs are still done by hand. Simply, much work must still be done by hand. To do good work by hand, you need good manual skills. This book can help you develop the manual skills you need to practice woodworking. In studying this information, remember that technology has been built on the manual skills you will be learning and practicing.

Well-learned woodworking skills offer several benefits. A woodworking class, for example can help you:

● *To discover your talents, interests, and career potential*. Well over two million people have found careers in woodworking. The wood industry is vital to the growth of our country. It has made possible the record-breaking building boom of homes and commercial buildings.

● *To learn how to use tools and machines to build and maintain wood products*. Learning to work with tools and machines can be a valuable skill. You may not earn a living in woodworking. Still, you will find the skills very useful as a "do-it-yourselfer." You may find making things of wood so fascinating that you will choose it as your hobby.

● *To develop good safety habits*. Using hand and machine tools safely and skillfully

is a most important part of your work. More accidents happen in the wood laboratory than in any other area of industrial technology. Learn to perform each task carefully. Do not become a statistic. Fig. 1-17.

● *To learn about good design*. You should learn to recognize good design in wood products. After you learn the difference between good and bad design, you will never again find poor design attractive. This ability to judge design will help you throughout life.

● *Explore the applications of English, science, mathematics, and social studies to the wood industries*. You can apply what you are learning in academic classes to wood technology. A woodworking class can include the reading of technical literature. This can help you understand the meaning of technical terms. The class can also help you develop math skills. The proper use of hand and power tools will help you understand the ways in which machines operate. You may

1-17. Safety should become a habit. Safety glasses are essential.

also have opportunities to study the chemistry of wood. You will be able to learn about the forestry industry. You will be able to see how it has helped shape the American economy.

● *Learn to judge the quality of wood products*. A home and furniture are two of the largest purchases you will ever make. Before you buy wood products, you should understand good design and construction. You should be able to judge if the product is good quality.

● *Enjoy the satisfaction of planning and building a product with your own hands*. Fig. 1-18. A real sense of accomplishment results from creating a wood product that is both attractive and well made. In completing the product you will learn to solve problems about materials and processes.

Review Questions

1. List the three major characteristics of technology.
2. List the five basic units of a computer.
3. Describe a computer chip.
4. What are the two types of memory chips?
5. List the advantages of CAD (computer-aided design).
6. Define *software*.
7. Name two programs used by architects and builders.
8. List the four basic parts of a numerical-control (N/C) machine.
9. For what types of jobs is a robot well suited?
10. What does the word *laser* mean?
11. How can a laser be used in surveying?
12. List five benefits offered by a woodworking class.
13. Refer to the list of terms headed "Look for These Terms" at the beginning of the chapter. Can you use these terms in a way that shows you understand them?

1-18. Careful project planning avoids waste. It also helps ensure a well-made product.

Chapter 2

Materials

After studying this chapter, you will be able to:
- List the main grades of lumber.
- List the main parts of a plywood panel.
- Describe the main defects in wood that affect lumber.
- List four types of manufactured lumber.

LOOK FOR THESE TERMS

bow	flat grained	plywood
check	hardboard	quarter-sawed lumber
common lumber	hardwood	rough lumber
conifers	honeycombing	softwood
crook	kiln	split
cross bands	molding	waferboard
cup	oriented strand board	warp
deciduous	particle board	wind
dressed (surfaced) lumber	plain sawed	yard lumber
factory (or shop) lumber	plies	

To build a project, many different materials may be needed. You may need, for example, moldings, veneers, and plastic laminates. You may also need fasteners (including dowel), adhesives, abrasives, hardware, and finishing materials. Materials vary greatly in cost, color, and use. Most wood projects combine several different kinds. For example, a small chest may include solid lumber, panel stock, plastic laminates, fasteners, and hardware in addition to the abrasives, and finishing materials required. Fig. 2-1. The first materials you will work with are solid lumber and panel stock. Other materials will be described later as you need them.

2-1. This small chest was constructed using many different materials. Lumber, plywood, hardboard, fasteners, and other hardware were used.

POINTS TO CONSIDER WHEN BUYING WOOD

Before selecting wood for a project, you should know something about the different kinds of wood available.

LUMBER

There are several points to remember in selecting lumber. Table 2-A. Remember the following:

● *Rough or dressed.* You can purchase lumber rough (specified "Rough") or dressed (specified S2S or S4S, surfaced on two sides or surfaced on four sides). *Rough lumber* comes just as it was cut at the sawmill. *Dressed (surfaced) lumber* has been put through a planer. When you buy dressed lumber, the actual dimensions will be less than the size indicated. For example, 1-inch hardwood will be about $^{13}/_{16}$ inch thick, and standard construction dry softwood which is 2 × 4 inches, will actually measure 1½ × 3½ inches.

● *Green or dry lumber.* When a tree is first cut down, its wood may contain as much as 30 to 300 percent moisture. *Softwood lumber* is cut into logs and placed in the open air to dry. Lumber treated in this way is called *air-dried lumber* (AD). If this lumber is sold with a moisture content of 19 percent or less, it is classified as *dry lumber*. Woods are dried in special drying rooms called *kilns* (often pronounced "kills"). Hardwood lumber used for furniture and interiors is *kiln dried* (KD) to about 6 to 12 percent moisture. This is the only type of lumber to buy for furniture and other fine projects.

Table 2-A. A Guide to Selecting Lumber

Standard Sizes of Softwood			Standard Thickness of Hardwoods		Grade	
					Softwood	Hardwood
Nominal or Stock Size	Actual Size		GREEN Rough	DRIED S2S	1. Yard lumber	FAS—Firsts and Seconds. Highest grade.
	Green	Dry			*Select*—Good appearance and finishing quality. Includes:	
1″	$^{25}/_{32}$″	¾″	⅜″	$^{3}/_{16}$″	Grade A—Clear.	
2″	$1^{9}/_{16}$″	1½″	½″	$^{5}/_{16}$″	Grade B—High Quality.	No. 1 Common and Select. Some defects.
3″	$2^{9}/_{16}$″	2½″	⅝″	$^{7}/_{16}$″	Grade C—For best paint	
4″	$3^{9}/_{16}$″	3½″	¾″	$^{9}/_{16}$″	finishes.	
5″	$4^{5}/_{8}$″	4½″	⁴/₄ (1″)*	$^{13}/_{16}$″	Grade D—Lowest Select.	No. 2 Common. For small cuttings.
6″	$5^{5}/_{8}$″	5½″	⁵/₄ (1¼″)	$1^{1}/_{16}$″		
7″	$6^{5}/_{8}$″	6½″	⁶/₄ (1½″)	1¼″	*Common*—General utility. Not of finishing quality. Includes:	
8″	7½″	7¼″	⁸/₄ (2″)	1¾″	Construction or No. 1—Best Grade.	
9″	8½″	8¼″	¹²/₄ (3″)	2½″	Standard or No. 2—Good Grade.	
10″	9½″	9¼″	¹⁶/₄ (4″)	3½″	Utility or No. 3—Fair Grade. Economy or No. 4—Poor.	
Surface	Method of Drying		Method of Cutting		No. 5—Lowest.	
Rgh. or Rough— as it comes from the sawmill.	AD—Air dried.		Plainsawed or Flat-grained.		2. Shop lumber—For manufacturing purposes. Equal to Grade B Select or better of Yard Lumber. Includes: No. 1—Average 8″ wide. No. 2—Average 7″ wide.	
S2S—surfaced on two sides.	KD—Kiln dried.		Quartersawed or Edge-grained.			
S45—surfaced all four sides.					3. Structural lumber.	

*Thicknesses are measured in ¼″ increments for hardwood lumber beginning at 1″. One inch (1″) is called *four quarter*. If you order ⁴/₄ lumber you will receive a board that actually measures $^{13}/_{16}$″. If you need a full 1″, then you should order ⁵/₄ lumber.

● The terms *hardwood* and *softwood* are botanical terms. They do not indicate actual softness or hardness. Some hardwoods are actually softer than some of the softwoods. *Softwoods* are those that come from conifers (evergreens), which are cone-bearing or needle-bearing trees. Common examples are pine, fir, cedar, and redwood. *Hardwoods* are cut from the broadleaf, *deciduous* trees. A deciduous tree is one that sheds its leaves annually. Some common hardwoods are walnut, mahogany, maple, birch, cherry, and oak.

● *Grade of lumber—softwoods.*

It is important to specify the grade of lumber you want. Grading softwoods (pine, fir, redwood, etc.) is little different from grading hardwoods. Softwood is classified first according to use: yard lumber, factory (or shop) lumber, and structural lumber.

Yard lumber is cut for a wide variety of uses. It is handled by all lumber yards. It is divided into two main classes: select and common.

Select grade lumber has a good appearance. It will take different finishes such as stain, paint, and enamel. It is the type of lumber you should choose for projects. Select lumber is available in four grades, as follows:

Grade A: Practically clear and suitable for natural finishes.

Grade B: High quality, generally clear, and also suitable for natural finishes.

Grade C: Suitable for a good paint finish.

Grade D: Lowest select grade; can be painted.

Common lumber is suitable for rough carpentry. It is not of finishing quality. It is graded Nos. 1, 2, 3, 4, and 5. Only Nos. 1, 2, and 3 are suitable for good, rough construction.

Factory (or shop) lumber is lumber that is to be cut up for manufacturing purposes. It is usually handled only by lumber yards that do millwork or sell to manufacturers and school laboratories. It is the grade that you would order for projects in place of one of the select grades listed above. There are two grades of shop lumber, Nos. 1 and 2. Both compare in quality to B select or better yard lumber. The grades differ only in the average width of the pieces. No. 1 averages 8 inches wide, and No. 2 averages 7 inches wide.

Structural lumber grading is based upon the strength of the pieces. Such grading is not of particular concern to the average woodworker.

● *Grade of lumber—hardwoods.*

The top grade is indicated by FAS, meaning "firsts and seconds." This is not perfect lumber, but it will produce about 90 percent clear stand cuttings. The next grade is called No. 1 common and select. It contains more knots and defects. The poorest grade is No. 2 common. This grade contains many defects and is suitable for small cuttings.

● *Method of cutting.* Most lumber is cut in such a way that the annular rings form an angle of less than 45 degrees with the surfaces of the piece. This is called *plain sawed* (when it is hardwood) or *flat-grained* (when it is softwood). Fig. 2-2.

Lumber is sometimes cut with the annular rings making an angle of more than 45 degrees with the surface of the piece. This lumber is called *quarter sawed* or *edge grained* or *vertical grained*. Quarter-sawed lumber usually costs more. It is more expensive to cut it this way. Quarter-sawed lumber is usually considered more attractive than plain-sawed or flat-grained lumber.

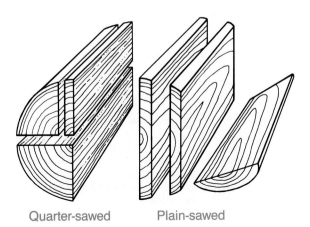

Quarter-sawed   Plain-sawed

2-2. The two most common types of cut lumber are plain sawed and quarter sawed. Plain-sawed lumber is also called flat-grained lumber.

PANEL STOCK

There are many different kinds and grades of panel stock. It includes plywood, hardboard, particle board, oriented waferboard, and strand board.

Plywood consists of panels made by gluing layers of wood together. The outside layers are single *plies* (thin sheets) of wood. They are called *faces* or *face and back*. The center layer, or *core*, may be one or more plies of wood, or it may be glued-up lumber or particle board. The plies between the faces and the core are called *cross bands*.

The layers are placed so that the grain of one runs at right angles to the grain of the next. When the core consists of more than one ply, these plies may be glued with their grains parallel. The entire core is considered one layer. It is glued with the grain at right angles to the adjoining layers. There are usually three, five, or seven layers.

Softwood plywoods are also called "construction and industrial" plywoods. They are divided into exterior (waterproof) and interior (not waterproof) types. For projects that are to be painted or enameled, interior plywood should be used. The more common grades of softwood plywood are A-A (both sides with a smooth surface), A-B (the face side smooth and the back side with a solid surface), and A-C (the back side of poor quality).

On hardwood plywoods, the outside ply is a good hardwood such as birch, mahogany, walnut, cherry, or gum. The grade of the entire panel is determined by the quality of the face and back. In order of quality, the grades are: (1) premium, (2) good, (3) sound, and (4) utility.

Plywood comes in standard thicknesses such as ¼, ⅜, ½ inch, etc. The most common size plywood sheet is 4 feet by 8 feet. Plywood is sold by the square foot. A piece 2 feet wide and 4 feet long has 8 square feet. The characteristics of the various grades of plywood are given in Table 2-B.

Hardboard is a manufactured wood board produced by "exploding" wood chips into wood fibers. The fibers are then formed into panels under heat and pressure. There are

---

Table 2-B. A Guide to Selecting Plywood

Hardwoods		Construction and Industrial (Softwoods)	
Grade	**Uses**	**Grade**	**Uses**
Premium grade	Best quality for very high-grade natural finish. Too expensive except for best cabinet work or paneling.	A–A	Best grade for all uses where both sides will show. Exterior or interior.
Good grade (1)	For good natural finish. Excellent for cabinets, built-ins, paneling, and furniture.	A–B	An alternate for A–A grade for high-quality uses where only one side will show. Exterior or interior. The back side is less important.
Sound grade (2)	For simple natural finishes and high-grade painted surfaces.	A–D	A good all-purpose "good-one-side" panel for lesser quality interior work.
Utility grade (3)	Not used for project work.	B–D	Utility grade. Used for backing, cabinet sides, etc.
Reject grade (4)	Not used for project work.		
Widths from 24″ to 48″ in 6″ multiples. Lengths from 36″ to 96″. Veneer-core panels in plies of 3, 5, 7, and 9 are available as follows: 3 ply—⅛″, 3/16″, ¼″; 5 ply—5/16″, ⅜″, ½″; 5 and 7 ply—⅝″; 7 and 9 ply—¾″. There are three types: Type I is fully waterproof, Type II is water resistant, and Type III is dry bond.		Many other grades for special uses in home construction are available in thicknesses of ½″, ⅜″, ⅝″, and ¾″; both exterior and interior; 1″ is also available in exterior grades. Common widths 3′4″, or 4′; common length is 8′. Be sure to specify exterior grade for outside work (including boats) and interior grade for interior construction.		

2-3. Moldings are available in many different shapes. A few of them are shown here. Molding is sold by the linear foot.

two types: standard, or untreated, and tempered, or treated. In tempering, the board is dipped in drying oils and baked. On some hardboard one face is smooth. The other face is rough and looks like screening. Other hardboard has two smooth surfaces. Tempered hardboard can be purchased with evenly spaced holes. Such board is used for hanger boards for tools, displays, and many other purposes. The standard sizes of hardboard are 4 × 6 feet (⅛ inch thick) and 2 × 12 feet (¼ inch thick).

Particle board is composition board made from wood chips held together by adhesives. Small pieces of wood are bonded together under heat and pressure with an adhesive or other binder. This material is something like hardboard. However, it is thicker and whole chips are used in making it. Particle board is available in common thicknesses of ⅜, ½, and ¾ inch and in a sheet size of 4 × 8 feet.

Waferboard is a panel made from wood wafers, rather than particles or strands. The wafers are bonded together with adhesives to form large panels. This panel stock is being used in housing to replace plywood.

Oriented strand board (OSB) is a panel stock made from wood strands that are arranged in a certain pattern for strength. The panels are bonded together with heat and pressure, using special adhesives.

MOLDINGS

A *molding* is a narrow strip shaped to a curved profile throughout its length. The materials used for moldings are available from lumberyards or home centers. They are available in many different sizes and shapes. The

molding material may be softwood, hardwood, or plastic. Plastic moldings have woodlike finishes that match most of the popular wood panels. Moldings are used to accent and ornament furniture and room interiors. They also conceal surface and angle joints. Fig. 2-3.

LUMBER DEFECTS

There are several defects that can affect the quality of lumber. Fig. 2-4. Some are natural defects that result from the growth of the tree itself. Others develop as lumber is cut, machined, and stored. You can use some defects (such as knots) to add interest to your project. However, most of the time you must work around defects when making a layout.

● A *knot* is a branch or limb of a tree that has been exposed as the log is cut into lumber. The knot may be solid and sound or loose and unsound. Knotty pine is often used for Early American furniture and for paneling.

● A *check* is a lengthwise separation of the wood, like a small crack or split. It often appears at the end of a board. *Honeycombing* is an area of checks that are not visible on the surface.

● A *split* is a lengthwise break or big crack in the board.

● *Decay* is rotting of wood.

● A *stain* is a discoloration of the wood surface.

● *Wane* is a lack of wood on the face of the piece.

● *Warp* is any variation from a true, or plane, surface. It includes crook, bow, cup, wind (twist), or any combination of these.

KINDS OF KNOTS

KINDS OF WARP

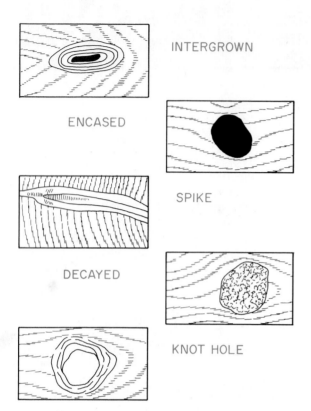

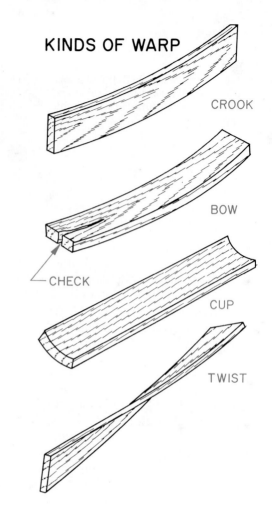

2-4. Common lumber defects.

- *Crook* is a deviation edgewise from a straight line drawn from end to end.
- *Bow* is a deviation flatwise from a straight line drawn from end to end of a piece.
- *Cup* is a curve across the grain or width of a piece.
- *Wind*, or *twist*, in a board indicates that the board is twisted throughout its length.

CHOOSING LUMBER FOR PROJECTS

The wood chosen for a project depends on three things:
- The type of project. For example, for outdoor furniture, you would want a wood that resists decay.
- The price of the wood.
- The appearance of the wood.

For beginning projects, select woods that are easy to work with hand tools and not too expensive. Basswood, willow, and pines are such woods.

For intermediate projects, select woods that are reasonable in price and fairly easy to work with hand tools and some machines. Soft northern elm or Philippine mahogany might be chosen. Woods recommended for the beginning project are also suitable.

For furniture projects, select quality woods such as walnut, ash, birch, maple, mahogany, cherry, and oak.

DESCRIPTION OF WOODS

The wood for each project should be selected with care. Each kind of wood has its own peculiar color, working qualities, and properties. Fig. 2-5 (pages 31-38).

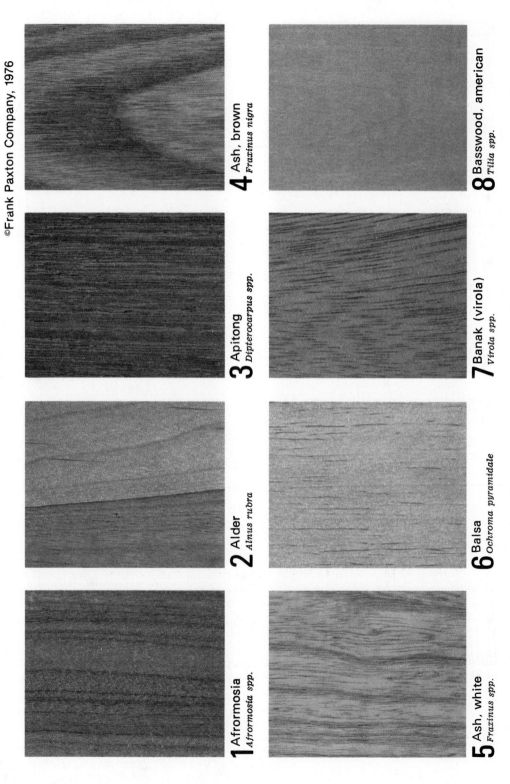

2-5. Some common kinds of wood.

1 Afrormosia
Afrormosia spp.

2 Alder
Alnus rubra

3 Apitong
Dipterocarpus spp.

4 Ash, brown
Fraxinus nigra

5 Ash, white
Fraxinus spp.

6 Balsa
Ochroma pyramidale

7 Banak (virola)
Virola spp.

8 Basswood, american
Tilia spp.

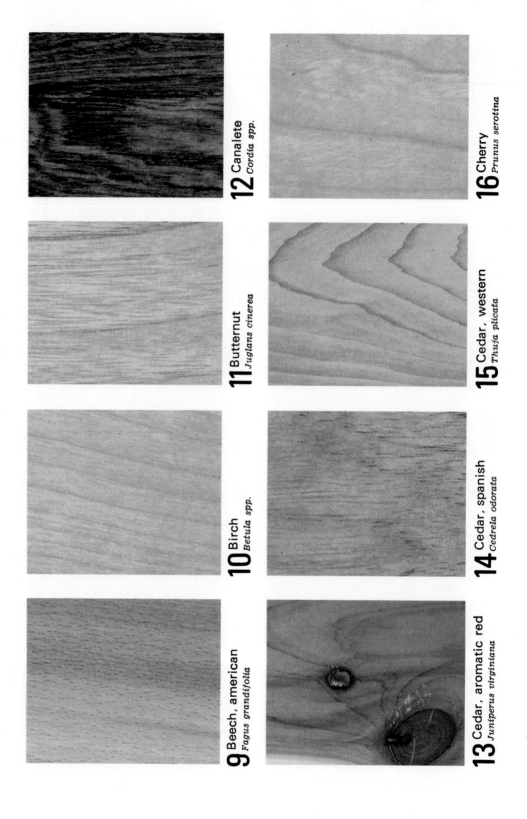

12 Canalete
Cordia spp.

16 Cherry
Prunus serotina

11 Butternut
Juglans cinerea

15 Cedar, western
Thuja plicata

10 Birch
Betula spp.

14 Cedar, spanish
Cedrela odorata

9 Beech, american
Fagus grandifolia

13 Cedar, aromatic red
Juniperus virginiana

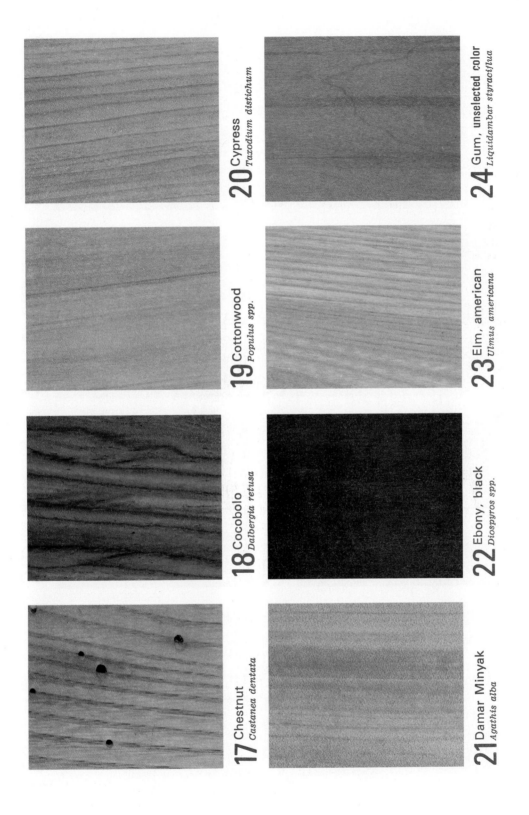

20 Cypress
Taxodium distichum

24 Gum, unselected color
Liquidambar styraciflua

19 Cottonwood
Populus spp.

23 Elm, american
Ulmus americana

18 Cocobolo
Dalbergia retusa

22 Ebony, black
Diospyros spp.

17 Chestnut
Castanea dentata

21 Damar Minyak
Agathis alba

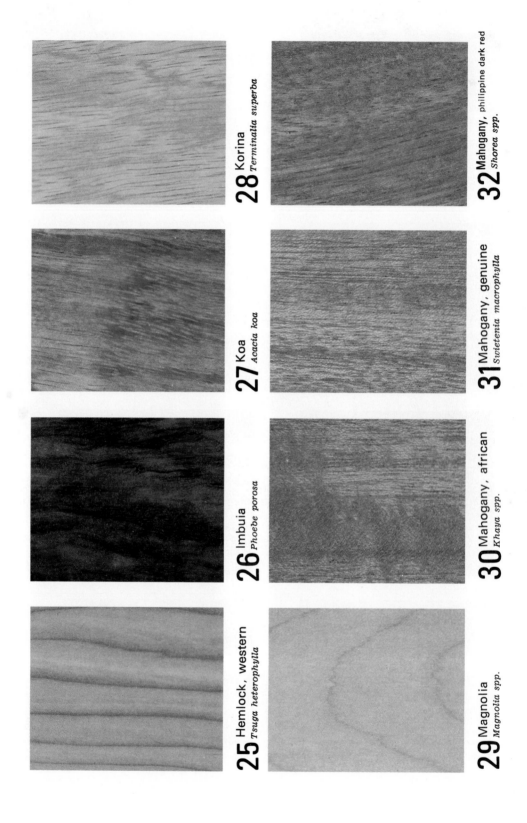

28 Korina
Terminalia superba

32 Mahogany, philippine dark red
Shorea spp.

27 Koa
Acacia koa

31 Mahogany, genuine
Swietenia macrophylla

26 Imbuia
Phoebe porosa

30 Mahogany, african
Khaya spp.

25 Hemlock, western
Tsuga heterophylla

29 Magnolia
Magnolia spp.

36 Maple, soft
Acer spp.

40 Obeche
Triplochiton scleroxylon

35 Maple, hard
Acer saccharum

39 Oak, plain white
Quercus spp.

34 Mansonia
Mansonia altissima

38 Oak, rift red
Quercus spp.

33 Mahogany, philippine light red
Shorea spp.

37 Oak, plain red
Quercus spp.

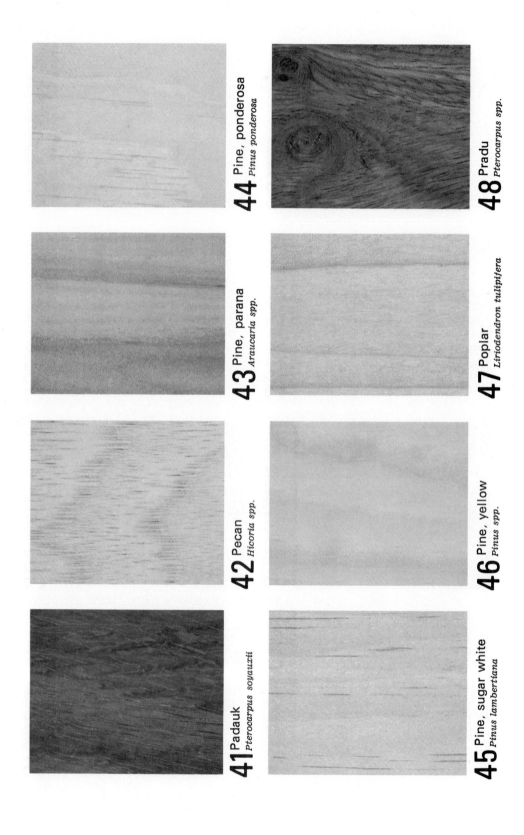

44 Pine, ponderosa
Pinus ponderosa

48 Pradu
Pterocarpus spp.

43 Pine, parana
Araucaria spp.

47 Poplar
Liriodendron tuliptfera

42 Pecan
Hicoria spp.

46 Pine, yellow
Pinus spp.

41 Padauk
Pterocarpus soyauxii

45 Pine, sugar white
Pinus lambertiana

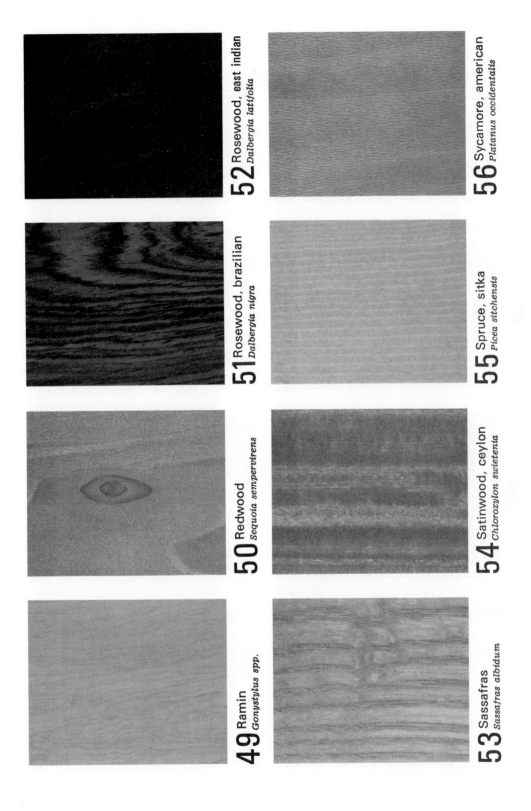

52 Rosewood, east indian
Dalbergia latifolia

56 Sycamore, american
Platanus occidentalis

51 Rosewood, brazilian
Dalbergia nigra

55 Spruce, sitka
Picea sitchensis

50 Redwood
Sequoia sempervirens

54 Satinwood, ceylon
Chloroxylon swietenia

49 Ramin
Gonystylus spp.

53 Sassafras
Sassafras albidum

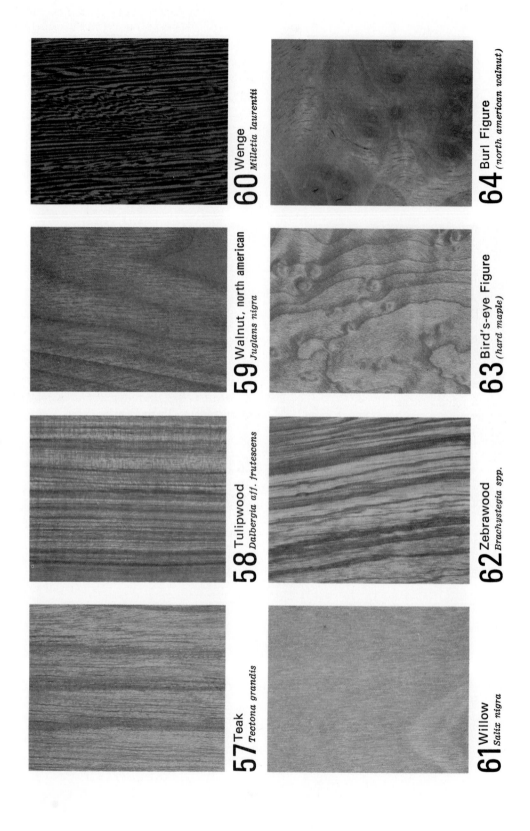

60 Wenge
Milletia laurentii

64 Burl Figure
(north american walnut)

59 Walnut, north american
Juglans nigra

63 Bird's-eye Figure
(hard maple)

58 Tulipwood
Dalbergia aff. frutescens

62 Zebrawood
Brachystegia spp.

57 Teak
Tectona grandis

61 Willow
Salix nigra

HARDWOODS (Broad-leafed Species)

Many woods are shown in Fig. 2-5. Some of these woods are discussed below. The number following each wood refers to the number of the wood in Fig. 2-5.

Ash, White (5)

The three most common types of ash are white, green, and black. White ash is very popular for furniture construction. It is also used widely for sports equipment such as skis, baseball bats, and toboggans because of its strength and hardness. Also, it holds its shape well after it has been formed.

Basswood, American (8)

The softest of commercial hardwoods, basswood is white with a few black streaks. It is fuzzy because of its long fibers. It is fairly strong for bending, is nonwarping, and has little or no grain marking. It is not durable for outside uses. It is used for drawing boards, moldings, and jigsaw work.

Beech, American (9)

Beech is one of the very best of the utility hardwoods. The wood is white or slightly reddish. It has no figure to make it ornamental. Thus, it is rarely used for the exterior of furniture, other than chairs. It is sometimes chosen as a substitute for more expensive birch or hard maple. Beech is strong and very durable.

Birch, Yellow and Curly (10)

Birch is a hardwood with fine texture and close grain. It comes primarily from the north-central states and Canada. Yellow birch is the most common. Curly birch is found only in occasional trees. It results from rare grain development. It has a delicate, wavy figure and is popular for fine furniture and panels. The heartwood is red. The sapwood is white. Therefore a single board may be either red or white, or red with white edges. It is a good wood for tabletops, doors, rails, and any furniture parts that require extra strength.

Birch will take practically any color of stain. It is sometimes finished to resemble mahogany, walnut, or maple.

Cherry, Black (16)

Black cherry is found in most parts of the United States. It is not abundant enough to be a common furniture wood. The heartwood is reddish brown and the sapwood is white. Cherry resembles unfinished mahogany. It is a very durable wood. It does not dent easily, and warps very little. Cherry darkens with age. It is best finished with shellac or lacquer.

Elm, American (23)

Elm grows throughout the eastern United States. It is moderately heavy and hard. The wood has large shrinkage and care must be taken to prevent warping. It has excellent bending qualities. This makes it good for many kinds of furniture work, particularly for the bent parts of chairs. The heartwood is brown to dark brown, sometimes containing shades of red.

Sweetgum or Red Gum (24)

Gumwood grows in river deltas throughout the South. Because it tends to warp in seasoning, gumwood was not commonly used for many years. It is recognized as a wood of great beauty with a wide range of usefulness. The heartwood, called red gum, ranges from light to deep reddish brown. The sapwood is light colored and is referred to as sap gum. Although gumwood is considered a hardwood, it is really a medium hardwood. It is not as hard as maple, but is harder than many pines.

Fine furniture and trim are made from gumwood. One of its unusual features is that no two long boards produce the same figure in the wood. The wood is close-grained and has a very fine texture. Gumwood is plain sawed, quarter sawed, or veneered. Selected gumwood finishes very well in the natural color. However, the best results come when it is given a light brown stain.

Mahogany, True or Genuine (30 and 31)

The two kinds of genuine mahogany most commonly used for furniture are the Honduras and African. True mahogany is considered the ideal cabinet wood. The heartwood of mahogany varies in color from pale to a deep reddish brown, becoming darker on exposure to light. It is tough, strong, easy to work, and polishes well. Mahogany is prized for its distinctive, fine grain figure, uniform texture, and natural color.

Mahogany, Philippine (32 and 33)

Philippine mahogany is the name given to a group of woods known as lauans that come from the Philippine Islands. Although they resemble genuine mahogany, these woods are coarser in texture and general appearance. They are usually classified as light red or dark red Philippine mahoganies. The dark red looks most like true mahogany. This wood is free from knots, checking, and shrinking. It is an excellent, inexpensive wood to use for furniture, cabinetwork, trim, and boats.

Maple (36)

Maple is a hard, tough, strong wood that wears very well and has good resistance to shock. The grain is usually straight and fine in texture. The heartwood is light reddish brown and the sapwood is white. Because of its wear-resisting qualities, maple is ideal for fine flooring. It is used extensively for both Colonial and contemporary furniture. A white, clear grade of maple, which comes from the sapwood, is especially light. The white wood can be made into furniture and fine floors on which natural finish is to be used. The brown heartwood makes a good base for a brown, mahogany, or dark stain. Curly maple results from twisted growth and the manner in which the lumber is sawed. Bird's-eye maple is cut from sugar-maple trees. Its texture is probably the result of thwarted bud growth.

Oak, Red (37 and 38)

There are nearly 300 kinds of oak in the United States. From the woodworker's standpoint, there are only two main kinds—red and white oak. Red oak is one of the most widely distributed trees in the United States. Because of its slightly reddish tinge and coarse grain, it is used very successfully for certain decorative effects. Red oak is used largely for furniture, flooring, interior finish, and construction. It is hard, heavy, and strong.

Oak, White (39)

White oak is preferred for furniture and other items that are to be given a natural finish. It is usually free of the reddish tinge. It has better color, finer texture, and more prominent figure than the red oak. White oak is a popular cabinet wood.

Poplar (47)

Poplar is a durable, soft, medium-strong hardwood. It is one of the largest native trees supplying lumber. The sapwood, which is frequently several inches thick, is white. The heartwood is yellowish brown with a green tinge. The wood is moderately light in weight, straight-grained, and uniform in texture. It is excellent for inexpensive furniture that is painted and enameled.

Walnut (59)

Walnut, a medium hardwood, is one of the most beautiful native woods. It is found in the eastern half of the United States. Its heartwood is brown and its sapwood is nearly white. Walnut is a strong, durable, and stiff wood. It is used chiefly for cabinetwork, furniture, veneers, and gunstocks. The veneer is cut from the best grade of walnut and is made into panel stock and plywood. Walnut is excellent for cabinetwork because it works well.

Willow (61)

Willow is a hardwood that is extremely light and soft textured. It is easy to work, glue, and finish. It is frequently used as a substitute for walnut. Willow is pale reddish brown in color. It is commonly used in furniture and for veneer cores. There is a wide color range in willow. It is much less expensive than walnut. Thus, it is a good wood to use for beginning projects.

SOFTWOODS (Cone-Bearing Species)

Cedar, Aromatic Red (13)

Cedar is a light, soft, fine-grained, pleasantly aromatic wood that is easily worked. The sapwood is white and the heartwood is reddish purple. The wood is in great demand for use in cedar chests and clothes closet linings. Because of its resistance to moisture, it is also used for canoes and fence posts.

Douglas Fir

Douglas fir is used extensively for lumber and plywood manufacture. The wood is moderately hard, heavy, and very stiff. It has a pronounced grain pattern, especially when made into plywood.

Pine, Ponderosa (44)

Ponderosa pine is used primarily for building lumber and to a lesser degree for post poles and veneers. The wood from this tree varies considerably in its properties. It is moderately lightweight, soft, and low in resistance. It is an excellent wood for home construction.

Pine, Sugar White (45)

Sugar pine is used almost entirely for lumber for building boxes, foundry patterns, and mill work. The wood is light in color, soft, smooth, straight-grained, and easily worked. It has very small shrinkage and seasons very readily. An oil stain or shellac finish can be used very easily on sugar pine.

Redwood (50)

Redwood is a widely used wood for home construction, fences, and outdoor furniture. It is lightweight, moderately hard, and strong. Redwood is very resistant to decay. This wood shrinks very little. It is quite easy to season and holds its shape well after seasoning.

SUMMARY

The characteristics of common woods are shown in Table 2-C.

Pine is often used for Early American furniture. Read about the properties of pine above. What characteristics make it a good choice for furniture?

Table 2-C. Characteristics of Common Woods

Species	Comparative Weights[1]	Color[2]	Hand Tool Working	Nail Ability[3]	Relative Density	General Strength[4]	Resistance to Decay[5]	Wood Finishing[6]
Hardwoods[7]								
Ash, tough white	Heavy	Off-white	Hard	Poor	Hard	Good	Low	Medium
Ash, soft white	Medium	Off-white	Medium	Medium	Medium	Low	Low	Medium
Balsawood	Light	Cream white	Easy	Good	Soft	Low	Low	Poor
Basswood	Light	Cream white	Easy	Good	Soft	Low	Low	Medium
Beech	Heavy	Light brown	Hard	Poor	Hard	Good	Low	Easy
Birch	Heavy	Light brown	Hard	Poor	Hard	Good	Low	Easy
Butternut	Light	Light brown	Easy	Good	Soft	Low	Medium	Medium
Cherry, black	Medium	Med. red-brown	Hard	Poor	Hard	Good	Medium	Easy
Chestnut	Light	Light brown	Medium	Medium	Medium	Medium	High	Poor
Cottonwood	Light	Grayish white	Medium	Good	Soft	Low	Low	Poor
Elm, soft, Northern	Medium	Cream tan	Hard	Good	Medium	Medium	Medium	Medium
Gum, sap	Medium	Tannish white	Medium	Medium	Medium	Medium	Medium	Medium
Hickory, true	Heavy	Reddish tan	Hard	Poor	Hard	Good	Low	Medium
Maghogany, African	Medium	Reddish brown	Easy	Good	Medium	Medium	Medium	Medium
Maghogany, Honduras	Medium	Golden brown	Easy	Good	Medium	Medium	High	Medium
Mahogany, Philippine	Medium	Medium red	Easy	Good	Medium	Medium	High	Medium
Maple, hard	Heavy	Reddish cream	Hard	Poor	Hard	Good	Low	Easy
Maple, soft	Medium	Reddish brown	Hard	Poor	Hard	Good	Low	Easy
Oak, red *(average)*	Heavy	Flesh brown	Hard	Medium	Hard	Good	Low	Medium
Oak, white *(average)*	Heavy	Grayish brown	Hard	Medium	Hard	Good	High	Medium
Poplar, yellow	Medium	Lt. to dk. yellow	Easy	Good	Soft	Low	Low	Easy
Walnut, black	Heavy	Dark brown	Medium	Medium	Hard	Good	High	Medium
Willow, black	Light	Medium brown	Easy	Good	Soft	Low	Low	Medium
SOFTWOODS[8]								
Cedar, Tennessee Red	Medium	Red	Medium	Poor	Medium	Medium	High	Easy
Cypress	Medium	Yellow to reddish brown	Medium	Good	Soft	Medium	High	Poor
Fir, Douglas	Medium	Orange-brown	Hard	Medium	Soft	Medium	Medium	Medium
Pine, ponderosa	Light	Orange to reddish brown	Easy	Good	Soft	Low	Low	Medium
Pine, sugar	Light	Creamy brown	Easy	Good	Soft	Low	Medium	Poor
Redwood	Light	Deep red-brown	Easy	Good	Soft	Medium	High	Poor

[1]Kiln-dried weight.
[2]Heartwood. Sap is whitish.
[3]Comparative splitting tendencies.
[4]Combined bending and compressive strength.
[5]No wood will decay unless exposed to moisture.
Resistance to decay estimate refers to heartwood only.
[6]Ease of finishing with clear or "natural" finishes.
[7]Leaf-bearing tree.
[8]Cone-and-needle-bearing trees.

FACTS ABOUT WOOD

Did you know that wood . . .

● is made up of thousands of hollow cells that form natural building blocks? If you could separate all the fibers in just one cubic inch of wood, you would have about three million.

● has greater strength per pound than steel? A wood block just one-inch square and two-and-one-quarter inches long can support 10,000 pounds of weight. This great strength helps wood houses withstand earthquakes and hurricanes better than buildings made of other materials.

● is a natural insulator? Wood insulates six times better than brick, 15 times better than concrete, and 1,770 times better than aluminum. Wood is an excellent insulator because of its cellular structure.

● will last for centuries? Many wood houses are over 300 years old. Wood piles under the streets of Venice, Italy, are over 1,000 years old. Timbers over 2,700 years old have been found intact in kings' tombs in the Middle East.

● is as varied as nature itself? Colors of wood range from greenish-black to creamy white. Wood's grain patterns come in as many varieties as the waves of the sea.

● can be worked by hand and power tools to take on forms and shapes limited only by the creativity of the woodworker?

● is our only renewable resource for construction and manufacturing? Modern forests make it possible to harvest trees much like any other crop.

Review Questions

1. What is green lumber?
2. What is dry lumber?
3. What is the actual thickness of 1 inch hardwood?
4. Are all hardwoods harder than all softwoods?
5. How is hardwood lumber cut?
6. What does "S2S" mean?
7. Name the three common types of ash. What are among the chief uses of ash?
8. Why is willow a good choice for beginning projects?
9. What is the color range of birch?
10. For what kind of wood is willow used as a substitute?
11. Cherry resembles what other kind of wood?
12. What are the characteristics of true mahogany that make it a desirable furniture wood?
13. Would you consider true mahogany a rather common wood? What are the chief sources of this wood?
14. Why is maple considered a very desirable material for flooring?
15. What style of furniture is usually made from maple?
16. How many kinds of oak are there?
17. Name the two large classifications of oak.
18. Yellow poplar is a very good selection for beginning woodworking projects. What are the reasons for this?
19. Give the color range for yellow poplar.
20. Name the chief uses for walnut. Why is walnut so often chosen for gunstocks and other articles that must be formed?
21. Describe the grain of walnut.
22. What are the uses of Douglas fir?
23. Describe the characteristics of redwood. Compare redwood with ponderosa pine.

Chapter 3

Design

After studying this chapter, you will be able to:
● List the three keys to good design.
● Identify the moods created by the use of various colors.
● Identify and give examples of the two kinds of balance.
● List the main steps in completing a simple project.

LOOK FOR THESE TERMS

balance	mass
design	primary colors
emphasis	proportion
function	texture

Every manufactured object has been designed. Your home, the furniture in it, cars, and even lead pencils have been developed from a design on paper.

WHAT IS DESIGN?

A *design* is the outline, shape, or plan of something. No one will agree completely with everyone else as to what is good or bad design. We all look at things in a slightly different way and see in them things we like or dislike. Fig. 3-1.

The three keys to good design are function, appearance, and solid construction. *Function* refers to the purpose of the product. A lamp, for example, should give the kind of light that is correct for a specific purpose. A lamp for reading would have a different function than a night-light. Fig. 3-2. The function, or purpose of a clock is to tell time. If the clock's face is poorly designed, it will be difficult to read. Fig. 3-3. *Appearance,* of course, refers to how the object looks. Are the materials and shapes combined to form an object that is pleasing to the eye? Sound construction means that the product is well built of the correct material so that it will last a long time with a minimum of maintenance.

As far as design, woodworking projects can be divided into three groups:
● Trinkets or gadgets that are made to satisfy your own interests and desires. Fig. 3-4.
● Practical objects that must be standard size if they are to be usable. For instance, a basketball backboard must be 4 × 6 feet.
● Artistically designed objects including furniture and accessories for the home. Figure 3-5 shows a clock with a traditional design.

3-1. In your opinion, are these turned bowls well-designed?

3-2. This lamp would be best for reading.

3-3. Compare the designs of these clock faces. Choose the clock face that is easiest to read. Which clock face is the most difficult to read?

3-4. Each of these designs might be used to make a set of salt and pepper shakers.

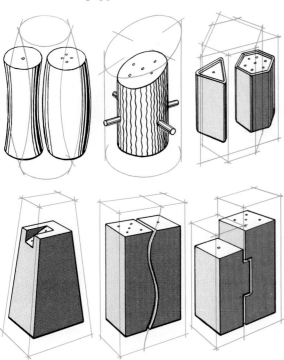

3-5. A traditional clock would be a fine accessory for any home. This clock is both decorative and useful.

3-6. This silverware chest is well designed.

One of the great mistakes made in the workshop is building furniture with no design or style.

WHAT MAKES UP DESIGN?

Design—good or bad—depends on several qualities. These qualities are line, shape, mass, texture, value, and color. Fig. 3-6.

- A *line* is a path moving through space. A line carefully drawn according to a plan makes for a good design. The basic lines are straight and curved. Straight lines suggest rigidity, precision, dignity, and strength. Slightly curved lines represent lightness, gracefulness, and softness. Curved lines that change direction rapidly show activity and forcefulness. Jagged or zigzag lines suggest nervousness or excitement. Lines can be vertical, horizontal, or at an angle. Fig. 3-7.
- *Shape* is a series of lines going in different directions, outlining an area. Some common shapes are square, rectangular, circular, and oval. Fig. 3-8.
- *Mass* is the solid form created by variations and combinations of the four basic shapes. The sphere, cone, cube, and cylinder are common solid forms. They have three dimensions, usually called depth, width, and height.
- *Texture*, or *surface quality*, adds to the surface design. Woods have textures of their own. Finishes are used to bring them out and protect them. Fig. 3-9.
- *Value* refers to the amount of lightness or darkness. The values used in design impart a feeling to the observer. Fig. 3-10. If the

3-7. Common types of lines. Note that the arrangement of the lines can prompt certain emotions.

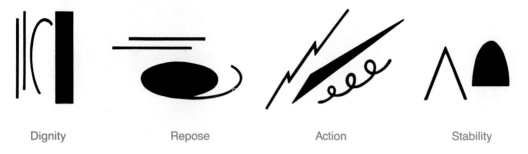

Dignity   Repose   Action   Stability

3-8. Four common shapes.

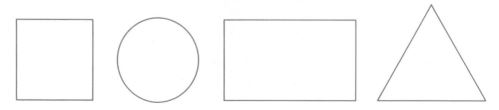

3-9. Inlay, veneers, and a fine finish add to the surface quality of this cedar chest.

contrast between the darkest and lightest values is great, the feeling is stimulating and cheerful. If there is little value contrast, the feeling is more dignified and perhaps depressed.

● *Color* is generally recognized as having an effect on mood. Fig. 3-11. Because color sets the mood, it must be appropriate to the

3-10. Reflection and absorption of light by white, gray, and black surfaces.

3-11. Color wheel.

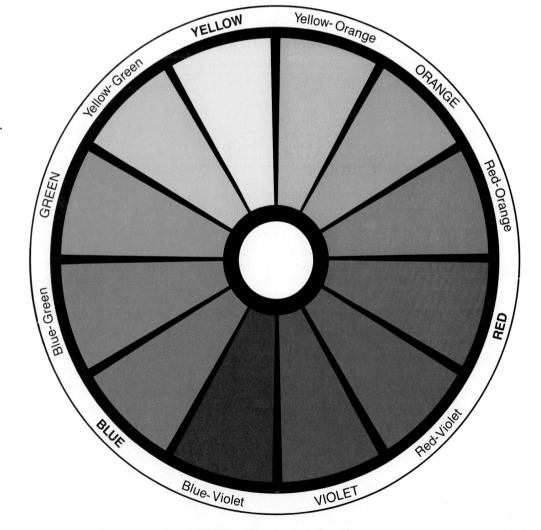

subject matter. In general, the warm colors (reds, yellows, oranges, and browns) stand out from their backgrounds. These colors are positive, aggressive, and stimulating. The cool colors (greens, blues, and violets) tend to recede more into the background. White reflects light, whereas black absorbs light.

Primary colors are the three colors from which all other colors are derived. The three primary colors are red, yellow, and blue.

Secondary colors are produced by mixing two primary colors:

Red and yellow—orange.
Yellow and blue—green.
Blue and red—violet.

Tertiary, or *intermediate*, *colors* are a mixture of one primary and one secondary color:

Red and violet—red violet.
Red and orange—red orange.
Blue and violet—blue violet.
Blue and green—blue green.
Yellow and orange—yellow orange.
Yellow and green—yellow green.

Neutrals are black and white and the many grays produced by mixing black and white in different amounts.

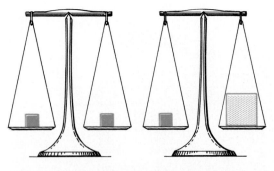

3-12. These balance scales illustrate formal and informal balance. The one on the left has units of equal size and shape. The scale on the right is balanced by units of different size but of the same weight.

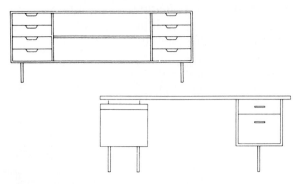

3-13. Each of these desk fronts illustrates a type of balance. A. Formal balance; B. Informal balance.

WHAT MAKES AN ATTRACTIVE PRODUCT?

In designing any item, certain principles should be followed:

● *Balance.* Exactly what it sounds like, balance makes things look stable. The human body, for example, is balanced. The human body has an arm on both sides, there are two eyes. The other body parts are in balance. Generally, lopsided or unstable things are not pleasing to the eye.

There are two kinds of balance, formal and informal. *Formal balance* is present when both sides of an object are exactly equal. The human body is an example of formal balance. *Informal balance* gives the impression of stability and balance by the "grouping" of the parts. Fig. 3-12. Formal and informal balance also are shown in the desk fronts in Fig. 3-13.

● *Proportion.* Proportion is the relation of one thing to another regarding size. A well-proportioned piece has a pleasing arrangement of parts.

In designing many wood projects, we use a rectangular shape instead of a square one. We do this simply because it looks better proportioned to us. Proportion in design is achieved when the object is not too fat, tall, thin, or square. Fig. 3-14.

Figure 3-15 shows one way of enlarging a 5-by-8 proportion. This proportion, shown by the jewelry box in Fig. 3-14, is thought by some to be the most pleasing.

● *Harmony.* When the parts, colors, shapes, and textures of an object seem to get along well together, we say the object has harmony.

● *Emphasis* is stress on one feature. For example, an accent, or special point of interest, is often used for emphasis.

3-14. The jewelry box, index card box, and paper towel holder shown here are award-winning projects. Each shows good proportion.

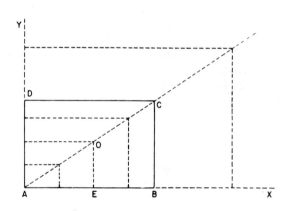

3-15. One way of enlarging a 5-by-8 proportion. This technique is useful in designing trays and picture frames. Make AB eight units long and BC five units long. Then lay off along the line AX any length you want—for example, AE. The distance for width, then, would be EO.

3-16. Though designed as a game table, this table can be used for other purposes.

In deciding whether something is well designed, ask yourself the following questions:
- Does the piece serve the purpose for which it is intended? Fig. 3-16.
- Does it perform its job efficiently? Fig. 3-17.
- Is it within your ability to construct and maintain? Fig. 3-18.
- Is it pleasing to the eye? Fig. 3-19.
- Does it satisfy you and the other people you want it to satisfy?

3-17. The top of this lazy susan must turn freely.

3-20. Are you interested in sailing or boating? You may want to build a model.

3-18. A pepper mill might be a good first project for the wood lathe.

3-19. Do you think this footstool has a traditional design?

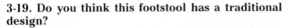

DESIGNING A WOODWORKING PROJECT

After you have reached a certain skill level, you may want to design a project of your own.

To design and make a project in wood, follow these steps:

1. Get the idea for the project you would like to build. Maybe you have something in mind that you have always wanted to make. If not, magazines and books with projects in them are good sources of ideas. Another way to get ideas is to visit stores selling furniture, hobby supplies, or sporting goods. You might like to build:

3-21. Each of these tables has a different style. You might want to select such a table for an advanced project.

3-22. A spice or condiment rack must be well designed. Be sure to measure the diameter and height of all containers to be stored on the rack.

- Toys, models, games, puzzles, and other hobby equipment. Fig. 3-20.
- Shelters for birds and pets.
- Things for your room or home such as lamps, bookends, shoe racks, and tie racks.
- Kitchen items such as cutting boards, salt and pepper shakers, and shelves.
- Sports equipment.
- Furniture, including chairs, tables, chests, and desks. Fig. 3-21.

2. After you've decided what to make, ask yourself, "What is the purpose of the object?" For example, a book rack is supposed to hold books conveniently. How large are the books? What must be the depth of the shelf? If there is to be more than one shelf, what should be the distance between the shelves? If the project is a spice rack, it must be able to hold the items efficiently. Fig. 3-22.

In designing a piece of furniture, certain standards, especially of height, must be observed.

3. Decide on the style or design of furniture. It should blend with your room or home.
4. Now make a sketch of what you would like to build to see how it will look. Suppose you decide to make a wall rack. Two sketches of possible designs are shown in Fig. 3-23. Let's suppose you decide on sketch A.
5. Make a working drawing of the project. Fig. 3-24. This will be necessary to determine the exact size of each part and how it is to be made.
6. Make a model. It is sometimes difficult to imagine what the finished article will look like with only sketches and drawings. It is helpful to see the three-dimensional appearance of the item by making

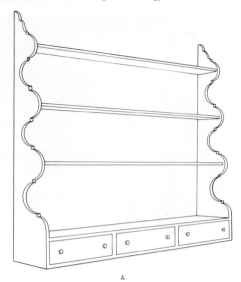

3-23. These two sketches are good examples of Early American design. Either of these would make a well-designed project.

3-24. A working drawing of wall rack A in Fig. 3-23.

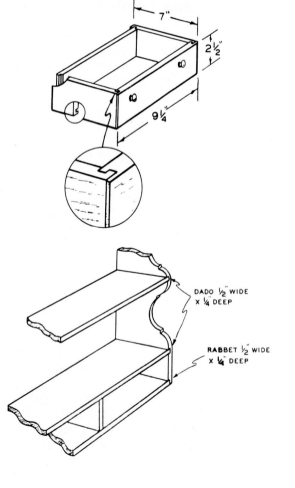

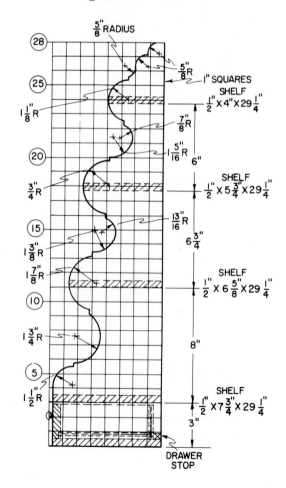

	Important: All dimensions listed above, except for length of dowel, etc., FINISHED size.				
No. of Pieces	Part Name	Thickness	Width	Length	Wood
2	Ends	½″	7¾″	28″	Knotty Pine
1	Shelf	½″	4″	29¼″	Knotty Pine
1	Shelf	½″	5¾″	29¼″	Knotty Pine
1	Shelf	½″	6⅝″	29¼″	Knotty Pine
2	Shelves	½″	7¾″	29¼″	Knotty Pine
2	Drawer Separators	½″	2½″	7¾″	Knotty Pine
3	Drawer Fronts	½″	2½″	9¼″	Knotty Pine
6	Drawer Sides	⅜″	2½″	7″	Clear Pine
3	Drawer Backs	⅜″	2½″	8⅞″	Clear Pine
3	Drawer Bottoms	¼″	6¼″	8¾″	Fir Plywood
6	Drawer Stops	½″	½″	1″	
1	Hardwood Dowel	¼″		36″	
6	Hardwood Knobs	¾″			

3-25. A bill of materials for the wall rack.

3-26. Plan of procedure for building the wall rack.

1. Lay out pattern of the ends on paper and trace on wood. Cut out on a jig saw.
2. Cut the dadoes for the shelves and the rabbet for the bottom board.
3. Saw the shelves and bottom board.
4. Dowel and glue the shelves and bottom in place. Before the glue sets be sure the entire structure is square.
5. Make drawer separators; install dowels and glue in place.
6. Cut the drawer fronts and fit into each opening. Then complete the drawers, using the joints suggested in the detailed drawing—or make a simple rabbet joint to fasten the sides and front, and a dado joint to fasten the sides and back. Glue drawer stops in place so the drawer fronts will be flush.
7. Sand edges to give a worn appearance.
8. Apply an antique pine finish, and add knobs.

a small model. This can be made of balsa wood or some other light material that is cut easily with a knife.

7. Make a bill of materials. A bill of materials is a list of the pieces needed, with their dimensions. Here you need to keep in mind the sizes and kinds of woods and plywoods and the kinds of fasteners to be used. Fig. 3-25.

8. Plan the building of the project. You must decide in what order each job will be performed. Fig. 3-26. Usually these jobs will include making a layout, cutting out the pieces and parts, shaping the parts, making the joints, fitting and assembling, and finishing.

9. Decide on what tools and machines you will need. Your future experiences in woodworking will help you decide on how to use the equipment.

10. Build the project. This is the time to display your skill by doing a fine job on each part.

11. Judge your work. Is the project useful, attractive, economical? Was it completed in a reasonable length of time? Did you learn by making it? If you can answer yes to these questions, the project was successful. Fig. 3-27.

3-27. The finished project.

Review Questions

1. Describe the meaning of design.
2. Name three keys to good design.
3. Name four kinds of lines.
4. What is mass?
5. Name the two kinds of balance.
6. Is a square in good proportion? Explain your answer.
7. What is emphasis?
8. Describe some of the kinds of things that you can build.
9. What is the value of making a model of the project you wish to build?
10. What is a bill of materials?

A variety of project plans are available. If you are interested, send for suppliers' catalogs.

3-28. Complete plans like these for making many interesting projects are available from many sources.

Chapter 4

Reading the Drawing or Sketch

After studying this chapter, you will be able to:
● Identify the three common kinds of pictorial drawing.
● Describe the five main types of lines used in drawings.
● Explain the system of dual dimensioning.

LOOK FOR THESE TERMS

cabinet drawing
center line
dimension line
dual dimensioning
exploded view

extension line
hidden line
isometric drawing
perspective drawing
pictorial

read-out chart
scale
visible line
working drawing

A *drawing* or *sketch* is the map you follow in making a project. Fig. 4-1. It tells you the exact size of the article, the number and sizes of its pieces, the design of each part, and the way in which the project fits together.

Understand the drawing *before* you begin to build the project. In industry, everything to be produced is first drawn by a drafter or on a computer. Pictorial and working (view) drawings are two types of drawings that are commonly used in woodworking.

PICTORIAL DRAWINGS

A *pictorial* is also called a picture drawing or sketch. It shows the project the way it looks in use. Fig. 4-2. The most common kinds of pictorial drawings are isometric (equal angle), cabinet, and perspective. All three are one-view drawings (the total object is shown in one view). An *isometric drawing* has parallel lines drawn at angles of 120 degrees to each other. In a *cabinet drawing*, the front of the object is drawn just like the front in a three-view drawing. However, the sides are drawn at an angle of 30 to 45 degrees.

4-1. Sketching a tool holder might be the first step in designing a project.

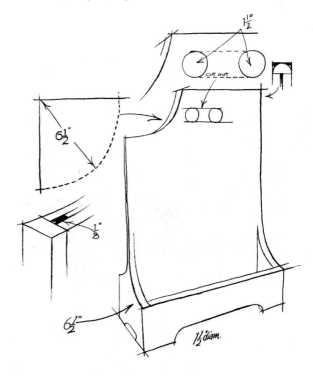

4-2. Pictorial drawings of several different plant containers.

The *perspective drawing* looks like a photo with either one or two vanishing points. The perspective with one vanishing point looks a great deal like a cabinet drawing. The perspective with two vanishing points looks somewhat like an isometric drawing.

WORKING, OR VIEW, DRAWINGS

Working drawings are used for construction. Fig. 4-3. These drawings have one, two, three, or more *views*. These views show the article from different sides. Most projects require two or three views. In the three-view drawing, the lower left-hand view shows the way the project looks from the front. The view above shows how the project looks from the top. The view to the right is the *right side* or *end view* of the project. Fig. 4-4. These views give the correct dimensions of each piece. The dimensions are placed on the views to be read from the bottom or right side. If only two views are included, either the front and top or front and side views are shown. Fig. 4-5.

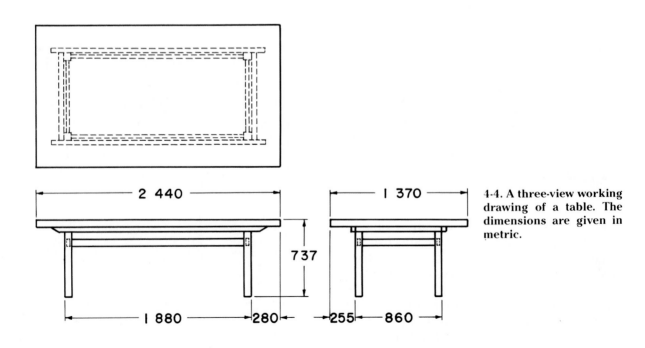

4-4. A three-view working drawing of a table. The dimensions are given in metric.

4-3. Three different drawings of a birdhouse. A. Working drawing; B. Isometric drawing; C. Cabinet drawing.

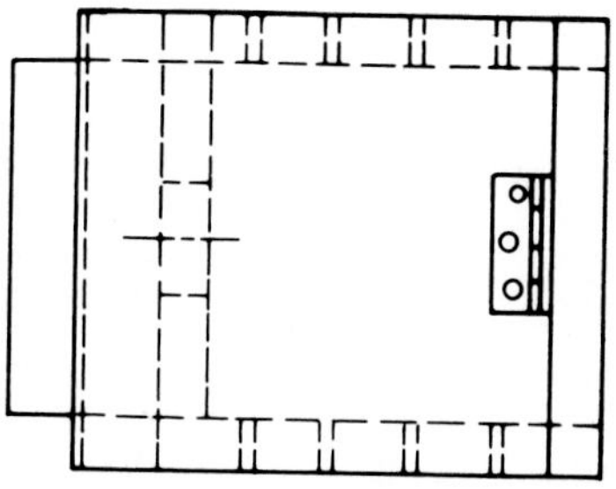

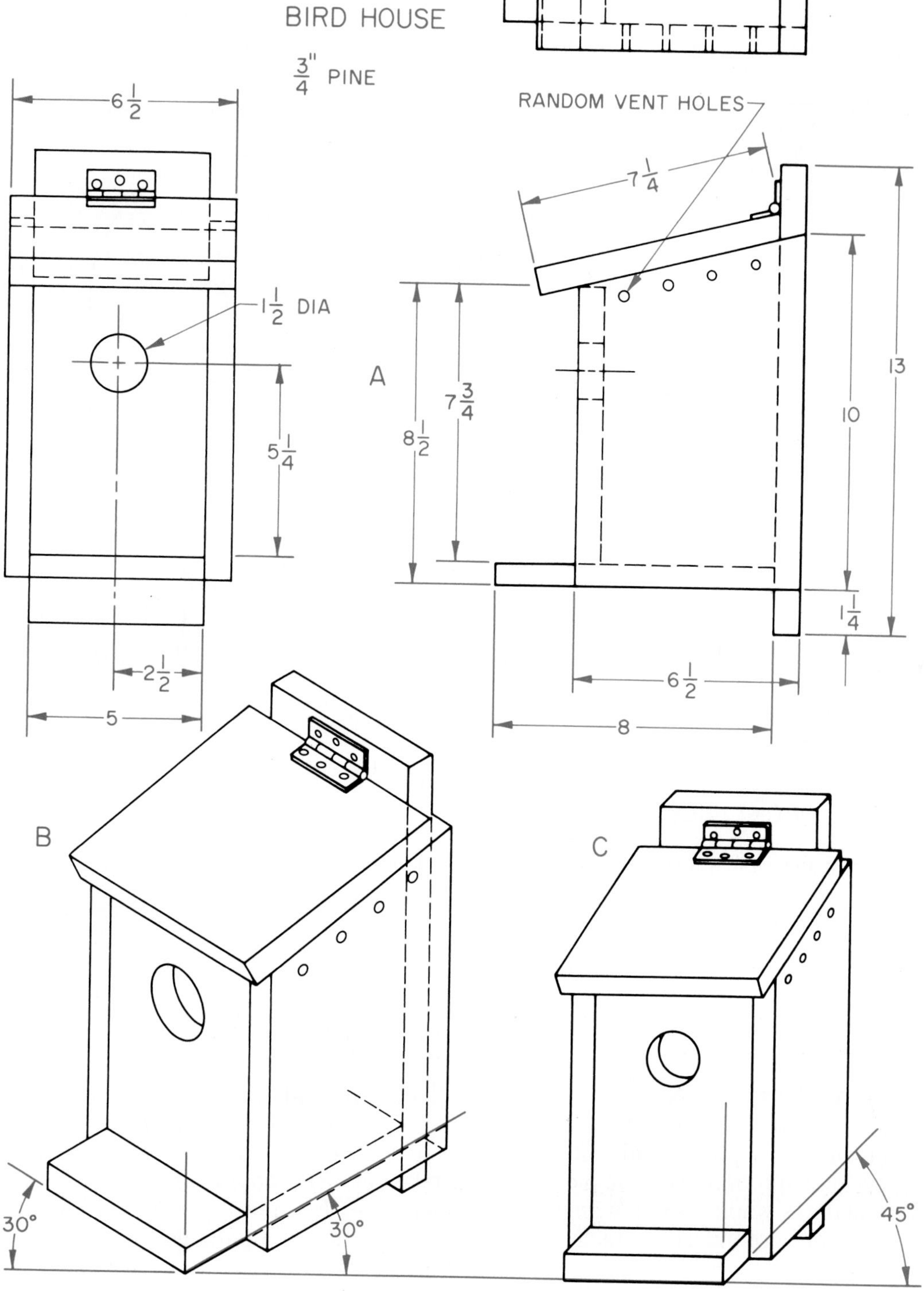

BIRD HOUSE

$\frac{3}{4}"$ PINE

RANDOM VENT HOLES

$6\frac{1}{2}$

$1\frac{1}{2}$ DIA

$5\frac{1}{4}$

$2\frac{1}{2}$

5

A

$7\frac{1}{4}$

$8\frac{1}{2}$

$7\frac{3}{4}$

13

10

$1\frac{1}{4}$

$6\frac{1}{2}$

8

B

30°

30°

C

45°

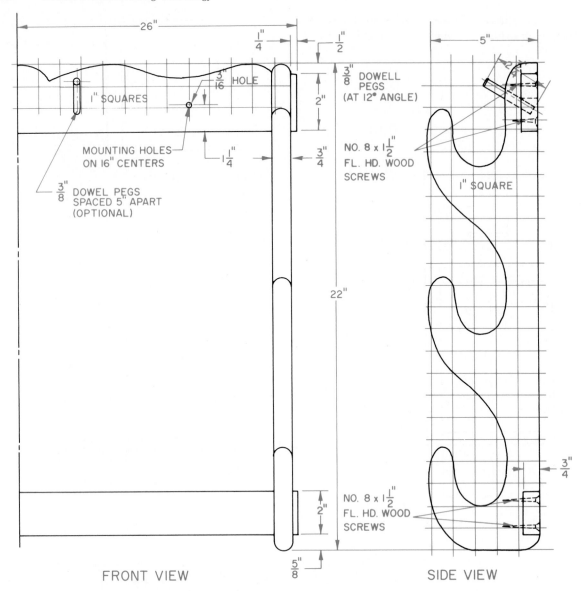

4-5. A two-view working drawing of a gun rack, showing the front and side views.

VARIATIONS

Drawings for woodwork do not follow rigid rules. A drawing for a project will often be partly a view drawing and partly a pictorial drawing. Sometimes when view drawings are used, the views are not placed correctly; that is, the right side or end view is not always to the right of the front view. Many isometric or perspective drawings are made as *exploded* (taken apart) *drawings*. Fig. 4-6. An *exploded view* clearly shows the dimension of each part and how the parts go together.

MEANING OF LINES

In a drawing or sketch, different kinds of lines indicate the following:

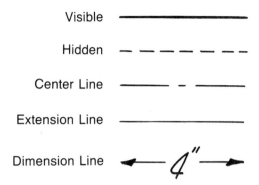

Visible

Hidden

Center Line

Extension Line

Dimension Line

Visible line: The major outline of the article.

Hidden line: Indicates the outline that cannot be seen from the surface.

Center line: Shows the center or divides the drawing into equal, or symmetrical, parts.

Extension line: Extends from the outline. It provides two lines between which measurements or dimensions can be shown.

Dimension line: Usually has arrowheads at each end and is broken in the center. These lines run between the extension lines. They give the measurements or dimensions.

SCALE OF THE DRAWING

When large projects must be drawn, the size of the drawing must be reduced so that it can be drawn on one page. In such a case, the drawing is made *to scale*. Frequently, for example, a customary drawing is made half size (6″ = 1′) and the scale is so stated. For larger projects, a scale such as ¼ inch to the foot (¼″ = 1′0″) may be followed, as in house plans.

On metric drawings, the common scales for reducing the size are 1:2 (half size), 1:5 (one-fifth size), 1:10 (one-tenth size), and 1:20 (one-twentieth size). In building drawings, a scale of 1:50 or 1:100 is often used. Note that all metric measurement is based on units of 10.

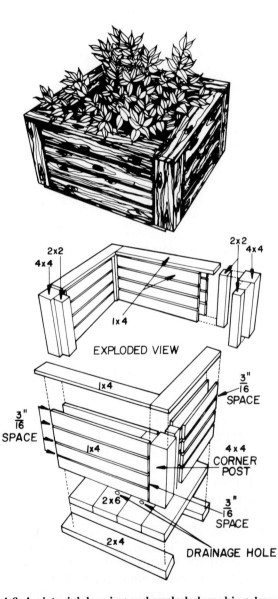

4-6. A pictorial drawing and exploded working drawing of a planter.

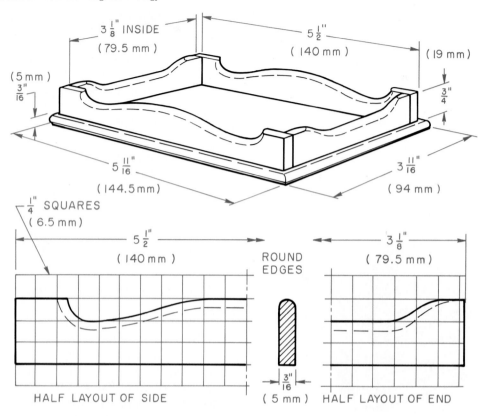

4-7. This drawing is dual dimensioned. This makes it possible to build the product using either customary (inch) or metric (millimetre) measurements.

READING DRAWINGS

In reading a drawing, it is important to read all dimensions. In making out the bill of materials, you must be sure to read these dimensions correctly. Then, after you have purchased the materials and are ready to begin, you must take equal care in transferring these measurements to the wood. Even if the drawing is made full size, never attempt to measure the drawing itself. Always use the dimensions stated.

There are two common ways to make drawings so they can be read either in metric or customary measurement:

● *Dual dimensioning.* In this method the customary measurement is placed first. The metric measurement is placed in parentheses directly behind or below it. Fig. 4-7. For example, if the dimension is 2 inches, it would read 2 inches (51 mm). Since both dimensions must be shown for each measurement, the drawing looks more complicated than it actually is.

● *Metric dimensioning with customary read-out chart.* Here all dimensions on the drawing are shown in metric. A small *read-out chart* is added to each drawing giving the equivalent sizes in the customary measurement. Fig. 4-8. For example, if the metric size is 12.7 mm, the chart would show that this equals ½ inch.

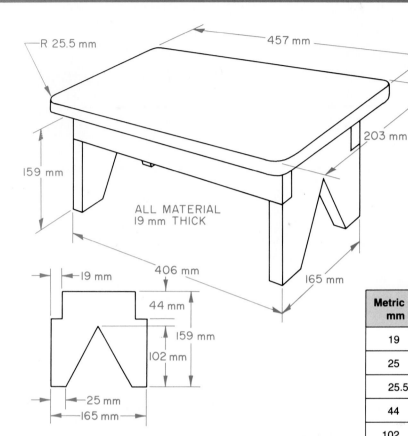

Metric in mm	Customary in inches	Metric in mm	Customary in inches
19	¾	159	6¼
25	¹⁵/₁₆	165	6½
25.5	1	203	8
44	1¾	406	16
102	4	457	18

4-8. This looks simple because only the metric measurements are shown. The customary sizes can be found in the chart.

Neither of these methods, however, solves the basic problem of designing in metrics. The change from customary to metric is only a mathematical change. Thus, all metric sizes are odd, such as 25.4 mm and 12.7 mm. If the original dimension is 1 inch, then the exact metric equivalent is 25.4 mm, or about 25.5 mm. If the drawing is to be truly metric, the product *should be designed in metric*, using the more common full numbers, such as 5, 10, 15, 20, and 25 mm.

Review Questions

1. What are the two types of drawings most commonly used in woodworking?
2. Name the kind of drawing that is similar to a photograph.
3. Does a working drawing always have three views?
4. How are invisible parts shown on a drawing?
5. If the drawing is full size, can you trace it to make the layout?
6. Describe the two common methods of dimensioning for drawings that must be read in metric or customary measurements.

Math Quiz

Print Reading

Drawing Dimensions

Figure A is an example of an *all-metric drawing.* Referring to the drawing, answer the questions below. Answer these questions on a separate sheet of paper. Do not write in this book.

1. The largest diameter of the turned bowl is _____ mm.
2. The diameter of the bottom of the turned bowl is _____ mm.
3. The height of the turned bowl is _____ mm.
4. The radius of the arc that forms the inside of the bowl is _____ mm.
5. The thickness of the handle is _____ mm.
6. The overall length of the handle is _____ mm.
7. The handle design is shown on _____ mm squares.

Conversions

Convert the metric dimensions to inch dimensions. Round the inch dimensions to the closest ¹⁄₁₆ inch.

mm	in.
9.5	
12.5	
19	
36.5	
44.5	
51	
77	
120	
127	
150	
168.5	
178	

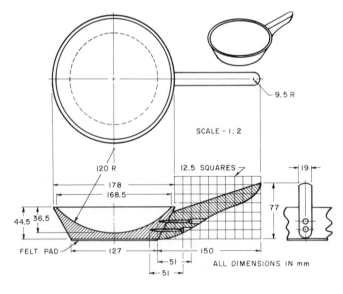

Skillet-Style Nut Bowl.

Answers

Drawing Dimensions

1. 178
2. 127
3. 44.5
4. 120
5. 19
6. 150
7. 12.5

Conversions

9.5 mm (⁶⁄₁₆ inch); 12.5 mm (⁸⁄₁₆ inch); 19 mm (¹²⁄₁₆ inch); 36.5 mm (1⁷⁄₁₆ inches); 44.5 mm (1¹²⁄₁₆ inches); 51 mm (2 inches); 77 mm (3 inches); 120 mm (4¹²⁄₁₆ inches); 127 mm (5 inches); 150 mm (5¹⁴⁄₁₆ inches); 168.5 mm (6¹⁰⁄₁₆ inches); 178 mm (7 inches).

Math Quiz

Dual Dimensioning

The drawing in Fig. B is **dual dimensioned.** The customary (inch) dimensions are the primary dimensions. The metric (millimetre) dimensions are the secondary dimensions. If the metric dimensions are to be rounded, the ½-inch thickness dimensions can be rounded up to 13 mm. However, it is better to convert this dimension to 12 mm since lumber thickness tends to be undersized. Referring to the drawing, answer the questions below. Answer the questions on a separate sheet of paper. Do not write in this book.

1. The overall size of the top is:
   A. Thickness _____ in; _____ mm
   B. Width _____ in; _____ mm
   C. Length _____ in; _____ mm

2. The thickness of the braces is _____ in.; _____ mm.
3. The radius of the arc on each leg is _____ in.; _____ mm.
4. The dadoes on the underside of the top are _____ inches from the end.
5. The chisel used to trim the dado will be exactly ½ inch in width. Therefore, the dado in metric measurement should be closer to _____ mm than to 12 mm.

Wooden Bench.

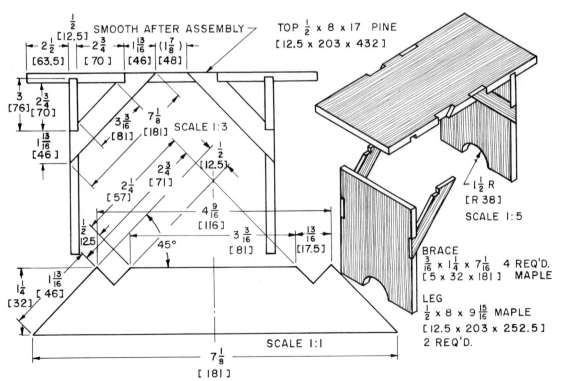

Facts about Wood

Common Fallacies about Wood

A fallacy is a false idea. There are several common fallacies about wood. Eight of these are discussed here. You may already be familiar with some of them.

Fallacy. In the course of time, all wood decays as a result of age.

Wood does not decay merely because it is old. Consider the following examples:

● The White House, when remodeled in 1949, was found to contain sound timbers that had been in place since 1816.

● The Fairbanks House, a wood structure in Dedham, Massachusetts, is standing intact after three centuries.

● Timbers several hundred years old have been found in the ruins of Amerindian pueblos in Arizona and New Mexico.

● A part of a Roman emperor's houseboat that sank nearly 2,000 years ago was sound enough to be identified as spruce.

● A log 7 feet in diameter was found during construction of a tunnel beneath the Yakima River in Washington. The wood was identified as an extinct species of sequoia. Geologists estimate that it was buried 12 million years ago.

These five examples prove that wood does not necessarily decay with age. Decay is the result of one thing only—the attack of wood-destroying fungus. A fungus is a plant. In each of the examples mentioned, the wood had been kept free of fungus attack in one of two ways. The wood had been kept dry, or it had been kept thoroughly and permanently saturated. If the wood is too dry for fungus to grow and spread, decay does not occur. Thorough saturation of wood also prevents the growth of fungus.

Fallacy. There is such a thing as dry rot of wood.

Any brown, crumbly rot is called dry rot. The term is not really correct. No fungus can grow without water. A fungus will feed on wood and destroy it. Wood is, then, a food for fungus. Fungus cannot use that food unless the wood contains at least 20 percent water. Some wood-destroying fungi can remain dormant in dry wood for years. If revived by moisture, they will continue their destructive work.

Fallacy. In a fire, a building supported by wood timbers will collapse before one supported by steel beams.

Wood, when exposed to fire temperatures, will burn and be converted to charcoal. Steel does not burn under similar conditions. When used in heavy timber construction, though, wood has a great advantage over unprotected steel. In a severe fire, the outside surfaces of thick beams will become charred. However, the core of the wood will remain at a low temperature. Because of its low heat conductivity, the center will remain uncharred and intact. It will retain most of its strength.

Under the same fire conditions, steel will quickly become heated throughout because of its good heat conduction. It will lose much of its rigidity and load-bearing capacity. This permits collapse of a steel-supported structure sooner than one using wood timbers of the same strength. For this reason, steel members are commonly required to be enclosed in concrete or some other protective material.

Fallacy. Oak, hickory, or other heavy hardwood has a higher fuel value than pine.

A cord of hickory weighs more than a cord of pine. A *cord* is a stack of wood 4 × 4 × 8 feet (128 cubic feet). Pound for pound, the pine gives off more heat. In general, resinous woods have a higher heat value per pound than nonresinous. For a quick, hot fire you would use pine.

Fallacy. The sap "rises" in a tree in the spring and "goes down" in the late fall.

Sap is circulating actively in the spring and summer. It is always "up," never "down." When weighed, logs are found to be heavier in the winter than in the spring. This proves that trees have more sap in the inactive season. If the sap were "down," trees could not freeze in winter—as they often do, with a loud crack.

Fallacy. Trees frequently exposed to storms and rough weather form stronger and better wood than sheltered trees.

Trees exposed to high winds and severe weather are apt to be deformed, twisted, and stunted. They will be fit mostly for firewood. Those grown under normal weather conditions provide the best lumber. Such trees are straight, with a regular grain. Their wood is as strong—if not stronger—than that taken from trees grown in the roughest weather.

Fallacy. Wood of a given species grown in one region is superior to that grown in another region.

You may have heard "Michigan maple" compared with "Vermont maple." Tests of more than 600,000 specimens by the Forest Products Laboratory prove that a tree's geographical location does not affect the strength of its wood. Moisture, drainage, and exposure have the greatest effect.

Fallacy. As the tree grows, the limbs rise higher from the ground.

For the limbs to rise, the wood would need to stretch where the limb is attached. Trees simply do not grow that way. In growing, a tree adds a new layer of wood every year. This layer covers the limbs, as well as the trunk. If a limb is now 10 feet from the ground, it will be at that height next year.

Chapter 5

Planning Your Work

After studying this chapter, you will be able to:
- List the three basic steps in planning a project.
- Define a bill of materials.
- Give the formula for finding board feet.
- Describe the method of finding the cost of lumber.

LOOK FOR THESE TERMS

bill of materials
board feet
stock cutting list

Before you begin to work with tools and machines, you must plan carefully the steps you will follow in making the project. Planning is an important part of any successful business. Like good business, you should "plan your work; then work your plan."

PLANNING AN INDIVIDUAL PROJECT

In planning a project, you should find out (1) what materials you need, (2) what tools and equipment are needed, and (3) what steps you will follow and in what order they will be done.

If you fail to plan your work, you may, for example, begin to sand project parts before completing all of the cutting tool operations. This could dull some of your tools. You might also waste lumber by forgetting to make the proper allowance for the joints needed. Many such mistakes can creep into your work.

METHOD OF PROCEDURE

In planning your job, you should first decide on the order in which the parts are to be made. Then list all of the things you will need to do to complete each particular part.

5-1. This corner shelf might be a good beginning project. Note the various parts of the project as you read through the plan of procedure.

5-2. Drawings for the corner box shown in Fig. 5-1.

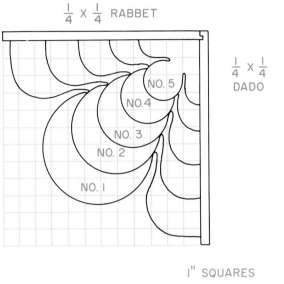

$\frac{1}{4} \times \frac{1}{4}$ RABBET

$\frac{1}{4} \times \frac{1}{4}$ DADO

I" SQUARES

WOOD SCREWS

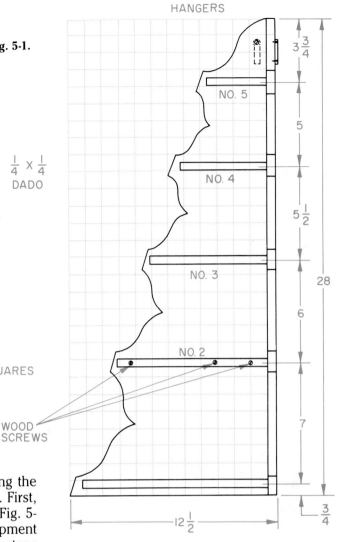

HANGERS

For example, suppose you are making the corner shelf shown in Figs. 5-1 and 5-2. First, decide on all of the materials needed. Fig. 5-3. Then, decide what tools and equipment will be needed. Think through all of the steps in cutting, shaping, fitting, and finishing the project. In written form, this might be as follows on the next page:

5-3. A bill of materials for the corner shelf.

BILL OF MATERIALS

STOCK: Pine

IMPORTANT: All dimensions listed below are FINISHED size.

No. of Pieces	Part Name	Thickness	Width	Length
1	Side	½″	12½″	28″
1	Side	½″	12¼″	28″
1	Shelf 1	½″	11½″	11½″
1	Shelf 2	½″	9¼″	9¼″
1	Shelf 3	½″	7¼″	7¼″
1	Shelf 4	½″	5⅜″	5⅜″
1	Shelf 5	½″	3¾″	3¾″
2	Flat Metal Hangers			
24	1¼″-8 Wood Screws			

CORNER SHELF

Tools and Equipment:

Crosscut saw, ripsaw, backsaw, plane, chisel, coping saw, twist drill, hand drill, scroll saw, rasp, sandpaper, try square, sliding T-bevel, ruler, pencil.

Procedure:

1. Draw patterns for the sides and shelves to full size and transfer to the stock. Cut on a scroll saw or band saw.
2. Smooth all edges by sanding.
3. Lay out and cut a rabbet along the left side for the rabbet-and-dado joint.
4. Lay out and cut the dado along the right side to complete the joint.
5. Glue the two sides together. Fit the shelves to the sides and fasten in place with small screws.
6. Apply the finish.
7. Attach hangers to the back.

This written plan, though not always absolutely necessary, is an excellent idea. You should at least think through each step you will take before you begin to work. In this way you avoid a great deal of trouble. Remember again: "Plan your work; then work your plan."

FINISHED BILL OF MATERIALS

Note the finished bill of materials shown in Fig. 5-3. A *bill of materials* is a complete description of the finished size of each piece of material used in making the project. There is always some waste in making the part. You must allow for this when cutting out the rough stock.

MAKING A STOCK-CUTTING LIST

The finished bill of materials must now be changed into what may be called a *stock-cutting list*. In this list you must add to the thickness, width, and length of the stock to allow for cutting, planing, chiseling, and other operations. Usually 1/16 to 1/8 inch (1.5 to 3 mm) is added to the thickness, 1/4 inch (6.5 mm) to the width, and about 1/2 inch (12.5 mm) to the length.

DETERMINING BOARD FEET OF LUMBER

After you have made a stock-cutting list, figure the number of board feet in each piece or group of identical pieces.

In the customary system of measurement, a board foot of lumber is a piece 1 inch thick, 12 inches wide, and 12 inches long. Fig. 5-4. Stock less than 1 inch thick is figured as 1 inch. Stock more than 1 inch is figured by actual measurement. For example, a piece of stock 1/4 inch × 6 inches × 4 feet would contain 2 board feet of lumber.

The formula used to find board feet is:

$$\text{Bd. Ft.} = \frac{T \times W \times L \text{ (all in inches)}}{144}$$

Board feet equals thickness in inches times width in inches times length in inches divided by 144.

Another formula that can be used is:

$$\text{Bd. Ft.} = \frac{T(\text{inches}) \times W(\text{inches}) \times L(\text{feet})}{12}$$

FIGURING THE LUMBER ORDER

You should make out the stock-cutting list and figure the board feet you need. Then you should decide on the number of pieces of standard size lumber required. Group together all of the pieces made from the same thickness of lumber. Then make an imaginary layout of these pieces on larger standard pieces of stock, as in Fig. 5-5.

5-4. Note the terms included in these drawings. Each piece is one board foot of lumber. The length of the board is always given *with* the grain. The width of the board is given *across* the grain. The *arrises* are the sharp corners where the edges, sides, and ends meet.

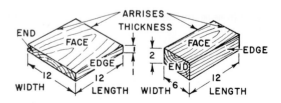

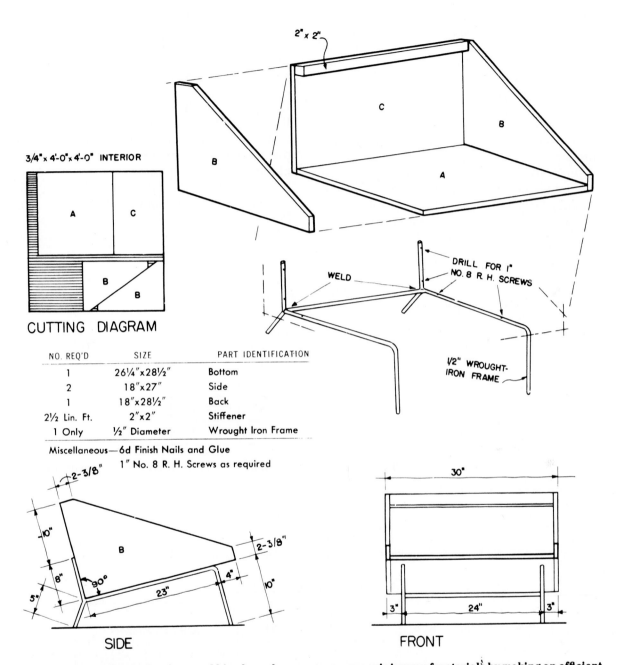

3/4" x 4'-0" x 4'-0" INTERIOR

CUTTING DIAGRAM

NO. REQ'D	SIZE	PART IDENTIFICATION
1	26¼"x28½"	Bottom
2	18"x27"	Side
1	18"x28½"	Back
2½ Lin. Ft.	2"x2"	Stiffener
1 Only	½" Diameter	Wrought Iron Frame

Miscellaneous—6d Finish Nails and Glue
1" No. 8 R. H. Screws as required

2" x 2"

DRILL FOR 1"
NO. 8 R. H. SCREWS

WELD

½" WROUGHT-
IRON FRAME

SIDE

FRONT

5-5. The cutting diagram for the wood bin shows how you can use a minimum of materials by making an efficient layout. This project is made from a 4' × 4' piece of plywood. Plywood is sold by the square foot. How many square feet are needed?

Softwood lumber in the customary system comes in standard widths from 2 to 12 inches, increasing by 2-inch intervals. It comes in standard lengths from 6 to 20 feet, increasing at intervals of 2 feet. Hardwood lumber comes in standard thicknesses. Because of its high cost, it is cut in whatever widths and lengths are most economical and convenient. If you are selecting lumber from a rack, use short pieces first. Cut the lumber as economically as possible. Never waste lumber.

Once you know the number of pieces of standard size lumber needed, you can make a lumber order to obtain the material from a lumber yard. Fig. 5-6. In addition, you will need a list of other supplies. Fig. 5-7.

DETERMINING COST OF LUMBER

When you buy lumber, the price is quoted as so much per board foot, per hundred board feet, or per thousand board feet (M). Fig. 5-7. To find the cost of each item on the rough bill of materials, multiply the number of board feet in each piece or group of identical pieces by the cost per board foot. When the cost of hardware items and finishing materials is listed, all items can be added to find the total cost of materials. Panel stock, including plywood, particle board, and hardboard is sold by the *square foot*. Molding and special pieces are sold by the *linear foot*. Prices vary according to quality.

LUMBER ORDER

No. of Pieces	T	W	L	Kind of Wood	No. of Bd. Ft.	Cost Per Bd. Ft.	Total Cost	Instr's O.K.

5-6. A lumber order. Instead of figuring board feet and the cost for each individual item in the materials bill, determine the size of the boards from which the cutout size pieces can be cut. Then figure the board feet and the cost of the boards.

5-7. A blank form such as the following can be used for ordering supplies such as hardware and finishing materials.

OTHER SUPPLY COSTS

Item	Quan.	Size	Unit Cost	Total Cost	Instr's O.K.	COST SUMMARY
						Lumber Cost _____
						Supply Cost _____
						Total Cost _____
						Less Allow. _____
						Amount Due _____
						Date Paid _____

Review Questions

1. What is a good motto to adopt in starting a project?
2. List the important parts of a plan sheet.
3. What kind of wood is used in the corner shelf?
4. How many different thicknesses of wood are needed to make the corner shelf?
5. How many parts make up the corner shelf?
6. What kind of drawing is shown in Fig. 5-2?
7. Describe a bill of materials.
8. How is the width of stock measured?
9. Is the longest measurement of a piece of stock always the length? Explain.
10. How many board feet of lumber are there in a piece 1½ inches thick, 8 inches wide, and 10 feet long?
11. If lumber costs $200.00 per M, what is the cost of five board feet?

Math Quiz

Figuring Board Feet

Answer the following questions by referring to the bill of materials in Fig. 5-3. Answer the questions on a separate sheet of paper. Do not write in this book.

1. How many board feet are there in the two sides of this project? Assume 10 percent extra for rough size. Remember, stock less than 1 inch is figured as 1 inch.
2. How much wider is shelf 1 than shelf 5?
3. How many square inches are there in the finish size of shelf 3?
4. If wood screws cost 4 cents each, what is the total cost for the wood screws needed?

Answers
1. 5.34 board feet
2. 7¾ inches
3. 52½ in.²
4. 96 cents

Chapter 6

Measurement and Marking Out

After studying this chapter, you will be able to:
- List the three main units in the metric system of measurement.
- Identify the common types of measuring rules.
- Identify the common measuring tools.
- Demonstrate the marking of stock that is to be cut to length.

LOOK FOR THESE TERMS

all-purpose measuring tool	framing square	sloyd knife
bench rule	kilogram	steel tape
bench stop	litre or liter	straightedge
bench vise	level	tape measure
caliper	metre or meter	try square
carpenter's square	metric system	utility knife
center square	sawhorse	vise dog
combination square	scratch awl	zigzag rule
customary system	sliding T-bevel	

CUSTOMARY AND METRIC MEASUREMENT

Noah was indeed a great carpenter. He built his wooden ark 300 cubits long, 50 cubits wide, and 30 cubits high, to hold many people and animals. Even by today's standards, this is a very large wooden ship. A cubit is roughly 18 inches. This means that Noah's ark was 450 feet from stem to stern. Noah built his ark according to instruction but without the aid of the yardstick. It had not yet been invented.

Although we no longer use the cubit as a unit of measure, many present-day standards originated in about the same way. A 1-foot rule started as the length of a man's foot. Since some men had bigger feet than others, the foot varied in length.

In the thirteenth century, King Edward of England had a permanent iron measuring stick made to serve as a master yardstick for the entire kingdom. It was called "the iron." He also decreed that the foot measure should be one-third the length of the yard and that the inch should be one-thirty-sixth.

Over the years, the system of measurement based on inches and pounds developed into what is known as the customary system (also called English, Imperial, or inch-pound). The United States has over 80 units of weights and measures—from pounds to tons and inches to miles.

In 1793, the French government adopted an entirely new system of standards. Called the *metric system*, it was based on what they called the *metre*. Note the spelling. "Metre" is the official spelling, even though "meter" is commonly used. The metre was supposed to be ¹⁄₁₀,₀₀₀,₀₀₀ of the distance from the North Pole to the equator when measured on a line running along the surface of the earth through Paris. When the metre was thus determined, the metric system was set up in decimal ratio. All units are in multiples of 10. There are 10 decimetres in a metre, 100 centimetres in a metre, 1,000 millimetres in a metre. Fig. 6-1.

In 1960, the current SI Metric System was developed. SI means System International. This system consists of seven base units and many derived units. Table 6-A.

Table 6-A. Base Units of the SI Metric System

Quantity	Unit	Symbol
Length	metre	m
Mass	kilogram	kg
Time	second	s
Electric current	ampere	A
Temperature*	degree Celsius	°C
Luminous intensity	candela	cd
Amount of substance	mole	mol

*For scientific work the kelvin scale (symbol K) is used.

6.1 Comparison of the metric and customary units of length measurement.

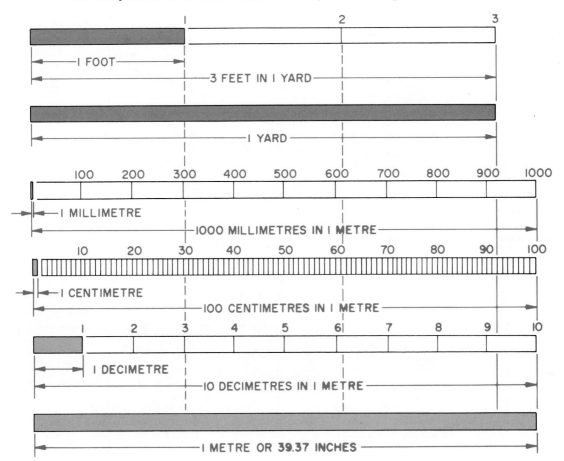

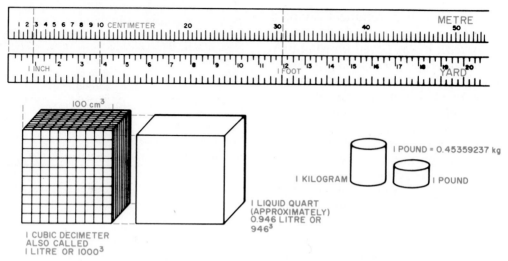

6-2. The three metric units most commonly used in industrial work.

6-3. In the metric system, there is a direct relationship between length, area, volume, liquid capacity, and weight.

LENGTH	AREA	VOLUME	LIQUID CAPACITY	WEIGHT (MASS) OF WATER
1 centimetre (cm)	1 square centimetre (cm²)	1 cubic centimetre (cm³)	1 millilitre (ml)	1 gram (g)
1 decimetre (dm)	1 square decimetre (dm²)	1 cubic decimetre (dm³)	1 litre (ℓ)	1 kilogram (kg)
1 metre (m)	1 square metre (m²) shower stall	1 cubic metre (m³)	Each barrel contains 42 gallons or about 160 litres. 6.25 barrels of oil. 1 kilolitre (kl)	1 tonne 1 metric ton or tonne (t)

6-4. A comparison of the metric rule with the customary rule.

For everyday use, only three metric measurements are important. They are the *metre* for length, the *kilogram* for weight, and the *litre* for volume. These units are fairly easy to remember. The metre is a little longer than the yard (39.37 inches). The kilogram is a little more than twice the pound (2.2 pounds). The litre is a little more than the quart. Fig. 6-2. For everyday use, only three prefixes are needed. They are *kilo* (1000 times the standard unit), *centi* (¹⁄₁₀₀ times the standard unit), and *milli* (¹⁄₁₀₀₀ times the standard unit). Figure 6-3 shows the relationship between the various units.

ACCURACY IN MEASUREMENT

The smallest division on a customary woodworking rule is ¹⁄₁₆ inch. The smallest division on a metric rule is 1 millimetre, or approximately ¹⁄₂₅ of an inch. Fig. 6-4. Remember that one millimetre is smaller than ¹⁄₁₆ inch but larger than ¹⁄₃₂ inch (one of the divisions found on a metal scale). Therefore for most work, you can measure to the nearest millimetre. For example, 1 inch equals exactly 25.4 mm, and 2 inches equals exactly 50.8 mm. You can mark these as 25 mm and 51 mm for most woodworking. However, for accurate work such as making patterns, it is just as easy to estimate distances between the division marks on the metric rule as on the customary rule when fine divisions are required. Therefore you can also mark off 1 inch as 25.5 mm. This will be particularly true when you use a 25-mm chisel to cut a dado, for example. The chisel will actually measure 25.4 mm. For a good fit, the second part of the joint should be finished to 25.5 mm.

The United States is moving towards use of the SI Metric System. Thus, it is important for you to be able to read a rule in both the customary and metric systems. You must also be able to convert liquid measures from pints and quarts to litres and to change weight (or mass) from pounds to kilograms. Some common conversions are given in Table 6-B.

Math Quiz

Refer to Table 6-B. Using the information in the table, solve the following short problems.

1. What is the length of a 14-inch board in millimetres?
2. If a piece of plywood contains 60 square feet, how many square metres is it?
3. If the width of a house measures 30 feet, what is its width in metres?
4. If a project weighs 35 pounds, how many kilograms does it weigh?
5. How many litres are in 8 quarts?

Answers
1. 355.6 mm
2. 5.57 m²
3. 9.14 m
4. 15.8 kg
5. 7.57 L

Table 6-B. Common Conversions

Length	
Customary to Metric	**Metric to Customary**
1 inch = 25.40 millimetres-mm 1 inch = 2.540 centimetres-cm 1 foot = 30.480 centimetres-cm 1 foot = 0.3048 metre-m 1 yard = 91.440 centimetres-cm 1 yard = 0.9144 metre-m	1 millimetre = 0.03937 inch 1 centimetre = 0.3937 inch 1 metre = 39.37 inches 1 metre = 3.2808 feet 1 metre = 1.0936 yards
Area	
Customary to Metric	**Metric to Customary**
1 sq. inch = 645.16 sq. millimetres-mm^2 1 sq. inch = 6.4516 sq. centimetres-cm^2 1 sq. foot = 929.03 sq. centimetres-cm^2 1 sq. foot = 0.0929 sq. metres-m^2 1 sq. yard = 0.826 sq. metre-m^2	1 sq. millimetre = 0.00155 sq. inch 1 sq. centimetre = 0.1550 sq. inch 1 sq. metre = 10.7640 sq. feet 1 sq. metre = 1.196 sq. yards
Mass (Weight)	
Customary to Metric	**Metric to Customary**
1 ounce (dry) = 28.35 grams-g 1 pound = 0.4536 kilogram-kg	1 gram = 0.03527 ounce 1 kilogram = 2.2046 pounds
Volume (Capacity)	
Customary to Metric	**Metric to Customary**
1 pint (liq.) = 0.473 litre = 0.473 cm^3 1 quart (liq.) = 0.9463 litre = 0.9463 dm^{3**} 1 gallon (liq.) = 3.7853 litres = 3.7853 dm^{3**}	1 litre = 1000 cm^{3*} = 0.5283 pint (liq.) 1 litre = 1 dm^{3**} = 1.0567 quarts (liq.) 1 litre = 1 dm^{3**} = 0.26417 gallon (liq.)

*cubic centimetre
**cubic decimetre

MEASURING TOOLS

READING A CUSTOMARY RULE

The most common customary rules are either a foot or a yard long. Each of these rules is divided into major inch divisions. Each inch is divided into either eighths or sixteenths as the smallest measurement. Let's look at a rule and find 1⁄16 inch. Notice that the longest line between 0 and 1 inch is the 1⁄2 inch mark. The next longest line is the 1⁄4 inch mark. The next longest is 1⁄8 inch. The shortest is 1⁄16 inch. Therefore, four-sixteenths (4⁄16) inch equals two-eighths (2⁄8) inch, or one-quarter (1⁄4) inch. Fig. 6-5.

6-5

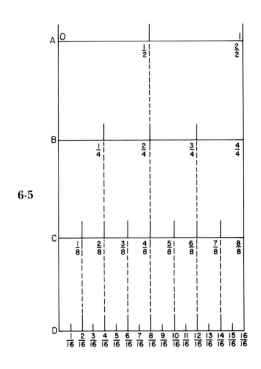

The rules shown in this chapter are shown only as examples. They are not shown actual size.

6-6. A 300-millimetre rule.

English

Metric Centimetre

Metric Millimetre

Metric (Centimetre) — English

6-7. Four forms of rule graduations available on steel tapes.

READING A METRIC RULE

A metric rule is usually available in metre, half-metre, or 300-millimetre lengths. Fig. 6-6. Remember that a metre is divided into 100 centimetres and 1000 millimetres. Generally the rule is marked with the centimetre divisions 1, 2, 3, 4, etc. There are 10 divisions in each centimetre. These divisions divide each centimetre into 10 millimetres. However, a rule with the numbered lines marked in millimetres, such as 10, 20, 30, 40, is easier to use. Remember that in the metric system, accurate measurements are always given in centimetres, millimetres, or metres. Figure 6-7 shows various steel tapes.

Accurate measurement and layout is a very important step to successful woodworking. In making measurements, you must answer these questions: How thick? How wide? How long? What are the angles? What are the diameters and depths? Avoid making mistakes by making sure everything is properly laid out and measured. Fig. 6-8.

6-8. Marking a line across the bottom of a door before cutting. To avoid mistakes, always measure twice before cutting.

6-9. The customary bench rule is 12, 24, or 36 inches long. Sometimes a 3-foot (36-inch) rule is called a yardstick. The rule is graduated in sixteenths of an inch on one side and eighths of an inch on the other. The illustration shows these graduations and larger ones for comparison.

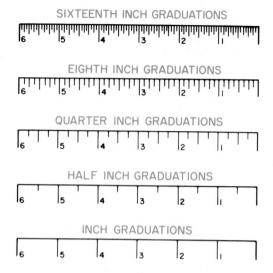

SIXTEENTH INCH GRADUATIONS

EIGHTH INCH GRADUATIONS

QUARTER INCH GRADUATIONS

HALF INCH GRADUATIONS

INCH GRADUATIONS

6-10. One-foot bench rule.

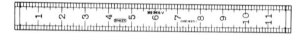

6-11. The top half of this rule is marked in inches and the bottom half in millimetres. It is easy to see that 1 inch is about 25 mm and 2 inches is about 50 mm.

RULES

Short Lengths

Rules are available with three kinds of graduation, namely: *customary* (English), *metric*, or a *metric-customary* combination. For measuring small pieces and marking short distances, use a *bench rule*. A customary rule is wooden, 1, 2, or 3 feet long, with a brass cap at both ends to protect it. Figs. 6-9 and 6-10. The metric rule is available in lengths of 300 millimetres (1 foot), ½ metre, and 1 metre. All metric rules are divided into millimetres. Every tenth millimetre is numbered 10, 20, 30, etc., to show millimetres. The metric-customary rule is usually divided into inches and fractions of an inch on the top half. It is divided into millimetres on the bottom half. Fig. 6-11. The *folding rule* is one that can be folded. A small wood *caliper* can be used to measure round stock conveniently. Fig. 6-12.

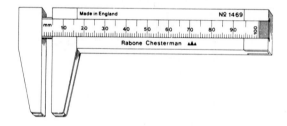

6-12. This wooden caliper is marked in millimetres only.

Rules for Measuring Long Lengths

The *zigzag rule* for long measurements is about 8 inches (203 mm) long when folded. It can be extended to its full length of 6 to 8 feet (2 to 3 m). Fig. 6-13.

Another rule for measuring long dimensions is the *steel tape*. Fig. 6-14. A small catch at its end slips over the end of a board. This makes it easier to pull out the tape. The steel tape has a length of 6 to 12 feet (2 to 4 m).

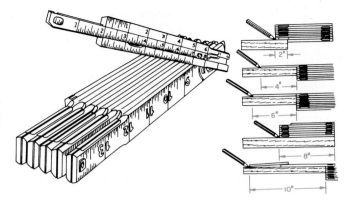

6-13. The zigzag extension rule is useful, mostly to carpenters, in measuring and marking lengths.

6-14. This push-pull steel tape rule is particularly adaptable as a shop rule. It will take inside and outside measurements accurately.

SQUARES

The *try square* has a metal blade and a handle of metal or wood. The blade is marked in eighths of an inch on one side. It is sometimes marked in millimetres on the other. Fig. 6-15.

The *carpenter's square* (framing square) is used in general building work. Fig. 6-16.

The *combination square* has many uses. Most models feature a level and a scratch awl. Fig. 6-17. Its sliding head adjusts for both 45- and 60-degree angle edges. The combination square can be used as a square, marker, or gauge. Fig. 6-18.

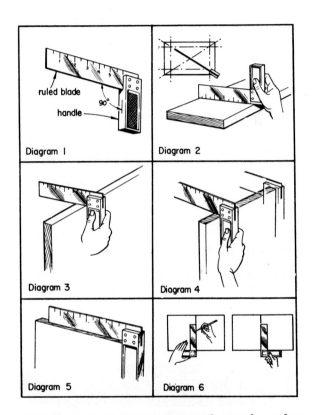

6-15. The parts of the try square and several uses for the square.

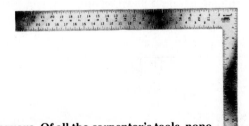

6-16. Carpenter's framing square. Of all the carpenter's tools, none is more nearly indispensable than this steel square. It has a table stamped on the body for figuring rafters. Other squares contain tables for figuring board measurements.

6-17. A combination square is a valuable tool for measuring and marking.

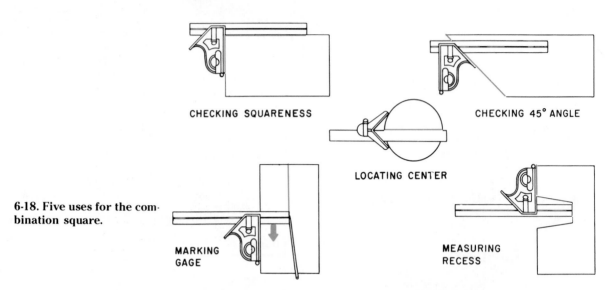

CHECKING SQUARENESS

CHECKING 45° ANGLE

LOCATING CENTER

6-18. Five uses for the combination square.

MARKING GAGE

MEASURING RECESS

OTHER MEASURING TOOLS

Levels have hardwood or aluminum frames. They are used to check true horizontal or vertical surfaces. Fig. 6-19.

6-19. A level is used to make sure the work is level or plumb (straight down or up).

6-20. A center square.

The *center square* can locate the center of any size circle. It can also be used for checking 90-degree measurements and as a protractor. Fig. 6-20.

The *all-purpose measuring tool* can be used as a rule, square, marking gauge, level, protractor, and for several other purposes. Fig. 6-21.

The *sliding T-bevel* is for laying out all angles other than those of 90 degrees. Fig. 6-22. It has an adjustable blade in a handle. To lay out a 45-degree angle, for instance, the adjustable T-bevel can be set with the framing square as shown in Fig. 6-23. To set the tool to such angles as 30 and 60 degrees, the bevel can be checked with the triangles used in drawing. It can also be set by laying out a right triangle with the hypotenuse (the side opposite the 90-degree angle) two units long and one side one unit long. Fig. 6-24. For other angles, the sliding T-bevel can best be set with a protractor. Fig. 6-25. The sliding T-bevel can be used to mark out a wood joint. Fig. 6-26.

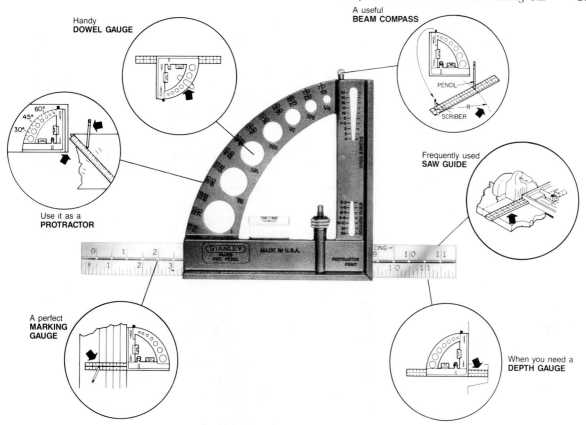

6-21. The all-purpose measuring tool (A) and some of its uses: B. as a marking gauge; C. as a protractor; D. as a dowel gauge; E. as a beam compass; F. as a saw guide; G. as a depth gauge.

6-22. This tool is called a sliding T-bevel. It gets its name from the fact that it can be adjusted to any angle desired. The blade, which slides back and forth in the handle, can be locked in position with a thumbscrew.

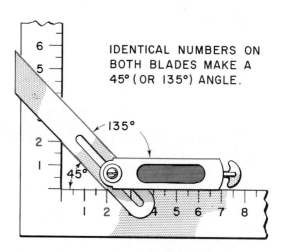

IDENTICAL NUMBERS ON BOTH BLADES MAKE A 45° (OR 135°) ANGLE.

6-23. A method of setting the sliding T-bevel by using a steel square. This shows the bevel set at an angle of 45 degrees.

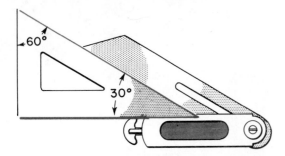

6-24. **Using a triangle to set a sliding T-bevel. By drawing a right triangle with the hypotenuse two units long and one leg one unit long, you have a triangle with 30- and 60-degree angles.**

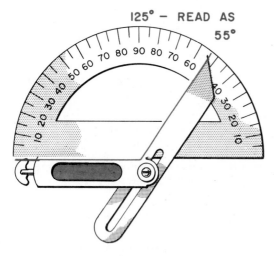

6-25. **Setting a sliding T-bevel by using a protractor. Any angle can be quickly and accurately established.**

6-26. **Using a sliding T-bevel to mark out a wood joint.**

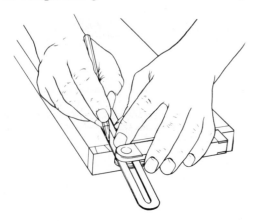

MARKING TOOLS

An ordinary *lead pencil* is the most common marking tool. Its mark can be seen easily on both rough and finished lumber. The mark is easy to remove, and the pencil does not scratch or mar the wood surface. Use a pencil with a rather hard lead for laying out fine, accurate lines. Keep the pencil sharpened in the shape of a chisel so the point can be held directly against the edge of the rule or square.

A *knife* is a good tool for very accurate marking. Fig. 6-27. Be careful, however, to use it only when you know that the mark will disappear as the wood is cut, formed, or shaped.

A *sloyd knife* is used for marking. Fig. 6-28. This is a very handy tool. It can be used for trimming a fine edge, slicing a piece of thin veneer, and whittling a small peg.

The *scratch awl*—a thin metal-pointed tool with a wooden handle—is good for marking and punching the location of holes to be drilled or bored. Fig. 6-29.

6-27. **The layout and cutting knife. This type has a blade that slides into the handle.**

6-28. **The sloyd knife is excellent for layout work and also for cutting, trimming, and whittling. This knife was so named because it was used in the sloyd system of teaching. This system was developed in Sweden.**

6-29. **The scratch awl is another layout tool that is very handy. It is used to lay out the positions for drilling and boring holes.**

HOLDING DEVICES

For good work, you must have a solid workbench with a sturdy bench vise. Figs. 6-30 and 6-31. The *bench vise* holds work to be cut, formed, or shaped. Line the metal jaws with wood inserts to protect the pieces to be clamped. The movable jaw of the vise has a small, sliding section called a *vise dog*. This, with a *bench stop*, can be placed in holes across the top of the bench. It is used for holding long, flat pieces of stock when planing, cutting, forming, or shaping. Fig. 6-32.

When handling large pieces for layout, sawing, and assembling, one or two wood sawhorses are needed. They should be about 20 inches (508 mm) high. The best kind to have is one like that shown in Fig. 6-33. Such a sawhorse is open down the center.

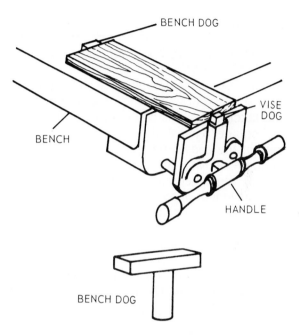

6-32. Use a vise dog and bench dog to hold the workpiece.

6-30. A sturdy woodworking bench is a requirement for doing good work. There are four bench vises on this table, one on each corner.

6-31. This excellent workbench has two vises, one on the side and the other on the end.

6-33. This kind of sawhorse is most practical for layout and cutting. Because it is open down the center, the sawing can be done with the blade free to move down the center of the opening.

MEASURING AND MARKING STOCK

● *Measuring thickness.* Check the lumber for thickness, width, and length. Measure the thickness of the lumber by holding the rule over the edge. Find the thickness by reading the two lines on the rule that just enclose the stock. Fig. 6-34.

● *Measuring width.* Measure the width by holding the left end of the rule (or the inch mark) on one edge of the stock. Slide your thumb from right to left along the rule until the width is shown. Fig. 6-35.

● *Measuring short lengths.* Select the end of the stock from which the measurement is to be taken. Check its squareness by holding a try square against the truest edge. Make sure that the end is not split or checked. If it is, square off and cut the end of the wood. Take the measurement from the sawed end. If a short length of stock is needed, hold the rule on edge. Mark the length with a pencil or knife. Fig. 6-36.

● *Measuring long lengths.* For measuring long stock, use a zigzag rule or a steel tape. This will eliminate measuring errors that come from moving a short rule several times. Fig. 6-37. Make a small mark at the point to be squared.

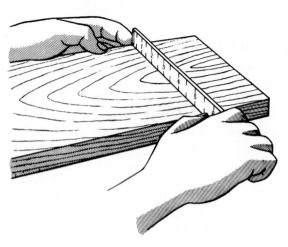

6-35. Checking the width of stock. The rule is held on edge for more accurate measurement. The left end of the rule is held even with the left side of the board with the forefinger of the left hand. The thumb is slid along the rule until the correct width is indicated.

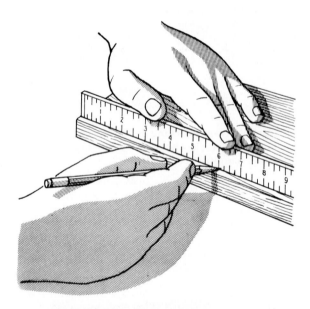

6-36. For measuring short lengths, place the end of the rule directly over the end of the stock, with the rule on edge. Then mark the correct length with a pencil.

6-34. Checking the thickness of stock with a bench rule. One end of the rule is held directly over one end, and the thumb is slid along until the thickness of the stock is shown.

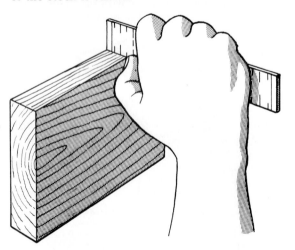

6-37. Using a steel tape to measure long lengths. This procedure is more accurate than using a short rule. With a short rule there is always the possibility of mistakes. A steel tape is especially convenient because the metal hook on the end can be dropped over the end of the stock and the tape drawn out easily to length.

6-38. Using a pencil to mark across the face of stock. Make sure it is sharpened to a point so it will make a thin, accurate line on the wood surface.

6-39. On wide stock the framing square is used to mark the line. The blade is tipped slightly and is held firmly against the edge of the stock as the knife marks across the face of the work.

MARKING STOCK FOR CUTTING TO LENGTH

● *Marking lengths on narrow lumber.* If rather narrow lumber must be marked for cutting, hold the handle of the try square firmly against the truest edge of the stock. Square off a line. Fig. 6-38.

● *Marking lengths on wide lumber.* Use a framing square on wide stock. The framing square is uniform in thickness. Therefore tip the blade slightly. Then hold it firmly against the truest edge while you make the mark across the stock. Fig. 6-39. To be sure of trueness, square a line across the edges with the face line.

● *Marking duplicate parts.* If a group of pieces must be measured and marked out to equal lengths, place them side by side. Make sure that the ends are lined up by holding a try square to correct length to mark the pieces. Fig. 6-40.

6-40. Frequently, several pieces of the same length are needed. It is easier and more convenient to mark them at the same time as shown here. Hold the try square over the ends to align them before marking the correct length.

MEASURING AND MARKING STOCK FOR CUTTING TO WIDTH

Decide on the width of stock you need. Hold the rule at right angles to the truest edge of the stock. Measure the correct width. This can also be done with a try square or combination square. Do this at several points along the stock. Then hold a straightedge over these points and connect them. You can also use a framing square to measure the width of stock needed.

DIVIDING A BOARD INTO EQUAL PARTS

To divide a board into two or more equal parts, hold a rule at an angle across the face of the stock until the inch marks evenly divide the space. Fig. 6-41. For this work, the board must be true along both sides.

6-41. The proper method of dividing a board into several equal parts. This piece, which is 3 5/8 inches wide, is divided into four parts. The end of the rule is held over one edge of the board and the rule shifted at an angle until the 4-inch mark is over the other edge. Then by placing a mark at the 1-, 2-, and 3-inch marks, the board is divided equally into four parts. This same technique can be used with a metric rule.

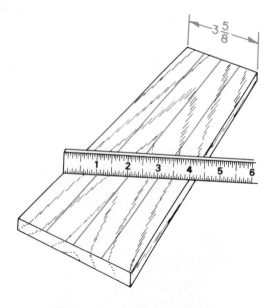

Review Questions

1. How long is a cubit?
2. Describe the two major systems of measurement.
3. What are the three major measurements used in the metric system? How do these measurements compare in size to the customary units?
4. Is a millimetre larger or smaller than $\frac{1}{16}$ inch?
5. In the term "SI metric," what does "SI" stand for?
6. Name two rules used for measuring short lengths.
7. For measuring long lengths, why is it better practice to measure with a zigzag rule or steel tape than with a bench rule?
8. Name one use of the center square.
9. Name three uses for the combination square.
10. Name four uses for the all-purpose measuring tool.
11. What kind of knife is best for marking wood before making a fine cut?
12. How many sixteenths of an inch are in $1\frac{1}{4}$ inches?
13. Why is the bench vise frequently lined with wood inserts?
14. To secure the most accurate measurement, should the rule be held flat or on edge?
15. Describe the method of dividing a board into equal parts.

Chapter 7

Safety

After studying this chapter, you will be able to:
● Identify the general and specific safety rules that must be followed in the workplace.
● Identify the purpose of the federal Occupational Safety and Health Act.

LOOK FOR THESE TERMS

OSHA
safety pledge card

START RIGHT, WORK RIGHT

First, think of the place in which you work as your laboratory. Fig. 7-1. Everyone working has an equal responsibility to see that the tools and machines are used correctly. If you don't, the others won't either. Then, the wood technology lab will not be a suitable workplace.

In carrying out the procedures, you learn to work accurately and correctly. The best way to complete a project and develop good woodworking skills is to do everything correctly. When you come into the laboratory, treat it as your own.

When you are taught to do a mechanical job properly, do not try to do it differently later. It is learning the hard way if you let a piece of wood kick back from a circular saw and strike you in the stomach. It is no joke to see a fellow student lose several fingers because he or she has tried to plane a piece that was too small on a jointer. In the school laboratory we learn by doing. Learning by doing means doing the job correctly.

DRESS CORRECTLY

For everything that you do, whether it is skating, playing baseball, or working, the right clothes should be worn. In the laboratory, you should remove all extra clothing, such as coats, sweaters, and jackets. Roll up your sleeves and put on a lab apron. Fig. 7-2.

7-1. Follow safety rules in all woodworking activities.

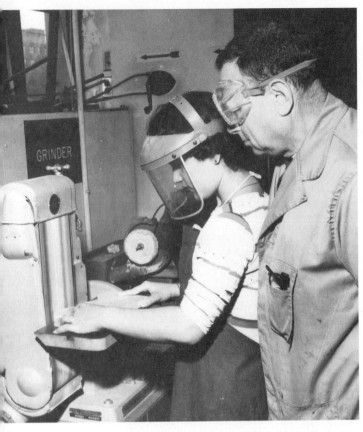

7-2. Each machine is designed for a specific job. Make sure you learn to use tools correctly and safely. Always wear the proper safety protection.

7-3. Use safety guards and wear eye protection when operating all machines.

The lab apron will protect your clothes from dust, paint, and dirt. Following these suggestions will help prevent accidents. Nothing is more likely to cause an accident than a loose sleeve hanging over a machine.

If your hair is long, tie it back. Make sure that it does not fall loosely where it can catch in a revolving machine. Also, wear approved eye protection for safety at all times while in a laboratory, except in safe areas designated by your instructor. Fig. 7-3.

DOING YOUR SHARE

Keeping up a laboratory requires cooperative effort. Everyone must do his or her part to maintain a safe and well-kept lab. Here are some of the things you can do:

● Pick up small pieces of wood on the floor and throw them in the waste box. Some student may turn an ankle on them.

● Keep the aisles clear by placing projects in their proper places.

● Keep your tools properly arranged on your bench. Don't allow sharp-pointed tools to stick out.

● Keep oil wiped up from the floor. Oil may cause a bad fall.

● Don't walk up behind a student who is working on a machine. He or she may be startled and move suddenly. If someone is using a machine, wait until he or she is finished.

● Be willing to sign a safety pledge card. A *safety pledge card* is your signed promise to use safe work habits. Your instructor provides this card to protect you, himself or herself, and your fellow students.

● Know the fire regulations in your laboratory. The woodworking laboratory is one of the places most likely to have a blaze. This is because wood dust and finishing materials present a fire hazard. Dust in the air can cause an explosion. Fig. 7-4. Such dust can be ignited by a spark from a loose wire on a piece of electrical equipment. The finishing room is a particularly dangerous place. The solvents used in applying finishes form a vapor. This vapor ignites easily and can cause an explosion.

7-4. This laboratory has a good exhaust system that will aid in keeping it clean and safe.

BE ATTENTIVE

Not many accidents occur in school woodworking labs. Each year, however, some students are injured. *Every one of these accidents can be prevented.* All of them occur because someone does something carelessly or incorrectly. To help prevent accidents, you should:

● Carefully watch your instructor's demonstrations on how to use each tool and machine. Fig. 7-5.

● Get your teacher's permission before using a power machine. Fig. 7-6. You may not be ready to use power machinery, so don't try it until you are. The machines may look harmless, but they are far from it.

7-6. Your instructor will want to check your use of all machines and tools to make sure you know how to operate them correctly.

7-5. Always follow good safety practices that your instructor has demonstrated.

AN OUNCE OF PREVENTION

Even when you are working correctly with tools and machines, small accidents can happen. The most common are slight cuts and bruises, a sliver in the finger, minor burns, and getting something in the eye. While none of these may be serious, they all *can* be. A sliver, for example, can cause blood poisoning. Your eyes can be permanently damaged if the injury is not treated immediately. Get immediate first aid from a nurse or doctor.

In the laboratory or on the job, you will be handling many different materials, including lumber, screws and nails, and unfinished projects. You should learn to handle them correctly.

When carrying lumber, be careful not to pinch your fingers. Always make sure that the lumber is kept in a neat pile. Poorly stacked lumber is dangerous.

Don't carry screws and nails in your mouth! You might swallow them. There is also danger of infection when you do this.

Store your project neatly. Never place it high on a locker or window ledge. It might fall and hurt someone. If you have a large finished project or a machine that should be moved, lift it correctly. There is danger of rupture from improper lifting.

HANDLING TOOLS

Many of the tools in the wood laboratory have sharp cutting edges. These tools are used for marking, shaping, and cutting stock. These tools can cause accidents. Some rules to follow are:

● Never carry pointed tools in your pockets.

● Always grind off a mushroom (flattened) head.

● Always cut and chisel *away* from yourself.

● Never use tools with loose handles. Fig. 7-7.

● Always carry cutting tools with the sharp edge down.

● Use tools for the proper purpose. Fig. 7-8.

In working with machines and hand tools, follow the instructions given in the units that follow. Always remember that the correct way is the safe way.

CAN YOU QUALIFY?

Before you are licensed to drive a car, you must be a certain age. You must also have received instructions and passed certain tests. These requirements protect you and others. The same rules apply to those working in the woodworking laboratory. You cannot expect to use power machinery until you are old enough to use it safely. You must also show that you know how to use the machine safely and correctly. You may have to prove your ability in a performance test. In this book you will find safety rules for using each machine.

The following general safety rules apply to the operation of power machinery. Specific safety rules for each machine are given later in this book.

7-7. Check your tools to see that the handles are in good condition. Cracked or rough handles on saws, chisels, planes, and gouges can cause blisters. These may become infected. Also, it is irritating to work with a tool that has a rough handle. You cannot do a good job with a poor tool.

7-8. In working with tools and power machinery, wear good eye protection.

⚠ General Safety Rules

- Secure approval from your instructor for all work that you plan to do.
- Never use any tool or machine on which you have not been properly instructed.
- Keep the lab clean and well organized.
- Keep the surface of large machines free from hand tools, scrap wood, sawdust, and oil.
- Keep all cutting tools sharp.
- Wear goggles or safety glasses.
- Do not wear any jewelry.
- Do not wear loose-fitting clothes. Wear short sleeves or roll up long sleeves. If you wear long sleeves, make sure they are fitted and buttoned at the cuffs.
- Keep hair away from moving parts. Wear a hair net if hair is too long.
- Keep all guards and other safety equipment in place and operating correctly.
- Report all injuries to your instructor.
- Fill out accident reports on all injuries.
- Know where to find first aid.
- Never leave a running machine unattended.
- Do not allow horseplay or roughhousing in the woodworking laboratory.

OCCUPATIONAL SAFETY AND HEALTH ACT

In April, 1971, the Congress of the United States made the federal Occupational Safety and Health Act (OSHA) an official part of the national labor law. The purpose of this law is ". . . to assure so far as possible every working man and woman in the nation safe and healthful working conditions and to preserve our human resources."

This law affects all employees in the woodworking trades where one or more workers are employed. For an individual employed in woodworking, it is just as important to develop the safe work attitudes and habits outlined by this law as it is to develop the skills of the trade. Employers are looking for people with these traits, for their benefit and welfare as well as yours. Thus it is important to know and follow safety rules.

Review Questions

1. Who is responsible for taking care of the tools and machines?
2. Why is the right attitude important before beginning to work?
3. Describe the proper clothes for the woodworking lab.
4. Why can long hair be dangerous in the workplace?
5. List five things you can do to keep the lab in order.
6. What causes most accidents?
7. List three rules to follow when using sharp cutting tools.
8. What is the purpose of OSHA?

SAFETY IS
- a habit.
- an attitude towards your work.
- planning your work—then working your plan.
- following directions.
- taking precautions.
- thinking ahead.
- learning to use tools and machines correctly.
- doing the job the right way.
- not being careless.

CAUTION

EYE PROTECTION REQUIRED

WARNING!!!

THIS COULD BE THE LAST THING YOU EVER READ

WEAR EYE PROTECTION!

Chapter 8

Careers

After studying this chapter, you will be able to:
- List seven steps that can help you identify a career choice.
- Identify the three major career levels in the wood industry.

LOOK FOR THESE TERMS

architect
apprentice
cabinetmaker
carpenter
forester
industrial technology teacher

interior designer and
   decorator
millwright
model maker
patternmaker
technician

It is not too early to begin to decide on a career. Even while you are still in school, you can gather information on a job that you think you might like. Many careers in construction, manufacturing, business, and sales require a knowledge of woodworking.

1. Refer to the *Occupational Outlook Handbook*. This book is published every two years by the U.S. Department of Labor. This book is available in your library.
2. Make the most of your school experience. Talk to your teachers or school counselor about which courses you should take. Choose specific courses related to the occupation you're considering. For example, if you are interested in becoming a carpenter, enroll in courses in woodworking and construction.
3. Broaden your learning outside of school. If a certain job interests you, read about it at the public library.
4. Develop your social and leadership skills. Become a member of the Vocational Industrial Clubs of America (VICA). Try to obtain a summer job. Fig. 8-1.

8-1. A job in the construction industry is a good way to find out if you like this kind of work.

5. Take vocational tests. These tests can alert you to your strong points. They also inform you of your weaknesses. This is valuable information. It can help you find the job for which you are best suited.

6. Learn how to fill out employment application forms properly. Filling out these forms is a necessary part of getting a job. The forms tend to be standard. Obviously, you will have a better chance for a job if your application is complete, legible, and accurate.

7. Develop job contacts. Talk to neighbors and relatives about their jobs. Of course, you should seek advice from your school counselor. Let these people know in advance about your job interests. They can then advise and help you more effectively. Find out about job opportunities in your community. Knowledge of the local job market can help you make your own plans. The offices of union locals can offer information. You can also check with the state employment service. The newspaper classified ads can sometimes indicate the skills needed in a community.

8-2. Many people in business and sales, including those who sell machinery, need to know about woodworking.

CHOOSING A CAREER

Finding a job you really like to do is one of the most important considerations in choosing a career. Here are some questions to ask yourself in that connection.

1. *Do I have the ability?* It is one thing to like a line of work—but it is another to be able to participate in it. Find out about your basic abilities by taking the courses and participating in the activities. You may want to share in technological advance. However, you may not be able to master the requirements for a professional career. Then, perhaps, you might want to consider becoming a technician.

2. *If I have the ability, do I also have the interest?* Ability, interest, and enthusiasm are essential if a person is to build a truly rewarding and successful career. There are many people with the necessary ability who would be miserable doing the work of an engineer. Such people will be happier—and will probably do more for themselves—if they go into some other line of work.

OPPORTUNITIES IN INDUSTRY

Many people work in and around forests and sawmills where logs are converted into rough lumber. Others are employed in the grading and seasoning of lumber. Many other workers are also needed to move lumber from the forest to the mill and from the mill to the factory.

In processing plants, people are needed to convert lumber into plywood, hardboard, particle board, and other manufactured products. The furniture and housing industries provide thousands of job opportunities. Workers in these and other industries use woodworking machines. Fig. 8-2.

Assembling and finishing operations supply jobs for many. The sash-and-door and box-making industries, for example, offer jobs of this type. Maintenance work is also important. Millwrights are needed to keep woodworking machines in good condition.

8-3. Carpenters make up the largest group of workers in the building construction industry.

8-4. You can learn to be a carpenter. With a skilled trade, you can always find a good job wherever you may want to live.

CAREER LEVELS

Throughout the wood industry, three major career levels are open to you. They are (1) craftspeople, (2) technicians, and (3) professionals. As you read about these three levels, think about which jobs appeal to you the most.

CRAFTSPEOPLE

Craftspeople have the knowledge and skill needed to build with wood. They build houses and furniture, for example. About 27 percent of the 10,000,000 workers employed as craftspeople and supervisors work in the construction trades. There is a need for approximately 46,000 new craftspeople each year. Construction craftspeople include such skilled workers as carpenters, bricklayers, electricians, and plumbers. Are you familiar with any of the skilled occupations that follow?

A *carpenter* is a person who builds or repairs wooden structures. Carpenters comprise the largest single group of craftspeople in the building trades. They number about one million. Fig. 8-3. Even though some housing is factory-built, there is still a great need for skilled carpenters. You can learn to be a carpenter by becoming a carpenter's helper. Here you will learn the trade informally by working with experienced carpenters. Still another method is to prepare in a trade vocational school. A small number of people complete a four-year apprenticeship in the trade. Fig. 8-4. The carpenter must have a knowledge of commercial and home construction. Carpenters are usually divided into two groups: the rough carpenter who does the basic framing and the finish carpenter who does the exterior and interior trim.

The *cabinetmaker* is a highly skilled woodworker. He or she may work as a finish carpenter. He or she may be involved in building kitchen cabinets, making furniture, or in remodeling. Fig. 8-5.

8-5. A cabinetmaker must be able to work carefully and precisely. A cabinetmaker uses all types of hand and machine tools.

The *millwright* takes care of the machinery in a plant and does repair work, resharpening of tools, and similar jobs. He or she must have a thorough knowledge of the construction and operation of all woodworking machines and be able to make machine setups.

Patternmakers make wood or metal patterns of the shapes needed for production. They must know and understand foundry work and how patterns are made.

Model makers build models for manufacturing and construction for such products as airplanes and buildings.

TECHNICIANS

The *technician* converts theories and ideas to products and processes. A technician works on a team with professional personnel and skilled craftspeople. Technicians hold many important jobs in manufacturing, building construction, and the lumber industry.

The technician is a graduate of a one- or two-year technical institute or community junior college. Two-year technical programs are available in many fields related to woodworking. These fields include forestry, building construction, model building, and manufacturing. Certain jobs, such as a real estate broker, can also be secured with technical training. Drafters are technicians. There are many opportunities to work in architectural drafting, furniture production, manufacturing, and other areas. Fig. 8-6. About one-third of a million drafters are now employed. About 16,000 new drafters are needed each year.

8-6. Computer skills are needed by many people who work in building construction. This person is using a computer to develop a list of materials needed to build a house.

PROFESSIONALS

The *professional* has a college degree in an area such as forestry, engineering, architecture, industrial technology, or industrial education. There are many professional opportunities available if you can secure a college degree and, in some cases, take graduate work. Are you familiar with the positions described here?

Foresters work for private owners of timber land and forest product industries, as well as for the federal government. A *forester* is a person trained to develop and care for forests. There are about 25,000 foresters now employed. There is a need for about 1,000 new foresters each year. Fig. 8-7.

Architects plan and design buildings and other structures. They work with other professionals such as engineers and landscape architects in designing buildings that are a part of major developments. There are about 34,000 registered architects. About 1,000 new ones are needed each year. Architecture is a very demanding profession. The architect must be an artist, an engineer, and a businessperson—all in one.

Interior designers and decorators do creative work to enhance the attractiveness of homes and other buildings. Designers and decorators plan the functional arrangement of interior space. They coordinate the selection of fabrics, draperies, and other materials to provide for a pleasant setting. There are about 80,000 people employed in interior designing and decorating. Fig. 8-8.

Industrial education teachers help students develop manual skills and familiarity with machines. These teachers are included in a group of approximately 100,000 industrial arts, vocational, and technical teachers. Fig. 8-9. At least one-third of these teach woodworking and building construction either full or part time. There will be a need for about 20,000 new industrial education teachers a year.

8-7. Foresters learn about the growing and harvesting of trees. They receive their instruction through classroom sessions and on-the-job training.

8-8. This designer is helping a customer choose fabric to cover a chair.

SELECTING AND PREPARING FOR A CAREER

In considering a career in woodworking, you should realize a few facts. Many of these jobs require that you work in noisy and somewhat dusty surroundings. In some jobs, you will be exposed to the elements. There is also danger of accidents.

All opportunities as a craftsperson offer great satisfaction to you as well as a chance to construct and build. An expert in any of the craft occupations will not only earn a good living but will also be doing a rewarding job. There are many opportunities for advancement. The carpenter, for example, can become a contractor. The patternmaker can become a supervisor.

Do you want to become a technician? If so, you must be willing to spend at least two years in a technical institute or community junior college. You will spend about half your time in classroom studies and the other half in laboratory work. Not all schools offer two-year programs in fields relating to wood and the construction industry. However, there are opportunities to get this kind of program.

To become a professional person, you must be ready to take a four-year college degree program and sometimes a one- or two-year internship beyond this. This, for example, is the program an architect must follow. To succeed in professional schools, you will need to have a good background in mathematics and science. You will need an above-average ability in written and spoken English. Each professional opportunity demands a different kind of personality and preparation. The forester should be interested in working outdoors. The architect must have creative talent, skill in math and science, and an understanding of people. He or she must be able to draw to communicate ideas and designs. If you want to become an industrial technology teacher, you must be interested in working with tools and machines as well as people.

Review Questions

1. Describe the three career levels in woodworking.
2. What is the largest skilled trade area in woodwork?
3. List three professional occupations in which an understanding of woodworking is important.
4. What training does a technician need?
5. What are some of the points to consider in selecting a woodworking trade?

8-9. Industrial education teachers must have a college degree with a teaching certificate.

Thinking about a Career

Carpenter

Ben Hwong is a carpenter who works for a large contractor in a Southwestern city. He has been employed as a carpenter for nearly ten years.

"I took a basic carpentry course in high school," says Ben. "And one summer, I helped my dad in some simple home repairs. I enjoyed the course and the home-repair work. That was in my senior year of high school. It was then that I thought that I might want to work as a carpenter.

"Though I thought about the idea, I still wasn't sure. A few months after graduation, I joined the Army. In the time I was in the Army—I was stationed in Germany—I gave serious thought to what I wanted to do after I got out. It was then that I finally decided to become a carpenter. After I got out, I enrolled in an apprenticeship program. I knew that I could have learned some of the carpenter's skills through on-the-job training. I selected the apprenticeship program, though. Such a program seemed to offer more thorough training. Also, I realized that the number of skills I would learn might depend on the contractor I was working for.

A carpenter's apprenticeship program consists of about 4 years of on-the-job training and 144 hours of related classroom instruction each year. "It was, I think, the on-the-job training that appealed to me," says Ben. "In the Army, I had been a supply room technician. I had hours of classroom instruction, but a good part of my training was on the job. I was in charge of issuing and inventorying helicopter parts.

"The on-the-job training was interesting, especially as I began to feel more comfortable with the skills I was learning. I learned a lot about elementary structural design. I also learned how to do basic carpentry jobs such as form building, rough framing, and finishing—both inside and outside. I think that I liked the on-the-job training more than the classroom instruction. Both, though, were equally valuable."

Classroom instruction in most carpentry apprenticeship programs includes instruction in safety and first aid. Blueprint reading, free-hand sketching, and carpentry techniques also are covered. The relationship between carpentry and other building trades is emphasized.

Many carpenters eventually go into business for themselves as general contractors. Because carpenters learn about the entire construction process in their work, they are well-suited to supervise the entire project.

"I think that I would like to go into business for myself at some point," says Ben. "Right now, I'm not sure when that will be. I know that I need to save more money. Also, I think that I would like to get just a little more experience."

Developing Science, Math, and Reading Skills

**Developing
Science Skills**

Wood—The Renewable Energy Resource

For more than a decade, scientists have been searching for sources of energy to replace fossil fuels. Although estimates by experts vary, it is generally agreed that petroleum and coal reserves will be used up in one to two centuries. Because fossil fuels require millions of years to form, scientists are investigating methods of producing fuels that can develop much more rapidly. These fuels are known as *renewable fuels.*

Today, renewable energy supplies provide approximately 18 percent of the world's energy. These are primarily in the form of water used to produce electricity *(hydroelectric power)* and wood fuel. These supplies also include steam produced in the earth *(geothermal energy)*, energy from agricultural products *(alcohols)*, energy from the sun *(solar energy)*, and energy from the wind. In recent years, all of these have been more widely used.

Currently, wood is the world's most frequently used renewable energy source. For example, both India and the United States burn about the same amount of wood—130 million tons. For India this represents over 25 percent of their total energy use. For the U.S., wood represents only 4 percent of the total fuel consumed. More than 100 million people in the developing nations of Africa and South America cannot get enough wood to cook their food. More than one billion people are meeting fuel needs by overcutting. Thus, they are depleting their wood resources. Many forests are being used up.

Extensive research is now being done to develop extremely fast-growing trees. Such trees will provide a renewable source of energy. Trees that can reach 30 feet in height in 10 years are now being planted. Instead of looking underground for fuel, future generations may be looking for open spaces in which fast-growing trees may be planted and harvested, to be burned as a renewable energy source.

ACTIVITY: Checking the Evaporation of Water from Wood
Materials
Several large freshly cut branches
A twin-pan balance. (This can be obtained from the science department.)

A. Assemble the materials.
B. A tree that is alive has a large amount of moisture in its fibers. If a tree is cut down and then burned shortly thereafter, much of the water is still present. This water is released as steam. To obtain as much heat as possible, firewood should be allowed to dry (or age) for at least a year before being burned. This allows much of its water weight to evaporate.
  1. Cut up a small tree branch with a mass of at least 500 grams. Weigh the pieces on the twin-pan balance. Record the mass.
  2. Allow the sample to dry undisturbed for at least one week, then reweigh. Record its mass. Compare this mass to the original mass. What do you observe? Why did this occur?

Activity One

On pages 13-24, the author introduced you to the many uses of technology in the woodworking industry. In discussing the development of technology, the author organizes the facts *chronologically*. This means that he organizes facts in the order of time. The earliest events are mentioned at the beginning of the discussion. The most recent events are mentioned towards the end.

As the author points out in the opening pages of the chapter, the development of technology—as related to tools—was slow. As the author mentions, the first tools were quite primitive, being made of stone. Note, though, that the author points out that metal tools were made later. These early tools were not designed for special uses. They were designed, then, for a general task such as cutting. For example, an axe would be used to cut wood and shape it in the simplest way. Later, different kinds of woodworking tools were developed for the various specialized trades. When were these tools developed?

Activity Two

The selection of the proper lumber for a project is critical to your success in building that project. On pages 26-27, the author discusses the various types of lumber. For example, he mentions that lumber can be rough or dressed, green or dry, or hardwood or softwood. He also discusses the various grades of lumber. Briefly review the author's comments on the various types of lumber. Using the information he presents, choose a wood for a corner cabinet to be placed in a living room.

Activity Three

On page 59, the author discusses the various types of lines used in a drawing. In particular, the author discusses visible lines, hidden lines, center lines, extension lines, and dimension lines. Review this discussion of the various types of lines. Then, close the book and write a brief explanation of each of the various types of lines. The explanation should be clear enough to enable someone to sketch the line and use it in a drawing.

Reading Plans

The dimensions for the ends and sides of the footstool in Figure A are shown on 1″ squares in the plan in Figure B. The wood is 1″ thick.

How wide are the end pieces?

How high are the end pieces?

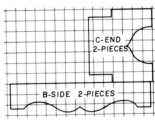

Fig. B.

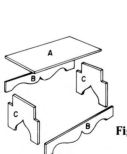

Fig. A.

Section II.

Hand Woodwork

Chapter 9

Cutting Out Rough Stock

After studying this chapter, you will be able to:
- Name the two types of saw used for cutting stock into unfinished pieces.
- Distinguish between points and teeth on a saw blade.
- Demonstrate the sawing of stock to length.
- Demonstrate the cutting of short pieces of stock to width.

LOOK FOR THESE TERMS

crosscut saw   points
kerf   ripsaw

SAWS

A *saw* is a wood-cutting tool that has a thin blade with sharp teeth. Fig. 9-1. For cutting stock into unfinished pieces to either width and/or length you will need a ripsaw or crosscut saw. Sometimes, you will need both.

CROSSCUT SAW

The saw used for cutting across grain is the *crosscut saw*. The teeth of the crosscut saw are shaped like small knife blades. Fig. 9-2. They are bent alternately to right and left.

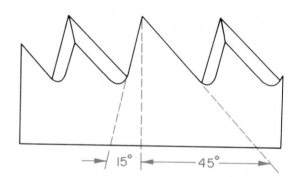

9-2. An enlarged view of a crosscut saw-blade section, showing the knifelike shape of the teeth. The teeth are bent alternately to the left and right. This can be seen when the blade is viewed from the top.

9-1. A high-quality handsaw. It is always wise to buy a good grade. With proper maintenance, such a saw will give years of service. Note the design of the saw handle. Such a grip makes the push-pull action easier.

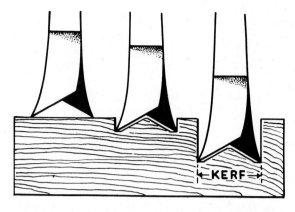

9-3. This illustration shows how the teeth of the saw blade form a kerf that is wider than the blade itself.

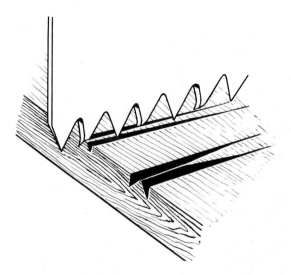

9-4. An example of how a crosscut saw performs its cutting operation. The beginning cut makes two grooves if drawn lightly over the surface.

This is called the "set" of the saw. When you use a crosscut saw with the proper set, the outside edges of the teeth cut the small fibers on either side. The center of the saw then removes these fibers to form the saw *kerf* (the slit or notch made in cutting). Fig. 9-3. The teeth are bent in this way to make them wider than the saw blade itself. This keeps the saw from buckling or scraping. Fig. 9-4.

Crosscut saws come in many different lengths. The easiest size to handle is about 20 to 26 inches (508 to 660 mm) long. If you are cutting rather wet, green wood, use a saw with about five or six points to the inch (25 mm). Note the difference between *points* and *teeth*. Fig. 9-5. There is always one more point to the inch than there are teeth, as you can see in Fig. 9-5. For hard, dry wood, a finer saw with perhaps seven, eight, or nine points to the inch is best.

RIPSAW

The *ripsaw* is used to cut with the grain. Fig. 9-6. It has chisel-like teeth that form the saw kerf by cutting the ends of the fibers. Figs. 9-7 and 9-8. A ripsaw used for ordinary woodworking ought to be 24 to 26 inches long with 5½ points per inch.

9-6. Ripsaw teeth cut like vertical chisels. First, on one side of the set, small pieces of the wood are cut loose across the grain and pushed out. Then, on the other side, the following tooth plows out a similar bit of material.

9-5. Here you see the difference between points and teeth on the saw. There is always one more point to the inch than there are teeth. The fewer the number of points to the inch, the rougher the cut.

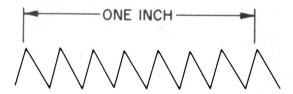

ONE INCH

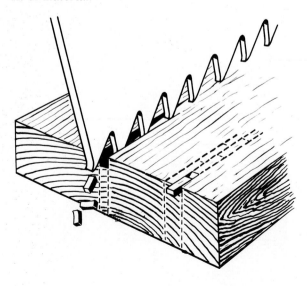

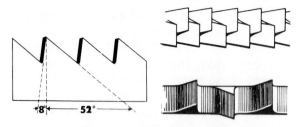

9-7. Ripsaw teeth are designed to cut with the grain. When you look at the edge of a ripsaw, the teeth appear as a series of chisel edges. Note that the teeth are filed straight across.

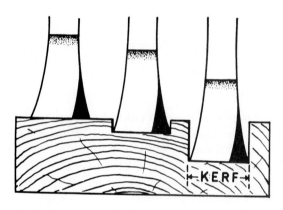

9-8. This shows the chisel-like action of ripsaw teeth.

SAWING STOCK TO LENGTH

Place the stock with the annular rings up (a). This will avoid splintering at the end of the cut. This might happen if the board is placed as shown in (b). Fig. 9-9.

● *Laying out the cutting line.* If the stock must be cut from stock 8 to 16 feet (2.44 to 4.88 m) long, the board should be laid across two sawhorses. Mark the cutting line. Place this point beyond the top of one of the sawhorses. Fig. 9-10.

● *Beginning the cut.* Place your left knee over the board to hold it. Then grasp the handle of the saw with the forefinger straight out on one side of the handle. Clamp the thumb and other fingers tightly around the handle opening. Put your left thumb against the smooth surface of the blade to guide the saw in starting. Fig. 9-11. Start the saw near the handle and draw up on it to begin the kerf. Hold the saw at an angle of about 45 degrees to the stock. Fig. 9-12. Make sure the cut is started just outside the measuring line. This will keep the kerf in the waste stock. Fig. 9-13.

● *Precautions to take in beginning the cut.* If you begin the cut on the downward stroke, the saw may jump out of place to cut your hand or nick the wood. Therefore draw up on the saw once or twice before you begin the cutting. When cutting, establish a steady, even movement. Do not force the saw. If it is sharpened properly, its own weight is enough to make the saw cut correctly.

9-9. The correct way of placing the stock on the sawhorse is shown in *a*.

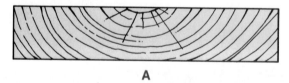

A

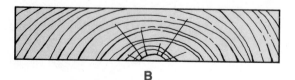

B

9-10. If long stock is to be cut, place it over two sawhorses with the cutting line extending just beyond one of the horses. Never try to make a cut between the supports.

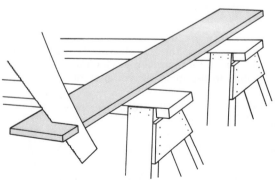

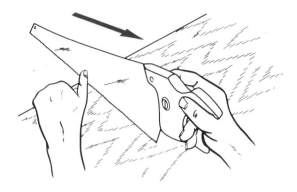

9-11. Starting a cut. Hold your thumb against the smooth surface of the blade. Draw the saw toward yourself slowly and carefully for several strokes. A slight groove will be formed. After the cut is started, take long easy strokes using light pressure on the push stroke. To start a cut when ripping, make short forward thrusts.

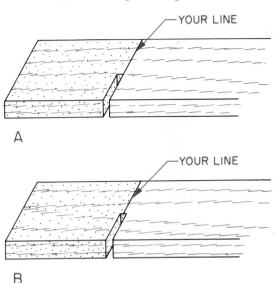

9-13. When cross-cutting stay on the waste side of the line, as shown in A. Never cut on the line, as shown in B. This will result in a board that is too short.

9-12. Hold the crosscut saw at an angle of about 45 degrees to the stock.

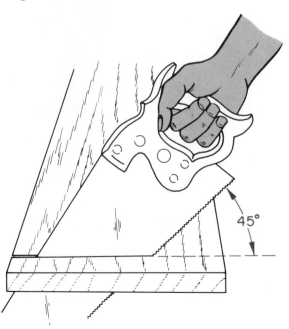

● *Making the cut.* Make sure that you are cutting square with the surface of the board. If you are a beginner, you should hold a try square against the side of the saw blade to check it. Fig. 9-14. As you saw, watch the line and not the saw itself. Blow the sawdust away from the line so you can see it. If the saw starts to go wrong, twist the handle slightly to get it back on the line. When you have cut almost through the board, hold the end of the board to be cut off while you make the last few cuts. This will keep the board from splitting off before the saw kerf is complete. Fig. 9-15.

CUTTING SHORT PIECES OF STOCK TO LENGTH

Before cutting short lengths of stock, place them in a vise. Fig. 9-16. Place the stock in the vise in a flat position with the cutting line extending slightly from the left side of the vise. Hold and start the saw in the same way as previously described. You will do a good job if you follow these directions.

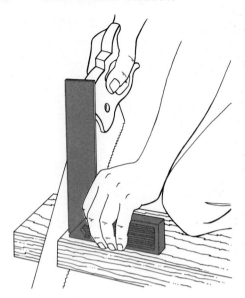

9-14. A way to keep the saw cut square with the face of the board. Place the handle of the try square firmly on the face of the wood. Then slide it along until the blade of the try square contacts the blade of the saw.

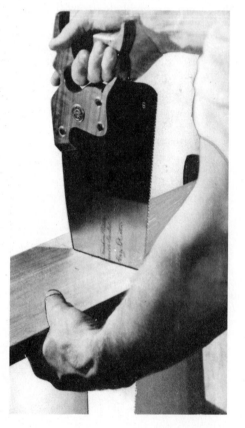

9-15. Taking the last few cuts in sawing off a board. Notice that you should hold the stock to be cut off in one hand while sawing with the other. In this way, the wood will not crack off before the saw kerf is completed.

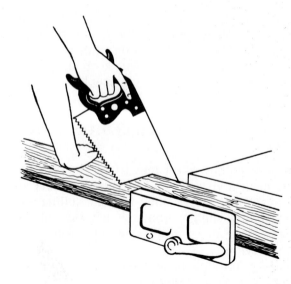

9-16. Cutting stock to length with the work clamped in a vise.

CUTTING LONG PIECES OF STOCK TO WIDTH

Lumber that is too wide must be cut to width. To cut along the grain of the wood, use a ripsaw. Short stock is easily handled, but if the stock is long, place it over two sawhorses. Hold the saw at an angle of about 60 degrees. Fig. 9-17. As you cut a long piece of stock to width, the saw kerf may close in behind the saw. This can cause binding. Fig. 9-18. Placing a small wedge at the beginning of the saw kerf will help keep it open. Move the wedge as you proceed. Fig. 9-19.

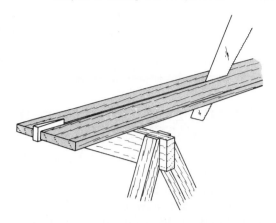

9-19. After a rip cut has extended a few feet, the kerf may close, causing the saw to bind. To avoid this, insert a small wedge at the start of the cut.

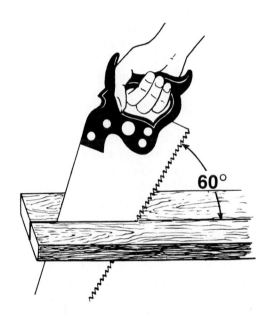

9-17. Hold a ripsaw at an angle of about 60 degrees when cutting to width.

9-18. Ripping a board with the work held over sawhorses.

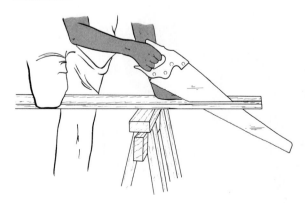

CUTTING SHORT PIECES OF STOCK TO WIDTH

If a short length is to be ripped, place it in the vise. Fig. 9-20. Do not saw too far from the side of the vise. This causes too much vibration. Begin with the board near the top of the vise. Move it up a little at a time as you continue your work.

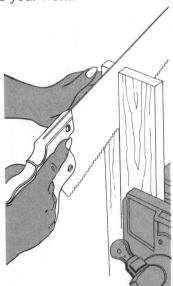

9-20. Ripping with the work held in a vise. Hold the saw at an angle of about 60 degrees to the work. Always do the sawing close to the vise jaws, so that the board will not vibrate. It is preferable to rip on a sawhorse. However, for cutting short pieces of stock, work can sometimes be done more conveniently in a bench vise. Make sure that the saw does not strike any other tools on the bench or cut the bench.

CUTTING PLYWOOD AND OTHER PANEL STOCK

To cut plywood or other panel stock, place the material on edge with guide boards securely clamped at the top and bottom. Make sure the distance between the guide boards is just equal to the width of the saw teeth. Also, be sure the finish (good) side of the material is facing you. Then as you saw with the blade between the guide boards, your cut will be straight and true. Fig. 9-21.

9-21. Cutting panel stock. Use a sharp saw having ten to fifteen points to the inch.

Review Questions

1. Name the type of saw used for cutting across grain.
2. Name the type of saw used for cutting with the grain.
3. Why must a saw have the proper set in order to cut correctly?
4. Why is a saw with five points to the inch best for cutting wet, green wood?
5. What does a ripsaw tooth resemble?
6. If you could have only one saw for your shop, which one would you choose?
7. Why shouldn't the cutting line on a long board be placed between the sawhorses?
8. At what angle to the stock should you hold the crosscut saw?
9. To start a cut, should you push down or draw up on the saw? Why?
10. Which should you watch, the action of the saw or the cutting line?
11. What is a saw kerf?
12. Why does the crosscut saw have knife-like teeth?
13. When a saw binds or sticks, what is the most likely cause?
14. What can be done to prevent a saw from binding or sticking?
15. How can you prevent the board from splitting off just before the saw cut is completed?
16. How is plywood handled in sawing?

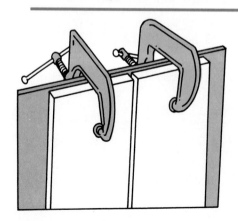

Facts about Wood

The Oldest Living Thing

The varied climate of North America has ensured a variety of forest types. Of course, these forests are not now what they once were. Of most of them, though, enough remains to give some idea of the types of trees that once flourished there. For example, for those living east of the Mississippi, the familiar trees are hardwoods such as maple and oak. While these are beautiful trees, they do not grow to a great height or a great age.

You probably have heard of the redwood and the sequoia. These trees were once widespread throughout the temperate regions of the northern hemisphere. Glaciers, however, destroyed most of them thousands of years ago. Today, redwoods and sequoias survive only in northwest California.

The redwood grows along the coast of northern California. There, in the beautiful isolation of Redwood National Park, the trees are protected. The world's tallest tree—named Libby—grows in this park. Libby is 367 feet tall. Its estimated weight is over one million pounds.

Sequoias grow to a greater age than redwoods. Hundreds of sequoias grow in the Sequoia National Park in central California. The largest sequoia, the General Sherman Tree, grows in this park. It is 272 feet high and 37 feet in diameter, with an estimated age of 3,500 years. The sequoia, incidentally, was named after Sequoyah, a Native American of the Cherokee tribe.

Though the sequoia grows to a greater age than the redwood, the oldest sequoia is not as old as the bristlecone pine, which grows in the White Mountains of California. Some of those trees are more than 5,000 years old.

You may wonder how the ages of the trees mentioned here compare with the ages of other living things. You might want to consider these facts:

- The largest land animal is the elephant. The African elephant can reach a shoulder height of about 13 feet and weighs 6 to 8 tons. Some elephants live to be about 70 years old.
- The largest sea animal is the blue whale. Some blue whales have reached a length of 100 feet, weighing about 120 tons. Blue whales may live as long as 50 years. The blue whale is the largest animal that has ever lived.
- The tallest sea plant is the giant kelp. Some of these have fronds that are 300 feet long.

The drawing below, which is done to scale, shows the relationship of these living things.

Chapter 10 | Assembling and Adjusting a Plane

After studying this chapter, you will be able to:
● Name the three common types of bench planes.
● Name the main parts of a plane.
● List the steps in assembling the double plane iron.
● Demonstrate the insertion of the plane iron in the plane.

LOOK FOR THESE TERMS

double plane iron   jack plane
fore plane   jointer plane
frog   smooth plane
hand plane

Most wood has been surfaced on two sides (S2S) at the mill. However, if you look closely at the surfaces, you will see small mill or knife marks (waves) made by the rotating cutter of the planer, or surfacer. Fig. 10-1. You must hand plane the wood to remove these mill marks completely. If you do not, these marks will show up after finishing.

KINDS OF BENCH PLANES

There are three common types of bench (hand) planes. Fig. 10-2. The *jack plane*, from 11½ to 15 inches long, is used for general planing. The *smooth plane* is the same, except that it ranges from 7 to 9 inches in length. The *fore* and *jointer planes* are much longer, from 18 to 24 inches. These are especially useful for planing long edges straight when making joints for (jointing) long pieces of stock.

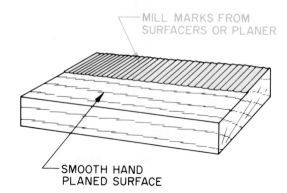

10-1. Exaggerated mill or knife marks that are made by the planer, or surfacer. These must be removed by hand planing.

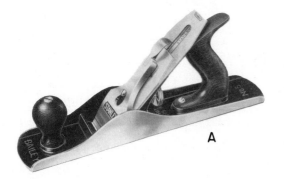

10-2. Three types of hand planes: A. This is a jack plane, which has a bed that is commonly 14 or 15 inches (355 or 380 mm) long. It can be used to true the edges of boards and for general planing. B. This is a smooth plane that can be purchased in lengths from 8 to 9 inches (203 to 228 mm). It is good for smoothing and finishing work for which a light plane is preferred. C. This is the fore, or jointer, plane. It is the type used to obtain a true surface on long edges in preparation for gluing up stock.

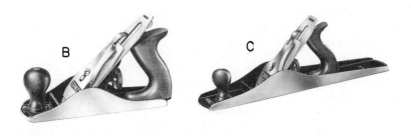

PARTS OF A PLANE

Figure 10-3 shows the major parts of a plane. Figure 10-4 shows these parts in more detail.

The *body* of the plane is made of cast steel. The *base*, or *bottom*, is either smooth or corrugated. Directly behind the opening in the bottom of the plane is a *frog*, which provides the support for the plane iron. This frog contains two adjustments. An *adjusting nut* (brass knurled nut) adjusts the depth of cut, regulating the thickness of the shavings. A long slender lever, called the *lateral adjusting lever*, provides for the sidewise adjustment of the cutter.

The *double plane iron* consists of the plane iron blade, sometimes called the cutter, and the plane iron cap (chip breaker). The most common sizes are 1¾, 2, and 2⅜ inches (45, 50, and 60 mm).

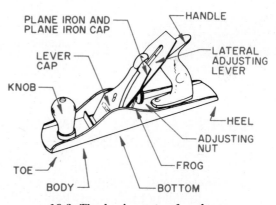

10-3. The basic parts of a plane.

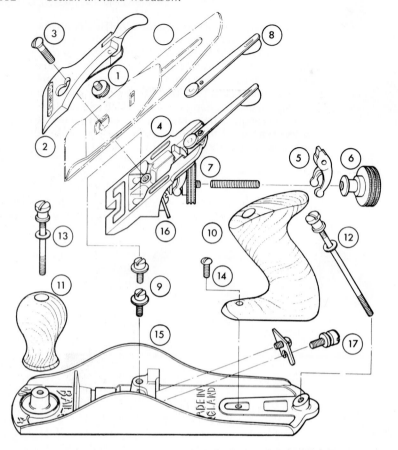

	Key No.
Cap Screw	1
Lever Cap	2
Lever Screw	3
Frog Complete	4
'Y' Adjusting Lever	5
Adjusting Nut	6
Adjusting Nut Screw	7
Lateral Adjusting Lever	8
Frog Screw and Washer	9
Handle	10
Knob	11
Handle Screw and Nut	12
Knob Screw and Nut	13
Handle Toe Screw	14
Plane Bottom	15
Frog Clip and Screw	16
Frog Adjusting Screw	17

10-4. An exploded view of a plane, showing its parts.

TESTING A PLANE IRON FOR SHARPNESS

Check the plane iron to be sure it is sharp in one of these ways: 1. Sight along the edge. A sharp blade will not reflect any light. 2. Cut a piece of paper with it. Fig. 10-5. 3. Let the cutting edge rest on your thumbnail and then push it lightly. If the blade clings to your thumbnail, it is sharp. If it slides easily, it needs sharpening, or whetting. (See Unit 26, "Sharpening Tools.")

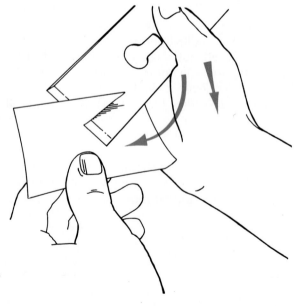

10-5. One method of checking a plane for sharpness. The blade will cut paper when it is sharp.

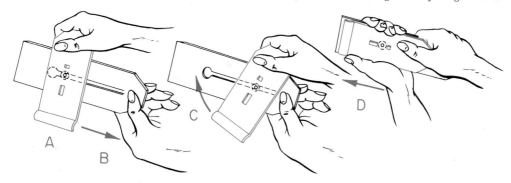

10-6. The correct method for assembling a double plane iron: A. Hold the plane iron in one hand, with the bevel side down and away from you. Place the plane iron cap at right angles to it and drop the setscrew through the large opening. B. Slide the plane iron cap back as far as it will go and then, C, turn it so it is parallel to the plane iron. D. Slowly move the plane iron cap to within about 1/32 to 1/16 inch of the cutting edge. Then tighten the setscrew with a screwdriver or the lever cap.

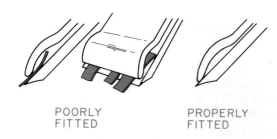

POORLY
FITTED

PROPERLY
FITTED

10-7. The plane iron cap must be properly fitted to the plane iron. This is necessary so that chips of wood do not get between the two parts. If necessary, file the edge of the cap so that it fits tightly against the blade.

ASSEMBLING THE DOUBLE PLANE IRON

Hold the iron in your left hand, with the bevel (slanted edge) away from you. Place the plane iron cap at right angles to the plane iron. Drop the setscrew into the plane iron through the large opening. With the plane iron cap still at right angles, slide it back and away from the cutting edge. Turn the plane iron cap parallel to the plane iron. Slip it up until it is about 1/16 inch (2 mm) away from the cutting edge for finish work. Fig. 10-6. Make sure that you do not injure the cutting edge of the plane iron by shoving the cap too far forward. Tighten the setscrew firmly.

The plane iron cap serves two purposes. It helps to stiffen and strengthen the plane iron blade. It also serves as a chip breaker. Fig. 10-7. The cap prevents the blade from tearing the surface of the wood.

INSERTING THE PLANE IRON IN THE PLANE

Insert the double plane iron in the plane with the bevel side down. Watch for the following:

● Do not hit the cutting edge on the body of the plane as you insert it over the frog.

● Make sure that the slot in the plane iron cap fits over the little Y adjustment.

● Check to see that the roller on the lateral adjustment slips into the slot of the plane iron.

Pull the little thumb-adjusting cam on the lever cap up at right angles. Fig. 10-8. Then slip the lever cap over the lever cap screw on the frog. Push the thumb-adjusting cam down to fasten the plane iron securely in the plane. If it must be forced, unscrew the lever cap screw just a little bit. Tighten it a little if it is too loose.

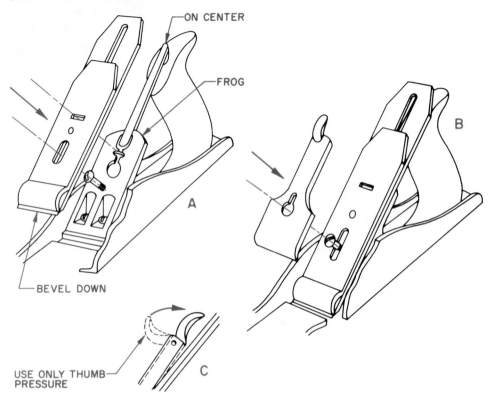

ON CENTER

FROG

BEVEL DOWN

USE ONLY THUMB PRESSURE

B

A

C

10-8. The basic steps in installing a double plane iron in the plane: A. The iron is assembled and placed over the frog. B. The iron is in place and the cap is inserted. C. The plane iron cap holds the other plane iron in place.

10-9. Adjusting the plane. Hold it with the bed or bottom at eye level. Turn the brass knurled nut until the plane iron just appears.

ADJUSTING THE PLANE

Turn the plane upside down with the bottom about eye level. Turn the brass knurled nut until the plane iron appears just beyond the bottom of the plane. Then, with the lateral adjustment lever, move the blade to one side or the other until it is parallel to the bottom. Fig. 10-9. The lateral adjustments that may need to be made are shown in Fig. 10-10.

Test the plane on a piece of scrap stock to see how it cuts. For rough planing and when much stock is to be removed, set the plane deeper. When truing up a surface and making it smooth, a light cut that forms a feathery shaving is best.

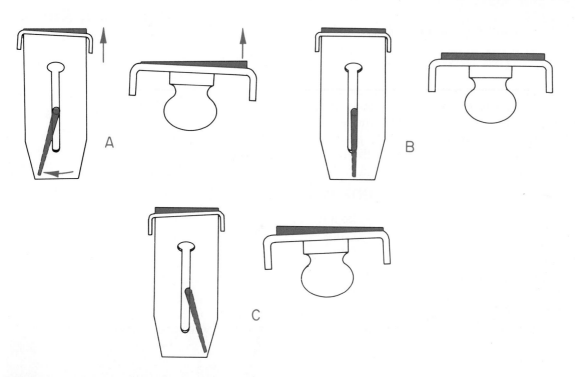

10-10. Move the lateral adjustment from left to right until the plane iron is parallel to the bed: A. Moving the lateral adjustment level to the left raises the right side of the plane iron. B. The plane iron is parallel to the bottom. C. Moving the lateral adjustment level to the right raises the left side of the plane.

Review Questions

1. Name the three common types of bench (hand) planes.
2. Name the important parts of a plane.
3. Tell three ways of testing for sharpness.
4. To do finish planing, how far should the cap be set from the cutting edge?
5. What is the purpose of the plane iron cap?
6. Describe in detail the steps to follow in fastening a plane iron in a plane.
7. Tell how to make the depth adjustment.

Chapter 11

Planing a Surface

After studying this chapter, you will be able to:
● Identify four flaws that can occur in stock.
● Describe the process used to remove wind from a board.
● Describe the basic steps used to plane a surface true and smooth.
● List the methods used to check the trueness of a surface.

LOOK FOR THESE TERMS

bench stop   warp
crook   wind
cup

The first surface to plane should be free of flaws and have the most interesting grain.

INSPECTING A SURFACE FOR WARP

Warp is any variation from a true, or plane, surface. It includes crook, bow, cup, wind (twist), or any combination of these. *Crook* is a deviation edgewise from a straight line drawn from end to end. *Bow* is a deviation flatwise from a straight line drawn from end to end of a piece. *Cup* is a curve across the grain or width of a piece. By using a straight-edge or the blade of a try or framing square, a beginner can check if a board is cupped. Fig. 11-1.

Wind, or *twist*, in a board indicates that the board is twisted throughout its length. Place two parallel pieces of wood across the grain, one on each end of the board. Then sight along the top of the first parallel. If you can see one end of the second parallel, you know that the board has a wind. Fig. 11-2. With a pencil, mark the high points of the board if it is warped or has a wind.

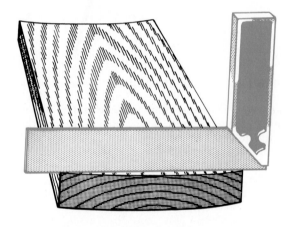

11-1. Checking the stock to see if it is cupped.

11-2. Sticks placed across the ends of the board will show wind or twist.

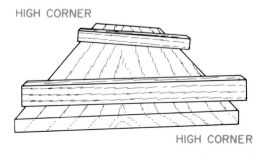

HIGH CORNER

HIGH CORNER

THE STICKS DO NOT LIE LEVEL

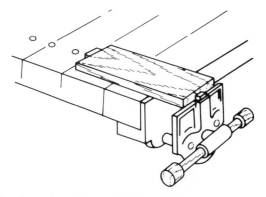

11-3. Note how the stock is held between a vise dog and a bench stop.

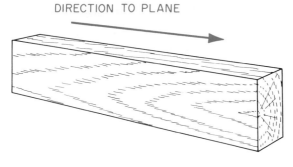

DIRECTION TO PLANE

11-4. The arrow indicates the direction in which the stock should be planed.

11-5. Planing the face of a board. Note that the work is locked securely between the bench stop and the dog of the vise. You can tell when the plane is cutting properly by the kind of shaving formed. The shaving should be uniform in thickness and width. The thickness of the shaving depends on the setting of the plane. For rough cutting, a heavy shaving should be taken. For finish work, shavings should be light and silky. Always plane with the grain of the wood.

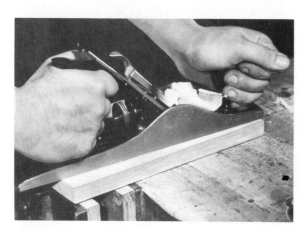

FASTENING A BOARD

Lock the board between the vise dog and the bench stop. Fig. 11-3.

PLANING THE SURFACE TRUE AND SMOOTH

Always plane with the grain. If you plane against it, you will roughen the surface. Fig. 11-4.

Grasp the knob of the plane in your left hand and the handle in your right hand. Fig. 11-5. Stand just back of the work with your left foot forward. Swing your body back and forth as you plane. At the same time, use a forward motion with your arms.

Place the toe or front of the plane on the board. Apply pressure to the knob at the start of the stroke. As the whole base contacts the wood, apply even pressure to the knob and handle. Then, as the plane begins to leave the surface, apply more pressure to the handle. Fig. 11-6.

Lift the plane off the board on the return stroke. Do not drag the plane back. This will dull the blade. Sometimes the plane will cut more easily if you take a shearing cut at an angle.

Work across the board gradually. High points will take more planing than other areas.

11-6. Proper method for applying pressure when planing. More pressure is applied to the knob at the start of the stroke and to the handle at the end of the stroke. This helps ensure that you don't cut a convex surface.

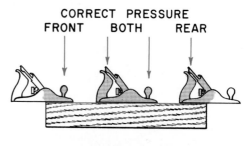

CORRECT PRESSURE
FRONT   BOTH   REAR

STRAIGHT EDGE

NO LIGHT SHOWS UNDER STRAIGHT EDGE

REMOVING WIND FROM A BOARD

Removing wind in a board requires taking a partial cut at either the beginning or end of the board.

To remove wind at the beginning of the board, take a partial cut there. Begin the stroke as before. Then as you plane along the board as far as you think necessary, slowly lift the handle to finish the cut.

To take the wind out of the end of the board, start the partial cut in the center of the board. Begin with the handle held away from the surface. Gradually lower the handle as you begin the forward motion.

CHECKING THE SURFACE

After the surface begins to get smooth, check it with a straightedge. The straightedge will touch the high points. Fig. 11-7. Check the total width and length every few inches and diagonally across the corners. Fig. 11-8. Use a pencil to mark the high points. Figs. 11-9 and 11-10.

The first planed surface is called the *face surface* or *face side*.

11-8. Check carefully the size of the material before proceeding to the next step.

11-7. Checking a board. Hold the board at about eye level and place a straightedge across it. Light showing through indicates a low spot. Mark the *high spot* on the board with a pencil. Then plane lightly over this area.

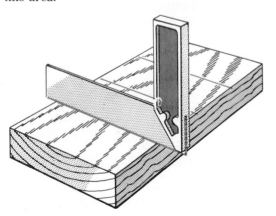

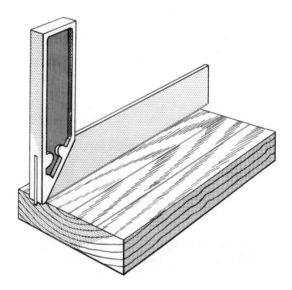

11-9. Check with a straightedge from one end to the other. Make sure that the surface is straight and true.

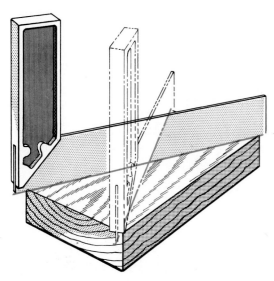

11-10. Checking across the corners.

Review Questions

1. Which surface of the board is the first to be planed?
2. Can you see if a board is warped?
3. What are the two ways of checking wind in a board?
4. What will happen if the plane is dragged backward?
5. Tell how you would go about removing wind from a board.
6. What is the surface that is planed first called?

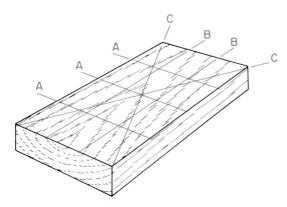

11-11. Checking the surface for flatness. Check from (A) edge to edge, (B) end to end, and finally (C) across the corners.

Chapter 12

Planing to Width and Thickness

After studying this chapter, you will be able to:
- Plane the face edge of a piece of stock.
- Set the marking gauge.
- Mark stock to width.
- Plane the second edge of a piece of stock.

LOOK FOR THESE TERMS

> face edge
> face surface
> marking gauge

In planing to thickness and width, take all measurements from the *face surface* or *side*. This surface should be marked with the number "1," or with a small mark, near the first edge to be planed.

SELECTING AND CHECKING THE FACE, OR JOINT, EDGE

Select the edge that is truest and best to plane first. This is called the *face*, or *joint*, *edge*. Test the edge for squareness at several points along the stock. Also check with a straightedge along the length. Mark with a pencil the high points where you must do most of the planing.

SELECTING THE PROPER PLANE

In planing an edge, especially a long one, it is better to use a plane with a long base such as the fore or jointer plane. The jointer plane tends to straighten the edge, whereas the shorter plane will follow any curve that may be in the edge. Fig. 12-1.

FASTENING THE WORK IN THE VISE

Lock the stock in the vise. If the stock is long, support one end in the vise and hold the other in place with a hand screw. Fig. 12-2. Sometimes the work is held against a V-block on the top of the bench.

12-1. This shows the reason for using a plane with a long bed to plane the edge of long stock. The longer plane tends to straighten out any irregularities, whereas the shorter plane tends to follow curves.

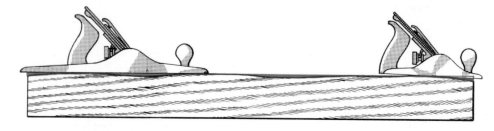

12-2. Supporting long pieces of stock when planing an edge. The hand screw is fastened to support the end of the stock while the front is locked in the vise.

12-3. Holding stock against a V-block to do edge planing. This is especially satisfactory for planing long stock or when a vise is not available. Note how the thumb is held around the back of the knob and the fingers are curled under the bottom of the plane to guide it.

HOLDING THE PLANE

In planing an edge you may hold the handle of the plane the same way as for surface planing. Fig. 12-3. To use a second method, place your thumb around the back of the knob with your other fingers curled under the bottom. In this way you can use your fingers along the face side to guide the plane. Fig. 12-4.

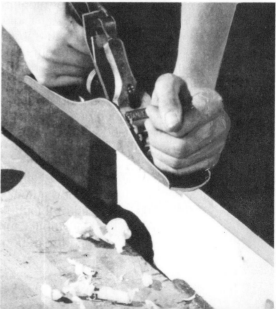

12-4. Starting the cutting stroke in planing an edge. Pressure is applied to the knob.

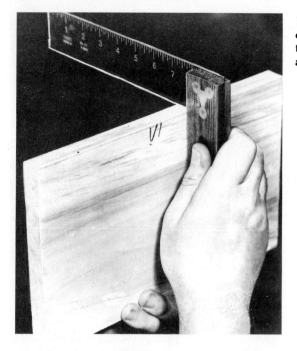

PLANING THE FACE EDGE

Plane with the grain. First remove any high spots that you have marked. Then take long, continuous strokes to remove a thin chip all along the edge. Be sure to apply pressure on the knob in starting the stroke and on the handle when finishing it. Fig. 12-4. In planing this first edge, cut the edge square with the face surface and straight along its entire length. Check with the try square and straight-edge as shown in Figs. 12-5 and 12-6. Mark this edge with two light pencil lines.

SETTING THE MARKING GAUGE

The *marking gauge* is used to transfer a measurement to the stock. Fig. 12-7. It has a scale along one surface. When the small spur is sharpened to a wedge shape, the starting point of the scale becomes inaccurate. Remember this as you set the gauge.

Set the head of the scale to the correct distance as shown on the beam. Then lightly turn the thumbscrew. Hold the marking gauge upside down in one hand. Use the rule to check the distance from the head to the point of the spur. Fig. 12-8. Then tighten the thumbscrew. Always recheck this measurement.

12-5. Checking the joint edge by holding the handle of a try square against the face side or surface. Move the try square to make certain that the edge is square along its total length.

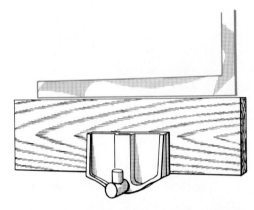

12-6. Checking an edge for straightness. This is especially important on long stock. The edge must be square with the face surface and not form a convex or concave curve. Hold the straightedge against the planed edge and sight at eye level to see if any light shows through.

12-7. Marking gauges are made of wood or metal. Gauges made from both materials are shown above. The essential parts are labeled on the wood marking gauge.

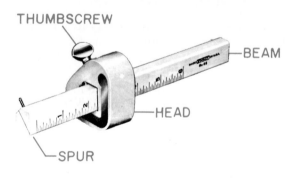

THUMBSCREW

BEAM

HEAD

SPUR

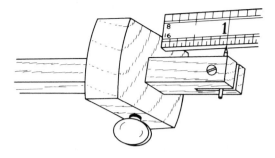

12-8. Setting a marking gauge. Note that the gauge is held upside down in one hand. A rule held in the other hand is used to check the distance from the point or spur to the head of the marking gauge.

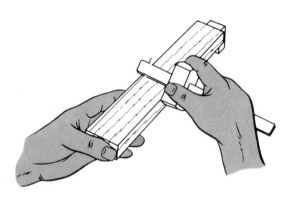

12-9. Using a marking gauge.

12-10. Using a combination square and pencil to mark for correct width. The carpenter uses this method.

MARKING THE STOCK TO WIDTH

Check the drawing for the width of stock needed. Then set the marking gauge to this width. Hold the stock to be marked with the face surface up and the face, or joint, edge to your right. Place the head of the marking gauge firmly against this joint edge. Then tip the marking gauge forward with a slight twist of your wrist until the spur just touches the surface of the wood. Push the marking gauge forward, applying pressure as shown in Fig. 12-9. The spur will make a fine layout line.

When widths too wide for the gauge must be marked, use a pencil and a combination square. Fig. 12-10.

PLANING THE SECOND EDGE

If much stock is to be removed, the board should be ripped to within ⅛ to 3/16 inch (3 to 5 mm) of the layout line.

Lock the stock in the vise and begin to plane the second edge. As the plane approaches the layout line, use the try square frequently to check the edge for squareness. Use a straightedge to check the length. Take special care at the layout line to take light, even shavings that are the total width and length of the edge. The last cut you take should just split the dent made by the marking gauge.

MARKING THE STOCK TO THICKNESS

Check the thickness of the stock. Then set the marking gauge to this measurement. Mark a line on both edges to indicate the proper thickness.

PLANING TO THICKNESS

Check the lines that show thickness to see if there are any spots that are higher than the rest of the board. These spots need extra planing. Plane these areas first. Then begin to plane the total length of the stock on the second surface. Work from one side to the other.

Planing to thickness is the same as planing the first surface. However, you must constantly check the two lines showing thickness.

Review Questions

1. When is a fore or jointer plane used?
2. The first planing should be done on which edge?
3. How can long stock be supported?
4. Describe the two ways of holding the knob of the plane in planing an edge.
5. What should be accomplished by planing this first edge? Should a large amount of stock be removed?
6. Describe a marking gauge and name its parts.
7. Should you depend on the marking gauge scale? Why?
8. Should the mark made by the marking gauge be deep?
9. Assume that considerable stock must be removed to bring the stock to width. How should this be done?
10. Should you completely remove the marking gauge line when you plane the second edge?

Chapter 13

Planing End Grain

After studying this chapter, you will be able to:
● Describe each of the three methods that can be used to cut end grain properly.
● Describe the lateral adjustment of a block plane.

LOOK FOR THIS TERM

end grain

End grain is produced when stock is cut across the grain. In planing end grain, you actually cut off the tips of the wood fibers. This takes a very sharp plane iron.

THE BLOCK PLANE

When the stock to be planed can be locked in a vise, a jack plane is used. For other jobs, choose a block plane. The block plane is much smaller than the others you have used so far. Fig. 13-1. It has a single plane iron that is placed in the plane with the *beveled side up*. The plane iron also rests in the plane at a much lower angle than the iron in a regular plane. This makes it easier to cut end grain.

Some block planes have a lateral adjustment. Others do not.

ADJUSTING THE BLOCK PLANE

The block plane is adjusted the same way as other planes, except when there may not be a lateral adjusting lever. To make a lateral adjustment, loosen the plane iron cap and sight along the bottom of the plane. Then, with your fingers, press the plane iron to the right or left until it is parallel to the bottom of the plane. Tighten the lever cap screw. The depth is controlled by the adjusting nut.

USING THE BLOCK PLANE

Make sure that the plane iron is very sharp. The iron cap should be set very close to the cutting edge, not over 1/32 inch (1 mm). Lock the stock firmly in the vise with the end showing a little.

Hold the block plane in one hand with the thumb on one side, the forefinger over the finger rest, and the other fingers on the other side. Take pains to hold the block plane square with the work. Fig. 13-2.

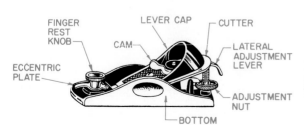

13-1. A block plane that can be used for planing end grain and for doing small forming and shaping work. The major parts are identified:

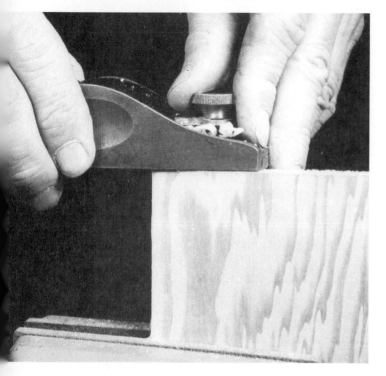

13-2. The cutter of a block plane rests at a much lower angle than on other types of planes. This makes it ideal for planing across grain.

13-3. Planing end grain with a hand plane by planing halfway across and then reversing the plane to finish the cut.

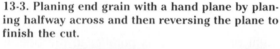

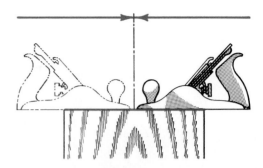

13-4. Planing end grain halfway across the stock.

13-5. Testing the end from the face surface. Move the try square back and forth.

13-6. Checking the end from the edge. Hold the try square against the joint edge to make sure that the end is square both ways.

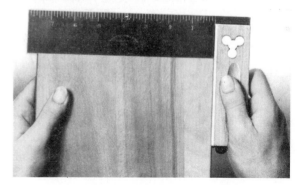

DO NOT PLANE BEYOND LAYOUT LINES

LAYOUT LINE

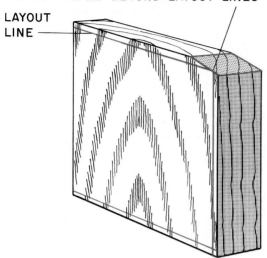

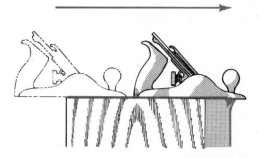

13-8. A third method for planing end grain. Place a scrap piece of the same thickness against the edge of the piece to be planed. With this method you are actually extending the end grain.

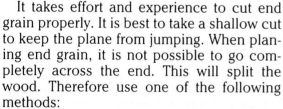

13-7. A second method for planing end grain. Note that a bevel is cut. This tends to prevent the wood from splitting out. You can, therefore, plane completely across the end.

It takes effort and experience to cut end grain properly. It is best to take a shallow cut to keep the plane from jumping. When planing end grain, it is not possible to go completely across the end. This will split the wood. Therefore use one of the following methods:

● Plane about halfway across the stock. Then lift the handle of the plane slowly. Fig. 13-3. Begin at the other end and do the same thing. Fig. 13-4. Check for squareness with the working face and working edge. Figs. 13-5 and 13-6.

● Plane a short bevel on the waste edge of the stock. Then begin from the other side to plane all the way across. Fig. 13-7.

● Get a piece of scrap stock exactly the same thickness as the piece you are working. Lock it in the vise just ahead of the piece you are planing. In this way you have actually extended the end grain. Then you can plane all of the way across the end grain without fear of splitting out the piece. Fig. 13-8.

Review Questions

1. Why is end grain difficult to plane?
2. How is a block plane different from other planes?
3. When would you choose a block plane to plane with the grain?
4. Describe the three ways of planing end grain.

Chapter 14

Cutting With a Backsaw

After studying this chapter, you will be able to:
- Demonstrate the laying out of a cutoff line.
- Demonstrate crosscutting with the backsaw.
- Distinguish between the backsaw and the dovetail saw.

LOOK FOR THESE TERMS

backsaw
bench hook
dovetail saw

A very fine saw cut is needed to square up stock or to make joints. For such a cut, use a backsaw or a dovetail saw.

THE BACKSAW AND DOVETAIL SAW

The *backsaw* has a very thin blade with fine teeth. Fig. 14-1. This saw is used to cut both across grain and with the grain. It gets its name from an extra band of metal across its back. This metal stiffens the saw. The *dovetail saw* is very similar except that it has a narrower blade and finer teeth. Fig. 14-2. It cuts a true, smooth, and narrow kerf. Fig. 14-3.

14-1. A backsaw. In hand woodworking, this is one of the most frequently used tools whenever an accurate cut is required. Because the blade is quite thin, it is strengthened on the back with a metal strip. This gives the saw its name. The backsaw comes in lengths from 10 inches (254 mm) to the most common length of 14 inches (356 mm).

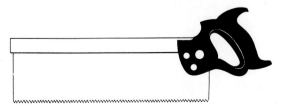

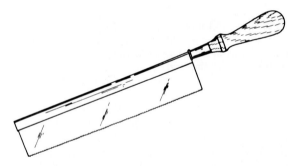

14-2. A dovetail saw. This is very similar to the backsaw, except that it is smaller and has a thinner blade. It is used for extremely accurate work. The common length is 10 inches (254 mm).

14-3. Dovetail saws are designed for cutting dovetails and for tenoning. They also are used for other types of precision work such as ship-model building and patternmaking.

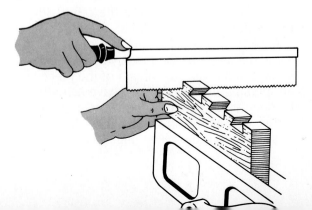

THE BENCH HOOK

A *bench hook* is a piece of wood with a hook or stop on opposite surfaces of each end. Fig. 14-4. When in use, the wide stop goes over the edge of the bench. The piece to be sawed is held against the shorter stop. This hook protects the bench top from damage.

LAYING OUT THE CUTOFF LINE

Accurately lay out the location of the cut to be made. Use a try square and pencil. For a very accurate layout, mark a line with a knife. If the stock is to be cut to length, lay out a line across the face side of the board and across both edges. If no planing is to be done, take the cut just inside or outside the layout line. The saw kerf should be *in the waste stock*. Fig. 14-5. However, if the edge is to be planed, allow about ⅟₁₆ inch (1.5 mm).

CROSSCUTTING

Place the bench hook over the edge of the bench. Hold your work with one hand firmly against the stop. Use the thumb of your left hand to guide the blade of the saw. Hold the s3w in a slanting position across the work. Draw it back once or twice to start the saw kerf. As the cut begins, gradually lower the saw until it is parallel to the wood. Fig. 14-6.

Make sure that you are holding the saw at right angles to the face of the work. Be careful to take light, easy cuts as the saw goes through the opposite side of the wood. Fig. 14-7.

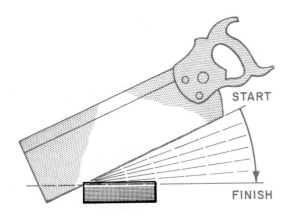

14-6. After starting the saw kerf, lower the handle slowly until it is parallel with the top of the bench.

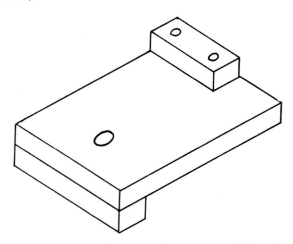

14-4. The bench hook is simply a piece of wood with wood cleats on both ends. It is used to protect the top of the bench during sawing, cutting, and other forming operations.

14-5. Always make sure that the saw kerf is in the waste part of the stock.

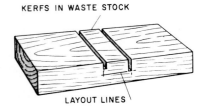

KERFS IN WASTE STOCK

LAYOUT LINES

14-7. Continuing the cut with the backsaw.

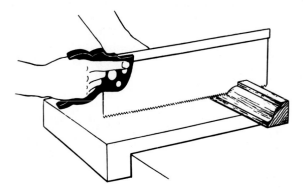

RIPPING

The backsaw is also used for cutting with the grain of stock, especially in making joints and in doing other fine cabinetwork. Begin the cut the same way you did in crosscutting. Continue to lower the handle until it is cutting the total width of the wood. Fig. 14-8. In cutting with the grain, be very careful not to allow the saw to creep in at an angle. This will make a crooked cut.

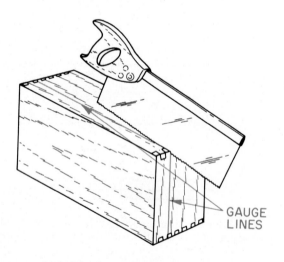

GAUGE LINES

14-8. Ripping with the backsaw.

Review Questions

1. How did the backsaw get its name?
2. In what ways does the dovetail saw differ from the backsaw?
3. What is a bench hook and how is it used?
4. Can the backsaw crosscut and rip?
5. When using the backsaw, how much stock must remain for planing?
6. Which saw most resembles the back-saw—the crosscut or the ripsaw?
7. Why must care be taken when sawing with the grain?

Facts about Wood

The Saw

All modern hand tools have developed from primitive tools. Usually, this process has taken thousands of years. Generally, every major change in tool design has been made to make work easier.

Flint tools with notched edges were used by human beings in the Stone Age, about 40,000 years ago. These were used for cutting hard materials. Though resembling knives, these simple tools would probably have been used with a sawing motion. In their use, then, they resembled saws. They were not, however, real saws. A real saw requires a blade with regularly shaped and evenly spaced teeth. Flint was not an appropriate material for a saw. Early human beings in the Stone Age were able to work flint with some skill. However, they would have had difficulty fashioning teeth of the same size at regular intervals.

The common saw was not developed until human beings learned to smelt metal. This discovery enabled them to separate metal from the ore containing it. From the metal obtained, they could make tools harder than the materials they wanted to cut.

Much of what we know about early tools comes from archeologists. *Archeologists* are scientists who study ancient cultures through the objects they have left. In studying the culture of ancient Egypt, for example, archeologists have learned that saws were used in Egypt in 4000 B.C. First, the saws were of copper. Later, they were of bronze. Their handles were of wood.

The blades of these early saws cut by being pulled through the material. The saw could not be pushed. If it was pushed, the soft metal blade would buckle. As well as being made of soft metal, the teeth had no set. Thus, the kerf (the cut made by the blade) was only as wide as the blade itself. This also caused these primitive saws to buckle in use. The teeth of these saws were irregular in shape and size. Their design made them difficult to use. Cutting with them was a slow process, requiring close attention and care.

The Minoans were a people who lived on the island of Crete in the Mediterranean between 3000 and 1000 B.C. The Minoans of the Bronze Age (1700 to 1400 B.C.) made important advances in saw design. Archeologists digging in Crete have unearthed two-handled saws. These were used both as crosscut saws and ripsaws. One saw found was about 5½ feet long and 5 inches high. The size of the saw and the evenness of the teeth indicate great advances in saw design. The teeth, for example, were cut at even intervals along the length of the blade. There are about 5 points to the inch.

As saws have changed, so have saw handles. For example, until the early 1700s the saws used in Europe had handles that resembled those found on a hammer or a screwdriver. The saw's handle was just a simple piece of wood. It offered the user little means of applying real pressure or control to the saw. The saw handle commonly found on crosscut saws and ripsaws was developed in 1760.

Saws today are precision cutting tools. However, their design and the materials used to make them reflect the latest state of technologies developed over thousands of years.

Chapter 15

Gluing Up Stock

After studying this chapter, you will be able to:
● List the eight common adhesives.
● Identify the various clamps used in woodworking.
● List the steps in gluing up an edge joint.
● List the steps in gluing up stock face to face.

LOOK FOR THESE TERMS

adhesive
animal glue
band clamp
C-clamp
cabinet clamp
casein glue
contact cement

double spread
edging clamp
epoxy cement
gluing
hand screw
hot-melt glue
liquid resin (polyvinyl) glue

pipe clamp
resorcinol
single spread
speed clamp
spring clamp
urea-resin adhesive
web clamp

An *adhesive* is a substance used to hold other materials together. Common adhesives include glues, cements, pastes, and mucilage. The term *gluing* means to assemble parts with adhesive. Fig. 15-1.

Two pieces of wood are held together with an adhesive because of *adhesion*. Adhesion also causes paint or enamel to stick to wood. Adhesives hold pieces of wood together because the molecules of glue adhere to the wood and also to the molecules of other adhesives.

KINDS OF ADHESIVES

There are eight common adhesives. They are available under many different trade names. Table 15-A.

15-1. Good wood gluing of this table means that the table will last a long time. The joints are stronger than the wood itself.

Table 15-A. Wood Adhesives

Type	Description	Recommended Use	Care in Using	Correct Use
Hide glue	Comes in flakes to be heated in water or in prepared form as liquid hide glue. Very strong, tough, light color.	Excellent for furniture and cabinetwork. Gives strength even to joints that do not fit very well.	Not waterproof; do not use for outdoor furniture or anything exposed to weather or dampness.	Apply glue in warm room to both surfaces and let it become tacky before joining. Clamp 3 hours.
Casein	From milk curd. Comes in powdered form. Must be mixed with water.	For inside and woodwork. Almost waterproof. Good for oily woods. Inexpensive. Good for heavy wood gluing.	Some types require bleaching. Will deteriorate when exposed to mold.	Mix with water to creamy consistency. For oily woods, sponge surfaces with dilute caustic soda one hour before gluing. Apply with brush. Clamp and allow to dry for three hours at 70 degrees.
Urea-resin adhesive	Comes as powder to be mixed with water and used within 4 hours. Light colored. Very strong if joint fits well.	Good for general wood gluing. First choice for work that must stand some exposure to dampness, since it is almost waterproof.	Needs well-fitted joints, tight clamping, and room temperature 70° or warmer.	Make sure joint fits tightly. Mix glue and apply thin coat. Allow 16 hours drying time. Dries in seconds with electronic gluer.
Resorcinol (waterproof)	Comes as powder plus liquid; must be mixed each time used. Dark colored, very strong, completely waterproof.	This is the glue to use with exterior type plywood for work to be exposed to extreme dampness.	Expense, trouble to mix, and dark color make it unsuitable to jobs where waterproof glue is not required.	Use within 8 hours after mixing. Work at temperature above 70°. Apply thin coat to both surfaces. Allow 16 hours drying time.
Liquid resin (white) polyvinyl glue	Comes ready to use at any temperature. Clean working, quick setting. Strong enough for most work, though not quite as tough as hide glue.	Good for indoor furniture and cabinetwork. First choice for small jobs where right clamping or good fit may be difficult.	Not sufficiently resistant to moisture for outdoor furniture or outdoor storage units.	Use at any temperature but preferably above 60°. Spread on both surfaces, clamp at once. Sets in 1½ hours.
Contact cement	Comes in a can as a light tan liquid.	Excellent for bonding veneer plastic laminates, leather, plastics, metal foil, or canvas to wood.	Adheres immediately on contact. Parts can't be shifted once contact is made. Position accurately. Temperature for working must be 70° F or above.	Stir cement. Apply two coats to both surfaces. Brush on a liberal coat. Let dry for 30 minutes. Apply second coat. Allow to dry for not less than 30 minutes. Test for dryness by pressing wrapping paper to surface. If paper doesn't stick, the surfaces are dry and ready for bonding.
Epoxy cement	Comes in two tubes, or cans, that must be mixed in exact proportions.	Excellent for attaching hardware and metal fittings to wood. Good for extremely difficult gluing jobs. Will fill large holes.	Epoxies harden quickly. Mix only what can be used in half hour. Use at temperatures above 60 degrees. Keep epoxy compounds separate. Don't reverse caps.	Mix small amounts. Clean and roughen the surfaces. Remove oil, dirt, and other loose matter. Apply to surfaces with putty knife. Clean tools immediately. Press parts together.
Hot-melt glues	Cream colored polyethylene based adhesive in stick form.	Quick bonding adhesive; best for small areas.	Glue hardens quickly. Work fast before glue cools.	Apply small amounts. Don't spread. Press surfaces together for 20 seconds.

● *Animal,* or *hide, glue* is made from hoofs, hides, bones, and other animal parts. It is refined, purified, and then formed into sticks or ground into powder.

Animal glue makes a stronger-than-wood joint, but it is not waterproof. It has long been used as an all-purpose furniture glue. If used dry, a glue pot or double boiler is needed to prepare it. It also comes in liquid form which does not need to be heated or mixed. Cold liquid animal glue eliminates tedious preparation and the need for speed and critical temperature control.

Stick or powder glue must be soaked in cold water for 6 to 12 hours. There are strict manufacturer's specifications as to the amounts of glue and water. However, a satisfactory mixture can be made by soaking the glue in just enough water to cover. The glue will absorb this water. After heating the mixture, add a small amount of water as needed. After animal glue is soaked, place it in the top of a double boiler or a regular glue pot. Heat it to steam temperature. The glue will dry out too much if heated directly over a flame. Animal glue is ready to use when it runs off the brush in a light stream.

Before applying hot animal glue, bring the wood to a temperature of about 80 to 90 degrees F. Apply quickly because it sets rapidly after cooling.

● *Casein glue,* made from milk curd, is available in powdered form. It is mixed with cold water to the consistency of cream. It is applied cold to the wood. It is easy to mix and makes a stronger-than-wood joint. Some types stain oak, mahogany, and other acid woods and must be bleached off. It is excellent for all indoor and outdoor gluing, with the exception of articles that require complete waterproofing.

Do not mix more than needed at one time because it loses its strength in a few hours. To mix, pour the powder in a container. Add a small amount of water, stirring until it becomes a heavy paste. Add more water until the mixture is about the consistency of thick cream. Allow the glue to set (takes about 15 minutes) before applying it with a stick or brush.

● *Urea-resin adhesive* is made from urea resin and formaldehyde. It comes in powder form and is mixed with water to the thickness of cream. It does not stain woods, is waterproof, and dries to a light color. It is used in the same way as casein glue. The manufacturer's directions must always be followed for mixing and drying. It is very good for cabinetwork and for bonding plywood. Fig. 15-2.

● *Resorcinol* is made by mixing liquid resin with a powder catalyst. It comes in a can divided into two compartments. This glue should be mixed only as needed, according to the manufacturer's directions. It does not require much pressure. It will fill gaps and can be used for gluing poorly fitted joints. It provides complete protection from both fresh and salt water.

● *Liquid resin (polyvinyl) glue,* white in color, is excellent for furniture making and repair. It is always ready for use, is nonstaining, economical, and odorless. It cannot be exposed to weather.

● *Contact cement* is a ready-mixed, rubbertype, bonding agent. It bonds practically all materials to themselves or in combination. There is no need for clamps, nails, or pressure.

15-2. With a high-frequency electronic gluer, urearesin adhesive dries in a matter of seconds. This equipment is used in industry to speed up production.

● *Epoxy cement* is a two-part adhesive that sticks to most materials. It can be used on wood, plastics, leather, metal, ceramics, and other materials. It produces a strong waterproof joint. Epoxy cements come in two containers consisting of a special resin and a chemical hardener. These are mixed together at the time of use. This cement produces superstrong joints without clamping.

● *Hot-melt glues* are supplied in stick or chunk form for use with an electric glue gun. A stick of hot-melt glue fits into the gun itself. Fig. 15-3. To use the glue gun, make sure that the flow-control valve in the gun tip is closed. Insert the hot-melt glue stick in the gun and plug in the cord. Allow about 3 minutes for the gun to heat. Clean the surface to be glued. Then soften the end of another glue stick on the hot tip of the gun. Insert the stick into the gun. It will fuse with the stick already in the gun. Open the flow valve by tapping the valve pin against any hard surface. Feed the glue onto the work by pressing the glue stick with your thumb. Then press the glued pieces together for 20 seconds.

TEN HINTS FOR SUCCESSFUL GLUING

● Make well-fitting joints.
● Make sure the surfaces are clean and dry.
● Choose the correct glue.
● Mix the glue to proper thickness.
● Mark the pieces for correct assembly.
● Have the proper clamps ready.
● Apply the glue to both surfaces of the joint.
● Remove extra glue before it dries.
● Allow plenty of time for the assembly to dry.

15-3. Using a small electric glue gun: A. Insert glue stick in gun; B. Open flow control valve by tapping nozzle; C. To feed glue, press glue stick with thumb; D. Press glued surfaces together for 20 seconds.

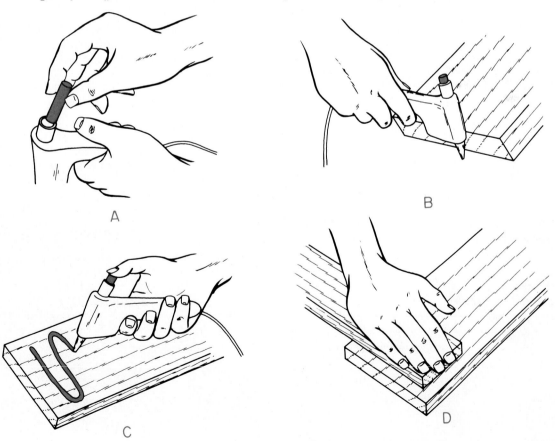

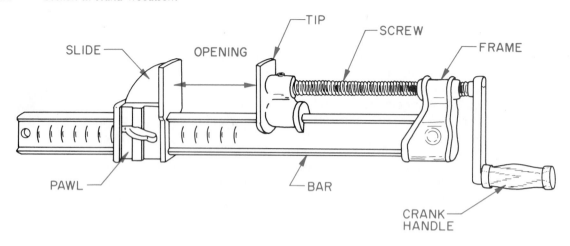

15-4. The parts of a cabinet, or bar, clamp.

KINDS OF CLAMPS

The *cabinet*, or *bar*, *clamp* is used for gluing up large surfaces edge to edge and for clamping parts together when assembling projects. Fig. 15-4. It is made in lengths from 2 to 10 feet (0.61 to 3 m) and in several styles. One end is adjusted to length by friction or by a pawl. The other end is moved in and out by a screw. When using a cabinet clamp, turn the screw out completely. Then move in the pawl or friction end until the clamp is slightly wider than the total width of the stock to be clamped. When using cabinet clamps on finished stock, protect the surface of the wood. Place small pieces of scrap stock between the clamp jaws and the wood or put plastic pads on the clamp itself.

● *Pipe clamps* are made with either a single or double pipe. The clamp units that fit the steel pipe are purchased so that the clamps can be made to any length. The double pipe clamps apply equal pressure to stock being glued up. Fig. 15-5.

● *Hand screws* are wooden parallel clamps about 6 to 20 inches (152 to 508 mm) long. They open from 4 to 20 inches (102 to 508 mm). Fig. 15-6. When using hand screws, hold the center screw in the left hand and the

15-6. Correct and incorrect ways of clamping with hand screws. The clamps on the left are not parallel. Therefore, they will not apply pressure correctly.

15-5. Pipe clamps are made with single or double pipes, as shown here.

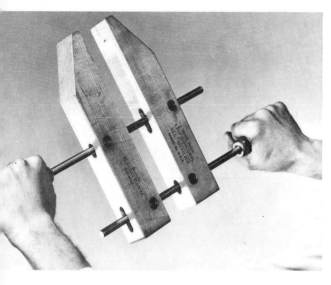

15-7. Hold the middle spindle and revolve the end spindle to open or close a hand screw.

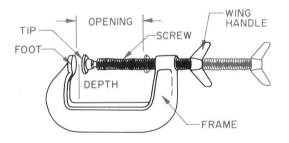

15-8. The C-clamp is used for clamping irregular or odd-shaped pieces and for many special jobs in the workshop.

15-9. Speed bar clamps such as this one are easily adjusted. This makes gluing a great deal easier.

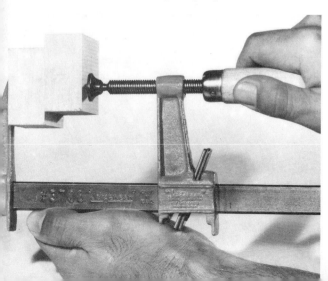

outside screw in the right hand. Open and close the clamp by twisting the handles in opposite directions. Fig. 15-7. The hand screw is for gluing stock face to face. It is also used for clamping together any work that is within the range of the clamp jaws.

● The *C-clamp* comes in many sizes. It is used to assemble and clamp parts. Fig. 15-8.

● *Speed (instant acting) clamps* are very convenient because they can be instantly adjusted for quick assembly. Fig. 15-9.

● *Spring clamps* are easy to use. Some types have pivoting jaws made of stainless steel with double rows of serrated teeth along the pressure edge. These toothed jaws hold the surface of parts so that miter joints and other odd shapes can be held together. Fig. 15-10.

● An *edging clamp* is designed to hold moldings, veneer, and laminates to the edge of a workpiece. It has three screws. There is a screw at the top and bottom of the jaw opening. An additional screw tightens in from the side. Fig. 15-11.

● A *band,* or *web clamp,* is a nylon strap that tightens around projects. It is used to glue up multisided projects such as a chair frame. Fig. 15-12.

15-10. A spring clamp is good for small work and delicate jobs. These come in assorted sizes. Some have rubber-covered jaws to protect the work.

15-11. An edging clamp.

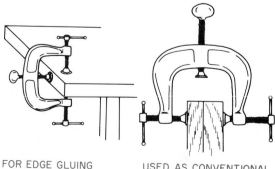

FOR EDGE GLUING

USED AS CONVENTIONAL "C" CLAMP

15-12. A band clamp.

SOME TIPS ON CLAMPING

● Dry-clamp all your workpieces before gluing. This will help you make sure the joints fit properly and that you have enough clamps for the job.

● Mark your pieces before final clamping and gluing-up.

● When gluing edge to edge, alternate bar clamps one above, one below every 10 to 15 inches to prevent buckling.

● Use *cauls*, small pieces of scrap wood, to prevent metal jaw faces from marring your workpieces.

● Don't apply too much pressure. This will force the glue out of the joint, causing a weak joint. Clamp down until the pieces are snug, but not too tight.

MAKING AND GLUING UP AN EDGE JOINT

Select stock that will form the larger surface. If it is wider than 8 to 10 inches (203 to 254 mm), rip into narrower strips to prevent warping when the pieces are glued together. After cutting the pieces, arrange them in their correct order. Remember the following:

● Make sure that the grain of all pieces runs in the same direction. After you have glued up the pieces, it will not be difficult to do the planing.

● Alternate the pieces so the annular rings face in opposite directions. Fig. 15-13. This will help to prevent the surface from warping.

● Try to match the pieces to form the most interesting grain arrangement.

Now mark the adjoining face of each matching joint with matching numbers, Xs, or lines. Make the marks in a place where they can be easily seen.

Plane one surface of each piece to remove wind or warpage and to help see grain direction. If any pieces are running in opposite directions, reverse them and re-mark the ends.

15-13. Note the proper method of arranging stock before gluing it together. Also, mark the adjoining boards so that they will be easy to assemble.

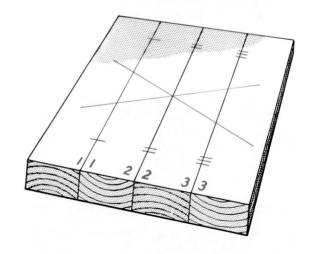

Plane both edges until they are square with the face surface. Hold a straightedge against the face surfaces of all the pieces to make sure they do not bow. Fig. 15-14. Tap the top piece with your finger to see that it does not rock. Finally, slide the top piece along the bottom one to see if it tends to have a suction action. Continue to plane one surface and the two edges of each piece. Match each of the joints.

ADDING DOWELS

When joints with additional strength are needed, dowels can be added. See Unit 27.

MAKING A TRIAL ASSEMBLY OF THE STOCK

After all joints have been constructed, place the pieces in position again on the top of a bench. Use a jig to hold the bar clamps. If the pieces are very long, place them over two sawhorses. Select three or more cabinet, or bar, clamps, depending on the length of the stock. Carefully set all cabinet clamps to the proper openings. They should be ready to clamp the stock as soon as the edges are glued. Cover the bench top with wrapping paper to protect the surface.

15-14. Holding a straightedge against the face surfaces of stock to see if the surfaces are straight and do not bow.

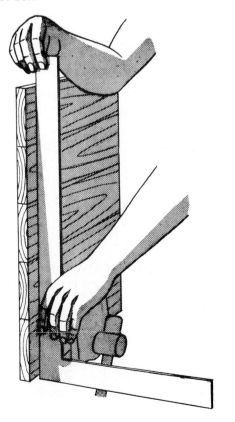

GLUING UP THE STOCK

Hold the two matching edges together so they are flush. Spread the glue with a brush, stick, or roller. Fig. 15-15. Make sure that both edges are completely covered. This is called *double spread*. When glue is applied to only one surface and the surfaces rubbed together, it is called *single spread*. Do not apply too much glue. It will squeeze out of the joint when it is put together. You will need to remove this glue later.

When you have glued all the edges, rapidly lay the pieces on the lower clamps till all are in place. If possible, rub the two pieces together to work the glue into the wood. Tighten the outside clamps lightly. Then place another clamp upside down on the stock at the midpoint. Clamp this lightly. Use a rubber mallet to tap the ends or the face surfaces to line them up. Check all the joints to make sure that the face surfaces are flush and the ends are in line. Then tighten each clamp until it applies firm pressure. Place a wood cleat above and below the surface at each end. Clamp these in place with hand screws. Fig. 15-16. This will help keep the surface true and free from warpage. A piece of waxed paper under the cleats will keep them from sticking. Before the glue begins to harden, wipe off the excess with a wet rag.

15-15. Two methods of spreading glue: A. Spreading cold glue with a roller after it is applied with a brush; B. Applying hot glue with a brush.

15-16. Bar clamps are holding glued-up stock together. Note the cleat that has been fastened to one end of the stock.

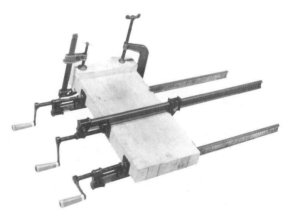

MAKING AND GLUING UP STOCK FACE TO FACE

Select and cut out several pieces of stock that will make up the correct size when glued together. Arrange the pieces with the annular rings alternating in direction. Also, make sure that the grain of the pieces runs in the same direction. Mark the ends and face surface so that you will know how the pieces should be arranged for gluing. Plane the face surface of the two outside pieces true and smooth. If more than two pieces are glued together, plane the center pieces to thickness.

Select several hand screws or C-clamps. Open them slightly wider than the stock to be clamped. Apply glue evenly. Then clamp as shown in Fig. 15-17. In tightening the hand screw, make sure the jaws are parallel.

DRYING AND REMOVING THE EXCESS GLUE

The drying time for glue varies with the kind of glue, the kind of wood, and the temperature. For white resin glue, about one-half hour is needed. In most cases, glues should be allowed to dry overnight. Remove excess glue with a scraper or sharp chisel.

15-17. Gluing up stock face to face. Cleats are fastened underneath the C-clamps to protect the surfaces of the wood.

Review Questions

1. Name eight kinds of glue and identify their ingredients.
2. Which glues are waterproof?
3. Which glue is best for a small repair job?
4. Tell what cabinet, or bar, clamps are needed for and how they are used.
5. Of what material are the clamps of hand screws made?
6. For what special kinds of gluing jobs can C-clamps be helpful?
7. To glue up a large board, wide stock is ripped into narrow strips. Explain the reason for this.
8. What three things must you consider when gluing up stock?
9. A trial assembly is always made before gluing. What is accomplished by it?
10. About how much glue should be applied to the edges?
11. With what kind of mallet should wood surfaces be pounded?
12. How can you keep the surface true and free from warpage?
13. Why must the jaws of hand screws be parallel?

Chapter 16

Squaring Up Stock

After studying this chapter, you will be able to:
● List the main steps in squaring up stock, using one of the three methods described in this chapter.

LOOK FOR THIS TERM

squaring up stock

You may need to plane several or all of the surfaces of the pieces for your project. Fig. 16-1. In some cases, you will plane only the edges of the stock. In other cases, such as in making a cutout design, you may plane the face surface, one edge, and the other surface. When parts are to be assembled, it may be better to plane the stock to thickness and width. You can then finish the ends by sawing.

Many times, however, you will need to plane all six surfaces of the board. This is called *squaring up the stock*. If machine tools are available, a planer and jointer can be used, following the same procedure as with a hand plane. There are several methods of squaring up stock. Three of these are discussed below.

16-1. The legs of this table are examples of stock that must be planed on all sides.

METHOD A

1. Plane the face surface or side (working face).
2. Plane the working edge.
3. Plane the stock to width (second edge).
4. Plane the stock to thickness (second surface or side).
5. Plane one end (working end).
6. Cut stock to length.
7. Plane other end (second end).

METHOD B

1. Plane the face surface (working surface).
2. Plane the working edge.
3. Plane one end square with the face surface and joint edge.
4. Plane stock to width.
5. Plane stock to thickness.
6. Cut off stock to length.
7. Plane other end.

METHOD C (RECOMMENDED)

1. Plane the face surface. Fig. 16-2.
2. Plane the working edge.
3. Plane one end square with the face surface and joint edge.
4. Cut off stock to length and plane other end.
5. Plane stock to width.
6. Plane stock to thickness.

After squaring up stock, use a cornering tool to remove the sharp corners. Fig. 16-3.

Review Questions

1. Must all six surfaces of the board be planed?
2. Name the machine tools that are useful in squaring up stock.
3. Describe the three methods of squaring up stock.
4. After squaring up stock, what tool is used for removing sharp corners?

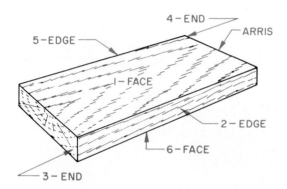

16-2. This is the recommended sequence for squaring up stock.

16-3. Cornering tool. This tool is used to trim the sharp edges from squared-up stock.

Chapter 17

Layout for Designs

After studying this chapter, you will be able to:
● Demonstrate the use of dividers in laying out small circles.
● Demonstrate the use of dividers in laying out an octagon or hexagon.
● Enlarge an irregular design.

LOOK FOR THESE TERMS

circle	hexagon
compass	octagon
dividers	template
ellipse	trammel points

Some projects have irregular designs or curved shapes that must be transferred to the wood. Figs. 17-1 to 17-4. If the design is geometric, the layout can usually be made directly on the wood. However, if the design is irregular, first draw a full-size pattern on paper and then transfer it to the wood.

17-1. Two tools for drawing circles and arcs: A. Dividers; B. Pencil compass.

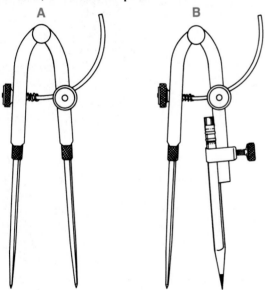

17-2. The parts for this weather station must be enlarged to full size. They must then be transferred to the wood before they can be cut out and finished.

DIVIDERS

Either *dividers* or a pencil compass can be used for laying out small circles, dividing space equally, transferring measurements, and scribing arcs. To set the tool, place one leg over the inch mark and open the other leg to the correct width. Lock the thumbscrew.

DRAWING CIRCLES

Set the dividers to equal half the diameter. Place one leg over the center. Tip the dividers at a slight angle. Working from left to right, scribe the circle. When drawing circles on finished wood, place a pencil eraser over the point to act as the center.

To lay out large circles, use a set of *trammel points*. Fig. 17-5.

LAYING OUT A ROUNDED CORNER

Check the drawing to get the radius of the arc and mark this distance from the corner on the side and end. Fig. 17-6. Hold a try square against edge and end. Draw two lines that intersect (cross) the center of the arc. Set the dividers to the proper radius. Draw the arc.

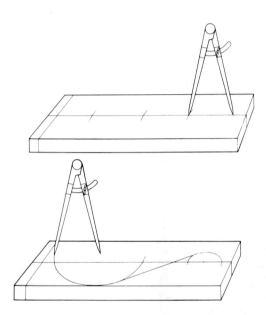

17-3. Dividers are used for marking out radius work and for stepping off measurements.

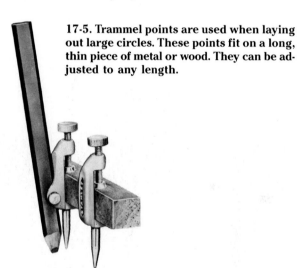

17-5. Trammel points are used when laying out large circles. These points fit on a long, thin piece of metal or wood. They can be adjusted to any length.

17-6. Locating the center for laying out a rounded corner.

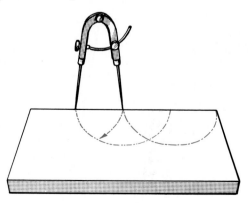

17-4. Set the dividers for the correct distance. Then step off these equal distances.

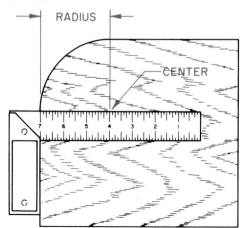

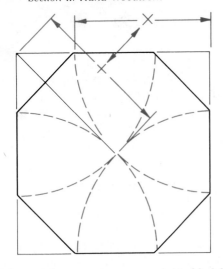

17-7. Layout for an octagon, an eight-sided figure.

LAYING OUT AN OCTAGON

An *octagon* has eight equal sides with all angles equal. Find the distance across the octagon. Lay out a square of this size. Set a dividers or *compass* to half the diagonal length across the square. Set the point of the compass at each corner of the square. Strike an arc from one side of the square to the other from each corner. Join the points where the arcs meet the sides of the square. Fig. 17-7.

LAYING OUT A HEXAGON

A *hexagon* has six equal sides with all angles equal. Find the length of one side. Set a compass or dividers to equal this measurement and draw a circle with this radius. Begin at any point on the circle and draw a series of arcs, moving the point to the place where the preceding arc has intersected the circle. Fig. 17-8. The last arc should intersect the circle at the first point. Join these points with a straightedge.

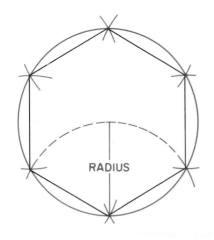

17-8. Layout of a hexagon, a six-sided figure.

DRAWING AN ELLIPSE

An *ellipse* is a regular curve that has two different diameters. Lay out the two diameters at right angles to each other. See, for example, AB and CD as shown in Fig. 17-9. Set a dividers equal to half the longest diameter. Place the point of the dividers on point C.

17-9. How to make an ellipse: A. Laying out the two diameters at right angles to each other; B. Striking an arc to intersect two points, X and Y, on the long diameter; C. Drawing the ellipse. Note that the outside thumbtack has been removed and a pencil put in its place. In forming the ellipse, be sure the pencil is held at right angles to the wood.

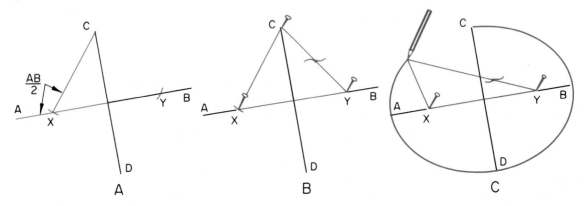

Strike an arc to intersect the longest diameter at points X and Y. Place a thumbtack at these two points and another at one end of the shortest diameter. Tie a string around the three thumbtacks. Fig. 17-9b. Remove the outside thumbtack and place a pencil inside the string. Hold the pencil at right angles to the paper. Carefully draw the ellipse. Fig. 17-9c.

ENLARGING IRREGULAR DESIGNS

Projects are seldom drawn full size. If the project contains irregular parts, make an enlarged drawing as a pattern in making the layout. Fig. 17-10.

1. Check how much smaller the original drawing is than full size. Drawings are usually one-half or one-fourth full size.
2. If the original drawing is not already on squared paper, lay out squares over the print. For example, if the pattern is one-fourth full size, draw ¼-inch (6.5 mm) squares.
3. On a large piece of wrapping paper, carefully lay out 1-inch (25.5 mm) squares.
4. From the lower left-hand corner of both the original drawing and the layout paper, letter all horizontal lines A, B, C, etc. Number all vertical lines 1, 2, 3, etc.

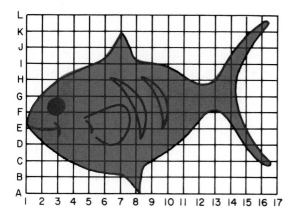

17-10. Enlarging an irregular design. Crosshatch paper is numbered the same, both in the original and the enlargement. This helps you locate the points needed to make an enlargement.

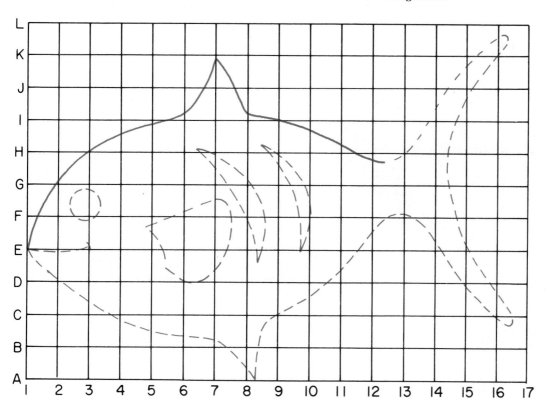

5. Using these letters and numbers, locate a position on the original drawing. Transfer this point to the full-size pattern.
6. Repeat the procedure in step 5 until you have enough points on the full-size pattern to complete the pattern accurately.
7. Sketch the full-size pattern. For curved lines, bend a piece of wire solder to use as a guide. (The piece may be symmetrical. If it is, you need to lay out only half the design. Then fold the sheet down the center and cut the full pattern.)
8. Place this paper pattern on the stock. Tape it to hold it in place. Trace carefully around the pattern. If many duplicate parts are needed, make a *template* of thin wood or sheet metal. Use this template to trace the layout. Fig. 17-11.

Review Questions

1. Name three uses for a dividers.
2. How should a dividers be set for transferring measurements?
3. What precautions should be taken when drawing a circle on a finished piece?
4. What are trammel points?
5. How many sides has an octagon? A hexagon?
6. Describe the procedure for laying out an octagon.
7. Define an ellipse. Describe how to draw one.
8. When is it necessary to enlarge an irregular design?
9. Why are most of the designs drawn on squared paper?
10. Is it always necessary to lay out the whole design?
11. What is a template?

17-11. Using a template to make a layout. When several pieces of the same design are to be cut, it is much simpler to use a template of thin wood or metal.

Facts about Wood

Petrified Wood

You may have seen a piece of petrified wood. It can have the texture, even something of the color, of natural wood. But, it will weigh more. Simply, petrified wood is wood that has been turned to rock. The way in which petrified wood is formed is similar to the way in which fossils are formed.

A *fossil* is the remains of a plant or an animal preserved from prehistoric times by natural means. For an object to be *fossilized*, or turned into a fossil, it must be quickly buried in a material that will protect it against oxygen and bacteria. Both of these will cause the object to decay. Slowly, then, the object is turned to stone. Consider the case of an insect buried in a layer of rock. Water may trickle in and dissolve the insect, leaving only a mold of its shape in the rock. If the water carried with it various minerals, these may fill in the mold, creating the fossil.

Petrified wood is formed in somewhat the same way as a fossil. Petrified wood is formed by a process known as *petrification*. Like a fossil, petrified wood was formed from material that was quickly buried. Then, exposed to underground mineral-bearing water, the wood was slowly petrified, or turned to rock. In this very slow process, each molecule of the wood is replaced by mineral matter. Since this replacement is molecule-for-molecule, the petrified object has the appearance of the natural object. You may, however, have seen pieces of petrified wood that are not very detailed. Sometimes, petrification results only in an object with the same shape. The texture and detail may be lacking.

The largest known display of petrified wood is in the Petrified Forest National Park in Arizona. The trees now petrified here were living things about 200 million years ago.

They died from causes such as fire and fungus. After they died, the trees were covered with earth that contained volcanic ash. This ash was rich in silica. Silica is a chemical compound found in quartzlike rocks, such as jasper and agate. As water seeped through the earth covering the trees, the silica was carried into the wood. Slowly, the silica replaced the individual wood cells. Finally, the logs are no longer wood but are instead silica, each of their cells being replaced by this substance.

The logs in the Petrified Forest National Park are of agate and jasper. They were exposed millions of years ago as the surrounding soil was washed away. Thousands of years ago, the site was occupied by prehistoric Amerindians. Remains of their dwellings are found in the forest. It was, though, a lost site, unknown until 1851, when it was discovered by an Army officer. The site has been a national park since 1962.

Chapter 18

Cutting Out Curves

After studying this chapter, you will be able to:
● Demonstrate the proper cutting of stock with a coping saw, the stock being held in a vise.
● Demonstrate the proper use of the compass saw.

LOOK FOR THESE TERMS

compass saw   keyhole saw
coping saw   saw bracket

Curved or irregularly shaped parts are cut with a thin blade coping or compass saw.

THE COPING SAW

The *coping saw* has a U-shaped frame, a wood handle and a replaceable blade with rip-saw like teeth. It is used for cutting internal and external shapes on thin wood. Fig. 18-1.

CUTTING WITH THE WORK SUPPORTED ON A SAW BRACKET

Thin wood (³⁄₈ inch or less in thickness) tends to vibrate as sawing is done when the stock is clamped in a vise. Therefore, a *saw bracket* is a better way to support the material.

Mount the blade in the frame with the teeth pointing *toward* the handle. If an internal opening is to be cut, drill a small hole in the waste material just large enough for the blade to pass through. Slip the blade through the hole. Fasten it into the frame.

Hold the work to the bracket with your left hand. Fig. 18-2. Grasp the handle in your right hand and move the saw up and down. Cut on the *downward* stroke, and then release the pressure. The workpiece can also be clamped to the bench top with a C-clamp. Fig. 18-3.

As you cut, it is better to move the work, keeping the saw blade inside the V-cut of the bracket. If the cutting is hard, apply a little soap or wax to the blade. Move the blade at a steady speed of about twenty to thirty strokes per minute. At sharp corners, turn the handle slowly in the direction of the line. Keep moving the saw up and down without applying any pressure to the blade. Begin cutting again as the blade is turned. Twisting or bending the blade at the corners usually breaks it.

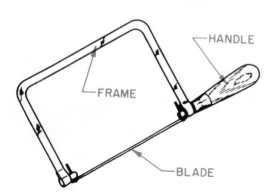

HANDLE

FRAME

BLADE

18-1. A coping saw. This type is tightened by screwing up the handle. The blade can also be adjusted at any angle to the frame.

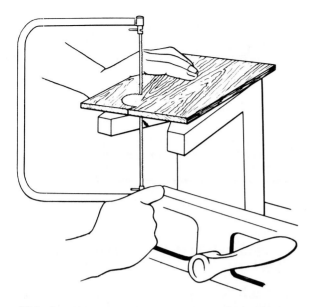

18-2. Cutting work with the stock held over a saw bracket. Shift the position of the work to accommodate the saw most easily. Secure the work. Take full and easy strokes. Guide the blade carefully. This will help prevent blade breakage. In cutting some types of wood, plywood in particular, draw the blade through beeswax at intervals during the cutting. This will ease the cutting.

CUTTING WITH THE WORK HELD IN A VISE

Put the blade in the frame with the teeth pointing *away* from the handle. Lock the work in the vise with the place to be cut near the top of the vise jaws. Begin the cutting in the waste stock. Make sure that the saw *kerf* is in the *waste* stock and that the blade is held straight up and down on the work. The saw can be supported with both hands as shown in Fig. 18-4.

THE COMPASS SAW

The *compass saw* is designed to cut a wide kerf for sawing curves or irregular shapes. It looks like any other handsaw except that it is much smaller and has a thin, tapered blade. Usually a compass saw comes with several different-sized blades to fit into the handle. The narrow point at the end makes it possible to start the tool in a small opening and to cut small curves and circles. The saw is made in lengths from 10 to 18 inches (254 to 457 mm) with eight points to the inch. Fig. 18-5.

A *keyhole saw* is similar, but smaller. It is named for its most common use. Fig. 18-6.

18-3. Holding a workpiece with a C-clamp.

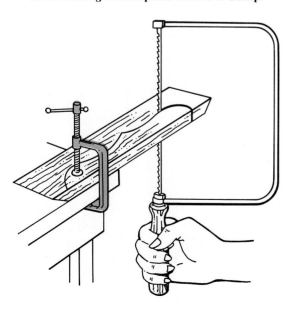

18-4. Cutting with a coping saw with the work held in a vise. In this type of work, the saw can be held in both hands. This gives it more support for cutting heavy stock. The blade should be inserted with the teeth pointing away from the handle.

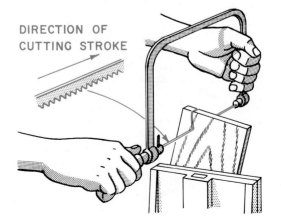

DIRECTION OF CUTTING STROKE

18-5. Compass saw. This one has several interchangeable blades for different types of jobs. Compass and keyhole saws have small, highly tempered blades. These blades have specially filed teeth designed for cutting curves and circles. In addition to the several types available for woodworking, special compass saws have been designed. These are used for cutting jobs such as those encountered by plumbers and electricians.

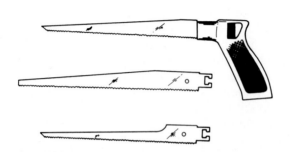

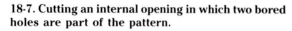

18-6. Keyhole saws are available with several different blades. One blade may be designed for cutting thin metal.

CUTTING WITH THE COMPASS SAW

Bore a hole in the waste stock large enough for the saw point. Fig. 18-7. Insert the point in the first hole. Take several short, quick strokes to force more of the blade to pass through the stock. Cut a curve by slightly twisting the handle of the saw to follow the pattern. Fig. 18-8.

18-8. Before starting to cut with a compass saw, clearly mark the line to be cut. Make certain that the work is securely supported. For best results, hold the saw almost perpendicular to the work. To get the saw to turn with the pattern, gently guide the saw by turning the handle in the direction of the cut. Forcing the blade too vigorously in the cut may cause it to bend, buckle or break.

18-7. Cutting an internal opening in which two bored holes are part of the pattern.

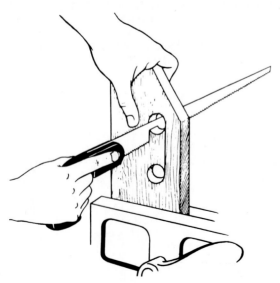

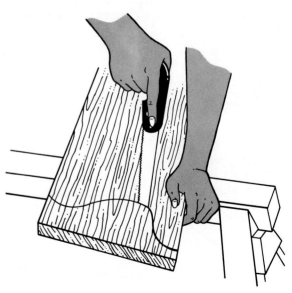

Review Questions

1. What hand tools will cut curves in wood?
2. The blades of a coping saw resemble those of what type of handsaw?
3. When work is cut on a saw bracket, should the teeth be pointed toward or away from the handle?
4. About how many strokes per minute should be taken with the coping saw?
5. Exactly where should the saw kerf be in regard to the layout lines?
6. Describe a compass saw and give its use.

This jar opener made of plywood could be cut with a coping saw.

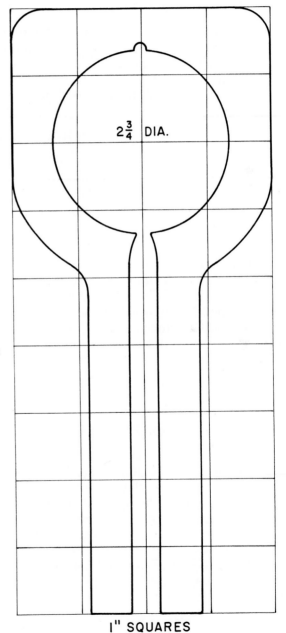

$2\frac{3}{4}$ DIA.

I" SQUARES

Chapter 19

Forming and Smoothing Curves

After studying this chapter, you will be able to:
- Demonstrate the proper use of the spokeshave.
- Demonstrate the proper use of a drawknife.
- Distinguish a rasp from a file.
- Discuss the design of the Surform® tool.

LOOK FOR THESE TERMS

chatter	solid-router drill
drawknife	spokeshave
file	Surform®
rasp	

After the curve has been cut, the edge is rough. Some stock must be removed to smooth the edge and to bring it down to the finished line. Sometimes it is necessary to form or mold a curved surface. Fig. 19-1. These jobs can be done with a cutting tool, such as a spokeshave or drawknife, or with a scraping tool, such as a file, rasp, or other forming tool.

THE SPOKESHAVE

A *spokeshave* has a frame with two handles that hold a small cutting blade. It is used to plane convex (dome-shaped) and concave (cup-shaped) edges. The depth of cut can be regulated with one or two small thumbscrews. The spokeshave was originally used for shaping the spokes of wheels. Now, however, it is a common tool for finishing the edges of curves and molding irregular shapes. Figs. 19-2 and 19-3.

19-1. The frame of this mirror requires forming.

19-2. A spokeshave is used to cut concave and convex edges and for molding and forming work. This type has two narrow nuts on the top for adjusting the depth of the cutter. The cutter is held in place with a cap, which is fastened by a thumbscrew.

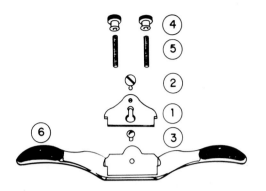

19-3. Parts of a spokeshave: 1. Cap; 2. Thumbscrew; 3. Cap screw; 4. Adjusting nuts; 5. Adjusting screw; and 6. Body.

19-4. Cutting with a spokeshave by drawing it toward you. The blade should be set just deep enough to form a thin shaving. If set too deep, the tool will chatter.

19-5. Cutting with a spokeshave by pushing it away from you. Even pressure must be applied to do the cutting.

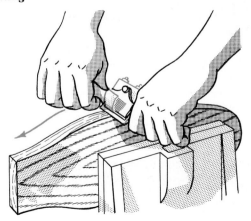

CUTTING WITH A SPOKESHAVE

Place the piece in the vise with the edge to be smoothed near the surface of the vise. Hold the tool with both hands. You can either draw the spokeshave toward you or put your thumbs behind the frame and push it as you would a small plane. Figs. 19-4 and 19-5. Place the cutting edge on the wood and apply even pressure. Work *with* the grain of the wood. If the blade is set too deep, the tool will *chatter* (vibrate and cut unevenly).

When shaping concave curves, cut from the top of the curve downward.

THE DRAWKNIFE

The *drawknife* is a U-shaped tool. It has a blade 8 or 10 inches (203 or 254 mm) long with a handle at each end. Fig. 19-6. This tool is very good for removing large amounts of stock rapidly. It is good for doing molding work such as shaping a canoe paddle or building a model boat. Be very careful in using this tool. The long, exposed blade *can be dangerous*.

CUTTING WITH THE DRAWKNIFE

Clamp the work in a vise in such a way that the cutting will take place *with* the grain of the wood. Hold the tool in both hands, with the blade firmly against the wood and the bevel side down. Turn the blade at a slight angle to the work. Carefully draw it into the wood until a thin chip forms. Then draw the knife steadily toward you. Fig. 19-7. Do not try to take too deep a cut at one time. This will split the wood.

19-6. A drawknife is especially useful when removing large amounts of stock rapidly.

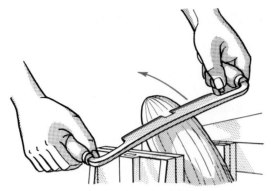

19-7. Using a drawknife to shape the hull of a model boat.

THE FILE AND RASP

The *file* and *rasp* are scraping tools. There are a great many kinds of files, in many shapes and sizes. The two files used most often are half-round cabinet and flat files. Fig. 19-8.

A rasp looks like a file, except that the face is cut with individually shaped teeth. Fig. 19-9. The rasp removes large amounts of stock quickly and leaves a rough surface. The file leaves a smoother finish. Always put a handle on the rasp and file when using them because the tang (the projecting point) can cause a bad injury. Fig. 19-10.

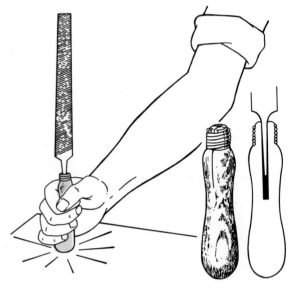

19-10. Always fit a handle on a file before using it.

19-8. A cabinet file. Be sure that the handle is attached when using it for smoothing operations. Never use a file without a handle.

19-9. A rasp. Notice the individually shaped teeth. This tool is used when removing large amounts of stock. The rasp leaves quite a rough surface.

SMOOTHING WITH A FILE OR RASP

Clamp the work tightly in the vise. Hold the handle in your right hand and the end of the tool in your left. Apply pressure on the forward stroke, making a slight shearing cut across the edge of the work. Fig. 19-11. Release the pressure on the return stroke. When you are using a half-round file for finishing a convex curve, twist the tool slowly as the forward stroke is made. Don't rock a file or rasp. This will round off the edge of the work. These tools should be cleaned often with a file card. Fig. 19-12.

THE SURFORM® TOOL

The *Surform® tool* is a cutting tool with a hardened, tempered tool-steel cutting blade. Fig. 19-13. This tool never needs sharpening, setting, or adjusting. The tool can be used for cutting, shaping, shaving, smoothing, filing, rasping, and forming. The teeth are shaped so that they bite into the material. They then allow the shavings to pass through the blade without clogging. Fig. 19-14. The blade makes it easy to cut wood, plastics, and other soft materials. The tool is available in a variety of types. The replaceable blade fits into a file, block plane, or plane-type holder. Fig. 19-15.

19-11. Using a file to dress an internal curve. Make sure that you hold the file flat against the stock and that you do not rock it.

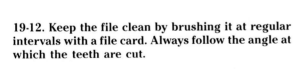

19-12. Keep the file clean by brushing it at regular intervals with a file card. Always follow the angle at which the teeth are cut.

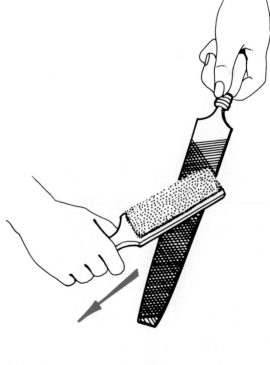

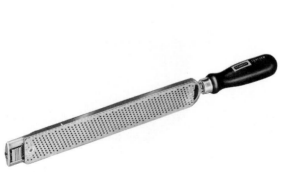

19-13. A file type of Surform® tool.

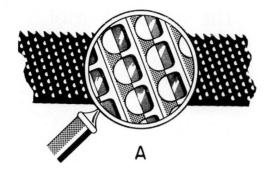

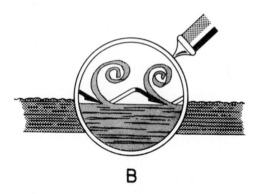

19-14. Notice the enlargement (A) of the Surform® tool. It consists of nearly 500 cutting teeth that are shaped in such a way as to bite into the material (B) and then allow the shavings to pass straight through.

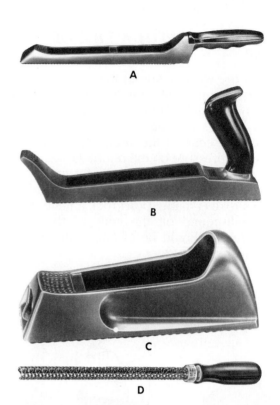

19-15. Common types of Surform® tools: A. File; B. Plane; C. Block-plane; and D. File type.

19-16. Using a plane-type Surform® tool to shape a table leg.

The Surform® tool is used like a rasp. To obtain best results, apply light pressure against the material. Fig. 19-16. This will produce a smooth, flat surface. It is a good repair tool for smoothing an edge or end that is chipped or splintered. It is also good for shaping gun stocks, canoe paddles, wooden tool handles, and other odd shapes. A rotary-type unit is also available that fits into a drill press or portable drill for shaping an edge. Fig. 19-17.

19-17. A rotary type of Surform® tool that can be used in a drill press or in a portable electric drill.

SOLID-ROUTER DRILLS

There are other types of tools for forming curves. The *solid-router drill* is ideal for enlarging holes, making circles and scrolls, and doing other types of shaping operations. Fig. 19-18.

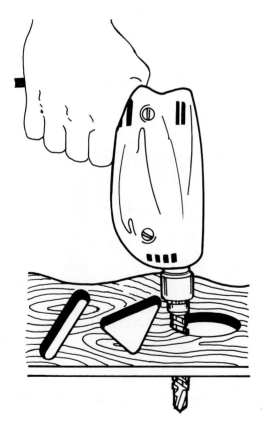

19-18. Note how the router-drill can be used to shape wood stock.

Review Questions

1. In what ways is a spokeshave like a plane?
2. Where did the spokeshave get its name?
3. Can a spokeshave be both drawn and pushed?
4. For what job is the drawknife best suited?
5. To make the cut, how should the drawknife be held against the wood?
6. What is the difference between a file and a rasp?
7. Does a good woodworker use a file or rasp very often?
8. What safety practice should be observed when using a file or rasp?
9. Describe how a Surform® tool is used.

Chapter 20

Chamfer, Bevel, and Taper

After studying this chapter, you will be able to:
● List the three methods for marking a through chamfer.
● Describe the method for cutting a stop chamfer.
● Describe the method for planing a bevel.
● List the main steps in cutting a taper.

LOOK FOR THESE TERMS

bevel   through chamfer
chamfer   taper
stop chamfer

The chamfer, bevel, and taper are three angular cuts made in much the same way. Each, though, is used for a different purpose.

The *chamfer* is an angular cut only part way across the corner or edge. It is used mostly as a decoration on an edge or end. Figs. 20-1 and 20-2. The *bevel* is an angle cut completely across the edge or end of a piece. Figs. 20-3 and 20-4. A *taper* is cut on the legs of tables and stools to make them appear more lightweight and graceful. Figs. 20-5 and 20-6. On some projects the taper is cut on all four sides. On others, only the two inside surfaces are cut.

20-1. The edge of this clock shows the use of a chamfer.

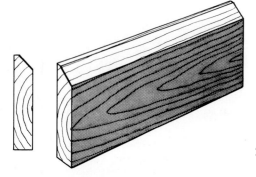

20-2. A chamfer.

20-3. A bevel was cut to form the joint on the two pieces at the roof line of this bird house.

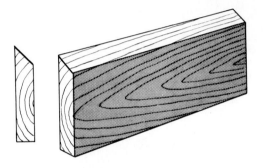

20-4. A bevel.

20-5. The inside of each leg of this table has a taper cut along its length.

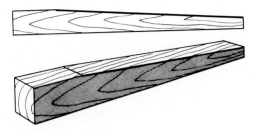

20-6. A taper.

MAKING A THROUGH CHAMFER

A *through chamfer* is one that extends the whole length of the board. First determine the amount of chamfer from the drawing. If this is not given, the usual practice is to cut a chamfer of about $\frac{3}{16}$ inch (5 mm) on stock 1 inch (25.4 mm) thick.

There are three methods for marking the chamfer. One is to hold a pencil between the fingers as a gauge and run it along the face surface and edge or end. Another way is to insert a pencil point in a marking gauge and use the marking gauge to lay out the line. Do not use a regular marking gauge. This would leave a rough edge on the chamfer. A third way is to use a combination square and pencil to mark the line.

Lock the stock in a vise. In some cases it may be easier to clamp the stock first in a hand screw as shown in Fig. 20-7. You should then lock the hand screw in the vise. In this way the plane can be held level as the cutting is done.

Plane the corner with the grain along the total length of the stock. Remove the stock evenly so that the chamfer will come to the marked line on both sides at the same time. Use the fingers of your left hand to guide the plane and hold it at the proper angle. In taking the last cut, form a chip that is the full width of the chamfer across the total length of the stock.

When cutting a chamfer on end grain, hold the plane or chisel at an angle to the surface. Take a shearing cut across the edge. Fig. 20-8. If this is not done, there is danger of splitting out the chamfer on the edge. Fig. 20-9. To check the chamfer, set a sliding T-bevel at an angle of 45 degrees. Hold it against the chamfer edge. Fig. 20-10.

20-7. Planing a chamfer with the wood held in a hand screw. By this means you can cut the chamfer with the plane held in a level position.

20-9. Using a block plane for cutting a chamfer on the edge of plywood.

20-10. Checking a chamfer with a sliding T-bevel set at 45 degrees.

20-8. Using a chisel to cut a chamfer on end grain.

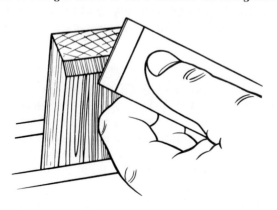

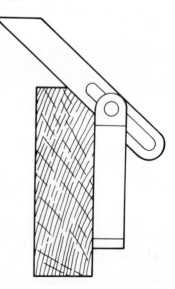

CUTTING A STOP CHAMFER

A *stop chamfer* is one that does not extend the whole length of the board. Mark the width and length of the stop chamfer with a pencil. Cut or pare with a chisel from one end of the chamfer to about half the length of the chamfer. Make thin cuts until you reach the layout line. Reverse the board and cut from the opposite end. Be careful not to cut into the stock that is not chamfered. Fig. 20-11.

PLANING A BEVEL

Determine the angle at which the bevel is to be cut. With a protractor, set a sliding T-bevel to this angle. Hold the sliding T-bevel against the face surface. Mark the angle of the bevel on both ends of the stock. Begin to plane the bevel as you would plane an edge. You must, however, tip the plane at about the angle at which the bevel is to be cut. Check this angle frequently with a sliding T-bevel. Continue to plane the edge until the bevel is formed.

CUTTING A TAPER

Lay the four legs side by side. Mark the position at which the taper is to start. Then square a line around all four sides of each leg. A taper may be cut on only one side of a leg. Fig. 20-12. However, most designs call for tapers on two adjoining sides or all four sides of the legs.

If tapers are cut on two or four sides, the layout and cutting must be done in two steps. The example in Fig. 20-13 shows the layout and cutting for tapers on two adjoining sides. Determine the amount of stock to be removed at the foot of the taper. Set a marking gauge to this amount. Mark a single line across the lower edge of the leg. Draw lines along opposite sides to show where the taper is to be cut. Cut the taper with a handsaw or, if one is available, a band or circular saw. Plane the tapered surface smooth and true. Fig. 20-14. Now mark the taper across the bottom of the leg on the adjoining side. Draw lines along opposite sides. Cut and smooth the second taper. If tapers are cut on all four sides, mark and cut the first two opposite tapers. Then mark and cut the second two opposite tapers.

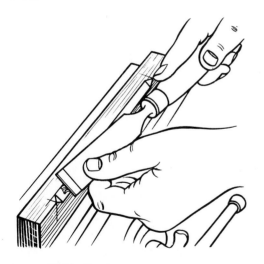

20-11. Cutting a stop chamfer.

20-12. Laying out a taper.

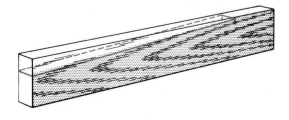

20-13. When the taper is to be cut on two adjoining surfaces, lay out one side and cut it before making the second layout.

FIRST TAPER MARKED

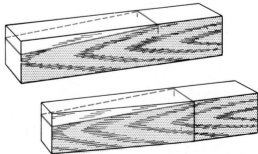

FIRST TAPER CUT, SECOND TAPER MARKED

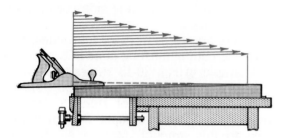

20-14. Planing a taper. Hold the plane on the angle of the taper. Make longer and longer strokes until you have planed the total length of the taper.

Review Questions

1. In what way is a chamfer different from a bevel?
2. Would you lay out a chamfer with a regular marking gauge? Discuss two methods of laying out an ordinary chamfer.
3. What precautions must be taken in cutting a chamfer on end grain?
4. How can you hold the plane level and still cut a chamfer?
5. Describe a stop chamfer.
6. Why is a sliding T-bevel necessary when making a bevel?
7. How should the planing strokes be taken when cutting a taper?

Chapter 21 | Shaping Stock With a Chisel or Gouge

After studying this chapter, you will be able to:
- List the two basic types of chisels.
- List the safety precautions to be followed when using a chisel.
- Demonstrate the proper use of the chisel.
- Demonstrate the proper use of a gouge.

LOOK FOR THESE TERMS

butt chisel	paring chisel
firmer chisel	socket chisel
gouge	soft-faced hammer
mallet	tang
mortise chisel	tang chisel

A *chisel* is a straight-edge cutting tool used to shape and trim wood. *Gouges* are similar to chisels but have curved cutting edges.

TYPES

There are two basic types of chisels, the *tang* and the *socket*. The most common *tang chisel* has a sharp-pointed shank. This shank, called a *tang*, fits into the wood or plastic handle. A heavy-duty tang chisel has a blade and tang forged in one piece. The tang goes completely through the handle and is fastened to a steel cap that covers the end of the handle. The *socket chisel* has a funnel-shaped socket at the top of the blade into which the handle fits. When using a *mallet* or soft-faced hammer for rough cutting or chiseling hardwood, use with a socket or a heavy-duty tang chisel. Fig. 21-1.

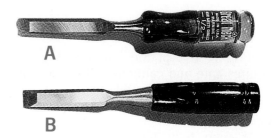

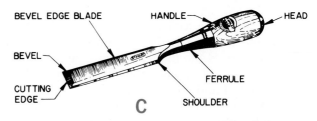

21-1. Types of chisels. A. A socket chisel is made in such a way that the handle fits into a socket of the blade; B. A tang-chisel has the tang of the chisel itself running into the handle. C. A heavy-duty tang chisel, with its parts labeled. A metal cap (head) is attached to the tang.

KINDS

Each chisel is designed for a certain type of cutting.

● *Butt chisels* have short blades about 3 to 4 inches long with beveled sides. They come in widths from ½ to 1½ inches. These chisels are used to shape joints and to cut recesses for hinges.

● *Firmer chisels* are all-purpose cutting tools with fairly thick, flat-sided blades. For rough cutting, these chisels are driven with a mallet or soft-faced hammer.

● *Paring chisels* are lightweight chisels for final trimming and fitting.

● *Mortise chisels* are very sturdy tools with thick blades ground flat on the sides. They come in widths from ⅛ to ⅝ inch. They are used for clearing out the mortise to fit a tenon. (See Chapter 32.)

You will need at least six chisels with blades from ¼ to 1½ inches wide, increasing at ⅛-inch intervals.

 Safety

Correct use of the chisel and gouge requires care and caution. Follow these guidelines when using these tools:

● Hold the workpiece so that it cannot move.

● Keep both hands behind the cutting edge and the chisel or gouge away from the body.

● Hold the tool correctly. The right hand should push with the handle while the left hand guides the blade. When using a mallet, the left hand should hold the handle, while the right hand taps the tool.

● Always hit the tool squarely on top of the handle.

● Never allow the edge to touch other tools. Avoid dropping the chisel or gouge on the floor or any other hard surface.

● Protect the handle by using a wood or plastic *mallet* or a *soft-faced hammer*. Figs. 21-2 and 21-3. Never use a metal hammer.

● When finished, store the chisel or gouge safely in a tool rack.

CUTTING HORIZONTALLY WITH THE GRAIN

Lock the work in a vise so the cutting can be done with the grain of the wood. Fig. 21-4. Never attempt to cut against the grain, as the wood will split out.

For rough cutting, hold the chisel with the bevel side against the stock. Grasp the chisel handle in your right hand and the blade in your left. Fig. 21-5. Use your right hand to apply pressure to the tool and your left hand to guide the cutting action.

You can apply the cutting action in two ways. You can force the blade into the stock parallel to the wood. You can also make a shearing cut, with the blade moving from right to left as it cuts. You will find that straight cutting takes more pressure. Also, it is more convenient to hold the tool in your left hand and pound with the mallet held in your right hand.

When making light, paring cuts with the chisel, turn the tool around with the flat surface next to the wood. Hold the blade between your thumb and forefinger to guide it in taking these cuts.

21-2. A mallet is used for pounding a chisel or gouge. The head should be wood, leather, or rubber.

21-3. A soft-faced hammer with replaceable plastic heads.

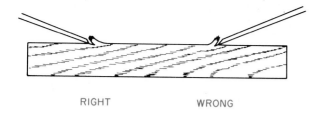

RIGHT   WRONG

21-4. Cutting action of the chisel when cutting horizontally with the grain. Always cut with the grain, never against it, for this procedure.

21-5. Holding a chisel for doing heavy horizontal cutting with the grain. The blade of the chisel is held firmly in the left hand.

21-6. Roughing out a cut across grain. Hold the chisel with the bevel side down. Use the mallet for driving. This illustrates the cutting of a lap joint.

21-7. Proper method of cutting a lap joint from both sides, leaving the center high and then trimming the center down.

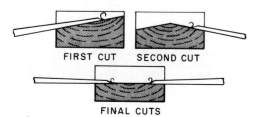

FIRST CUT   SECOND CUT

FINAL CUTS

CUTTING HORIZONTALLY ACROSS THE GRAIN

Lock the work in a vise or clamp it to the top of the bench. Rough cutting can be done with the bevel down or by paring with the flat side down. In cutting across the grain to make a rabbet, dado, or lap joint, work from one side to about halfway across the stock. Fig. 21-6. Never go completely across the stock. This will chip out the opposite side. Work from both sides to the finished line, leaving the center higher. Fig. 21-7. Then, with light paring cuts, bring the center down to the line. Fig. 21-8. To clean out the corners, hold the chisel in one hand with the flat side toward the shoulder. Draw the chisel across as you would a knife. Fig. 21-9.

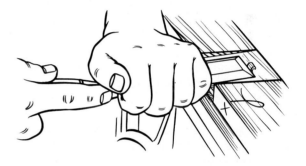

21-8. Horizontal cutting across grain for heavy cuts. Support the chisel with your left hand resting on the bench or vise. Cut with a slicing action.

21-9. Cleaning out the corners of a lap joint by pulling the chisel across with the flat side held against the shoulder of the joint.

CUTTING CONVEX CURVES HORIZONTALLY

When you lock the work in the vise, remember that you will be cutting with the grain. Begin by taking straight cuts that tend to follow the convex (dome-shaped) curve. Fig. 21-10. Remove most of the extra stock with these straight cuts until the curve is almost formed. Then hold the chisel with the flat side down. Carefully cut the curve by applying forward pressure and raising the handle to follow the curve. Fig. 21-11. Move the chisel sideways across the work, making a series of cuts close together.

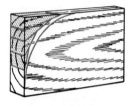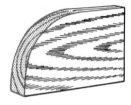

21-10. Cutting a convex curve. Note that several straight cuts can be taken to pre-form the curve to the approximate arc.

21-11. Finishing a convex curve. Apply forward pressure and raise the handle gradually to follow the proper curvature.

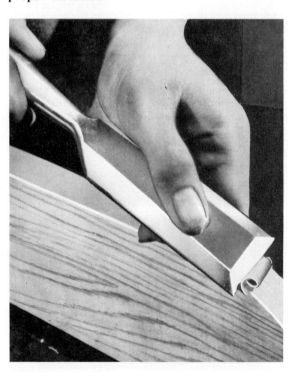

CUTTING VERTICALLY ACROSS THE GRAIN

Hold the stock over a bench hook, clamp it over a scrap piece of wood, or place it over a bench stop. Never do vertical chiseling directly on the top of a bench. This would damage the bench.

Hold the chisel in a vertical position with the handle in your right hand and the blade guided between your left thumb and forefinger. Take a shearing cut, working from right to left. On wide stock, you can regulate the depth of the cut by holding the flat side of the chisel against the surface that has already been cut. Fig. 21-12.

21-12. Cutting vertically across the grain. A. Notice how the left hand guides the chisel as the right hand applies pressure. The chisel should be tilted slightly to give a sliding action. B. Cut with the grain so that the waste wood will split away from the layout line.

CUTTING END GRAIN VERTICALLY

Lay the work flat over a bench hook or piece of scrap stock. Clamp it firmly in place. Beginning at one corner of the stock, begin the cut by tipping the handle to one side. Rotate the handle to get a shearing cut. Fig. 21-13. Always start from the corner and work toward the center. Working the other way would split out the end grain.

CUTTING CONCAVE SURFACES VERTICALLY

Lock the work in a vise with the concave (cup-shaped) surface to be removed just above the end of the vise. Take straight cuts until most of the waste stock is removed. As always, work from the edge toward the end to avoid splitting out the stock. To form the concave curve, hold the chisel with the bevel side toward the stock. Apply forward pressure, at the same time moving the handle in an arc (curve). Fig. 21-14.

GOUGES

Gouges are chisels with curved blades. They are sharpened either with the bevel on the inside or the outside. Fig. 21-15. Gouges range in size from ¼ to 2 inches (6 to 51 mm).

CUTTING WITH A GOUGE

Gouges are used in the same general way as chisels. Outside bevel gouges are handled in the same way as a chisel is handled when the bevel side is down. An inside bevel gouge is used as a chisel, with the bevel turned up.

21-13. Cutting end grain vertically. Note that the stock is held over a bench hook. Pressure is applied to the handle at the same time that it is rotated slightly to obtain a shearing cut. The left hand should rest on the wood, with the first finger controlling the chisel.

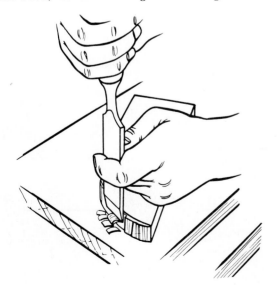

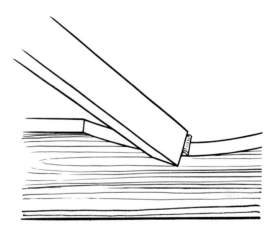

21-14. Cutting a concave curve. Hold the chisel with the bevel side down. Take the cut from the edge to the end grain. In this way you are cutting with the grain of the wood.

21-15. Types of gouges: A. Gouge with a bevel on the outside; B. Gouge with a bevel on the inside.

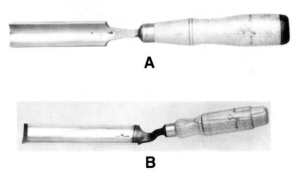

A

B

To do heavy gouging with an outside bevel gouge, hold the handle in your right hand and the blade in your left hand. Push the gouge forward, rocking it slightly from side to side to make a shearing cut. Fig. 21-16. For very heavy work, the gouge can be held in the left hand and the force applied with a mallet. If a large surface is to be gouged out, it is better to work across the grain. Directed this way, the gouge is less likely to dig in than when cutting in the direction of the grain.

To do light gouging, hold the blade in your left hand and take a long, thin shaving. Force the tool into the wood lightly. Then push on the handle to finish it.

Gouging is done to form recesses and to do veining and decorating work. Fig. 21-17. It is also used to shape such articles as boat hulls. It is used to give the appearance of age—as on a treasure chest.

Review Questions

1. Describe a butt chisel.
2. Do you cut with the grain of the wood?
3. How should a chisel be held for making heavy cuts?
4. What are the two ways to do rough cutting with a chisel?
5. When making light paring cuts, how should the blade be held?
6. Give the procedure for cutting a rabbet, dado, or lap joint.
7. How can the corners be chiseled out?
8. Should vertical chiseling be done directly on the top of a bench?
9. In cutting convex curves, why are straight cuts made first?
10. What kind of chisel action is best for cutting end grain vertically?
11. Can a concave surface be cut with a chisel?
12. How does a gouge differ from a chisel?
13. How are gouges sharpened?
14. What kind of gouge is best for heavy gouge work?
15. To remove a great deal of stock with a gouge, is it better to work with or across the grain?

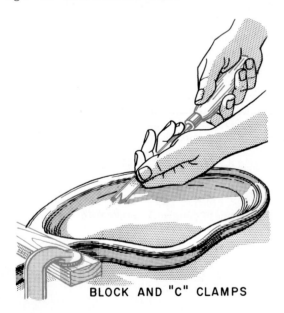

BLOCK AND "C" CLAMPS

21-16. Doing heavy gouging to shape out the inside of a tray. The left hand holds the blade firmly, while the right hand applies the pressure.

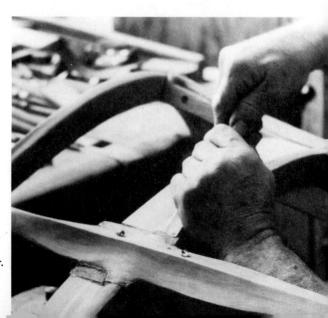

21-17. Using a gouge to shape the back of a chair.

Chapter 22

Wood Carving

After studying this chapter, you will be able to:
- List five main types of carving.
- Select woods suitable for carving.
- Describe the PEG treatment.
- List the main steps in carving.

LOOK FOR THESE TERMS

carving tools	knives	skew chisel
chase carving	PEG treatment	whittling
chip carving	parting tool	wood sculpture
fluters	relief carving	veiner

Wood carving is an ancient art, examples of which can be seen in museums, churches, and public buildings all over the world. Fig. 22-1. It is also one of the most interesting woodworking hobbies. Many artistic and attractive objects can be made with very simple tools.

22-1. Carving is an ancient art.

KINDS OF CARVING

There are several kinds of carving. These include the following:
- *Whittling* is freehand carving done with knives. Many interesting and useful projects can be made by using only the knife as a cutting tool. Fig. 22-2.
- *Chip carving* is a method of forming a design by cutting shapes in the wood surface. It is used mostly for cutting geometric shapes such as triangles, squares, and curved variations of these. Chip carving can be done with carving tools or knives.
- In *chase carving*, a design is laid out and gouges are used on the surface with long, sweeping cuts. Fig. 22-3. Carved free-form bowls and a variety of other items can be made in this manner.
- In *relief carving*, the background is cut away to form the surface design. This is one of the most difficult kinds of carving. The design stands out in three-dimensional form. If the carving is fairly shallow, it is called *low relief;* if the design has greater depth, it is known as *high relief*. In high relief the design is undercut so that it seems to stand away from the background. Fig. 22-4.

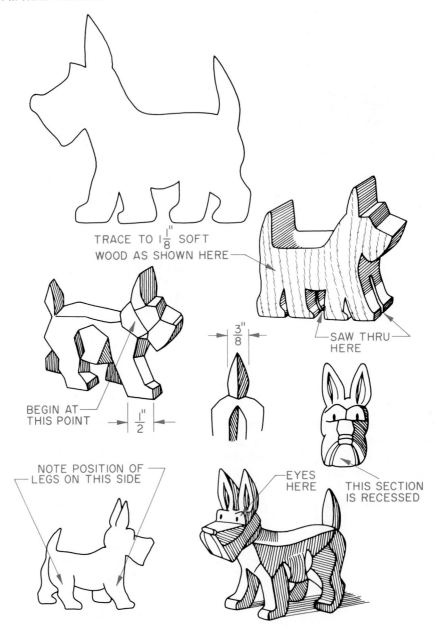

TRACE TO 1⅛" SOFT
WOOD AS SHOWN HERE

SAW THRU
HERE

¾"

½"

BEGIN AT
THIS POINT

EYES
HERE

THIS SECTION
IS RECESSED

NOTE POSITION OF
LEGS ON THIS SIDE

22-2. This type of whittling can be done with simple knives.

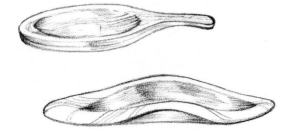

22-3. Chase carving was used in the hand-carving of these trays.

22-4. High relief carving on domestic buckwood. Carving is a wood activity in which you can use your creative ability.

● *Wood sculpture,* or "carving in the round," is perhaps the most difficult kind of wood carving. This method is used in forming a figure such as an animal or a person. The design is first traced on two sides of the wood. The outline can be jigsawed on one face. The block can then be turned around a quarter-turn and the side view cut out with the jigsaw. Fig. 22-5. The work is completed with knives and gouges. Routing bits or milling rasps can be used on a drill press or portable power carver to do some of the rough shaping. Figs. 22-6 and 22-7.

22-6. To do freehand carving on the drill press, use a high speed of at least 5,000 RPM. Be sure to wear a mask.

22-5. These delicate, sculptured pieces illustrate careful work and creative design ability.

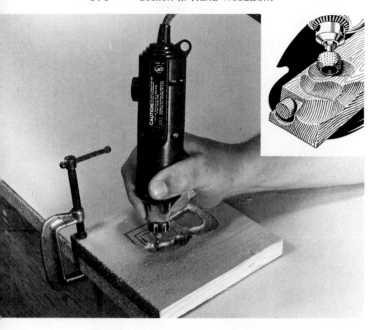

22-7. Carving with a small portable power tool. Various shapes of cutters are available to do the shaping. The inset shows a close-up of a work area.

TREATING WOOD FOR CARVING AND WOOD TURNING (PEG TREATMENT)

One of the problems in making wood carvings and turning thin bowls on the lathe is that later on the project often will split, check, or warp. This may happen when the wood dries out. This is especially true if the moisture content of the wood is higher than that of the room where it is used. However, a relatively simple chemical treatment can prevent these defects, even when you are starting with green or partially dry wood.

The first step is to rough-shape the carving or rough-turn the bowl to about ⅛ inch (3 mm) oversize. Then make a watertight container of plywood or line a wood box with a thin plastic sheet. Place a 30-percent solution of polyethylene glycol-1000 (PEG) in the tank. Soak the rough carving or bowl in the solution at room temperature for about three weeks. The water-soluble, waxlike chemical is absorbed by the wood. This prevents checking, splitting, and warping. Allow the rough carving or bowl to air-dry on shelves in a heated shop for several weeks. Now complete the carving or bowl to final size.

The only finish that works well on the treated wood is a polyurethane resin.

WOODS FOR CARVING

Many kinds of woods can be used for carving. Some of the best are described here.

White pine is a good choice for the beginner. Its fibers are close together, yet are easily cut clean, both with and across grain. Pine is relatively straight-grained. It has a rather even structure with few hard and soft spots.

Both *genuine mahogany* and *Philippine mahogany* are excellent woods for carving. Genuine mahogany has a deep brown color that gives it a rich appearance. It also has an interesting grain pattern. Philippine mahogany is also easy to work. It has, though, a less interesting grain.

Walnut is somewhat more difficult to work. It is, nevertheless, an excellent wood for carving. It is especially good for such projects as handles for sports equipment.

CARVING TOOLS

Gouges, knives, and carving tools are needed for wood carving. There are many special carving tools that can be purchased. However, only a few are required for basic work. Fig. 22-8. These include:

● A *skew*, or *chisel*, which is ground on both sides to a sharp edge. Fig. 22-9A.

● A *parting tool*, which is V-shaped. This is used to cut triangular shapes in the wood. Fig. 22-9B.

● A *veiner*, a very small gouge with a sharp V cutting edge. Fig. 22-9C.

● *Gouges* and *fluters* that are ground on the outside in sizes from ⅜ to ⅝ inch (10 to 16 mm) and with cutting edges of different radii. Some are quite flat—almost chisel shaped. Others are shaped like half an ellipse. Fig. 22-9D.

● *Knives* for whittling. Fig. 22-10.

22-8. A matched set of carving tools.

22-9. Patterns of cutting edges of carving tools: A. Chisel; B. V parting tool; C. Veiner; D. Gouges and fluters.

22-10. A complete set of knives and other cutting tools for whittling.

GENERAL SAFETY HINTS AND SUGGESTIONS FOR CARVING

● Always work out a pattern before starting the carving. Enlarge the pattern to the size you want. Then carefully transfer the design to the wood.

● Clamp the work securely. It is much better to work with the wood in a vise or clamped to the top of the bench. In this way both hands are free to do the carving. For some work, the tool is held in one hand and the end struck with a mallet. For other cutting, one hand applies the pressure while the other hand guides the tool.

● Keep your fingers and body away from the front cutting edge as much as possible. There is always danger that the tool will slip and cut you severely. In whittling, it isn't always possible to keep your hands away from the front of the cutting edge. At those times, try to keep your fingers below so that if the knife slips it will not cut you.

● The first cut should always sever or cut apart the grain. After drawing the outline (in chip carving, for example), outline the design with a sharp V parting tool. Fig. 22-11. After this is done, you can work up to the cut by removing clean-cut chips.

● Try to cut with the grain as much as possible. Cutting with the grain is always easier. Also, there is less chance that the tool will cut in and chip out a piece of your design. When cutting against the grain, roll the tool to the right and left to cut the fibers. This will help prevent tearing into the fibers and gouging out.

● When cutting the raised portion (on relief carving, for example), cut so that the base will be slightly wider than the upper part. Don't undercut until all of the carving is completed. This will cause problems.

● Start with a simple design so you can practice the art of tool control.

● Remember that sharp cutting tools are best for all kinds of carving.

22-11. A parting tool used to outline the design.

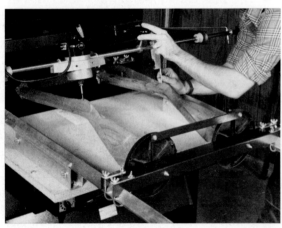

(a)

USING A DUPLICATOR-CARVING MACHINE

A duplicator-carving machine consists of a frame that holds a router and a duplicator pin. Both the original model and a rough piece of wood are mounted in the machine. The duplicator pin follows that original model and the router does the carving. Fig. 22-12.

Review Questions

1. Describe low relief carving.
2. What kind of carving is done to produce a carved animal?
3. Tell what kinds of wood are best for carving.
4. List the common cutting tools needed for wood carving.
5. Is the procedure for all carving the same? Explain.
6. Tell how to treat wood to prevent warping and checking.

22-12 (a & b). The duplicator pin moves over the original carving and the router follows.

(b)

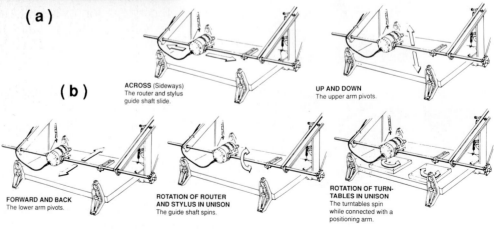

ACROSS (Sideways)
The router and stylus guide shaft slide.

UP AND DOWN
The upper arm pivots.

FORWARD AND BACK
The lower arm pivots.

ROTATION OF ROUTER AND STYLUS IN UNISON
The guide shaft spins.

ROTATION OF TURN-TABLES IN UNISON
The turntables spin while connected with a positioning arm.

Facts about Wood

Lignin

Most of the materials you use in this class are woods. Wood is composed of three chemicals—cellulose, hemicellulose, and lignin. About 25 percent of hardwood and 30 percent of softwood is lignin. Lignin is the "wood glue" that holds the wood cells together. Lignin increases the strength of the wood cells. In doing this, it gives rigidity to the tree. It is the thin, cementing layer between the wood cells themselves.

Lignin can be separated from wood by a complicated process requiring high temperatures and high pressures. It then becomes quite a different material. When dried, lignin is a cream-colored powder consisting of carbon, hydrogen, and oxygen. These are the same chemical elements that make up cellulose. However, lignin is a very different chemical from cellulose. Lignin expands and contracts the same amount in all directions. Cellulose expands and contracts different amounts in each direction. Cellulose makes up the great majority of wood. That is why wood expands more in width than in length when it gets wet.

Lignin is a mysterious chemical material. In the early 1960s, a researcher was working in a laboratory with a material called DMSO (dimethyl sulfoxide), a product made from lignin. He accidentally spilled some on his hands. A few minutes later, he was amazed to find that he could taste the sweetness in his mouth. The liquid apparently had spread through his body very rapidly. It was discovered that this clear liquid could be used on animals to relieve sore muscles. Soon it became the "miracle medicine" for athletes. Often, when a football or basketball player developed a sore and aching joint, DMSO was applied to relieve the pain. Many were convinced that this was a "cure-all." The medical community, however, has never approved the treatment.

Lignin has many commercial uses. For many years, it has been used to make about half of all the vanilla flavoring. An excellent lubricant, it is used in making the mud used in oil drilling. It also is used in the artificial sand used for making sand castings. It is used as a binder in cement and roadbuilding materials. Lignin is the tanning agent for curing leather. The full chemical uses of lignin are still quite limited. Possible uses for lignin are still being explored.

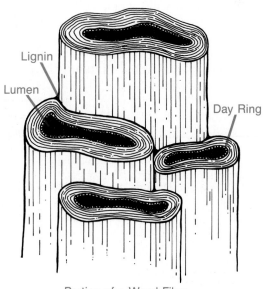

Portion of a Wood Fibre

Chapter 23

Bending Solid Wood

After studying this chapter, you will be able to:
● Describe the technique used to bend solid wood, using hot water.
● Describe how to bend wood without heat or moisture.

LOOK FOR THESE TERMS

form
heating tube

To make sports equipment such as toboggans, skis, and surfboards, stock must be bent. Fig. 23-1. Sometimes stock is bent to form a curved furniture part such as the front of a drawer. There are many kinds of wood suitable for building such projects. Ash, hickory, birch, and oak are the best.

Wood can be bent more easily when it is steamed or made soft by soaking in hot water. This makes the wood cells more plastic so they can be stretched or compressed. Most of the bending is due to compression (squeezing the cells on the inside curve). Much less is due to the stretching of the cells (on the outside curve). The outside will stretch only 1 to 2 percent. The inside will compress as much as 25 percent. Properly moistened and heated, wood will bend ten times more easily than when it is dry.

EQUIPMENT

The most popular method of bending wood is to soften it by steaming or boiling in hot water. A necessary piece of equipment is the *heating tube*. It is closed on the lower end and has a cover on the upper end. Fig. 23-2. The lower end of this tube is placed directly above a gas flame. Water is poured into the tube and the end closed. The heat and moisture soften the wood, as explained later.

A form for bending the wood is also needed. A *form* is a shape over which the wood can be bent. The wood will take on the shape of the form. A form like the one shown in Fig. 23-3 can be used for the staves of a toboggan. Another form is satisfactory for bending the tips of water skis. Fig. 23-4.

23-1. A toboggan is only one of the many pieces of sports equipment that require bending. It can be made in a length to suit your needs.

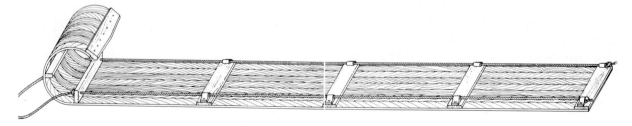

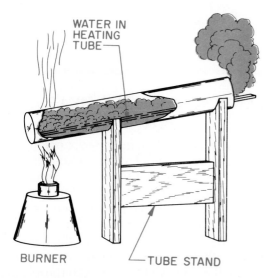

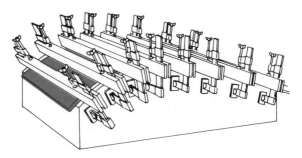

23-4. A form similar to this is needed to bend the tips of water skis. Each clamp must be tightened a little at a time.

23-2. This is the type of heating tube you will need for bending wood. An old hot water heater can also serve this purpose. A tube is fastened to the wall or on a stand at a slight angle. A burner is then placed under the low end.

23-3. A form similar to this one is required to shape the front of the toboggan staves or slats.

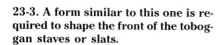
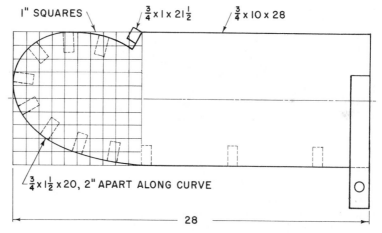

HEATING THE WOOD

Fill the heating tube about half full of water. Light the gas flame and close the end of the tube with a tight cover. There should be a tiny hole in the cover to keep it from blowing off. Prepare the staves at the same time. These should be cut to thickness and width. Their edges should be chamfered or rounded off with a radius of ⅛ inch.

When the water in the tube is boiling, put in the wood pieces. Don't add too many at one time, as the water should completely surround the end of each one. Leave the wood in the tube for two to three hours.

Prepare the bending equipment while the wood is heating. You need the form for bending these pieces, several C-clamps, and parallel handscrews. Also have ready a piece of thin sheet metal the same width as the staves and the length of the bend.

BENDING THE WOOD

When the pieces have been heated, remove them from the tube. Insert the heated end under the protecting bar at the top of the form. Insert the thin sheet metal directly under it. Then begin to draw the stock around the form. Work slowly. Clamp the staves at each cross support with a C-clamp.

Do not try to pull the stave around the form too rapidly. This will split the wood. Continue to clamp the stave to the form, as shown in Fig. 23-5. Allow each piece to dry for at least twenty-four hours before removing it from the form. You are now ready to sand, shape, and assemble the pieces.

BENDING WITHOUT HEAT AND MOISTURE

Water skis can be made by bending flat stock to shape without steam or soaking. Fig. 23-6. Make the skis of mahogany, spruce, or ash. A bending form is needed. Cut the stock to size and square it up. Saw one or more kerfs, 13 to 15 inches in length from one end. Fig. 23-7. Then cut veneer the thickness of the kerf, slightly wider than the stock and as long as the saw kerf. Apply waterproof glue to both sides of the veneer and slip it into the kerf. Clamp the stock in the form and allow it to dry at least twelve hours. Then shape and complete the skis.

Review Questions

1. Toboggans, skis, and surfboards are most commonly made from what kinds of wood?
2. List the equipment needed for bending wood.
3. What can happen if wood is bent too rapidly?

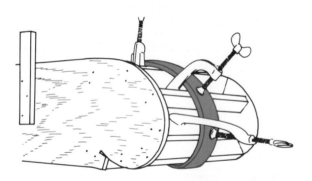

23-5. Clamping a stave or slat to the form with C-clamps. A piece of sheet metal is placed directly over the wood to protect it.

23-6. Only the tips of skis need to be bent to shape.

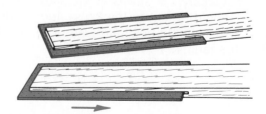

23-7. Waterproof adhesive has been applied and the veneer has been slipped into the saw kerfs.

Chapter 24

Wood Lamination

After studying this chapter, you will be able to:
● List the steps in making a simple laminated wood project.

LOOK FOR THESE TERMS

lamination
veneer

Lamination is the process of building up the thickness or width of material by gluing together several layers. The grain of all the layers must run in approximately the *same* direction. Fig. 24-1. Veneers are used in lamination. A *veneer* is a thin layer of wood of good quality. Laminating is done to produce a wide variety of products. Arches, beams, and furniture parts are a few examples of lamination. Fig. 24-2.

Wood laminations resist warpage and reduce the number of splits and checks. They also produce a part that is stronger than regular wood.

Laminating can be done in the school woodworking laboratory. There, small formed projects such as salad servers and bent bookends can be made. Figs. 24-3 and 24-4.

24-1. The legs of this stool are formed of bent laminated veneers.

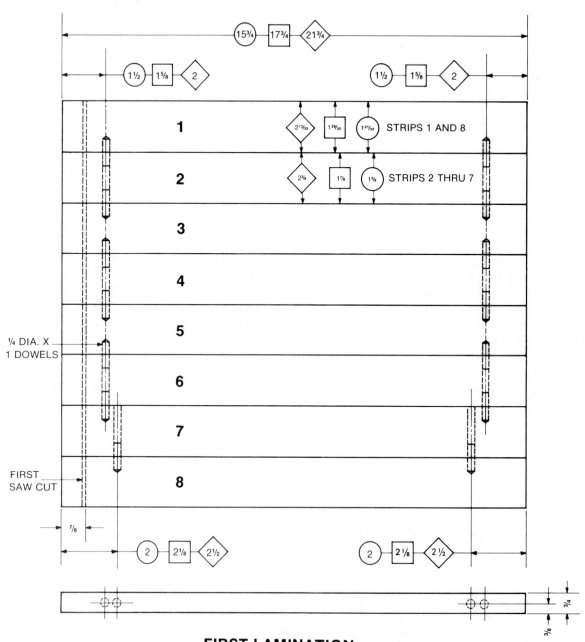

FIRST LAMINATION

A

BILL OF MATERIALS

13″ x 13″ (1⅝″ Squares)

QTY.	DESCRIPTION
6	3/4 x 1⅝ x 15¾ hardwood (3 light, 3 dark)
2	3/4 x 1²¹/₃₂ x 15¾ hardwood (1 light, 1 dark)
36″	1/4″ dowel
—	scrap wood for sanding frame
—	wax paper
—	white glue

BILL OF MATERIALS

15″ x 15″ (1⅞″ Squares)

QTY.	DESCRIPTION
6	3/4 x 1⅞ x 17¾ hardwood (3 light, 3 dark)
2	3/4 x 1²⁹/₃₂ x 17¾ hardwood (1 light, 1 dark)
36″	1/4″ dowel
—	scrap wood for sanding frame
—	wax paper
—	white glue

BILL OF MATERIALS

19″ x 19″ (2⅜″ Squares)

QTY.	DESCRIPTION
6	3/4 x 2⅜ x 21¾ hardwood (3 light, 3 dark)
2	3/4 x 2¹³/₃₂ x 21¾ hardwood (1 light, 1 dark)
36″	1/4″ dowel
—	scrap wood for sanding frame
—	wax paper
—	white glue

B

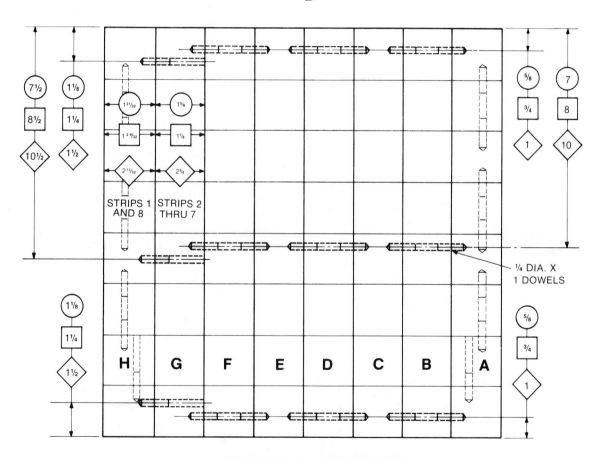

SECOND LAMINATION

C

24-2. Plans for making a chessboard or checkerboard in three different sizes using strips of light and dark hardwoods such as birch and walnut. A. Make the first lamination by joining the strips of solid wood with edge dowel joints; B. Bill of materials needed for each different size; C. After cutting the first lamination into strips, join these with edge dowel joints to complete the game board.

24-3. This laminated fireplace log holder can be made in the school shop.

STEPS IN MAKING A LAMINATED WOOD PROJECT WITH SIMPLE EQUIPMENT

1. Decide on the project and design you want.
2. For a curved project like a salad server, draw a full-size pattern of the curve on a piece of heavy paper.
3. Decide on the number of thicknesses needed. Usually the number is odd, such as three, five, or seven. Fig. 24-5.
4. Select a piece of hard maple or birch that is wide enough and long enough to enclose the veneer sandwich needed to make the project. The form must have at least 1 inch of material on each side of the curve. You will make the mold from the hard wood. These molds are placed between presses or clamps to shape the laminated surface.
5. Transfer the full-size curve to the side of the form, following the grain direction.
6. Cut the curve on the band saw. Eliminate as many irregularities as possible. The two halves of the form or die should fit perfectly. Fig. 24-6.
7. Sand very lightly with fine paper to remove saw marks, if necessary.
8. Apply a thin coat of flexible material such as thin rubber or plastic to both sides of the form. This is not necessary, but it helps to provide a better rough lamination. If rubber is used, it should be tacked onto the form. The surface should then be covered with wax.

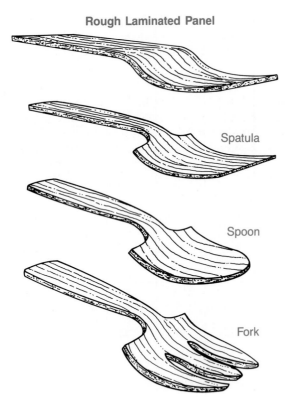

Rough Laminated Panel

Spatula

Spoon

Fork

24-4. These projects are typical of the laminated products that can be made. The rough laminated panel can be made into any of the objects shown beneath it.

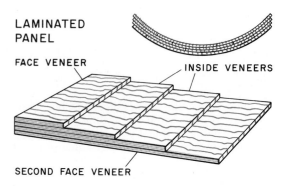

LAMINATED PANEL

FACE VENEER

INSIDE VENEERS

SECOND FACE VENEER

24-5. Four-ply laminated panel for curved furniture parts.

9. Cut several pieces of veneer, ¹/₃₂ to ¹/₂₈ inch thick and large enough to make the project. One type of wood, such as mahogany or walnut, may be used. The layers might be alternated with a lighter wood, such as birch or maple, for contrast.
10. Select a good-quality casein glue or white resin glue. Spread the glue evenly on both sides of each piece of veneer with, of course, the exception of the two outside pieces. The finished sides of these must be free of glue.
11. Place a piece of waxed paper over one side of the form.
12. Stack the layers of veneer on the form.
13. Place another piece of waxed paper over the last piece.
14. Place the other half of the form over the pieces. Clamp the two forms together with standard wood clamps. Fig. 24-7.
15. Allow the sandwich to remain under pressure for at least twenty-four hours.

24-6. This is the kind of form needed to make the rough blank for a salad-server set.

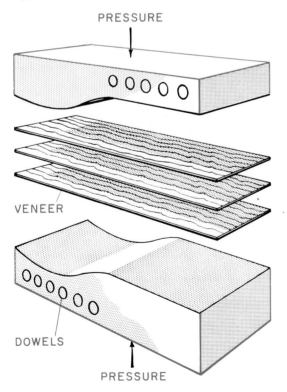

PRESSURE

VENEER

DOWELS

PRESSURE

16. Remove the lamination from the form and pull off the waxed paper.
17. Trace the outline of the project on the rough lamination.
18. Cut on a band or scroll saw.
19. Sand and smooth the edges.
20. Apply penetrating finish to the object as soon as possible.

Caution *If the laminated project is to be used around food, use mineral oil as a sealer.*

MAKING A LAMINATED SERVING TRAY

BILL OF MATERIALS

One piece, 7 × 13 inches (178 × 330 mm), ¹/₃₂-inch vertical grade plastic laminate or .050 postforming grade laminate; color, pattern, and surface finish are optional.

Four pieces, 6½ × 12½ inches, approximately ¹/₃₂-inch wood veneer; the bottom veneer should complement or match the color of laminate used on the surface.

Two pieces, ³/₁₆ × ³/₁₆ × 7 inches, solid wood rails; choice of wood should complement or match the color of laminate used on the surface.

Urea-resin adhesive.

Paste wax.

Clear wood finish.

24-7. A simple lamination clamped over a form.

PLAN OF PROCEDURE

1. Construct the two dies used to form the tray shape. Refer to the drawing for dimensions. The die should be 1 inch deeper than the height of the finished ends. Figs. 24-8 and 24-9.
2. Cut the plastic laminate and wood veneer to correct size.
3. Glue up the plastic laminate and wood veneer.
   a. Use a urea-resin adhesive. Follow the manufacturer's directions for mixing and curing.
   b. Some adhesive will squeeze out. To keep it from sticking to the laminate surface, wax the surface with a good grade of wax. You can also apply masking tape to the surface and veneer.

24-8. Laminated serving tray.

   c. Apply glue with a stiff bristle brush. Coat both sides of the center veneers, the back side of the bottom veneer, and the back of the plastic laminate.
   d. Place waxed paper between the plastic laminate and bottom veneer and the surfaces of the dies to prevent the adhesive from sticking.

24-9. Drawings for the laminated serving tray in Fig. 24-8. The basic design of this tray may be altered by changing its shape or the angles to which the wood is bent. Legs and handles might also be added.

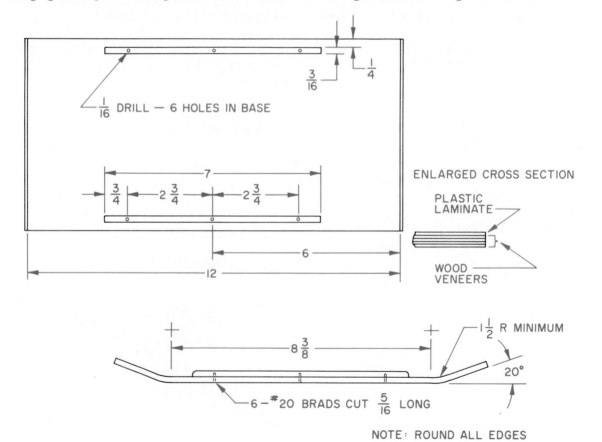

e. Clamp with a veneer press, jaw clamp, or bar clamp. Fig. 24-10.
4. Lay out the shape of the finished tray on the plastic laminate assembly with a soft pencil.
5. Rough-cut to shape with a band saw.
6. Sand on a belt or disc sander or with a hand file. If the finished shape is rectangular, edges may be jointed and circular sawed to make them parallel. For final smoothing, hand-sand edges and bottom with 150-grit abrasive paper. Be sure to protect the laminate surface.
7. Cut the rails from solid wood.
8. Sand and finish with the same finish as the bottom veneer.
9. Drill holes in the base according to the dimensions on the drawing.

10. With a brad driver or hammer, install the rails on the base.
11. Apply finish to the wood veneer.
12. Attach felt pads to the bottom.

Review Questions

1. What is lamination?
2. Describe some of the advantages of wood lamination.
3. Describe the steps for making projects by wood lamination.
4. Describe the procedure for making a laminated serving tray.

24-10. This type of veneer press can be constructed in the laboratory.

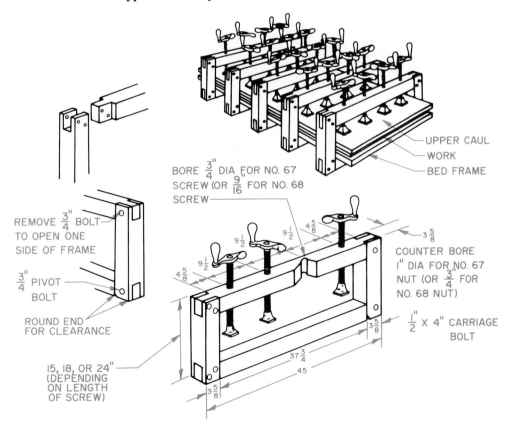

Chapter 25

Hand Drilling and Boring

After studying this chapter, you will be able to:
- Distinguish drilling from boring.
- Demonstrate the use of a hand drill.
- Describe the technique of boring with an auger bit.
- Describe the technique of boring with an expansive bit.
- Describe the technique of boring with a Forstner bit.

LOOK FOR THESE TERMS

auger bit	depth gauge	screw
automatic drill	drilling	shank
bit brace	expansive bit	speed bit
blind hole	Forstner bit	spur
boring	hand drill	twist drill

Holes are made by drilling and boring. It is usually called *drilling* when drills are used for holes ¼ inch or smaller. It is called *boring* when bits are used to make holes larger than ¼ inch.

DRILLING HOLES

TOOLS

Twist drills come in sets from 1/64 inch to ½ inch, in steps of 1/64 inch. Fig. 25-1. These drills can be used for both metal and wood. Drills ⅜ inch and smaller can be held in a hand drill. Larger sizes can be used in a drill press.

Automatic Drill

An *automatic drill* with drill points is handy to have when many small holes must be drilled. Fig. 25-2. The drill points are numbered from one to eight. Number 1 is 1/16 inch, 2 is 5/64 inch, 3 is 3/32 inch, 4 is 7/64 inch, 5 is ⅛ inch, 6 is 9/64 inch, 7 is 5/32 inch, and 8 is 11/64 inch.

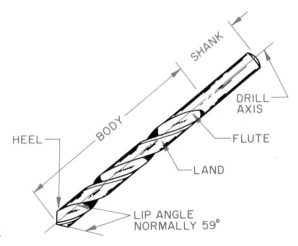

25-1. A twist drill, with its parts labeled.

To use the automatic drill, first insert the drill in the chuck. Tighten the chuck. Place the drill point where the hole is needed. Then simply push down a few times, allowing the handle to spring back after each stroke. This will give a good, clean hole.

25-2. The automatic drill is very efficient for drilling many small holes, such as those needed for installing. Here, its important parts are labeled. The proper technique for using it is also shown.

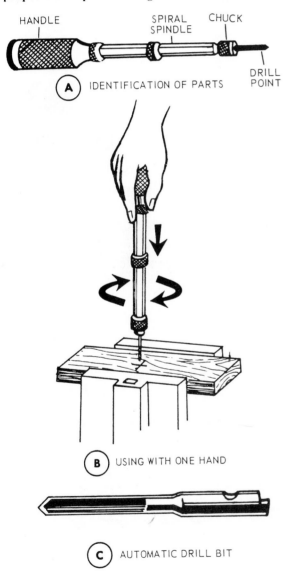

Hand Drill

The *hand drill* is used to hold twist drills for drilling holes. It has three jaws in the chuck for holding round shanks. Fig. 25-3.

Select a twist drill of the correct size. Hold the shell of the chuck in your left hand. Pull the crank backward until the jaws are open slightly wider than the shank. Place the shank in the chuck. Tighten the chuck by pushing the crank forward. Make sure the drill is in the chuck straight. Locate the position of the hole. Mark it with a scratch awl. Hold the handle in your left hand and turn the crank with your right hand. Make sure the drill is square with the work. Fig. 25-4.

25-3. Hand drill.

25-4. Vertical drilling with a hand drill. Grasp the handle in one hand and turn the crank with the other. Be sure to hold the drill square with the work. Control the feed by the pressure you apply. Here, the important parts of the drill are labeled.

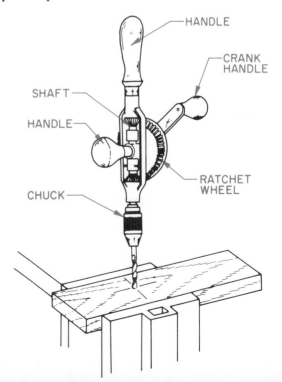

Never bend the hand drill to one side or the other. Small drills will break. Continue to turn the handle until the hole is drilled. If holes of a certain depth are needed, make a depth gauge from a piece of scrap wood or dowel rod. Fig. 25-5. You can also use a commercial depth gauge. Fig. 25-6.

BORING

For cutting out a design, making a mortise-and-tenon joint, fitting dowel rods, and many other construction procedures, you need to know how to bore holes.

BITS

For holes that are ¼ to 1¼ inches, an *auger bit* is used. Figs. 25-7 and 25-8. The size of the auger bit is stamped on the tang, always as a single number such as 4, 5, or 6, etc. Fig. 25-9. This shows that it will bore a hole ⁴⁄₁₆, ⁵⁄₁₆, ⁶⁄₁₆, etc., inch in diameter. Figs. 25-10 and 25-11.

For holes larger than 1 inch, you need an expansive bit. Fig. 25-12. This tool can be adjusted with different cutters for diameters from ⅞ to 3 inches.

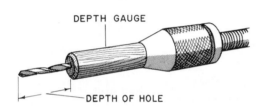

25-5. A depth gauge made from a piece of dowel rod, which covers a part of the drill. Cut the piece until the drill extends the correct amount.

25-6. A ring depth gauge that can be used on drills to control the depth of the hole.

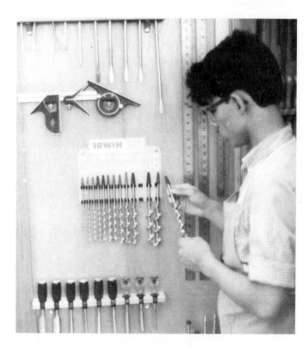

25-9. Check the size of the auger bit carefully. It is stamped on the tang.

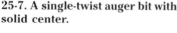

25-7. A single-twist auger bit with solid center.

25-8. A double-twist auger bit.

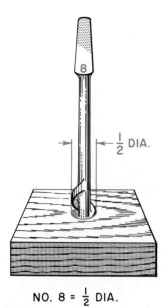

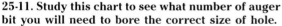

NO. 8 = $\frac{1}{2}$ DIA.

25-10. The number 8 on this auger bit indicates that it will bore a 1/2-inch hole.

25-11. Study this chart to see what number of auger bit you will need to bore the correct size of hole.

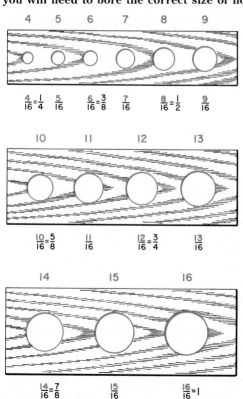

THE SET CONTAINS 13 AUGER BITS.

25-12. An expansive bit. There are usually two cutters, a small one for holes of 7/8 to 2 inches in diameter and a larger one for holes 2 inches and more in diameter.

25-13. A Forstner bit is used to enlarge existing holes or to cut a hole partway through thin stock. Both hand and machine types are shown.

25-14. A speed, or flat, bit is an excellent cutting tool to use, especially in a portable electric drill.

When you want to bore a hole partway into thin board or when you want to enlarge an existing hole, a *Forstner bit* is the tool to choose. Fig. 25-13.

Speed, or *flat*, *bits* are also useful for boring holes, especially when using an electric drill. Fig. 25-14.

BORING WITH AN AUGER BIT

Installing an Auger Bit in a Brace

The auger bit is held in a bit brace. Figs. 25-15 and 25-16. To install the bit, hold the shell of the chuck in your left hand. Turn the handle to the left until the jaw is open slightly larger than the shank of the bit. Fig. 25-17. Then insert the bit and turn the handle to the right to fasten it in the brace. Most bit braces have a ratchet attachment. This makes it possible to drill in corners or other tight places.

25-15. The bit brace is used for holding auger bits, Forstner bits, and other tools with rectangular-shaped shanks. Most braces have a ratchet arrangement, making it possible to bore in corners and otherwise inaccessible places.

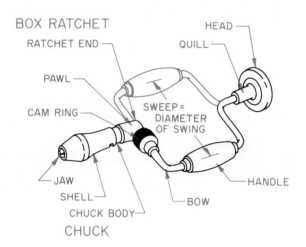

25-16. Parts of a brace.

25-17. Inserting the shank into the two jaws. The corners should be in the V-grooves of the jaws.

Horizontal Position

Be sure that the center of the hole is properly located. Punch the center with a scratch awl. Fig. 25-18. Place the stock in a vise so that the brace can be held in a horizontal position. Fig. 25-19. Hold the head of the brace with your left hand cupped around it. Hold your body against the head for added pressure. Turn the handle with your right hand to start the hole. Fig. 25-20. Be careful to keep the auger bit square to the work. It is easy to

sight the top to see if it is square to the right and left. If another person is present, have this person sight to make sure it is straight up and down. Do not press too hard on the brace. The auger bit tends to feed itself into the wood. Fig. 25-21. Continue to bore the hole until the point of the bit just comes through the opposite side. Then turn the wood over to complete the hole. If this is not done, the hole will split out on the opposite side as the auger bit comes through. Another way to keep from splitting the wood is to put a piece of scrap wood in back of the piece you are boring. Then you can go all the way through from one side. Fig. 25-22.

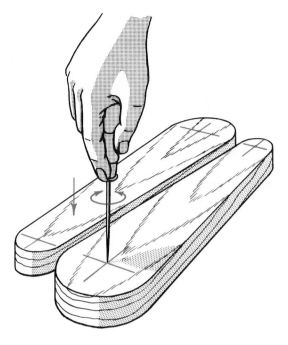

25-18. Marking the center of the hole with the scratch awl.

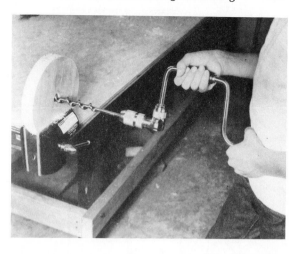

25-20. Horizontal boring with a bit and brace. Make sure that the auger bit is held at right angles to the stock.

25-19. The proper setup for a hole to be bored. The center has been accurately located. On thin stock a piece of scrap wood should be fastened to the back to support the wood while boring, as shown.

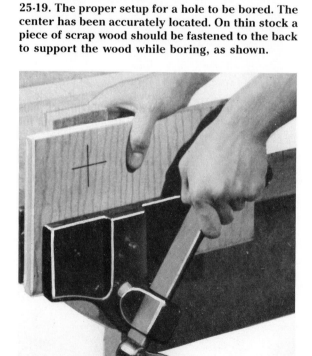

25-21. A bit bores a hole as follows: (1) The screw point pulls the bit into the wood; (2) The spurs scribe the diameter of the hole in advance of the cutter; (3) The cutter lifts the chips, which then pass through the twist.

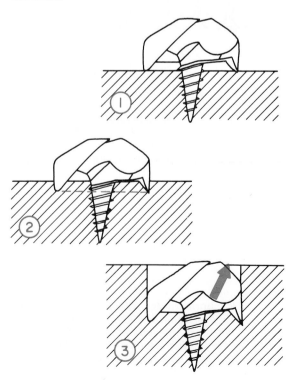

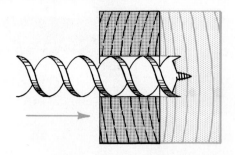

A. CORRECT

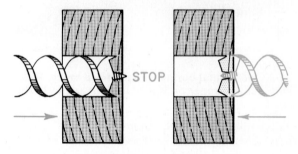

STOP

B. CORRECT

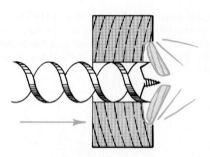

C. INCORRECT

25-22. The correct and incorrect methods of boring a hole: A. Use a piece of scrap wood; B. Stop when feed screw pricks through and bore from the other side; C. Never bore straight through without scrap wood.

Vertical Position

Holes sometimes have to be bored with the auger bit held in a vertical position. Lay out and locate the position of the hole as before. Put one hand over the head of the brace. Use your other hand to turn the handle. Fig. 25-23. Sometimes you will find it natural to rest your chin on the handle to steady it. To make sure that you are boring square with the surface, sight along the board or use a try square. Fig. 25-24.

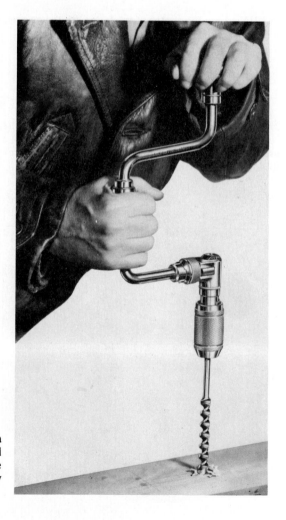

25-23. Boring holes with a bit and brace held in a vertical position. The hand is cupped over the head of the brace. Sometimes the chin is rested on the hand to steady the tool. Most boring in the laboratory will be done in a vertical position.

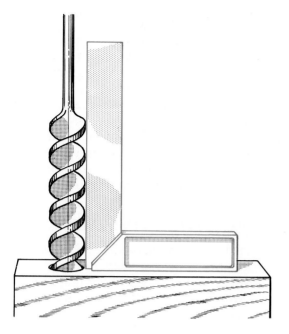

25-24. Checking to make sure the auger bit is square with the work.

In some construction you will need to bore only partway through the stock. For this, you need a *depth*, or *bit*, *gauge*. There are two commercial types that can be clamped on the auger bit to the proper depth. Figs. 25-25 and 25-26. A depth gauge also can be made by boring through a piece of wood or dowel rod, exposing the auger bit to the correct depth.

Angle Boring

To bore a hole at an angle, first adjust a sliding T-bevel to the required angle. Use this as a guide. Start the auger bit as you would for straight boring until the screw feeds into the wood. Then tilt the bit so that it is parallel to the blade of the T-bevel. If several holes must be bored at an angle, it is a good idea to use a simple wood jig. First, bore a hole at the correct angle through a piece of scrap stock. Slip this jig over the auger bit. Place the feed screw of the auger bit on the center of the hole. Slip the jig against the wood and clamp it with a hand screw. This will guide the bit. Fig. 25-27.

25-25. Spring-type bit, or depth, gauge. This type will not mar the surface of the wood when the tool reaches the correct depth.

25-27. Using a small wood jig to bore a hole at an angle.

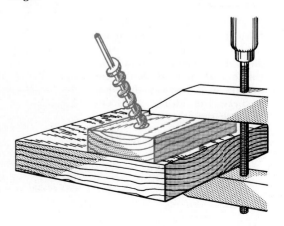

25-26. Solid-type bit, or depth, gauge.

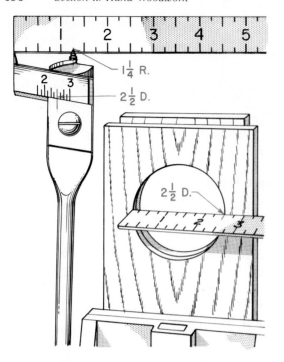

25-28. Notice that the diameter of this expansive bit is set to 2 1/2 inches.

BORING WITH AN EXPANSIVE BIT

Choose a cutter of the correct size and slip it in the bit. Adjust the cutter until the distance from the spur to the feed screw equals the radius of the hole. Fig. 25-28. Fasten the bit in a brace. Then make sure the work is held tightly. It's a good idea to put a piece of scrap stock behind the work. As you rotate the tool, use just enough pressure to make a cut. Fig. 25-29. After the feed screw shows through, reverse the stock and cut from the other side.

BORING WITH A FORSTNER BIT

Forstner bits are numbered in the same way as auger bits. The sizes range from ¼ to 2 inches. Locate the center of the hole. Draw a circle with a dividers the same size as the hole. Clamp the stock securely. Carefully guide the bit over the circle to start the boring. Fig. 25-30.

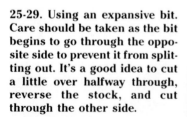

25-29. Using an expansive bit. Care should be taken as the bit begins to go through the opposite side to prevent it from splitting out. It's a good idea to cut a little over halfway through, reverse the stock, and cut through the other side.

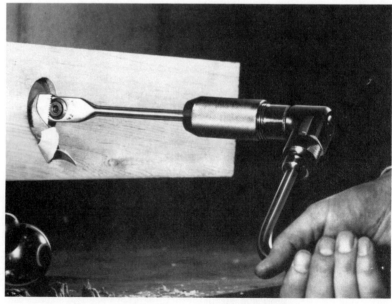

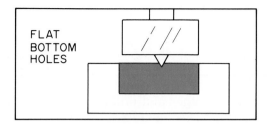

FLAT
BOTTOM
HOLES

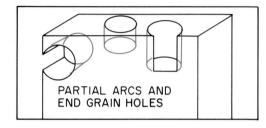

PARTIAL ARCS AND
END GRAIN HOLES

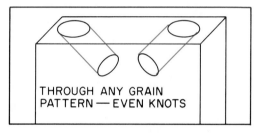

THROUGH ANY GRAIN
PATTERN — EVEN KNOTS

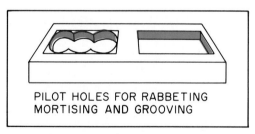

PILOT HOLES FOR RABBETING
MORTISING AND GROOVING

25-30. Boring holes with a Forstner bit.

Review Questions

1. Name the kind of cutting tool used for drilling holes in wood.
2. Describe a hand drill.
3. How is the hand drill held for drilling?
4. What is an auger bit?
5. Where is the size marked on the auger bit?
6. What is an expansive bit and how is it used?
7. What is the primary use for the Forstner bit?
8. Name the parts of a brace.
9. Why do some braces have a ratchet attachment?
10. To bore holes in a vertical position, how can the brace be kept square with the work?
11. Should you bore the hole completely through the stock from one side? Explain.
12. Describe a depth gauge and tell how it is used.
13. How is a depth gauge made?
14. Tell how to do angle boring.
15. How do you adjust an expansive bit to cut a 2½-inch hole?

Facts about Wood

The Mechanical Advantage of Machines

Machines are used in woodworking. You may think of a machine as a complex device—a circular saw or lathe. These are machines, but so are a hammer, a screwdriver, and a screw. A *machine* is any device that allows its user to get the most force from the energy applied. We use machines to:

● *Transform energy*. Example: The motor on a drill press transforms electrical energy into mechanical energy, which turns the spindle.

● *Multiply force*. Example: A pry bar can be used to lift a heavy load. The pry bar increases the user's applied strength.

● *Multiply speed*. Example: The belt and pulley on many machines increases the speed of the tool.

● *Change the direction of a force*. Example: Turning the handle on a vise moves the jaws together.

A circular saw and a lathe are *compound machines*. Compound machines contain two or more simple machines. There are six simple machines: the lever, wheel and axle, pulley, inclined plane, wedge, and screw.

A *lever* is a bar that turns or pivots on a point called a fulcrum. The *fulcrum* is the point at which a lever pivots. Levers make it possible to exert a great deal of force for cutting, holding, or lifting. There are three kinds of levers. Fig. A. In the first-class lever, the fulcrum is between the load and the force. Examples of first-class levers are pliers and pry-bars. In the second-class lever, the load is between the fulcrum and the force. Examples are the nutcracker and the wheelbarrow. The third-class lever has the force between the fulcrum and the load. Tweezers and shovels are examples of the third-class lever.

The *wheel and axle* consists of a wheel fastened to a shaft. Fig. B. This makes it possible to multiply or reduce the force exerted to do work. The control and adjustment wheels on lathes and drill presses are examples of the wheel and axle.

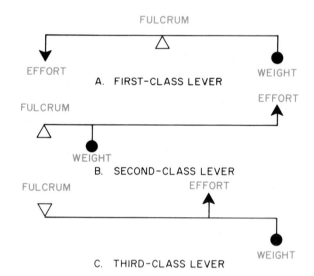

Fig. A. The three types of levers.

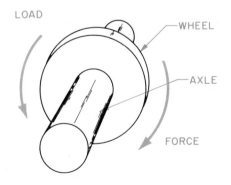

Fig. B. A wheel on an axle can multiply the force needed to move a load.

The *pulley* is a lever that acts continuously. Figure C shows a fixed wheel acting as a fulcrum between a load and a force. The pulley makes it possible to lift loads by changing the direction of the force or increasing the force. The electric motors that run lathes and drill presses have pulleys. A belt connects the motor pulley and the drive pulley. This transmits power from one place to another.

The *inclined plane* is a slanted surface used to raise objects. Fig. D. Less force is needed to lift an object using an inclined plane. However, the object is moved through a longer distance than if it were moved straight up. A ramp used to roll a barrel onto a truck is an inclined plane. It takes less force to roll the barrel up the ramp than it does to lift it straight up onto the truck.

The *wedge* is made up of two inclined planes placed back to back. Fig. E. Because it moves easily into the load, a wedge multiplies force greatly. All knives, chisels, saws, and axes have wedges.

The *screw* is an inclined plane centered on a cylinder. Fig. F. The screw multiplies force like a wedge. A bolt moves only a short distance through a nut with one turn. But the force that pulls this bolt through the nut is much greater than the effort required to turn it. For this reason, objects fastened with a nut and bolt are drawn together very tightly. Threaded fasteners, vise screws, and wood screws are examples of the screw. The screw is a simple machine that has many uses. The vise on a workbench makes use of the great mechanical advantage of the screw.

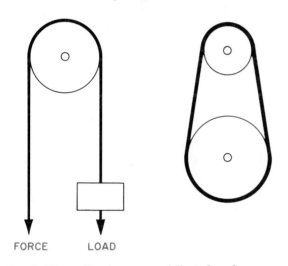

FORCE   LOAD

Fig. C. The pulley is a type of first-class lever.

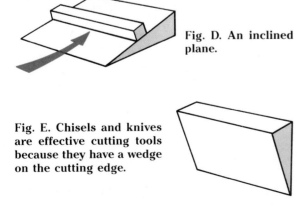

Fig. D. An inclined plane.

Fig. E. Chisels and knives are effective cutting tools because they have a wedge on the cutting edge.

Fig. F. Cut a sheet of paper in the shape of a right triangle—an inclined plane. Wind it around a pencil, as shown. You can see that the screw is actually an inclined plane wrapped around a cylinder. As the pencil is turned, the paper is wound up. It forms a spiral thread similar to the thread on the screw shown at the right. The pitch (P) of a screw, and of the paper, is the distance between adjacent and corresponding points on the same thread. The pitch is measured along the length of the screw.

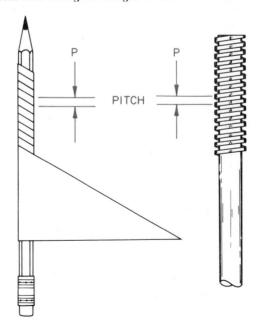

P   P

PITCH

Chapter 26

Sharpening Tools

After studying this chapter, you will be able to:
● List the safety rules that must be followed when operating the grinder.
● Describe the machine sharpening of single-edged tools by machine.
● Describe how to use a whetstone.
● Describe the sharpening of an auger bit.

LOOK FOR THESE TERMS

burnisher	whetstone
fast-speed grinder	whetting
grinding	wire edge
oilstone	

One rule that is very important in woodworking is this: *Successful woodworking depends on good cutting edges.*

For example, if you have used a plane that digs in, sticks, is hard to push, or leaves grooves in the work, you will understand why good cutting tools are so necessary. Time spent on tool sharpening is well rewarded in better and easier work.

GRINDER

A *fast-speed grinder* with a plane iron grinding attachment is used for sharpening all kinds of cutting tools and for grinding metal. Fig. 26-1.

 Safety

In using the grinder, always observe the following safety rules:
● Always wear proper eye protection.
● Adjust the tool rests to within 1/16 inch of the grinding wheel.
● Adjust the spark deflectors to within 1/16 inch of the grinding wheel.

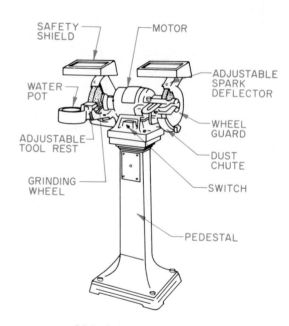

26-1. A fast-speed grinder.

● Do not grind on the side of the grinding wheel.
● Stand to one side when starting the grinder.

- If a grinding wheel is too small or is cracked, don't use it. Report this to your instructor.
- Hold small workpieces with vise-grip pliers.
- Do not leave the machine until the grinding wheels have come to a full stop.

SHARPENING SINGLE-EDGED TOOLS

Several single-edged tools, such as plane irons, chisels, and spokeshave blades, are sharpened in the same general way. A description of sharpening a plane iron will show how to sharpen all of these tools.

A plane iron needs to be reground if it is badly nicked or untrue or if the bevel is rounded, too blunt, or too thin. Before regrinding the plane iron, decide what the shape of the cutting edge should be. For most general work the cutting edge should be straight, with the corners slightly rounded to keep them from digging into the wood. For rough planing, the entire edge should be slightly rounded with the center of the cutting edge about ⅓₂ inch higher than the corners.

REMOVING THE OLD EDGE

Leave the plane-iron cap fastened to the iron to act as a guide. Hold the plane iron at right angles to the grinding wheel. Move it back and forth to grind off the old cutting edge until all nicks are removed and the edge is square with the sides. (This last reshaping needs to be done only when the plane iron is in very poor condition.) Check the edge for squareness with a try square. Hold the handle against the side of the plane iron. After the edge is square, remove the cap.

GRINDING

The plane iron, chisel, and other single-edge tools usually are ground with a bevel that is two or two and one-half times longer than the thickness of the blade. Figs. 26-2 and 26-3. The smaller angle, about 20 degrees, is used on softwoods. The more blunt angle, about 25 to 30 degrees, is used on hardwoods. Before grinding the bevel, check the wheel to make sure that it is true and that the face is square. Also, the wheel must turn toward the cutting edge.

If a grinding attachment is available, use it to hold the plane iron. This will assure you that the correct bevel will be ground. Fig. 26-4. If you don't have a grinding attachment, hold the plane iron in both hands. Fig. 26-5. Carefully move the plane iron back and forth across the grinding wheel. Do not apply too much pressure, as this will overheat the edge. Frequently remove the blade and dip it in water to cool it. This also will prevent the temper from being drawn from the steel.

26-2. A plane-iron blade should be ground at an angle of 20 to 30 degrees. The length of the bevel should be about two to two and one-half times the thickness of the blade.

26-3. The correct and incorrect cutting edges for a chisel. The cutting angle will depend on the kind of work to be done. Use a sharper angle (about 20 degrees) for final trimming.

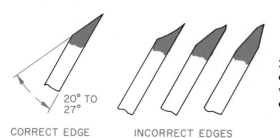

CORRECT EDGE   INCORRECT EDGES

26-4. Grinding a plane-iron blade held in an attachment. This is the simplest method since, once the angle has been set, it is easy to keep the bevel even. However, care must be taken not to burn the cutting edge, especially when using a dry grinder, as shown here.

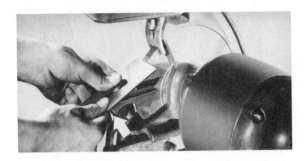

26-5. Grinding a plane-iron blade without the use of a guide. In using this method, the plane iron should be moved from right to left constantly. It should be cooled frequently in water. It takes considerable skill to keep the bevel even when grinding in this manner.

26-6. Fine and coarse oilstone.

If you are grinding freehand, move the tool slowly back to the wheel to get the "feel" of the angle. Be sure that you continue grinding at the same angle as before. As the cutting edge is formed, a slight burr may appear. This will be removed later. As the final grinding is done, make sure that you have a single surface on the bevel and that the bevel is at the correct angle. This can be checked with a sliding T-bevel or the protractor head of a combination set.

WHETTING OR HONING THE EDGE

Whetting is sharpening. A *whetstone* is a stone used for sharpening a tool by whetting or honing. An *oilstone* is a whetstone that is used with oil.

Select an oilstone with a flat, true surface. There are two classes of oilstone for this purpose. The natural stones, such as the Arkansas and Washita, are white. The artificial oilstones are made either of aluminum oxide, which is brownish, or silicon carbide, which is grayish. A combination artificial oilstone is best. One surface is coarse and the other surface is fine. Fig. 26-6.

Wipe off the stone. Then apply a mixture of half kerosene and half machine oil to the surface. Hold the plane iron on the oilstone with the bevel side down. Fig. 26-7. First apply pressure on the heel of the bevel. Then slowly raise the plane iron until the bevel is in contact with the oilstone surface. Fig. 26-8. Keep the whetting angle between 30 and 35 degrees. Move the tool back and forth on the face of the oilstone or in a circular motion to form a figure 8. Fig. 26-9. A *wire*, or *feather*, *edge* will form on the cutting edge. To remove this, turn the plane iron around. Hold the side opposite the bevel flat against the oilstone. Move it back and forth a few times. *Make sure that you hold the tool flat.* Figs. 26-10 and 26-11. The slightest bevel on this side will prevent the plane-iron cap from fitting properly. Chips can then get between the cap and the iron.

If the wire edge is not completely removed, push the cutting edge across the corner of a piece of softwood. The finer side of the oilstone can be used to sharpen the plane iron to an even keener edge.

26-7. A chisel-sharpening holder can be used to keep the tool at the correct angle. The holder can be adjusted to provide the correct bevel angle.

26-8. Whetting a plane iron. Hold the iron with the bevel side down at a slightly greater angle than that at which it is ground. Apply oil to the stone and move the plane iron back and forth or in a figure-8 movement.

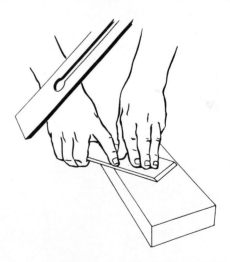

26-9. A figure-8 movement of the tool will distribute wear evenly on the stone.

26-10. Remove the burr or wire edge from the cutting edge by holding the plane iron flat on the stone.

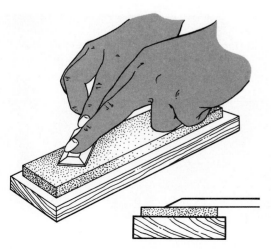

26-11. Honing produces a *wire edge*, which must be removed. Hold the chisel flat on the stone when you remove this edge.

TESTING FOR SHARPNESS

To test for sharpness, hold the plane iron with the cutting edge down and allow the edge to rest lightly on the thumbnail. As you move the tool, it will tend to "bite" into the nail if it is sharp. It will slide across easily if it is dull. Another method is to look carefully at the edge. If it is sharp, the edge cannot be seen. If it is dull, a thin, white line can be seen.

Be careful when assembling the plane iron and cap and when inserting them into the plane so as not to nick the cutting edge.

26-12. Drawfiling the hand scraper. Use a fine file in this manner until the edge is square with the sides of the scraper.

26-13. Whetting the edge of the scraper. Hold the scraper at right angles to the stone and move it back and forth.

SHARPENING A HAND SCRAPER

A hand scraper must be sharpened frequently. The good woodworker sharpens it before every use. Place the tool in a vise with the cutting edge showing. To remove the old cutting edge, hold a file flat against the side of the scraper and take a few strokes. Then use a fine file to drawfile the edge until it is square with the sides of the scraper. Fig. 26-12.

Whet the cutting edge by moving it back and forth across an oilstone. Hold the blade at right angles to the surface. Fig. 26-13. Then hold the sides of the blade flat against the stone, again working it back and forth, to remove the wire edge. Fig. 26-14.

Place the scraper flat on the bench, with the cutting edge extending slightly over the edge of the bench. Hold a burnisher flat on the side of the scraper. Take a few firm strokes toward you to draw the edge. Fig. 26-15.

Then hold the scraper on edge as shown in Fig. 26-16. Use the *burnisher*, held at an angle of about 85 degrees, to turn the edge of the scraper. Fig. 26-17. Do this by drawing the burnisher up with a firm, brisk stroke. The edge is sharp when it will catch your thumbnail as it is drawn across it.

26-14. Hold the scraper flat against the stone on both sides to remove any burr.

26-15. A burnisher.

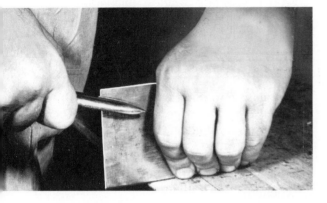

26-16. Drawing out the edge. Use a burnishing tool. Hold the scraper on the bench top as you work.

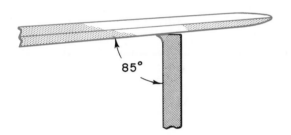

85°

26-17. After the edge is drawn out, hold the burnishing tool at an angle of about 85 degrees to the side of the scraper and turn the edge.

26-18. Sharpening the spur. Hold the bit with the feed screw uppermost. Place the twist against the bench. File the inside of the spur only—never the outside.

SHARPENING AN AUGER BIT

To obtain the best results, keep the auger bit sharp. Sharpening is done by filing the spur and the lip with a small half-round or three-cornered file. Figs. 26-18 and 26-19. File the spur on the inside to keep the same general shape. Never file the outside. File the lip on the underside or the side toward the shank until it has a sharp cutting edge. Keep the bits in good condition by cleaning off the pitch with solvent. Use steel wool to polish the surface. Sharpen a speed bit on the two cutting edges. Fig. 26-20.

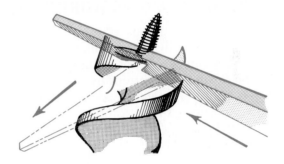

26-19. Sharpening the lip of an auger bit, using a triangular-shaped file.

26-20. Sharpen a speed bit with a small slipstone or dead-smooth file. Make sure that the original angles are maintained and that each side of the nose is sharpened equally. Do not file the sides of the blade or the boring diameter will be reduced.

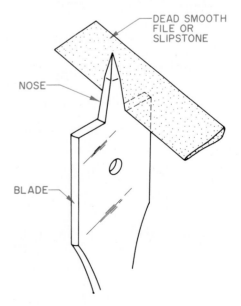

DEAD SMOOTH FILE OR SLIPSTONE

NOSE

BLADE

SHARPENING A DRAWKNIFE AND SMALL KNIVES

The drawknife can be sharpened on the grinding wheel in the same general way as a plane iron. Hold the drawknife with one handle against the top of the bench and the other handle in your hand. Hold a small oilstone in the other hand and move it back and forth along the bevel to make a keen edge.

GRINDING A SCREWDRIVER

The screwdriver is one of the most badly misused tools in the woodworking lab. Fig. 26-21. Very often it is not ground properly, with the result that a burr forms when screws are set. These burrs in screws are both dangerous and unsightly. Grind the screwdriver with a slight taper on each side and the end flat, as shown in Fig. 26-22.

SHARPENING TURNING TOOLS

Proper grinding angles for woodturning tools are shown in Fig. 26-23. Sharpening is done the same as for a chisel.

Review Questions

1. Why is it important to keep tools sharp?
2. What can be done to correct a badly nicked cutting edge?
3. At what angle should a plane iron be ground for softwood? For hardwood?
4. At what angle should a plane iron be whetted?
5. How is the edge of a hand scraper shaped? At what angle should the burnishing tool be held?
6. Tell how to test a plane iron for sharpness.
7. Describe the correct way to grind a screwdriver.

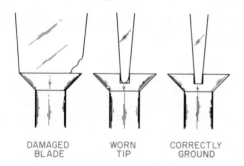

DAMAGED BLADE   WORN TIP   CORRECTLY GROUND

26-21. Good and bad tips: a damaged tip that needs regrinding; a worn tip that should be reground; and a correctly ground screwdriver.

26-22. Grinding the tip of the screwdriver.

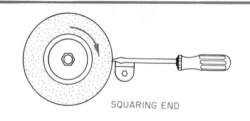

SQUARING END

GRINDING SIDES

26-23. Grinding angles for woodturning tools.

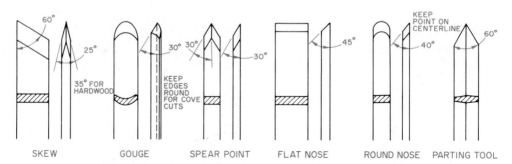

SKEW   GOUGE   SPEAR POINT   FLAT NOSE   ROUND NOSE   PARTING TOOL

Thinking about a Career

Teacher

Mary Amarel is a technology education teacher at a large high school in the West. She teaches three woodworking technology classes and one graphic arts class. She also is the sponsor for VICA, a club for students in vocational classes.

"When I was in high school, I took a woodworking course," says Mary. "I enjoyed it so much that I would have taken a second course—but only one was offered. When I enrolled in the local branch of the state university, I studied liberal arts at first. But I wasn't sure exactly what I wanted to do. In the summer after my freshman year, I got a summer job with a local contractor. Even the few simple tasks I did that summer helped me realize how much I liked working with my hands. When I returned to school, I enrolled in a woodworking course. I liked it as much as I thought I would. I decided to declare my major as Industrial Sciences/Technology Education."

The demand for industrial technology teachers is met by graduates of the nation's colleges and universities. A variety of subjects are taught in the area of industrial education. These include wood technology, metalworking, graphic arts, electronics, drafting, and environmental and energy technologies. In high school, some of the students in technology education classes are taking them only to gain some general knowledge of the subject. Others take the subjects to obtain background knowledge of a field they might be considering as a career.

"In teaching my classes, I need to be aware that many students have no intention or desire of using the knowledge beyond that class. But, I also know there are some students considering careers in, say, carpentry. I find the same differences in students in the graphic arts class. I need to balance my teaching to offer as much knowledge and practice as possible to each type of student.

"I know that some industrial technology teachers teach on the college level. I've been working on my master's degree for over two years now. I hope to have it completed in another two years. It has taken me longer than usual because I have been able to go only at night and during the summers. After I obtain my master's degree, I plan to continue to teach here at the same high school."

Mary has the qualifications a successful teacher needs. She has the necessary educational requirements. She also has a willingness to communicate her knowledge to her students. She has a keen interest in her special subjects—woodworking and graphic arts. She has the ability to motivate her students. Her combination of knowledge and interest has helped her find a satisfying career.

Developing Science, Math, and Reading Skills

How Do Glues Hold Wood Together?

All substances have particular properties that are helpful in describing them. For example, woods may be described in terms of color, odor, hardness, and density. Those properties that may be observed without creating a new substance are called *physical properties.* However, some properties, such as the ability to burn or react with acids, are more difficult to observe. Properties that can only be observed by allowing materials to react are known as *chemical properties.*

Chemicals and physical properties are extremely important in understanding the forces that cause glues to bond well. Some glues pour very slowly. The rate at which a liquid pours is a measure of the substance's *viscosity.* This would be a physical property. Very viscous glues pour very slowly—like "molasses in January." This is due to high cohesive attraction between the particles that make up the glue. *Cohesion* is the force that holds like molecules together.

As mentioned earlier in the unit, *adhesion* is the force that cause unlike molecules to bond together. When the woods are joined by glues, the glue is forced into the hollow air spaces of the walls of the cell cavities. The pieces are held together by both adhesion and cohesion. However, for most glues, the property of adhesion to the wood molecules is stronger than the property of cohesion to other glue molecules. Consequently, a thin layer of glue will hold things together better than a thick layer will.

ACTIVITY: Investigating Properties of Materials
Materials
Plastic drinking straws
Water
3 or 4 different types of glue
Stopwatch
Optional: A stalk of fresh celery with leaves attached, at least 10″ (15 cm) long

A. Obtain the listed materials.
B. An Investigation of Cohesion, Adhesion and Viscosity.
   Add about 1″ (2.5 cm) of glue samples to each of four cups with paper beneath them. Have your stopwatch ready. Have helpers turn each of the samples over at the same time. Have them record the time it takes for the first drop of glue to hit the paper. Rate the glues as to high, moderate, or low viscosity, cohesion, and adhesion. The glue that flowed most quickly probably had the lowest viscosity, lowest cohesion, and lowest adhesion to the paper cup (as explained above).
C. An Investigation of Capillarity.
   Another important property of matter is the ability of liquids to rise and fall in thin tubes. Liquids will rise in a tube if the liquid has a high adhesion to the tube. Liquids will fall in tubes if the cohesion between liquid molecules is stronger than the attraction of the molecules to the tube. This concept is known as *capillarity.* It is the reason

that liquids are drawn up into a tree to feed it. To observe capillarity, do the following experiment:

1. Slice the celery about 6″ (15 cm) up the stalk. Place this piece in a jar of water and red food coloring. Place the other piece in a jar of water and blue food coloring.
2. Leave the celery in the liquid for at least 24 hours and observe. What do you notice about the color of the celery leaves? Why did this occur?
3. Place an ordinary drinking straw in one of the jars. Why does the colored water rise above the level of water in the jar?

Activity One

On page 109, the author provided you with some facts about wood. Varieties of wood types, as well as the heights, sizes, and ages of various trees were described. You were told, for example, that the world's tallest tree is a redwood named Libby. It is 367 feet tall and weighs over one million pounds.

How does the size of this tree compare with the size of the largest land animal, the largest sea animal, and the largest plant?

Activity Two

Many woods are suitable for carving. On page 174, the author mentions three kinds of wood that are best for carving. He also tells you how to treat wood to prevent splits, cracks, or warping.

Developing Reading Skills

Review those pages and then briefly describe the type of wood that you would select for handles for sports equipment. Describe how you would treat the wood to prevent cracking.

Activity Three

On pages 200-206, the author tells you that successful woodworking depends on good cutting edges. He then discusses methods of sharpening various tools to accomplish this work.

Review these pages and, in your own words, describe how you would sharpen a hand scraper for successful woodworking.

Measurement Conversion

What is the length of the brace and bit shown in Fig. A? The length is _____ mm, or _____ inches.

What is the length of the saw shown in Fig. B? The length is _____ mm, or _____ inches.

Developing Math Skills

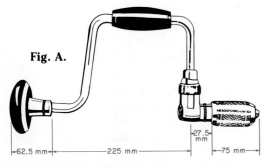

Fig. A.

62.5 mm 225 mm 27.5 mm 75 mm

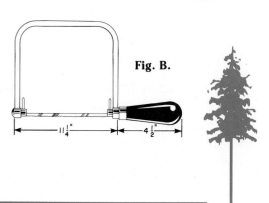

Fig. B.

11¼″ 4½″

Section III.

Joinery and Assembly

Chapter 27

Butt, Dowel, and Biscuit Joints

After studying this chapter, you will be able to:
● Distinguish an end butt joint from an edge butt joint.
● Describe the technique for making an edge dowel joint.
● Describe the technique for making a dowel joint on a frame.
● Describe the technique for making a dowel joint on a leg and rail.
● Tell how to make a biscuit joint.

LOOK FOR THESE TERMS

biscuit joint	dowel joint
dowel	dowel rod
dowel bits	dowel sharpener
dowel center	edge butt joint
dowel drill guide	end butt joint
doweling jig	

The simplest joints to make are the end and edge butt joints. Both can be strengthened by adding dowels.

END BUTT JOINTS

In an *end butt joint*, the end of one piece is connected to the flat surface, edge, or end of the second piece. Figs. 27-1 and 27-2. This joint is weak unless strengthened with a corner block, dowels, or some kind of metal fastener like screws or nails. Fig. 27-3.

The ends of a butt joint must be square to the side and edge. The two parts must fit flush against each other.

Before assembly, clean the surface. Apply a coating of glue to the mating parts. Position the pieces so that they will line up perfectly. Always use fasteners that will give the greatest holding strength.

27-1. This simple footstool is assembled with a butt joint.

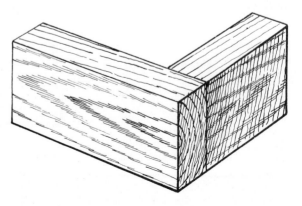

27-2. A butt joint like this one is used to join the ends and rails of the footstool.

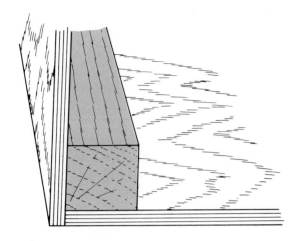

27-3. A corner block is added to the thin plywood corner to give added strength.

EDGE BUTT JOINTS

In an *edge butt joint* (edge-to-edge), the edges of two pieces are fastened together. Fig. 27-4. The edge butt joint is used for joining narrow boards to make wider widths for tabletops and other large parts. Strengthening this joint with dowels or a spline is a good idea. See Chapter 15.

DOWEL JOINTS

Dowels are wood or plastic pins placed in matching holes where the two pieces of a joint join. Fig. 27-5. They add strength to the joint and may be used on a miter joint or an end or edge butt joint. When dowels are added, the joint may be called a *dowel joint*. Fig. 27-6.

DOWEL TOOLS AND MATERIALS

Dowel rod is usually made of birch in diameters from $1/8$ to 1 inch in 3-foot lengths. Small dowel pins are made with spiral or straight grooves and pointed ends. Fig. 27-7. The grooves allow the glue to flow more freely. A *dowel sharpener* points the ends of the dowels. Fig. 27-8. *Dowel centers* are small metal pins used for spotting the location of holes on two parts of a joint. Fig. 27-9.

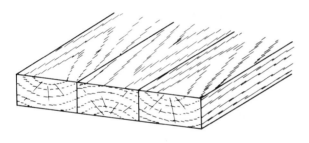

27-4. An edge butt joint.

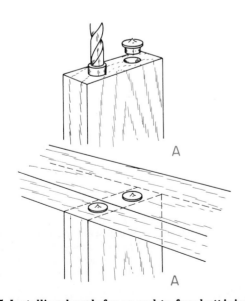

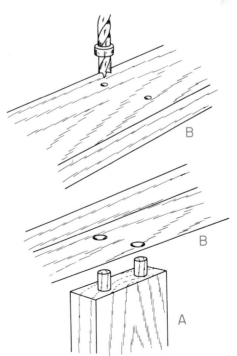

27-5. Installing dowels for an end-to-face butt joint. A. Note that the holes are bored in the end pieces first. B. Then place dowel centers in the holes to locate the holes in the face pieces. Bore these holes to the proper depth.

A *doweling jig* will help locate the position of the holes and guide the auger bit for boring the holes. There are several kinds of these jigs. Fig. 27-10. *Dowel bits* are auger bits for boring the dowel holes. They are shorter than regular auger bits. Fig. 27-11.

MAKING AN EDGE DOWEL JOINT

To make this joint, clamp the two pieces to be joined with the edges flush and face surfaces out. With a try square, mark across the edges of both pieces at the several points where the dowels will be. Next, set a marking gauge to half the thickness of the wood. Mark the center locations of the dowel joints. Make sure that you mark these from the face side.

Decide on the size of the dowel you want to use and the depth to which the dowel will go. The diameter of the dowel should never be more than half the thickness of the wood.

Usually the dowel should be no longer than 3 inches (76 mm). Therefore, the holes will be drilled about $1^5/8$ inch (30 mm) deep. This provides about $^1/8$ inch (3 mm) clearance at the bottom on each side to help hold glue and prevent a dry dowel joint.

27-7. Dowel pins usually have a spiral groove that helps the glue flow.

27-8. A dowel sharpener. This is used to cut a slight bevel at the end of dowel rod.

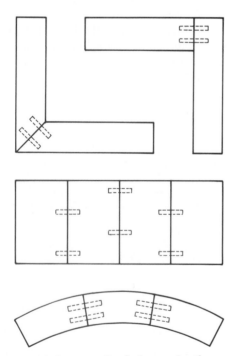

27-6. Dowel joints are simple to construct.

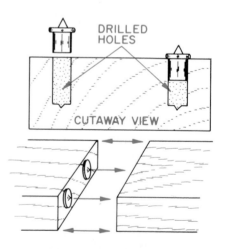

27-9. The locations for the dowels are marked on the first piece and drilled. Then the dowel centers are put in place. When the two pieces are held together, the dowel centers show the hole locations on the second piece.

After locating the points, make a small dent with a scratch awl. Select an auger bit the same size as the dowel rod. Carefully bore the hole to the proper depth, making sure that you are working square with the edge of the stock. Use a depth gauge as a guide. Use a doweling jig if one is available. Figs. 27-12 and 27-13. With this tool you will always be able to bore the holes square and in the right place.

After boring the holes, saw off the dowel. Cut a slight bevel at each end to make the dowel pieces slip into the holes easily. When gluing, dip the dowels about halfway in glue. Drive them into the holes on one edge. Then coat the other half and the edges and assemble. Fig. 27-14.

MAKING A DOWEL JOINT ON A FRAME

One way to strengthen a butt joint on a simple frame is to install two or more dowels at each corner. Do this in the following manner:
1. Square up pieces of wood that are to go into the frame. Carefully saw and sand the ends.
2. Lay out the frame. Mark the corners with corresponding numbers.
3. Indicate on the face surfaces the location and number of dowels. Fig. 27-15.

27-10. A doweling jig with a rotating head. Select the correct size of bit to be used. Then turn the head until the hole that fits the bit is centered over the stock. Line up the lines on the jig with the lines on the face of the stock.

27-11. A dowel bit is shorter than an auger bit because it is not used to bore deep holes. Their sizes match the common dowel diameters.

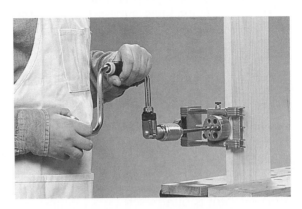

27-12. A dowling jig that will help locate the position of holes and guide the auger bit for boring. This jig comes with several metal guides in sizes 3/16, 1/4, 5/16, 3/8, 7/16, and 1/2 inch. This jig has been clamped to the stock and the proper size guide fastened in it. An auger bit of the correct size is being used. A depth gauge is attached to control the depth of the hole.

27-13. A self-centering dowel drill guide. This holds the material like a vise. When the workpiece is clamped in the tool, the guide holes for the drill are automatically centered over the work. The jaws will clamp on work up to 2 inches in thickness. The guide accommodates five bit sizes.

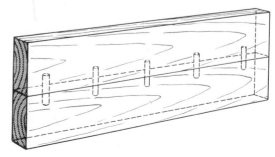

27-14. Edge dowel joint with the dowels installed.

4. Place the two pieces that are to form one of the corners in a vise. Have the butting end and the butting edge sticking out a little, with the face surfaces of the two pieces out and the end and edge flush.
5. Hold a try square against one of the face surfaces. Mark lines across to show the location of the dowel rods. Fig. 27-16.
6. After setting a marking gauge to half the thickness of the wood, hold it against the surface of each piece. Mark the exact location.
7. Mark these points with a scratch awl. Bore the holes as described above.

MAKING A DOWEL JOINT ON A LEG AND RAIL

A dowel joint is often used on a leg and rail instead of a mortise-and-tenon joint. Fig. 27-17.

Square up the leg and rail as for any joint, making sure that the end of the rail is square. Next clamp the leg and rail in a vise with the butting end and the butting edge sticking out and the face surface of each turned out. Hold a try square against the face surface of the rail. Mark the location of the dowels on the end of the rail and the edge of the leg.

Next set a marking gauge to half the thickness of the rail. From the face surface of the rail, mark the crossline that will show the location of the dowel joints. Then decide how far back you want the rail to be from the face surface of the leg. Add this amount to the setting you already have on the marking gauge. From the face surface of the leg, mark the crossline that will show the exact location of the dowel. Bore the holes, cut the dowels, glue, and assemble as before.

BISCUIT JOINTS

Biscuit joinery is the ideal way to strengthen many kinds of joints. Fig. 27-18. A machine is used to cut the slots for the wood "biscuits" that fit into those slots. The machine looks like a hand-held grinder with a saw blade mounted on the arbor. Fig. 27-19.

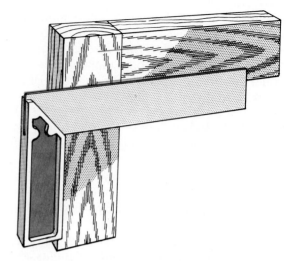

27-15. Using a try square to mark the locations of the dowels on the face surfaces.

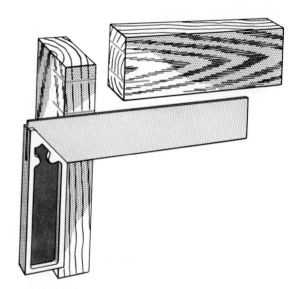

27-16. Squaring a line across the edge and end of both pieces.

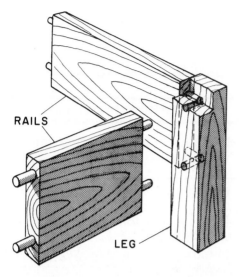

27-17. Notice that the rails are thinner than the leg. The dowels are centered on the ends of the rails and on the legs. If the rails must be flush with the surface of the legs, then the dowel holes on the legs must be closer to the outside surface.

The head is spring-loaded and has adjustable stops for different depths of cut. The fence can be adjusted to angles other than 90 degrees. The biscuits are football-shaped pieces of compressed beech available in three sizes. Fig. 27-20.

There are three steps in making a biscuit joint. First, lay out the location of the joint on the two adjoining surfaces. Adjust the fences for vertical location of the slots. For most joints the fence should be at 90 degrees. Adjust for depth of cut, depending on the size of biscuits that are selected.

Next, clamp the two pieces of wood securely to the top of the bench using a vise or clamp. Align the red mark on the front of the fence or face plate with the layout lines on the wood. Turn on the machine and, with a steady forward motion, push the blade into the wood. Repeat for each adjoining slot.

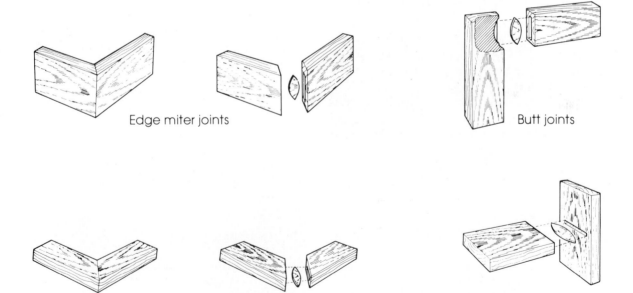

Edge miter joints

Butt joints

Flat miter joints

T joints

27-18. Many joints can be strengthened using biscuits.

Finally, assemble the joint. Select the correct size of biscuits for the slots. Because the slots are cut slightly longer than the biscuits, the two parts can be shifted slightly for alignment. (This isn't possible when using dowels.) Apply water-based glue to the slots and the surfaces to be joined. Insert the biscuits into the slots of the first piece and then fit the second piece to it. Clamp the pieces together until the glue is dry. The compressed biscuits begin to expand as moisture permeates the wood, making a tight, perfectly aligned joint.

27-19 The fence on the biscuit machine can be adjusted to different angles and also reversed for making miter joints. All the equipment needed is shown here. Standard and junior models, a glue dispenser, and band clamps are included.

Review Questions

1. How can a butt joint be strengthened?
2. From what kinds of wood is dowel rod usually made?
3. Why are dowels used in making an edge joint?
4. State the rule for choosing the correct dowel diameter.
5. Should there be clearance at the bottom of a dowel hole? Why?
6. What is a doweling jig? Explain how it is used.
7. List the steps in making a dowel joint on a frame.
8. What would happen if the dowel holes of two joint pieces were not aligned perfectly?
9. Describe how to make a biscuit joint.

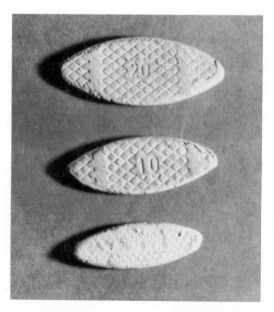

27-20. Biscuits are available in three sizes.

Chapter 28

Rabbet Joint

After studying this chapter, you will be able to:
● Identify a rabbet joint.
● Describe how to make a rabbet joint.

LOOK FOR THESE TERMS

rabbet joint
superimposing

The *rabbet joint* is a slot cut at the end or edge of one piece into which the end or edge of a second piece fits. Fig. 28-1. It is made with the end grain hidden from the front. This joint is found in drawer construction, boxes, and cabinet frames. Figs. 28-2 and 28-3.

28-1. A rabbet joint is a simple type of construction found in much modern furniture.

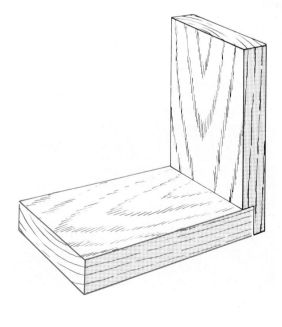

28-2. The lower shelf of this medicine cabinet is attached with a rabbet joint.

28-3. Note how the back of a cabinet or case fits into a rabbet joint.

LAYING OUT A RABBET JOINT

Make sure that the end on which the joint is to be made has been squared properly. Place the first board on the bench with the face surface down. Hold the second piece directly over the first, with the face surface of the second piece flush with the end grain of the first. Fig. 28-4. This is called *superimposing*.

With a sharp pencil or knife, mark the width of the rabbet. Then remove the second piece. With a try square held on the joint edge, square a line across the surface of the first piece. Then mark a line down each edge. From the face surface, mark the depth of the rabbet on the sides and end with a marking gauge. Cut the rabbet one-half to two-thirds the thickness of the piece. Fig. 28-5.

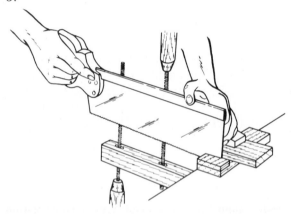

28-6. Making a shoulder cut on a rabbet joint. Notice that a piece of scrap stock is clamped over the layout line with hand screws. Then the backsaw is held against the edge of the scrap stock. This prevents the saw from jumping out of the kerf and damaging the wood.

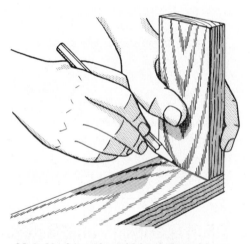

28-4. Marking the width of the rabbet.

28-5. The width of the rabbet must be equal to the thickness of the stock. The depth of the rabbet is usually one-half to two-thirds the thickness.

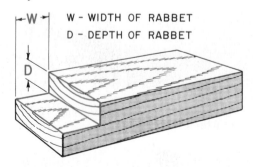

W – WIDTH OF RABBET
D – DEPTH OF RABBET

28-7. After cutting the rabbet, trim it with a chisel. Hold the blade of the chisel between thumb and forefinger to trim the excess stock.

CUTTING THE RABBET

In cutting the rabbet joint, the piece should be held firmly against a bench hook. It is better for the beginner to clamp the wood directly to the bench top. Use a backsaw to make the cut in the waste stock or inside the layout line. The beginner should clamp a square piece of scrap stock directly over the layout line. Then the backsaw can be held against this edge to make the saw cut. Fig. 28-6. Cut the joint to the proper depth, as indicated by the layout line.

The excess stock from the joint can either be sawed out or pared out with a chisel. If you saw it out, lock the wood in a vise with the joint showing. With a backsaw, carefully saw out the excess stock. If you use a chisel, leave the wood clamped to the top of the bench. Pare out the excess stock with a chisel. Fig. 28-7.

It is a good idea to mark this joint on both edges with corresponding numbers. A final check with a try square will show if the joint is square.

ASSEMBLING THE JOINT

This type of joint is usually assembled with glue or with both glue and nails (or screws). Fig. 28-8. If the joint is nailed, drive the nails in at a slight angle to help them fasten the joint more tightly. Fig. 28-9. Screws should be long and thin, as they will have to go into end grain.

Review Questions

1. What is a rabbet and how is it used?
2. Explain superimposing.
3. What tools should be used to mark a rabbet?
4. How can the pieces of several different rabbet joints be kept in order?
5. What saw should be used for cutting a rabbet?
6. When can a chisel be chosen for making a rabbet joint?
7. If you decide to assemble a rabbet joint with nails, how would you insert them?

28-8. Nailing a rabbet joint so that the front has no visible joint. Since the nails must be fastened in end grain, it is a good idea to drive them at a slight angle. This will give them more holding power.

28-9. Rabbet joints are neat, strong, and easy to make. You will find them the ideal choice for drawers, chests, and cupboards.

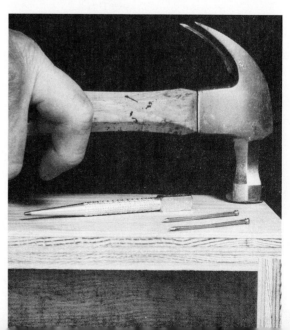

Chapter 29

Dado Joint

After studying this chapter, you will be able to:
● Describe how to cut a dado.
● Describe how to make a rabbet-and-dado joint.
● Describe how to make a blind dado joint.

LOOK FOR THESE TERMS

blind dado joint	dado joint
dado	rabbet-and-dado joint

A *dado* is a groove cut across the grain of wood. Fig. 29-1. The *dado joint* is fairly easy to make. When snugly fit, it is quite strong. This joint is found in bookracks, drawers, cabinet shelves, ladders, and steps. Fig. 29-2.

29-1. A dado joint is used if the crosspieces must support considerable weight, such as for shelves, stairsteps, or ladders.

29-2. This wall shelf was a prize winner in a mass production contest. Can you count the number of *dado* joints in the project. The bottom and back are attached with *rabbet* joints.

LAYING OUT A DADO JOINT

From the end of the board, measure in the correct distance to one side of the dado. Then square off a line across the surface of the piece at this point. Superimpose the other piece with one edge directly over the line. With a sharp knife or pencil, mark the correct width of the dado.

Remove the second piece and square off a line across the surface to show the proper width. Continue both lines down both edges. Fig. 29-3. Lay out the correct depth of the joint to one-half the thickness of the work-piece.

CUTTING A DADO

Using a backsaw, cut the dado to the proper depth at both layout lines. Make sure that the kerfs are in the waste stock and not outside the layout line. Fig. 29-4.

With a chisel, cut and trim the dado to proper depth. A router plane may be used to remove the waste stock. Figs. 29-5 and 29-6.

If the dado is very wide, you may need to make several saw cuts to depth so that the waste stock can be easily trimmed out. With a combination square, check the dado to make sure that it has the same depth throughout. Fig. 29-7. Check the dado joint by inserting the piece in the joint. Fig. 29-8.

You may have to plane the side of the second piece slightly to make it fit into the joint.

29-3. Making the layout for a dado joint. One line is laid out on the face surface and then, by superimposing, the width of the dado is marked. Finally the lines are drawn across the surface and down the edge of the stock.

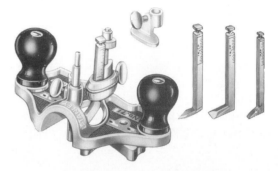

29-5. A router plane is equipped with blades of different widths. It is used for surfacing the bottom of a groove or other depression.

29-6. Using the router plane to trim out the bottom of a dado joint. Select a cutter that is the same width or slightly narrower than the width of the dado. Adjust the thumbscrew to the proper depth. Take the cut by holding the router plane firmly on the surface of the work and applying pressure with both hands. Don't attempt to cut the total depth with one setting.

29-4. Make sure that the saw kerfs in the dado joint are inside the waste stock.

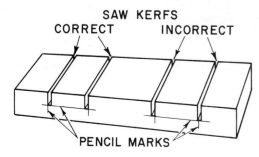

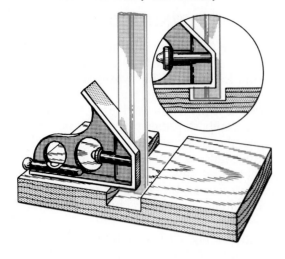

29-7. The depth of a dado joint can be checked by setting the blade of a combination square to the correct depth.

ASSEMBLING THE JOINT

The dado joint is usually assembled either with glue alone or with glue and nails or screws. Fig. 29-9.

MAKING A RABBET-AND-DADO JOINT

A *rabbet-and-dado* joint is used when additional strength and stiffness are needed. Fig. 29-10. This joint is popular for drawer construction. The joint consists of a rabbet with a tongue. The tongue fits into the dado. To make this kind of joint, lay out and cut the rabbet first. Then lay out the position of the dado joint by superimposing the tongue of the rabbet. Mark the width of the dado. Make the dado as described earlier. Fit the tongue of the rabbet into it.

29-8. Checking a dado joint. The second piece is inserted in the dado. If it is necessary to fit the joint, it is simpler to remove a little stock from the second piece than to cut the dado wider.

29-9. Assembling a shelf with dado joints.

MAKING A BLIND DADO JOINT

In a *blind dado joint* the dado is cut only partway across the board. Fig. 29-11. The piece that fits into the dado is notched so that the joint does not show from the front. Lay out the width of the dado as described before. Mark the depth of the dado on the back edge only. Also lay out the length of the dado from the back edge to within ½ to ¾ inch of the front edge. The dado can be cut by boring a series of holes in the waste stock and then trimming out with a chisel.

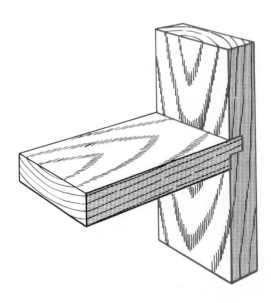

29-10. A rabbet-and-dado joint gives added strength and rigidity. It is commonly used for the back corner of drawers.

Review Questions

1. What is a dado?
2. Point out the difference between a dado and a rabbet.
3. When cutting a dado, where should the saw kerf be formed?
4. Explain a router plane. What is it used for?
5. How could you make a depth gauge to check a dado?
6. In fitting a dado joint, is it better to plane the side of the second piece or to cut a wider dado?
7. What advantage does a rabbet-and-dado joint have? Where is it frequently found?
8. Sketch a blind dado joint.
9. Why would a blind dado joint be found in expensive furniture?

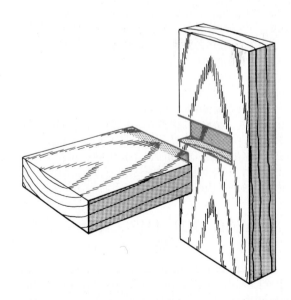

29-11. A blind dado joint has the same strength advantage as the dado joint. In addition, it does not show the joint. It is built into bookcases and other projects of this type when a neat appearance at the front of the shelves is desirable.

Chapter 30

After studying this chapter, you will be able to:
- Identify the four main types of lap joints.
- List the main steps in making a lap joint.

LOOK FOR THESE TERMS

cross-lap joint   lap joint
end-lap joint   middle-lap joint
half-lap joint

All *lap* joints have one thing in common—namely, an equal amount of wood is cut from the two parts to be joined.

There are many different lap joints. Fig. 30-1. The *end-lap* is used on screen doors, chair seats, frames, or any type of corner construction in which the surfaces must be flush. The *middle-lap* is used in screen-door construction, in making cabinets, and in framing a house. The *cross-lap* is used in furniture whenever two pieces must cross and still be flush on the surface. The *half-lap* is used to make a longer piece of stock from two shorter pieces. Fig. 30-2. The cross-lap is by far the most common. To make any of the other types, follow the same general directions as for the cross-lap.

LAYING OUT THE CROSS-LAP JOINT

The cross-lap joint is usually made in the exact center of the two pieces that cross at a 90-degree angle. However, a cross-lap joint can be made at any angle.

The two pieces must be exactly the same thickness and width. Lay the two pieces on the bench side by side, with the face surface of one (piece A) and the opposite surface of

the other (piece B) upward. Divide the length of each into two equal parts. Lay out a center line across the two pieces. Measure the width of the stock and divide this measurement in half. Lay out a line this distance on each side of the center line. Fig. 30-3.

Now check this measurement by superimposing piece B over piece A at right angles. Be sure to place it in the position that the joint will be when assembled. Fig. 30-4. The layout line should just barely show beyond the edge of each piece.

Now continue the lines showing the width of the joint down the edge of each piece. Next, set a marking gauge to half the thickness of the stock. From the face surface of each piece, mark along the edge on each side to show the depth of the joint. If you make this measurement from the face surface, the two pieces will be flush when the joint is made. This is because you will be cutting the joint from the face surface of one piece and the opposite surface of the other.

EDGE CROSS LAP

END LAP

HALF LAP

MIDDLE LAP

30-1. Several types of lap joints that are used for various purposes.

30-2. This attractive serving tray is made by joining many pieces of stock with edge cross-lap joints. When this many joints must be cut, it is almost a necessity to use a circular saw.

30-3. Correct layout for a lap joint. Both pieces should be marked at the same time.

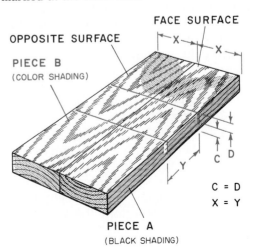

FACE SURFACE

OPPOSITE SURFACE

PIECE B
(COLOR SHADING)

X   X

C   D

Y

C = D
X = Y

PIECE A
(BLACK SHADING)

30-4. The layout has been made and the lap joint is checked. A try square keeps the pieces at right angles. The lines on the lower piece, which indicate the width of the lap joint, should be just visible.

CUTTING THE LAP JOINT

Hold the piece in a bench hook or clamp it to the top of the bench. Cut with a backsaw to the depth of the joint just inside each of the layout lines, as you did to make a dado joint. If the joint is wide, you should make several cuts in the waste stock. This helps to remove the waste. It also acts as a guide when you chisel it out.

Next, use a chisel or router plane to remove the waste stock. Work from both sides of each piece, tapering up toward the center. If you chisel across the stock from one side, you will chip the opposite side.

After you have brought the joint down to the layout line on either edge, continue to pare (cut) the high point in the center of the joint. (See Chapter 21.)

Complete this on both pieces. Then fit them together. Fig. 30-5. The pieces should fit snugly. They should not be so loose that they fall apart or so tight that they must be forced together. If the fit is too tight, it is better to plane a little from the edge of one piece rather than to try to trim the shoulder.

ASSEMBLING THE JOINT

When assembled, the surfaces of both pieces should fit flush with one another. Both glue and nails or screws are used. If the nails or screws are installed from the underside, they will not show and the joint will be neat.

Review Questions

1. Name four types of lap joints. What are the common uses of each?
2. Which type of lap joint is most common?
3. At what angle do the pieces of a cross-lap joint usually cross?
4. How can you make sure that the two pieces will be flush when the joint is assembled?

30-5. Fitting a lap joint. The lap joints should fit together with a moderate amount of pressure. It is simpler to trim off a little from the edges of the stock than it is to make the joint wider.

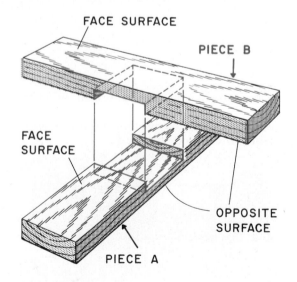

Chapter 31

Miter Joint

After studying this chapter, you will be able to:
● List the main steps in the cutting of a miter joint.
● Describe the making of a picture frame, using standard wood moldings.

LOOK FOR THESE TERMS

miter box and saw
miter and corner clamp
miter joint

A *miter joint* is an angle joint that hides the end grain of both pieces. The ends of each piece are usually cut at 45 degrees to form a right angle. A simple miter can be *flat* or *on edge*. Because it is a relatively weak joint, it is often strengthened with a spline, dowel, key, or feather. Fig. 31-1. Some uses of miter joints are shown in Figs. 31-2 and 31-3.

31-1. The miter joint is weak by itself. It can be strengthened by adding dowels, a spline, or a key.

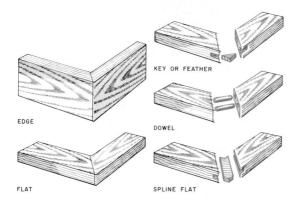

31-2. Odd-angle miter joints are part of the design of this prize-winning clock. Note also that the top frame uses open and tenon joints. (See Unit 32.)

31-3. A polygon miter with an angle of more or less than 45 degrees must be cut to form certain objects. To form a three- to ten-sided object, the correct gauge setting can be found as follows: Divide 180 by the number of sides. Then subtract this amount from 90 degrees. A twelve-sided polygon miter would be cut at an angle of 75 degrees.

MITER BOXES

The *miter box and saw* has a metal box in which a saw can be adjusted to any angle from 30 to 90 degrees. Fig. 31-4. If one is not available, it is simple to make one. This can be done by fastening two pieces of stock to a base. Then, with a sliding T-bevel, lay out a 45-degree angle in both directions. Usually, only this and a 90-degree angle cut are needed. Figs. 31-5 and 31-6. Cutting a frame is the most common use for the miter joint, so this will be described.

31-4. A miter box and saw. This box consists of a frame and a saw that can be adjusted to various angles.

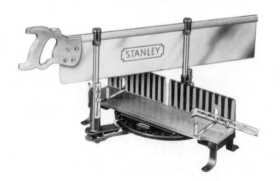

CUTTING A FRAME

If a metal miter box is available, swing the saw to the left and set it at 45 degrees. If a wood box is used, use the cut that is to the left as you face it. Place the edge of the frame in the box with the rabbet edge down and toward you. Hold the stock firmly with the thumb of one hand against the side of the box. Fig. 31-7. Then carefully bring the miter saw (or backsaw or fine crosscut saw if the box is homemade) down on the stock and cut the angle. Be especially careful not to let the stock slip when starting the cut. This could ruin the surface of the frame.

Next, determine the length of the glass or the picture. Add to this length twice the width of the frame, measured from the rabbet edge to the outside edge. Lay out this measurement along the outside edge of the stock. Fig. 31-8. Then swing the miter-box saw to the right and set it at 45 degrees. Hold the stock firmly with one hand. Cut the stock to length, using your other hand to operate the saw. If you find this awkward, clamp the stock to the box with a hand screw. Then operate the saw with your favored hand. Repeat this for the second side and the ends.

31-5. A simple miter box that you could make for cutting 45- to 90-degree angles.

31-6. Cutting a miter joint with a homemade miter box and backsaw. Be certain that the line to be cut is directly under the saw teeth. Hold the work tightly against the back of the box. Start the cut with a careful backstroke.

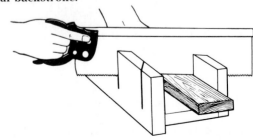

31-7. In using a metal miter box, make sure the stock is held firmly against the back of the box. This will keep it from slipping when the saw kerf is started.

ASSEMBLING THE MITER JOINT

Check the joint to make sure the corners fit properly. The miter joint is usually put together by gluing and nailing. Dowels, a spline, or a key may be added to strengthen the joint. To nail a miter joint, drive the nail partway into one piece. Lock the other piece in a vise in a vertical position. Hold the first piece over the vertical piece with its corner extending somewhat outside the edge of the vertical piece. Fig. 31-9. As you nail the corners together, the top piece will tend to slip down until it fits squarely.

A *miter and corner clamp* is the ideal clamp for assembling frames. This clamp allows you to fasten the corners with the two pieces held firmly in place. Figs. 31-10 and 31-11. A wooden frame clamp can be made to use in assembling picture frames. Figs. 31-12 and 31-13. There are also special spring clamps that will hold a miter corner together. Fig. 31-14.

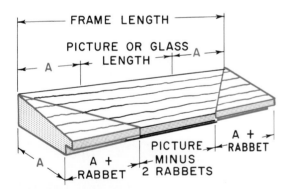

31-8. Laying out the proper measurement for cutting miter joints on a picture frame. The length as marked on the outside of the frame is equal to the length of the glass plus twice the width of the stock measured from the rabbet to the outside edge.

31-9. Nailing a miter joint. One piece is locked in a vise and the second piece held over it, with the corner extending slightly.

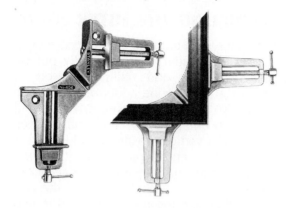

31-10. This miter and corner clamp holds the corners together as they are fastened.

MAKING PICTURE FRAMES WITH STANDARD WOOD MOLDINGS

Standard wood moldings can be used in one design or in a combination of designs to frame pictures. Fig. 31-15. Moldings are available in over 250 patterns and 400 sizes. Fig. 31-16. The tools needed are the same as those available for making any kind of frame.

To make the frame, first select the molding pattern and size. Purchase enough to make the frame. Produce the frame as follows: Glue up the molding strips that will make the complete frame. Clamp them together until the glue is set. The extra piece that is glued onto the first piece will form the rabbet into

31-11. A miter vise with tilting base. This vise can clamp moldings up to 4 inches wide. It will join any frame larger than 3 1/2 x 3 1/2 inches.

31-12. This adjustable frame clamp can be made. The major disadvantage is that it does not permit nailing the corners together when the frame is in the clamp.

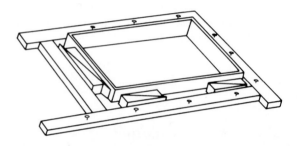

31-13. You can make a simple frame clamp by fastening pieces of wood to a piece of scrap and then using wedges to hold the frame securely until the glue dries.

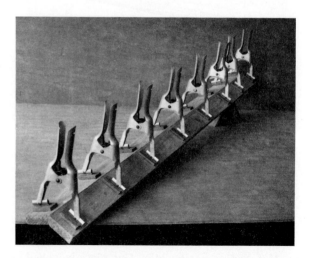

31-14. Spring clamps with special grooved teeth will hold a miter joint together after fastening.

which the glass and picture fit. When dry, cut one end of each piece of molding at 45 degrees. Fig. 31-17. Carefully measure the bottom edge of the picture and add ⅛ inch to this measurement. Fig. 31-18. Transfer this measurement to the moldings. Start from the edge of the miter at the point where the picture inserts into the frame. Mark and cut a 45-degree angle at the opposite end of the first cut. Measure the second piece from the first so that you will have two identical pieces.

31-17. Cut one end of each of the pieces of molding at a 45-degree angle using a metal miter box.

31-15. Wood molding can be used to make a very attractive picture frame.

31-18. Measure the second cut along the picture rabbet. Add 1/8 inch for clearance for the glass and picture.

31-16. These moldings are typical of the more than 250 patterns and 400 sizes available for picture framing.

Measure the side edge of the picture. Cut two pieces of molding to this length, making sure to add the extra ⅛ inch. Assemble the frame one corner at a time. If you have four corner clamps, this can be done in one operation. Cover the ends of one side piece and one bottom piece with glue and insert them in a corner clamp. Align the miter joint carefully and then tighten the clamp. Fig. 31-19. Drive two or more brads through the corner from each side. Fig. 31-20. Allow the heads of the brads to protrude slightly. Now carefully drive the heads of the brads about 1/16 inch below the surface of the frame with a nail set. Fig. 31-21.

Fill the nail holes with plastic wood. When necessary, use a flat corner plate at each corner of a large frame to give it added strength. Complete each of the other corners and then allow the glue to dry thoroughly. After the frame is dry, sand lightly.

Review Questions

1. What is one disadvantage of a miter joint?
2. Name the common uses of a miter joint.
3. Briefly explain the construction of a miter box.
4. At what angle is a miter joint made?
5. What precaution should be observed in starting a miter cut?
6. Name two ways in which a miter joint can be strengthened.
7. What implements would you choose for holding a miter joint after it is glued?
8. Explain how to build a picture frame with standard wood moldings.

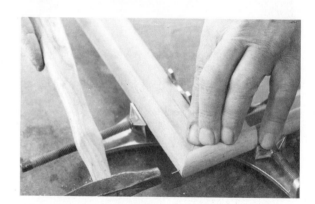

31-20. All finishing nails are nailed from both edges. Allow the heads to protrude 1/16 inch so that you do not mar the frame.

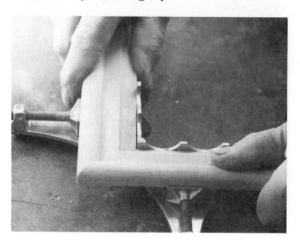

31-19. Clamp the corner tightly. Then wipe off the excess glue with a warm, damp rag.

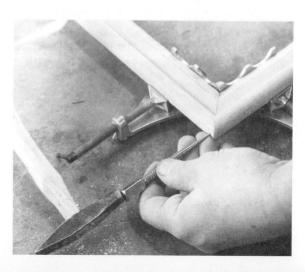

31-21. Use a nail set to drive the nail heads 1/16 inch below the surface. Then fill the nail holes with plastic wood.

Chapter 32

Mortise-and-Tenon Joint

After studying this chapter, you will be able to:
- List the three common types of mortise-and-tenon joints.
- List the main steps in making a mortise-and-tenon joint.

LOOK FOR THESE TERMS

blind mortise-and-tenon joint
mortise
open mortise-and-tenon joint

tenon
thru mortise-and-tenon joint

Mortise-and-tenon joints are very strong joints found in fine furniture. A *mortise* is a rectangular hole cut in wood. The *tenon* is a projecting piece of wood shaped to fit the mortise. Making this joint by hand is difficult and time-consuming. Figs. 32-1 and 32-2.

MAKING THE PRELIMINARY LAYOUT

A project such as a chair needs several mortise-and-tenon joints. For a small table, hold the several pieces to be assembled in the position they will be in when finished. Place the face surface of the rails and the face surface and joint edge of the legs outward. Begin at one corner to mark No. 1 on the leg and No. 1 on the adjoining rail, No. 2 on the next, etc. Do this until you have marked with matching numbers the pieces that make up each mortise-and-tenon joint. In this way, you will be sure the pieces will fit together in the proper order when you are ready to assemble them.

32-1. This desk was built using several kinds of mortise-and-tenon joints. The cross rail between the legs was assembled with a keyed mortise-and-tenon joint. This joint is made like a thru mortise-and-tenon joint, except that the tenon is longer to extend through and beyond the mortise. An opening is cut in the tenon for the key (wedge).

32-2. Common types of mortise-and-tenon joints.

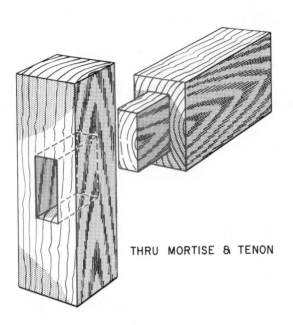

THRU MORTISE & TENON

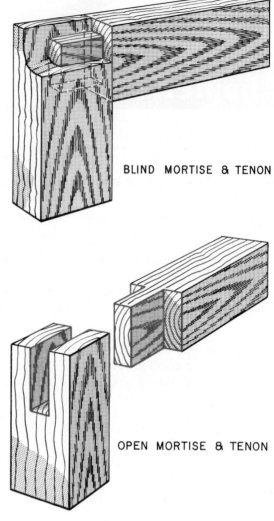

BLIND MORTISE & TENON

OPEN MORTISE & TENON

LAYING OUT THE TENONS

The size of the mortise-and-tenon joint is usually given on the drawing. If no size is given, the tenon is made half as wide as the total thickness of the piece and about ½ to ¾ inch narrower than the total width.

Mark the length of the tenon from the end and square a line completely around each piece. Do this on all pieces. Then check to see that all of the rails are the same length from shoulder to shoulder. Set the marking gauge to half the thickness of the stock to be removed. Mark a line across the end and down each edge.

Add to this measurement the thickness of the tenon. Check the gauge. Again mark a line across the end and down the sides. Subtract the width of the tenon from the total width of the stock. Divide this amount in half and set this measurement on a marking gauge.

From the joint edge of the rail, mark a line across the end and down the side. Add to this measurement the width of the tenon and set the gauge again. Repeat the mark across the end and down the side. Fig. 32-3. If several tenons are needed, mark them at the same time.

32-3. Proper layout for a tenon. These lines should be made accurately so the tenon will be the correct size and shape.

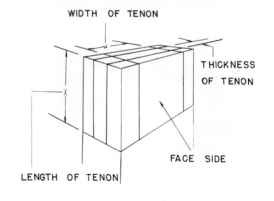

WIDTH OF TENON

THICKNESS OF TENON

FACE SIDE

LENGTH OF TENON

LAYING OUT A MORTISE

Use a pencil point in your marking gauge to make all lines on the legs at the same time. From the top end of each leg, lay out two lines on the inside surfaces (opposite the face side and joint edge) that indicate the total width of the rail.

Lay out two more lines on these surfaces to show the width of the tenon. Decide how far back the rail is to be set from the outside edge of the leg. Add to this measurement the thickness of the stock removed from one side of the tenon. Set the marking gauge to this measurement. Hold the marking gauge against the face side and joint edge. Mark a line between the lines that indicate the width of the tenon. Add to this measurement an amount equal to the thickness of the tenon. Mark another line to complete the outline. This will be exactly the same as the thickness and width of the tenon. Fig. 32-4. If an auger bit is to be used to remove the waste stock from the mortise, lay out a line down the center of the outline.

32-4. The proper layout of a mortise. Only the part indicated by the shading is absolutely essential to the layout.

X — DISTANCE FROM EDGE OF LEG TO FACE SIDE OF RAIL

Y — THICKNESS OF RAIL

Z — WIDTH OF RAIL

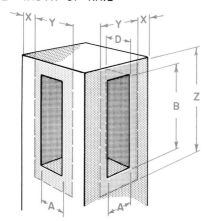

A — WIDTH OF MORTISE (TENON THICKNESS)
B — LENGTH OF MORTISE (TENON WIDTH)
C — LENGTH OF TENON
D — MORTISE DEPTH = C + $\frac{1}{8}$ (3mm)

CUTTING THE MORTISE

The most common way to remove most of the stock is with an auger bit and brace. Bore a series of holes to remove most of the stock from the opening. Fig. 32-5. Use a depth gauge set to make the holes slightly deeper than the length of the tenon. With a chisel trim the side and ends of the opening to the layout line. Finish the ends with a narrow chisel.

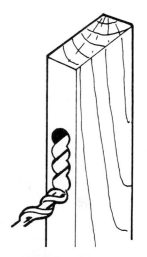

32-5. Boring out a mortise. Note that the bit selected has the same diameter as the thickness of the tenon or the width of the mortise. A depth gauge controls the amount of stock removed. The inset shows this step in detail.

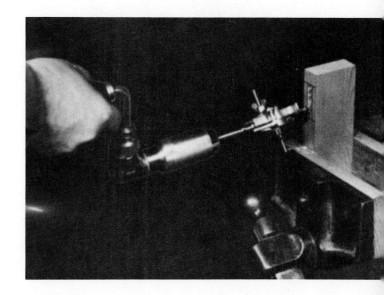

Some woodworkers prefer to remove all of the stock with a mortise chisel. The width of the blade should be exactly the width of the opening. Clamp the workpiece firmly to the bench. Fig. 32-6. Begin to cut at the center of the mortise. Hold the chisel in a vertical position with the bevel side toward the end of the mortise. Cut out a V-shaped notch to the depth required. Then continue to remove the stock by driving the chisel down with a mallet. Draw down on the handle to remove the chips. Stop when you are within about ⅛ inch of the end of the opening. Turn the chisel around with the flat side toward the end of the mortise and cut out the remainder of the stock. Fig. 32-7.

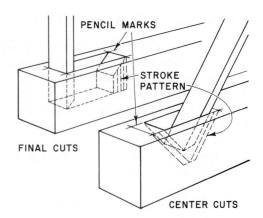

32-7. Proper method of cutting a mortise with a mortising chisel. The center cuts are taken with the chisel held with the bevel toward the outside. Other cuts are taken with the bevel turned in.

32-6. Make sure the workpiece is clamped securely when cutting the mortise with a mortising chisel.

CUTTING THE TENON

Lock the stock in a vise with the marked tenon showing. Using a backsaw or fine crosscut saw, make four saw cuts in the waste stock. These marks will shape the thickness and width of the tenon. Fig. 32-8.

Next, remove the stock from the vise and clamp it on the top of the bench. Make the shoulder cuts to remove the waste stock that forms the thickness and the width of the tenon. Fig. 32-9. *Be especially careful.* It is essential that these saw marks be accurate for a tight-fitting tenon.

Cut a small chamfer around the end of the tenon to help it slip easily into the mortise opening.

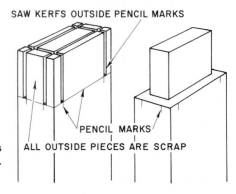

32-8. Cheek cuts completed. This shows the four cuts that will shape the thickness and width of the tenon. *Make the cuts in waste stock.*

ASSEMBLING THE MORTISE-AND-TENON

Use a chisel to pare off stock from the thickness and width of the tenon until you can force the tenon into the mortise with a moderate amount of pressure. Make sure that the shoulder of the tenon fits squarely against the face of the mortise.

This joint is usually fastened permanently with adhesives.

Review Questions

1. Is a mortise-and-tenon joint found on better-quality furniture? Why?
2. Which part is the mortise? The tenon?
3. Name three common types of mortise-and-tenon joints.
4. How many mortise-and-tenon joints could be found on a simple table?
5. What is the rule for the thickness of the tenon? What should the length of the tenon be?
6. Tell how to lay out a tenon.
7. Could a marking gauge be used to lay out a mortise?
8. How do the width of the mortise and the thickness of the tenon compare?
9. Should the shoulder cuts be made first? Why?
10. Describe the two methods of cutting a mortise.
11. How are mortise-and-tenon joints fastened?

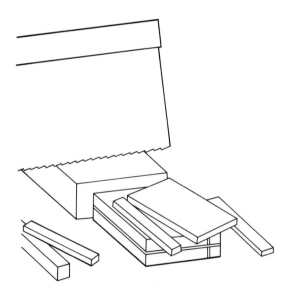

32-9. Making the shoulder cut with a backsaw.

Facts about Wood

Wood in Shipbuilding

Shipbuilding became an important industry along the Eastern seaboard of the United States during the early seventeenth century. By 1775, over one-third of all the ships in the British merchant marine were being built in American shipyards.

After the Revolution, shipbuilding continued to be important to commerce and trade. In the mid-nineteenth century, two significant boat designs were developed. One, the paddlewheel, was adapted for inland waterways. The other, the clipper ship, was designed for the high seas.

In nineteenth-century America, the railway system was not complete. Roads were generally poor. Much cargo was moved by boat along the major rivers—the Ohio, the Mississippi, and the Missouri. Traffic on these rivers included flatboats and paddlewheel steamboats, a boat that was developed especially for use on America's rivers. Steamboats were built of woods such as oak and walnut. A steamboat could float in such a small amount of water that some joked that it could run on a wet handkerchief. Their design ensured that they would not scrape bottom in shallow rivers. Their boilers were fired by wood. Each steamboat had along its route a series of stations at which fresh supplies of wood could be taken on. From the early 1830s until the early 1880s, the steamboat was a common sight on America's major rivers. An excellent account of life on board a paddlewheeler is given in Mark Twain's *Life on the Mississippi*.

With the completion of transcontinental railway systems in the years following the Civil War, the paddlewheel steamboat lost popularity. There are still a few steamboats on our nation's rivers. They are, however, like the older ones only in design. Most of the present models are modern, with metal hulls. Rather than carrying cargo, they are used mainly for short passenger excursions.

The clipper ship was being developed at the same time as the paddlewheel steamboat. Designed to sail the high seas, the clipper ship has a smooth and narrow streamlined hull. This was a commercial sailing ship designed for speed. Its three tall masts were crowded with sails. The first true clipper ship was built in 1833. You may have heard these ships referred to as "China clippers." They received this name because many of them were used in the trade with China. They were used especially to carry tea. The names of a few of these ships may be familiar to you. The *Cutty Sark* and the *Flying Cloud* are two of the most famous. The short era of the clipper ships came to an end in the 1880s. Then, improvements in the steamship enabled it to exceed the speeds reached by even the fastest clipper ships. Even after that, though, clipper ships still found a limited use. Because they were fast and powered by the wind, clipper ships were used for voyages to distant ports where coal was unavailable.

Chapter 33

Simple Casework

After studying this chapter, you will be able to:
- List three methods of installing fixed shelves within a bookcase.
- List two techniques for installing adjustable shelves within a bookcase.

LOOK FOR THESE TERMS

casework
shelf standards

Simple *casework*, such as a bookcase or storage cabinet, is a box turned on its end or edge. Figs. 33-1 and 33-2. The box is easily assembled using a butt, rabbet, or miter joint at the corners. There are many ways of fitting a back to the case. The most common is to cut a rabbet around the back edge. You can then fit a back of thin plywood or hardboard into the recess. Advanced casework is fitted with dividers, shelves, web frames, face frames (sometimes called face plates), drawers, and doors. Such casework is often used for cabinets in kitchens and bathrooms. Figs. 33-3 and 33-4. It is used also for bookcases. Fig. 33-5.

Most simple casework is constructed of soft wood and plywood or particle board. The case can be painted or covered with plastic laminate.

33-1. A box is an example of simple casework. These boxes can be used for all types of storage.

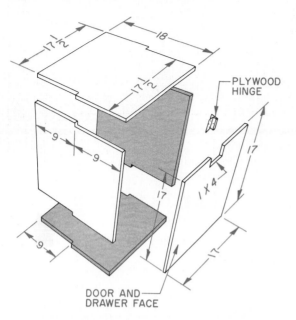

33-2. Note the simple construction of a box.

33-3. Advanced casework, such as this kitchen cabinet unit, is built like fine furniture.

33-4. Typical construction for quality kitchen cabinets.

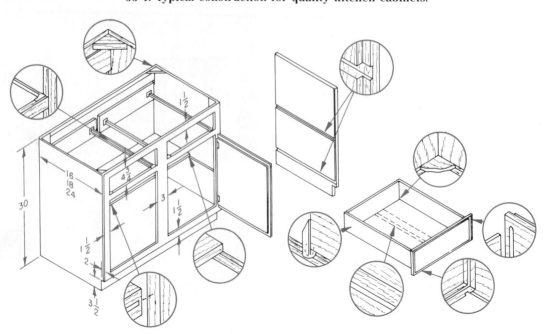

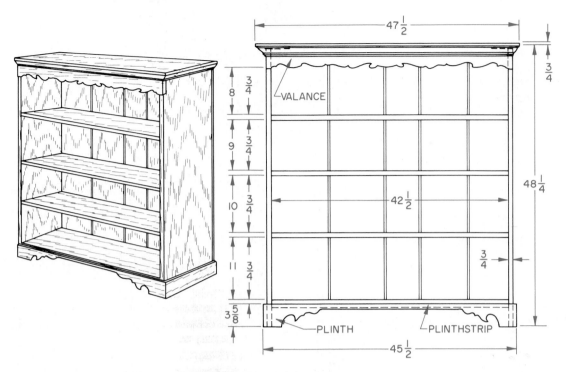

33-5. This bookcase is a good example of casework.

INTERIOR CONSTRUCTION

Interior construction of simple casework usually includes either fixed or adjustable shelves. Fixed shelves are installed with dado joints, wood cleats, or shelf brackets. Figs. 33-6 and 33-7. There are many methods of providing for adjustable shelves. Fig. 33-8. One way is to buy adjustable metal *shelf standards* with snap-on clips. These can be purchased in any length. You will need two for each side. The best way to install standards is to cut a groove along the inside of the side into which the standards fit. Figs. 33-9 and 33-10. Then cut the shelves to the correct lengths. If you mount the standards without a groove, the ends of each shelf must be notched to fit around these standards. Another common method is to drill a series of holes in the sides of the case for metal or plastic shelf pins or dowels to hold the shelves in place. Various metal and wood commercial standards and brackets are available for all kinds of shelving.

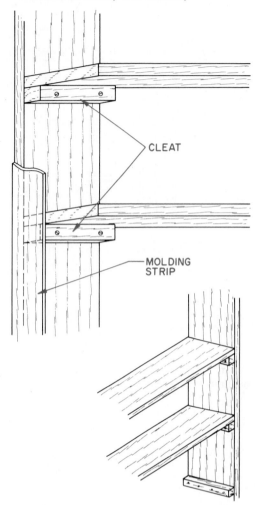

33-6. Wood cleats can be used to hold fixed shelves in place.

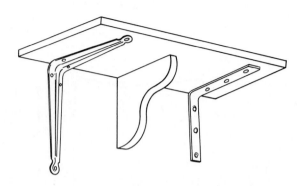

33-7. Three ways of supporting fixed shelves.

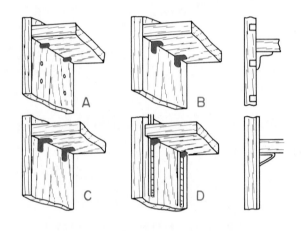

33-8. Ways of installing shelves: A. Dowel pins; B. Metal shelf pins; C. Fixed shelf brackets; D. Adjustable shelf brackets.

33-9. The standard, bracket, and shelf used in the assembly of a free-standing adjustable shelf.

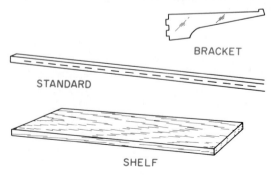

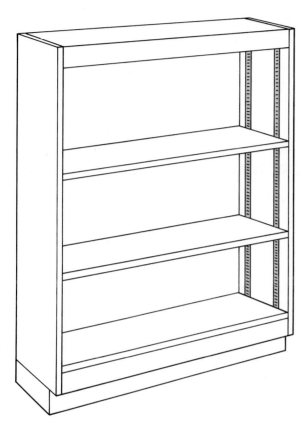

33-10. A bookcase with adjustable shelves. The metal brackets are recessed into grooves so that the ends of the shelves can be cut square.

Review Questions

1. Why is casework like a box?
2. What are the three common joints used in assembling simple casework?
3. Describe three ways of installing fixed shelves in a case.
4. Name four methods of installing adjustable shelves in a case.

Chapter 34

Building Furniture

After studying this chapter, you will be able to:
- List the main steps in constructing a drawer.
- Distinguish a lip drawer from a flush drawer.
- List the three common types of drawer guides.

LOOK FOR THESE TERMS

drawer guide	rail
flush drawer or door	sliding door
lip drawer or door	stile

Small furniture you can build includes a table, stool, or cabinet. Fig. 34-1. In advanced woodwork, larger furniture for a living room, dining room, or bedroom can be constructed.

34-1. A small footstool is a project you might want to build.

TABLE AND STOOL CONSTRUCTION

Most tables or stools are made with four legs joined by rails. Fig. 34-2. The legs and rails are usually fastened together with either dowel construction or mortise-and-tenon joints. Fig. 34-3. To strengthen the joining parts, a wood or metal corner block is inserted. Figs. 34-4 and 34-5. The corner blocks help to hold the table square. They also add support at its weakest points. Table legs can be made of wood in various designs. Matching wood, metal, or plastic legs can be purchased. Usually, these are sold in pairs. Fig. 34-6. The tabletop is usually made of plywood or particle board. It is often covered with either wood veneer or plastic laminate. The edge of the tabletop may be trimmed with solid wood or with plastic laminate or veneer. See Fig. 34-2. Figure 34-7 shows three common methods of attaching a tabletop to the rails.

34-2. This simple table has four legs and rails joined with dowels. The corners are strengthened with corner blocks. The top is a piece of plywood covered with plastic laminate.

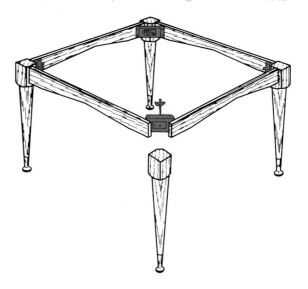

34-5. Metal corner blocks can be purchased to strengthen the corners.

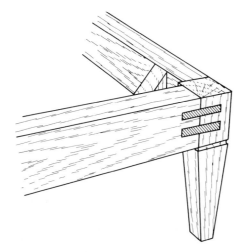

34-3. Double dowel joints are installed between the rail and the leg.

34-4. All corner blocks should be glued and screwed.

34-6. Typical leg shapes used in constructing a stool or table.

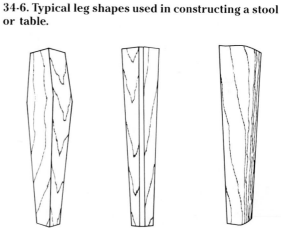

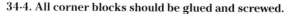
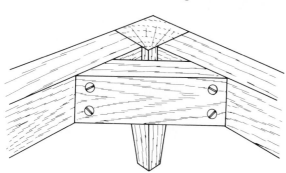

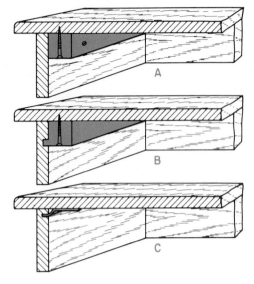

**34-7. Several ways of attaching a tabletop to the rails:
A. Square cleat; B. Square cleat with rabbet and
groove; C. Metal tabletop fastener.**

CABINETS, CHESTS, AND DESKS

Most cabinets, chests, and desks include
drawers and doors. There are three steps in
installing a drawer in a table: cutting the rail
to receive the drawer, making the drawer,
and making the drawer guide. In desk and
chest construction, only the last two steps
are needed.

DRAWER CONSTRUCTION

CUTTING THE RAIL FOR A DRAWER

Before cutting the rail to receive the drawer,
first decide on the exact size of the drawer.
Then cut an opening that is $\frac{1}{16}$ inch wider
and $\frac{1}{8}$ inch longer than the drawer front.

34-8. Two basic types of drawer fronts: A. Flush drawer; B. Lip drawer.

A

B

MAKING THE DRAWER

The drawer may be made to fit flush with the opening, or it may be a *lip drawer* (fit over the frame). Fig. 34-8. To make a lip drawer, a ⅜-inch rabbet is cut around the inside edge of the drawer front. Then the lip drawer overlaps the frame.

The front is usually made of ¾-inch material. The grain and color usually match the material used in the project. The sides and back are made of ½-inch stock such as pine, birch, or maple. The bottom is usually made of ¼-inch fir plywood or hardboard. Fig. 34-9.

A common way of joining the front to the sides is with a rabbet joint. The rabbet is cut to a width of two-thirds the thickness of the sides. This will allow some clearance for the drawer. Other kinds of drawer joints can also be used.

The back is joined to the sides with a butt or dado joint. The back should be cut so that the drawer is slightly narrower at the back than at the front.

Cut a groove ¼ inch by ¼ inch about ½ inch above the bottom on the inside front and sides. Sometimes a groove is also cut across the back.

Cut the drawer bottom about ¹⁄₁₆ inch smaller than the width between the grooves. This will allow for shrinkage and swelling.

Assemble the drawer. Glue and nail the sides to the front. Never put glue into the grooves for the bottom. Slip the bottom in place. Then glue or nail the sides to the back.

MAKING THE DRAWER GUIDE

The three most common *drawer guides* are the slide-block guide and runner (simple drawer guide), the side guide, and the center guide. Drawer guides support the drawer. They keep it from slipping from one side to the other and allow it to open and close more easily.

To make a slide-block guide and runner for a table drawer, cut a rabbet in a piece of wood. This piece will fit between the rails at the lower corner of the drawer. Fig. 34-10.

Figure 34-11 shows plans for a footstool. The drawer has a side guide. Here, there is a groove in the side of the drawer. The runner is attached to the project itself. Another method is to attach a runner to the side of the drawer and then cut a groove in each side of the project. Fig. 34-12.

34-9. Drawer construction. A. Simple ways of fastening the sides to the front and back in drawer construction. B. Parts of a drawer.

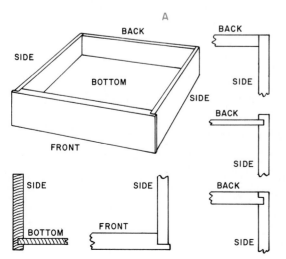

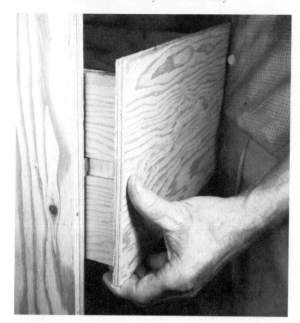

34-10. A simple drawer guide. This type can be easily made and will work well when fitting a drawer between rails.

34-11. This beautifully crafted footstool has a small drawer installed in the rail.

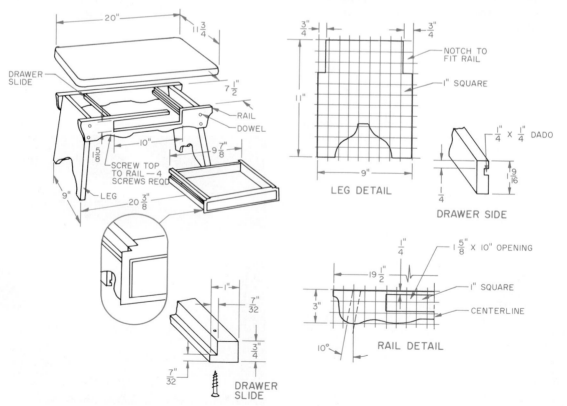

DRAWER SLIDE

20"

11 3/4"

7 1/2"

DRAWER SLIDE

RAIL

DOWEL

10"

5/8"

SCREW TOP TO RAIL—4 SCREWS REQD

9"   LEG   20 3/8"

9 7/8"

3/4"

3/4"

11"

NOTCH TO FIT RAIL

1" SQUARE

9"

LEG DETAIL

1/4" X 1/4" DADO

1/4"

9/16"

DRAWER SIDE

1"

7/32"

3/4"

7/32"

DRAWER SLIDE

1/4"

1 5/8" X 10" OPENING

19 1/2"

3"

1" SQUARE

CENTERLINE

10°

RAIL DETAIL

34-12. Side guide and runner with the dado cut in the case and a strip attached to the drawer.

34-13. A center guide is fastened to the bottom of the drawer. Notice the small glue blocks placed along the two adjoining surfaces.

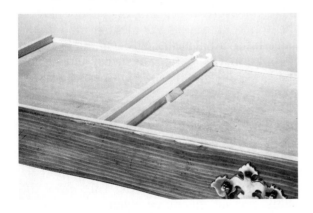

On better-quality furniture a center rail is attached to the project. Then a guide is attached to the bottom of the drawer. A groove is cut in the guide that is fastened to the bottom of the drawer. Fig. 34-13. If a drawer sticks, rub a little paraffin at the tight points.

DOORS

Common hinge doors are made of either plywood or particle board. This is often covered with plastic laminate or veneers. Better-quality doors are of panel construction. They have the advantage over solid construction. They warp less. Only the frame can change in size, while the panel inside is free to expand or contract.

MAKING A PANELED DOOR

Lay out and cut the stock for the frame. Allow extra length to provide for making the joint. Square up the stock. Select the panel to be used to fill the frame. Check this thickness. Then cut a groove along the joint edges of each piece into which the panel will fit. This groove should be as deep as it is wide. The simplest way of cutting it is to use the circular saw, although it can be done with a hand combination plane.

The mortise should be far enough away from the ends of the stiles to keep it from breaking out under pressure. The mortise should be made the same width as the width of the groove. The length should be about two-thirds the width of the rail. The tenon should be cut as thick as the width of the groove. The length of the tenon should equal the depth of the mortise plus the depth of the groove. Fig. 34-14.

Fit the panel temporarily into the frame to check it. Take the frame apart. Cover the edge of the panel with soap or wax. This will help keep glue from getting into the groove or edge of the panel. Apply glue, and clamp the frame together.

The two most common methods of mounting a swinging door are the flush door and the lip door. The *flush door* fits inside the frame of the cabinet or case. The *lip door* has a rabbet that has been cut around the inside edge of the door on three or four sides so that the door covers part of the frame of the cabinet.

Sliding doors are used in areas in which it is difficult to have doors that swing open and shut. Sliding doors are usually made of plywood, hardboard, or glass. Fig. 34-15.

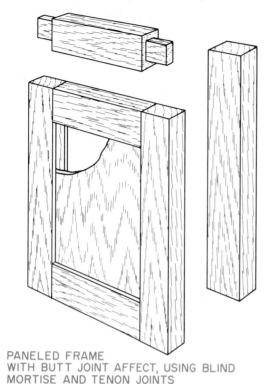

34-14. A mortise-and-tenon joint is often made for a panel door. The side pieces are called *stiles*. The top and bottom pieces are called *rails*.

PANELED FRAME
WITH BUTT JOINT AFFECT, USING BLIND
MORTISE AND TENON JOINTS

FITTING A FLUSH DOOR

Check the opening for the door. Plane the edge that will fit against the frame. Have the hinges straight and true. After the edge has been planed true, hold the door against the opening as close as possible to get a rough check on how well it fits. Make sure that each *stile*, or side piece, will be about the same width when the door is fitted.

Use a framing square to check the frame. If the frame is square, then square off a line on the upper rail. Cut and plane this end square with the edge that has been fitted. Continue to check and plane until the door fits properly. The frame sometimes is a little "out of square."

Measure the height of the opening. Lay out and cut the bottom *rail*. If the frame is square, plane this end square with the first edge. Measure the width of the opening at the top and bottom. Sometimes the frame opening will not be exactly parallel from top to bottom. Lay out these measurements on the top and bottom rail. Join these lines, using a straightedge.

Cut and plane the edge until the door fits properly. The door must not be too snug. After the hinges are installed, it must still have some "play" to swing open. Fig. 34-16. This edge should be planed at a slight bevel toward the back of the door. This gives the stiles proper clearance when the door is opened and closed.

34-15. One method of installing sliding doors.

34-16. Make sure the door swings freely. Note that two butt hinges are used on each door.

Review Questions

1. How can the corners of a table be strengthened?
2. What are three ways of fastening a tabletop to the rails?
3. Describe the three common types of drawer guide.
4. List the three basic steps in installing a drawer in a table.
5. What things should you think about when choosing the wood for the front of a drawer?
6. Why are some doors and frames made of panel construction?
7. What kind of joint is found most frequently in panel construction?

Chapter 35

Assembling With Nails

After studying this chapter, you will be able to:
● Identify the main types of common nails.
● Demonstrate the correct technique for driving nails straight into the wood.
● Describe the technique of toenailing.

LOOK FOR THESE TERMS

box nail	corrugated fastener	spike
brad	escutcheon nail	tack
casing nail	finishing nail	toenailing
claw hammer	nail set	upholstery nail
clinch	penny number	wire nail
common nail	ripping bar	

Nails are easier to use and less expensive than any other way of joining wood.

TOOLS FOR NAILING

The *claw hammer* has a head of drop-forged steel and a handle of hickory, steel, or fiberglass. Fig. 35-1. The metal handle is covered with hand grips of plastic, leather, or rubber. The face of the hammer should be slightly domed to prevent hammer marks. Fig. 35-2. Hammers come in weights ranging from 5 to 20 ounces. The 16-ounce hammer is best for everyday use.

A *nail set* is a short metal punch with a cup-shaped head used to drive the head of the nail below the surface of the wood. Fig. 35-3.

A *ripping bar* has a gooseneck with a nail slot on one end and a chisel-shape on the other. It is used for ripping down buildings, opening crates, and similar jobs. Fig. 35-4.

35-2. The head of the hammer is domed slightly. This helps keep the nail from bending if you don't strike it exactly square. It also concentrates force at the contact point.

35-1. The parts of a claw hammer.

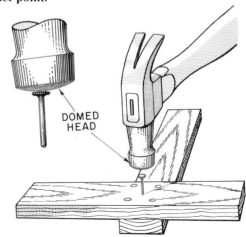

35-3. The nail set is used to drive the nail head below the surface of the wood. This hole is then filled with putty or similar material before the project is finished.

35-4. Ripping bar.

KINDS OF NAILS

There are nails to meet every specific need. Fig. 35-5. Nails are distinguished by their heads, shanks, points, surface finish, and the material from which they are made. The common materials are steel, aluminum, stainless steel, copper, brass, and monel metal. The surface finishes include bright, galvanized, cement-coated, and blued. Fig. 35-6. Nails are ordered by the *penny number*, or "d". Once based on the price per nail, this number now relates to length. Nail sizes start at 2d, which is 1 inch long, and range up to 60d, which is 6 inches long. Table 35-A. The 2d through 10d nails are in ¼-inch increments. A 4d common nail has a larger diameter than a 4d finishing nail.

35-5. Several of the many different kinds of nails available. Three of the most commonly used are numbers 2, 6, and 12. 1. Wood Siding, Box (Plain & Anchor); 2. Finishing; 3. Insulating, Plastic Siding; 4. Asphalt Shingle (Anchor, Plain & Screw); 5. Cedar Shake (Plain & Anchor); 6. Casing; 7. Cribber; 8. "Split-Less" Wood Siding (Plain & Anchor); 9. Asbestos; 10. Cedar Shingle; 11. Hardboard Siding; (Plain & Screw); 12. Common (Anchor & Plain); 13. Aluminum, Steel & Vinyl Siding (Screw & Plain); 14. Insulation Roof Deck (Plain & Anchor); 15. Gutter Spike (Plain & Anchor).

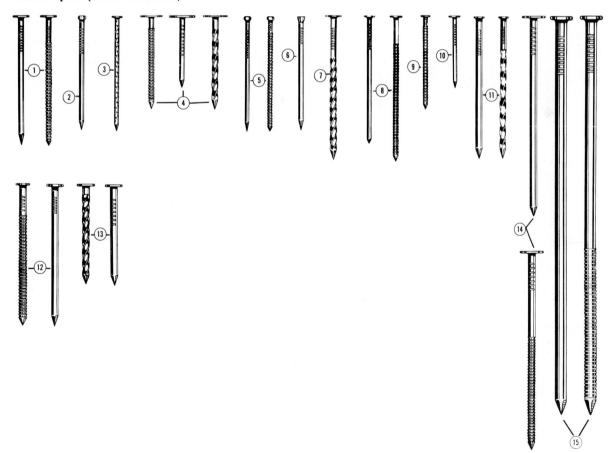

Common nails with large flat heads are used in building construction. The larger sizes are called *spikes*. *Box nails* are similar to common nails. They are used mostly for construction of packing cases. The *casing nail* has a small head. It is a rather heavy nail for more finished carpentry. The *finishing nail*, the finest of all nails, is used for all fine cabinet and construction work.

Other kinds of small metal fasteners include *wire brads, wire nails, tacks, staples*, and *upholstery nails*. Fig. 35-7. *Escutcheon nails* are small brass nails with round heads used to decorate small projects. Fig. 35-8. *Corrugated fasteners* are used in rough construction. Fig. 35-9.

SELECTING NAILS

Choose nails with small diameters for thin stock and large diameters for heavy stock.

35-6. Nails are made with different types of heads, shanks, and points.

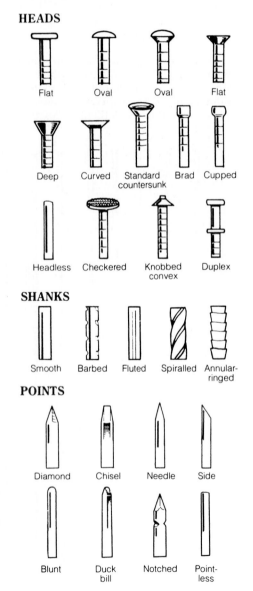

HEADS

Flat Oval Oval Flat

Deep Curved Standard countersunk Brad Cupped

Headless Checkered Knobbed convex Duplex

SHANKS

Smooth Barbed Fluted Spiralled Annular-ringed

POINTS

Diamond Chisel Needle Side

Blunt Duck bill Notched Point-less

Table 35-A. Nail Sizes

Penny Number	Length in Inches	Number Per Pound		
		Common Nails	Box Nails	Finishing Nails
2	1	876	1010	1351
3	1¼	568	635	807
4	1½	316	437	548
6	2	181	236	309
8	2½	106	145	189
10	3	69	94	121
12	3¼	64	87	113
16	3½	49	71	90
20	4	31	52	62
30	4¾	20		
40	5			
50	5½			
60	6			

35-7. Small metal fasteners. A. wire brad; B. wire nail; C. tack; D. staple; and E. upholstery nail.

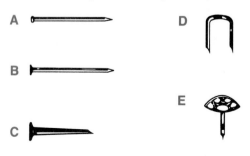

A

B

C

D

E

DRIVING NAILS

Nails can be driven straight into the wood. For a tighter joint, they may be driven at a slight angle. If two pieces are to be nailed together, as on the corner of a box, first drive one or two nails through the first piece. Then hold this piece over the other piece to drive the nails in place.

Hold the nail in one hand between thumb and forefinger and close to the point. To start the nail, grasp the hammer near the head. Fig. 35-10. Tap the head with the hammer to get it started. Fig. 35-11. Remove your fingers from the nail as you continue to strike it with firm, even blows. To hammer, hold the handle near its end. Use wrist as well as elbow and arm movement, depending on the size of the nail being driven.

35-8. This chest is decorated with brass. Escutcheon nails are used to hold the metal in place.

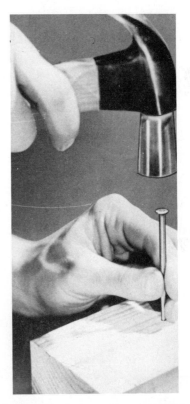

35-10. Starting a nail. Hold the nail between the thumb and forefinger. Grasp the hammer close to the head.

35-9. Corrugated fasteners, or "wiggle" nails, are used in place of standard nails for certain purposes. These include repair work and box-and-frame construction. They are also used to hold miter and butt joints together.

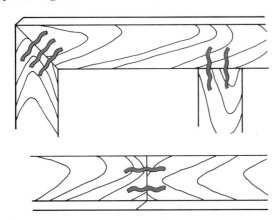

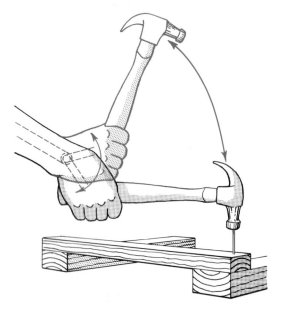

35-11. Use wrist movement for driving small nails. For driving large nails, use elbow movement, as well.

35-12. Using a nail set. Hold the nail set between the thumb and forefinger. Guide it with the other fingers. This helps keep it from slipping off the nail head and marring the wood surface.

Watch the head of the nail, not the hammer. Drive the nail with a few well-placed blows, rather than with many quick taps. If a nail begins to bend, remove it. Start over with a new nail.

Choose the location for the nails wisely. Do not put several nails along the same grain. This will split the wood. A few well-placed nails in a staggered pattern will hold more strongly than a larger number placed carelessly.

When using casing or finishing nails, do not drive the heads completely down to the surface. Complete the driving with a nail set. Hold the nail set in your left hand with the middle finger against the surface of the work and the side of the nail. Then drive the nail in until it is about 1/16 inch below the surface. Fig. 35-12. Cover the small hole with a wood filler.

When nailing hardwood, drill holes that are slightly smaller than the diameter of the nail. Apply a little wax to the nail and drive it in.

When nails are longer than the total thickness of both pieces, drive them completely through the pieces. Then bend, or *clinch*, them. Bend the nails over *with the grain* so they can be flattened easily. Fig. 35-13.

To nail the end of one piece of wood to the side of another, drive the nails into the wood at an angle from both sides. This is called *toenailing*. Fig. 35-14.

REMOVING NAILS

To remove nails, force the claw of the hammer under the head of the nail and pull on the handle. When the nail is drawn partway out, slip a piece of scrap wood under the hammer head (to protect the surface) before continuing to draw out the nail. Fig. 35-15.

35-13. Clinching a nail. It is better to clinch a nail with the grain than across. The nail will sink into the wood more easily since it does not have to break the fibers.

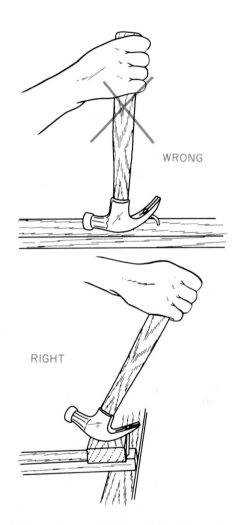

WRONG

RIGHT

35-14. Toenailing. When it is necessary to nail the end of one piece to the side of another piece, the pieces should be toenailed together by driving the nails in at an angle on each side.

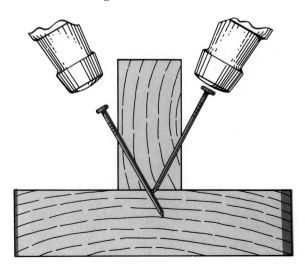

35-15. Removing a nail. After the nail is partway out, do not continue to pull it out. It will bend the nail and ruin the surface of the wood. Place a scrap of wood under the hammer head. This will provide leverage for drawing the nail out straight. It will also protect the surface of the wood.

Review Questions

1. Name the parts of a claw hammer.
2. Explain how to use a nail set.
3. Name and describe the four most common nails.
4. What are the larger sizes of common nails called?
5. How is a brad different from a finishing nail?
6. How is a nail started?
7. In hammering a nail, should you watch the head of the hammer or the nail?
8. How are finishing and casing nails set?
9. Hardwood is very difficult to nail. What would you do to overcome this difficulty?
10. Tell how to clinch a nail.
11. Explain the technique of toenailing.

Math Quiz

By referring to Table A, answer the following questions.

1. What is the weight (in pounds) of 212 8d nails?
2. How much larger in diameter is a 16 common nail than a box nail of the same size?
3. How much longer is a 20d nail than a 7d nail?
4. What is the weight (in ounces) of one 40d box nail?

Answers
1. 2 pounds
2. .031
3. 1¾"
4. .457

Chapter 36

Assembling with Screws

After studying this chapter, you will be able to:
- List the guidelines to be followed when working with screws.
- Describe how to drill a clearance hole.
- Describe how to countersink for flathead screws.
- Demonstrate the driving of a wood screw.

LOOK FOR THESE TERMS

American Screw Wire Gauge	Phillips-head screwdriver
counterbore	plain screwdriver
countersink	screwdriver bit
countersinking	screw-mate drill
offset screwdriver	wood screw

A *wood screw* is a fastener with a groove twisting around part of its length. The screw cuts its own threads. It is a strong fastener that can be removed to take the product apart. Fig. 36-1.

SCREWDRIVERS

The *plain*, or *regular*, *screwdriver* is used to install *slotted-head screws*. The size depends on the length and diameter of the blades. Fig. 36-2. Make sure that the tip of the screwdriver is the same width as the diameter of the screw head. If it is wider, it may mar the surface of the wood as it is set in place. Fig. 36-3. The *Phillips-head screwdriver* is made for driving screws with recessed heads. Fig. 36-4. The spiral ratchet screwdriver is usually sold in a set with several plain bits and a Phillips bit. Fig. 36-5.

36-1. Screws were used in assembling this bookcase. The holes for the screws were recessed and fancy wood plugs used to cover the heads.

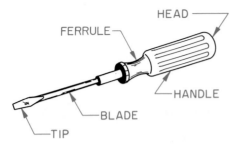

36-2. Parts of a plain screwdriver.

Offset screwdrivers are used to install or remove screws located in tight places where a standard screwdriver cannot be used. They are available for slotted or Phillips-head screws. Fig. 36-6.

Figures 36-6, 36-7, and 36-8 show properly ground screwdriver tips. If ground to a sharp edge, the tip tends to slip out of the slot. This would mar the surface of the wood or damage the head of the screw.

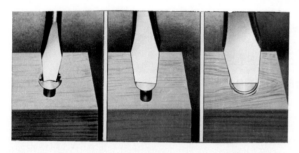

36-3. Selecting the proper size of screwdriver. Note the following: A. The screwdriver is too narrow with the result that it causes a burr on the head; B. The screwdriver is the correct width; C. The screwdriver is too wide. It would mar the wood surface.

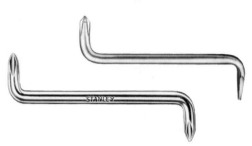

36-6. Offset screwdrivers.

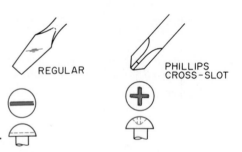

36-4. Choosing a screwdriver of the correct size.

SIZE OF DRIVERS TO USE FOR DIFFERENT SIZE SCREWS																			
SCREW NUMBER	0	1	2	3	4	5	6	7	8	9	10	12	14	16	18	20	24	7/16"	1/2"	9/16"
REGULAR BLADE	3/32"			1/8"		1/8"-5/32"	3/32"-3/16"		3/16"		1/4"	1/4"-5/16"	5/16"	5/16"-3/8"	3/8"	3/8"-7/16"	7/16"	1/2"	1/2"-9/16"	9/16"
CROSS-SLOT BLADE		NO. 1					NO. 2					NO. 3				NO. 4				

36-5. The spiral ratchet screwdriver is excellent for quick installation of screws.

SPIRAL RATCHET SCREWDRIVER.
Drives screws when handle is depressed.

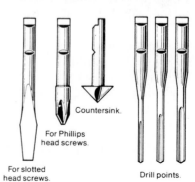

Countersink.

For Phillips head screws.

For slotted head screws.

Drill points.

TIPS FOR RATCHET SCREWDRIVERS.

Here are some hints for using screwdrivers:

● Select a screwdriver with a length and tip fitted to the work. The tip should fit the slot snugly. It should not be wider than the screw head.

● Use the longest screwdriver convenient for the work. More power can be applied to a long screwdriver than to a short one. Also, there is less danger of it slipping from the screw slot.

● Hold the handle firmly in the palm of the right hand with thumb and forefinger grasping the handle near the ferrule. Use one hand to steady the tip and keep it pressed into the slot. Keep your other hand on the handle. Fig. 36-9.

In working with screws, follow these guidelines:

● When screws must be driven into "hard-to-get-at" places, use a screwdriver with steel jaws that hold the screw firmly in place for easy starting. Fig. 36-10.

● When driving brass screws into hardwood, use the same size steel screw to complete pilot holes. This reduces damage and the risk of shearing the head off brass screws.

● If the screw tends to bind, back off and enlarge the pilot hole or rub paraffin or wax on the screw.

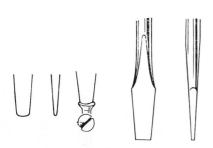

36-7. If the tip is rounded or beveled, the driver will raise out of the slot, spoiling the screw head. Regrind or file the screwdriver tip to make it as shown above on right.

36-8. If the tip is too wide, it will scar the wood around the screw head. If the screwdriver is not held in line with the screw, it will slip out of the slot and mar both the screw and the work. The driver and screw should fit as shown on right.

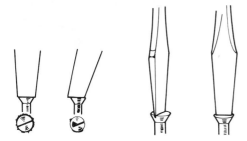

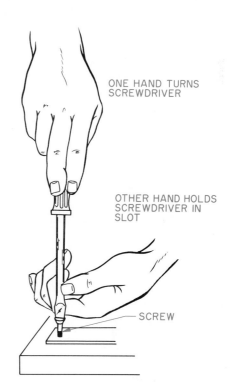

ONE HAND TURNS
SCREWDRIVER

OTHER HAND HOLDS
SCREWDRIVER IN
SLOT

SCREW

36-9. Hold the screwdriver properly to start the screw.

36-10. Steel jaws hold the screw firmly for easy starting. After the screw is started, pull back the screwdriver and the jaws will automatically withdraw from the screw. This screwdriver is ideal for driving and seating screws in hard-to-get-at places.

• Heating the top of a screw head with a soldering iron will make it easier to remove after it cools.

• Use wood screws instead of nails: (a) to avoid splitting; (b) for greater holding power; (c) if you want to take the product apart later; (d) for better appearance.

• Never try to install screws partway with a hammer.

• Screw length should be as close as possible to ⅛ inch less than the combined thickness of the parts.

WOOD SCREWS

Wood screws vary in length, driver type, head style, material, finish, and gauge size. Fig. 36-11. Most screws are made of mild steel. Screws made of brass, aluminum, stainless steel, and silicon bronze are used primarily for boat construction or wherever moisture would rust other screws. Most flat-head screws have a bright finish. Roundhead screws are usually finished in a dull blue. Sheet-metal screws are ideal for fastening thin metal to wood products. They are used, for example, to attach metal legs to a plywood top. The sheet-metal screw has excellent holding power. Unlike wood screws, the threaded shank is the same diameter through its length. Fig. 36-12.

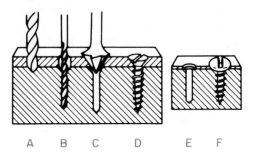

A   B   C   D   E   F

36-12. Installing a flathead sheet-metal screw: A. Drilling the clearance hole; B. Drilling the pilot or anchor hole; C. Countersinking; D. Screw installed; E. Hole for roundhead sheetmetal screw; F. Screw installed.

36-11. Screws vary in length, driver types, head styles, materials, finishes, and sizes.

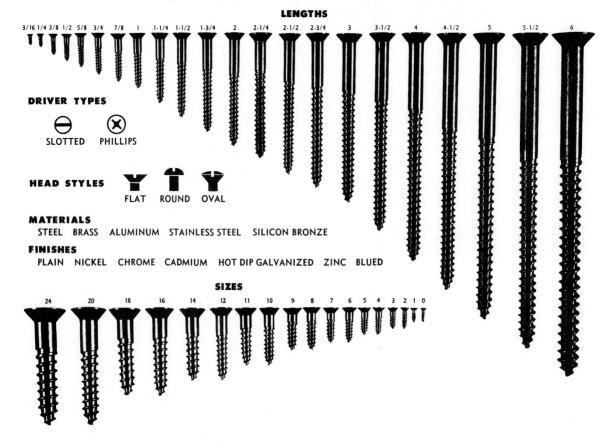

LENGTHS

3/16 1/4 3/8 1/2 5/8 3/4 7/8 1 1-1/4 1-1/2 1-3/4 2 2-1/4 2-1/2 2-3/4 3 3-1/2 4 4-1/2 5 5-1/2 6

DRIVER TYPES

SLOTTED   PHILLIPS

HEAD STYLES

FLAT   ROUND   OVAL

MATERIALS

STEEL   BRASS   ALUMINUM   STAINLESS STEEL   SILICON BRONZE

FINISHES

PLAIN   NICKEL   CHROME   CADMIUM   HOT DIP GALVANIZED   ZINC   BLUED

SIZES

24   20   18   16   14   12   11   10   9   8   7   6   5   4   3   2   1   0

Wood screws are indicated by the *American Screw Wire Gauge* with numbers from 0 to 24. The smallest number is 0, which has a diameter of .060. The diameter of each succeeding number is .013 larger. For example, a number 5 screw is .125, or ⅛ inch in diameter. The shank clearance hole is always about this diameter. Table 36-A. Two screws can be the same length but have a different gauge size. Fig. 36-13. The size of the screw is usually shown on the drawing. For example, No. 8 R.H. 1½ means that the screw is No. 8 gauge size, roundhead, and 1½ inches long. If the size isn't shown, choose a screw that will go at least *two-thirds* of its length

into the *second* piece. If the second piece is end grain, the screw should be even longer, since end grain does not hold well. Specialty screw devices are shown in Fig. 36-14.

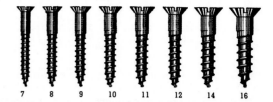

36-13. Different gauge sizes of 1 1/4-inch screws. Wood screws range in length from 1/4 to 6 inches and in gauge sizes from 0 to 24. Of course, each length is not made in all gauges, as shown by the 1 1/4-inch screw.

Table 36-A. Common Wood Screw Sizes

The bottom part of the table shows the correct size of drills and/or auger bits needed to install the screws.

Length	Number of Screw Size																	
¼ inch	0	1	2	3														
⅜ inch			2	3	4	5	6	7										
½ inch			2	3	4	5	6	7	8									
⅝ inch				3	4	5	6	7	8	9	10							
¾ inch					4	5	6	7	8	9	10	11						
⅞ inch						6	7	8	9	10	11	12						
1 inch						6	7	8	9	10	11	12	14					
1¼ inch							7	8	9	10	11	12	14	16				
1½ inch						6	7	8	9	10	11	12	14	16	18			
1¾ inch								8	9	10	11	12	14	16	18	20		
2 inch								8	9	10	11	12	14	16	18	20		
2¼ inch									9	10	11	12	14	16	18	20		
2½ inch												12	14	16	18	20		
2¾ inch													14	16	18	20		
3 inch														16	18	20		
3½ inch															18	20	24	
4 inch															18	20	24	
Diameter In Inches At Body	.060	.073	.086	.099	.112	.125	.138	.151	.164	.177	.190	.203	.216	.242	.268	.294	.320	.372
Shank Hole Hard & Soft Wood	¹⁄₁₆	⁵⁄₆₄	³⁄₃₂	⁷⁄₆₄	⁷⁄₆₄	⅛	⁹⁄₆₄	⁵⁄₃₂	¹¹⁄₆₄	³⁄₁₆	³⁄₁₆	¹³⁄₆₄	⁷⁄₃₂	¼	¹⁷⁄₆₄	¹⁹⁄₆₄	²¹⁄₆₄	⅜
Pilot Hole Soft Wood	¹⁄₆₄	¹⁄₃₂	¹⁄₃₂	³⁄₆₄	³⁄₆₄	¹⁄₁₆	¹⁄₁₆	¹⁄₁₆	⁵⁄₆₄	⁵⁄₆₄	³⁄₃₂	³⁄₃₂	⁷⁄₆₄	⁷⁄₆₄	⁹⁄₆₄	⁹⁄₆₄	¹¹⁄₆₄	³⁄₁₆
Pilot Hole Hard Wood	¹⁄₃₂	¹⁄₃₂	³⁄₆₄	¹⁄₁₆	¹⁄₁₆	⁵⁄₆₄	⁵⁄₆₄	³⁄₃₂	³⁄₃₂	⁷⁄₆₄	⁷⁄₆₄	⅛	⅛	⁹⁄₆₄	⁵⁄₃₂	³⁄₁₆	¹³⁄₆₄	⁷⁄₃₂

| CUP HOOK | SCREW HOOK | "L" SCREW HOOK | SCREW EYE |

36-14. *Cup hooks* (usually of brass) come in sizes from 1/2 to 1 1/2 inches. *Screw hooks* are made in lengths from 1 1/4 to 2 1/2 inches. *"L" (squarebent) screw hooks* come in lengths from 1 to 2 1/4 inches. *Screw eyes* are made with either small or medium eyes in many sizes.

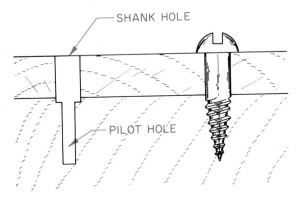

SHANK HOLE

PILOT HOLE

36-15. Here the shank hole and pilot hole are properly drilled and the screw is installed.

36-16. Two types of 82-degree countersinks: A. For use in a brace; B. For use in a drill press.

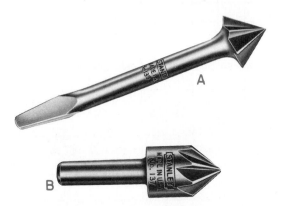

A

B

DRILLING CLEARANCE HOLES

Select the kind and size of screw needed. Note in Fig. 36-12 the two drill sizes required. The first one is for the shank clearance hole, drilled in the first piece. The second one is for the pilot hole, drilled in the second piece. Fig. 36-15. The shank clearance hole should be the same size or slightly smaller than the shank of the screw. In this way the screw can be inserted in the first piece without forcing.

Drill the shank clearance hole in the first piece of stock. Then hold this piece over the second. Mark the location for the pilot hole with a scratch awl. When assembling softwood pieces, drill the pilot hole only about half the depth to which the screw will go. When drilling hardwood, make sure that it is drilled to the total depth of the screw.

COUNTERSINKING FOR FLATHEAD SCREWS

Countersinking is a way of enlarging the top portion of a hole to a cone shape so that the head of a flathead screw will be flush with the surface of the wood. If flathead screws are installed, countersink the upper surface of the first piece. This will allow the head of the screw to be flush with the surface. Fig. 36-16. Check the depth of the countersunk hole by turning the screw upside down and fitting it in the hole. Fig. 36-17. A *screw-mate drill* and *countersink* can be used with flathead screws. Fig. 36-18. A *counterbore* will do all the operations performed by the screw-mate drill and countersink plus drill plug holes for wooden plugs. Fig. 36-19.

PLUGGING SCREW HOLES

In most furniture construction, screws are not supposed to show. Choose a drill or auger bit the same size as the head of the screw. Counterbore a hole in the first surface about ⅜ inch deep. The screw will then be below the surface of the wood. After the parts are assembled, this hole can be filled with plastic wood or surface putty. Or you can make a little screw plug with the tool shown in Fig. 36-20. Furniture supply companies can supply fancy, decorated plugs. Fig. 36-21.

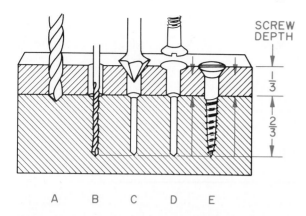

36-17. Steps in installing a flathead screw: A. Drill the shank hole; B. Drill the pilot or anchor hole; C. Countersink; D. Check the amount of countersink with the screw head; E. Install the flathead screw.

36-20. If you do much furniture work where screws are countersunk or counterbored, it will pay to use a plug cutter. These tools permit cutting perfect plugs from the same stock of which the item is built. The plug cutters are made in sizes, 6, 8, 10, and 12 to match the commonly used screw sizes. The plugs are a snug fit in the counterbored holes.

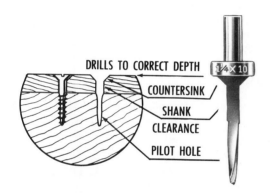

36-18. The screw-mate drill and countersink will do four things: (1) Drill to the correct depth; (2) Do the countersinking; (3) Make the correct shank clearance; and (4) Drill the correct pilot hole.

36-19. A screw-mate counterbore does five things at once, as shown in the illustration. A wood plug can be used to cover the screw head.

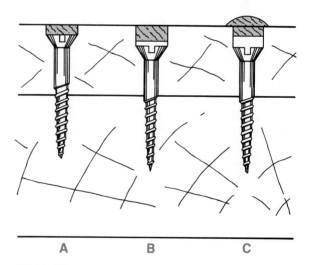

36-21. Three methods of covering the heads of screws: A. With plastic wood; B. With a plain wood plug; and C. With a fancy wood plug.

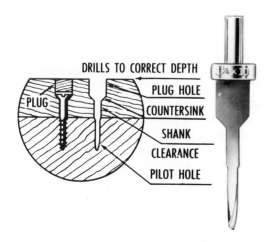

DRIVING THE SCREW

To install a screw, hold the blade between your thumb and forefinger. Refer again to Fig. 36-9. Grasp the handle of the screwdriver in the palm of your hand. Let your thumb and forefinger point toward the shank. Start the screw and then move your left hand up just back of the point of the screwdriver. This will guide the tool and keep it from slipping off the head as the screw is set in place. Continue to turn the screw until it is firmly set, but don't strip the threads or shear off the screw from the wood. Be especially careful if the screws are small or made of brass. A *screwdriver bit* used in a brace will provide more leverage in setting screws. Fig. 36-22.

36-22. A screwdriver bit to use in a brace.

SPECIAL FASTENERS

Standard wood screws do not work well in composition panels, such as particle board, waferboard, and oriented-strand board. They tend to chew up the particles rather than groove them for holding power. Special wood screws that have widely spaced threads are available for these materials. When driven into the material, the thread allows more of the particles to remain between the turns. Fig. 36-23. These screws may have either a square drive, Phillips-head drive, or a combination of both. Another good screw for this purpose is the drywall screw that is threaded throughout its length.

Several other kinds of special fasteners are used in assembling wood projects. The chevron wood fastener has permanent spring tension. When it is driven into a joint it holds the joint together without warping and twisting.

The most common T-nut has a round base with prongs and a threaded hole in the center. A hole is bored into the underside of a table top, for example. The hole is just large enough for the center portion. Then the nut is driven into the wood. A hanger bolt has a wood screw on one end and a metal screw on the other. The wood screw thread is installed

Math Quiz

Refer to Table 36-A. Answer the following questions.

1. What is the diameter in decimal inches of a No. 14 wood screw?
2. What size twist drill is needed for the shank hole for a No. 7 screw?
3. How much larger in diameter is a No. 10 screw than a No. 5 screw?
4. What size of twist drill is needed for the pilot hole for hardwood when using a No. 7 screw?
5. The distance between the threads of the screw in Fig. A is $\frac{3}{32}$". How far does the screw travel if it is turned six times?

Answers
1. .242"
2. $\frac{5}{32}$"
3. .065"
4. $\frac{3}{32}$"
5. $\frac{9}{16}$"

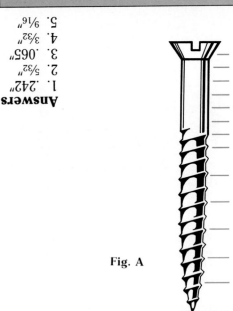

Fig. A

in the end of the table leg and the metal screw thread is fitted into the T-nut. This makes it possible to take such things as tables apart for shipping or storage.

A dowel screw has a wood screw thread on each end. Matching holes are drilled into two pieces to be assembled. The screw is driven an equal distance into both pieces. Fig. 36-24.

36-23. This heat-treated steel wood screw for composite materials has a combination square and Phillips head. The thread surfaces are nearly at right angles to the screw, the body diameter is small, and the point is sharp.

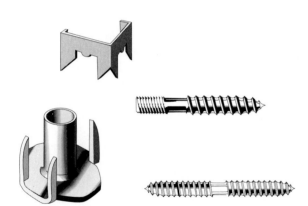

36-24. Fasteners for special uses.

Review Questions

1. Name several advantages the screw has over a nail.
2. How do you know what size screwdriver to choose?
3. Describe the proper way of grinding a screwdriver.
4. What information must you have to secure the proper kind and size of screw for your work?
5. As the gauge number increases, how is the diameter of the screw affected?
6. What is the general rule for selecting screw lengths?
7. Name two types of screws.
8. What is the shank clearance hole and what purpose does it serve?
9. Is the pilot hole drilled in softwood in the same way it is drilled in hardwood?
10. When is it necessary to countersink the hole?
11. How can you check the depth of the countersink hole?
12. What is the purpose of screw plugs?
13. Describe the proper method of holding a screwdriver when starting a screw.
14. Why is it important to set the screw with the correct size of screwdriver?

Facts about Wood

"The Spruce Goose"—The World's Largest Flying Boat

During World War II, metals were in short supply. The federal government needed to develop a large military transport plane that could be built from non-metal materials. They asked Howard Hughes to design such a craft. An industrialist and filmmaker, Hughes was an inventive genius. Assembling a team of engineers, he directed work on the design of the giant aircraft. The work proceeded slowly. In 1945, when World War II ended, the plane was unfinished. Finally, having spent $8,000,000 on the project, the government cancelled the Hughes contract. Convinced of his idea, Hughes continued his work. It took him another three years to finish the plane.

The plane is unusual in many ways. Its structure is of wood. Its outer surface is covered with 3-ply birch plywood. The physical dimensions of the craft are awesome. It has a wingspan of 319 feet—19 feet longer than a football field. The plane is designed to carry 130,000 pounds. It can hold 14,000 gallons of fuel.

The amount of wood used in building the plane caused some to nickname it "The Spruce Goose." Because of its enormous size, many thought the airplane would never fly. Hughes, however, was determined to silence the plane's critics. An aviator—and the holder of three aviation speed records—Hughes decided to fly the plane himself. On November 2, 1947, Hughes boarded the plane, along with 26 selected passengers. He started the plane's eight engines and taxied the plane in Long Beach Harbor. Gradually, he increased the speed of the plane until it reached 70 knots. Then, Hughes slowly lifted the craft off the water.

The plane flew one mile before he gently set it down again. Hughes had proved his point: the Spruce Goose could fly. That was the only flight the plane made. It also was the public's only view of the plane. After its flight, the Spruce Goose was taken to a specially constructed hangar. Because the hangar was temperature controlled, the aircraft was maintained in a remarkable state of preservation. After Hughes' death, the plane was placed on display inside the world's largest clear-span aluminum dome.

Some measure of the progress of aviation can be made by comparing the distance of the first airplane flight with the wing span of the Spruce Goose. The first powered sustained flight was made by Orville Wright at Kitty Hawk, North Carolina. Lasting only 12 seconds, it covered a distance smaller than one-half the wingspan of the Spruce Goose.

<table>
<tr><td>Chapter 37</td><td>Scraping a Surface</td></tr>
</table>

Chapter 37

Scraping a Surface

After studying this chapter, you will be able to:
● Demonstrate the use of the hand scraper.
● Demonstrate the use of the cabinet scraper.

LOOK FOR THESE TERMS

cabinet scraper
hand scraper

For a really fine surface on open-grain wood such as oak, mahogany, and walnut, plane the wood first. Then scrape it with a *hand scraper* or *cabinet scraper*. Figs. 37-1 and 37-2. Scraping removes the small imperfections left by the plane. A scraper will take a wide shaving that is so thin you can see through it. It will smooth irregularities prior to sanding. Some woods, such as curly maple and cedar, can't be planed very well. However, they can be scraped very smooth. It is always necessary to sharpen the scraper before each use—and frequently during its use. See Chapter 26.

37-2. A cabinet scraper.

USING A HAND SCRAPER

Clamp the stock firmly in a vise or on top of the bench. Using both hands, hold the hand scraper between the thumbs and forefingers, with the cutting edge toward the surface of the wood. Fig. 37-3. Turn the blade at an angle of about 50 to 60 degrees to the wood surface. Apply firm pressure to the scraper blade. Push or draw it across the surface.

Be careful to keep the cutting edge flat against the wood so that the corners do not dig in or mar it. Always scrape with the grain. Sometimes the scraper is turned a little and a shearing cut made across the surface. When working on curly maple or other burly-type wood, keep changing the direction of the scraping action to match the grain direction.

37-1. A hand scraper.

STANLEY
ALLOY STEEL
SCRAPER No.O
MADE IN U.S.A.

37-3. Scraping a surface with a hand scraper. Note that the scraper is held in both hands and tipped at an angle to the wood surface.

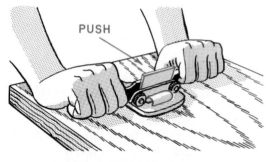

PUSH

SCRAPE WITH GRAIN

37-4. Using a cabinet scraper.

USING A CABINET SCRAPER

The cabinet scraper is simpler to use than the hand scraper. To adjust it, first loosen the adjusting thumbscrew and the clamp thumbscrews. Insert the blade from the bottom, with the bevel side toward the adjusting screw. Make sure the edge of the blade is even with the bottom. This can be done by placing the tool on a wood surface and pressing the blade lightly against the wood. Tighten the clamp thumbscrews. Bow the blade slightly by tightening the adjusting thumbscrew. Apply equal pressure with both hands as you push the scraper along the wood. Fig. 37-4.

Review Questions

1. What kinds of wood must be scraped to produce a smooth surface?
2. At what times should a scraper be sharpened?
3. The hand scraper is held at what angle to the surface of the wood?
4. How can you prevent the corners of the hand scraper from marring or digging into the wood?
5. Tell how the hand scraper should be used on burly woods.
6. Explain how to adjust a cabinet scraper.

| Chapter 38 | Sanding a Surface |

After studying this chapter, you will be able to:
● List the characteristics of four abrasives commonly used on sandpaper.
● Describe the preparation of an abrasive sheet for use.
● Demonstrate the sanding of the flat surface, end, and edge of a piece of stock.

LOOK FOR THESE TERMS

aluminum oxide	sanding
coated abrasives	sanding block
flint	silicon carbide
garnet	

Sanding is the finishing of wood by rubbing it with an abrasive. Sanding is done to finish the wood surface, not to form or shape it. All planing, cutting, and forming should be completed before using sandpaper. Sanding should never be done in place of using cutting tools. Fig. 38-1.

38-1. Sanding is an important step in completing any project.

KINDS OF ABRASIVES

There is really no such thing as "sand" paper, though the name is given to several types of coated abrasives. *Abrasives* are made in a wide range of grades from very coarse to very fine. Abrasive sheets are produced by bonding (gluing) abrasive material to paper or cloth backing.

● *Flint*, or *quartz*, which has a yellowish cast, is an inexpensive natural abrasive. It is commonly used for the hand sanding of woods.

● *Garnet* (made from natural rock) is reddish brown. It is harder, sharper, and better for most woods, especially hard woods. It is long lasting and fast cutting.

● *Aluminum oxide* is a manufactured abrasive, either reddish brown or white. It is used for both hand and machine sanding.

● *Silicon carbide* is shiny black, almost diamond hard, and very sharp. It is used for sanding lacquers, shellac, and varnishes. It is also used for sanding between finishes. It is made in wet or dry types.

Abrasive materials come in chunk form. These must first be crushed into fine particles and sorted. These abrasive grains pass through screens of different sizes. For example, one screen may have 36 openings per inch. The next screen may have 40 openings per inch. The grains that pass through the screen with 36 openings and not through the next are numbered 36. The higher the number, the smaller the grain and, therefore, the finer the sandpaper. Abrasive papers are sold in many forms including sheets, discs, and belts. The common abrasive used in the wood shop is garnet paper. This comes in sheets measuring 9 × 11 inches. Table 38-A.

PREPARING ABRASIVE SHEETS

To soften an abrasive sheet, first draw it over the edge of the bench. A sheet is usually divided into four or six pieces. Their size depends on the work to be sanded and the size of the sanding block. To tear the sheet, fold it lengthwise with the abrasive surface inward. Hold one-half of the sheet over the bench and tear along the folded line. You can also tear the piece by holding a straightedge or the cutting edge of a hacksaw blade over the folded line. Fig. 38-2.

A *sanding block* is a good backing for most sanding. If the sheets are torn into six pieces, the block should be 1½ inches thick, 3 inches wide, and 5 inches long.

A piece of foam rubber or felt glued to the base gives a better surface.

SANDING TIPS

● Always sand with the grain except on end grain.

● Sand end grain in only one direction. Lift the sandpaper on the return stroke.

● Take special care to prevent a round corner or wavy appearance on edges and corners. Use a sanding block.

● Never use a grit coarser than necessary. Always work from a coarser paper to a finer one.

● Always dust, wipe, or blow off the stock being sanded when changing grits. Projects that are to be finished must be absolutely dust free.

● Exert even pressure over the entire surface being sanded. This is especially necessary on thin veneers.

38-2. Standard sandpaper (9 x 11 inches) can be cut into smaller sizes by tearing it along a hacksaw blade nailed to a wood jig.

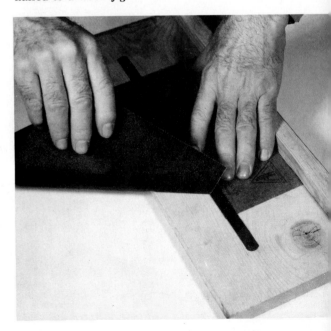

Table 38-A. The Grading of Common Abrasives

Coarseness	Flint (Common Sandpaper)	Garnet (Old Grit Numbers)	Garnet, Silicon Carbide and Aluminum Oxide (New Symbols Numbers)
Very fine	Extra fine	8/0 7/0 6/0	280 240 220
Fine	Fine	5/0 4/0 3/0	180 150 120
Medium	Medium	2/0 0 ½ 1	100 80 50
Coarse	Coarse	1½ 2	40 36
Very coarse	Extra coarse	2½	30

38-3. Two kinds of sanding blocks. On the left is a commercial block with a foam-rubber base. The one on the right is homemade. It has a piece of leather tacked in place under the sandpaper.

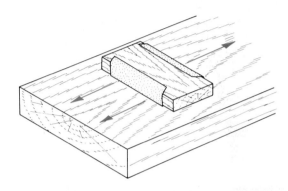

38-4. Sanding a surface. Hold the sanding block firmly against the surface. Move it back and forth in the direction of the grain.

38-5. Sanding an edge. Grasp the sanding block in both hands with the thumbs on top and the fingers curled underneath. This will keep the block square with the surface. If this is not done, there is danger of rounding the edge.

SANDING A FLAT SURFACE

Fasten the piece between the vise dog and bench stop or hold it firmly against the surface of the bench. If the piece is held in the vise, grip the sanding block as shown in Fig. 38-3. Apply even pressure to the block. Sand the surface *with the grain* of the wood. Move the block back and forth. Work slowly from one side to the other to get an even surface. Fig. 38-4. Take special care to keep from sanding the edges too much.

After coarse paper has been used, substitute finer and finer grades.

SANDING AN EDGE

Lock the work in a vise with the edge showing. Grasp the sanding block in both hands. Place your forefingers on each side of the edge to keep it square with the sides. Figs. 38-5 and 38-6. It is just as important to sand an edge square as it is to plane it square. After the edge has been sanded, round the sharp edge slightly by drawing the sandpaper over the edge.

SANDING AN END

Convex surfaces can usually be sanded with a block in the same way as an edge is sanded. A convex surface such as a rounded end can be sanded more satisfactorily by holding the paper in your fingers or the palm of your hand. Fig. 38-7.

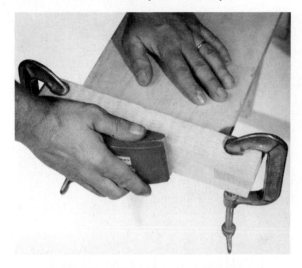

38-6. Sanding end grain. Sand in *one direction*. Notice the guide boards clamped over the end to keep the sanding square with the face surface.

SANDING CONCAVE OR OTHER INSIDE SURFACES

Concave and other inside surfaces are most easily sanded by wrapping the paper around a stick such as part of a broomstick or the handle of a tool. The half-round surface of a file also makes a good backing. Fig. 38-8.

SANDING SMALL PIECES

To sand small pieces of wood, fasten a full sheet of abrasive paper to a jig board. Clamp this to the top of the bench. Then hold the small pieces on the abrasive paper and move them back and forth. Fig. 38-9.

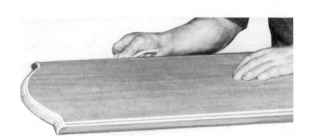

38-7. When sanding a molding by hand, hold the sandpaper in your fingers and guide it along the edge.

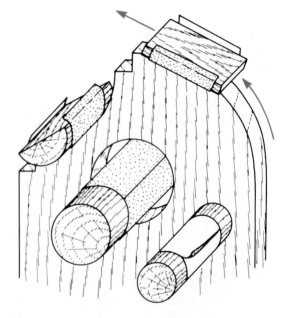

38-8. Sanding inside and outside curved surfaces.

SANDPAPER

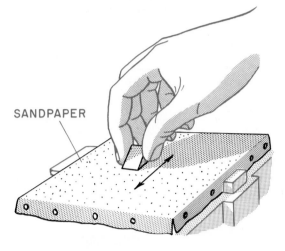

38-9. Sanding small pieces.

Review Questions

1. At what point in building the project should the sanding be done?
2. Is there any sand on sandpaper? What are the abrasives used in sandpaper?
3. How is sandpaper usually sold?
4. What number would you ask for when buying very coarse sandpaper? Very fine sandpaper?
5. How would you soften a sheet of sandpaper before using it? How would you tear it into smaller pieces?
6. How is a sanding block useful?
7. Is it correct to sand across grain? Explain.
8. How can you keep the edge square when sanding?
9. Describe how you would sand a convex surface.
10. How would you sand a concave surface?

Chapter 39

Fitting, Assembling, and Gluing Up a Project

After studying this chapter, you will be able to:
● List the various checks needed to ensure that the parts are properly finished.
● Discuss the advantages of a trial assembly.

LOOK FOR THIS TERM

trial assembly

You are now ready to assemble your project. How difficult this is, of course, depends on the kind of project and its size. For a small project such as a shelf, the assembly is fairly simple. Fig. 39-1. For an end table, bookcase, or a desk with drawers, assembly is much more complicated. Fig. 39-2. However, certain things must be done regardless of the size of the project.

COLLECTING THE PARTS

Get together all the parts that are to go into the finished project. If they were carefully made, your identification marks will still show. You will know how each part, joint, and piece fits to the next. This is very important. You will find yourself in a very unhappy position if, when you begin to glue, the joints do not fit or the parts do not match. This can easily happen unless you are careful.

39-1. A small project such as this shelf is easy to assemble since it can be done in one operation.

39-2. Assembling a desk with drawers requires careful planning. Such assembling requires several steps.

CHECKING ALL THE PARTS TO SEE THAT THEY ARE FINISHED

To be considered completed, the parts should be scraped and sanded. If there are duplicate parts, rails, or legs, check each one of them to make sure that they are all exactly the same in size and shape. If the project has joints, try each joint to see that it fits properly. Fig. 39-3. Check whether it is clearly marked in a place that can be seen after glue is applied and after the joint is assembled. This checking is especially important. You will usually need to make some small correction before assembling the project. Parts that have been stored for some time may have swelled slightly. Therefore the joints may not fit.

Your plan of procedure or the drawing shows whether the project is to be assembled with glue, screws, or nails. If screws or nails are used, carefully check to see that you have the correct type and number to complete your job. You should have a few more screws or nails than necessary. If glue is to be used, decide whether it is to be animal glue, casein, or plastic resin glue. Be sure that you have enough glue and that it is ready to apply.

MAKING PROTECTIVE PIECES

Before attempting to clamp the pieces together, cut some softwood pieces to place between the clamps and the project. Fig. 39-4. It is a good idea to plane the surface of the pieces. These protective pieces are not needed if you use hand screws or if the metal clamps have plastic clamp pads. Fig. 39-5. It may be necessary to cut special shapes if the project is not square—for example, if you are clamping a table with legs that taper outward. Of course, you will know when this is necessary. Figs. 39-6 and 39-7.

39-4. Using scrap pieces of wood to protect the surface during gluing.

39-5. Bar clamp pads of plastic slip onto the faces of bar and pipe clamps. They provide a protective cushion between the finished wood and the metal of the jaw clamps.

39-3. Before gluing a joint, check that its parts fit properly.

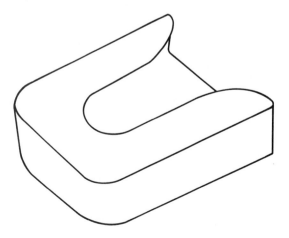

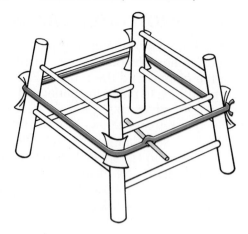

39-6. A windlass clamp made of rope. A dowel is turned to apply the pressure. Note the protective cardboard around each leg. This is a good type of clamp to use when gluing the legs of a chair.

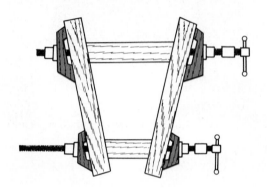

39-7. When clamping awkward angles, make protective blocks to fit.

39-8. Checking the project for squareness.

ASSEMBLING THE PROJECT TEMPORARILY

A *trial assembly* will allow you to see if the parts fit properly. Use cabinet clamps and hand screws to clamp all parts together temporarily. This will give you an idea of how the pieces fit together. Also you can see if any small corrections need to be made. This step is simple if you are assembling a project such as a bookcase or a hanging wall shelf made with parallel sides and crosspieces with dado or rabbet joints. Then, all you need are flat pieces of scrap stock, cabinet clamps that fit across the project on the front and back, and a pair of clamps for each shelf. Such projects as end tables, stools, and small desks usually have legs and rails with corners made with mortise-and-tenon joints or dowel joints. In either case, you will need clamps to go across the ends and cabinet clamps to go across the sides.

After assembling the project with clamps, check with a square to make sure that the project is squared up. Fig. 39-8. Using a steel tape or rule, measure across the corners and up and down to check that the sides and ends are parallel and that the project has the same height throughout. Fig. 39-9. By shifting a clamp or tapping a side or leg with a mallet, you can bring it into place.

This trial assembly will allow you to adjust all clamps to the correct width. It will prepare the project for final assembly.

ASSEMBLING WITH NAILS AND SCREWS

Follow the directions given in Chapters 35 and 36.

ASSEMBLING WITH GLUE

It is helpful if a glue bench or gluing room is available. If not, place wrapping paper over the bench or floor where the gluing is to be done. If the project is to be glued, carefully remove the clamps from top to bottom. Lay the clamps on the bench in definite order so that you can pick them up easily. Place the scrap pieces of wood next to the clamps so that everything will be on hand as needed.

If the project can be assembled at one time, do it that way. If the project is a desk, table, or stool, you may assemble and glue the end section one day and assemble the rest later.

In addition to the project parts, clamps, scrap pieces, and glue, have ready a rubber mallet, a rule or tape measure, and a square. If hot animal glue is used, heat the wood parts before assembling. Work very rapidly, as the glue sets quickly. If cold liquid glue is used, you do not need to work quite so fast.

With a brush, bottle, stick, or glue gun, carefully apply the glue to both parts of the joint. Fig. 39-10. Do not use too much glue. Any excess is a problem to remove later. Animal glue, especially, tends to dribble. As quickly as possible, fasten the joints.

Place the scrap pieces over the proper places. Lightly screw up the clamps. Do this until all the clamps are in place. Then turn up all clamps, each a little at a time. Check often to see that the project is squared. Fig. 39-11. Check that it measures the same distance wherever there are parallels. Using a straightedge, check for flatness. Fig. 39-12. Check also that edges are parallel. Fig. 39-13. You may need to use the rubber mallet to tap a joint in place or change the position of a clamp.

As soon as the project is clamped together, clean off the excess glue with a damp sponge. Do this before the glue dries. *Be careful not to mar the surface of the project.* Place the project in a safe place where no one will bump it. Allow most work from twelve to twenty-four hours to dry. Carefully remove each of the clamps and scrap pieces.

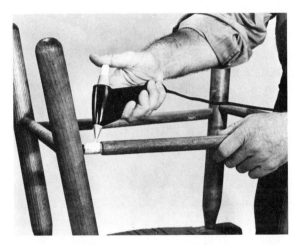

39-10. Applying glue to chair rungs with an electric glue gun.

39-9. Checking the project for levelness.

39-11. Checking the assembly with a square.

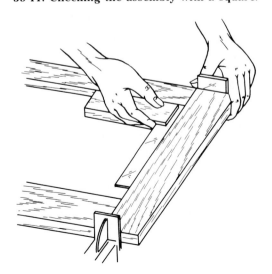

39-12. Check across several places with a straight-edge to make sure the surface is flat.

39-13. Checking across corners to make sure the measurement is equal in both directions.

Review Questions

1. Why should identification marks be kept on all pieces before they are assembled?
2. What processes must be completed before the parts of a project can be considered ready for assembly?
3. Should joints be checked again just before assembly? Why?
4. Name the three fasteners most commonly used for fastening parts together permanently.
5. Why are protective wood pieces unnecessary when hand screws are used for assembly?
6. Name two projects that would require specially shaped protective pieces.
7. Why is it necessary to make a trial assembly first?
8. Would you always assemble a project completely in one operation?
9. Describe the checks that should be made when the project is temporarily assembled.
10. How much glue should you apply?
11. How long should a project be allowed to dry?

Chapter 40

Installing Hardware

After studying this chapter, you will be able to:
- Identify the two types of hardware needed to build a project.
- List the steps in installing a butt hinge.
- Identify four types of repair plate.

LOOK FOR THESE TERMS

bent-corner iron	gain
cabinet hardware	mending plates
catches	repair plates
drawer pulls	structural hardware
flat-corner iron	T-plates

Two kinds of hardware are needed:

● *Cabinet hardware* (such as hinges, handles, and catches) is used to complete a project with drawers and doors. It can be used to decorate and add interest to a project. Figs. 40-1 and 40-2.

● *Structural hardware* (such as repair plates and corner blocks) is used to strengthen joints and hold unseen parts together.

Cabinet hardware should be selected to match the style of furniture. Hardware catalogs are available that show many different styles of hardware.

If the hardware including metal fasteners must be cut, use a hacksaw with 32 teeth per inch. Fig. 40-3.

KINDS OF CABINET HARDWARE

There are many different types of *cabinet hinges*. Figs. 40-4, 40-5, 40-6, and 40-7. The butt hinge requires that a recess, or *gain*, be cut. In most cases, a gain is cut both in the door and in the frame on which the door is fastened. Sometimes a deeper gain is cut ei-

40-1. The large drawer pulls on the ends of this adjustable book rack are both functional (for opening and closing the rack) and decorative.

ther in the frame or in the door. Thus, the hinge is recessed in only one part of the two surfaces.

Figure 40-8 illustrates different types of *drawer pulls* and *knobs* suited to different furniture styles. The most common *catches* are shown in Fig. 40-9.

40-2. Two pairs of hinges and two doorknobs are needed to complete this wall cabinet.

40-3. A hacksaw is necessary when hand-cutting any metal parts in the woodshop.

40-4. Common types of hinges. The main parts of a hinge are identified on the butt hinge.

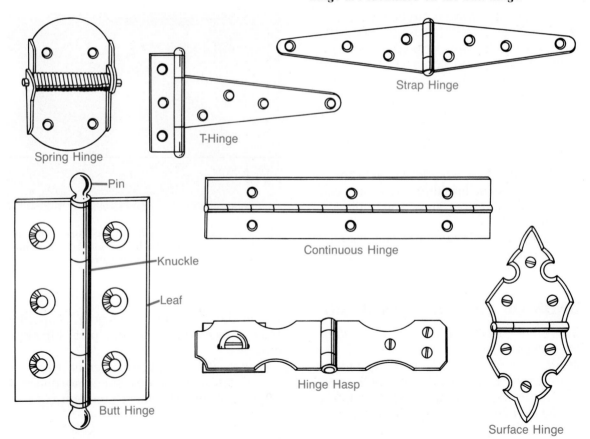

Spring Hinge

T-Hinge

Strap Hinge

Pin

Knuckle

Leaf

Continuous Hinge

Butt Hinge

Hinge Hasp

Surface Hinge

40-5. Hidden hinge for lip doors.

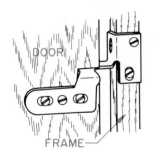

40-6. Hidden hinge for flush overlay drawer.

3/8 Inset

Flush Overlay

Reverse Bevel.

40-7. Semiconcealed ornamental hinges adaptable to several door styles as shown in the drawings. For a 3/8 inset lip door, A is the depth of the rabbet, B is the width of the rabbet, and C is the width of the leaf.

40-8. Choose drawer pulls and knobs that match the design of your project.

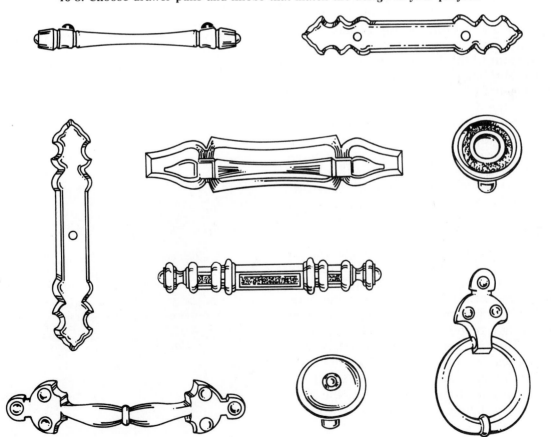

DOUBLE ROLLER CATCH—
Steel with wrought strike—

PLASTIC POST CATCH—
Steel strike with plastic post—

ROLLER CATCH—Steel with
two strikes

DOUBLE ROLLER CATCH—
Steel strike with white plastic—

MAGNETIC CATCH—
Aluminum for under shelf & flush
doors

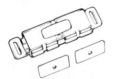
**DOUBLE MAGNETIC
CATCH**—Aluminum with two
strikes—

MAGNETIC CATCH—
Aluminum, reversible·

FRICTION CATCH—Steel
with ball screw strike—

40-9. Eight of the most common catches.

INSTALLING A BUTT HINGE

Select the proper size and kind of hinge for the door. The hinge size is indicated by its length. A 1-inch hinge is for a cabinet door for a desk.

Fit the door into the opening. Place a thin piece of wood under the door, on the side away from the hinges to hold the door in place. Measure from the top of the door to the upper location of the top hinge and from the bottom to the lower point of the bottom hinge. The hinges should be located just inside the upper and lower rail. Make a mark on both the door and the frame.

Remove the door and place it on the floor or bench with the hinge edge upward. Hold the hinge over the edge of the door with one end flush with the mark. Draw another line to show the length of the hinge. Mark this length on the door frame also. Then, square off these lines across the edge. Repeat on the door frame.

Determine how far in the hinge will be from the face of the door. Set a marking gauge to this measurement. Hold the marking gauge against the face side of the door. Mark a line between the two lines to show the position of the hinge. Repeat on the door frame. Then set a marking gauge to the thickness of one leaf of the hinge. From the edge, mark a line indicating the depth to which the stock must be removed, both on the door and on the frame. This cut in the wood is called a gain.

With a chisel, outline the gain on the door as shown in Fig. 40-10. Then make several V-cuts in the stock to be removed. Fig. 40-11. Pare out the stock to the depth of the gain. Try the hinge in the recess to see whether it fits flush with the edge of the door.

Mark the location of the screw holes. Drill the pilot holes as needed. Fasten half the hinge to the door section.

Cut out the gains in the frame of the door. Locate the position of the holes. Drill, and insert one screw. Put the door in position and place the pins in the hinges. Try the door

40-10. After laying out the gain on the edge of the door, outline it with a chisel.

to see how it operates. It may be necessary to shift the position of the hinge or cut the gain a little deeper or to raise it by putting a piece of paper under it. After any needed correction has been made, drill the other pilot holes. Fasten the hinge securely.

INSTALLING DRAWER KNOBS AND PULLS

Locate the position of the knobs or pulls. Drill a hole the same size as the machine screws used to fasten the knob or pull. Install the knob or pull. Fig. 40-12.

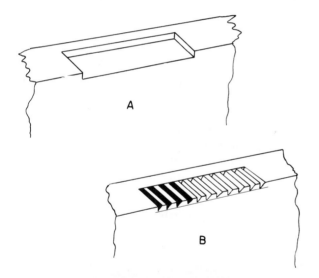

40-11. A. Chisel cuts in the stock to be removed to form the gain. B. The gain is cut and ready to have the hinge installed.

40-12. Attaching a handle to a drawer.

USING REPAIR PLATES

Repair plates come in many sizes and shapes. Fig. 40-13. *Mending plates* are used to strengthen a butt or lap joint. The *flat-corner iron* is used to strengthen corners of frames such as a screen door or window. The *bent-corner iron* can be applied to shelves and the inside corners of tables, chairs, and cabinets. It can also be used to hang cabinets and shelves. *T-plates* are used to strengthen the center rail of a frame.

Review Questions

1. Name three common types of hinge.
2. Define a gain.
3. What indicates the size of a hinge?
4. Describe the method of laying out a gain.
5. What tool is used to trim out a gain?
6. How can you test a hinge to make certain that it has been installed correctly?

40-13. Four types of repair plates: A. Mending; B. Flat corner; C. Bent corner; D. T-plate.

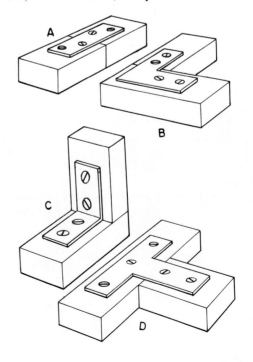

Chapter 41

Veneering Small Projects

After studying this chapter, you will be able to:
- Describe the basic techniques used for each of the four common veneer cuts.
- Identify four patterns of veneer matching.
- Describe the binding of veneer using veneer adhesive.

LOOK FOR THESE TERMS

book match
flat-sliced
flitch
half-round
quartered

random match
rotary-cut
slip match
veneer

veneer adhesive
veneer knife
vertical butt and horizontal
   bookleaf match

Veneer is a thin layer or sheet of wood (usually ⅟₂₈ inch) that is sliced from a log. Decorative veneers are cut from exotic woods such as rosewood, teak, or fine cabinet woods such as walnut or cherry. These veneers can be used to cover projects of less expensive woods as well as those made from plywood or particle board. Fig. 41-1.

VENEER CUTS

In the furniture industry, veneered parts such as tabletops are made in the factory by building up the part to size, using core stock, cross bands, and veneers. Fig. 41-2. Four different veneer cuts are used. Fig. 41-3.

41-2. The top of this table is built of lumber-core plywood with matching veneer.

41-1. A veneered box made of basswood and decorated with a small casting.

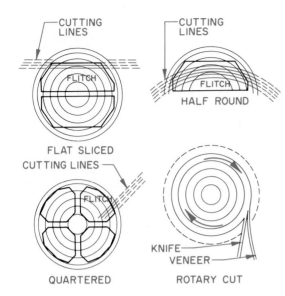

41-3. Four common methods of cutting veneers.

FLAT-SLICED

Flat-slicing is the method of cutting veneer used most frequently. The half log, or *flitch* (section of a log), is mounted so that slicing begins at a tangent to the growth rings of the tree.

HALF-ROUND

Half-round cuts normally display a broader and stronger grain pattern than flat sliced. This is because the half log, or flitch, is rotated against the veneer knife in such a way that the cut goes across the annual growth rings more gradually.

QUARTERED

Quartered veneer is produced from log quarters. Quarter-cut flitches are sliced approximately at right angles to the growth rings. This produces a straight, or so-called pencil stripe, grain pattern.

ROTARY-CUT

Rotary-cut hardwood is now uncommon. The full log turns on a lathe against a knife to produce a continuous sheet of veneer. This method is used for making softwood plywood.

VENEER MATCHING

In many furniture designs, face veneers have patterns made by some type of matching. The pieces of veneer must be cut and glued edge to edge before being applied to the core. Fig. 41-4. For small projects such as jewelry boxes and chessboards the veneering can be done in a much simpler way. Figs. 41-5 and 41-6. The project is built of some relatively inexpensive material such as softwood plywood, particle board, or inexpensive solid wood such as pine or poplar. Then it is covered with fine veneer.

VENEER THICKNESSES

Most veneers are cut $\frac{1}{28}$ inch thick. The normal flitch is about 12 to 14 inches wide and 16 feet long. However, veneers are also available in standard sizes such as 18×24 inches, 18×36 inches, and 24×48 inches. These sizes are designed specifically for veneering small projects. Veneer edging is available in matching woods in widths of $\frac{1}{2}$ inch, $\frac{5}{8}$ inch, $\frac{3}{4}$ inch, 1 inch, and 2 inches.

VENEER EDGING

Veneer edging is available as follows:
● Plain edging that must be attached with adhesive.
● Edging with pressure-sensitive adhesive covered with paper. Fig. 41-7. To glue this edging, the cover paper is stripped away and the edging fastened in place.
● Edging coated with adhesive that must be heated with an electric iron to make it stick.

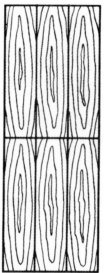

41-4. Basic veneer matching effects.

VERTICAL BUTT AND HORIZONTAL BOOKLEAF MATCH
Panels can be matched vertically and horizontally when additional height or width is desired.

SLIP MATCH
In slip matching, veneer sheets are joined side by side, repeating the flitch figure. All types of veneer may be used, but this type of matching is most common in quarter-sliced veneers.

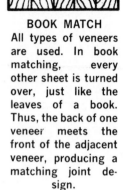

BOOK MATCH
All types of veneers are used. In book matching, every other sheet is turned over, just like the leaves of a book. Thus, the back of one veneer meets the front of the adjacent veneer, producing a matching joint design.

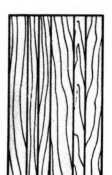

RANDOM MATCH
Veneers are joined to create a casual, unmatched effect. Veneers from several logs may be used in a set of panels.

41-5. This handsome chess set was built on a base of fir plywood with solid wood for the edging.

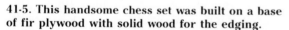

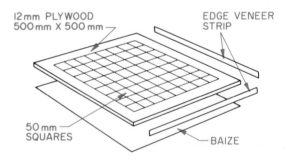

12mm PLYWOOD
500mm X 500mm

EDGE VENEER STRIP

50mm SQUARES

BAIZE

41-6. A drawing of a checkerboard or chessboard. This board is made of plywood covered with veneer. To make the squares, use veneers of two different colors. One veneer should be light, the other dark.

41-7. Thin strips of real veneer edging are available coated with pressure-sensitive adhesive. Simply peel off the backing paper and apply the edging to the plywood edge according to the manufacturer's recommendations. This photograph shows one edge already covered with a strip of wood matching the plywood surface.

TOOLS

A *veneer knife* is used to cut veneer. Fig. 41-8. A paper cutter or heavy-duty shears can also be used. A veneer roller is used to apply pressure to veneer surfaces. Fig. 41-9. A household iron is needed for heating the veneer to set veneer adhesive.

APPLYING VENEER WITH ADHESIVES

Two adhesives can be used to attach veneer, namely, contact cement and veneer adhesive. *Contact cement* produces an instant bond. The material cannot be moved once contact is made. With *veneer adhesive*, the permanent bond does not occur until heat is applied.

USING CONTACT CEMENT

Cut sheets of veneer slightly larger, about ¼ inch on each side, for each major surface of the project. Coat the surface of the project and one surface of the veneer with contact cement, brushing thoroughly. Allow to dry about 30 minutes or until the gloss is gone. Hold the veneer over the surface and align it. Then lower it in place. Remember that it cannot be moved once it touches the surface. If a relatively large area is to be cemented, use strips of scrap plastic laminate or plastic. Lay them lightly across the cement-coated surface of the project with the smooth surface down. Place the veneer on the scraps. Then remove one strip of scrap at a time and press the veneer to the surface. Roll the surface with a small roller. Place a block of softwood over the veneer and strike with a hammer until the veneer is in complete contact with the surface. Trim excess material with a knife. Then sand lightly for a square edge. Make sure all sawdust is removed from the edge before applying contact cement for the edging.

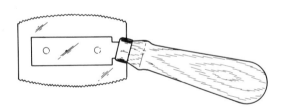

41-8. A veneer knife can be used to cut thin veneer.

41-9. A veneer roller can be used to make sure the veneer is tightly fastened to the base material.

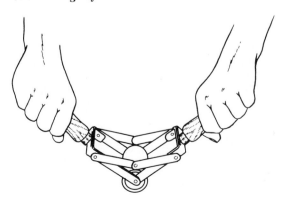

USING VENEER (THERMO-SET) ADHESIVE

In making small projects, the main advantage of using veneer adhesive instead of contact cement is that the pieces can be cut and fitted for a design before adhesive is applied. Even after adhesive is applied to both surfaces, the design can be assembled and moved around until heat is applied. Also, a design can be built up piece by piece since the veneer will not adhere until heat is applied.

Apply veneer adhesive directly from the container by brushing it on both surfaces. Allow it to dry to a clear gloss. Now place the veneer over the surface and align it. Use a regular household iron set at a high heat. Start at one corner, moving the iron slowly. The heat must penetrate the veneer to liquify the adhesives so they will fuse. Cover the surface with a very smooth block of wood to hold the veneer in place while the cement dries. Trim any excess veneer at sharp right angles to the edge. Make sure that the edge is square, smooth, and free of sawdust.

If heat-adhesive edging is used, remove the paper liner and apply the veneer tape to the edge with hand pressure. Apply a hot iron to the tape until the heat penetrates the veneer, activating the adhesive. Follow directly behind the iron with a block of wood to hold the adhesive until it cools. Fig. 41-10.

41-10. Using a home electric iron set at a high heat to apply the veneer. Move the iron slowly, allowing the heat to penetrate the wood and the adhesive. After the heat has been applied the full length of the veneer tape, allow the veneer to set until it is cool to the touch.

Review Questions

1. Name the four different methods of cutting veneer.
2. What is the most commonly used method of cutting veneer?
3. Describe the three kinds of veneer edging available.
4. What two types of adhesive can be used?
5. Describe the process of using contact cement.
6. What is the main advantage in using veneer adhesive?

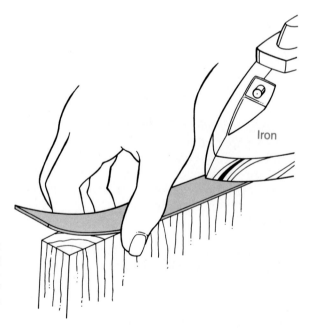

Iron

Chapter 42

Plastic Laminates

After studying this chapter, you will be able to:
● Describe the basic steps in the cutting and bonding of plastic laminate.
● Demonstrate the proper use of a laminate trimmer for bevel finishing.

LOOK FOR THESE TERMS

laminate
laminate trimmer
plastic laminate

A *laminate* is a material made up of several different layers. The tops of tables, cabinets, and chests are often covered with an extremely hard material called *plastic laminate*. Fig. 42-1. On some furniture, plastic laminates give the appearance of wood grain. Plastic laminates are also made with patterns.

You may know this material by one of its trade names: Panelyte®, Formica®, or Texolite®. Plastic laminate is made from layers of materials. They consist primarily of kraft paper that has been impregnated with resin and a rayon surface paper covered with another kind of resin. The laminates are placed under high heat and pressure to produce a 1/16-inch sheet of material that is very hard, but brittle. Tea, coffee, ink, iodine, alcohol, and crayon wax have no effect on this surface. Soap and water can be used to clean it.

WORKING WITH PLASTIC LAMINATES

Because plastic laminates are brittle, they must be well supported before being cut. Since a sheet is only 1/16 inch thick, it cracks very easily. Plastic laminates are usually applied to plywood, solid wood, or particle board. They can be cut with any of the standard woodworking tools. However, the carpenter or cabinetmaker prefers carbide-tipped tools. These are very hard and remain sharp longer than ordinary tools.

42-1. Plastic laminates were used in the construction of these cabinets.

The following is an example of the use of plastic laminate to cover the top of a dressing table:

1. Place a piece of wrapping paper on a bench to make a pattern.
2. With a grease pencil, trace the size of plastic laminate needed by placing the tabletop over it. Fig. 42-2. Allow about 3/16 inch oversize, since the material may chip slightly at the edges when sawed. This extra material is removed after the laminate is fastened to the tabletop.
3. Attach the paper pattern to the *good side* of the plastic laminate with masking tape. Cut out the laminate with a compass saw and a hacksaw. Always cut with the good side up. Make sure that it is firmly supported to keep it from cracking. Fig. 42-3. Then place the laminate on the bench with the good side down.
4. Make sure that the surface to be bonded is clean, dry, sound, and level. On an old surface, remove any varnish and sand the surface smooth.

5. Apply a coat of contact cement to both the tabletop and the back of the plastic laminate. Fig. 42-4. This is the best adhesive for attaching the plastic laminate to the wood. It can be applied with a brush or a metal spreader with a serrated edge. Make sure that both surfaces are completely and evenly covered with the cement. An adequately coated surface will have a glossy film when dry. Any dull spots after drying indicate that too little cement was used. These spots must have a second coat.

42-3. Using a compass saw to cut along the edge of the laminate.

42-4. Applying contact cement to the back of the laminate.

42-2. Tracing the shape of the tabletop on a paper pattern with a grease pencil. With a larger table or kitchen counter, the top can be removed.

6. Allow both surfaces to dry at least 30 to 40 minutes. Test for dryness by applying a small piece of wrapping paper lightly against the cemented surface. If no cement sticks to the paper, the cement is dry and ready for bonding.

7. Bond the two surfaces. This can be done any time within 3 hours after the contact cement is applied. Do not rush the job. It is better to wait a little longer and be sure. Remember, there is a complete bond immediately when the two surfaces come in contact. Therefore no adjustment can be made. To avoid any mistake, use the following technique.

   Place a piece of heavy wrapping paper lightly over the entire base surface. Fig. 42-5. Now place the plastic laminate in position over the wrapping paper and align it carefully. Raise one side of the laminate slightly. Draw the paper away 2 or 3 inches. Now check that the parts are still aligned. Press down where the paper has been withdrawn. Then remove the paper completely.

8. Roll the entire surface with a rolling pin or roller. Fig. 42-6.

9. Trim the edge with a *laminate trimmer*. Fig. 42-7. You might also use a file. Fig. 42-8. Hold the tool at an angle of about 20 to 25 degrees for bevel finishing.

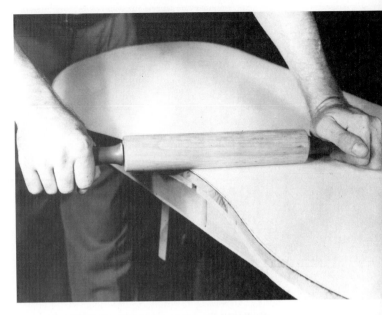

42-6. Using a rolling pin to flatten the surface.

42-7. The best way to trim the edge is with a laminate trimmer (or router) using carbide-tipped cutters to produce a clean edge without chipping. A. laminate trimmer; B. flush trimmer cutter will trim the laminate flush and square with the edge; C. 22-degree bevel trimmer cutter will give the top a neatly trimmed bevel.

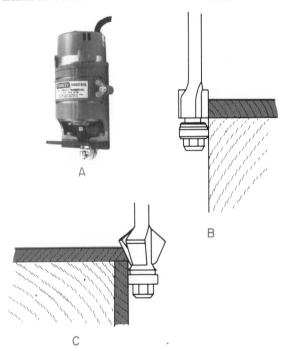

42-5. Fastening the plastic laminate to the tabletop. Do not press down. Notice the wrapping paper that is placed between. Remove this slowly after properly positioning the material.

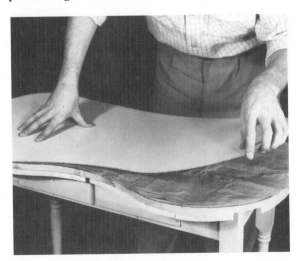

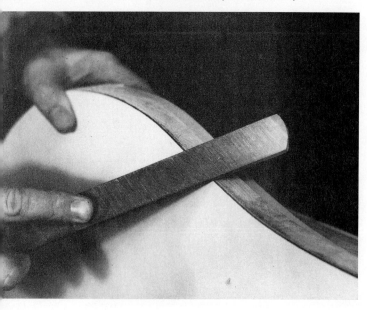

42-8. Beveling the edge of the plastic laminate with a file. Use light, regular strokes to keep the bevel even.

42-9. Types of edge treatment: A. Wood tape or veneer edge; B. Plain facing of solid wood; C. Bevel edge; D. Self edge.

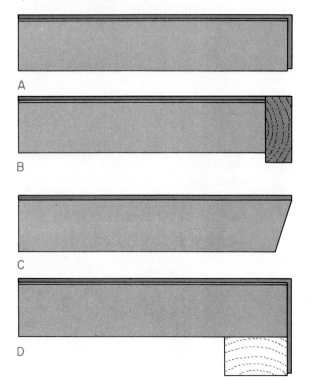

A

B

C

D

10. Finish the edge of the tabletop. It can be covered with a metal or plastic laminate edge. Edge-banding material to match the plastic laminate is available. It can be easily bent around a curved surface. A more pleasing appearance can be obtained on the edge of a tabletop by adding a strip of wood to the underside for added thickness. Fig. 42-9.

MAKING A COFFEE TABLE

Drawings for the coffee table in Fig. 42-10 are shown in Fig. 42-11.

1. Cut the particle board to exact size. Corners must be square. Using the circular saw or shaper, cut the groove in the edge of the board.
2. Cut the plastic laminate to 15¼ × 45¼ inches.
3. Adhere the plastic laminate to the particle board, using contact cement and following manufacturer's directions. Trim the laminate even with the substrate (base).
4. Where necessary, cut and joint the long and short edge pieces to size. Cut 45-degree miter corners to fit around the particle board.
5. Glue the edge pieces to the particle board, using polyvinyl glue. Make sure excess glue is removed from the edge pieces and laminate.

42-10. A handsome coffee table with a plastic laminate top.

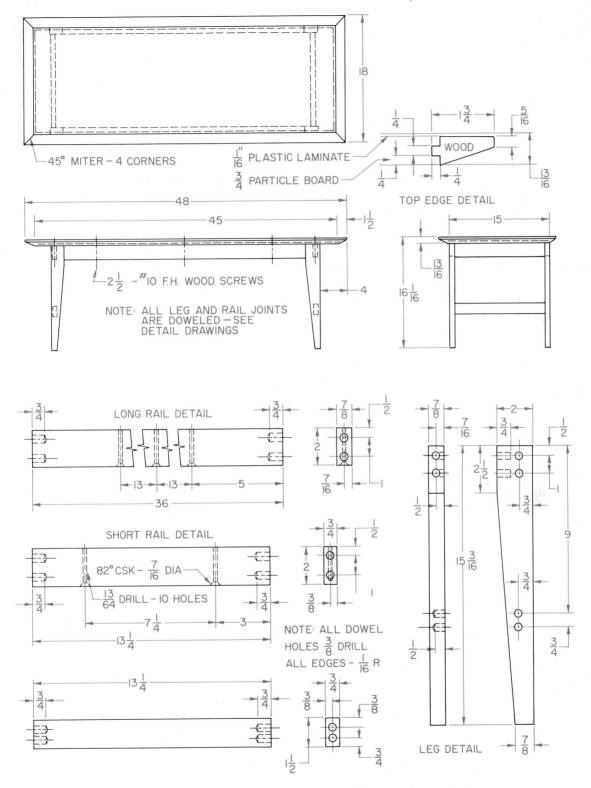

45° MITER – 4 CORNERS

$\frac{1}{16}$" PLASTIC LAMINATE

$\frac{3}{4}$ PARTICLE BOARD

TOP EDGE DETAIL

WOOD

NOTE: ALL LEG AND RAIL JOINTS ARE DOWELED – SEE DETAIL DRAWINGS

$2\frac{1}{2}$ – #10 F.H. WOOD SCREWS

LONG RAIL DETAIL

SHORT RAIL DETAIL

82° CSK – $\frac{7}{16}$ DIA

$\frac{13}{64}$ DRILL – 10 HOLES

NOTE: ALL DOWEL HOLES $\frac{3}{8}$ DRILL ALL EDGES – $\frac{1}{16}$ R

LEG DETAIL

42-11. Drawings for the coffee table shown in Fig. 42-10.

6. Sand the edge pieces, stain if desired, and finish. Care should be taken to protect the laminate surface when sanding.
7. Cut and joint the legs and rails to the correct dimensions.
8. Lay out the dowel locations on all rails. Drill dowel holes. Mortise-and-tenon joints may be substituted for dowel joints.
9. Lay out the location of dowel vertical centers on the legs. Using dowel centers, mark the holes on the legs for the top rails. Measure the height of the bottom rail and mark with the dowel centers.
10. Drill dowel holes in the legs.
11. Lay out, drill, and countersink holes to fasten the rails to the tabletop.
12. Dry assemble the parts. Make adjustments, if necessary.
13. Sand all parts, rounding all exposed edges to a ⅛-inch radius.
14. Assemble, using polyvinyl glue.
15. Remove excess glue. Sand, stain, and finish to match top edging.
16. Assemble top to base with 2½-inch No. 10 wood screws.

Review Questions

1. What is a plastic laminate?
2. Why is plastic laminate so popular for kitchen cabinet tops?
3. What is the best adhesive for gluing plastic laminate to the project?
4. How can you tell when the cement is ready for bonding?
5. Can you move the plastic laminate a little if you don't have it in the right place the first time? Explain why or why not.
6. Describe the method of trimming the edge of the plastic laminate after it is in place.

Thinking about a Career

Cabinetmaker

John Duncan is a cabinetmaker. He makes finely detailed cabinets, bookcases, and desks. He also makes paneled doors, mantelpieces, and countertops. Because John Duncan is in business for himself, he also is an entrepreneur.

An *entrepreneur* is anyone who organizes and manages a business. This person also assumes the risks of the business. This means that the entrepreneur is responsible for paying the business expenses. All responsibility for the success of the business rests with the entrepreneur.

The role of entrepreneur in American business has been important to the development of the nation's economy. In an age of large corporations and heavy international trade, it may be hard to realize that many of today's largest businesses developed from small beginnings. The spirit of the entrepreneur has been essential to the economic health of the nation.

Self-employment is not for everyone. To be successfully self-employed, a person must be able to supply a service or product that the public needs. The products John Duncan makes are keenly sought by his many customers. These customers include individuals, as well as large businesses.

In his shop, John is relaxed. Though he started in business alone in a small basement workshop, he now has four employees. The shop has all of the basic woodworking power tools, most of them bought used.

What advice would John give someone interested in pursuing a career in fine cabinetmaking? Asked this question, John replied quickly and enthusiastically. "Take all the woodworking courses you can. Join the student clubs—such as VICA and AIASA. Read about woodworking. There are several excellent woodworking magazines that have been started in the last ten years. Take a course in drafting. Take a course in design. Get a good set of hand tools and practice your craft. Work to develop your skills. Skill development is important. Ultimately, it is the most important aspect. Only the quality of your work will bring in customers in the first place—and keep them coming back.

"If you attend a school that does not offer a woodworking program, learning the basic skills will be a bit more difficult. You might, however, be able to find a cabinetmaker in your town who might give you a job in his or her shop. I held such a job in my junior and senior years of high school. It was a valuable experience. It taught me much I could not have learned in any other way. I learned exactly what makes the difference between a piece of fine cabinetwork and several boards nailed together. I developed an eye for detail. I don't think I've lost that, because my customers tell me that's what they like about my work."

Developing Science, Math, and Reading Skills

What Causes Wood to Rot?

While walking through wooded areas, you have probably stopped to examine pieces of limbs and logs. Have you ever picked up what appeared to be a heavy, solid-looking hunk of wood only to have it crumble in your hand? Why did this happen? The wood was decayed by microscopic organisms known as *bacteria.* Many bacteria are harmful to humans. These harmful bacteria cause diseases such as tuberculosis and tetanus. However, other bacteria are beneficial. Some of these, for example, cause cheeses to ripen. Others break down foods in our digestive tract.

When working with woods it is very important to be aware of ways to prevent wood from decomposing. After all, what good would be the strongest wood foundation if it rotted in only a year? Some conditions will slow the decay of woods. For example, Venice, Italy, is constructed on wooden piles buried in the shallow sea. Yet these supports have lasted for centuries. As you might have guessed, the salt water has killed any bacteria that might attack the wood piles. In addition, areas that are very dry or very cold seem to be harmful to bacteria that decompose wood. Wood decays most quickly in moist, warm regions where bacteria can readily grow and reproduce.

In the southern United States, trees such as the bald cypress grow in swamps. This particular tree easily resists attacks from harmful bacteria and insects. Its wood is remarkably hard. Because of its natural tendency to avoid rotting, the bald cypress is commonly used for railroad ties, dock piers, and fence posts. Human beings have learned to copy nature by applying to wood substances that slow down decay in trees. These substances are called *preservatives.* Usually, they are substances that trees produce naturally to prevent rot. Common examples are creosote and wood tar. These, however, are now being replaced by materials that are considered to be safer for humans to use.

ACTIVITY: A Computer Investigation of the Reproductive Rates of Wood-Decaying Bacteria

Materials
Microcomputer
Monitor

A. Obtain access to a microcomputer.
B. The following program is written in a computer programming language known as BASIC. It is one of many languages that can be used to program a computer to accomplish a specific task. Here, you will type in and run a program. This program illustrates how rapidly wood-decaying bacteria can reproduce. This mathematical exercise can also be modified and done with a hand calculator.

As discussed, bacteria are responsible for decaying wood. They reproduce at an incredible rate. Before long, they are abundant enough to be seen without a microscope. When this occurs, a *colony* has formed. Most bacteria split by a process known as *fission.* In our computer simulation, we will assume that all new bacteria live and go on to reproduce every 15 minutes. Thus, one bacterium becomes two, two become four, and so on.

1. Type in the following and press the RETURN (or ENTER) key after each line.

   10   REM program to calculate total number of bacteria that would reproduce in 24 hours.

   20   PRINT "IN A 24-HOUR TIME PERIOD, THERE ARE 96 TIMES THAT REPRODUCTION WOULD OCCUR."

   30   PRINT "AFTER 24-HOURS, THERE WOULD BE "; 2^{96}; " BACTERIA IF ALL BACTERIA LIVED."

   40   PRINT "PLEASE DO NOT BE TOO NERVOUS! NOT ALL OF THE BACTERIA WILL BE ABLE TO LIVE AND REPRODUCE. IF THEY DID, THEY WOULD WEIGH OVER 2000 TONS!

2. Type RUN and press the RETURN (or ENTER) key when finished.

Activity One

On pages 224-226, you are introduced to lap joints. The author tells you that all lap joints have one thing in common—an equal amount of wood is cut from the two parts to be joined. After describing the many different kinds of lap joints, the author describes in detail the cross-lap joint. This is the most common of all lap joints.

You are told how to lay out, cut, and assemble the lap joint. You also are told what tools to use.

What is the most common use of a lap joint in the industry?

Activity Two

The section on building furniture gives you the necessary information for making tables, stools, drawers, and doors. On pages 244-249, the author mentions the kinds of construction, joints, guides and rails that can be used in making furniture.

> **Developing Reading Skills**

Review this section of the text. Then choose the correct way to make a footstool. Write a brief step-by-step description of the procedure.

Activity Three

The goal of any project is to have an acceptable finished product. All of the effort you put forth in planning, measuring, cutting, and fitting is reflected in your final product. Only your best work should be your objective.

On pages 276-280, you are told how to fit, assemble, and glue up a project. Review that section. Then write a step-by-step description of how you would work from trial assembly to finished product.

Measuring Square Feet and Board Feet

You want to make the ping-pong table shown in Fig. A. The top is made of 1″ plywood. The legs are made of 1½″ square oak.

How many square feet of plywood are needed for the top?

How many board feet of oak are needed for the four legs?

> **Developing Math Skills**

Fig. A.

Section IV. Finishing

Chapter 43 Wood Finishing and Finishing Supplies

After studying this chapter, you will be able to:
- List the three general types of finishes.
- List the basic steps in applying a fine finish.
- Identify those qualities it is important to look for in selecting a brush.
- List those finishing supplies that are commonly used in finishing.
- List the safety habits that must be followed when working with finishing supplies.

LOOK FOR THESE TERMS

bleaching	paraffin oil	sealing
filling	paste wax	solvents
linseed oil	penetrating finish	staining
mineral oil	pumice	steel wool
mineral spirits	rottenstone	tack rag
opaque finish	rubbing oil	transparent coating

The beauty of any fine wood project can be greatly enhanced by a proper finish correctly applied. The appearance of less attractive woods can also be greatly improved by applying a suitable finish. To apply these finishes, specific steps must be taken. Certain techniques must be learned. Fig. 43-1.

There are only two reasons for finishing wood—to protect it and to add to its beauty. Many different finishes can be used. You should select the one best suited to your project. Table 43-A.

All finishes can be grouped into three general types:
- *Transparent coatings* such as shellac, varnish, and lacquer. Transparent coatings can be seen through.
- *Penetrating finishes* such as oil and penetrating oil-resin finishes. Penetrating finishes penetrate the surface of the wood.
- *Opaque finishes* such as paint, enamel, and colored lacquer. Opaque finishes cover the surface completely. They cannot be seen through. Table 43-B.

43-1. The fine finish on this pine blanket chest adds to its beauty and durability.

Table 43-A. Wood Finishing Characteristics

Name	Relative Hardness[1]	Grain	Finish
Ash	Hard	Open[2]	Requires filler.
Basswood	Soft	Close[3]	Paints well.
Beech	Hard	Close	Poor for paint, takes varnish well.
Birch	Hard	Close	Stains and varnishes well.
Cedar	Soft	Close	Paints well. Finishes well with varnish.
Cherry	Hard	Close	Requires filler.
Fir	Soft	Close	Can be painted, stained, or finished natural.
Gum	Soft	Close	Can be finished with variety of finishes.
Mahogany	Hard	Open	Requires filler.
Maple	Hard	Close	Takes any type finish.
Oak	Hard	Open	Requires filler.
Pine	Soft	Close	Takes any type finish.
Walnut	Hard	Open	Requires filler. Takes all finishes well.

Notes: [1]"Hard" and "soft" refer to the relative hardness of wood; no relation to hardwoods or softwoods.
[2]"Open grain" is associated with varying pore sizes between springwood and summerwood.
[3]"Close grain" is associated with woods having overall uniform pore sizes.

Table 43-B. Finishes

Finish (solvent)	Application	Drying Time	Durability	Color	Appearance	Notes
Wax (none)	Hand rub with soft cloth.	30 minutes	Good moisture resistance.	Tends to yellow with age.	Soft sheen	Paste wax can be used for sealer.
Shellac (alcohol)	Wide brush or hand wipe.	30-60 minutes	Poor. Water turns shellac white. No outdoor use.	Orange shellac dries honey-colored. White shellac dries clear.	Sheen to gloss	Good as a liquid wood filler on some woods. Better as a sealer.
Oil: Boiled Linseed (turpentine or mineral spirits)	Rub with soft cloth.	Indefinite	Will not peel or crack.	Darkens quickly.	Soft sheen	Driers can be added to increase hardness.
Oils: Sealacell, Watco, Tung (mineral spirits)	Rub with soft cloth.	2 days	Will not peel or crack. Better moisture resistance.	Dull, but shines to satin luster when steel wool is used between coats.	Soft sheen	Finish is more durable than boiled linseed oil.
Varnish (turpentine or mineral spirits)	Bristle brush or foam polybrush.	1-1½ days	Good weather and wear resistance.	Spar varnish tends to darken.	Sheen to gloss	Avoid shaking varnish. Apply several thin coats. Finish in dust-free place.
Lacquer brushing (lacquer thinner)	Brush (sable or camel).	4 hours	Fair moisture resistance, good durability.	Will not discolor wood.	High gloss	Foam polybrush can be used.
Lacquer spraying (Lacquer thinner)	Spray.	Dries quickly.	High durability.	Clear. Slight yellowing with age.	Gloss. Can be steel-wooled to soften sheen.	Use spray booth.
Enamels and paints (turpentine or water)	Brush or pad.	2-4 hours	Closs is very durable. Can be washed.	Any color or tint.	Opaque. Covers surface completely.	Adds beauty to soft woods.

BASIC STEPS IN ACHIEVING A FINE SURFACE FINISH

Although the materials may vary, all finishing is done in about the same way. There are several basic steps to follow. Not all are necessary, however, for finishing every piece of wood. Choose from the following only the steps needed for the finish you want.

1. *Bleaching.* Bleaching is done to lighten or to even out the color of unfinished wood. Very light, natural wood finishes are popular for contemporary furniture. For natural and darker finishes, bleaching, of course, is not necessary.
2. *Staining.* Staining is done to enhance the grain and to achieve the color you want.
3. *Sealing.* Sealing is done to seal the stain to prevent bleeding (running of the stain). A wash coat (one part shellac to seven parts alcohol) is good for most stains. If lacquer is used, a lacquer sealer can be applied.
4. *Filling.* Filling is required for porous and semiporous woods. Wood from some broad-leaf trees such as oak, mahogany, and walnut contains large cells. Such wood is, therefore, very porous. When the lumber is cut and planed, the cells are ruptured. This reveals tiny troughs running lengthwise. These must be filled to obtain a smooth finish. Some woods such as birch, maple, and gum have smaller cells. These require a thinner filler or no filler at all. Nonporous woods such as pine, cedar, and redwood do not require a paste filler.
5. *The second sealing.* A sealer should again be applied over a filler. It can be a commercial lacquer sealer or a wash coat of shellac.
6. *The standard finish.* A shellac, varnish, lacquer, or synthetic finish is applied after sealing. Usually two or more coats are needed. Always sand the surface with 5/0 (180) sandpaper after each coat is dry. The final coat may be gloss or satin—a duller gloss.
7. *Rubbing, buffing, and waxing.* To get a hand-rubbed finish, the normal gloss is removed and reduced by using an abrasive material. The surface to be rubbed should have at least three or four coats of the final finish to withstand the rubbing. The common method of rubbing is to use a felt pad and pumice. Several layers of felt should be tacked to a piece of wood. Then mix the pumice in water to a paste consistency. Wet the surface. Dab the pad in water, then in pumice paste. Rub the surface with the grain. Use long strokes with moderate pressure.

For an even finer polished surface, rub with a felt pad or cloth, using powdered rottenstone and water or rottenstone and rubbing oil.

Another method of rubbing the surface is to use wet-or-dry sandpaper. Lubricate the surface with soapy water. Then rub with the grain, using long strokes. Use very fine wet-or-dry sandpaper, grades 360 to 380. When uniformly dull, polish with a clean, soft felt pad or cloth.

A simpler method of getting a rubbed surface is to rub with 4/0 steel wool until the surface is uniformly dull. The final step is to apply a good coat of paste wax and rub vigorously with a soft cloth.

BRUSHES

To get a good finish, choose a brush carefully. Fig. 43-2.

Natural bristle brushes are made with hog hair. This type of brush was originally recommended for applying oil base paints, varnishes, lacquers, and other finishes, because natural fibers resist most strong solvents.

43-2. Parts of a brush.

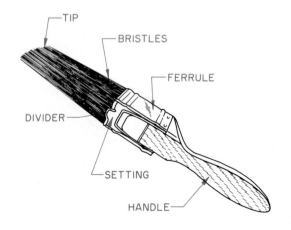

Synthetic bristle brushes are made from synthetic fiber, usually nylon. Today's nylon brushes are recommended for both latex (water-soluble) and oil-base paints. This is because the fiber absorbs less water than natural bristles do, while also resisting most strong paint and lacquer solvents. In addition, nylon bristles are easier to clean than natural bristles.

Foam polybrushes are very inexpensive. They can be used to apply most finishes. These brushes come in many different sizes. They are made of a plastic foam tapered on both sides to a sharp point. These brushes cost so little that they can be discarded after use.

Brush quality determines painting ease, plus the quality of the finished job. A good brush holds more paint, controls dripping and spattering, and applies paint more smoothly to minimize brush marks. To assure that you are buying a quality brush, check the following factors:

● *Flagged bristles* have split ends that help load the brush with more paint, while allowing the paint to flow more smoothly. Cheaper brushes will have less flagging or none at all. Fig. 43-3.

● *Tapered bristles* also help paint flow and provide smooth paint release. Check that the base of each bristle is thicker than the tip. This helps give the brush tip a fine painting edge for more even and accurate work.

● *Fullness* is important, too. As you press the bristles against your hand, they should feel full and springy. If the divider in the brush setting is too large, the bristles will feel skimpy. There also will be a large hollow space in the center of the brush.

● *Bristle length* should vary. As you run your hand over the bristles, some shorter ones should pop up first. This indicates a variety of bristle lengths for better paint loading and smoother paint release.

● A *strong setting* is important for bristle retention and maximum brush life. Bristles should be firmly bonded into the setting with epoxy glue. Nails should be used only to hold the ferrule to the handle.

● *Size and shape* of a brush are also important. Choice of brush width is determined by the amount of open or flat area to be painted. Table 43-C can be used as a guide for choosing a brush of the right size. This information, though, should not be considered a limiting factor when selecting a brush.

GOOD USE OF BRUSHES

The following are some general suggestions for using brushes:

● Revolve a new brush rapidly by its handle to dislodge loose bristles. Remember that all new brushes have them. Fig. 43-4.

● Dip the brush into the finishing material about one-third the bristle length. Tap the excess against the side of the can. Fig. 43-5. Never scrape the brush against the rim of the can.

● When using a brush, always hold it at a slight angle to the work surface.

● Never apply finish with the side of the brush.

● Never use a wide brush to finish small round surfaces such as dowel rods.

43-3. Two types of bristles.

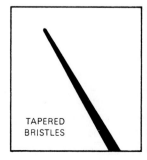

TAPERED BRISTLES

FLAGGED BRISTLES

Table 43-C. Selecting the Proper Brush for the Job

Size	Application
1" to 1½"	Touch-ups and little jobs, such as toys, tools, furniture legs, and hard-to-reach corners.
2" to 3"	Trim work, such as sashes, frames, molding, or other flat surfaces. An angular-cut brush helps do clean, neat, sash or narrow trim work and makes edge cutting easier.
3½" to 4"	For large flat surfaces, such as floors, walls, or ceilings.
4½" to 6"	Large flat areas, particularly masonry surfaces, barns, or board fences.

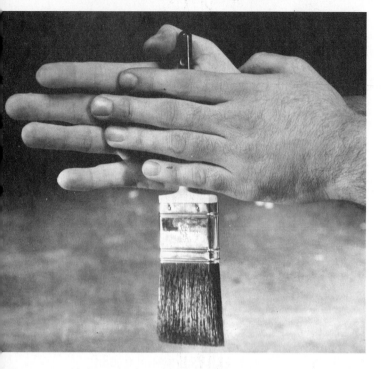

43-4. Twirling a brush to get rid of the loose bristles.

43-5. Tapping a brush on the side of a can. Never rub the bristles on the edge of the can. A larger mouthed container is better.

● Never let the brush stand on its bristle end. Its own weight bends and curls the bristle. Fig. 43-6. This would make finishing difficult.

● When not in use, brushes should be put into a solvent suited to the material used on the brush. The proper solvents for finishing materials are listed in Table 43-D.

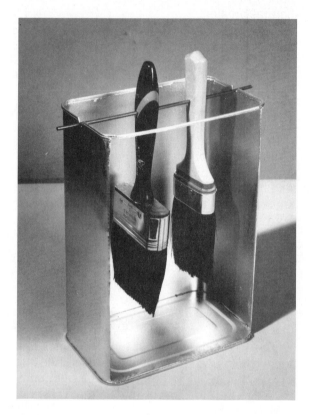

43-6. One method of suspending brushes to make sure that the bristles do not become bent.

Table 43-D. Solvents to Be Used with Certain Finishing Materials

Solvent	Finishing Material
Turpentine	Oil stain Filler for varnish and shellac finish Varnish Enamel
Turpentine and linseed oil	Paint
Alcohol	Shellac
Lacquer thinner	Filler for lacquer finish Lacquer

CLEANING BRUSHES

It pays to clean brushes immediately after they have been used. The solvents used to thin down finishes are generally recommended for cleaning brushes. There are also special brush and roller cleaners that can be used. Work the cleaner thoroughly into the heel of the brush. With your fingers, open the bristles to clean out the waste material. Wipe the brush dry. If the brush is to be stored longer than overnight, wash it in good commercial cleaning solvent mixed in water or a good grade of detergent. Wash the brush thoroughly. Comb the bristles with a metal comb. Rinse well, shake out the excess water, and allow to dry. Then wrap the brush in heavy waxed paper. Fig. 43-7.

FINISHING SUPPLIES

Linseed oil is made from flaxseed. This oil is obtained by compressing the seed under high pressure to squeeze out the oil. The oil is used either in its raw state or is boiled to improve its drying qualities as a paint ingredient. Linseed oil is used by itself to finish certain types of furniture. The oil is applied with a rag and then rubbed into the surface. Several coats are applied in this manner. After the oil is dry, a paste wax is applied and rubbed to a high polish.

Solvents are liquids that dissolve another substance to create a solution. Most solvents are used as thinners. Table 43-E.

The best *alcohol* for mixing shellac is made from wood drippings or chemicals, if available. The government has established a standard alcohol mix that is called Formula Special No. 1 denatured alcohol. This contains ethyl alcohol and wood alcohol.

Benzene, used as a solvent and a cleaning fluid, is made from coal tar.

Mineral spirits is a pure distillation of petroleum that will do everything that turpentine will do. It can be used as a thinner or solvent.

Waxes can be either liquid or paste. Both are made from a base of beeswax, paraffin, carnauba wax, and turpentine.

43-7. Steps in wrapping a brush that is to be stored.

STEP 1

STEP 2

STEP 3

Table 43-E. Characteristics of Solvents

Kind	Flammable	Source	Uses	Comments
Turpentine	Yes	Sap of pine trees.	Thinning oil and alkyd-base paints. Cleaning brushes. A final finish on certain woods.	Costly. Strong odor.
Mineral spirits	Yes	Refined petroleum product.	Thinner for oil and alkyd paints and varnish. Cleaning brushes.	Cannot be used to clean hardened paint brushes.
Naphtha (Benzene)	Highly	From coal tar.	Thinning oil-based paints. Removing spots.	Makes paint dry very fast. Wear gloves and mask when using.
Denatured alcohol (Ethyl)	Highly	From wood drippings and chemicals.	Thins shellac. Cleans shellac brushes.	Softens shellac. Dangerous to drink. Affects certain finishes.
Acetone	Highly	From various alcohols and acetic acid.	Paint, varnish, and lacquer removers.	Attacks all finishes. Wear gloves and mask.

Paste wax forms a protective overcoat for most other finishes. Wax gives wood a durable sheen that resists everyday dirt and scuffs. Wax can also be used by itself as a sealer/finish on most woods. To make sure it penetrates the wood pores, melt the wax. Hand rub several coats along the grain with a soft cloth. Waxes do not darken the wood as do most oils. However, wax can yellow over time, so the surface should be renewed once a year. Remove the old wax with a cloth dipped in mineral spirits. Allow the wood to dry. Then repeat the waxing.

Mineral oil is a clear nontoxic oil that comes from a petroleum base. It is also known as *paraffin oil*. This material can be used as an oil finish on projects that will hold food.

Steel wool is made of thin metal shavings. It comes in pads or rolls and can be purchased in grades from 000, very fine, to 3, coarse.

Pumice is a white powder made from lava. It is available in several grades. The most common for wood finishing are FF and FFF. Pumice is combined with water or oil to rub down the finish.

Rottenstone is a reddish brown or grayish black iron oxide vehicle that comes from shale. It is much finer than pumice. It is used with water or oil to produce a smoother finish after the surface has been rubbed with pumice.

Rubbing oil is a pale, medium-heavy mineral oil used with pumice or other abrasives as a lubricant for rubbing the dried film of finishing material.

Abrasive papers needed are garnet or aluminum oxide finishing papers in grades No. 4/0 (150) and No. 6/0 (220). Number 4/O (150) is used for sanding after staining, after applying the first coat of shellac, and before applying the filler coat. Number 6/0 (220) is used for final smoothing after shellac coats or other finish. These grades may be used dry or with oil.

Waterproof (wet-or-dry) abrasive papers in grades from 240 to 400 grit are used with water for hand sanding between lacquer coats or for rubbing enamel or lacquer.

A *tack rag* is cheesecloth or cotton rag moistened with thinned varnish. It is used to pick up dust from the wood before the finish is applied.

Finishing Safety

Keep safety uppermost in your mind when working with finishing materials. All finishing materials have some danger associated with them. In working with finishing materials, be sure to observe the following cautions:

Personal Safety
- Wear approved eye protection.
- Cover your clothing with a suitable apron.
- Wear a respirator when spraying finishing materials.
- Avoid breathing fumes from toxic materials.
- Wear rubber gloves to minimize risk of skin irritations when applying paint removers, bleaches, and finishing materials with a cloth or pad.
- Wash your hands after using any finishing materials.

Materials Safety
- Read labels on containers carefully before using any material. Follow directions exactly as stated on the container.
- Keep all solvents away from smoke, fire, or sparks.
- Whenever possible, store all thinners and solvents in their original containers. Make sure they are clearly marked.
- Keep all used rags in a fireproof container.
- Dispose of all excess combustible materials immediately or store the excess in approved containers.
- Close all cans and containers tightly after use.
- Store aerosol containers in a cool place.
- Keep all finishing materials in a fireproof cabinet.

Finishing Room Safety
- Do all finishing in a separate, well-ventilated area specifically designed for finishing.
- Make sure the proper types of fire extinguishers are available in the room.
- For spraying, use a properly installed spray booth that is kept clean and well maintained.
- Keep the total area clean and free from spills.
- Store all brushes and other utensils in approved containers.
- Never leave opened finishing materials unattended.
- Never use tools or machines that can cause sparks or fire in the finishing area.

Review Questions

1. List the basic steps in achieving a fine finish.
2. What are the bristles for most finishing brushes made from?
3. What is linseed oil? How do raw and boiled linseed oil differ?
4. What are waxes made from?
5. What is pumice?
6. What is rottenstone?
7. What safety precautions should be followed when finishing?

Chapter 44

Preparing the Project for Finishing

After studying this chapter, you will be able to:
- Identify the three most common defects in wood.
- Describe the methods used to correct the three most common defects in wood.
- List the basic steps in refinishing.

LOOK FOR THESE TERMS

bleaching	mill marks
chips	refinishing
dents	scratches
gouges	wood dough

After assembling the project, check it carefully to make sure the surfaces are smooth and free from defects. A finish never covers up dents, chips, gouges, or scratches. Instead, these defects will show more clearly after the finish is applied. Fig. 44-1.

REMOVING EXCESS GLUE

Before finishing, remove excess glue around joints and on flat surfaces. Make sure that every fleck of glue has been removed. Glue will not take stain. Use a sharp chisel to remove glue around joints. Fig. 44-2. Remove glue from flat surfaces with a paint scraper or hand scraper. If casein glue has been used, you may need to apply bleach to the glue spots. Certain kinds of casein glue will darken the wood, especially porous woods with an open grain. Bleach these spots before staining. Fig. 44-2.

44-1. Much of the beauty of a project lies in its fine finish.

e laque.
e tous les rebords en cas de rétrécissement.
est suggéré de décoller graduellement.

n outil à lame droite ou d'un chiffon
ner les bulles ou les plis.

de la tablette.

ir un côté puis faire le coin. Répéter pour l'autre côté.

d'intervalle.

à cheveux peut faciliter la tâche.
ces, avec de l'alcool dénaturé ou un nettoyant ménager.
nt. Quand la surface est sèche, aplanir de nouveau le revêtement.

avonneuse. Rincer et bien sécher.

ón. Aclarar y secar totalmente.

ble encojimiento.

ies, se sugiere remover pequeñas partes de cada vez para hacer el trabajo más fácil.

elina o paño.
dor para evitar burbujas de aire o arrugas.

abajo y alrededor de la esquina. Repetir con el otro lado.

Printed in U.S.A. Imprimé aux E.U. Impreso en los EE UU
D.R. © 1992 Rubbermaid Incorporated, Wooster, OH, U.S.A. 44691 6000

ayudar.
vado/artículos de limpieza para el hogar para residuos más resistentes.
superficie debajo del revestimiento. Cuando se haya secado, volver a alisar el revestimiento.

 **CASTON RECYCLES**

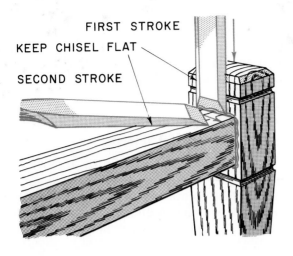

FIRST STROKE

KEEP CHISEL FLAT

SECOND STROKE

44-2. Removing hardened glue around a joint with a sharp chisel. Wipe away as much glue as possible while it is still wet. Hardened glue is difficult to remove.

REMOVING OIL AND GREASE SPOTS

Oil and grease spots will prevent stains from penetrating the wood surface. Remove these spots by rubbing them with naphtha or benzine.

REMOVING MILL MARKS

Mill marks are the uniform ridges that run across the width of planed lumber. These result from the revolving cutter head of a planer or jointer. Most of these marks should have been removed by hand planing as the project is built. However, some may be missed. These must be removed or they will show up after the finish is applied. These mill marks are hard to see. To see them, hold the wood at a very low angle to your eyes. Remove them with several light passes of a sharp plane or by scraping the surface.

CORRECTING DEFECTS

The three most common defects are *shallow dents* (the wood cells have been crushed), *chips* (wood is missing), and *gouges* or *scratches* (the wood cells are severed). Look at the wood surfaces from different angles and under very strong light to find these defects. If it appears there is a defect, highlight it by wiping with a cloth dipped in naphtha or alcohol.

Shallow dents. Often a dent can be raised by applying a drop of water to it. Place a wet cloth or paper towel over dents. Then press with a hot iron. Keep the iron moving so that the wood is not scorched. The moisture in the cloth or paper will raise the dent. Make sure the surface is dry before sanding. Fig. 44-3.

Deep defects. Clean the defect to remove loose or crushed wood fibers. To repair a chip, try to find the splinter and reglue it in place. To repair a deep dent or gouge, fill it properly. First, fill the defect to just below the surface with natural plastic wood or wood putty. Allow it to dry. Fig. 44-4. Then fill the defect with wood dough, plastic wood, stick shellac, or a lacquer stick of a color that matches the wood. These materials come in clear and natural. Plastic wood comes in natural, mahogany, walnut, oak, and other colors. You can make your own filler by mixing equal parts of wood sanding dust and powdered glue. Add water to make a paste. Stick shellac and lacquer stick are flammable.

44-3. Swelling a dent in wood with a damp cloth or paper placed beneath a household iron set on "high." Steam will penetrate the dent and swell it to the surface of the wood.

They should be used only in a well-ventilated room. Place masking tape around the defect to keep the filler from flowing away. Use an electric burn-in knife, soldering iron, or very hot putty knife to apply the material. Apply enough to flow into the defect until it is a little higher than the surrounding areas. Fig. 44-5. After the patch has hardened, remove the tape. Cut off the excess material with a razor blade or sharp knife. Rub with an oiled felt pad dipped in rottenstone or burn the area until it is even with the surface.

44-4. Filling a crack with plastic wood. A natural shade can be tinted with colors in oil. Remember that plastic wood shrinks when it dries, so fill the hole above the level of the wood.

44-5. Filling a crack with stick shellac, using a warm putty knife.

Wood dough, a synthetic wood, can also be used to fill holes and cracks. Fill and sand knots. Then cover them with a knot sealer such as white shellac. If the project is to be painted, filling can be done with putty.

REMOVING HARDWARE FOR FINISHING

Before applying a wood finish, remove all items such as knobs, hinges, locks, and catches that do not require a finish. You may also want to paint or enamel the metal hardware so that everything matches.

REFINISHING

To completely *refinish* wood furniture, you may need to remove all of the old finish. You must do this before bleaching, staining, or other wood finishing operations can be properly carried out. For finish removal, use a good grade of paint and varnish remover. Many brands and types are available. Use a nonflammable, wax-free type. It will be safest and easiest to use. This type eliminates the fire hazard. Also, it leaves no wax residue. Therefore, it does not require after-rinse or neutralizing when the job is done. However, it must still be used with caution. It must be used in a well-ventilated room, since the vapors are harmful. Wear rubber gloves.

Apply the remover with a brush. Spread it on liberally by stroking in only one direction. Fig. 44-6. Apply to one small section at a time. Then allow to soak on the surface until the finish is soft down to the wood. (This may require from 5 to 15 minutes.) When the finish has been thoroughly softened, scrape it off with a dull putty knife. Take care not to gouge or scratch the wood. Fig. 44-7. In some cases, one or more repeat applications may be needed. On carved or grooved surfaces use steel wool, pointed sticks, or an old toothbrush to remove the softened finish.

After removing the old finish, wipe the wood dry with clean cloths. If you used a wax-based remover, an additional rinse with denatured alcohol, turpentine, or a similar solvent will be needed. A new finish can then be applied after bleaching and/or staining.

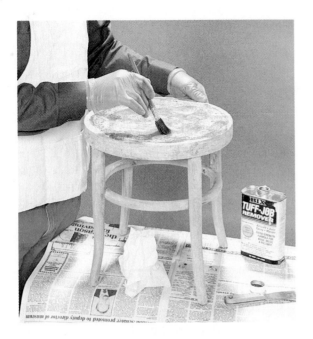

44-6. Applying commercial paint remover to a finish.

BLEACHING

Bleaching is needed only when the color of the wood must be lightened, or when stains must be removed. Use commercially prepared wood bleaches. Most are two solution preparations that must be intermixed or applied in successive steps. Fig. 44-8. All contain strong chemicals, so it is important that you wear rubber gloves to protect your hands. An apron or old clothing should also be worn to protect your clothing.

Apply the bleach with a brush or sponge. Allow it to dry on the surface until the desired effect is reached. The instructions will tell whether neutralization or rinsing is required. Fig. 44-9. After bleaching and rinsing, allow the piece of furniture to dry thoroughly. Then sand it lightly with very fine sandpaper to remove the raised grain. However, do not sand more deeply than the bleach has penetrated.

44-7. Removing the old finish with a dull putty knife. Take care not to damage the wood.

44-8. There are several kinds of bleaches. Some require the application of two liquids—a bleach followed by a neutralizer. Others consist of two liquids that are mixed in equal parts at the same time of use and applied as a single material. Use a glass or porcelain jar for mixing.

44-9. A commercial bleach can be applied with a synthetic rubber sponge or a brush. Remember always to wear rubber gloves to protect your hands when working with bleaches.

FINAL SANDING

The smoother the wood, the finer the finish it will take. Therefore, it is especially important to sand the wood as smooth as possible before applying any finish. Fig. 44-10. Of the different types of sandpaper, open-coat aluminum oxide paper cuts faster and lasts longer. It is generally preferred for sanding furniture. Sand with progressively finer grits, starting with medium or fine (100 to 180) grades. Finish off with very fine (220 to 280).

When sanding, remember to rub with the grain. Sanding across the grain will cause scratches that will show through the finish. On flat surfaces, use a sanding block to prevent unevenness and round edges. For curved or irregular surfaces, tear the paper into strips and use it without a block. Pads of medium to fine steel wool are excellent for smoothing difficult areas. Fig. 44-11.

After sanding, remove dust by wiping the wood with a *tack rag*. This is a cloth that has been treated to attract and hold dust. You can purchase tack rags. You can also make them from lint-free cotton cloth. To make a tack rag, sprinkle the cloth with varnish that has been diluted with about 25 percent turpentine. Fold tightly, then wring the cloth out until it is almost dry.

Review Questions

1. Why must every bit of glue be removed from the project before sanding?
2. When is it necessary to bleach glued surfaces?
3. Name three different kinds of defects.
4. How can shallow dents in wood be raised?
5. What must be done to refinish wood?
6. When must bleaching be done?
7. Why is final sanding important?

44-10. A tack rag, several grades of sandpaper, and a sanding block are needed for final sanding.

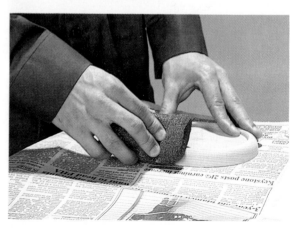

44-11. Steel wool can be used to smooth carved surfaces and other irregular areas that need to be smooth before finishing.

Chapter 45

Staining

After studying this chapter, you will be able to:
- List the two common kinds of oil stains.
- Describe the application of oil stain.
- Describe the application of water stain.
- Describe the way in which synthetic sealers are applied as stains.

LOOK FOR THESE TERMS

penetrating oil stains   synthetic sealers
pigment stains   water stain
staining

Staining is changing the color of wood without changing its texture. This is done by applying transparent or semitransparent liquids made from dyes, pigments, and/or chemicals. Aniline dyes are colors made from aniline oil or coal tar materials. Pigments are fine solid particles used for coloring and adding body to the oil base. Stains are applied to enrich the natural beauty of some woods and to color less expensive woods to resemble the more expensive woods. Fig. 45-1.

To check the color of the stain, apply the stain first to scrap wood of the same kind or to an inconspicuous part of the project. Fig. 45-2. For a true idea of the final color, apply the total finish (filler plus varnish, shellac, oil, or lacquer) to the test spot. If the stain is too dark, lighten it by thinning with turpentine or mineral spirits. If the test area is blotchy or uneven, apply a wash coat of clear penetrating sealer first. Allow this to dry thoroughly before staining.

There are oil stains and water stains.

45-1. The finish on this corner shelf was obtained by applying the right color of stain as a base.

45-2. When staining, check the color of the stain on a spot that will not show when the piece is finished.

Table 45-A. Pigment Colors in Oil for Finishing

Color	Directions
White	Use zinc oxide ground in oil.
Golden oak	Use white zinc tinted with yellow ochre and raw sienna.
Medium oak	Use raw sienna and burnt sienna.
Light brown	Use Vandyke brown.
Dark brown	Use Vandyke brown and drop black.
Walnut	Use half Vandyke brown and half burnt umber.
Black	Use drop black.

OIL STAINS

The two common kinds of oil stains are pigment and penetrating. *Pigment stains* are made by adding color pigments to boiled linseed oil and turpentine. These stains can be purchased ready-mixed in a wide variety of colors. They can also be made in the shop. Table 45-A. *Penetrating oil stains* are made by mixing aniline dyes in oil. These can also be purchased in many different colors. Shades can be made by intermixing stains of the same type or by adding tinting colors. The common colors used to tint oil stains are listed below.

Light yellow	Light green
Medium yellow	Medium green
Raw sienna	Dark green
Burnt sienna	Blue
White	Toluidine red
Raw umber	Deep red
Burnt umber	Chrome orange
Ochre	Lampblack
Orange	

WATER STAIN

A *water stain* is made by mixing aniline dye with hot water. The dye usually comes in powdered form. You can mix water stains yourself. The strength of the stain can be changed by increasing or decreasing the amount of dye.

Water stains also come ready mixed. Water stain has three advantages. It is cheaper than other stains, has a more even color, and is less likely to fade. However, it raises grain.

APPLYING OIL STAIN

Choose the color stain you want and test it on a scrap piece. When you find the right color, mix up enough for the entire job. For example, it will take about 1 pint of stain to cover about 25 square feet of porous wood such as oak.

End grain of wood absorbs more stain than the surface grain. Therefore, it looks darker. To prevent this, soak a lint-free rag in some linseed oil and rub the end grain before applying the stain. Now you are ready to apply the stain to the surface.

Pour out about one-third cup of stain into a porcelain, glass, or enamel container. Use a good brush. A sponge or lint-free rag can be used also, although not as easily.

If possible, apply the stain with the wood held in a horizontal position. This will help avoid streaking caused by gravity flow. Always stain the lower surfaces first, beginning at the corner and working out. To stain a large, flat surface, dip about one-third of the brush into the liquid. Wipe off the excess stain on the side of the jar, and begin at the center of the surface. Fig. 45-3. With light strokes, work out toward the edges, brushing on the stain evenly. With each new brushful, begin on the unfinished surface and stroke toward the stained surface. As you near the edges and ends of the wood, brush carefully to keep from spattering the stain. Apply the stain to one small area at a time. Wipe off the excess with a clean, dry cloth. Fig. 45-4.

45-3. Applying stain. Dip the brush into the stain about one-third of the bristle length. Brush on a uniform coat, following the wood grain.

45-4. After the stain loses its wet appearance and looks flat, wipe lightly until the depth of color or desired effect is obtained. Use a clean, lint-free cloth formed into a pad. Follow the grain of the wood. This will bring out the full beauty of the dark and light highlights of the grain.

One reason oil stains are less satisfactory is that they are slow to dry. Be sure to cover and wipe off the total surface evenly. Allow the work to dry from 12 to 24 hours before continuing with the finishing operation. Then apply a wash coat of shellac (6 parts of alcohol to 1 part shellac). When this is dry, resand lightly with 6/0 sandpaper.

APPLYING WATER STAIN

Before applying water stain, sponge the surface of the wood lightly with water. Do not saturate the surface. After the surface is dry, sand with 2/0 sandpaper. This will help the stain flow on evenly and give a clear, transparent color. Apply the water stain in the same general way as the oil stain. Wipe off the excess with a cloth. Let it dry from 12 to 24 hours. Apply a wash coat of shellac. Then use a small piece of 6/0 sandpaper to sand the surface lightly, removing the high surfaces of the wood. Wipe clean of dust.

USING SYNTHETIC SEALERS AS STAINS

Synthetic sealers can be used for both the stain and the final finish. These sealers give a close-to-the-grain appearance. They are partly penetrating and partly surface finishes. The sealers are usually available in clear and satin. The stain can be made by mixing a tube of tinting color (pigments) with the sealer. For example, ochre added to the sealer produces a pleasing, light walnut stain. The stain is brushed on and then wiped off with a cloth. If necessary, a filler is added.

Sand between coats. Wipe the surface with a tack rag before applying the final coat. The same sealer without the coloring is used as the final finish. With this material, avoid excessive brushing strokes. Flow it on the surface, rather than brushing it on.

Review Questions

1. Name the two common types of oil stains.
2. How can the strength of water stain be varied?
3. Name three advantages of water stain.
4. How can you judge the amount of oil stain needed?
5. Tell how water stain is applied.
6. How can you prevent the end grain of wood from taking up too much stain?
7. Describe the brushing technique for staining.
8. What should be done to prepare the wood surface before applying water stain?
9. Explain how to use a sealer finish as a stain.

Chapter 46

Wood Filler

After studying this chapter, you will be able to:
- Describe the function of fillers in finishing wood.
- Describe the application of paste filler.

LOOK FOR THESE TERMS

filler
liquid filler
paste filler

Fillers are used to seal the pores of wood and to add beauty to the finish. Open-grained woods, such as oak, walnut, chestnut, hickory, pecan, and mahogany, need a medium or heavy paste filler. For closed-grained woods like birch, fir, and pine, the best filler is a *liquid filler* such as shellac. Fig. 46-1.

46-1. The filler needed depends upon the wood used. A paste filler was used on this table.

Paste filler is made of ground silicon, linseed oil, turpentine, drier, and coloring. It comes in a natural color or in colors to match wood stains. The natural can be tinted with oil colors to match the color of the wood (or the stain). It is best, however, to buy the shade you wish to be sure your filler has permanent colors. Most fillers stain the flake of the wood as well as coloring the pores, so stains may not be necessary. The paste is thinned a little with turpentine, but if applied under a lacquer finish, the filler must be thinned with a lacquer thinner. On bleach finishes, white lead or pure zinc paste is sometimes the filler. Either of these can be colored by adding burnt umber, raw sienna, or other pigment. The types of fillers needed for various woods are listed in Table 46-A.

Add turpentine until the paste is a thin cream. Remember, the filler should be thick for open-grained woods such as oak, elm, or chestnut. It should be thinner for medium open-grained woods like cherry, red gum, soft maple, and redwood. If the filler is to be applied over a stained surface, apply a wash coat of shellac (1 part shellac to 6 or 7 parts of alcohol) on the stain to prevent any bleeding. Then sand the surface with No. 6/0 sandpaper before the filler is applied.

Table 46-A. Paste Fillers for Various Woods

No Filler Needed	Thin Filler*	Medium Filler	Heavy Filler
Basswood	Beech	Butternut	Ash
Cedar	Birch	Korina	Chestnut
Cypress	Cherry	Mahogany	Elm
Ebony	Gum	Rosewood	Hickory
Fir	Maple	Walnut	Lauan (Philippine
Pine		Zebrawood	mahogany)
Poplar			Oak
Redwood			Teakwood
Spruce			

*Liquid filler may also be used.

Apply paste filler with a stiff brush, thoroughly covering the surface. Brush first with the grain, then across it. Do not cover too large an area at one time, as the filler dries very rapidly. Rub in the paste filler with the palm of your hand, going over the entire surface in a circular motion. Allow the filler to dry (about 20 minutes) until the surface loses its wet, shiny appearance.

To test for proper dryness, drag your finger across the surface. If a ball is formed, it is time to wipe. If the filler slips under the pressure of your finger, it is still too wet for wiping. Wiping too soon will drag the filler from the pores. Allowing it to set too long will make it very difficult to wipe off the excess.

When the filler is ready for wiping, rub off the excess by wiping across the grain with a pad of burlap or other coarse cloth. Rub with a circular motion, trying to force the filler into the pores. Rub across the grain until you have removed practically all excess filler. Then finish up by giving a final light wipe with the grain, using a clean cloth. Allow filler to dry 24 hours or more before continuing.

Burn used rags or store them in a fireproof container.

Review Questions

1. Name the two kinds of wood filler.
2. What kind of filler is applied to open-grained woods?
3. What solvent is used to thin filler?
4. What filler is chosen for modern bleached finishes?
5. How can you make a wash coat of shellac?

Chapter 47

Shellac

After studying this chapter, you will be able to:
- Describe the manufacture of shellac.
- List three main uses for shellac.
- List the main steps in applying a shellac finish.

LOOK FOR THESE TERMS

cut	shellac
lac	wash coat
sealer	

Shellac is a resinous substance (lac) from the lac bug. The lac is ground and mixed in denatured alcohol. Standard shellac, called a 4-pound (1.8 kg) *cut*, is a mixture of 4 pounds (1.8 kg) to a gallon (3.8 litres) of alcohol.

Shellac is a good finish because it is easy to apply, dries quickly, and produces a hard surface. It is not good for wood that is to be exposed to moisture. Shellac turns a cloudy color in dampness. Shellac is frequently used as a finish by itself. It is also used as a sealer over a stain or filler coat before varnish is applied. It is also applied to knots before painting to seal in the *pitch* (resin in the wood). Fig. 47-1.

Natural shellac is orange and provides a tough finish. However, natural shellac gives to many light woods an unattractive, yellow-orange tint. Shellac in a bleached form is called white shellac. This is more satisfactory for general use.

SHELLAC USES

Shellac is used as a sealer, a wash coat, and a top coat.

Sealer. A *sealer* forms a barrier between coats. A sealer is used as a first coat on closed-grained woods and over the filler on open-grained woods. When thinned, shellac forms an excellent, tough, softwood sealer under other finishes (except polyurethane). For a sealer use a mixture of one part shellac (4-pound cut) to two parts of alcohol.

47-1. Applying shellac over a wood knot. This seals the knot and prevents resin in the wood from leaking out and discoloring the paint or enamel.

Wash coat. A *wash coat* is a thin solution of shellac applied over stain. This coat enriches the stain and stiffens the fibers of the wood so they can be easily sanded. In some cases, a wash coat is applied to bare wood to prevent succeeding coats from discoloring it.

Top coat. Shellac produces a strong, smooth, and durable finish. It is flexible enough to resist marring. It dries so quickly that it is dustproof within minutes. Other coats can be applied within hours. It is a good finish for all interior projects except tabletops, where water or alcohol will discolor it. Fig. 47-2.

APPLYING A SHELLAC FINISH

The wood should be wiped clean with a lint-free cloth that has been dipped in alcohol. Pour a small amount of shellac into a glass or porcelain container. Add an *equal* amount of alcohol to thin it.

It is far better to apply several thin coats than a few heavy coats. Thinned shellac sinks into the surface providing a smoother finish. Apply the shellac with a clean varnish brush about 1½ to 3 inches wide. Dip about one-third of the brush length into the shellac and wipe off the sides of the brush on the container. Begin at the center of a flat surface or near the top of a vertical surface and work out toward the edges. Work quickly and evenly, taking light, long strokes. Do not brush over the same surface several times, as shellac dries very rapidly and becomes sticky.

On the edges, be careful to keep the shellac from piling up and running. After the entire surface has been covered, soak the brush in pure alcohol. Allow the project to dry 2 to 4 hours.

Now go over it with steel wool or 5/0 sandpaper. *Rub with the grain of the wood.* Steel wool will follow the surface better and cover both high and low spots. If sandpaper is used, hold it in your fingers.

47-2. Shellac is an excellent finish for projects such as this rocking chair.

Before applying the second coat, wipe the surface with a clean tack rag. This second coat is applied the same way as the first coat but may have only about 40 percent alcohol. Again, go over the surface with steel wool or sandpaper. Then apply a third coat with even less alcohol, perhaps 25 percent.

After the last coat, rub the surface lightly with fine sandpaper. To get a very even, smooth surface, mix some ground pumice in oil. Rub down the surface with a felt pad. After this, a still smoother surface can be obtained by mixing rottenstone with oil and rubbing it in.

Clean the surface with a clean cloth dipped in benzine. Allow it to dry about one-half hour. Apply a good coat of wax and let it dry thoroughly. Then rub briskly with a soft cloth.

Clean the shellac brush immediately with alcohol.

Review Questions

1. What is the source of shellac?
2. How is shellac made?
3. What is meant by a 4-pound cut?
4. What is the natural color of shellac?
5. Why is bleached shellac available?
6. Describe the special brushing technique for applying shellac.
7. List the steps to follow in applying a shellac finish.

Facts about Wood

The Making of Shellac

Shellac is a preparation of lac dissolved in acetone or alcohol. *Lac* is a resinous secretion that comes from the body of a small insect. Common to India, this insect is found also in Southeast Asia. India is the principal source of the world's shellac.

Lac is obtained by a relatively simple process. The female insects eat the sap that flows from certain tropical trees. (In some regions, these trees are cultivated to attract the insects.) The insects then release a sticky substance. This substance hardens around the mother insect and its young. It forms a protective capsule, fixing the insects fast to the twig.

This lac encrusted on the wood is then scraped away by hand. Known as *stick lac*, this is lac in its crudest form. This stick lac is crushed. Foreign matter such as bits of twigs and leaf particles are then removed. The shellac is still, however, colored with a red coloring matter produced by the lac-producing insects. This red matter is filtered out. The filtered and purified lac is then dried. Dried, it is known as *seed lac*.

Seed lac is melted and filtered again. It is then poured out to dry in thin sheets. After being dried, the sheets are broken into flakes. Shellac is made from these flakes by dissolving them in alcohol. While you may be familiar with the use of shellac in furniture finishing, you may not know of its other uses. Shellac is, for example, an ingredient in several products, such as abrasives and hair sprays. Before 1930, it was used to make molds for phonograph records. In that use, though, it has now been replaced by various plastics.

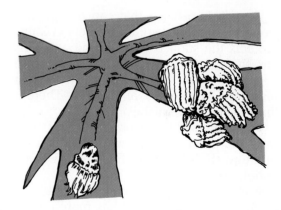

Chapter 48

Varnish

After studying this chapter, you will be able to:
● List the characteristics of each of the three common varnishes.
● List the basic steps in applying a varnish finish.

LOOK FOR THESE TERMS

alkyd resin
arris
phenolic resin
polyurethane varnish

spar varnish
varnish
varnish stain

Varnish is a finish that can be spread on wood to form an even, transparent coating. It protects the surface of the wood and brightens the color of the stain. Varnishes are a combination of natural and synthetic resins dissolved in thinners and driers. There are three common varnishes:

● *Alkyd resin* (soya or linseed oil) is the most common prepared varnish. It is a good furniture varnish that is resistant to water, alcohol, and other liquids.

● *Phenolic resin* is commonly called *spar varnish*. It is tougher and has more moisture resistance than alkyd varnishes. It is excellent for finishing outdoor furniture and sports equipment. These varnishes yellow and darken with age, therefore they are not good for fine indoor furniture.

● *Polyurethane varnish* is closer to being a true plastic than any other synthetic finish. It gives a finish that is extremely durable and flexible.

Varnishes are available in high gloss, medium gloss, satin finish, and flat. The number of coats determines the "depth" and smoothness of the finish. Fig. 48-1.

APPLYING VARNISH

Find a dust-free place. If no finishing room is available, wait to do varnishing until no woodworking machines or tools have been used for some time. Then sprinkle the floor with water to settle the dust. Also, do not varnish anything on cold and damp or hot and humid days. Make sure that the temperature is between 70 and 80 degrees Fahrenheit (21 and 27 degrees Celsius). Wipe the project completely with a tack rag to remove dust.

48-1. A varnish finish can be used successfully on a small accessory.

Open a small can of quick-drying (synthetic-resin) varnish. Pour some into a porcelain or glass container. For a first coat, add about 25 percent turpentine. Select a 2- to 3-inch brush with long bristles.

Dip the brush in the varnish to about one-third the length of the brush. Do not overload it. *Do not wipe the brush on the side of the can.* The varnish will dry on the rim and on the inside. Apply the varnish with long, easy strokes. Brush first with the grain and then across the grain. Figs. 48-2 and 48-3. When the brush is "dry," brush out the varnish with the grain, using only the tip of the brush. You can do more brushing out with varnish than you can with shellac. Continue to brush from the center toward the outside edges. As you near the edges, have very little varnish on the brush. This will keep it from running over the edges or from piling up along the corners.

After applying the first coat, soak the brush in turpentine. Also, cover the varnish left in the can to keep scum from forming. Allow the varnish coat to dry about 24 hours or until all tackiness has gone. After it is dry, rub the surface with the grain, using No. 6/0 sandpaper.

Make sure that the varnish is perfectly dry before applying another coat.

For the second and third coats of varnish, use the varnish just as it comes from the can. Lightly sand each dried coat before applying the next one. Do this sanding with a very fine grade of aluminum oxide paper, or with "super-fine" (#400) waterproof sandpaper. Use aluminum oxide paper after the first coat is dry. Use waterproof paper after the second coat is dry. With the latter, soapy water is often used as a lubricant.

Very fine steel wool can also be used between coats of varnish.

Always sand the finish by working parallel with the grain. Sand with *light* pressure only. Use just enough pressure to dull the sheen and produce a uniform, satin-smooth finish. When sanding is complete, wipe with a tack rag before applying the next coat.

48-3. Brush across the grain to level out the varnish.

48-2. Apply varnish generously, brushing with the wood grain.

FINAL RUBBING

No matter how carefully it is applied, the final coat of varnish may have a few dust specks or "pimples" to mar its finished appearance. If a high-gloss furniture varnish was used, it may also have too much gloss. Correct these conditions by a final rubbing and polishing with special abrasives.

Before the final rubbing, allow the last coat of varnish to harden for about one week. When ready, mix a paste of powdered pumice stone and oil, such as machine oil. Do not use linseed or drying oils. Then rub with a folded pad of heavy, lint-free cloth or a felt pad. Rub with straight strokes, parallel to the grain. Use only moderate pressure. Continue until the surface feels perfectly smooth. Then wipe off all remaining powder and oil with a clean, dry cloth.

To restore the high luster that some prefer, a second rubbing or polishing is required with a still finer powdered abrasive. Mix a second paste of powdered rottenstone and crude oil. Again, rub in parallel strokes following the grain. After polishing the surface to the luster desired, wipe off all paste and oil. Do this by rubbing repeatedly with clean cloths until the surface is so dry that it "squeaks" when rubbed.

After the varnish has dried thoroughly, apply a good paste wax. Polish with a clean piece of cheesecloth.

VARNISH STAINS

A *varnish stain* will give the desired color and finish in one coat. Varnish stain finish is especially satisfactory for simple woodworking projects. It is also useful when time cannot be given to applying many coats of regular varnish. Varnish stains can be purchased in different colors. Apply these stains in the same way as varnish. Drying time varies between 2 and 8 hours.

Review Questions

1. What is the most common prepared varnish?
2. Should spar varnish be used for indoor furniture?
3. What conditions must prevail to obtain a good varnish surface?
4. Describe the technique for applying varnish.
5. List the steps to follow in applying a varnish finish.
6. How can a dull finish be obtained?
7. What is a varnish stain? Why is it commonly used by beginners?

Chapter 49

Oil and Wipe-On Finishes

After studying this chapter, you will be able to:
● List three natural oils that are used for finishing.
● List the steps in the application of a French-style oil finish.
● List three commercial penetrating oil finishes and discuss their qualities.

LOOK FOR THESE TERMS

commercial salad bowl finish
French-style oil finish
linseed oil

penetrating resin-oil
tung oil

Oil finishes and penetrating resin-oil finishes such as Watco® and Minwax® add a finish *in the wood*, not on the surface. These oil finishes emphasize the grain and leave a flat, natural appearance. They darken slightly with age and take on a rich glow. Most can be applied with a small soft cloth, brush, sponge, or pad. These finishes do away with the dust problem. These finishes can be natural oils or commercially prepared penetrating finishes that become permanently hardened. Fig. 49-1.

NATURAL OILS

Linseed oil is a yellowish oil obtained by crushing the seeds of flax. After heating and filtering, the raw material becomes raw linseed oil. When heated to higher temperatures so as to admit small amounts of metallic driers, the oil becomes boiled linseed oil. Boiled linseed oil can be used as a final finish. It is applied after bleaching or staining (if either of these steps is required). It tends to darken wood in most cases. Though not highly water-resistant, a linseed oil finish will withstand hot dishes. It is also less likely to show scratches than a varnish finish.

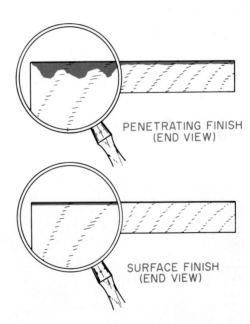

49-1. These two drawings show the difference between a penetrating finish and a surface finish.

Spread the oil liberally over the surface with a thick pad or folded cloth. Fig. 49-2. Allow this to soak in until no more is absorbed by the wood. This may take from a few minutes to an hour. Then rub again with the same pad, working additional oil into the pores of the wood. Then wipe off surplus oil with a clean cloth. Allow to dry overnight. Then repeat the process. The more coats applied, the more attractive and durable the finish. A minimum of three coats is recommended. This finish may turn sticky in damp weather. Store used rags in a fireproof container.

When finishing open-grained woods like oak or walnut, filling the pores will create a smoother finish. Apply the first coat. While it is still wet, sand the surface with 400-grit waterproof abrasive paper. This will produce a slurry of wood dust and finish that will fill the pores of the wood. After sanding, allow the finish to dry about 20 minutes. Then wipe off the excess slurry with the grain. Some of the slurry will remain in the wood's pores. Allow this coat to dry overnight. Then apply one or more coats. This procedure can be followed with all wipe-on finishes.

Tung oil is obtained by pressing the nuts of the tung tree, which grows in China. This oil is not used in the raw state because it dries to a flat nonlustrous film. However, when it is heat-treated it dries to a gloss finish. It penetrates deep into the wood and forms a long-lasting moisture barrier. It can be applied in the same way as boiled linseed oil.

Vegetable oils can be used on eating utensils, but these become rancid and can affect the taste of food. Use a *commercial salad bowl finish* that is odorless, tasteless, and will not spoil. These finishes are approved by the U.S. Food and Drug Administration for use on wood tableware such as salad bowls and cutting boards. This finish is excellent for wooden toys. The main ingredients are tung oil and alkyd resins.

COMMERCIAL PENETRATING OIL FINISHES

Resins, driers, thinners, and natural oils have been combined into commercial penetrating oil finishes. These are easy to use and give a beautiful finish.

Minwax® is a penetrating finish, a combination wood seal and wax. It is applied directly to raw wood. Two coats will complete the job. The natural beauty of the wood is preserved because this finish penetrates and seals. The finish is in the wood, with very little on the surface. Minwax® is available in natural, light oak, pine, dark walnut, colonial maple, and red mahogany. It dries rapidly. This makes it possible to apply more than one coat in a day. This finish does not need to be rubbed after each coat. However, by rubbing with 4/0 steel wool, a very fine finish can be obtained.

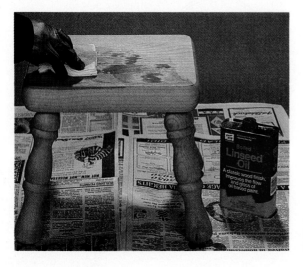

49-2. Use a pad soaked in boiled linseed oil to apply the finish. Wear thin plastic gloves to protect your hands.

Watco® Danish oil finish is a penetrating resin-oil. This finish improves the wood without hours of hand rubbing. Danish oil requires only a simple application. It is long lasting and it seldom needs replenishing. One of its big advantages is that a marred surface is relatively simple to refinish.

Apply Danish oil finish as follows:
1. After sanding, apply a quick-dry, alcohol (or water-base) wood stain with a clean cloth or brush.
2. Let stand to dry for about 45 minutes.
3. Apply liberal amounts of the oil.
4. Allow the oil to soak into the wood for about 30 minutes, or until penetration stops. Flow on another coat, allowing it to penetrate for about 15 minutes.
5. Wipe the surface completely dry with a soft, absorbent cloth.
6. For more luster, let the surface dry for 4 hours.
7. Dry the wood thoroughly with a clean cloth.
8. Polish briskly with another cloth.
9. For additional sheen, apply a stain wax after the oil has dried about 24 hours.

OTHER SIMPLE FINISHES

Deft is a semigloss, clear, interior wood finish made of tung oil with urethane (plastic) for greater durability. It is easy to use and requires no thinning. This material seals, primes, finishes the wood, and dries in 30 minutes. Three coats are recommended. The first coat seals the wood. The second adds depth. The third coat results in a mirror-smooth, fine furniture finish. The third coat can be sanded with 6/0 wet-or-dry sandpaper or rubbed mirror-smooth with pumice and rottenstone. All three coats can be applied in a few hours. Deft can also be applied from an aerosol spray can.

Sealacell® is a three-step process requiring three different materials to complete the finish. Each can be applied with a cloth. The materials are as follows:
1. Sealacell® is a moisture-repellent, penetrating wood sealer that is applied over the raw wood. (Ground-in-oil pigments can be mixed with the Sealacell® to serve as a stain). Stain and filler can be applied in one step by mixing paste filler in the Sealacell® and then adding ground-in-oil pigment to get the desired color. Apply very liberally with a cloth. The depth of penetration depends upon the amount applied. Let dry overnight. Buff lightly with fine steel wool.
2. *Varno-wax* is a blend of gums and waxes. To apply, make a small cloth pad about 1 × 2 inches. Coat with wax. Rub first with a circular motion. Then wipe out with the grain. Buff lightly with 3/0 steel wool.
3. *Royal finish* is the final coat. It is applied in the same manner as Varno-wax. Two or more applications of Royal finish increase the depth and luster. A soft, eggshell finish can be obtained by buffing the finish with fine steel wool.

Review Questions

1. Tell how to apply a linseed oil finish.
2. Why is tung oil not used in the raw state?
3. List the steps in the application of a Sealacell® finish.
4. How many coats of Deft should be used?
5. List the steps in the application of a Danish oil finish.

Chapter 50

After studying this chapter, you will be able to:
- List the steps in the application of a clear lacquer finish.
- Identify the pieces of spraying equipment needed for the spray application of lacquer.
- Describe the proper technique for spraying a project, listing the important steps.

LOOK FOR THESE TERMS

air compressor	lacquer thinner
air transformer	respirator
brushing lacquer	spray booth
fluid needle adjustment screw	spray gun
lacquer	spreader adjustment valve

Lacquer is a finish composed of nitrocellulose, resins, and solvents. Lacquers are sold in both clear and colored forms. Fig. 50-1. They dry quickly and produce a hard finish. Most commercial lacquer finishes are applied by spraying, but the brush finish is usually done in most small shops. Always use *lacquer thinner* for thinning the materials and for cleaning the brushes.

APPLYING A CLEAR LACQUER FINISH

1. Apply the stain and filler coats the same as you would for shellac and varnish finishes. It is better to use a water stain than an oil stain. A water stain will not bleed so much. Apply a thin coat of lacquer sealer before using the lacquer.
2. Open a can of clear, brushing lacquer and stir it well. Lacquer usually does not have to be thinned. If it does, use lacquer thinner of the same brand. Select a brush with soft bristles, such as a camel's-hair brush. Dip it about one-third of the way into the lacquer, but do not wipe it on the side of the container. Load the brush heavily. Ap-

50-1. A clear lacquer finish brings out the grain in wood objects.

ply with long, rapid strokes. Lap the sides of each stroke. Do not attempt to brush the lacquer in as you would paint or varnish. Remember that lacquer dries very quickly.

3. Allow the lacquer to dry about 2 hours. Then go over the surface lightly with No. 6/0 sandpaper.
4. Apply the second and third coats in the same way. After the third coat is dry, rub and polish the surface.

APPLYING A COLORED (OPAQUE) LACQUER FINISH

Sand the wood surface with No. 2/0 sandpaper. Then apply a thin coat of shellac to the wood as a base for the lacquer. Apply two or three coats of the colored lacquer. To finish the surface, rub it down with rottenstone and oil after the lacquer is dry.

USING AEROSOL PRODUCTS

Many finishing materials—including lacquers, paints, and enamels—are available in *aerosol (spray) cans*. Read the directions on the can carefully. Some aerosols require shaking, while others do not. Most are held upright when using the product, but some are not. Fig. 50-2.

GENERAL SUGGESTIONS

- Place the item to be sprayed on a bench that has been covered with newspapers.
- Do the spraying in a well-ventilated room or outdoors.
- Start at the front (side nearest you) and spray back and forth, moving towards the rear.
- Overlap each stroke. Turn the project a quarter of a turn and spray again. Spray several light coats rather than one heavy one. Fig. 50-3.

- When finished, turn the can upside down. Press the spray head for a few seconds to clean out the line. If the spray head becomes clogged, remove it. Use a pin to clean out the small opening and a knife to clean out the small slot at the bottom. Fig. 50-4.

APPLYING LACQUER FROM AN AEROSOL CAN

The aerosol can contains about half lacquer and half liquid gas. In using a spray can, hold it so the valve is about 12 to 15 inches from the surface. Move the can back and forth, keeping it an equal distance from the surface. If sags or runs develop, you are covering the surface too quickly. Remember that the hiding power of lacquers varies with the color. If you are spraying light-colored lacquer, apply a series of several light coats.

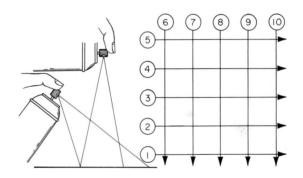

50-3. Here is the pattern for spray painting. Spray as shown in steps 1 through 5. Then turn the work one-quarter turn to the left and repeat.

50-4. Cleaning the spray head. Another method is to soak it in the proper solvent.

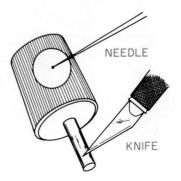

50-2. Do not hold this spray can in a horizontal position since the tube must always be in the liquid.

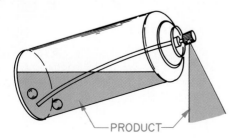

SPRAYING EQUIPMENT

The spray method is most commonly used in industry. Typical equipment used in a well-equipped school laboratory consists of the following:

● An *air compressor* takes the air at atmospheric pressure and delivers it at a higher pressure through pipe and hose to operate a spray gun. Fig. 50-5. The high air pressure breaks up the finishing material into a fine spray.

● A *metal pipe* or an *air hose* connects the compressor to the transformer.

● An *air transformer* removes all the oil, dirt, and moisture from the compressed air. It also filters and regulates the air.

● A *hose* carries the air from the transformer to the spray gun.

● The finishing material is fed through a *spray gun* by means of a suction cup attached directly to the gun. A suction- or siphon-fed gun, on which a container is directly mounted, uses a stream of compressed air to create a vacuum. Fig. 50-6.

● Spraying should be done in a *spray booth* whenever possible. The dry spray booth is found mainly in smaller shops.

There, quick-drying material like lacquer is used and spraying is not done continuously. Fig. 50-7.

● A *respirator* or *mask* is worn over the nose and mouth to prevent inhaling finishing materials. The organic vapor mask that covers only the nose and mouth is the most common. It comes with replaceable cartridges that remove the organic vapors.

● The simplest spraying equipment consists of a small portable compressor, a length of air hose, and a suction-fed spray gun. Fig. 50-8.

When there is no spray booth, the spraying must be done outdoors on a very quiet day. The operator must wear a respirator.

USING A SPRAY GUN IN A BOOTH

If a small portable unit is being used, lacquer is usually thinned half and half with lacquer thinner. For spray outfits that have greater air pressure, lacquer can be used just as it comes from the can.

50-5. This compressor and storage tank is the stationary type, commonly found in school and industrial shops. Portable units also are available.

50-6. With a suction- or siphon-fed gun, the compressed air passes over the fluid tube inside the nozzle, creating a vacuum that draws the finishing material up from the container. A suction-fed gun always has an air hole in the paint container cover. This type is recommended for finer atomization where an extra-fine finish is required.

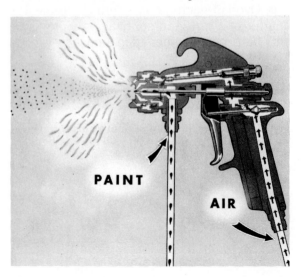

PAINT

AIR

There are two common adjustments on the suction-fed spray gun. The *fluid needle adjustment screw* controls the amount of fluid flow. Flow can also be controlled by limiting the amount the trigger is pulled. The *spreader adjustment valve* changes the spray pattern.

SPRAYING TECHNIQUES

1. Hold the gun about 6 to 8 inches from the surface being sprayed. This distance can be determined by following the technique shown in Fig. 50-9.
2. Move your arm, not your wrist, when spraying. Keep the gun at right angles to the surface at all points along the stroke. Fig. 50-10.

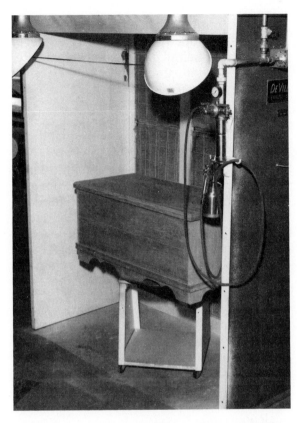

50-7. The dry booth is simpler to install and is most common in school shops. Note the transformer mounted on the right side of the booth.

50-8. A portable spraying unit is satisfactory for small projects.

50-9. Keep the spray gun the correct distance from the surface.

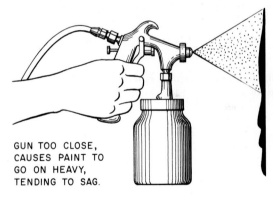

GUN TOO CLOSE, CAUSES PAINT TO GO ON HEAVY, TENDING TO SAG.

GUN TOO FAR AWAY, CAUSES EXCESSIVE DUSTING AND A SANDY FINISH.

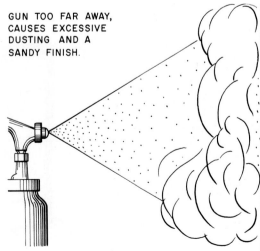

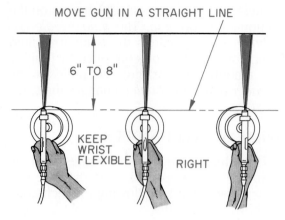

MOVE GUN IN A STRAIGHT LINE

6" TO 8"

KEEP WRIST FLEXIBLE

RIGHT

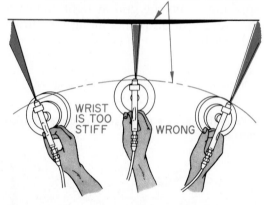

ARCING GIVES AN UNEVEN COATING

WRIST IS TOO STIFF

WRONG

50-10. Move the spray gun in a straight line, never in an arc.

3. Feather out the ends of the stroke by triggering the gun. To trigger correctly, begin the stroke before pulling the trigger. Release it before ending the stroke. Never move the gun in an arc. This will make the spray uneven.
4. Spray corners by holding the gun so that these surfaces will be sprayed equally and at the same time. Fig. 50-11.
5. Overlap strokes about 50 percent as the gun moves back and forth across the surface. This will eliminate the need for double strokes or cross strokes. Fig. 50-12.
6. When spraying curved surfaces, use the same spraying techniques as for other surfaces. Use vertical strokes for small-diameter surfaces, such as table legs. Use horizontal strokes with a curved motion when spraying larger, rounded surfaces. Fig. 50-13.

SPRAYING A PROJECT

1. Clean the surface with a tack rag.
2. Check the gun to make sure that it is clean.

50-11. Spray the edges and corners in "bands" before spraying the flat surfaces. Aim the gun directly at an edge so that the adjoining surfaces receive equal amounts. Hold the gun from 5 to 7 inches from a corner and aim so that each side receives an equal amount of spray.

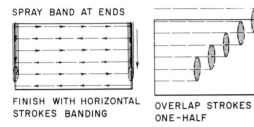

SPRAY BAND AT ENDS

FINISH WITH HORIZONTAL
STROKES BANDING

OVERLAP STROKES
ONE-HALF

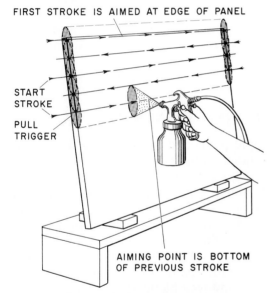

FIRST STROKE IS AIMED AT EDGE OF PANEL

START
STROKE

PULL
TRIGGER

AIMING POINT IS BOTTOM
OF PREVIOUS STROKE

50-12. Banding. Vertical bands sprayed at the ends of a panel prevent wasted spray from the horizontal strokes. When spraying a panel, use alternate right and left strokes. Release the trigger before the end of each stroke. Spray long work in sections of convenient length, each section overlapping the previous one by 4 inches.

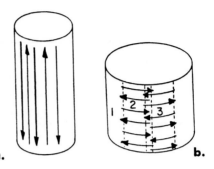

a.   b.

50-13. Use vertical strokes for small-diameter curved surfaces. Use horizontal strokes for large-diameter curved surfaces.

3. Fill the spray container about half full of lacquer and one-fourth full of lacquer thinner.
4. Test the spray gun on a piece of scrap stock or wrapping paper. It should spray with a fine, even mist.
5. Spray on four or five coats of thin lacquer. Usually the first two coats are gloss or bright. The last two coats are made dull or semigloss by rubbing.
6. After you have finished spraying, clean all the equipment with lacquer thinner.

Review Questions

1. What is lacquer?
2. Can lacquer be applied over a painted or varnished surface?
3. How is lacquer most often applied commercially?
4. Describe the correct brushing technique for applying lacquer.
5. Describe the correct method for spraying.

Chapter 51

Paints and Enamels

After studying this chapter, you will be able to:
● List the two basic ingredients in all paints and enamels.
● List the basic steps in applying paint or enamel.

LOOK FOR THESE TERMS

cool colors
enamel
flat
gloss
high gloss

latex paint
oil-based paint
opaque finish
paint

pigment
semigloss
vehicle
warm colors

Paints and enamels are *opaque finishes*. This means that they cannot be seen through. They cover the wood. Paints and enamels are used to cover less expensive woods and to add beauty to a project. All paints and enamels consist of a *pigment* (the color) in a *vehicle* (the liquid). There are two basic types, *oil-based* and *latex* (latex acrylic), which is water-based. Oil-based can be thinned with a *solvent* such as turpentine or mineral spirits. Latex paints and enamels are easier to apply. Also the brushes and other tools can be cleaned with water. Paints are available in *flat*, *semigloss*, and *gloss* finish. (*Gloss* refers to the amount of surface brightness. Flat paint, for example, has little gloss.)

Enamels are *high-gloss* paints, either latex or oil-based. Enamels are easily washed. Therefore they are used for most small projects. Enamels and paints are also available in aerosol-spray cans that make it easy to spray-paint small projects.

Paints and enamels are available in a wide range of colors—literally thousands of colors if the paints are custom-mixed at the store. Remember that reds, yellows, and oranges are *warm colors*. Blues and greens are *cool colors* that are calm and restful.

APPLYING PAINTS AND ENAMELS

Apply paint and enamel by following the directions on the can.
● Prepare the wood by sanding, scraping, and filling dents so that the surface is smooth.
● If the directions call for a primer coat, use a type that matches the final coat. Do not mix oil- and water-based paints and enamels.
● Stir the paint or enamel until it is smooth and well blended.
● If the paint or enamel needs to be thinned, use the recommended thinner.
● Apply the paint or enamel with a brush that is full, but not dripping. Use long, even strokes. The surface should be well covered. Do not apply too much paint or enamel. This will cause the paint to run on the surface. Figs. 51-1 and 51-2.
● Allow the surface to dry thoroughly. Sand smooth with fine sandpaper. Clean with a cloth to remove the dust.
● Apply the second coat in the same manner, but do not sand the final coat.

51-1. Dip the brush into the paint at least one-third the length of the bristles. When the brush is well filled, remove and tap lightly against the inside of the can.

● When painting two or more colors on the same project, use masking tape for color separation. Masking tape eliminates the time-consuming job of clean-up. The tape is readily stripped off afterwards.

ENAMELING FURNITURE

Remove all knobs and handles. Finish these separately, using a small brush. Fig. 51-3. Always paint the hard-to-reach furniture parts first—legs, cross spindles, and backs.

TABLES

Begin by turning the table upside-down and painting the bottom and its edges. Then paint the legs. Paint the inner sides first. Finish them with smooth, lengthwise strokes. When enameling round or turned legs or braces, brush around them without finishing with lengthwise strokes. Turn the table right side up. Enamel all the top edges and frame sides. Finally, finish the tabletop, enameling across the narrowest dimension. Follow with long, light strokes the length of the tabletop. Use only the tip of the brush to achieve a smooth, even finish.

51-2. Hold the brush comfortably near the base of the handle, exerting light pressure with your fingertips. Do not bear down. Exert only enough pressure to flex the bristles slightly toward the top as you begin the brush stroke.

51-3. Finish all knobs at the same time, using a small brush.

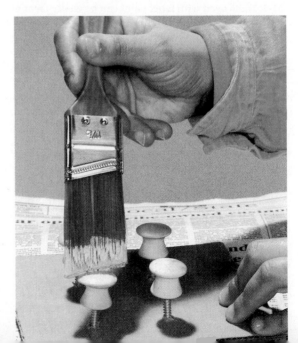

CHAIRS

Turn the chair upside-down. Place the seat of the chair on a box or table. Paint all bottom surfaces, seat bottom, legs, and cross braces. Stand the chair upright. Enamel all top surfaces, finishing with the seat.

51-4. Tools used with latex paint can be easily cleaned in water. Tools used with oil-based paint are cleaned with paint brush cleaner.

CHESTS AND CABINETS

Remove any drawers. Paint the moldings (if any) surrounding trim panels. Then paint the panels, picking up any runs or sags at the corners. Paint the frame and then the top, using a cross-brushing technique.

In painting drawers, first paint the sides about 6 inches back from the front panel. Next, paint all exposed edges and the front panel. (If painting the entire drawer inside, do that before the exposed edges and the front.) Stack all painted drawers with the bottom edges in an upright position.

Clean brushes and other tools used in latex paint and enamel by rinsing them well in warm, soapy water. Fig. 51-4.

Review Questions

1. How does enamel differ from paint?
2. Name the two basic kinds of paints.
3. Why is a gloss enamel best for most small projects?
4. List the order in which the parts of a table are painted.

Facts about Wood

The Violins of Stradivari

Wood is used to make musical instruments. Many musical instruments are made entirely or partially of wood. Some of these instruments, such as the guitar and the violin, are known as *stringed instruments*. A stringed instrument produces sound by means of vibrating strings. On a guitar, the strings are plucked. The strings on a violin are played with a bow.

The making of fine stringed instruments is a difficult craft. The work of the best instrument makers has always been prized. Formerly, as today, the best instruments were made entirely by hand. One of the most famous and skilled violin makers was Antonio Stradivari (1644-1737). An Italian, he made his finest violins around 1700. In his long career, he made about 540 violins, as well as other stringed instruments. These include violas and cellos. He was recognized as a master violin maker in his own lifetime. For example, James II of England and Charles III of Spain commissioned him to make violins. His violins are now worth hundreds of thousands of dollars. Today, a violin made by Stradivari is a priceless possession of some concert violinists.

Stradivari was an innovator. He set the proportions for the modern violin. The violins made by Stradivari have never been surpassed for sweetness of tone. Though modern violin makers have sought to imitate the instruments made by Stradivari, they have not been entirely successful. The quality of his violins depended, of course, on several factors. Among these were the type of wood, its grain, and the varnish used. Stradivari used woods such as well-aged spruce, maple, sycamore, and rosewood. The wood is important. This is known by modern violin makers,

who prefer to use wood that has been aged from 20 to 60 years. The excellence of Stradivari's violins depended on other factors, as well. Many think that the excellence of tone in a Stradivari violin results from the special varnish that was used. Modern violin makers have been unable to duplicate this varnish.

Violins are still made by hand. There are, in fact, small schools where people can begin a program of apprenticeship in violin-making. In these schools, students average about 30 hours a week in the shop. They also study a musical instrument and attend concerts and recitals. This apprenticeship program can last two years. There may then be a period of probation. This might be followed by courses in the making of violin bows, guitars, and other stringed instruments.

Chapter 52

Antiquing

After studying this chapter, you will be able to:
● Identify the characteristics of a surface treated by antiquing.
● List the basic steps in the antiquing process.

LOOK FOR THESE TERMS

antiquing
color glazing

Antiquing is a refinishing method that develops a soft, mellow surface tone normally associated with age and many hours of hand rubbing. Antiquing is sometimes called *color glazing*. It is one of the simplest and most attractive wood finishes that can be applied. Fig. 52-1. Because it is opaque, it can be used successfully on relatively inexpensive woods like pine and poplar.

Antiquing is done in two simple steps. First, a paintlike undercoat is applied to cover the entire project (including any old paint or varnish). This provides a base color for the second step—the application of the color glaze. Wood tones and other special effects are achieved by wiping or texturing the color glaze before it dries. The result is a soft-toned luster plus a tough finish. For added protection, a finish coat of varnish can be applied.

Antiquing can be used on chests, tables, picture frames, and almost all decorative items.

52-1. This small chairside chest has an antique white finish with gold inserts.

PROCEDURE FOR ANTIQUING

Select an antiquing kit that contains the color base undercoat and the color glaze. These kits are available in light and dark tones and in wood-tone effects. Most of the light tones have an undercoat base of white with a glaze of blue, gold, olive, red, or pink to produce an antique-white finish. The deeper tones use a base color of gold, blue, olive, green, or red with a glaze of similar or contrasting color. For wood-tone effects, select an undercoat of cherry, fruitwood, walnut, butternut, or beechwood with a glaze to match. In addition to the antiquing kit, other materials and tools may be needed. Fig. 52-2.

Prepare the project for antiquing by removing all of the hardware, including knobs and pulls. If there are any imperfections in the surface, fill these with patching plaster or plastic wood. Then sand the surface lightly. Make sure that all oil, grease, or wax has been removed with paint thinner.

Stir the undercoat thoroughly and apply to the clean surface. Apply a generous coat, working it well into the surface by brushing in all directions. Make the final smoothing brush strokes in the direction of the wood grain without cross-brushing. Fig. 52-3.

Allow the undercoat to dry overnight. On new or unfinished wood, two coats of undercoat may be needed. The first coat will be partly absorbed in the wood pores, sealing them. The second coat will remain on the surface to give a full, rich color effect. Allow the second coat to dry overnight also.

Apply the color glaze with a brush, in a thin, even coat. Fig. 52-4. Make sure all indentations, crevices, and other low places are covered. The glaze will remain in these places, giving the project its antique appearance. Let the glaze stand about 15 minutes.

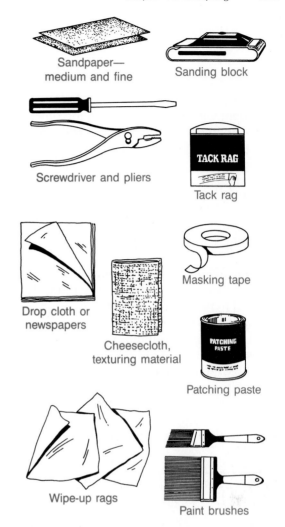

Sandpaper—
medium and fine

Sanding block

Screwdriver and pliers

TACK RAG

Tack rag

Drop cloth or
newspapers

Cheesecloth,
texturing material

Masking tape

PATCHING PASTE

Patching paste

Wipe-up rags

Paint brushes

52-2. Some tools and materials that may be needed in antiquing.

52-3. Apply the colored undercoat with a brush. Make sure that this is dry before applying the glaze.

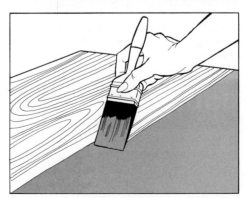

Wipe lightly with cheesecloth in the direction of the grain. The amount of glaze removed can vary. Wipe heavily in areas that you want highlighted, such as the center panels or the high points of carvings or other features. Fig. 52-5. Allow the glaze to remain in the crevices and corners. If you are finishing a large piece of furniture, glaze only one section at a time. Wipe that section before going on to the next.

When using wood-tone glazes, apply the glaze to only one section at a time. Then proceed to the wiping operations. Brush on a very light, thin coat of glaze. Spread it as far as it will go before dipping the brush again. As soon as you have applied the glaze to one section, wipe it with cheesecloth in the direction of the wood grain. Remember that grain usually runs the long way on a project. After the glaze is completely dry, preserve the finish by applying a coat of varnish.

Review Questions

1. Discuss the two basic steps in antiquing a product.
2. Is it necessary to remove the old finish before applying an antique finish?
3. In what direction should a wood-tone glaze be wiped?
4. What is the best method of preserving an antique finish?

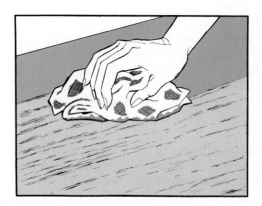

52-5. Continue to wipe the glaze until you have achieved the antique effect desired. Highlights can be contained by working the glaze into the corners with the cloth.

52-4. Apply the glaze with a brush. Before it dries, wipe the surface with cheesecloth to create the antique effect.

Thinking about a Career

Patternmaker

Glenda Hayes is a patternmaker with a manufacturer of heavy equipment in the Midwest. There are basically two types of patternmakers—metal patternmakers and wood patternmakers. *Metal patternmakers* prepare patterns from metal stock or from rough castings. *Wood patternmakers* prepare patterns from wood stock. Glenda is a wood patternmaker.

"As you may know, every cast part that goes into the tractors we make requires a pattern. It is my job to make some of those patterns. I select the wood and lay out the pattern. Some of the patterns are quite big. I may need to assemble these patterns from several pieces of wood. For such a large pattern, I need to cut each piece of wood to the correct size. Then I need to shape the pieces. To do this, I use various power tools, such as wood lathes and power sanders. I also use a variety of hand tools. Finally, after I have completed work on the various segments of the pattern, I assemble them. I fasten them together using glue, nails, and screws.

"I graduated from a local high school. There I had taken a woodworking course, plus courses in mechanical drawing and general mathematics. Even in high school, I knew that I liked working with detail. I also knew that I did not like repetitive work. Much of the work in this factory is repetitive. In talking to my high school guidance counselor, I learned about patternmaking. When I applied for work here at the factory, I asked about the possibility of getting into that field. The personnel manager told me about their apprenticeship program for patternmakers."

An apprenticeship program provides the best experience for a patternmaker. The apprenticeship period usually lasts about 5 years. The program consists of on-the-job work experience and classroom instruction.

"I like my work," says Glenda. "There is a variety to it that does not exist in several of the other jobs here in the factory. I never make the same pattern twice. When I first considered patternmaking as a career, I think I underestimated the need for precision and attention to detail. It did not take me long to realize that these are essential in patternmaking. The pattern has to be exact. If it's the wrong size, the mold from which the casting is made will be the wrong size. This means that the part will not fit. A mistake in patternmaking can be an expensive error. A mistake I make in a pattern can affect the entire assembly process. That's why I carefully check and double-check all of my measurements.

"Careful reading of blueprints is one of my main job responsibilities," says Glenda. "I think that one of the great satisfactions of this job is fashioning a three-dimensional pattern, using a set of blueprints as a guide."

Glenda has been on the job for 17 years now. In that time, she has advanced to head patternmaker. She supervises the work of four other patternmakers and one apprentice patternmaker.

Developing Science, Math, and Reading Skills

Duplicating the Techniques of Stradivari

Antonio Stradivari was a seventeenth-century Italian violin maker. Joseph Nagyvary, a professor of biochemistry at Texas A&M University, uses modern methods to reproduce musical instruments similar to those of Antonio Stradivari. Nagyvary attempts to duplicate the wood preservation techniques of the seventeenth century. He is discovering that even with the help of twentieth-century science and technology it is difficult to achieve Stradivari's results. Nagyvary has found that wood used for classic violins has been through a "pickling process." This process left small amounts of gold, iron, manganese, and other metals in the wood. The substance in the sap that fills the wood pores, pectin, has been removed. This treatment seems to prevent the undesired overtones that rob a violin of its fullness of sound.

One other difference between classic and modern violins seems to be in the finish. Stradivari finished his instruments with a varnish containing a material known as *chitin.* This is the hard part of insect exoskeletons. Compared to finishes used today, chitin is very stiff. In Nagyvary's opinion, this may be one reason that classic violins have a big sound that can fill a concert hall.

ACTIVITY: Determining the Presence of Metallic Elements
Materials
Candle
Matches
Water
10-gram samples of potassium chloride, barium chloride, sodium chloride (table salt), and lithium chloride. (You should be able to obtain all of these from the chemistry teacher.)
A 10″ length of nichrome or hard steel wire

A. Gather all materials.

It is possible to analyze a certain chemical sample for the presence of certain metallic elements by using a simple technique known as a *flame test.* This test is based upon the fact that the electrons in various metals take in and give off energy in unique amounts. These electrons produce different colors in a flame.

Procedure: Light the candle. Clean the wire in the flame by heating it. Dip the wire in water (distilled, if possible) and dip it in one of the chemicals. Then place the wire in the flame and observe. What color is the flame? Clean the wire thoroughly in water. Repeat for each of the other samples. Did the flame produce the same color each time? The metal in each chemical causes the color. (The metal is the first element in the name—such as sodium or potassium.) Some stores sell a fireplace log that produces beautiful colors when burned. Can you guess how the colors are produced?

Note: If dilute hydrochloric acid is available, it should be used to clean the wire between each test.

Activity One

This section of your text deals with wood finishing. Since you want every project you do to look its best, the type of finish you select is important. It will either help or hinder you in your efforts toward getting a superior product. On pages 300-307, various finishes are described, along with the basic steps in applying finish.

There are three general types of finishes. Review the qualities of each. Tell which of the three types can be seen through.

Activity Two

Staining is changing the color of wood without changing its texture. As you have read on pages 313-316, different types of stain are used to enrich the natural beauty of wood.

Review the material. Then tell how you would check the color of the stain before spreading it over your entire project.

Activity Three

Antiquing is a refinishing process that is becoming more and more popular. At some time, you may want to antique some previously finished furniture.

On pages 338-340, the author discusses the process of antiquing. Review this section on antiquing. Then close your book and write your own brief description of the procedure for antiquing.

Determining Finish Coverage

Containers of finishing materials list the approximate square feet of coverage per quart or gallon. Typical coverages are:

Stain: 400 square feet per gallon
Filler: 250 square feet per gallon
Lacquer: 200 square feet per gallon

Refer to Fig. A. The measurements of the dresser shown there are as follows:

	Square Inches
Front, 44″ × 36″	1584
Left end, 36″ × 20″	720
Right end, 36″ × 20″	720
Top, 20″ × 44″	880
	3904

For square feet, divide by 144.

$$\frac{3904}{144} = 27.1 \text{ square feet}$$

Determine the number of dressers that can be covered by one gallon of stain, filler, and lacquer.

Stain _____ exact number; _____ rounded to nearest full number.

Filler _____ exact number; _____ rounded to nearest full number.

Lacquer _____ exact number; _____ rounded to nearest full number.

How many square feet are there in a dresser that has a top measuring 22″ × 60″ and a height of 36″?

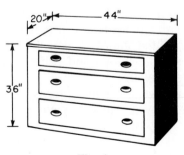

Fig. A.

Section V.

Machine Woodwork

Chapter 53

Planer, or Surfacer

After studying this chapter, you will be able to:
● Identify the major parts of the planer.
● List the safety precautions that must be followed in operating the planer.
● List the steps in surfacing a board to thickness.

LOOK FOR THESE TERMS

backing board	hand wheel	pointer
chip breaker	in-feed roll	pressure bar
clip (snipe)	out-feed roll	rate-of-feed control
cutterhead	planer	surfacer
feed control lever		

Machine Safety Rules

Chapters 53-61 cover the operation of stationary power machinery.

In operating power machinery, observe the following rules:
● Wear eye protection for all machine operations.
● Never use woodworking machinery until you have been given proper safety instruction. Always get your teacher's permission before using a machine.
● Keep all safety guards in proper position. There are few operations on the circular saw for which it is necessary to remove the guard. Make sure that you use special setups and extreme care for these operations.
● Always wear clothes properly. Roll up your sleeves. Tuck in your tie, and put on a shop apron.
● Always remove rings, wristwatches, pins, and other jewelry before operating a machine.
● Plan your work before you start to use the machine.

● Never start or stop a machine for another student.
● Keep your fingers and hands away from moving parts of machines.
● Keep the floor around the machine clear of lumber scraps, waste pieces, and oil.
● Never force material into the machine faster than it can be cut.
● Never stand in line with a revolving blade or wheel.
● Make sure that all clamps are securely fastened before turning on the power.
● Never remove or change a guard without getting your teacher's permission.
● Inspect wood carefully for nails, screws, and knots before machining.
● Keep the table of the machine and other work surfaces clear of excess materials and tools.
● Never feed stock into a machine until it has reached full speed.
● Never hurry when working on a machine.

- Always make sure that the machine has come to a dead stop before oiling, cleaning, or adjusting.
- Always clean sawdust and scraps of wood from the machine with a brush.
- Turn off the power immediately if the machine does not sound right.
- Never attempt cutting with a dull blade.
- Never stand around a machine that is operated by other students.
- Use hand tools and processes for very simple operations or for work on very small pieces of wood.
- For special setups make sure that all clamps are securely fastened. It is a good idea to have the instructor check the setup before doing the machining.
- Keep your mind on your work. Do not become distracted by other students in the class. Be careful not to bother other students who are operating a machine.
- If a machine is not operating properly, always report it to your instructor.
- Take your time when working with a machine. Most accidents happen by not following instructions or by trying to do things too fast.
- Never try to stop a machine after the power is off by forcing a piece of wood into the blade or knives.
- Always stay next to a machine until it has come to a dead stop.
- When you are through using a machine, always remove any special setups. Clean off the waste stock and place it in the scrap box. Leave the machine in its normal operating condition with the power shut off.

The thickness *planer*, or *surfacer*, is designed to surface boards to thickness and to smooth rough-cut lumber. Fig. 53-1. *It will not straighten a warped board.* The cutting head is mounted above the table so only the top of a board is surfaced. This machine is self-feeding. After stock has been fed into it, it will continue through the machine by itself. The size is indicated by the maximum width and thickness that can be surfaced. For example, if the capacity is 18 by 6 inches, the largest piece that can be surfaced is 18 inches wide and 6 inches thick.

PARTS OF THE PLANER

The major parts of the planer include a motor, cutterhead, in-feed and out-feed rolls, chip breaker, pressure bar, table, and feed control wheel.

As the stock is fed in, the upper corrugated *in-feed roll* grips the stock and moves it toward the cutterhead. Fig. 53-2. The *chip breaker* presses firmly on the top of the wood to prevent the grain from tearing out. The *rotating cutterhead* surfaces the board much like a jointer. The *pressure bar*, back of the cutterhead, holds the stock firmly against the table. The *out-feed roll* helps move the stock out the back of the machine.

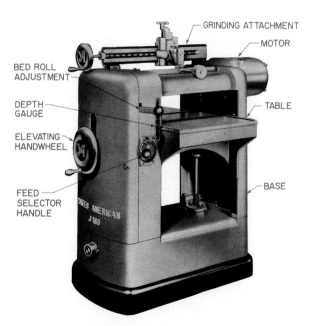

53-1. An 18-inch thickness planer, or surfacer.

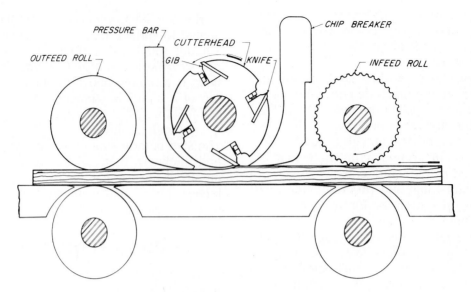

53-2. Cross section of a planer head.

On small planers, the controls are relatively simple. They consist of the following:

- A *switch* to turn on the machine.
- A *hand wheel* that elevates or lowers the tables.
- The *pointer* on the table that indicates thickness of the stock after it has been fed through the machine.
- A *feed control lever* that operates the feed control.
- A *rate-of-feed control* that regulates the rate of feed from slow to fast. (Some machines do not have this feature.) Fig. 53-3.

The planer/surfacer should be connected to a dust collection system to carry away the chips. Fig. 53-4.

 Safety

In operating the planer, take the following precautions.

- Check the board to be sure it is free of nails, loose knots, and other imperfections.
- Always stand to one side when planing. Never stand directly behind the board.
- Never attempt to plane more than one thickness at a time. If several boards of different thicknesses are to be surfaced, always plane the thick one first until it is about the same thickness as the others.

- Never look into the planer as the board is passing through. Loose chips may be thrown back with great force, causing an eye injury.
- Plane a warped board only when one surface has been trued on a jointer.
- Make sure that the board is at least 2 inches longer than the distance between the feed rolls. For a small planer, this usually means a board should be at least 14 inches long.
- Keep your hands away from the board after it starts through the planer.
- If a board sticks, turn off the switch. Wait for the cutterhead to stop. Then lower the table.
- Have a helper take the stock away from the planer. *Never reach over the planer.*
- Whenever helping to ""tail off," hold the board up and allow the out-feed rollers to feed the stock out of the planer.
- Never pull on a board being planed.
- Stop the planer to make any adjustments or to clean or oil it.

53-3. The variable speed cutting feed makes it possible to select any feed range from 15 to 36 feet per minute.

53-4. The dust collection system helps keep the area around the machine free of sawdust.

SQUARING LEGS

The planer is used to square stock to be used for legs. Fig. 53-6.

Begin the squaring operation by cutting the stock to rough size. Joint one face and then one edge 90 degrees to the jointed face. (This face and edge are shown as sides A and B, Fig. 53-7.) Mark these surfaces for identification.

Place the stock with the jointed surface on the planer table and the jointed edge to the right. Set the planer for the necessary cut. Fig. 53-7, side C. Make the cut. When taking the stock from the out-feed table, take care not to alter the position of the pieces. Place the stock on the in-feed table in the same position as for the first cut. Turn each piece one-quarter turn clockwise. Do not change the thickness setting. Feed the stock through the planer for the second cut. Fig. 53-7, side D. Measure the stock. If necessary, repeat the two cuts on sides A and B. It may also be necessary to make additional cuts on sides C and D, continuing until the stock is the correct size. Plan your cuts so an equal amount of material is removed from all sides.

53-7. Squaring stock on the planer.

PLANING THIN STOCK

If very thin stock must be planed, it is a good idea to use a *backing board*. This is true for all stock 3/8 inch (10 mm) or less in thickness. Make sure that the backing board is true, smooth, and at least 3/4 inch (19 mm) thick. Place the backing board on the bed. Then put the thin stock on it. Adjust for the correct depth of cut, taking into consideration the thickness of the backing board. Then run the two boards together through the surfacer. Fig. 53-8.

53-6. Table legs made with a planer.

53-8. Surfacing thin stock. Use a backing board so that the piece will not split.

SURFACING SEVERAL SHORT PIECES

If several short pieces of the same thickness are to be surfaced at the same time (such as four rails for a table), butt the ends together as they are fed through the planer. This helps keep the wood moving. It also eliminates the possibility of a clip or snipe dip. A *clip* or *snipe* is a small, concave cut at the end of the stock.

The last board should always be a longer board. It should be equal to at least 2 inches more than the distance between the feed rolls. Feed the pieces at a slight angle to improve the quality of the surface. Fig. 53-9.

53-9. Surface short stock by feeding one board behind the other at a slight angle.

Review Questions

1. What is the purpose of a planer?
2. List eight safety rules to follow when using the planer.
3. What is the maximum amount of stock that should be removed at one cut?
4. Tell what to do if the board sticks in the planer.
5. Explain how to plane thin stock.

Chapter 54

Circular Saw

After studying this chapter, you will be able to:
- Identify the main parts of the circular saw.
- List those precautions that must be followed in operating the circular saw.
- Describe how to rip with the circular saw.
- Describe how to perform a crosscutting operation on the circular saw.
- Describe how to cut a miter with a circular saw.
- Describe how to cut a groove on the circular saw.
- Describe how to cut a rabbet with a circular saw.
- Describe the use of a dado head with the circular saw.

LOOK FOR THESE TERMS

antikickback pawls	guard	saw-raising handwheel
arbor	miter gauge	saw-tilt handwheel
carbide tip	push stick	splitter
circular saw	ripping fence	table saw
dado head		

The *circular saw*, or *table saw*, is a machine for cutting wood. Ripping and crosscutting are the chief cutting operations. The machine parts are shown in Fig. 54-1. In addition, the machine should have a *guard*, a *splitter*, and *antikickback pawls* (fingers) to protect the operator from injury. Fig. 54-1. Saw size is indicated by the largest diameter of saw blade that can be used on the machine. The most common sizes are 8- and 10-inch tilt arbor saws. The *saw-raising handwheel* is usually under the front of the table. It is used to raise and lower the saw blade. The *saw-tilt handwheel*, usually on the left side, is used to tilt the arbor for cutting at an angle.

SELECTING A SAW BLADE

There are many kinds of circular saw blades. The most common are ripsaw (rip-tooth), crosscut, and combination. Fig. 54-2. When many different operations are done one after another, it is a good idea to use a combination blade. Fig. 54-3. Many saw blades have *carbide tips*. Carbide is extremely hard. It keeps the blade sharper for a longer period of time.

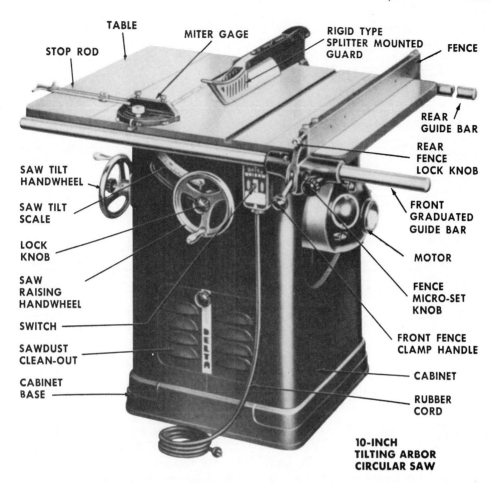

TABLE
STOP ROD
MITER GAGE
RIGID TYPE SPLITTER MOUNTED GUARD
FENCE
REAR GUIDE BAR
REAR FENCE LOCK KNOB
FRONT GRADUATED GUIDE BAR
MOTOR
FENCE MICRO-SET KNOB
FRONT FENCE CLAMP HANDLE
CABINET
RUBBER CORD

SAW TILT HANDWHEEL
SAW TILT SCALE
LOCK KNOB
SAW RAISING HANDWHEEL
SWITCH
SAWDUST CLEAN-OUT
CABINET BASE

10-INCH TILTING ARBOR CIRCULAR SAW

54-1. A 10-inch, floor-type, circular saw. Study the names of the parts. You should become familiar with them.

Crosscut tooth   Standard combination tooth   Rip tooth   Chisel combination tooth   Extra fine tooth crosscut

54-2. Kinds of circular saw blades.

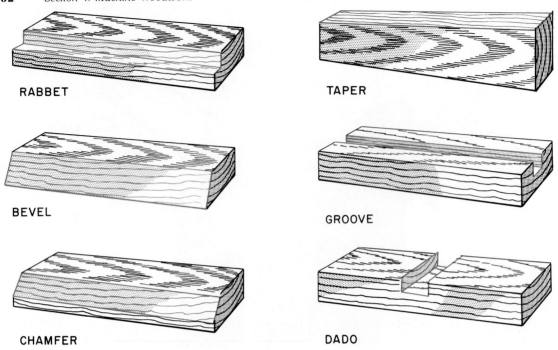

RABBET

TAPER

BEVEL

GROOVE

CHAMFER

DADO

54-3. Common cuts that can be made on the circular saw.

Safety

- Raise the saw blade from ⅛ to ¼ inch higher than the thickness of the stock to be cut.
- When changing saw blades or using a dado head, make sure the main switch is off. When possible, pull the plug from the receptacle to prevent accidental starting.
- Hold the stock to be sawed against the fence or miter gauge. Never try to saw "freehand" (without holding the stock against the fence or miter gauge). Use a ripping fence for ripping operations. Use a miter gauge for all crosscutting operations.
- Keep the saw guard down over the saw blade while operating the saw.
- Make all adjustments when the saw is at a dead stop. These adjustments include height of the saw blade, angle setting, fence adjustments, and all special setups. Always stop the saw before changing any adjustments.
- When setting up the saw for any sawing operation, check to see that the saw blade revolves freely in the correct direction.

Check that it is securely fastened to the arbor. Check that any clamps or knobs on the fences are properly tightened.
- Make sure that the antikickback pawls (fingers) behind the saw blade are always in place. These resist the tendency of the saw to throw the stock upward and toward the operator.
- Use the splitter guard and antikickback pawls or fingers when ripping. Wood cut with the grain tends to spring the kerf closed and bind the blade. Fig. 54-4. The splitter prevents this from happening. If the splitter is not used, stop the machine and insert a wedge in the kerf just as soon as the cut has passed the back of the blade. Fig. 54-5.
- Always use the saw guard. The saw guard covers the blade and the area around it, while allowing the stock to slide under it. Never operate the saw without the guard in place unless a special jig or fixture is used as a guard.
- Use a *push stick* to push the stock past the blade if the space between the saw blade and the fence is 6 inches or less.

- Stand to one side of the saw blade. No one should ever stand in line with the blade where kickback could cause serious injury.
- Stock to be ripped must have a straight, true edge and must lie flat on the table. Never cut stock on the saw if it is warped, "in wind," or has a rough or bowed edge.
- Whenever helping to "tail-off," hold the board up and allow the operator to push the stock through the saw. Never pull on a board being ripped. Fig. 54-6.
- Fasten a clearance block to the ripping fence when cutting off short lengths of stock. Make sure the block is clamped ahead of the blade. Use a sliding miter gauge to hold the stock. Never use the ripping fence as a stop when crosscutting. It will cause kickback.
- Do not force stock into a saw blade faster than it will cut.

- Never reach over the saw blade! Have a helper take the stock away.
- Do not allow your fingers to come closer than 5 inches to the saw blade when cutting stock.
- Use a stick or board to clear away scraps close to the saw blade. Do not use your hand.
- Have your instructor check all special setups and blade changes before the saw is started.
- Remove all special setups and the dado head from the saw after use.
- Do not try to cut cylindrical (round) stock on the saw.

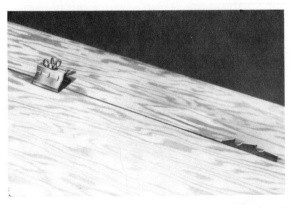

54-5. Some old types of saws do not have splitter and antikickback pawls or fingers. When making a long rip cut with these saws, stop the saw after the front edge has cleared the blade by a few inches. Use a commercial device or a wedge of wood to keep the kerf open so that the kerf will not close and bind on the saw.

54-4. Resawing using a guard, splitter, and antikickback pawls or fingers. Resawing is making a thick board thinner by cutting with the grain. To resaw very wide stock, set the blade 1/8 inch higher than half the thickness. Make one cut. Then turn the board over and make the other cut.

54-6. When ripping long stock, have someone help you.

CHANGING A BLADE

Snap out the throat plate around the saw. Obtain a wrench that will fit the arbor nut. On most circular saws, the arbor has a left-hand thread and must be turned clockwise to loosen. Fig. 54-7. However, some manufacturers use a right-hand thread on the arbor. If so, you must turn the arbor nut counterclockwise to remove it. Always check the thread before loosening. If the nut does not come off easily, force a piece of scrap wood against the blade to keep the arbor from turning. Remove the nut, the collar, and the blade. Now mark the arbor with a slight file cut or prick-punch mark. Always turn the arbor so the mark is "up" before putting on a new blade. Place the trademark on the blade at the top, in line with the mark on the arbor. Replace the collar and nut.

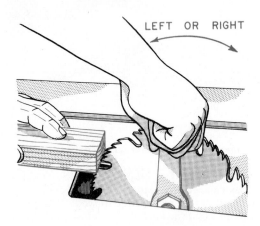

54-7. Removing a blade. Hold a piece of wood against the blade to keep it from turning. Then turn the nut with a wrench of the proper size. On most saws the arbor has a left-hand thread and must be turned clockwise to loosen it. However, some arbors have a right-hand thread. If so, you must turn it counterclockwise to remove it.

54-8. Adjust the stock to extend 1/8 to 1/4 inch above the stock.

RIPPING

Before you rip stock to width on the circular saw, make sure that one edge of the stock is true. If it is not, plane one edge. Then, with the power off, adjust the saw blade to a height of ⅛ to ¼ inch more than the thickness of the stock. Figs. 54-8 and 54-9. Adjust the ripping fence to the correct width. Do this by holding a rule or try square against the fence and measuring the distance to the saw blade. On many machines, the width for ripping is found directly on a scale mounted on the front edge of the saw table. Lock the ripping fence so it is tight. Make sure the guard, splitter, and antikickback pawls or fingers are in place.

Turn on the power. Place the stock on the table. Stand to one side, not directly in back of the saw blade. To start the cut, apply forward pressure with one hand as you hold the stock against the fence with the other. Do not apply too much forward pressure on a small saw. This will make the saw burn or stop altogether. Continue to feed the work into the saw with even pressure. Figs. 54-10 and 54-11.

54-9. A blade gauge can be made or purchased with notches accurately cut in 1/8-inch steps. Raise the blade until it touches the gauge. This jig saves time when adjusting the blade to different heights.

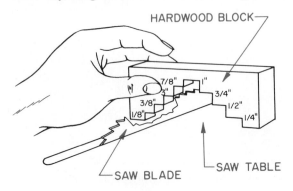

54-10. The fence for ripping can be placed either on the left side as shown here or on the right side as shown in Fig. 54-11. Most operators prefer to place the fence on the right side.

If the stock is hardwood and quite thick, you may need to begin with the saw set at less than the total thickness. You may need to run it through several times rather than trying to cut through the thickness in one operation.

When cutting to narrow widths, hold the push stick in your right hand. As the rear edge of the stock clears the table, apply forward pressure with the push stick until the cut is completed. Figs. 54-12 and 54-13.

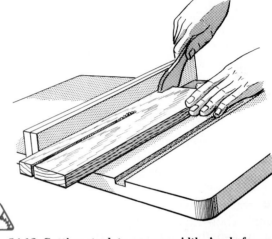

54-12. Cutting stock to narrow width. Apply forward pressure with a *push stick*. Never run your hand between the revolving blade and the fence if narrow widths are being ripped. The guard has been left out in order to show the operation.

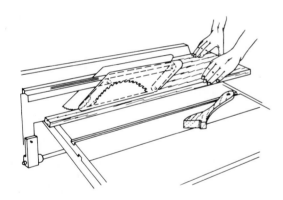

54-11. Ripping stock. Push with your right hand and hold the stock against the fence with your left hand. If the stock is narrow, have a push stick handy for finishing the cut. Keep your hands away from the blade.

54-13. This push block, which slides along the fence, makes it easy to cut thin pieces safely.

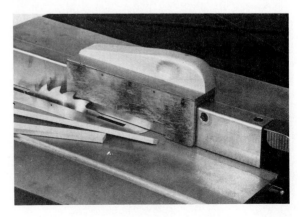

CROSSCUTTING

The miter gauge fits into either groove of the table but is most often used in the left groove. Some operators attach a squared piece of stock the same width as the miter gauge to its face to better support the work. To make a square cut, set the gauge at a 90-degree angle. Check by holding a try square against the gauge and the saw blade. Mark the location of the cut clearly on the front edge or face of the stock. Fig. 54-14. Set the blade to the correct height. Hold the stock firmly against the gauge and slide both the work and gauge along the table to complete the cut. Fig. 54-15. If you must cut several pieces to the same length, use one of the following methods:

● Set the stop rod that is attached to the miter gauge to the correct length. Fig. 54-16.

● Clamp a small block of wood to the ripping fence just in front of the saw blade. The fence with block attached acts as a length guide. Fig. 54-17. Never use the ripping fence only as a length guide. If you do, the piece will lodge between the revolving saw and the ripping fence. It may kick back with terrific force.

● Fasten a wood extension to the miter gauge. Then clamp a stop block to it to control the length of cut. Fig. 54-18.

54-15. Crosscutting. The miter gauge is set at a right angle to the blade. An even forward pressure should be applied to the stock and gauge.

54-16. Using a stop rod to cut identical pieces to length. This miter gauge is equipped with a clamp to hold the stock. Note that a piece of abrasive paper has been glued to the miter gauge to keep the stock from slipping.

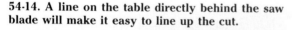

54-14. A line on the table directly behind the saw blade will make it easy to line up the cut.

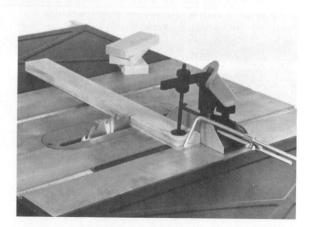

54-17. Cutting stock to length with a block attached to the ripping fence. This is one of the simplest methods of cutting many pieces of stock to the the same length. Note that as the stock is cut off there is plenty of clearance between the saw blade and the fence. In this way there is never a danger of kick-back. *The guard has been removed to show the operation.*

54-18. An auxiliary wood fence has been fastened to the miter gauge. Then a stop block is clamped to this fence. *The guard has been removed to show the operation.*

CUTTING SHEET STOCK

Sheet stock, such as plywood, particle board, and hardboard, comes in large sizes (usually 4 × 8 feet). These are hard to handle. It is often a good idea to cut the large sheets into smaller sizes with a hand saw or portable power saw. However, some circular saws have extension tables that make it possible for one person to handle large sheets safely. Fig. 54-19. Use a fine-toothed crosscut saw to cut plywood. Use a carbide-tipped saw to cut the other materials. Place plywood on the table with the good side up.

54-19. Extension tables make it easier to handle sheet stock.

MITERING

To make a miter cut, adjust the miter gauge to the correct angle and proceed as in crosscutting. Hold the stock firmly against the miter gauge because it tends to creep toward the revolving saw as the cut is made. Figs. 54-20 and 54-21. To make a compound miter cut, set the gauge to the correct angle and tilt the blade. Fig. 54-22.

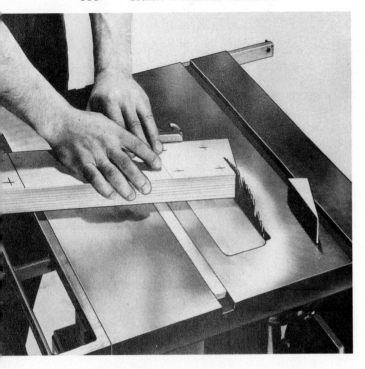

54-22. Making a compound miter cut. The miter gauge is set at an angle and the blade is tilted. The stop rod on the miter gauge is used to control the length of cut.

54-20. Making a miter cut with the gauge set in an open position—cutting from the outer edge of the miter towards the inside edge. You must hold the stock firmly against the gauge since the stock tends to "creep." The guard has been removed to show the operation.

54-21. Cutting a miter in the closed position—cutting from the inner edge towards the outside. This is a preferred method, since the stock can be held in place more easily. Note that the combination of abrasive paper on the miter gauge plus the clamp will keep the stock from moving.

BEVELING AND CHAMFERING

To cut a bevel or chamfer when you are either ripping or crosscutting, you must tilt the saw blade to the correct angle for the cut. The gauge, which shows the angle of tilt of the saw blade, is on the front of the saw just below the table. After making the adjustment, check the angle by holding a sliding T-bevel against the tabletop and saw blade. After you have the correct angle, you can proceed as for ripping or crosscutting. Fig. 54-23.

GROOVING

Cutting a groove on the circular saw will simplify the making of a spline joint. Fig. 54-24. Lay out the groove on the edge of the stock. Set the circular saw to a height equal to the depth of the groove. Adjust the ripping fence to allow the cut to be made just inside the layout line. Hold one surface of the stock firmly against the fence and make a cut. Reverse the stock and make a second cut. If necessary, you can make several cuts in the waste stock of the groove. Clean out the groove with a sharp chisel. A groove can also be cut with a dado head.

54-23. Be particularly careful where you place your hands when cutting stock at an angle with the arbor tilted (either to the right or left). The danger zone is much wider than you think. *The guard has been removed to show the operation.*

54-24. Here you see the difference between a groove and a dado.

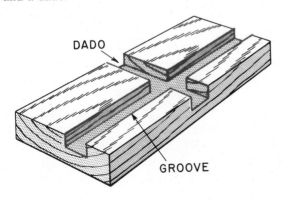

RABBETING

A rabbet can easily be cut on the end or edge of stock with a circular saw. Lay out the rabbet joint. (See Chapter 28.) Set the saw blade to a height equal to the depth of the rabbet. If the rabbet is to be cut at the end of the board, hold the stock against a miter gauge and make the shoulder cut. Fig. 54-25. Then set the saw blade to a height equal to the width of the rabbet. Set the ripping fence to a position that will permit the saw kerf to be just inside the layout line. Hold the stock on end with the surface opposite the rabbet firmly against the ripping fence. Make the second cut.

An edge rabbet is cut in the same way, except that the ripping fence is used for making both cuts.

54-25. Making the first cut of a rabbet. *The guard has been removed to show the operation.*

TENONING

Making mortise-and-tenon joints is quite simple when the tenon is cut on the circular saw. Lay out the tenon. (See Chapter 32.) Set the saw blade to a height equal to the thickness of stock to be removed from one side of the tenon. Hold the stock against the miter gauge and make the shoulder cuts. After this is done, set the saw blade to a height equal to the length of the tenon. Now select a homemade or commercial tenoning jig. Figs. 54-26, 54-27, and 54-28. The simplest method of cutting the cheek is to clamp the stock to the tenoning jig and position the jig and fence so as to cut out the cheek on the side away from the jig. Fig. 54-29. Then turn the stock around and cut the other cheek without changing the location of the fence.

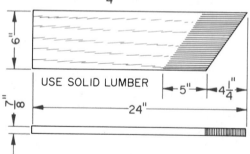

54-26. A feather board can be used for many different purposes. For example, it can be clamped to the table to hold the stock against the fence when ripping. It can also be used as a guard when the standard guard cannot be used for a particular operation, such as making the shoulder cut in a rabbet.

54-27. If the shoulder cut is made freehand, use a feather board saw guard to protect your hands while cutting the tenon.

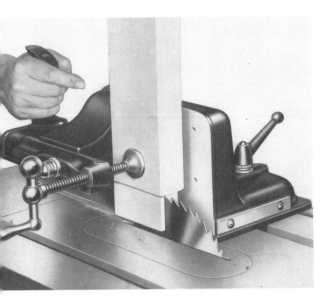

54-28. A commercial tenoning jig is an excellent accessory for cutting tenons and grooves. This one will take stock up to 2 3/4 inches thick and any width within the capacity of the saw.

54-29. Making the cheek cut with a hand-made tenoning jig.

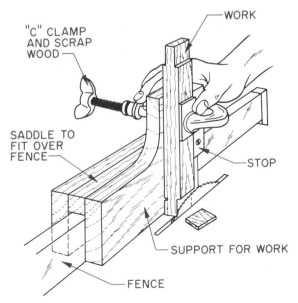

"C" CLAMP AND SCRAP WOOD

WORK

SADDLE TO FIT OVER FENCE

STOP

SUPPORT FOR WORK

FENCE

USING A DADO HEAD

A *dado head* will cut grooves or dadoes from ⅛ to 2 inches in width. Figs. 54-30 and 54-31. This head is equally adapted to cutting with or across the grain. One dado blade will cut a groove ⅛ inch thick. Two will make a cut ¼ inch thick. Cutters of different widths can be put between these two dado cutters to cut a groove of any width. This attachment is especially useful for cutting grooves, tenons, dadoes, and lap joints. Figs. 54-32 and 54-33.

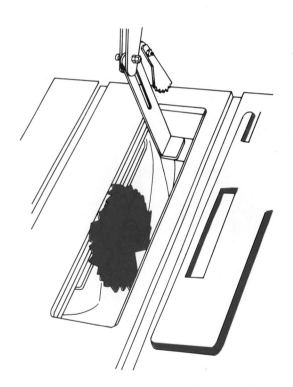

54-30. A dado head attached to the saw arbor in preparation for use. The plate that must be used over the head has a wider opening than that used with the regular saw blade.

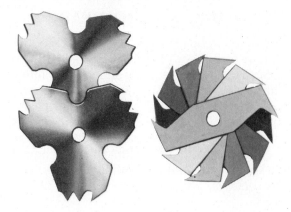

54-31. A typical dado head has two outside blades that are 1/8 inch thick. It also has four chipper blades: one that is 1/16 inch thick, two that are 1/8 inch thick; and one that is 1/4 inch thick. With this assortment, you can cut grooves from 1/8 to 13/16 inch in intervals of 1/16 inch.

54-33. Cutting a series of dadoes. *The guard has been removed to show the operation.*

54-32. Cutting a groove with a dado head. Note how simple it is to cut a groove of any width and depth with this attachment. When the groove is cut across grain, it is called a dado. This is a common type of joint construction. *The guard has been removed to show the operation.*

USING AN ADJUSTABLE DADO HEAD

An adjustable dado head gives a good, clean cut and is easy to use. Figs. 54-34 and 54-35. Set the width by loosening the arbor nut and rotating the center section of the head until the width mark on this part is opposite the correct dimension. This adjustable dado head will make cuts from ¼ to 13⁄16 inch wide and up to ¾ inch deep. It can be used for making all kinds of cuts.

54-34. A 6-inch adjustable dado cutter.

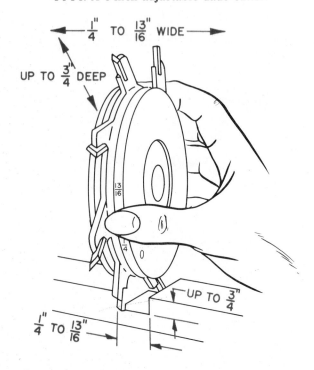

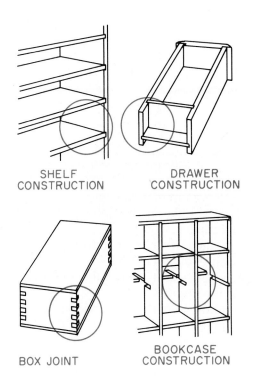

SHELF
CONSTRUCTION

DRAWER
CONSTRUCTION

BOX JOINT

BOOKCASE
CONSTRUCTION

54-35. A few of the cuts that can be made with an adjustable dado cutter.

54-36. A simple adjustable taper jig. Detail drawings are at top and lower left.

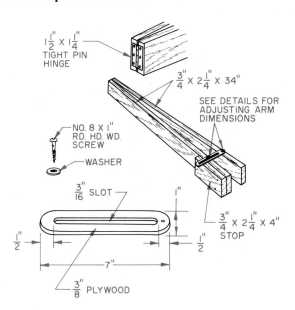

$1\frac{1}{2}" \times 1\frac{1}{4}"$ TIGHT PIN HINGE

$\frac{3}{4}" \times 2\frac{1}{4}" \times 34"$

SEE DETAILS FOR ADJUSTING ARM DIMENSIONS

NO. 8 X 1" RD. HD. WD. SCREW

WASHER

$\frac{3}{16}"$ SLOT

$\frac{3}{4}" \times 2\frac{1}{4}" \times 4"$ STOP

$\frac{1}{2}"$

$1"$

$\frac{1}{2}"$

$7"$

$\frac{3}{8}"$ PLYWOOD

CUTTING A TAPER

The best way to cut a taper is to use an adjustable *taper jig*. Fig. 54-36. Mark a line to indicate the taper to be cut. Then adjust the jig until the line of the taper cut is parallel to the fence. Fig. 54-37.

54-37. Using an adjustable taper jig. *The guard has been removed to show the operation.*

Math Quiz

A circular saw blade that is sharp and rotating at the correct speed will cut wood easily.

To find the rim speed of a blade, use the following formula:

$$\text{Rim speed in FPM} = \frac{3.14 \times \text{dia. of blade in inches} \times \text{RPM of motor}}{12}$$

What is the rim speed in feet per minute cf a 10-inch circular saw blade being turned by a motor operating at 3600 revolutions per minute?

Remember, a 12-inch blade operating at 3600 RPM is traveling at more than 120 miles per hour—a racing speed. Can you see why kickback can make a piece of wood a deadly missile?

Answer
9,420 feet per minute.

Review Questions

1. Sketch a circular saw and name its parts.
2. Name the three common types of circular saw blades.
3. List the safety precautions to observe when using a circular saw.
4. At what height should the saw blade be set for ripping?
5. Tell how to make a cut on hardwood that is quite thick.
6. At what times should a push stick be used?
7. Name the gauge used in crosscutting.
8. Relate the three methods of cutting several pieces to the same length.
9. How can a compound miter cut be made?
10. What difficulty is frequently encountered when making a miter cut?
11. How can a groove be cut?
12. Tell how to make the cheek cut in tenoning.
13. What is a dado head? What is it used for?
14. Tell how to cut a taper.

Chapter 55

Radial-Arm Saw

After studying this chapter, you will be able to:
● Describe the operation of the radial arm saw.
● List those safety precautions that must be followed in operating the radial arm saw.
● Make a straight crosscut on the radial arm saw.
● Perform a ripping operation on the radial arm saw.

LOOK FOR THESE TERMS

cut-off saw   radial-arm saw
overarm   yoke

The *radial-arm saw* is ideal for crosscutting operations. It is sometimes called a *cut-off saw*. While it can be used for ripping, it is better to use the circular saw for that operation. For all crosscutting operations, including straight cutting and cutting a miter, bevel, dado, or rabbet, the stock is held firmly on the table in a stationary position. The saw is moved to do the cutting. For all ripping operations, the saw is locked in a fixed position and the stock moved into the revolving blade.

There are several designs for the radial-arm saw. On one type the saw unit moves back and forth under the overarm. Figs. 55-1 and 55-2. Another type has an extra track under the overarm on which the saw moves. Fig. 55-3. The size of the machine is determined by the size of the blades. The common size for the school laboratory is 9- to 10-inches.

55-1. On this radial-arm saw, the saw moves back and forth under the overarm.

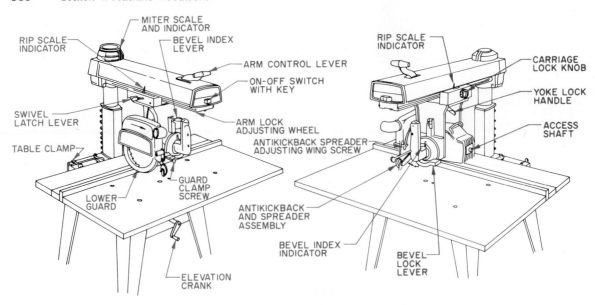

55-2. The controls for a radial-arm saw. Each different model has a slightly different arrangement. Study the manufacturer's manual for complete instructions on how to use the saw.

55-3. On this radial-arm saw, the saw moves back and forth under a track that is attached to the overarm.

BASIC MACHINE

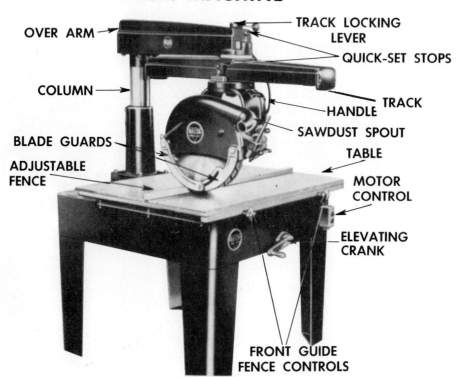

ADJUSTMENTS

The *overarm* or *track* can rotate in a complete circle. The *yoke* that holds the motor can be turned in a 360-degree circle. The blade can be tilted to the right or left 90 degrees. There are three principal adjustments:

• The *depth of cut* is made by turning the elevator crank that is located either directly above the column or on the front of the machine.

• The *angle of cut* is adjusted by turning the overarm or track to the correct angle. There is a *locking lever* at the column or the outer end of the overarm for making this adjustment.

• *Bevel cuts* are made by tilting the motor to the right or left.

 Safety

Observe the following precautions:
• Get personal instruction on the use of the radial-arm saw before operating it.
• Make sure a sharp blade of the correct kind is installed. The same blades are used on the radial-arm saw as on the circular saw.
• Mount the blade on the arbor so that the cutting edges turn toward you.
• Make sure the guard is always in place.
• See to it that all clamps are tight before starting the motor.
• Hold the stock firmly against the table for crosscutting operations.
• Keep your hands away from the danger area—the path of the blade. Maintain a 6-inch margin of safety.
• Make sure the saw is at full speed before starting the cut.
• Return the saw to the rear of the table after completing the cut. Never remove stock from the table until the saw is returned.
• When ripping, always feed stock into the blade so that the bottom teeth are toward you. This will be the side opposite the antikickback fingers.
• Do not try to stop the blade after turning off the machine by holding a stick or similar item against it.
• *Make all adjustments with the motor at a dead stop.*

CROSSCUTTING OPERATIONS

To make a straight crosscut, make sure that the arm or track is at right angles to the guide fence. Adjust the depth of cut so that the teeth of the blade are about 1/16 inch below the surface of the wood table. Set the *antikickback device* about 1/8 inch above the work surface. This will act as a safety device to keep your fingers away from the rotating blade. Hold the stock firmly on the table with the cutoff line in line with the saw blade. Start the machine and allow it to come to full speed. Now pull the motor slowly so that the blade cuts into the stock. Figs. 55-4 and 55-5. This will take very little effort.

After making the cut, return the saw to its place behind the guide fence and turn off the machine. To make a miter cut, simply adjust the arm or track to the angle you want. Cut as you would for straight crosscutting. Fig. 55-6. To cut a bevel, adjust the track or arm for straight crosscutting. Then tilt the saw to the desired angle. Fig. 55-7. The angle is 45 degrees for most bevel or end miter cuts. To make a compound miter, adjust the arm or track to the correct angle and then tilt the saw. Fig. 55-8. To cut a rabbet or dado, install a dado head on the arbor and use it as you would a saw blade.

55-4. To do straight cutting, pull the saw smoothly through the stock.

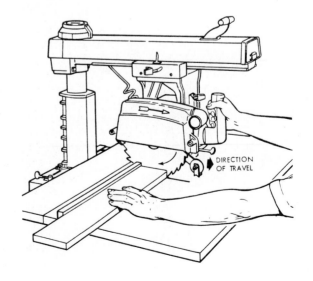

55-5. To cut duplicate parts, clamp a *stop block* to the table with a C-clamp.

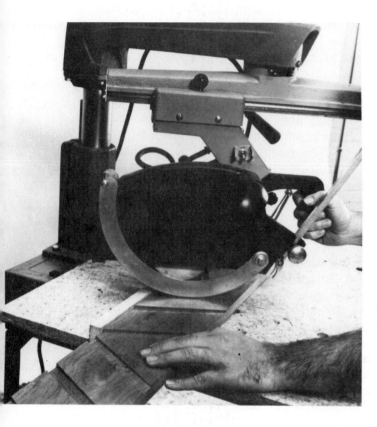

55-6. The track of the machine is adjusted to make a miter cut. Note that a dado head is used to cut dadoes at an angle.

55-8. Making a compound miter or hopper cut.

55-7. Making a bevel cut.

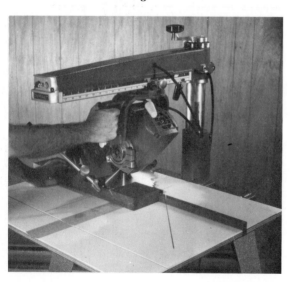

RIPPING OPERATIONS

Set the track or overarm at right angles to the guide fence. Turn the saw so that the blade is parallel to the guide fence. Then move the saw in or out until the correct distance between the guide fence and blade is obtained. Lock it in position. Set the depth of cut. Adjust the guard so that it is close to the work. Set the antikickback device so that the fingers rest firmly on the wood surface and hold it against the table. Check to make sure that the saw is rotating up and toward you. Turn on the power and move the stock slowly into the blade. Figs. 55-9 and 55-10.

Review Questions

1. Describe the three principal adjustments that are made on a radial-arm saw.
2. List five safety precautions to follow when using the radial-arm saw.
3. Tell how to adjust the saw for straight crosscutting.
4. Tell how to adjust the saw for ripping.

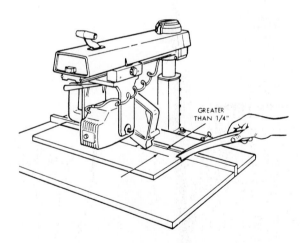

55-9. In-ripping. The motor is turned so that the blade is towards the fence guide. Adjust the upper guard so that it just clears the thickness of the stock. Note that the stock is fed from the right side. Use a push stick to complete the cut when ripping narrow pieces.

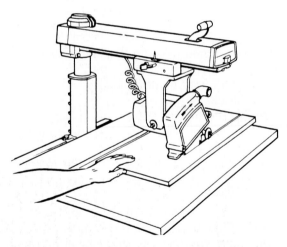

55-10. Out-ripping. The motor is turned so that the blade is away from the fence guide. Adjust the upper guard so that it just clears the stock. Note that the work is fed from the left side.

Chapter 56

Band Saw

After studying this chapter, you will be able to:
● List the advantages of the band saw.
● List those safety rules that must be followed in the operation of the band saw.
● Demonstrate the changing of a blade on the band saw.
● List those guidelines that must be followed in cutting with the band saw.
● Demonstrate the cutting of simple and compound curves on a band saw.

LOOK FOR THESE TERMS

band saw
pad sawing
resawing

The *band saw* is a very versatile cutting machine. It can perform the following operations:
● It will cut wood, plastics, metal, and panel stock.
● It will make long, sweeping curves much more accurately than can be done with any hand saw.
● It has a large depth of cut that makes it perfect for resawing and cutting duplicate parts.

The saw has two wheels mounted on a *frame*. It also has a *table*, *guides*, a *saw blade* and *guards*. Fig. 56-1. In addition, a ripping fence and miter gauge are sometimes used. The table can be tilted to different angles. The size of the band saw is indicated by the diameter of the wheels. It is used mostly for cutting curves, circles, and irregular designs. Fig. 56-2. It can also be used for straight crosscutting, ripping, and resawing. Fig. 56-3.

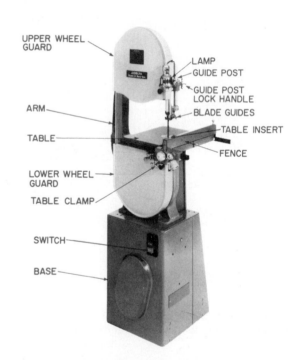

56-1. A 14-inch band saw that can be mounted on a table or bench. It has all the features of a large machine, such as a tilting table, ball-bearing guides, and an adjustable upper wheel. It differs only in that it has a smaller capacity.

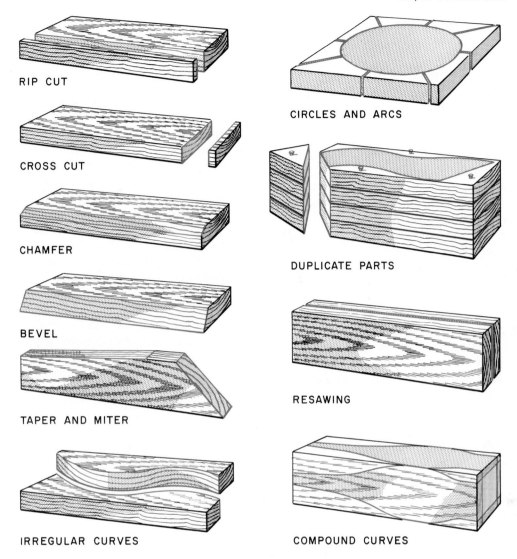

RIP CUT

CROSS CUT

CHAMFER

BEVEL

TAPER AND MITER

IRREGULAR CURVES

CIRCLES AND ARCS

DUPLICATE PARTS

RESAWING

COMPOUND CURVES

56-2. Common cuts that can be made on the band saw.

56-3. The legs of this table can be cut on a band saw.

Safety

In using the band saw, observe the following precautions:

- Use the correct blade. Choose the largest one with the coarsest teeth that will cut the stock cleanly. Follow the sharpest curve in the pattern.
- Before operating the saw, check the blade for proper tension and proper mounting. The teeth should point down on the downward stroke.
- Be sure the wheels turn clockwise as viewed from the front of the saw. The arrow on the motor pulley indicates the direction of rotation.
- Make sure the blade is sharp and in good condition. A clicking noise may indicate a crack in the blade.
- Be sure wheel guards are closed before turning on the machine.
- Adjust the upper guide assembly so it is ¼ inch above the stock.
- Allow the saw to reach full speed before starting the cut.
- Hold the stock flat on the table.
- Keep your fingers at least 2 inches from the blade.
- Keep your fingers to the side of the blade, never in front of it.
- Feed (push) work into the band saw blade firmly and at a rate that will not overload the saw.
- Keep from twisting the blade or crowding it beyond its cutting capacity.
- Clean sawdust from the table frequently.
- If you need to back the saw blade out of a long cut, first turn off the power and allow the machine to come to a dead stop.
- Clear away scraps close to the saw blade with a stick, not with your fingers.
- Cut cylindrical (round) stock by holding it in a special "V" fixture.
- Stop the band saw before making any adjustments.
- If you hear a clicking noise, turn off the band saw at once. This indicates a crack in the blade. If the blade breaks, shut off the power and move away from the machine until both wheels stop.
- Turn off the band saw as soon as you have finished your work. If the machine has a brake, apply it smoothly. Do not leave the machine until it has stopped running.

56-4. Folding or coiling a band-saw blade.

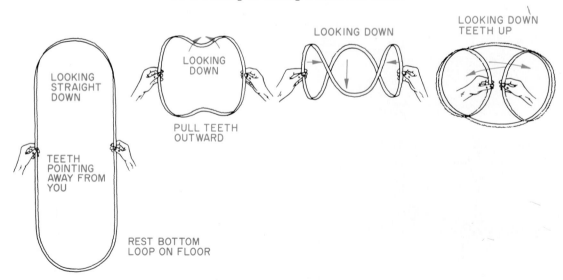

CHANGING SAW BLADES

Change saw blades as follows:
1. Disconnect the machine.
2. Open upper and lower guard doors. Remove pin in table slot, and loosen vertical adjustment screw.
3. Remove the old blade. If it has been broken, pull it off very carefully. It is "springy" and may flip around and cause an injury. If the blade is in one piece, pull the steel pin out of the slot in the table. Lower the upper wheel by turning the vertical adjustment wheel. Grasp the saw blade with both hands; lift it off of the upper and lower wheels. Coil it into three loops. Fig. 56-4.

4. Slip the new blade onto the upper and lower wheels with the teeth pointing downward. Fig. 56-5. The guides should be back out of position. Fig. 56-6. Tighten the vertical adjustment screw. Revolve the wheels by hand to see how the blade "rides." If the blade does not run in the center of the wheels, tilt the upper wheel with the tilt adjustment screw. The rear edge of the saw blade should be perpendicular to the table.
5. Adjust the tension of the saw with the vertical adjustment screw. If the saw does not have a tensioning spring, the blade should bend ⅛ to ¼ inch when pushed lightly on the side of the saw blade.

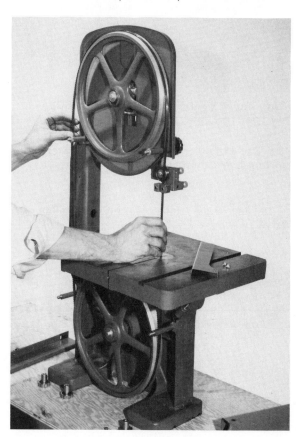

56-5. Installing a band-saw blade. The guards have been removed and the upper wheel released to permit the new blade to be slipped over the two wheels. There are adjustments on the reverse side of the upper wheel for tension and for tilting the wheel back and forth. This will, of course, move the blade.

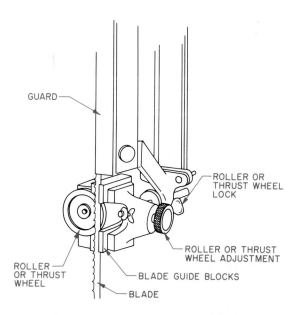

56-6. The roller or thrust wheel should just clear the back of the blade. The blade guide blocks should just clear the blade. They must not run on the blade. The front of the blocks should be just back of the teeth.

CUTTING WITH A BAND SAW

In cutting with a band saw, follow these general suggestions:

● *Watch the feed direction.* Before making the cut, think through the path that the blade must make. Some pieces will swing in such a way as to hit the upper arm if the plan is not correct. Fig. 56-7.

● *Make short cuts before long cuts.* It is much easier to backtrack out of a short cut than a long one. Fig. 56-8.

● *Make use of turning holes.* Depending on the design, a round or square hole can first be cut in the waste stock before bandsawing. Fig. 56-9.

● *Break up complicated curves.* Look at each job to see if a combination cut can be completed by making several simpler cuts. Fig. 56-10.

● *Rough-cut complex curves.* Make a simple cut through the waste stock to follow as much of the line as possible. Then cut to the layout line. Fig. 56-11.

● *Backtrack out of corners.* Cut out narrow grooves by "nibbling" at the closed end. On large rectangular openings, cut to one corner. Then backtrack slightly before cutting to another corner. Fig. 56-12.

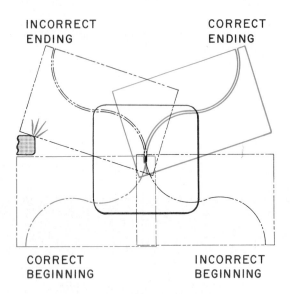

56-7. Checking the feed direction so that the work does not hit the saw arm.

56-8. Make short cuts before long cuts.

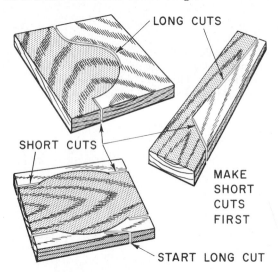

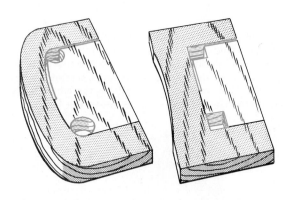

AN AUGER AND MORTISING CHISEL
USED TO MAKE TURNING HOLES

56-9. Use the auger bit and mortising chisel to cut starting holes shown.

56-10. The correct sequence in cutting a combination curve.

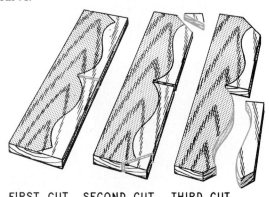

FIRST CUT   SECOND CUT   THIRD CUT

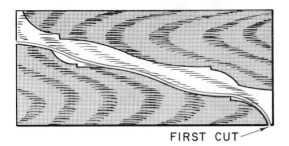

FIRST CUT

CUTTING CURVES

Select a band-saw blade for cutting curves, following this general rule: A ⅛-inch blade will cut down to about a ½-inch circle. A ⅜-inch blade will cut down to about a 2-inch circle. Fig. 56-13. The width of blade depends on the thickness and kind of wood to be cut and also on the sharpness of the curve.

In cutting curves, apply even forward pressure. Carefully guide the work with your left hand to keep the cut just outside the layout line. Fig. 56-14. In cutting sharp curves, make many relief cuts from the outside edge to within less than the thickness of the blade from the layout line. Fig. 56-15. Then, as you cut along the layout line, the waste stock will fall away freely. Cut circles freehand or with a circle jig. Figs. 56-16 and 56-17.

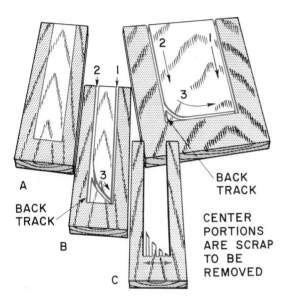

A

BACK TRACK

B

C

2 1

2 1

3

3

BACK TRACK

CENTER PORTIONS ARE SCRAP TO BE REMOVED

56-12. Sequence in cutting rectangular openings.

56-14. Cutting a curve on a band saw. The stock is carefully guided along the layout line.

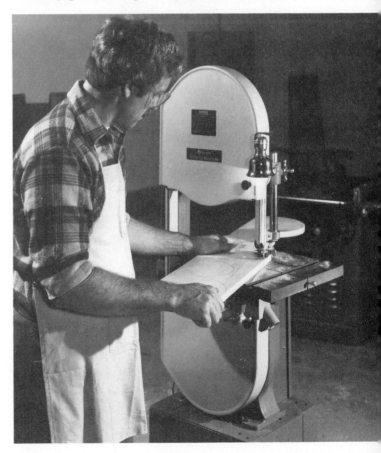

56-13. This chart shows how to select the right blade. For example, a 1/2-inch blade cannot cut a circle smaller than 2 1/2 inches in diameter. (Remember, radius is half of diameter.)

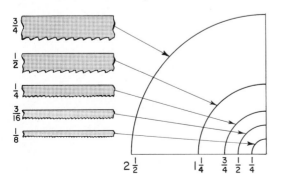

¾

½

¼

3⁄16

⅛

2 ½   1 ¼   ¾   ½   ¼

56-15. Cutting a sharp curve. When the blade on the band saw is a little too wide, a "closer" cut can be made with the aid of relief cuts.

COMPOUND CUTTING

Cut compound curves from two sides of the stock. Make a pattern and trace it on two adjoining faces. Then cut the waste stock from two sides of the stock. Then fasten the waste stock back in place, using small nails or masking tape. Turn the stock one-quarter turn and make the other two cuts. Fig. 56-18.

56-18. Make a compound cut. Step 1, trace the pattern on two adjoining sides. Step 2, make two cuts from one side. Step 3, fasten the scrap wood back on the piece and make two cuts from the adjacent side.

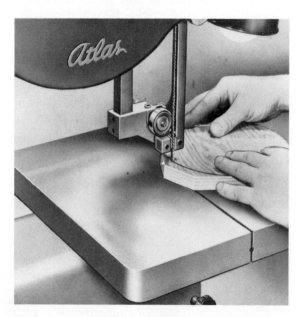

56-16. Cutting a circle freehand on the band saw.

56-17. Using an extension guide bar type of circle jig for cutting a true circle.

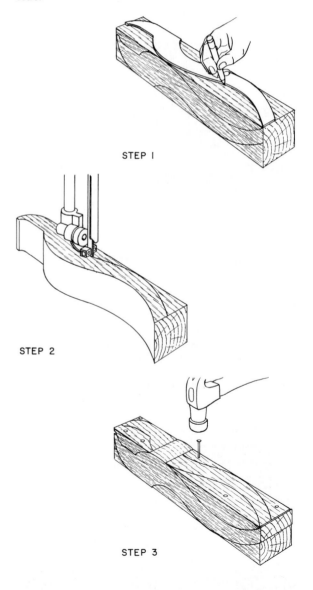

STEP 1

STEP 2

STEP 3

RESAWING

Resawing is sawing stock to reduce its thickness. When stock is much thicker than needed, it is resawed. This can be done on the band saw. The widest possible blade should be selected and a fence or pivot block attached to the table. A layout line across the end and edge of the board is helpful. Hold the stock against the fence or block and slowly feed the work against the blade. Fig. 56-19.

For very wide boards, it is better first to resaw partway from either edge on a circular saw and then complete the cut on the band saw.

PAD SAWING

Pad sawing is the cutting of several pieces at one time. On projects that require duplicate pieces such as flat scroll work, you can nail several thin boards together and make the scrolls with one cut. Or you can use a thick piece of stock. Cut your pattern. Then resaw it into thinner pieces. See Fig. 56-2.

56-19. Resawing stock. Fasten a pivot block to the table with a C-clamp to control the thickness of the cut. A band saw is better for resawing than a circular saw because less stock is wasted with the thinner blade and because the exposed blade is longer. Notice the tension nut for tightening the upper wheel and the adjustment for tilting the wheel.

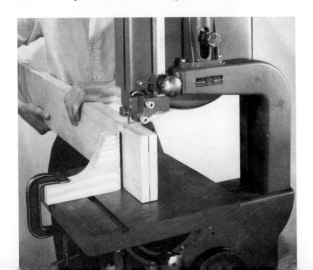

RIPPING

If a circular saw is not available, stock can be ripped to width by fastening a fence or pivot block to the table and proceeding in the same way as with a circular saw.

CROSSCUTTING AND MITERING

The table of the band saw has a groove into which a miter gauge will fit. Stock can be held against this miter gauge to do accurate crosscutting or miter cutting on a band saw.

TILT-TABLE WORK

The table can be tilted to do many jobs such as beveling and chamfering on curves and irregular designs.

Review Questions

1. Name the parts of the band saw.
2. How is the size of the band saw determined?
3. Describe the method followed for installing a saw blade.
4. Where should you stand when cutting with a band saw?
5. How can a sharp curve be cut?
6. What is the rule for selecting a band saw blade for cutting curves?
7. What is resawing?
8. What is the advantage of resawing on a band saw over resawing on a circular saw?
9. How can ripping be done on the band saw?

Chapter 57

Scroll (Jig) Saw

After studying this chapter, you will be able to:
- List the three types of blades used in the scroll saw.
- Describe how to install a scroll-saw blade.
- List those safety precautions that must be followed when operating the scroll saw.
- Demonstrate cutting with the scroll saw.

LOOK FOR THESE TERMS

inlaying
marquetry
scroll (jig) saw

The *scroll (jig) saw* is designed to cut sharp curves on both outside edges and interior sections of a workpiece. Fig. 57-1. The saw moves up and down to do the same type of cutting that can be done by hand with a coping or compass saw. Figs. 57-2 and 57-3. It differs from the band saw because it can make inside cuts without cutting through the stock.

PARTS OF THE SCROLL SAW

The saw consists of a *frame* with *overarm* and *base*, a *driving mechanism* to convert rotating action into up-and-down (reciprocating) action, *table, guide,* and *saw blade.* A tension sleeve is mounted in the end of the overarm, through which a plunger moves.

The size of the saw is indicated by the distance between the blade and the overarm, measured horizontally. The speed of the saw can be adjusted by shifting a belt to various positions or by turning the variable speed control handle.

There are three types of blades. *Power jig-saw blades* are used for many kinds of cutting on wood. The *saber blade* is fastened only in the lower chuck. *Jeweler's piercing blades* are used to cut thin metal. The saber blade is used for heavier stock. Table 57-A.

57-1. The fine scroll work on this mirror frame is typical of the cutting done on a scroll saw.

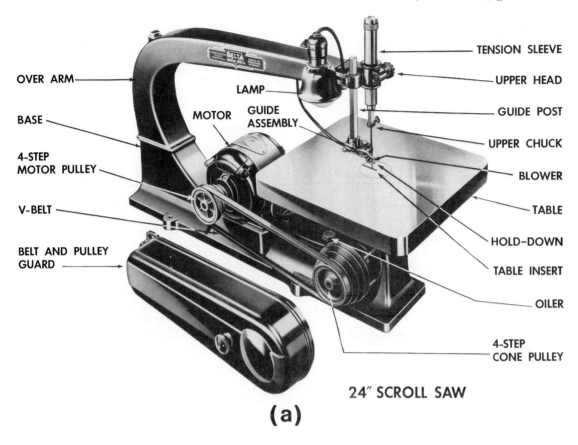

OVER ARM

BASE

4-STEP
MOTOR PULLEY

V-BELT

BELT AND PULLEY
GUARD

LAMP

MOTOR

GUIDE
ASSEMBLY

TENSION SLEEVE

UPPER HEAD

GUIDE POST

UPPER CHUCK

BLOWER

TABLE

HOLD–DOWN

TABLE INSERT

OILER

4-STEP
CONE PULLEY

24" SCROLL SAW

(a)

(b)

57-2. (a) A 24-inch scroll saw with a four-step pulley. (b) This 18" electronic variable-speed scroll saw can be adjusted for speeds from 40 to 2000 cutting strokes per minute.

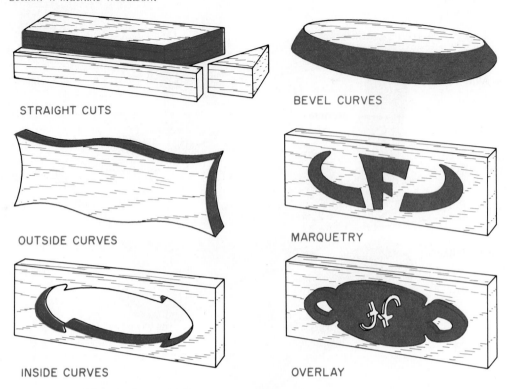

STRAIGHT CUTS

BEVEL CURVES

OUTSIDE CURVES

MARQUETRY

INSIDE CURVES

OVERLAY

57-3. Common cuts that can be made on the scroll saw.

INSTALLING A SCROLL-SAW BLADE

Select the correct type and thickness of blade. All are usually about 5 inches long. Remove the table insert.

Tilt the table so that you can see the lower chuck. Place the lower end of the blade in the lower chuck with the teeth pointing down. Fig. 57-4. Tighten the setscrew (thumbscrew), making sure that the blade is held securely in the chuck. Fig. 57-5. Remember, the lower chuck does the driving. If external cutting is to be done, fasten the blade in the upper chuck. Fig. 57-6. This upper chuck controls the tension. Pull down on the upper chuck and attach the other end of the blade in this chuck. If necessary, loosen the tension sleeve knob and move the sleeve up and down. Replace the table insert. If a saber blade is used for internal cutting, it is held only in the lower jaw. Fig. 57-7. Now adjust the guide post until the hold-down will apply light pressure on the workpiece.

Adjust the roller guide to touch the back of the blade lightly. Tighten it in position. Use the hand wheel without power to turn the machine to make sure that the blade moves freely. Now recheck with the power on. If the speed is too fast, readjust the variable speed hand control. If the machine does not have such a control, turn off the power. Remove the belt guide, and move the belt for a lower speed. Fig. 57-8.

Table 57-A. Blade Selection

Material Cut	Thick In.	Width In.	Teeth Per Inch	Blade Full Size

Wood
  Veneer
Plus Plastics
Celluloid
Hard Rubber
Bakelite
Ivory
Extremely
  Thin
  Materials
	.008	.035	20	

Plastics Celluloid Hard Rubber Bakelite Ivory Wood	.019 .019 .020 .020	.050 .055 .070 .110	15 12 7 7	
Wall Board Pressed Wood Wood Lead Bone Felt Paper Copper Ivory Aluminum	.020	.110	15	
Hard and Soft Wood	.020 .028 .028	.110 .187 .250	10 10 7	

Pearl
Pewter
Mica
Pressed
  Wood
Sea Shells
Jewelry
Metals
Hard
  Leather
	.016
	.016
	.020
	.020
		.054
		.054
		.070
		.085
			30
			20
			15
			12	

57-4. Clamp the blade firmly in the lower jaw, using a hexagon wrench or a thumbscrew to tighten the jaws. Tilt the table so that you can see what you are doing. Do not clamp too tightly or you may shear the threads or break off the thumb control. The lower chuck does the driving, while the upper chuck controls blade tension.

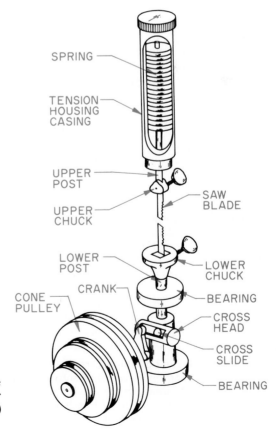

57-5. The correct way to install a jeweler's blade. The blade must be fastened in both the lower and upper chuck. The tension housing casting (tension sleeve) must apply the tension to the blade.

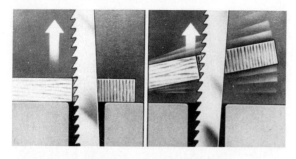

57-6. Install the blade with the teeth pointed down. Slant the blade toward the work to clear the stock on the upstroke. If it slants away, the teeth will catch and lift the stock.

 Safety

In operating the scroll saw, take the following precautions:

● Be certain the blade is properly installed in a vertical position with the teeth pointing down.

● Roll the machine over by hand to see if there is clearance for the blade and if the tension sleeve has been properly set.

● Check the belt guard to see that it is closed and tight.

● Adjust the hold-down to the thickness of the stock being cut. This will prevent the work from moving up and down with the blade.

● Do not allow your fingers to come any closer to the blade than 2 inches when cutting stock.

● Keep your fingers to the side of the blade, never in front of it.

● Cut cylindrical (round) stock by holding it in a special "V" fixture.

● Stop the scroll saw to make any adjustments.

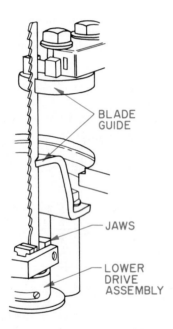

57-7. Fastening a saber blade in the lower chuck. Notice that the chuck has been turned a quarter turn and the blade fastened in the V-jaws. An extra support bracket has been fastened in place.

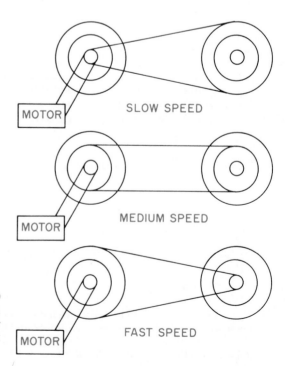

57-8. Speeds can be adjusted from 600 rpm to 1750 rpm. The fast speed is for cutting softwoods and then hardwoods. Medium speeds are for cutting thicker hardwoods (from 1/2 to 3/4 inches). The slowest speed is for cutting soft metals like aluminum.

CUTTING WITH A SCROLL SAW

Adjust the guide so that the small spring tension holds the stock firmly against the table. Fig. 57-9. Hold the workpiece with thumb and forefinger of both hands. Apply even, forward pressure. Fig. 57-10. Do not force the stock into the work. Turn the stock slowly when cutting a curve. If the stock is turned too sharply, the blade will break. If rather complicated cuts must be made, plan the cutting carefully before you proceed. Figs. 57-11 and 57-12.

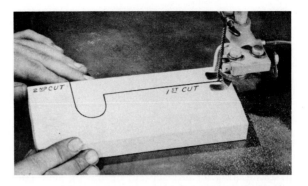

57-11. The proper method of making complicated cuts on the jig saw. In cutting out this design, make a straight cut first. Then back the stock off the saw and make a curved cut until it joins the straight cut. This eliminates the necessity of trying to cut a sharp corner.

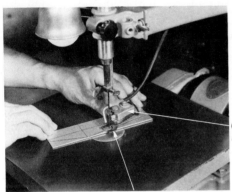

GUIDE ASSEMBLY

HOLD DOWN

57-9. The saw guide properly adjusted. The small spring tension in the bottom of the saw guide holds the stock firmly against the table of the saw.

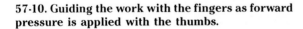

57-10. Guiding the work with the fingers as forward pressure is applied with the thumbs.

57-12. Break up combination curves. A continuous line should not always mean a continuous *cut*. Most complex curves can be broken into simple curves for easier cutting.

CUTTING INTERNAL CURVES AND DESIGNS

Drill a relief hole in the center of the waste stock. Fig. 57-13. If a jeweler's blade is to be used, remove the throat plate. After the blade is fastened in the lower chuck, put the stock over the blade. Fasten the other end of the blade to the plunger chuck. Then replace the throat plate. Adjust the guide to the correct height. Then make a circular cut from the relief hole to the layout line. Fig. 57-14.

TILT-TABLE WORK

The table of the jig saw can be tilted to cut a bevel on a straight, circular, or irregular design.

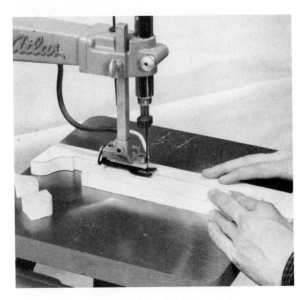

57-13. Making an internal cut on the jig saw. The relief hole has been drilled in the center of the waste stock and the cut is made to the layout line.

MAKING AN INLAY OR SIMPLE MARQUETRY

Inlaying (or *marquetry*) is a way of forming a design by using two or more different kinds of wood. To make a simple inlay, first fasten two pieces of wood together in a pad. Nail them together with small brads at each corner. Drill a small hole at an inside corner of the design to start the blade. Now tilt the table of the saw 1 or 2 degrees. Make all necessary cuts, with the work always on the same side of the blade. Fig. 57-15.

Take the pad apart and assemble the design. When pieces with a beveled edge are fitted together, there will be no space caused by a saw kerf. Fig. 57-16.

57-14. Doing internal cutting on the jig saw.

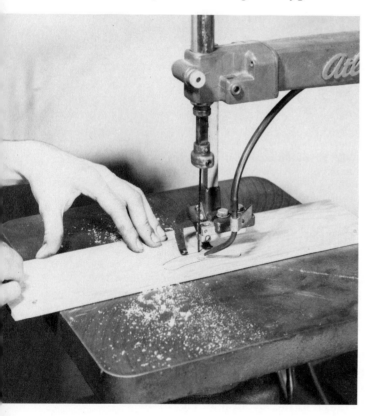

57-15. The pad of material has been nailed together in the corner as the design is cut out.

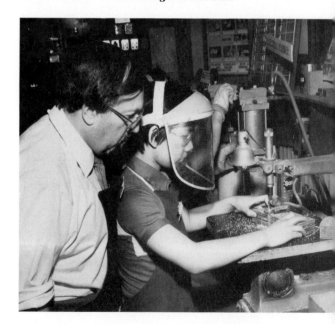

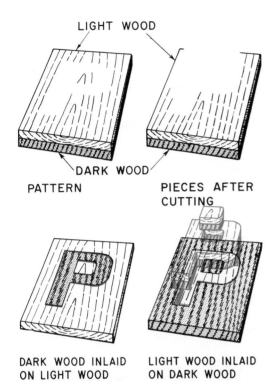

LIGHT WOOD

DARK WOOD

PATTERN

PIECES AFTER
CUTTING

DARK WOOD INLAID
ON LIGHT WOOD

LIGHT WOOD INLAID
ON DARK WOOD

57-16. The basic steps in making a simple inlay.

Review Questions

1. Sketch a scroll saw and locate its parts.
2. How is the size of the scroll saw indicated?
3. Name the three types of blades.
4. How is internal cutting done on the scroll saw?
5. Explain how to make an inlay.

Chapter 58 | Jointer and Rotary Jointer-Surfacer

After studying this chapter, you will be able to:
● Identify the main parts of the jointer.
● List those safety precautions that must be followed in operating the jointer.
● Describe face planing.
● List the steps in jointing an edge.
● Describe how to cut a bevel on a jointer.
● Describe how to cut a rabbet on a jointer.
● List the advantages of the rotary jointer-surfacer.

LOOK FOR THESE TERMS

face planing
jointer
rotary jointer-surfacer

The *jointer* is used for surfacing or face planing, jointing an edge or end, beveling, chamfering, tapering, and rabbeting. Figs. 58-1 and 58-2. Parts are shown in Fig. 58-3.

The circular cutterhead holds three knives firmly mounted with wedges and setscrews. The size of the jointer is determined by the length of these knives. The most common sizes are the 6- and 8-inch machines.

The in-feed and out-feed tables are mounted on sliding ways so that they may be raised and lowered to make adjustments. The out-feed table supports the work after it has been cut. Therefore, it should be the same height as the cutting knives at their highest point. Fig. 58-4. The in-feed table supports the work before it is cut. Therefore the height of this table determines the thickness of the cut to be taken.

Once the out-feed table has been adjusted to the proper height, it can be locked in position and does not need to be changed. Fig. 58-5. Only the in-feed table should be moved up or down to change the thickness of the

58-1. A jointer is used for getting out stock, squaring up stock, and making joints like those used on this table.

cut. The fence of a jointer is usually set at right angles to the table. However, it can be adjusted to any angle when you want to plane a bevel or chamfer.

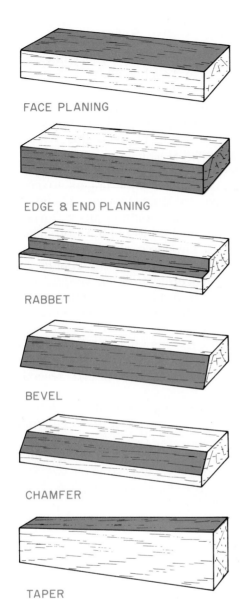

FACE PLANING

EDGE & END PLANING

RABBET

BEVEL

CHAMFER

TAPER

58-2. Common processes that can be done on the jointer.

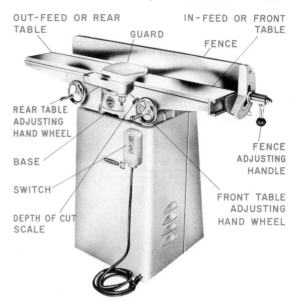

OUT-FEED OR REAR TABLE

GUARD

IN-FEED OR FRONT TABLE

FENCE

REAR TABLE ADJUSTING HAND WHEEL

BASE

FENCE ADJUSTING HANDLE

SWITCH

DEPTH OF CUT SCALE

FRONT TABLE ADJUSTING HAND WHEEL

58-3. A jointer with a fence and guard. The parts include a base, the cutterhead, the infeed (or front) table, and the outfeed (or rear) table. This is a 6-inch jointer.

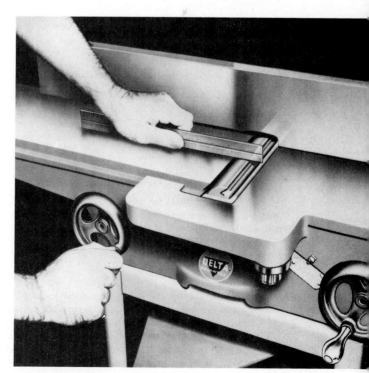

58-4. Using a straightedge to check the position of the outfeed table so that it is level with the knives.

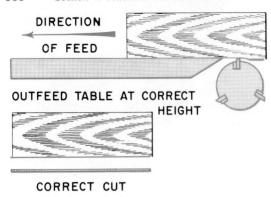

DIRECTION OF FEED

OUTFEED TABLE AT CORRECT HEIGHT

CORRECT CUT

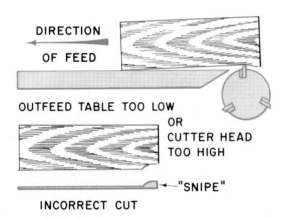

DIRECTION OF FEED

OUTFEED TABLE TOO LOW
OR
CUTTER HEAD TOO HIGH

← "SNIPE"

INCORRECT CUT

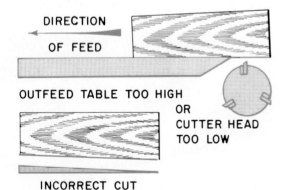

DIRECTION OF FEED

OUTFEED TABLE TOO HIGH
OR
CUTTER HEAD TOO LOW

INCORRECT CUT

58-5. The jointer must be adjusted so the outfeed table is at exactly the same height as the cutterhead knife at its highest point.

58-6. Stock should be fed into the cutterhead opposite the grain direction so that the revolving knives (rotating clockwise) will cut *with* the grain. The cutting action is the same as when using a hand plane with the grain. Place the stock on the jointer with the grain pointing toward the *infeed* table.

Safety

- It is dangerous to use a jointer for stock less than 2 inches wide or 12 inches long or ½-inch thick.
- Always have the guard in place over the knives while the jointer is being operated. The only exception to this rule is when rabbeting stock.
- Feed the stock with the grain. Fig. 58-6.
- Do not allow your fingers to come any closer to the revolving blades than 5 inches when jointing stock. Always keep your hands on top of the work. Fig. 58-7.
- Adjust the depth of the cut before turning on the power. The front table adjusting handwheel controls the vertical movement of the front table and regulates the depth of the cut. Stop the jointer to make any adjustments.
- Do not use the jointer for cuts heavier than ⅛ inch. A cut that is too heavy may cause kickback. It is safer to take several lighter cuts.
- Hold the work face of the stock flat against the fence throughout the edge jointing operation.
- Use a push block when planing the face of a board. Fig. 58-8.

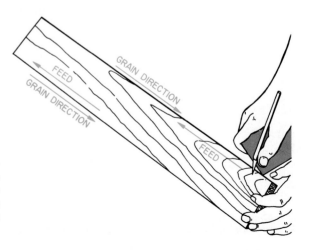

GRAIN DIRECTION
FEED
GRAIN DIRECTION
FEED

- Feed (push) work into the revolving blade firmly and at a rate that will not overload the machine.
- Keep your hands on top of the stock and not on the ends. A sudden jar, caused by a knot, might dislodge your hands or jab the corners of the stock into your palms.
- Stand to the left of the jointer, never directly in back of it.

58-7. The danger zone of a jointer is the area directly over the revolving cutter. This is the area you must guard against.

58-8. Using a push block. Never attempt to surface thin stock or joint the edge of narrow pieces without using a push block to keep your fingers away from the revolving cutter.

FACE PLANING OR SURFACING

Face planing, or *surfacing*, means planing the surfaces of stock true. Only stock that is less in width than the knives of the jointer should be face planed. *Generally speaking, the jointer is not used for face planing.* If it is used, set the in-feed table to take a very thin cut. Hold the stock firmly against the front of the table. With one hand, push the stock as the other hand holds the front of the stock down. Slowly push the board through the cutterhead. As in hand planing, apply most of the pressure to the front of the board as the cutting is started. Then apply equal pressure to both front and back as the board passes across the cutter. Finally, apply more pressure to the rear of the board as the major portion of it has passed the out-feed table. Figs. 58-9 and 58-10.

58-9. The correct method of face planing. 1. Start the cut by applying pressure on the stock with both hands against the infeed table. 2. As the stock passes over the cutter head, move one hand to the outfeed table and apply pressure. *Never allow your hand to pass directly over the cutter head.* 3. Now apply pressure on the outfeed table using both hands.

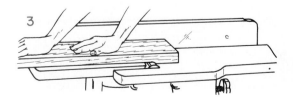

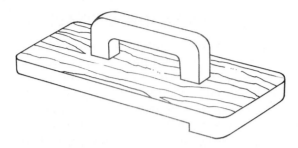

58-10. A push block can be used to move the stock. If a push block is used, your hand can pass directly over the cutter head without danger of injury.

JOINTING AN EDGE

The most common use of the jointer is to square an edge true with the face surface. To do this, make sure that the fence is at right angles to the table. Check this with a try square. Hold the stock on the in-feed table with the face surface against the fence. Use one hand to guide the stock and the other hand to apply forward pressure. Fig. 58-11. Do not push the stock through the jointer too fast. This will cause little ripples to be formed by the revolving cutter.

BEVELING AND CHAMFERING

To cut a bevel or chamfer on an edge with a jointer, set the fence at the proper angle to the table. The fence may be tilted in or out. Fig. 58-12. Check this angle with a sliding T-bevel. Then proceed as in jointing an edge.

58-11. Jointing an edge. Hold the stock firmly against the infeed table at the beginning of the cut. Then apply even pressure. Finally, apply pressure on the outfeed table.

58-12. Cutting a bevel or chamfer. The fence of the jointer can be tilted for the operation.

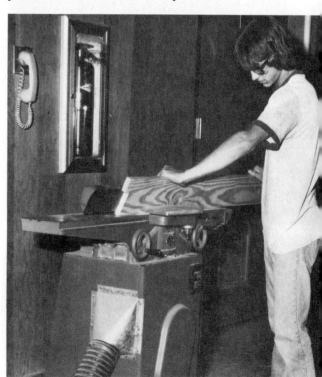

RABBETING

A rabbet can be cut with the grain by first adjusting the fence to an amount equal to the width of the rabbet. Then the in-feed table is adjusted to an amount equal to the depth of the rabbet. If the rabbet is quite deep, it may be necessary to cut it in two passes. *Caution: The guard must be removed for this process, so be especially careful.* Fig. 58-13. However, you can clamp a scrap piece to the fence to cover the cutterhead.

58-13. Cutting a rabbet on the jointer.

ROTARY JOINTER-SURFACER

The *rotary jointer-surfacer*, which is sold under the trade name Uniplane®, will perform many operations not easily done on the conventional jointer. Fig. 58-14. It will safely and accurately plane, joint, bevel, chamfer, trim, and taper. This machine can surface stock up to 6 inches wide. It can plane pieces as small as ⅛-inch square. Fig. 58-15.

The cutterhead has eight cutters. Mounted alternately are four scoring cutters and four shearing cutters. The cutterhead operates at 4000 RPM.

The depth-of-cut control is located on the front of the machine. It is calibrated in sixty-fourths of an inch, with even finer settings possible to five-thousandths of an inch.

By loosening the two table-locking handles, one in the front and one in the rear, the table can be positioned at 90 degrees to the cutterhead or at any angle up to 45 degrees. The table has a slot in which a miter gauge can be used to support the stock for trimming narrow pieces or for cutting miters, chamfers, or compound miters. Fig. 58-16.

With a rotary jointer-surfacer you can work on much smaller pieces of stock than with a jointer. This machine will also do a good job on end grain. However, keep in mind that the safety precautions used for the jointer must be followed. Fig. 58-17.

58-14. Parts of a jointer surface.

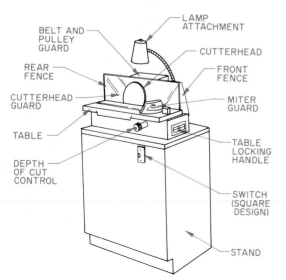

LAMP ATTACHMENT
BELT AND PULLEY GUARD
CUTTERHEAD
REAR FENCE
FRONT FENCE
CUTTERHEAD GUARD
MITER GUARD
TABLE
TABLE LOCKING HANDLE
DEPTH OF CUT CONTROL
SWITCH (SQUARE DESIGN)
STAND

58-15. Thin stock up to 6 inches wide can be planed smoothly.

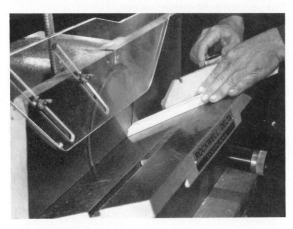

58-16. Trimming end grain for a compound miter.

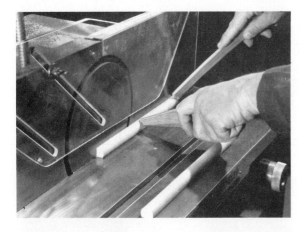

58-17. Cutting a flat side on round stock. Note the use of the push stick—to keep your fingers at a safe distance from the cutters. Note also the plastic guard that can be lowered to cover most of the cutterhead.

Math Quiz

If the jointer is set to cut at .125 inch and the board is passed through three times, by how much is the board reduced in size?

Answer
.375

Review Questions

1. Name the parts of a jointer.
2. What determines the size of a jointer?
3. How is the depth of cut controlled?
4. List the safety precautions for the jointer.
5. Is the jointer commonly used for face-planing?
6. How can the fence of the jointer be checked for squareness?
7. What causes ripples to be formed on a board when it is run through the jointer?
8. How can you check the fence for cutting a bevel?
9. What are some of the advantages of a jointer-surfacer?

Facts about Wood

The Building of Jamestown

Jamestown was the first permanent English settlement in North America. Established in May, 1607, by Captain John Smith and a band of about 100 settlers, it was located on a peninsula in the James River. The marshy site was to prove unhealthy for the settlers. The small settlement was surrounded by forest on three sides. But, from this forest came the raw materials that enabled the English settlers to build the shelters they needed to survive. Smith himself directed the building of the houses. Smith was a man of considerable energy and talent. A former soldier, he also was an expert mapmaker.

To cut the wood needed for the houses and the fort, Smith established a crude sawmill at Jamestown. Though it was simple, it gave the settlers a means of cutting the wood they needed for their shelters. As well as needing shelter for themselves, the settlers also needed shelter for their animals. They needed also to build a fort to provide them with protection. All of these structures were built of wood. The building of all of them was directed by Captain Smith.

Wood was used to make barrels and buckets. It was used as fuel during the grim winters—especially during the "starving time"—the winter of 1609-1610.

Knowledgeable and resourceful, Captain Smith also directed the making of tar and pitch. (Tar and pitch are similar. Tar is more fluid than pitch.) Both of these were made from trees growing in the surrounding forest. They were essential products if the ships were to be well-sealed against leaks. Tar also was used to prevent ropes from deteriorating and to seal barrels. The forest also provided wood from which ships' masts and spars might be fashioned. As the settlement became more firmly established, outlying forts were built. Again, these were of wood.

Jamestown was the capital of Virginia until 1699. In that year, the capital was moved to Williamsburg (then named Middle Plantation). Shortly after that, Jamestown fell into decay. In the last two hundred years, the marshy peninsula has become an island, Jamestown Island. Incorporated into the Colonial National Historical Park, it contains exhibit pavilions and a replica of the first fort. It also has other 17th-century replicas that offer some suggestion of life on the first English frontier in North America. Jamestown Island is the property of the federal government.

Williamsburg is less than 20 miles from Jamestown. In Williamsburg, the more elaborate architecture and the greater use of brick as a building material indicated the progress that was made in the years since the founding of the first settlement. Brick, though, is a building material for a more settled, more established settlement. As the frontier pushed west, it was wood that was the principal building material.

Chapter 59

Drill Press

After studying this chapter, you will be able to:
- List those safety precautions that must be followed in operating a drill press.
- Identify the cutting tools that can be used in the drill press.
- Identify the adjustments that can be made on a drill press.
- Demonstrate the proper operation of a drill press.

LOOK FOR THESE TERMS

drill press
expansive bit
fly cutter
Forstner bit
hole saw

machine spur bit
mortising attachment
multispur machine bit
plug cutter
sanding drum

solid center auger bit
spade bit
spur machine bit
twist drill

The *drill press* is used primarily for drilling and boring holes. With proper speeds, it can also be used for shaping, routing, carving, sanding, and mortising. Fig. 59-1. The *size* of the machine is determined by the largest diameter stock that can be drilled through the center. If the distance from the column to the center of the table is 8 inches, then the size of the drill press is 16 inches. Machines equipped with step pulleys usually have four speeds of 470, 780, 1,300, and 1,950 RPM. Fig. 59-2. Machines with variable speed pulleys can operate at any speed from 450 to 4,700 RPM. Fig. 59-3. The higher speeds are needed for such operations as routing and shaping.

⚠ Safety

In operating a drill press, observe the following precautions:
- Use a drill or bit with a straight shank—never a square one.
- Check the speed. Use a slow speed for large holes and a faster speed for smaller holes. On a step pulley machine, change the speed with the switch *off*. On a variable speed machine, change the speed with the machine operating.
- Keep your hair and loose clothing away from all moving parts.
- Place the drill or bit in the chuck straight and tighten it securely.
- Always remove the chuck key before starting the machine.
- When making the setup, make sure the bit or drill will not mar the vise or table. Place a piece of scrap stock under the work to be drilled.
- Clamp round stock in a V-block before drilling.
- Keep your fingers at least 4 inches away from the rotating tool.
- Remove chips and shavings with a brush or stick of wood—never your fingers.
- Feed the drill or bit smoothly into the workpiece. When the hole is deep, withdraw it often to clear the shavings. Fig. 59-4.
- Check the setup carefully before doing special operations such as routing or shaping.

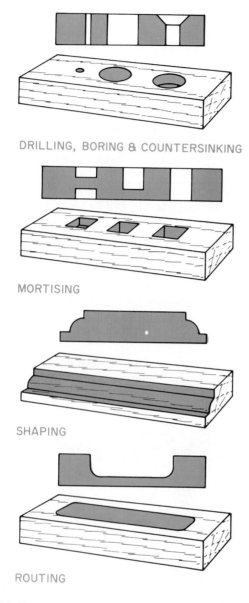

DRILLING, BORING & COUNTERSINKING

MORTISING

SHAPING

ROUTING

59-1. Common operations that can be performed on the drill press.

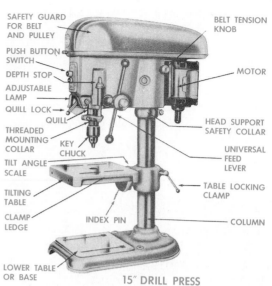

SAFETY GUARD FOR BELT AND PULLEY

PUSH BUTTON SWITCH

DEPTH STOP

ADJUSTABLE LAMP

QUILL LOCK

QUILL

THREADED MOUNTING COLLAR

KEY CHUCK

TILT ANGLE SCALE

TILTING TABLE

CLAMP LEDGE

INDEX PIN

LOWER TABLE OR BASE

BELT TENSION KNOB

MOTOR

HEAD SUPPORT SAFETY COLLAR

UNIVERSAL FEED LEVER

TABLE LOCKING CLAMP

COLUMN

15″ DRILL PRESS

59-2. A bench-type drill press with step pulleys showing the major parts. Size is indicated by the largest diameter of stock through which a hole can be drilled.

59-3. Drill press with variable speed pulleys. The range of speed is from 450 RPM to 4,700 RPM. The speed is changed by moving the dial lever while the drill press is running. Never change the speed when the machine is off. This is the ideal machine for doing a wide variety of drill-press operations.

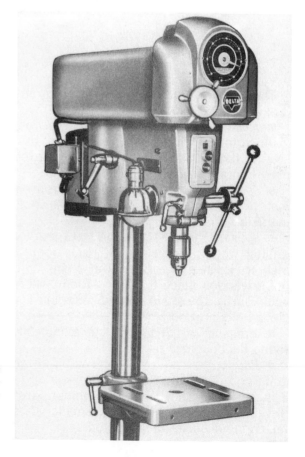

59-4. Follow good safety practices when using the drill. Be sure to wear proper eye protection.

CUTTING TOOLS

The following cutting tools are used in the drill press:

- *Twist drills* are available in sizes from ¹⁄₁₆ inch to ½ inch by 64ths. Some twist drill sets all have ½-inch shanks so they can be used in portable electric drills. Fig. 59-5.
- *Spade bits* come in diameters from ³⁄₈ inch to 1½ inch. They are fast-cutting tools that leave a rather rough hole.
- *Spur machine bits* are the ideal tool for drilling wood. They come in sizes from ¹⁄₈ inch to ½ inch by 16ths. The sharp brad point lets you place the hole exactly where you want it. The sharp cutting spurs make a clean hole in wood.
- *Multispur machine bits* cut a perfectly round flat-bottomed hole.
- *Plug cutters* are used for cutting cross-grain and end-grain plugs and dowels up to 3 inches long. They come in common sizes of ³⁄₈, ½, ⁵⁄₈, ¾, and 1 inch. The smaller sizes match the diameter of dowel rods.

- *Twist drills* with an adjustable countersink attachment are used for installing flat head screws. They do the same job as the screw-mate drill and countersink. See Chapter 36.
- *Solid center auger bits* with straight shanks can be used for boring larger holes.
- *Expansive bits* are adjustable to different diameters. When using this tool, make sure the workpiece is fastened securely with clamps.
- *Fly cutter*, sometimes called a circle cutter, can be adjusted to cut holes from 1 inch to 4 inches.
- *Hole saws* come in sizes up to 3½ inches. Saws of several different diameters can fit the same mandrel.
- *Forstner bits* are used to cut flat-bottom holes, even through knots, end grain, and veneer. See Chapter 25.

59-5. Cutting tools used on the drill press. A. Twist drill; B. Space bit; C. Spur machine bit; D. Multispur machine bit; E. Forstner bit; F. Expansive bit; G. Countersink.

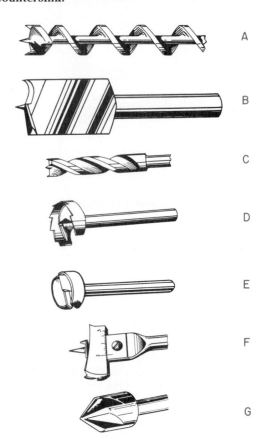

ADJUSTMENTS

The following adjustments are made on a drill press:

● *Speed*. Speed is adjusted by either changing the belt on the pulleys or by turning the handle on the front of the variable speed control. Before changing speeds on a belt and pulley machine, first make sure the power is disconnected. Then raise the cover over the pulleys. To adjust to the fastest speed (for holes under ¼ inch) place the belt in the top position with the belt on the largest

pulley on the motor (driving pulley) and on the smallest pulley on the spindle (driven pulley). Fig. 59-6.

● *Installing a drill or bit*. Place a piece of scrap wood on the table. Use the key to open the chuck slightly larger than the shank of the tool. Hold the tool in the chuck, making sure it is straight. Then tighten securely with the key. A common mistake is not to have enough pressure on the tool shank. If this happens, after drilling begins, the tool itself begins rotating in the chuck instead of cutting the hole. Fig. 59-7.

Math Quiz

On a machine that uses pulleys and a belt to transmit power, the speed of rotation is changed by moving 297he belt from one set of pulleys to another. The highest speed is obtained when the belt is on the largest pulley on the motor (driving pulley) and the smallest pulley on the spindle (driven pulley). The relationship between the pulley diameters and the speed is as follows:

$$\frac{\text{speed of driven pulley}}{\text{speed of driving pulley}} = \frac{\text{diameter of driving pulley}}{\text{diameter of driven pulley}}$$

Assume that a driving pulley with a diameter of 6 inches and a speed of 1,400 RPM is connected to a driven pulley with a diameter of 9 inches. Using the formula above, the speed of the driven pulley is found as follows:

$$\frac{s}{1,400} = \frac{6}{9}$$

$$9 \times s = 1,400 \times 6$$
$$9s = 8,400$$
$$s = \frac{8,400}{9}$$
$$s = 933 \text{ RPM}$$

What would be the speed of the driven pulley, if a 10-inch driving pulley turning at a speed of 1,600 RPM is connected to a 5-inch driven pulley?

Answer
3,200 RPM

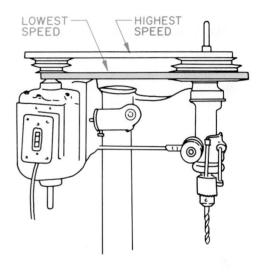

59-6. In this position, the belt will provide the highest speed of about 1950 RPM.

59-7. Make sure the cutting tool is centered in the three jaws of the chuck. *Always remove the chuck key.*

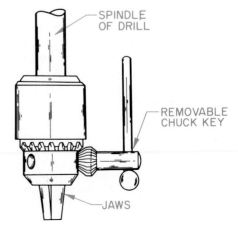

● *Adjusting the table.* Release the table-locking clamp. Raise the table so that the space between the top of the workpiece and the point of the tool is about ½ inch. Tighten the clamp.

● *Setting the depth gauge or stop.* This device on the side of the drill press controls how far the cutting tool can move. If you wish to drill a hole only partway through a piece of wood, draw a line on the side indicating this depth. Pull down on the handle until the point of the tool is at this line. Then move the two adjusting nuts that limit the drilling to this point.

GENERAL PROCEDURES

1. Select the correct bit or drill and fasten it securely in the chuck. *Caution: Always remove the key before turning on the power.*
2. Make sure the proper layout has been made and that the position of the hole is well marked.
3. Make sure the drill or bit is free to go through the table opening in the drill-press table. Also, place a piece of scrap wood under the material. This will help prevent splintering when the drill goes through the underside of the work.
4. Adjust the drill press for the correct cutting speed. The speed should vary with the type of bit, the size, the kind of wood, and the depth of the hole. In general, the smaller the cutting tool and the softer the wood, the higher the speed. Select the approximate speed. Then use good judgment when feeding the tool into the material. If the tool smokes, reduce the speed and the feed.
5. Clamp the work securely when necessary, especially when using larger drilling and boring tools, hole cutters, and similar cutting devices. Clamping is a must if the tool has only one cutting edge, such as a hole cutter. Fig. 59-8.

59-8. When drilling holes for dowels, place one piece over the other so that the holes will align. Note how the workpiece is clamped in a vise.

DRILLING SMALL HOLES IN FLAT STOCK

To drill or bore a hole that is ¼ inch or smaller, use a twist drill. Locate the center of the hole and mark it with a center punch or scratch awl. Place it on the table over a piece of scrap wood. Turn on the power and slowly move the point of the bit into the stock. Hold the stock firmly and apply even pressure to the handle. If the stock is hardwood or the hole is deep, back up the bit once or twice to remove the chips before finishing the hole. Always bore through the hole and into the scrap wood.

CUTTING MEDIUM-SIZED HOLES IN FLAT STOCK

Holes from ¼ inch to 1¼ inch can be cut with a variety of drilling and boring tools. For example, a twist drill, auger bit, Forstner bit, or spade bit could be used. Figs. 59-9 and 59-10. There are two methods for boring a through hole. The simplest is to place a piece of scrap wood under the hole so that the tool will cut through the stock and into the scrap piece. This keeps the underside from splintering. The second method is to cut until the point of the bit shows through the stock, then drill from the other side. To bore a hole to a specific depth, adjust the depth stop *with the power off.* Bring the cutting tool down to the side of the work where the depth is marked. Then set the depth stop.

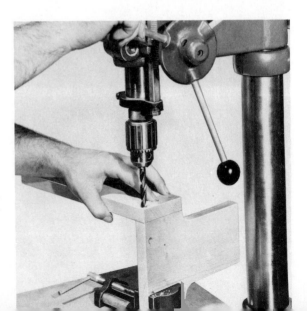

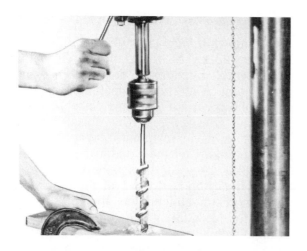

59-9. Boring a hole with an auger bit. Stock is clamped to the bed with a C-clamp. The auger bit must have a straight shank in order to be used in a three-jaw chuck.

BORING LARGE HOLES IN FLAT STOCK

Holes larger than 1¼ inch are best cut with a hole saw or a circle cutter. Make sure that the work is firmly clamped, especially when using a hole cutter, since any tool with a single point tends to rotate the work.

OTHER DRILLING OPERATIONS

Holes can be drilled or bored in round stock by holding the workpiece in a V-block. Fig. 59-11. To drill or bore holes at an angle, adjust the table to the right or left to the correct angle. Fig. 59-12. Countersinking is necessary when installing flat head screws. Fig. 59-13.

59-11. Drilling holes in a cylindrical piece of stock, using a V-block. The table has been turned at a 90-degree angle to its original position and a V-block clamped to the table with two C-clamps.

59-10. Using a power Forstner bit with the work securely clamped to the table.

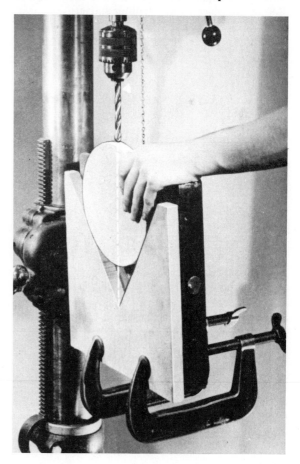

TABLE TILTS ALL ANGLES LEFT OR RIGHT THRU 90°

59-12. Drilling a hole at an angle. Make sure to center-punch the location so that the drill will not slide out of place as the drilling starts.

59-13. Countersinking holes on the drill press.

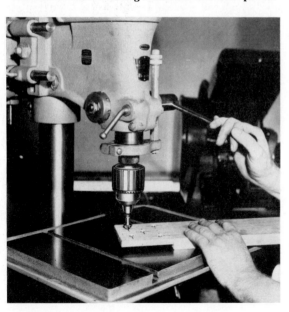

MORTISING

If much furniture construction is done, a *mortising attachment* should be available. This greatly simplifies cutting a mortise-and-tenon joint. A mortising attachment consists of a hollow, square mortising chisel in which an auger bit revolves. The chisel itself is ground to a sharp point at each corner. These points enter the wood just after the revolving bit. They cut the square opening after the bit has removed most of the stock. On most mortising attachments, the chisel is fastened to the quill of the drill press and a straight-shank auger bit fastened in the chuck. The chisel should be the same width as the width of the mortise to be cut. A fence should be attached to the table to guide the stock. Fig. 59-14.

59-14. Using a mortising attachment. The part for holding the chisel is locked to the quill of the drill press. The auger bit is fastened in the chuck. A fence is locked to the table, and clamps are attached to hold the stock in place.

SHAPING

For shaping, a spindle speed of 4,700 RPM is needed. This speed can be attained by using the variable-speed pulley or a high-speed motor. It is also necessary to have a special adapter that will hold the shaper cutter. Fig. 59-15. This adapter can be attached to the spindle of the drill press. Then an inexpensive set of shaper cutters will enable you to construct setups that will cut a variety of shapes. Never use a shaper cutter in a chuck. Select the shaper cutter for the particular shape you want to make.

The depth of the cut can be controlled by placing a collar of the correct diameter just above or below the cutter or by using a fence. Fasten the cutter and collar to the special adapter. Raise the table to the correct position and lock it in place. Make a trial cut in a piece of scrap stock of the same thickness as the finished piece. In using a shaper attachment, force the wood into the cutter very slowly. Sometimes it is a good idea to cut the design to partial depth and then go over it again. If the design is cut on three or four edges, finish the ends first and then the sides. If the trial cut is satisfactory, cut the edge. Fig. 59-16.

59-16. Using the drill press as a shaper. When doing shaping operations, a high spindle speed is required.

59-15. An adapter for holding the shaper cutters. This one is fastened to the spindle of the drill press so that side pressure can be exerted on the shaper cutters. Never attempt to hold shaper or router cutters in a drill-press chuck unless you are sure that the chuck is a part of the spindle assembly as a unit.

ROUTING

A routing tool is fastened in a special router attachment. The spindle speed must be about 5,000 RPM. Various types of routing such as grooves, slots, and irregular openings can be done on the drill press. Fig. 59-17.

SANDING

Sanding drums are available in several sizes that can be used in the drill press to do edge sanding. Manufacturers supply sanding sleeves in grits and sizes to fit the drums. Fig. 59-18.

59-17. Doing router work on a drill press. Router cutters are fastened in a special adapter. Make sure that the stock is held firmly against the table and a fence when doing the routing. Notice the guides that have been clamped to the machine to hold the stock in place.

59-18. Sanding can be done using a sanding drum.

Review Questions

1. Drilling is not the only operation performed on the drill press. Name several others.
2. What spindle speed is needed for shaping?
3. Name the parts of a mortising attachment and describe how it is used.
4. How do you control the depth of cut for shaping?
5. What spindle speed is needed for routing?

Chapter 60

Sanding Machines

After studying this chapter, you will be able to:
- List safety precautions for sanding machines.
- Change a belt on a stationary belt sander.
- Describe the basic steps in removing worn abrasive and applying new abrasive to an abrasive disk.

LOOK FOR THESE TERMS

narrow belt sander-grinder	stationary belt sander
rotary sanding attachments	stationary disk sander

There are sanding machines for every type of cutting and finishing operation. In the school laboratory, there are four common pieces of sanding equipment.

 Safety

- Be certain the belt or disk is correctly mounted. The belt must track in the center of the drums and platen. Do not operate the disk sander if the abrasive paper is loose. Make sure an adhesive is holding the abrasive disk tightly to the revolving platen.
- Check the guards and table adjustments to see that they are securely locked.
- Use the table, fence, and other guides to control the position of the work, whenever possible. The table should be adjusted to ¹⁄₁₆ inch of the belt or disk.
- Small or irregularly shaped pieces should be held in a hand clamp or special jig or fixture.
- When sanding the end grain of narrow pieces on the belt sander, always support the work against the table.

- Sand only on the side of the disk sander that is moving down toward the table. Check the rotation of the disk. Some rotate clockwise, others counterclockwise.
- Always use a push block when sanding thin pieces on the belt sander.
- Do not use power sanders to shape parts when the operations could be better performed on other machines.
- Sand only clean new wood. Do not sand work that has excess glue or finish on the surface. These materials will load and foul the abrasive.
- Feed the stock directly against the abrasive belt. Never feed it in from the left or right as it may catch and rip or pull the belt off.
- Keep the stock in motion when sanding to prevent burning due to friction.

STATIONARY BELT SANDER

The *stationary belt sander* can be used in vertical, horizontal, or slant positions. Fig. 60-1. It is set in the desired position by loosening the hand lock and moving the entire unit. The table will tilt 20 degrees toward the belt and 40 degrees away from the belt. A miter gauge can also be used on the machine. With the machine in the horizontal position, a fence can be attached to guide the work for surface sanding.

To change a belt, first remove the guards. Then release the tension by turning the belt-tension knob. Remove the old belt and slip on a new one. Apply a slight amount of tension. Then center the belt on the drums by adjusting the idler pulley with the tracking handle. Next, increase the tension and replace the guards. Check the centering adjustment again by moving the belt by hand. Readjust when necessary. If the sander is to be used in a tilted position, the centering should be done after this adjustment.

For surface sanding, place the machine in a horizontal position. The work can be fed freehand across the belt by steadily applying light pressure. However, for more accurate edge sanding, use a fence to guide the work. Fig. 60-2. Beveling and angle sanding can be done by tilting the fence and sander. Fig. 60-3.

Sanding can also be done on the open end of the machine when it is in a horizontal position. Fig. 60-4.

For end-grain sanding, the unit should be in a vertical position and the table should be used as a guide. Fig. 60-5. Bevels and chamfers can also be sanded in this manner by using a miter gauge as a guide.

60-1. Parts of a belt sander. This is sometimes called an abrasive-belt finishing machine since it can be used for many kinds of finishing.

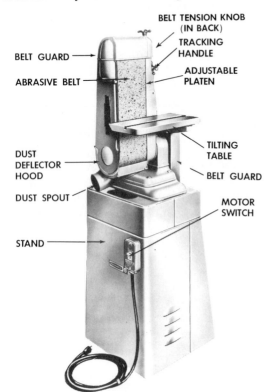

BELT TENSION KNOB (IN BACK)
TRACKING HANDLE
BELT GUARD
ABRASIVE BELT
ADJUSTABLE PLATEN
DUST DEFLECTOR HOOD
TILTING TABLE
BELT GUARD
DUST SPOUT
MOTOR SWITCH
STAND

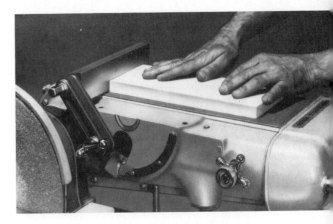

60-2. Using the belt sander in a horizontal position with the stock held against the fence.

60-3. Sanding a miter with both the belt sander and the table tilted to the correct angle.

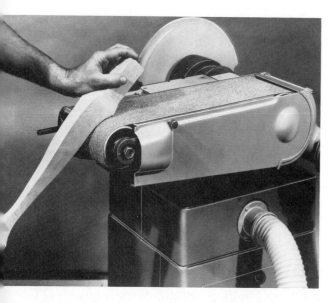

60-4. Sanding a concave shape using the end of the belt sander. Note that the belt guard has been removed for this operation.

60-5. Using the belt sander in a vertical position. Note how the abrasive belt moves toward the work, tending to hold it to the table.

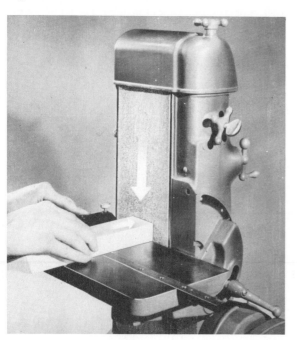

STATIONARY DISK SANDER

The *stationary disk sander* is used for some types of rough and end-grain sanding. Fig. 60-6. It has rather violent action. This makes it effective for fast, rough work.

If the abrasive disk is worn, remove it. If the abrasive disk is attached with glue, soak it in hot water until loose. Then remove it with a putty knife. If rubber cement or stick cement was used, turn on the sander and hold the end of a hardwood stick against it. Move the stick back and forth to loosen the old adhesive. Be sure the metal disk is dry before mounting the new abrasive.

To apply the new abrasive, hold the adhesive stick against the metal disk and move it back and forth. Make sure that there is a uniform coat of adhesive on the metal. Then turn off the power and carefully apply the abrasive. Let dry a short time. Clamp on a flat piece of wood to prevent wrinkles.

Abrasive disks can be purchased already cut to exact size and with an adhesive coating on the back. All that is needed is to make sure the metal disk is clean. Strip the cover paper off the abrasive and install.

60-6. The parts of a disk sander.

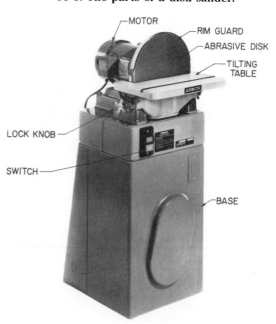

Work can be held on the table for end-grain sanding. The table can be used in combination with a miter gauge to sand a chamfer or bevel. Fig. 60-7. It can also be used to sand the edge of a circular piece. Fig. 60-8. Always sand on the "down" side of the disk. Also, move the stock back and forth on this side. Holding it in one position tends to burn the wood.

Most disk sanding is done freehand. Remember that the edge of the disk is moving much faster than the center. Allow for this. To sand circles or arcs, hold the work firmly on the table and revolve it slowly.

NARROW BELT SANDER-GRINDER

The *narrow belt sander-grinder* is a table-top machine. It uses a narrow belt that moves around three or four pulleys. Fig. 60-9. This machine is excellent for sanding small parts and for getting into hard-to-reach places. Fig. 60-10.

ROTARY SANDING ATTACHMENT

Rotary sanding attachments consist of strips of abrasive paper or cloth attached to a metal wheel. Fig. 60-11. They can be purchased in several types. Some have rectangular pieces of abrasives. Others have very thin strips of abrasives. They are fastened to a grinder, buffer, or portable electric drill. They are used to sand rounded or intricate surfaces. The brushes force abrasive strips over and around irregular surfaces. It is an excellent tool for sanding wood carvings. Fig. 60-12.

60-7. Sanding a chamfer using a miter gauge. The sanding disk is rotating *clockwise*.

60-9. A narrow belt sander-grinder. The table can tilt 10 degrees in and 90 degrees out.

60-8. Sanding the edge of an irregularly shaped piece on a disk sander.

60-10. Sanding the edges of stock using a narrow belt sander. There is a metal plate (platen) directly behind the belt and just above the table. This can be removed so that the belt is flexible for sanding internal and external surfaces.

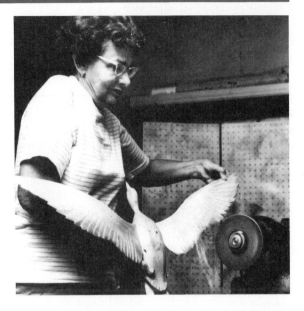

60-12. Sanding a large wood carving. A wheel with very thin strips of abrasives is best for this type of sanding.

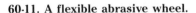

60-11. A flexible abrasive wheel.

Review Questions

1. Name three sanding machines commonly found in the laboratory.
2. Why is it important to check the disk rotation?
3. List five safety precautions when using sanders.
4. In what different positions can a stationary belt sander be used?
5. Describe the method for mounting new abrasive on a disk.

Chapter 61

Wood Lathe

After studying this chapter, you will be able to:
- Identify the main parts of a wood lathe.
- Identify the common turning tools.
- Describe the two basic methods of turning.
- List safety precautions for the wood lathe.
- Demonstrate rough turning with a gouge.
- Demonstrate finish turning with a skew.
- Demonstrate the procedure for cutting a shoulder.
- List the main steps in turning on the faceplate.

LOOK FOR THESE TERMS

bed
caliper
cup center
faceplate
gouge
headstock assembly

parting tool
roundnose tool
scraping
shearing
skew

spear
spur
swing
tailstock
wood lathe

The *wood lathe* can do many basic operations that cannot be done by hand. It also has important industrial uses. You will find a variety of uses for it in making turned parts for your projects. Fig. 61-1. Some common cuts that can be made on the wood lathe are shown in Fig. 61-2.

The wood lathe consists of a *bed*, the *headstock assembly* that is permanently fastened to the bed, a *tailstock* that slides along and can be locked in any position on the bed, and a *tool rest*. Fig. 61-3. The *headstock spindle* has a hollow-ground *taper* into which is fastened the *spur*, or *live center*. The outside of the spindle is threaded to receive the *faceplate*. The speed of the lathe is controlled by changing the belts to the various positions. The tailstock is also taper-ground and a dead or cut center is inserted in the spindle.

61-1. The base of this lamp was turned on a wood lathe.

CYLINDER

CONCAVE & CONVEX

TAPER

BEADS & COVES

SHOULDERS & V'S

EXTERIOR
&
INTERIOR
FACE PLATE
TURNING

61-2. Common cuts that can be made on the wood lathe.

61-3. Parts of a gap-bed lathe.

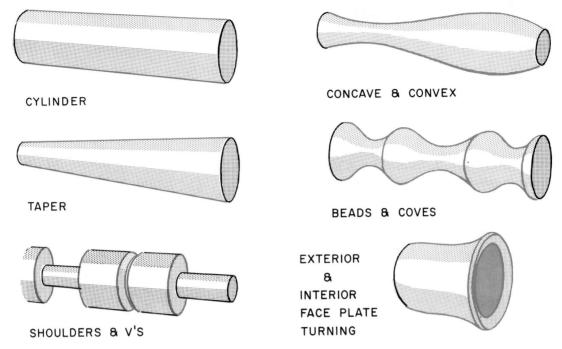

HEADSTOCK
SPINDLE

CALIBRATED
TOOL SUPPORT

TAILSTOCK
LOCKING CLAMP

SWITCH

TOOL SUPPORT
BASE

LOCKING
HANDLE FOR
TOOL SUPPORT
BASE

SPINDLE

HEADSTOCK

SPINDLE
LOCK

INDEXING
PIN

BED GAP

THREAD
PROTECTOR

HAND
WHEEL

HAND
WHEEL
AND INDEX

TAILSTOCK

BED

SPEED
CONTROL
HAND
WHEEL

STEEL
CABINET

VARIABLE
SPEED DIAL

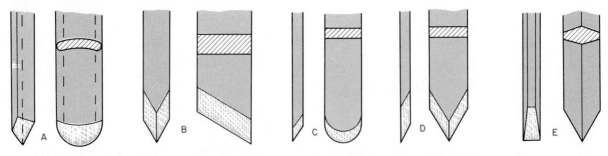

61-4. The common turning tools include: A. A large gouge for roughing cuts and a smaller gouge for small concave cuts; B. A large skew for smoothing and a smaller skew for squaring ends, cutting shoulders, V-grooves, and beads; C. A roundnose for cutting out concave curves; D. A spearpoint for finishing V-grooves and beads; E. A parting tool for cutting off and for cutting to specific diameters.

61-5. Some tools needed for measuring.

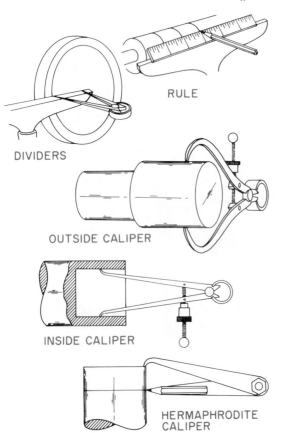

RULE

DIVIDERS

OUTSIDE CALIPER

INSIDE CALIPER

HERMAPHRODITE CALIPER

TURNING TOOLS

The common tools for turning are shown in Fig. 61-4. In addition, the operator must have a good *bench rule*, a pair of inside and outside *calipers*, a *pencil, dividers*, and *hermaphrodite caliper*. Fig. 61-5.

METHODS OF TURNING

There are two basic methods of turning wood—cutting and scraping. In *cutting*, the tool actually digs into the revolving stock to peel off the shaving. Fig. 61-6. This is a faster method, but it requires much skill. It produces a smooth surface that requires very little sanding. In *scraping*, the tool is held at right angles to the surface. Fine particles are worn away, instead of shavings. Fig. 61-7. Scraping is easier to do and is accurate, but the surface is rougher and requires more sanding. All faceplate turning is done by the scraping method.

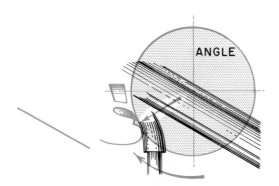

61-6. The chisel cuts away the chips, using a cutting action.

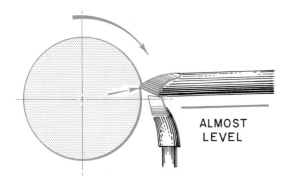

61-7. Action of the chisel in scraping fine particles, instead of shavings.

61-8. Some lathes are equipped with a metal and plastic guard. Always wear safety goggles or glasses, even when the lathe has a safety guard.

⚠ Safety

- Wear proper eye protection for lathe operation. Fig. 61-8.
- Make sure the wood is free of checks, knots, or other defects.
- All glued-up work must dry at least 24 hours before being turned on the lathe. If the glue has not set properly, the pieces may fly apart during turning.
- Use wood-turning tools for lathe work.
- Hold all turning tools firmly with both hands.
- Maintain a firm, well-balanced stance on both feet.
- Taking too heavy a cut or scraping too long in one spot will "burn" lathe tools.
- Lubricate the dead-center (in the tailstock) with oil or beeswax.
- Securely lock the tailstock before starting the lathe.
- Check for end play (left or right movement) by rotating the stock.
- Set the tool rest as close as possible to the stock being turned.
- Turn rough stock a few times by hand (after centering it) to make sure it will clear the tool rest.
- If the lathe chatters (makes noise due to excessive vibration), turn off the power and tighten the dead center.
- Start all lathe turning jobs at the lowest speed until the stock is roughed down to cylindrical (round) form before increasing to a higher speed.
- Always stop the lathe when checking the diameter of the stock with calipers.
- Do not turn large-diameter stock at high speed.
- Screw the faceplate securely to the wood. Avoid cutting too deeply so as not to strike the screws.
- When sanding or polishing on a lathe, remove the tool rest to prevent accidents.

PREPARING STOCK TO BE TURNED

Choose a piece of wood with a rectangular measurement larger than the diameter to be turned. It should be about 1 inch longer than the finished piece will be. Mark a line across the corners of each end to locate the center of the stock. Fig. 61-9. Place the live center over the stock. Tap it with a wooden mallet to force the spur into the wood. Fig. 61-10.

With hardwood, it may be necessary to make two saw kerfs across the corners so that the wood will hold. Fig. 61-11. If the stock is over 3 inches thick, the corners should be trimmed off to form an octagon shape before inserting the wood in the lathe.

Hold the wood against the live center and bring the tailstock to within about 1½ inches of the end of the stock. Lock the tailstock to the bed. Then turn up the tailstock handle, forcing the *cup center* into the wood about ½₃₂ inch. Back off the cup center. Rub a little oil or wax on the end of the stock to lubricate it. Then tighten up the tailstock handle and lock it in position. Adjust the tool rest to clear the stock by about ⅛ inch and about ⅛ inch above center. If the stock is rather large

in diameter, adjust the lathe to its lowest speed; if medium diameter, to medium speed; if small diameter, to the highest speed. Table 61-A.

Rotate the stock by hand to see if it has enough clearance.

ROUGH TURNING WITH A GOUGE

The blade of a large gouge can be held in two ways. It can be grasped close to the cutting point with the hand underneath and the thumb over it. The forefinger then serves as a stop against the tool rest as shown in Fig. 61-12. Another way is to place your hand over the tool with your wrist bent at an angle to form the stop, as shown in Fig. 61-13.

61-10. One method of setting a spur, or live center, is to drive it into the wood with a mallet.

61-9. Here a line is drawn across the corners to locate the center of the stock.

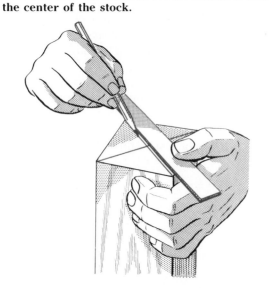

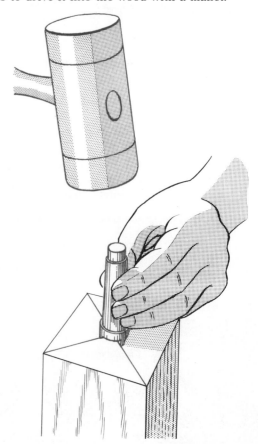

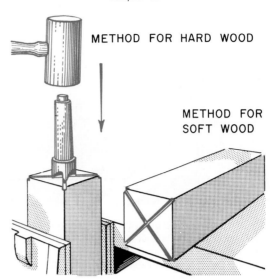

METHOD FOR HARD WOOD

METHOD FOR SOFT WOOD

61-11. On hardwoods it is a good idea to cut a saw kerf across the corners. This can also be done on softwood, but it is not necessary.

Table 61-A. Speeds for Woodworking

Diameter of Stock	Roughing to Size	General Cutting	Finishing
Under 2″	900 to 1300 RPM	2400 to 2800	3000 to 4000
2″ to 4″	600 to 1000 RPM	1800 to 2400	2400 to 3000
4″ to 6″	600 to 800 RPM	1200 to 1800	1800 to 2400
6″ to 8″	400 to 600 RPM	800 to 1200	1200 to 1800
8″ to 10″	300 to 400 RPM	600 to 800	900 to 1200
Over 10″	200 to 300 RPM	300 to 600	600 to 900

CAUTION Do not exceed these recommended speeds. Serious injury can result if parts being turned are thrown from the lathe

61-12. The first method of holding a gouge. The thumb is placed over the tool and the other fingers under it. The forefinger is used as a guide against the rest.

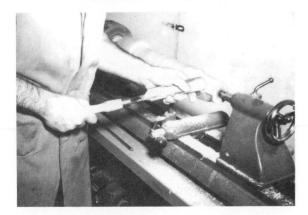

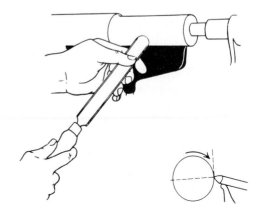

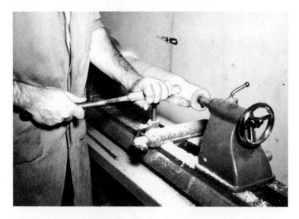

61-13. The second method of holding a gouge. Here, the left hand is placed over the tool with the wrist bent. The hand is held against the tool rest to steady the tool. The right hand raises the tool to the cut and moves it along the workpiece.

Grasp the handle of the gouge in the other hand. Tilt it down and away from the direction in which the cut is to be made. Be sure to hold the tool tightly against the tool rest. Begin about one-third of the way in from the tailstock. Twist the gouge to the right so that a shearing cut will be taken. Then move the cutting edge toward the dead center. Hold the tool firmly; the revolving corners could throw the tool out of your hand. After each cut, begin about 2 inches closer to the live center.

Stop the lathe to see if the stock is nearly round. If wide flat sides are still visible, further rounding with the gouge is necessary.

When round, stop the lathe and move the tool rest closer to the work. Then set the calipers to about 1/16 inch more than the finished diameter is to be. Hold the calipers loosely in the left hand and a parting tool in the right hand.

Make a cut with the *parting tool* near one end. At the same time hold the calipers in the groove formed. Fig. 61-14. When the correct depth is reached, the calipers will slip over the stock. Make similar cuts about 2 inches apart throughout the length of the cylinder in order to obtain the correct diameter. Figs. 61-15 and 61-16.

Using the scraping method, smooth the cylinder with a square-nose chisel. Run the lathe at its maximum speed. Fig. 61-17. Hold the chisel flat on the tool rest. Move the chisel back and forth until the grooves made by the parting tool have disappeared and the cylinder is smooth and of uniform diameter.

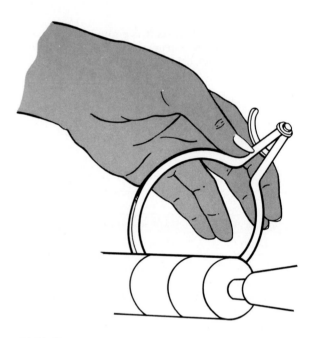

61-14. The caliper should just slip over the cylinder.

61-15. The parting tool has two purposes—the cutting of diameter grooves and the cutting of stock, particularly in faceplate turning. It is a scraping tool and should be held as shown—tool upright with narrow edge on the tool rest. Push the tool slowly into the work with the point slightly above center. As the tool advances into the work, raise the handle slightly until the desired diameter is obtained.

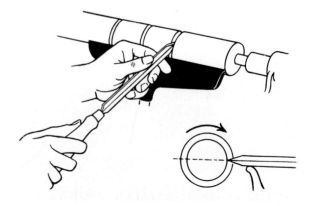

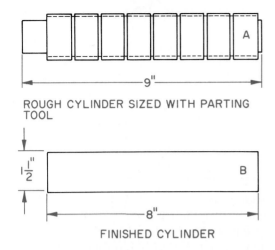

ROUGH CYLINDER SIZED WITH PARTING TOOL

FINISHED CYLINDER

61-16. Using a parting tool to make a series of grooves before turning to rough size.

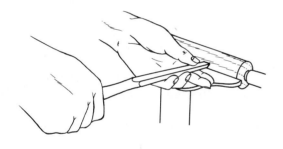

61-17. Cutting the cylinder to rough size with a square-nose chisel.

FINISH TURNING WITH A SKEW

The skew is more difficult to handle. Its cutting edge is tapered. The uppermost point is called the toe and the lower point the heel. Grasp the tool, holding it firmly against the tool rest with the cutting edge well above and beyond the work. Then slowly draw the skew back, turning it at a slight angle until the center of the cutting edge comes in contact with the wood. Fig. 61-18. Lift the handle slightly and force the cutting edge into the wood. Work from the center toward the live and dead centers, taking a shearing cut. *Caution: Never attempt to start at the ends of the stock to do the cutting. Make sure that the toe does not catch in the revolving stock, since this could easily throw the tool out of your hands.* A little practice will tell you when you are getting a good cut. If the skew is properly sharpened, the surface will be so smooth and true that it needs no sanding.

To scrape stock to finish the sides, use a square-nosed tool or a large skew. Adjust the lathe for high speed. Hold the cutting edge parallel to the cylinder and force it into the stock until the scraping begins. Fig. 61-19. Then move it from one side to the other. Always start the scraping some distance in from the ends. This will prevent the tool from catching and splitting the wood.

On long cylinders or tapers, smooth down the work accurately with a small block plane. Hold the plane at an angle of approximately 45 degrees with the axis of the work. Fig. 61-20. Make sure that the tool is adjusted for a very light cut so that there will be a clean, continuous shaving and a smooth surface. The plane can be supported on the tool rest.

61-18. Using the skew as a cutting tool.

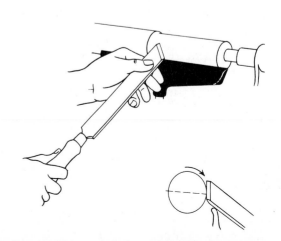

61-19. Using the skew as a scraping tool. This is the simplest method of using turning tools. It is satisfactory, however, only for making a straight cut.

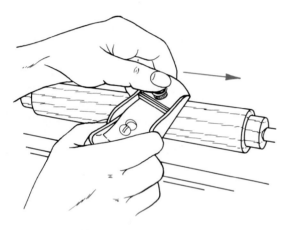

61-20. Using the block plane to smooth a cylinder.

61-21. Squaring one end with a skew chisel using the scraping method.

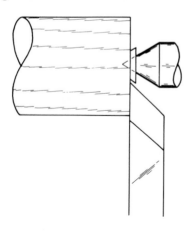

SQUARING OFF THE ENDS

Square the end that runs on the dead center with the parting tool or with the point of the skew chisel. Hold it so its side is flat on the tool rest. Fig. 61-21.

Measure the length of the cylinder from the squared end. Cut down with the toe of the skew chisel at this point. Hold the chisel so that this cut will be square to the cylinder. With the toe or heel of the skew chisel, make a series of sloping cuts against this square surface. Make the cut deeper gradually until only ¼ inch of the stock remains.

Measure the length of the cylinder from the squared end. Cut down to this point from the parting tool until only ¼ inch of stock remains. This may then be cut through with the toe of the skew chisel.

The end that runs on the dead center is squared with the point or toe of the skew chisel when its edge is held on the tool rest. The bevel of the chisel must be parallel to the end to make a square cut. Fig. 61-22.

CUTTING A SHOULDER

The procedure for cutting a shoulder is similar to that for squaring off the end. First use a parting tool to cut a groove. Fig. 61-23. Cut down the diameter at this point to slightly more than the smaller size. Then, with a small gouge, remove most of the stock from the smaller diameter. Cut the vertical part of the shoulder, using the toe of the skew. Cut the horizontal part of the shoulder with the heel of the skew in a manner similar to finish-turning. Fig. 61-24. The scraping method can also be used for this. Figs. 61-25 and 61-26.

61-22. Squaring one end of the stock and cutting the other to length using the cutting method.

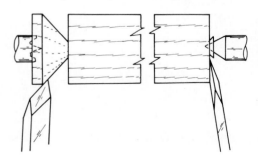

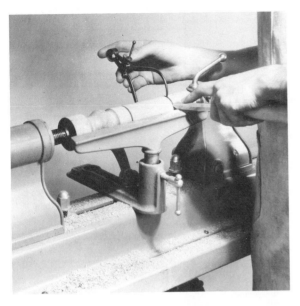

61-25. Forming a shoulder by the scraping method.

61-23. Using a parting tool. It is held with the narrow edge against the rest and forced into the wood. At the same time, the diameter is checked with an outside caliper. In using the caliper on revolving stock, be careful not to apply any pressure. This will cause it to spring over the stock.

61-24. Using the skew to make a horizontal cut of a shoulder. The heel of the skew is doing most of the cutting.

CUTTING A TAPERED SURFACE

Turn the stock to the largest diameter. Then use a parting tool to mark the smallest diameter. Make several grooves, each of lesser depth, as guides for the turning. Rough out the taper with a gouge. Then finish-turn the taper with a skew, using the heel to do most of the cutting. Fig. 61-27.

CUTTING V'S

Use a small skew to do the cutting. Force the heel into the stock a small amount. Then work in at an angle as shown in Fig. 61-28 to cut one side of the V. Continue to the correct depth. Then turn the skew in the opposite direction to finish the V on the other side.

CUTTING BEADS

Cutting accurate beads is rather difficult. With the toe of a small skew, mark the point at which the beads are to join. Continue to cut a V-shape in the stock with the toe of the skew. Now turn the skew around and use the heel to cut the bead. Hold the tool high on the stock to start the bead. Then slowly draw the handle back. At the same time turn the cutting edge to form the arc. Figs. 61-29 and 61-30. Repeat in the opposite way to form the other half of the bead.

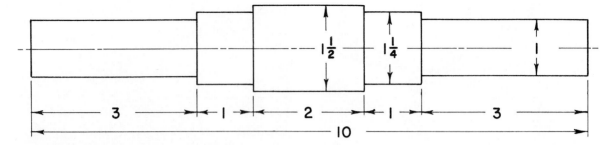

61-26. A shoulder-turning exercise.

61-27. Using the skew to cut a taper.

61-28. Cutting V's with the heel of the skew. The tool is forced into the stock at the angle of the V.

61-29. Cutting beads. Here again the skew is used. The cut is started with the tool held fairly high. As the bead is formed, the tool is drawn back and turned at the same time.

TURNING CONCAVE SURFACES

Concave surfaces (coves) can be turned either by scraping with a roundnosed tool or by cutting with a small gouge. The simplest way is to force a roundnosed tool into the wood and work the handle back and forth to form the concave surface. If a small gouge is used, tip it on edge. Begin the concave cut by rolling the gouge as pressure is applied. Continue to take shearing cuts, first from one side and then the other, until the concave surface is formed. Figs. 61-31 and 61-32.

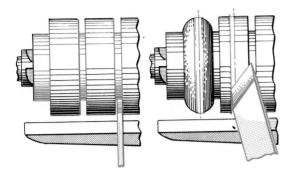

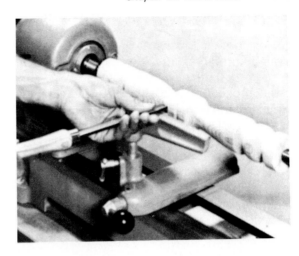

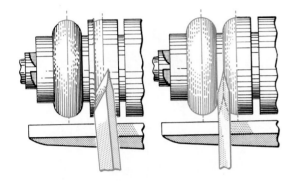

61-30. Correct steps in cutting beads.

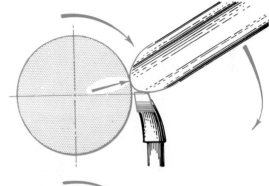

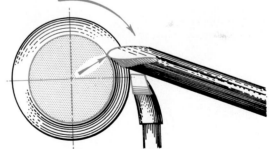

61-31. Using a small gouge to turn a concave surface. The tool should be rolled to form the curve.

61-32. A cove-turning exercise.

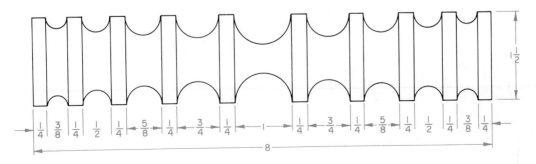

TURNING CONVEX DESIGNS

Most turned pieces are a combination of straight turning, beads, V's, and long concave or convex surfaces. For convex work, the usual procedure is to turn the piece to the largest diameter to be finished. Then, with a parting tool, mark points along the stock where extra material is to be removed. In many cases the parting tool is used at several points to show where stock is to be removed and to what depth. Then the gouge, skew, and roundnosed tool are used to form the design. If necessary, use a file and sandpaper to smooth the surface. Fig. 61-33.

DUPLICATOR ATTACHMENT

Many types of *duplicator attachments* can be used to make duplicate parts with relative ease. Fig. 61-34. The template, or pattern, to use for other parts can be either the original turning done by hand or a flat template that has been cut on the scroll saw. If it is necessary to make a part in repair work, one good part can be used as the pattern. Figs. 61-35, 61-36, and 61-37.

61-34. The best way to make duplicate parts for a product such as this globe is with a lathe duplicator. Using this device will give you an understanding of how industry produces parts for a short-run production. A student made this prize-winning project.

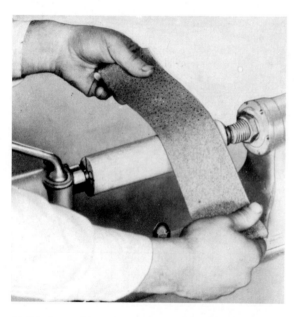

61-33. Smoothing the surface with abrasive paper.

61-35. Lathe duplicator attachment.

61-36. A flat pattern, or templet, can also be used as the guide.

TURNING ON THE FACEPLATE

To turn many small articles such as bowls, fasten the stock to a faceplate. Do all of the cutting by the scraping method. Figs. 61-38, 61-39, and 61-40. Two common types of faceplates are the *screw center* for small work and the *standard faceplate* with screw holes for larger work. Figs. 61-41 and 61-42. The cutting tools most commonly used for faceplate turning include the roundnose, spear, and gouge.

61-37. Making an identical wood turning from a round pattern. A follower stylus touches the pattern. As it moves in and out, the cutting tool follows the same path.

61-38. Turned jewelry boxes with matching tops.

61-39. Drawing for a nut bowl.

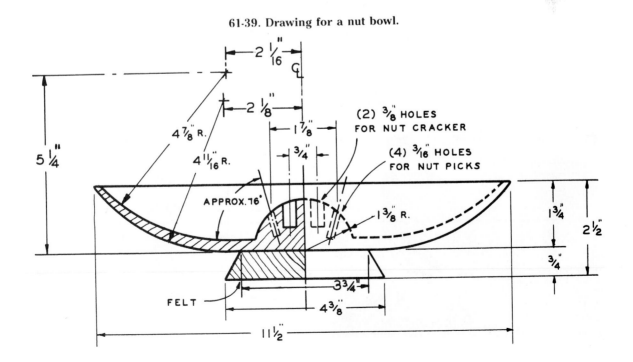

61-40. Nut bowl to be turned on a faceplate.

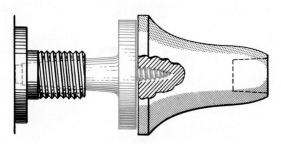

61-41. Screw center for holding small work.

61-42. Fastening stock to the headstock spindle. The work has been fastened to the faceplate with short wood screws. The faceplate is attached to the headstock spindle.

To make a small bowl, first cut out stock of correct thickness on a band or scroll saw to a circle slightly larger than the project itself. See Chapter 22 for treatment of wood to prevent splits, checks, or warping. If the back of the stock will be damaged greatly by screws, protect it with a piece of scrap stock. Cut a piece of scrap stock at least an inch in thickness and about the same size as the base of the bowl. Glue the two pieces together with a piece of brown wrapping paper between them so that they will separate easily later. Figs. 61-43 and 61-44.

Fasten the material to the faceplate with about ¾-inch screws. Make sure that they are not so long that they will mar the bottom of your bowl. Remove the live center and fasten the faceplate on the headstock spindle. Adjust the rest parallel to the outside of the round stock about ¼ inch away. Set the lathe to a slow speed and dress the outside edge of the stock. Fig. 61-45. Once the circle is trued, increase the speed.

Now make a cardboard template that will match the interior and exterior shape of the bowl. Turn the tool rest parallel to the face of the bowl and begin to shape the inside. Fig. 61-46. Use a gouge or a roundnose tool. Always work from the outside edge nearest you to the center. Figs. 61-47 and 61-48. Never try to cut across the entire diameter. Once you pass the center, the tool will move up and away from a tool holder.

61-43. How a piece may be glued to waste stock to do the turning.

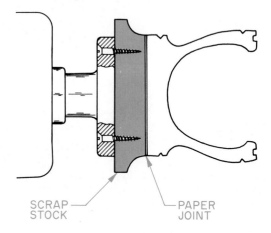

SCRAP STOCK   PAPER JOINT

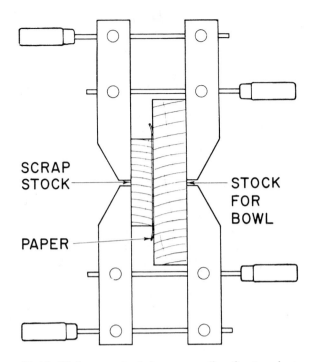

61-44. Gluing up stock in preparation for turning.

SCRAP STOCK

STOCK FOR BOWL

PAPER

61-46. Using a roundnosed tool to shape stock on the faceplate.

61-45. Turning the outside of stock fastened to the faceplate.

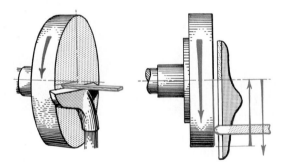

61-47. Keep the cutting tool on the side nearest you. Never try to cut across the entire diameter.

61-48. Turning a trinket box with a small gouge doing the internal work. The box has been glued to a piece of scrap stock. That piece has then been fastened to the faceplate with short screws.

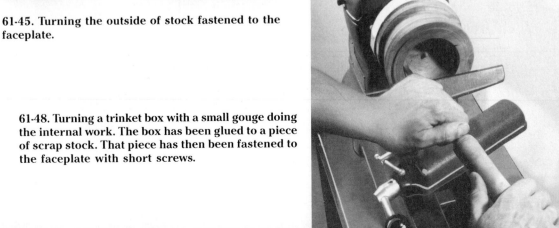

After the inside is shaped, sand it with 2/0 or 1/0 sandpaper. Now move the tool rest around and shape the bowl exterior. Sand this surface and apply a finish.

After completing the turning, cut or split away the scrap stock from the finished product with a sharp chisel. Fig. 61-49. To do turning in which the base must be formed, use a recessed wood chuck to hold the stock while it is turned. Figs. 61-50, 61-51, and 61-52.

61-49. Using a parting tool to cut off the project after it has been turned.

61-50. This shows a bowl that has been fastened in a wood chuck to turn the back.

FINISHING ON THE LATHE

There are several ways to apply a finish as the piece revolves in the lathe. A simple method is to apply paste wax to a folded cloth and hold it on the revolving stock. Repeat this application about a dozen times.

To apply a French-type oil polish, fold cotton or linen cloth into a pad. Apply about one teaspoon of white shellac to the pad. Then add several drops of linseed or mineral oil. Hold the pad over the spinning work, moving it back and forth. As the pad gets dry, apply shellac and oil to keep it moist until the wood has a mirrorlike finish.

Still another method of finishing a bowl is to apply several coats of clear lacquer before removing the bowl from the faceplate. Then return the piece to the lathe. Apply a little rubbing oil and rottenstone to the cloth, then polish.

61-51. A recessed wood chuck for turning the bottom of a dish.

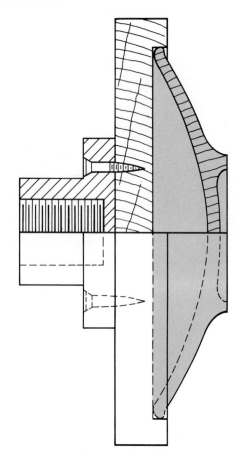

61-52. Turning a shallow tray with the piece held in a wood chuck. When it is necessary to turn both the front and back of a piece, make a chuck to hold the stock for turning the second side.

Review Questions

1. Describe a wood lathe and name its parts.
2. What tools are needed for wood turning?
3. Describe the two basic methods of turning wood.
4. Name five safety rules that must be followed in using the wood lathe.
5. What are the two methods of fastening a live center to the stock?
6. What is the largest size stock that can be turned from a square without first trimming the corners?
7. What is the relation between the diameter of the stock and the speed of the lathe?
8. What are the two ways in which a gouge can be held?
9. What makes the skew a difficult tool to use?
10. Describe how to square off the ends of stock.
11. What tools are used for cutting a shoulder?
12. When a tapered surface is to be produced, what part of the skew should do most of the cutting?
13. What tool is used to cut V's?
14. What kinds of work are turned on a faceplate?

Chapter 62

Portable Electric Drills

After studying this chapter, you will be able to:
- Identify the uses of the portable electric drill.
- List those safety precautions that must be followed in the operation of the portable electric drill.
- Identify the accessories that can be used with the portable electric drill.
- Demonstrate the proper use of the portable electric drill.

LOOK FOR THESE TERMS

disk
drill guide
drill jig
grinding wheel
hole saw

portable electric drill
router drill
screwdriver bit
wire brush

Safety Rules for Portable Power Tools

In operating all portable power tools, observe the following safety rules:

- Know your tools. Read the owner's manual or instructions carefully before using a tool. Learn the tool's correct application and its limitations.
- Ground all power tools, unless they are double insulated. If the tool is equipped with a three-prong plug, it should be plugged into a three-hole electrical outlet. If an adapter is used to connect the three-prong plug to a two-hole outlet, the adapter wire must be attached to a known ground. Never remove the third prong.
- If you need to use an extension cord, use one that has a suitable heavy-duty gauge (wire size) for its length and the ampere rating of the tool. Use a three-wire extension cord with three-prong plugs. Two-wire cords are suitable with double-insulated tools.

- Wear eye protection at all times.
- Clamp workpieces properly or secure them before cutting.
- Make sure you do not cut through the power supply and/or extension cord.
- Keep your fingers away from the blades or cutters.
- Remove all keys and adjusting wrenches from a power tool before turning it on. If the tool has a guard, keep it in place and in working order.
- Disconnect a tool befcre changing accessories, such as blades, bits, or cutters. Never leave a tool running unattended. After you have disconnected the tool, make sure it has stopped running before you leave. Disconnect tools that are not in use.
- When disconnecting, never yank a tool by its cord. Do not carry a tool by its cord.
- Avoid accidental starting. Make sure the switch is in *off* position before plugging

it in. Never carry a plugged-in tool with your finger on the switch.

- Use clamps or a vise to hold work when it is practical. It is safer than using your hand.
- Don't overreach. Maintain your footing and balance at all times when working with tools.
- Keep the work area clean and well lighted. Do not use power tools in a damp or wet location. If working outside with a power tool, wear rubber gloves and footwear.
- Wear proper apparel when working—no loose clothing or jewelry to get caught in moving parts.
- Keep other people at a safe distance from your work area.

The *portable electric drill* is a portable power-driven device used primarily for drilling and boring holes. Fig. 62-1. With accessories, it can also be used for installing and removing screws, cutting holes, sanding, grinding, and polishing.

Drill size is shown by the largest twist drill it will hold. The most common sizes are ¼, ⅜, and ½ inch. Light-duty, ¼-inch electric drills may develop as little as ⅛ horsepower. A good ½-inch electric drill should develop at least ⅔ horsepower.

For most jobs, a single-speed drill is adequate. However, a two-speed or variable-speed model is more suitable for drilling at slow speed or for use with accessories. A drill with both variable speed and reverse can be used to drive and remove screws.

Most drills have a pistol-grip handle. Some models also have a side handle. These drills can be held with both hands for heavy work or for drilling in an unusual position. Fig. 62-2. A trigger switch on the pistol-grip handle starts the drill. On variable-speed drills you can change the speed by varying the pressure on the trigger. The harder you press, the faster the speed.

 Safety

In operating the portable electric drill, observe the following precautions:

- Disconnect the drill from the power source before installing drills, bits, and other tools.
- Make sure all bits and drills are properly ground before installing in the chuck.
- Use a chuck key to tighten the drill, bit, or other tool. Rotate the chuck by hand to make sure the tool runs straight.
- Always remove the chuck key before starting the drill.
- Mark the hole location with a center punch or awl.
- Clamp the workpiece in a vise or to the top of a bench before drilling. If the bench is used, make sure a piece of scrap stock is under the location of the hole.

62-1. Parts of a portable electric drill.

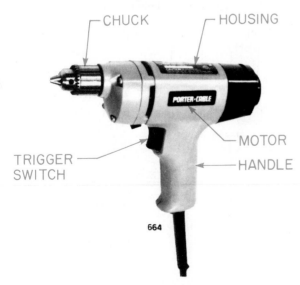

CHUCK
HOUSING
MOTOR
HANDLE
TRIGGER SWITCH
664

62-2. Larger drills usually have a side handle. This allows added pressure to be applied during the boring of large holes.

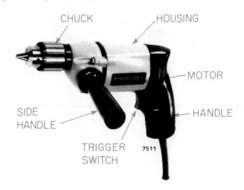

CHUCK
HOUSING
MOTOR
HANDLE
SIDE HANDLE
TRIGGER SWITCH
7511

- Work with a steady even pressure and let the drill do the work.
- Make sure the cutting tool does not catch in your clothing or shop apron.
- When the work is complete, disconnect the drill from the power before removing the tool from the chuck.

ACCESSORIES

Several accessories can be used with the portable electric drill. Accessories make it possible to use a drill for jobs other than drilling.

- The *screwdriver bit* attaches to drills with variable speed and reverse drive to install and remove screws. On single-speed or two-speed drills, the bit must be used with a screwdriver attachment. Fig. 62-3.
- *Hole saws* can be used to cut circular holes. Fig. 62-4.
- *Disks* are used with either abrasive cloth for sanding or with a soft bonnet for polishing. Fig. 62-5.
- *Grinding wheels* are used for sharpening tools and grinding metal. Fig. 62-5.
- *Wire brushes* remove paint, rust, and dirt from wood and metal. Fig. 62-5.

- *Polishing and sanding disks, grinding wheels, wire brushes,* and *hole saws* are usually fastened to a drill with an arbor adaptor. Fig. 62-5. One end of the arbor goes through the center hole of the wheel or disk and is fastened by a washer and nut or by a screw and washer. Some disks, wire brushes, and hole saws have built-in shanks that fit directly into the chuck.
- *Router drills* can be used for sawing, drilling, routing, and filing. Fig. 62-6.

62-4. Here, a portable electric drill with a hole saw is being used to install hardware in a door.

62-3. On drills with variable speed and reverse action, screws can be installed and removed without a special driving attachment.

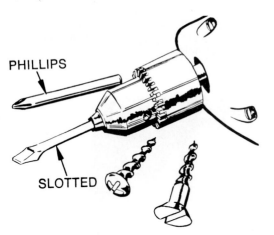

PHILLIPS

SLOTTED

62-5. A wire brush usually has a shank that is installed directly into the chuck. Grinding wheels and abrasive and polishing devices must be attached to an arbor adapter before being installed in the chuck.

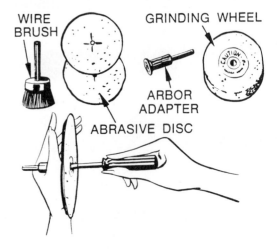

WIRE BRUSH

GRINDING WHEEL

ARBOR ADAPTER

ABRASIVE DISC

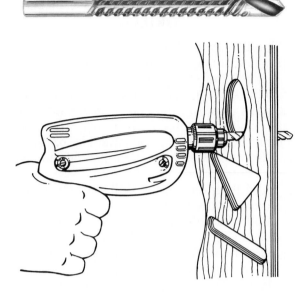

62-6. A router drill has several uses. Here, it is being used for filing.

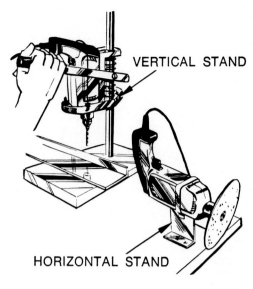

62-7. The two main types of drill stands.

STANDS

A drill stand holds an operating drill in place while you manipulate workpieces. Fig. 62-7. It is permanently attached to a workbench. It is designed, however, so that the drill can be easily inserted or removed.

The *vertical stand* holds the drill with the bit pointing down. A handle lowers and raises the drill bit into the work. Adjustments allow you to drill precisely spaced and positioned holes.

The *horizontal stand* holds the drill so that the operator can conveniently control and position work against revolving accessories.

DRILL JIGS AND DRILL GUIDES

A *drill jig* is a hand-held device used to guide the drill. A dial is rotated to the correct drill size. Then the device is held directly over the location of the hole. Fig. 62-8.

A *drill guide* enables you to drill holes absolutely straight, time after time, to a predetermined depth or at any preset angle. The base slides on rods to position for drilling 90-degree or angled holes. It also allows you to drill precise holes in round stock exactly on center. Many of these jobs are extremely difficult to do. Fig. 62-9.

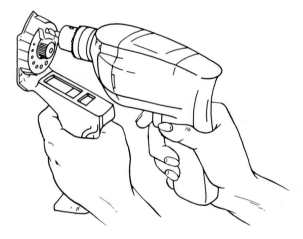

62-8. A drill jig can be used with a portable electric drill. Mark the location of the hole. Rotate the dial to the correct drill size. The jig will hold the drill straight so that the hole is drilled accurately.

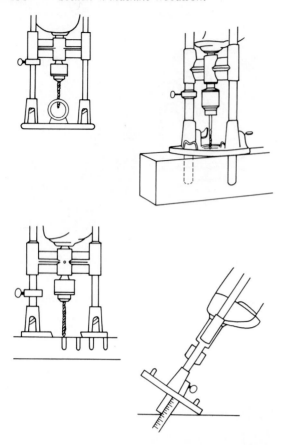

USING A PORTABLE ELECTRIC DRILL

To put a twist drill or a bit in the electric drill, first unplug the drill. Open the chuck and insert the shank of the twist drill or bit. Turn the outside of the chuck clockwise until the jaws close on the shank. Make sure the drill or bit is centered in the chuck. Then use a chuck key to tighten the jaws. Fig. 62-10.

1. Mark the location of the hole with an awl or center punch.
2. Hold the point of the drill over the place you want the hole.
3. Guide the drill with one hand on the housing or side handle. Apply pressure with the other hand. The drill cuts a hole quickly. Be careful that it does not go in too far. If the revolving chuck touches the wood surface, it will mar the wood. Fig. 62-11.
4. It is easy to break small bits in an electric hand drill. Hold the drill steady. Do not force it into the wood.
5. A good method of controlling the depth of the hole is to attach a piece of masking tape to the drill bit. Fig. 62-12.

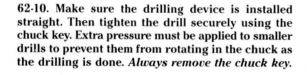

62-9. This heavy-duty cast aluminum guide is fastened to the housing of the portable electric drill. With this device, the portable electric drill can be used for many of the jobs done on the drill press.

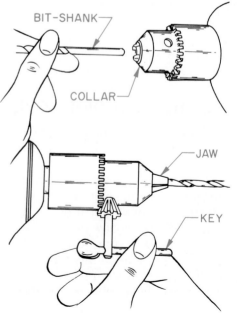

62-10. Make sure the drilling device is installed straight. Then tighten the drill securely using the chuck key. Extra pressure must be applied to smaller drills to prevent them from rotating in the chuck as the drilling is done. *Always remove the chuck key.*

62-11. Most drills have a pistol-grip handle. Some models also have a side handle. The side handle is attached so that the drill can be grasped with both hands when used for heavy work.

Review Questions

1. Why is the portable electric drill such a valuable tool?
2. List five safety rules that must be observed when using this tool.
3. Name four accessories that can be used with the portable electric drill.

62-12. Attached to the drill bit, a piece of masking tape will indicate the depth of the hole.

Chapter 63

Portable Saws

After studying this chapter, you will be able to:
- Identify the main parts of the portable power saw.
- List necessary safety precautions for using the portable power saw.
- Demonstrate the proper use of the portable power saw.
- List safety precautions for using the motorized miter box.
- Identify the safety precautions that must be observed in the operation of the portable saber saw.
- Demonstrate the proper use of the portable saber saw.

LOOK FOR THESE TERMS

motorized miter box
pocket cut
portable power (cutoff) saw

portable saber (bayonet) saw
reciprocating saw

A portable electric saw can cut materials ranging from thin hardboard to thick lumber. With the correct change of blades, it can also cut metal, cement, and ceramics.

The *portable power (cutoff) saw* is designed primarily for straight cutting of heavy lumber and plywood. It is used by the carpenter for pre-sizing lumber or for trimming off uneven ends of boards that are already nailed in place. In this way, the cutoff saw eliminates much measuring and fitting. The *portable saber (bayonet) saw* is the best choice for making curved and internal cuts. Some of these saws can cut right up to a vertical wall, a convenience for cutting openings for electrical outlets.

The *reciprocating saw* is an all-purpose saw that operates with a back-and-forth movement. Fig. 63-1.

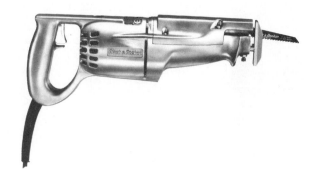

63-1. The reciprocating saw is used for remodeling and heavy cabinetwork because it can cut wood, plastics, metal, and other materials.

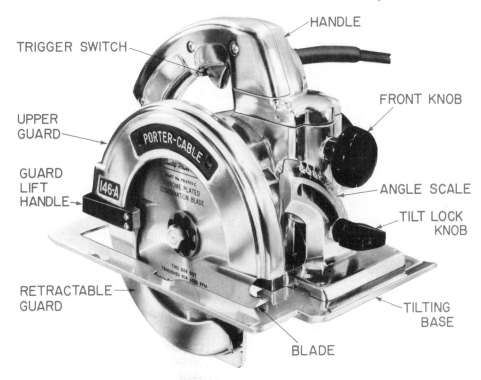

63-2. Parts of a portable power saw.

THE PORTABLE POWER SAW

The main parts of the saw are shown in Fig. 63-2. The saw is rated by the size of the blade, which determines the maximum depth of cut. A good size for most work is a 6- or 8-inch blade size with at least a ¾-horsepower motor. Before connecting the saw, make sure that it is grounded to protect from possible shock. If an extension cord must be used, make sure that it is 12-gauge or larger—up to 100 feet—and 10-gauge or larger—up to 150 feet. Unlike the regular circular saw, the portable saw cuts with the thrust upward. Fig. 63-3. Because of this, the good side of plywood and other materials should be placed facedown for cutting. Fig. 63-4.

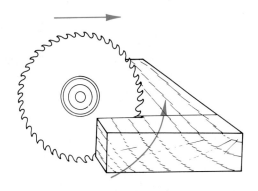

63-3. The cutting action of the portable power saw is exactly opposite that of the regular circular saw.

63-4. The saw should be used with the good face of plywood and other materials down.

⚠️ **Safety**

- Be alert. Sawing with the portable circular saw is so quick and easy that it is possible to be careless and inattentive when operating it.
- Select the proper saw blade for the work.
- To prevent accidental starting, always pull the plug from the electric power source when changing saw blades or making adjustments.
- Check to see that the saw blade is mounted properly, revolving freely, and is securely fastened to the arbor. Be sure nuts and knobs are tight.
- Be sure that all adjustments are properly made.
- Keep the saw guard down over the saw blade except during the cut. Always let the workpiece move the guard away from the blade.
- Stock to be sawed should be clamped to a bench, or held in a vise, except large sheets of plywood or hardboard. These should be laid on sawhorses.
- Allow the saw to reach full speed before sawing.
- Stand to one side of the line of cutting and allow no one to stand in line with the saw. The blade rotates counterclockwise with the teeth cutting in an upward direction.
- Keep the portable circular saw cutting in a straight line. Any twisting will bind (jam) the saw blade and cause it to kick back. If this happens, turn off the switch immediately.
- Guide the saw along the line of cutting with one hand on the handle and the other on the knob.
- Never force the saw into the stock faster than it will cut.
- Avoid distractions. Keep your attention on your work.
- Cylindrical (round) stock should be held securely in a vise.
- Stop the saw to make any adjustments.
- When you shut off the portable circular saw, wait for it to stop before laying it down.

CROSSCUTTING AND RIPPING

Place the work to be cut over two or more sawhorses with a scrap piece of wood on top of each horse. Adjust the saw to a depth slightly more than the thickness of the stock. Fig. 63-4. Rest the front of the base plate on the work and in line with the layout line. A combination blade is usually installed for crosscutting and ripping.

Hold the tool firmly against the work. Squeeze the switch and allow the blade to come to full speed before starting the cut. There is a line or guide edge on the front of the base plate which is exactly in line with the saw blade. Use this as a guide. Move the saw slowly along the line. If the blade slows down, back it out and re-start it. If the motor should stall, always back the blade out and let it run free. *Do not turn off the machine.*

Ripping can be done freehand, but it is better to use a guide attached to the saw. Fig. 63-5. When making a long cut that is beyond your arm's reach, either walk with the saw or stop the saw and pull it back a few inches. Then take a new position and resume the cutting. If a rip guide is not available, clamp a board over the work so that the base plate will ride against it.

63-5. Ripping with a fence. Note the ruled guide to assist in setting the width of cut.

For more accurate crosscutting, a simple guide strip can be held against the edge of the stock and used as a guide for the saw. Fig. 63-6. Bevels can be cut by adjusting the base plate to the correct angle. A miter can be cut freehand or by using a miter gauge. Fig. 63-7.

POCKET (PLUNGE) CUTTING

To make a *pocket cut*, swing the guard out of the way. Fig. 63-8. Then place the front edge of the base plate on the work with the blade aligned over the line to be cut. Start the saw and slowly lower the blade into the stock. Then clean out the corners of the saw.

63-7. Making a miter cut with the portable power saw.

63-6. A good way to make an accurate straight cut is to clamp a guide strip to the material being cut. The insert shows such a procedure in detail.

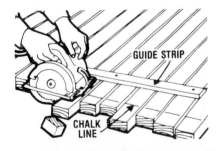

GUIDE STRIP

CHALK LINE

63-8. Starting a pocket cut.

MOTORIZED MITER BOX

The *motorized miter box* is a portable power saw fastened to a miter box. Fig. 63-9. It makes accurate crosscuts and miter cuts to any angle between 90 and 45 degrees.

⚠ **Safety**

- Make sure all guards are in place and operating correctly.
- Always use proper eye protection.
- Be sure power is disconnected before making angle adjustments or changing blades.
- Hold the work firmly against the fence and table.
- Install a new table when support has been cut away.

- Allow the motor to reach full speed before cutting.
- Use the brake to stop the blade before removing scrap or chips from the work area.
- Be sure guard parts are functioning properly.

USING THE SAW

Adjust the saw to the correct angle using the positive stop/handle. Pull out the handle and move to the correct position. Then tighten the lock just above the handle. Place the stock on the table and align the layout line directly under the blade. Hold the stock firmly against the fence with one hand. *Keep your hand at least 4 inches from the blade.*

63-9. Parts of a motorized miter box.

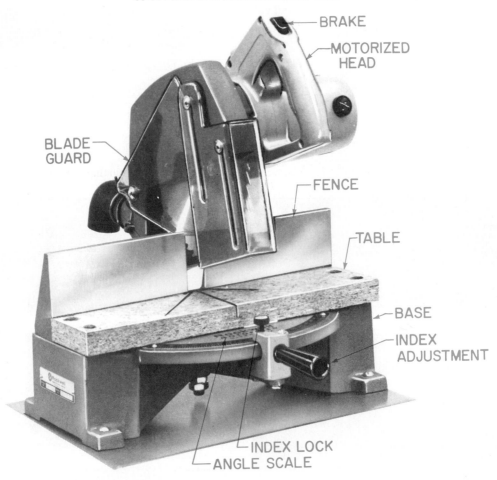

Turn on the saw and allow it to come up to full speed. Pull down on the handle slowly to make the cut. Fig. 63-10. Raise the handle and release the switch. Push the brake button to stop the saw. *Do not move either hand until the saw blade comes to a complete stop.*

PORTABLE SABER SAW

The *portable saber (bayonet) saw* is used for straight or irregular cutting. It will do the same kind of work as the floor-type saw. The main parts are shown in Fig. 63-11. On some machines the plate can be adjusted for making bevel cuts. The saw blades are designed to do many different kinds of cutting. Blade selection is shown in Table 63-A. The blade should have at least two teeth in contact with the work at all times.

To install the blade, loosen the setscrews or clamp and slip the blade in the slot. Fig. 63-12.

63-10. Making a miter cut on a piece of trim. Note that the material is held firmly against the fence. The table is a piece of replaceable particle board. Whenever too many saw kerfs are cut in the table it should be replaced.

63-11. The main parts of the portable saber saw.

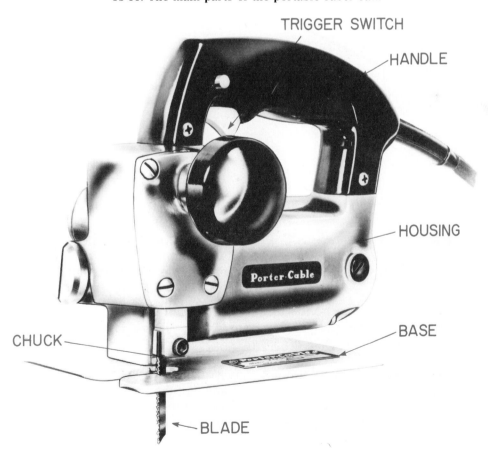

TRIGGER SWITCH

HANDLE

HOUSING

Porter-Cable

CHUCK

BASE

BLADE

Table 63-A. Blades for the Portable Saber Saw

Blade Type	Speed	Type of Cut	Material	Thickness
Approx. 7 Teeth Per Inch	Med	Rough Plunge	Wood	1/4"-2 1/4"
	High	General	Wood	1/4"-2 1/4"
Approx. 8 Teeth Per Inch	Med	Smooth	Wood	1/4"-2 1/4"
	Med	Extra Smooth	Plastic	1/4"-1"
	Med	Extra Smooth	Plywood	1/4"-1"
Approx. 10 Teeth Per Inch	High	Scroll	Wood	1/4"-2 1/4"
	Med	Smooth Plunge	Wood	1/4"-2 1/4"
	Med	Scroll	Composition Board	1/4"-5/8"
Approx. 14 Teeth Per Inch	High	Straight	Plywood	1/4"-1/2"
	Med. High	General	Thin Wall	1/8"-3/8"
	Med	General	Ferrous Thin Wall	3/16"-1/4"
Approx. 32 Teeth Per Inch	Med	General	Metal, Thin Wall Tubing	3/32"-1/4"

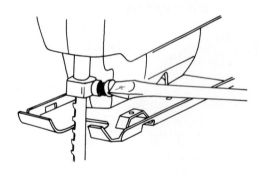

63-12. Insert the blade into the chuck as far as it will go. Then tighten securely.

 Safety

- Make sure the blade is the correct type for the material and that it is tightly clamped in the chuck.
- Be sure the switch is off before connecting the saw to the power source.
- Hold the material securely with a vise or clamps.
- Keep the cutting pressure constant. Do not force the blade into the work.
- When finished, turn off the power and allow the saw to come to a dead stop before setting the saw down. Lay it on its side.

STRAIGHT CUTTING

Straight cutting can be done freehand but it is always best to use a guide. Some machines come equipped with a rip guide which simplifies the job. Fig. 63-13. If a standard guide is not available, clamp a piece of extra material over the stock as a guide. For crosscutting, a simple T-board is best.

BEVEL CUTTING

The base can be tilted to allow bevel cutting at any angle up to 45 degrees. To change the angle of the base, loosen the screw or clamp and tilt the base. Check the angle with a protractor held between the blade and the base. Fig. 63-14.

63-13. Using a fence for ripping.

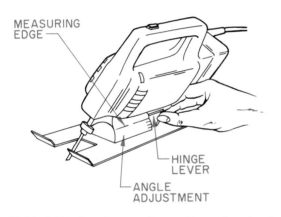

MEASURING EDGE

HINGE LEVER

ANGLE ADJUSTMENT

63-14. Adjusting the saw for making a bevel cut.

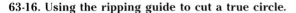

63-16. Using the ripping guide to cut a true circle.

CUTTING CURVES

Regular and irregular curves can be cut. Remember that the smallest radius to be sawed should be at least three times the width of the blade. Fasten the work firmly to a bench. Allow the saw to come to full speed. Then carefully guide it along the layout line. Fig. 63-15. Circles can be cut by using the rip guide as a jig. Fig. 63-16.

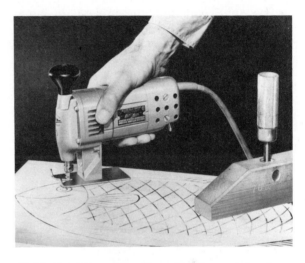

63-15. Cutting a curve. Note that the work has been firmly clamped to the top of the bench.

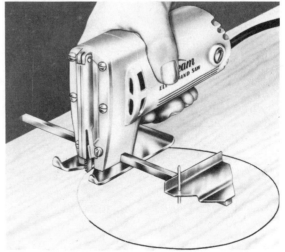

CUTTING INTERNAL OPENINGS

The simplest method of cutting internal openings is to drill a clearance hole in the scrap stock. However, the cut can be made without first drilling the hole. This is called *pocket*, or *plunge, cutting*. Mark the opening to be cut. Then hold the tool at an angle, with the base resting on the surface. Turn on the power. Slowly lower the saw blade into the work until the blade cuts through the material. Then cut the opening. Fig. 63-17.

Review Questions

1. Name the three kinds of portable power saws.
2. Why should plywood be cut with the good face down when using portable saws?
3. What is pocket cutting?
4. Describe the methods of guiding portable saws for ripping.
5. Describe the process of plunge cutting with the portable saber saw.

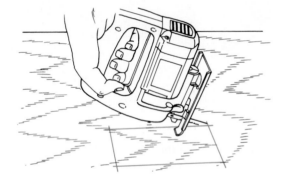

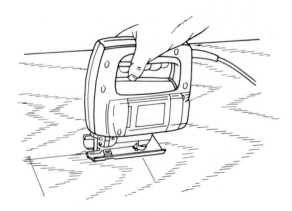

63-17. Pocket cutting is a good way of making an inside cut. The saw is inserted directly into the stock without first drilling a clearance hole. Measure the opening to be cut. Mark it clearly with a pencil. Tip the saw forward until the front edge of the base is firmly on the work. Turn on the switch and allow the blade to come to maximum speed. Grip the handle firmly. Lower the blade into the stock until the blade cuts completely through the material. Then complete the cut.

Chapter 64

Portable Router

After studying this chapter, you will be able to:
- List those safety precautions that must be followed in the operation of the portable router.
- Identify the two basic types of router bits.
- List those guidelines that should be followed in the operation of the portable router.
- Discuss the use of the portable router in inlaying.

LOOK FOR THESE TERMS

freehand routing   portable router
inlaying   router bit
pilot end

The *portable router* has a high-speed motor that screws into a base fitted with two handles. A collet-type chuck at the end of the motor holds the router bits. A threaded-collar device for raising and lowering the motor relative to the base changes the depth of cut. The sub-base (base plate) is the square or round metal or plastic surface that "rides" on the surface of the wood. A good general-purpose router should have a 1¼- to 2-horsepower motor. Fig. 64-1.

Figure 64-2 shows some of the cuts that can be made with the portable router.

 Safety

In using the portable router, observe the following precautions:
- Follow all general safety rules for power tools.
- Select the proper bit or cutter for the specific job.
- Tighten the bit or cutter with the proper wrenches.
- Adjust the cutter to the proper depth.
- Fasten the workpiece firmly in a vise or with clamps.

64-1. The main parts of the portable router.

- Check to see that the bit revolves freely and that all adjusting nuts and knobs have been tightened.
- Hold the router firmly while switching to an "on" position.
- Make a trial cut on a scrap piece of the same thickness before attempting the final cut.

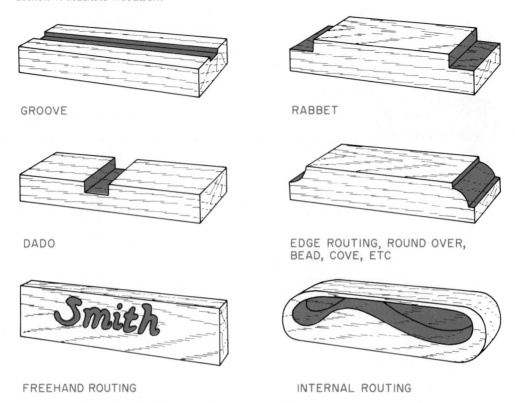

GROOVE

RABBET

DADO

EDGE ROUTING, ROUND OVER,
BEAD, COVE, ETC

FREEHAND ROUTING

INTERNAL ROUTING

64-2. Several examples of the types of cuts that can be made with a router.

64-3. Common types of router bits. Note that seven of the bits have a pilot end, which rides against the edge of the workpiece during cutting.

STRAIGHT	V-GROOVE	CORE BOX
CHAMFER	COVE	CLASSICAL
CORNER ROUND	DOVETAIL	RABBET
ROMAN OGEE	OGEE	TRIM

● Keep your hands clear of the revolving cutters. Hold the router firmly in both hands. Feed the router into the workpiece firmly and at a rate that will not overload it. Never force the router into the stock faster than it will cut.
● Follow the proper cutting direction.
● Turn "off" the power switch and wait until the machine comes to a complete stop. Rest the machine on its side after the cut has been completed.

ROUTER BITS

There are two basic types of router bits: those with a pilot end and those without. Fig. 64-3. Bits with a *pilot end* are designed so that the pilot rides against the edge of the workpiece during cutting. Fig. 64-4. Therefore, at least ⅛ inch of the original edge must remain for the pilot to follow. Some pilots are solid, while others have a ball-bearing end. Bits with pilot ends are used to shape the inside or outside edges of the workpiece. For example, they can be used to cut a fancy edge on a tabletop. Bits without a pilot end are used for such operations as grooving and dadoing. The cutting must be controlled either freehand or with a guide. Bits are made of either high-speed steel or carbide. Carbide bits are used primarily for production work. Fig. 64-5.

INSTALLING A ROUTER BIT

The *router bit* is that part of the router that does the cutting. Turn the router upside down to install the bit. The exact method of installing the bit depends on the design of the router. Some routers have a push button to lock the motor shaft. Others have two nuts, one on the shaft and one on the collet. Two open-end wrenches are needed. One is used to hold the nut on the shaft. The other is used to tighten the nut on the collet. Insert the shank of the bit as far as possible. Then pull it out about ⅛ inch. Hold the shaft to keep it from turning and tighten the nut on the collet. Fig. 64-6.

64-4. The pilot on the end of the cutter controls the amount of cut. It rides on the edge and does no cutting.

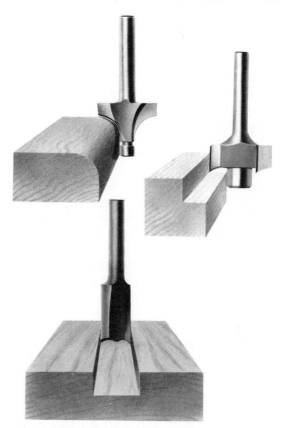

64-5. The three most common router bits in use.

64-6. Installing a bit. Note that one open-end wrench keeps the motor shaft from turning while the other wrench tightens the collet nut.

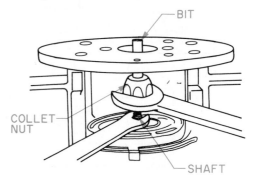

OPERATION

In operating the portable router, observe the following precautions:

- Make sure the workpiece is clamped down and stable enough to support the router during cutting.
- Control the router with both hands.
- Adjust the depth of cut.
- Try the router on a piece of scrap stock that is the same thickness as the finished piece.
- Since the bit rotates clockwise, cleaner cutting will result if you move the router from left to right as you face the workpiece.
- Move the router counter-clockwise when cutting outside edges. Move the router clockwise when routing inside edges. Figs. 64-7 and 64-8.
- Because the router bit rotates at a very high speed, it may heat up if the router is moved too slowly through the material. The wood will also show burn marks.
- Do not feed the router too fast or with too much cutting depth, especially with decorative bits. This will overload the motor and cause the edge of the wood to chip out. When necessary, make two or more passes. Adjust the guide or depth of cut after each pass.

- Get to know the "feel" and "sound" of the router as you practice on scrap wood. When you turn on the router, it may sound like it is operating too fast. As the cutting starts, the sound decreases. If you feed the router too fast it will begin to "moan." Also, you may smell burnt wood.

FREEHAND ROUTING

Freehand routing is routing that is done without guides. A good example of this would be routing out a name plate or numbers for an address. Sometimes the numbers or letters are formed by the cutter bit. In other cases, the background around the letters and numbers is routed so the numbers and letters stand out. Use a narrow router bit for inside routing. Carefully trace the words or letters on the workpiece. For inside routing, place the base of the router at a slight angle to the outline. Then lower the cutter into the wood. Carefully guide the router to form the letter or number. It will take some practice to cut sharp, smooth, even letters or numbers. Fig. 64-9.

T-SQUARE GUIDE

A homemade T-square is a simple device for guiding the router when making straight cuts on flat workpieces. This device can be made of scrap stock. Make sure the edges are perfectly smooth and straight. Place the square on the surface being routed and clamp in place. Hold the base of the router firmly against the edge of the T-square when making straight cuts. Fig. 64-10.

64-7. Use the correct direction of feed in cutting with a router.

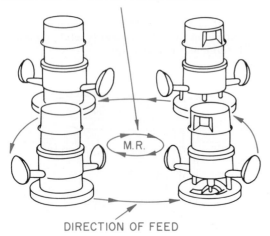

DIRECTION OF MOTOR ROTATION (M.R.)

M.R.

DIRECTION OF FEED

64-8. The correct direction of router travel for routing outside edges and inside edges.

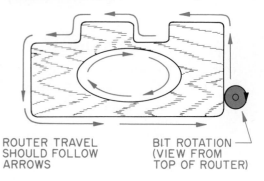

ROUTER TRAVEL
SHOULD FOLLOW
ARROWS

BIT ROTATION
(VIEW FROM
TOP OF ROUTER)

64-9. In freehand routing, the router is moved and controlled by the operator.

MAKING STRAIGHT CUTS

There are two ways of decorating the edge of straight pieces. One is by using a bit with a pilot on the end. This will control the amount of the cut. Another method is to use a commercial guide that is held against the edge of the work as the router is fed along.

MAKING RABBET CUTS

A rabbet is cut with a straight bit that is adjusted to the required depth of cut. The width of the rabbet is controlled by the guide attached to the sub-base of the router. When making a rabbet cut completely around a piece, it is usually better to make the cuts across the end grain first and then along the grain. This will help prevent chipping at the corners.

CUTTING GROOVES AND DADOES

To cut grooves and dadoes, use a T-square guide or attach a commercial guide to the router. Adjust so that the groove or dado will be in the correct location. Make sure the bit is set to the proper depth. Hold the base firmly on the surface so that it will not rock. For wide dadoes or for making a cross lap joint, several passes may be necessary. Fig. 64-11. To cut a groove in a narrow piece, clamp it between two other pieces to provide support for the router base. Fig. 64-12.

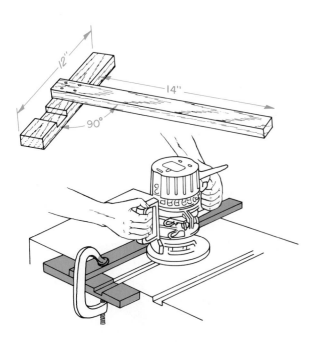

64-10. A T-square guide is a useful device in making straight cuts.

64-11. Using a guide attachment for cutting a dado.

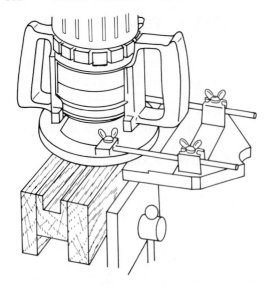

64-12. Cutting a groove in a narrow piece. Clamping the piece between two boards will provide support for the router base.

64-13. Using a router equipped with a small diameter bit and a guide to cut the groove. The diameter of the bit is equal to the width of the inlay.

INLAYING

Inlaying is the setting of a material into a surface to form a decoration. To add a strip of inlay, first cut a groove the desired distance from the edge, using a left-hand spiral bit. Use a gauge to guide the router. Set the bit for the correct depth. This should equal the thickness of the inlaying material. Carefully cut a groove around the edge of the material. Figs. 64-13 and 64-14. The corners will be rounded and must be trimmed out with a chisel. The groove must be cut to the exact width of the inlay strip. Then cut the strip of inlay material with a miter corner. Fit each piece in to check the final design. Then apply glue to the back of the inlay and fasten it in the groove. Place a piece of wood over the inlay. Clamp it until the glue is dry.

Interesting block inlays can be purchased for mounting in tabletops and other projects. Place the piece of inlay material over the location. Trace the outline with a sharp pencil. Then mark it with a sharp knife. Set a bit to the correct depth. Rout out the area in which the block inlay is to be placed. Clean out the sharp corners with a knife. Then glue the inlay in place.

64-14. Inlaying. A. A router has been used to cut the groove for the inlay; B. The inlay has been glued in place.

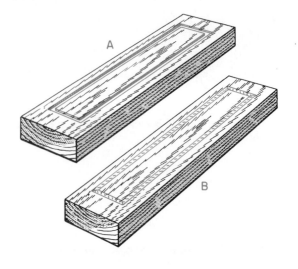

OTHER ROUTER CUTS

Many other kinds of router cuts can be made using various guides and attachments. The procedure differs slightly with each model of router. Therefore it is a good idea to check the manufacturer's instruction manual for details. Fig. 64-15.

Review Questions

1. Name the major parts of the router.
2. What is freehand routing?
3. Is a guide necessary in shaping an edge?
4. Name some of the common router bits.
5. Describe the technique of inlaying.

64-15. Making a dovetail joint, using a dovetail attachment. The dovetail joint is the best one to use for drawer construction.

Chapter 65

Portable Sanders

After studying this chapter, you will be able to:
● Identify the two common types of portable sanders.
● List the safety precautions that must be followed in the operation of the portable sander.
● Demonstrate the operation of the portable belt sander.

LOOK FOR THESE TERMS

belt sander
finishing sander
orbital motion

portable sander
reciprocating motion

A *portable sander* is a power tool that moves the abrasive mechanically. The two most common types of portable sanders are the *belt sander* and the *finishing sander*. On the belt sander, the abrasive belt runs continuously over pulleys at both ends. On the finishing sander, an abrasive pad moves in an orbital or straight line motion.

 Safety

In operating portable sanders, observe the following precautions:
● Make sure the abrasive sheet or belt is in good condition and properly installed.
● Use a dust mask to filter out the harmful, fine particles produced by sanding.
● Wear goggles or a face shield.
● Be sure the switch is off before connecting the sander to a power source.
● Keep your hands and body clear of the moving pad or belt.
● Start the tool above the work. Then set it down and move it slowly over a wide area. With a belt sander, let the rear of the belt touch first. Then level the machine.
● Hold the sander firmly, but let the weight of the sander do the work.

● Use successively finer grit abrasive sheets or belts until the desired finish is obtained.
● When through sanding, lift the sander off the work before turning off the switch.
● Never place a sander on the bench top when it is running. The moving disk or belt may propel the sander onto the floor. This could cause personal injury. It could also damage the sander.

PORTABLE BELT SANDER

Portable belt sanders are excellent for sanding assembled cabinetwork and furniture pieces. Fig. 65-1. The size of the machine is determined by the width and length of the belt. The most common sizes are 2 inches x 21 inches, 3 inches x 24 inches, 3 inches x 27 inches, 4 inches x 22 inches, and 4½ inches x 26 inches. The belt should be so installed that the splice runs off the work. An arrow stamped on the back of each belt indicates the direction the belt should run.

To change a belt, first retract the front, free-turning roller of a belt sander. Then, after the new belt is on and the front roller returned to operating position, align the belt so it will not run off to one side during sanding. Fig. 65-2.

65-1. Parts of a portable belt sander.

Operate the portable belt sander as follows. Place the cord over your right shoulder or out of the way. Hold the machine firmly with both hands. Turn on the power. Lower the sander so that the heel touches the work first. Fig. 65-3. Then move the sander back and forth in a straight line. Sanding is actually done *on the pull stroke*. Fig. 65-4. Never allow the sander to stand still for any length of time. This would cut deep grooves in the wood. It is particularly important to watch this when sanding plywood. Always machine slowly and evenly.

When you want to remove material quickly, sand cross-grain. Once you have reached the proper dimension, sand *with the grain* for a smooth finish.

To sand the edges of boards, allow the belt to extend beyond the edge a little. Be careful that the sander does not tilt.

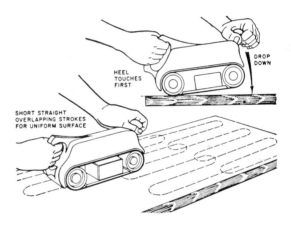

65-3. The correct method to begin sanding with a portable belt sander.

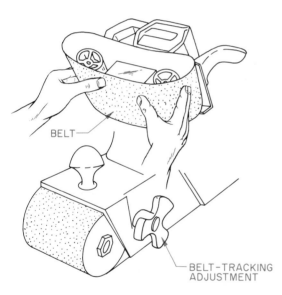

65-2. Replacing an abrasive belt. Make sure the arrow on the belt points in the same direction as the rotation of the pulleys.

65-4. Using a portable belt sander. Note how the material is clamped firmly to a sawhorse so it will not move as the sanding is done.

FINISHING SANDER

The finishing sander is used primarily for final sanding on the assembled product and for sanding between finish coats. There are many sizes and styles. Fig. 65-5.

The least expensive models commonly have vibratory motors and *back-and-forth*, or *reciprocating, sanding motion*. (This also is known as straight-line motion.) Models that are moderately priced usually have rotary motors and a *circular*, or *orbital, sanding action*. More expensive models with rotary motors are capable of both motions. Fig. 65-6.

Orbital action is best for rapid sanding and fast stock removal. However, it leaves swirl marks that show up under a finish. Reciprocating action leaves the least amount of cross-grain scratches.

To replace a worn abrasive sheet on the pad of a finishing sander, you must operate a special mechanism. On some models a lever opens and closes clamps at the front and back of the sanding pad. Fig. 65-7. On others, a special key or a screwdriver loosens and tightens pad clamps. Some have spring-loaded clamps that must be held open while the abrasive sheet is inserted.

Finishing sanders are relatively easy to use. Lower the pad to the surface and move it back and forth slowly.

Review Questions

1. List five safety rules to follow when using sanders.
2. Describe the technique for operating the portable belt sander.
3. When should a portable belt sander be used to sand across the grain?
4. Describe how to replace a belt on a portable belt sander.
5. Describe the two common sanding actions on finishing sanders.

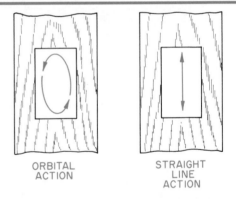

ORBITAL ACTION   STRAIGHT LINE ACTION

65-6. Sanding motions on a portable finishing sander. The more expensive machines have a switch that changes the sanding action from orbital to straight-line.

65-7. Installing a sheet of abrasive paper on a finishing sander that has spring-loaded clamps to hold the abrasive paper to the pad.

65-5. With a finsihing sander you can sand to a corner. It is a good machine to use for sanding a project after it is assembled.

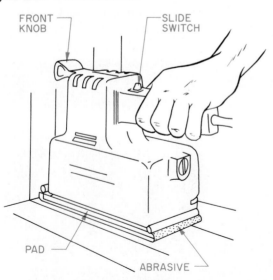

FRONT KNOB
SLIDE SWITCH
PAD
ABRASIVE

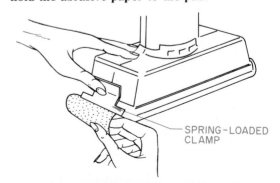

SPRING-LOADED CLAMP

Thinking about a Career

Lathe Setup Worker

Jim Mancuso is a lathe setup worker with a large furniture manufacturer in the South. He sets up wood lathes that turn spindles and other furniture parts. A setup worker adjusts a machine tool to manufacture a particular part.

"When I started here I had no training, beyond what I had picked up in a high school wood technology course. So, my first jobs were somewhat repetitive. I was able to learn the operation of the lathe fairly quickly. But I really didn't care for the work. I really had nothing to do with the setup of the machine or the calculations needed to ensure that it would cut the wood correctly. All of that was done by a skilled lathe setup worker. I decided that that was the job I wanted. It is the job I now have.

"I knew that I could develop the ability to become a lathe setup worker. This person has more responsibility for the manufacturing of the product. For example, the lathe setup worker sets up the correct sequence of operations. To do this, I need to refer to blueprints and the designer's notes and instructions. I select the proper cutting tools for each sequence of the operation. I am responsible for the adjustment of the speed, feed, and other controls. In my work, I use micrometers and other precision gauges. These are essential. All of the work has to be completed within the tolerance limits given in the specifications. After I make the necessary adjustments, I turn the operation of the lathe over to a semiskilled lathe operator."

In becoming a lathe setup worker, Jim was helped by some classes he took at the local junior college. A course in blueprint reading and one in general mathematics were especially helpful.

"It took me nearly 2 years before I was qualified as a lathe setup worker," says Jim. "I was helped, I think, by my natural mechanical aptitude. I was also determined to succeed."

Many people find factory work boring, especially when it involves doing the same job over and over again. Even though some of Jim's work involves repetitive tasks, he enjoys his job. "There is just enough variety in what I do to make each day a little bit different. The company I work for produces furniture in a wide variety of designs. They use many different woods in manufacturing their furniture. Because of these different designs and the different woods used, I am sure of something different every day."

Some of the machines in Jim's plant are controlled by computer programs. To learn more about the operation of these machines, Jim has begun to take computer programming courses at the local junior college. "Computer technology is affecting manufacturing," says Jim. "Eventually this technology may have a greater effect on my job. I need to understand what is going on in my workplace."

Developing Science, Math, and Reading Skills

Studying Trees Helps Find Dates of Volcanic Eruptions

For many years scientists have known that a single tree ring indicates one year's growth of a tree. However, a researcher at the University of Washington in Seattle, David Yamaguchi, is the first to examine tree rings to date volcanic eruptions.

Yamaguchi studied small sections of trees that were growing in the region of Mount St. Helen's. He was able to establish that a major volcanic eruption had occurred in 1480. He discovered that trees that had survived that volcanic blast had extremely narrow growth rings for that particular year. This was probably due to damage of the trees by volcanic ash and pumice (volcanic rock). In addition, enormous amounts of ash probably darkened the sky. This prevented normal amounts of sunlight from reaching the trees. This was another factor that seemed to slow down tree growth.

However, in the years immediately following a volcanic eruption, trees seemed to grow more quickly. This was observed in wider-than-normal growth rings. This faster growth probably resulted from the "fertilizer effect" caused by nitrogen and phosphorous compounds in the volcanic ash.

ACTIVITY: Studying Tree Rings

Materials
Several cuts from the trunks of trees ranging from 4" (10 cm) to 12" (30 cm) in diameter
Hand lens (magnifying glass)
Ruler

A. Collect materials.
B. Most trees grow larger each year by adding a layer around the trunk, just below the bark. When the tree is cut across, it shows the number of rings, one inside the other. Each ring is approximately one year's growth.
  1. Examine each of the samples of wood. Complete the following table:

Sample Number	Diameter	Number of Rings
1.		
2.		
3.		

  2. Using a magnifying glass, carefully examine several sets of rings with different distances between rings in any two consecutive years. Use a ruler to measure the width of each selected ring. What conditions could dramatically affect the growth rate of a tree in two consecutive years?

Activity One

One of the primary tools that you will use in any project is a circular saw. Circular saws are also called table saws. They are used mostly for ripping or crosscutting. Most common table saws are 8-inch or 10-inch. This size is indicated by the largest diameter of the saw blade that can be used on the saw.

The most important factor in using a table saw is safety. On pages 352-353, a number of table saw safety rules are presented. Review these rules until you are thoroughly familiar with them. Why would you always keep the antikickback pawls in place?

Activity Two

The wood lathe is a tool that can do many operations that cannot be done by hand. In addition to the kinds of projects you will undertake, the lathe has many important industrial uses. You will find a variety of uses for it in making turned parts for your projects.

On pages 408-425, the author presents several methods of using wood lathes. He also discusses the types of products you can produce using a lathe. Review these pages. Pay particular attention to the methods of turning. Using that information, decide which turning method is faster and requires less sanding.

Activity Three

On pages 432-440, the book tells you about different types of portable power saws and the various uses of each type of saw. Of equal importance are the safety rules to be followed while using each of these tools.

Review these pages. Then put your book away. Write a short description of each type of saw and when you would use it.

Finding Cutting Speed

Cutting speeds are usually given in feet per minute (FPM). However, the diameters of cutting tools (such as grinding wheels or circular saw blades) are given in inches. The formula for finding cutting speed is:

$$\text{Cutting speed} = \frac{3.1416 \times \text{diameter (in inches)} \times \text{rpm (revolutions per minute)}}{12}$$

Because $\dfrac{3.1416}{12} = .2618$, the formula can be simplified, as follows:

$$\text{Cutting speed} = .2618 \times \text{diameter (in inches)} \times \text{rpm}$$

Example: A grinding wheel 10″ in diameter revolves at 1725 rpm. What is the cutting speed?
Cutting speed = .2618 × d × rpm
Cutting speed = .2618 × 10 × 1725
Cutting speed = 4516

Find the cutting speed of each of the following. (These are actual tool sizes and rpm's taken from a power tool catalog.)
1. An 8″ grinding wheel that operates at 3450 rpm.
2. A 10″ circular saw blade that operates at 3450 rpm.
3. A ½″ twist drill in a direct drive drill press operating at 900 rpm.
4. A planer with a cutter head that is 4:72″ in diameter operating at 5000 rpm.

Section VI. Wood Science

Chapter 66 Nature of Wood

After studying this chapter, you will be able to:
- Distinguish deciduous trees from coniferous trees.
- Identify the main parts of a tree as they would be identified in a cross section cut through the trunk.
- List the two classifications of lumber according to moisture content.
- Identify the three major air pollutants and their sources.
- Describe the use of trees in soil conservation.

LOOK FOR THESE TERMS

annual growth rings
bark
bending strength
cambium
cellulose
coniferous trees
deciduous trees
density
dry lumber

ethylene
figure
green lumber
hardwood
heartwood
lignin
medullary ray
ozone
pith

pollution
porosity
resilience
sapwood
shock absorption
softwood
specific gravity
sulphur dioxide

A tree is a woody plant growing at least 20 feet tall, with a single self-supporting stem or trunk. Wood makes up most of the tree stem.

Table 66-A. Woods Classified by Hardness

Hard	Medium Hard	Soft
Ash	Fir, Douglas	Basswood
Beech	Gum	Pine,
Birch	Mahogany, true	ponderosa
Cherry	Mahogany,	Pine, sugar
Maple	Philippine	Poplar
Oak, red	Walnut	Redwood
Oak, white		Willow

HARD AND SOFT WOODS

Deciduous (di-SIJ-uh-wus) *trees* are trees that shed their leaves. These trees—such as oak, walnut, and maple—are called *hardwoods*. They have broad leaves.

Coniferous (koh-NIF-ehr-us) *trees* are cone-bearing trees. These trees—including fir and pine—are called *softwoods*. They have needles or scalelike leaves.

Woods are classified according to their actual hardness, or ability to resist wear. Table 66-A. Another method of classification is based on whether the wood has open or closed grain. Open-grain woods have larger pores than closed-grain woods. Table 66-B.

Table 66-B. Common Woods Classified by Grain

Open Grain	Closed Grain
Ash	Basswood
Mahogany, true	Beech
Mahogany,	Birch
Philippine	Cherry
Oak, red	Gum
Oak, white	Maple
Walnut	Poplar
Willow	Fir, Douglas
	Pine, ponderosa
	Pine, sugar
	Redwood

STRUCTURE OF WOODS

A chunk of wood is an intricate arrangement of tiny, but strong, cells. Most of these cells, which are about as fine as human hairs, are lined with spiral-wound strands of *cellulose*. The cells themselves are held together with a substance called *lignin*.

The arrangement of cells in a piece of softwood is shown in Fig. 66-1. There are three faces of wood—the cross sectional, radial, and tangential. The cross sectional face is the surface you see if you cut across a tree stem.

HOW A TREE GROWS

The cells provide the passageways into the tree for water and other growth-giving materials from the earth. During the spring and early summer there is much moisture. Then, the tree grows rapidly. Springwood, or early wood, is formed at this time. In the summer and fall, the tree develops more slowly. Summerwood, or late wood, forms during this time. When you look at a cross section of a tree, you can see the dark summerwood rings, called *annual growth rings*. These are the dark rings shown in Fig. 66-2. Some idea of the age of the tree can be obtained by counting these rings.

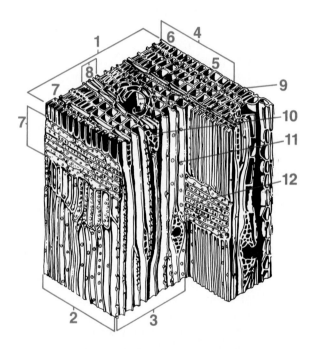

66-1. This microscopic view of a thin section of wood shows a block of softwood measuring about 1/4 inch on a side. (1) Cross-sectional face, (2) radial face, (3) tangential face, (4) annual ring, (5) earlywood, (6) latewood, (7) wood ray, (8) fusiform ray, (9) vertical resin duct, (10) horizontal resin duct, (11) bordered pit, (12) simple pit.

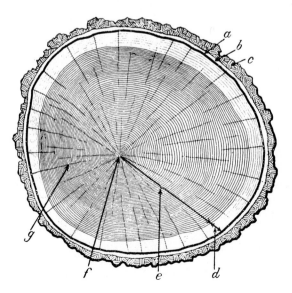

66-2. Cross section of a tree trunk showing: A. cambium; B. phloem; C. bark; D. sapwood; E. heartwood; F. pith; G. medullary ray.

PARTS OF A TREE

Figure 66-2 shows the cross section of a tree trunk. A porous material called the *pith* is at the center. Around the pith is the mature wood, the *heartwood*. Beyond the heartwood is the newer growth of *sapwood*. Between the sapwood and the inner bark is a pitchlike material called *cambium*. Here, the cell formation takes place to form more sapwood. Radiating from the pith of the tree are ray cells or *medullary rays*. These form passageways for food in feeding the tree. The *outer bark* is a dead, corky covering. The *inner bark* (bast or phloem) carries the food made in the leaves down to the branches, trunk, and roots.

MOISTURE CONTENT AND SEASONING

When a tree is cut down, it contains moisture. Before the wood can be used, a large part of this moisture must be removed. This is done by air and/or kiln drying. In drying, the free water inside the cell cavities is removed first. When all of this is gone, the wood is said to be at the *fiber-saturation point*. The wood will still contain about 23 to 30 percent moisture.

Lumber for house framing construction dried to 19 percent, or less, moisture is called *dry lumber*. That above 19 percent is called *green lumber*. Lumber for furniture construction, however, should have only about 6 to 10 percent moisture content. If wood has too much moisture when the project is built, the wood will continue to dry out, causing warpage and cracked joints.

FIGURE IN WOOD

A *figure* in wood is a pattern. It is formed by the coloring matter, by annular rings, and medullary rays, and by cross grain, wavy grain, knots, and other irregularities. The woods that have a distinct figure are considered superior for fine furniture.

PROPERTIES OF WOOD

SPECIFIC GRAVITY

The *specific gravity* of wood is the ratio of the weight of a wood to the weight of an equal volume of water at a standard temperature. For example, the specific gravity of ash is .50. This means that it weighs half as much as an equal volume of water. This figure is determined by expressing the ratio and dividing to get the specific gravity. If the weight of the ash were 10 pounds and the weight of an equal volume of water were 20 pounds, the ratio would be 10:20, or $^{10}/_{20}$. When the bottom number is divided into the top, the resulting answer is the specific gravity, or .50. Specific gravity is not followed by any units (like pounds) because it is purely a mathematical expression.

Will ash float in water? If your answer is yes, you are correct. Any wood whose specific gravity is lower than 1.0 will float because these woods weigh less than equal volumes of water. Any wood whose specific gravity is greater than 1.0 will sink because the wood weighs more than an equal volume of water.

Specific gravity tells you something about the density of wood. *Density* is quantity per unit volume. In general, the higher the specific gravity, the more dense, heavy, strong, and hard the wood will be.

You can measure the specific gravity of wood with a simple procedure. Cut pieces of wood that measure $1 \times 1 \times 10$ inches. Mark ten equal divisions along the length of each piece. Place each piece of wood end down in a tube of water. Each will sink to a depth in proportion to its specific gravity.

WOOD POROSITY

Wood is made of pores that have open spaces. The number of pores in the wood is a measure of that wood's *porosity*.

To test for porosity, cut blocks of wood measuring about $2 \times 2 \times \frac{1}{2}$ inch. These should be three different kinds of wood. For some pieces, have the wood grain running parallel to the ½-inch dimension. On other pieces, have the grain at right angles to the ½-inch dimension. Now place some alcohol, a wetting agent such as detergent, and some colored dye in a shallow pan. Carefully place the pieces of wood in the liquid with the ½-inch dimension at right angles to the bottom of the pan. The liquid should not cover the wood. In a short time the liquid will penetrate the wood. You can judge the porosity of the different pieces of wood by observing how long it takes the liquid to rise through the wood.

BENDING STRENGTH OF WOOD

The capability of wood to bend without breaking is known as its *bending strength*. You can test this. Cut several pieces of hardwood and softwood measuring ½ × ½ × 45 inches. Obtain a piece of metal wire or rod 45 inches in length and equal in weight to one of the hardwood pieces. Now support the wood pieces at points about 2½ inches from each end. This can be done by clamping two pieces of angle iron to a bench with the ends extending out from the bench. Place the hardwood piece across the two pieces of angle iron. At the center of the wood sample, loop a heavy metal hook that will hold a bucket. Pour sand into the bucket. Measure the amount of bending deflection as the bucket weight increases. Continue until the wood breaks. Now load the steel wire or rod in the same way. Determine the load it will take before it bends. This will show the relative strength of the hardwood piece.

INSULATING PROPERTY OF WOOD

Get a piece of ¼-inch dowel rod and a steel rod 12 inches long. Place one end of each in boiling water for a few minutes. Now touch the opposite end of each of the two materials. You can easily feel the difference in heat conductivity.

USE OF GLUE IN LAMINATED CONSTRUCTION

Cut nine pieces of softwood, ¼ × 1 × 18 inches. Glue three pieces together and allow the glue to set. Nail three other strips together, one on top of the other. Do nothing to the other three pieces. Make two V-supports and place a cardboard backdrop on a bench. Place the loose strips together over the supports. Add a heavy weight to determine how far the beam will bend. Mark this point on the cardboard. Then place the three pieces that have been nailed together over the supports. Check the amount of bend with the same weight. Mark this point on the cardboard. Finally, do the same with the pieces that have been glued together. By looking at the marks on the cardboard, you can compare strengths. Of the three techniques used, which would be best for heavy construction?

SHOCK ABSORPTION OF WOOD

Shock absorption, or *resilience*, is the ability of wood to absorb shock without permanent change in size. Select several pieces of wood of different species. Each piece of wood should be about ½ × 4 × 10 inches. Lay them on a flat surface. Now, from a height of approximately 2 feet, drop a hard rubber ball onto each piece. Allow it to bounce off each piece. Measure the height of the bounce from each of the test pieces. The more resilient the wood, the shorter the distance the ball bounces.

TREES AND POLLUTION

Two major problems facing our society are providing enough energy and reducing pollution. *Pollution* is the contamination of the environment by manufactured materials. Trees play a key role in helping to solve both of these problems.

TREES AND AIR POLLUTION

Our atmosphere is primarily a mixture of invisible, odorless, tasteless gases. These gases are mainly oxygen, nitrogen, and carbon dioxide. Pollution makes air unfit for breathing in two basic ways. Pollution adds foreign substances to air. It also changes its proportional makeup. This diminishes the supply of oxygen.

All known forms of combustion consume oxygen and release carbon dioxide. This includes power plants, home heating systems, and automobile engines. Trees reverse this process by consuming carbon dioxide and releasing the oxygen that men and animals need. Fig. 66-3. Every ton of living wood consumes 1.47 tons of carbon dioxide and releases 1.07 tons of oxygen. Trees filter the air of impurities. They also slow air currents and wind. In this way, they cause dust particles and other solid pollutants to settle out of the air.

Too much air pollution can cause trees to die. The three major air pollutants are *sulphur dioxide* (which comes from burning coal), *ozone* (a photochemical product caused by automobile exhaust gases), and *ethylene* (a gas from the burning of certain gasolines).

TREES AND WATER POLLUTION

Soil, trees, and water are the three greatest renewable natural resources. They depend on each other for their existence. If there were no trees, the uncontrollable runoff of rain or melted snow would wash away valuable topsoil and cause serious flooding downstream. Although trees will not help clear up a polluted lake or stream, they do prevent additional pollution. Soil and timber conservation practices make it possible for the land to absorb and store water. This helps prevent erosion and floods.

TREES AND NOISE POLLUTION

During the past thirty years the noise level in the average urban community has increased over eight times. Proper placement of trees and shrubs can reduce noise level up to 50 percent.

66-3. The trees and oceans absorb the carbon dioxide from burning fossil fuels. They return oxygen to the air we breathe. Four tons of oxygen per year are produced by one acre of growing forest. This is enough oxygen for eighteen people a year. About 40 percent of Earth's oxygen is produced by forests and green land plants. Photosynthesis by ocean plant life produces most of the remaining supply. Trees consume only solar energy. They convert carbon dioxide, moisture, and solar energy into wood fiber at the rate of four tons per acre annually.

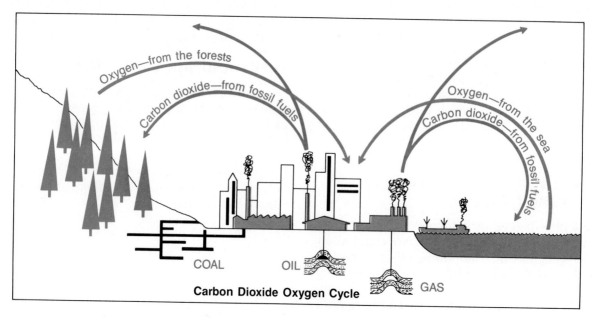

Carbon Dioxide Oxygen Cycle

POLLUTION IN THE LUMBER AND PAPER INDUSTRY

Modern technology gives us the good things of life. It also causes many of our pollution problems. To use trees for wood and pulp for paper making, it is necessary to process the materials. Using trees for lumber and paper products has increased air and water pollution. Now industries have become conscious of their responsibility to society. Pollution control systems are now installed in all new plants. Many older plants are adding devices to remove or reduce pollutants.

WOOD AND ENERGY

Wood makes a substantial contribution to energy conservation. Expanding the use and thickness of insulation in homes and increasing the use of wood-frame construction in other types of buildings can result in even greater energy savings. Consider the following facts:

● Wood is the only renewable industrial raw material.

● Trees, while growing, consume only solar energy.

● Conversion of wood from the raw to the finished state consumes very little energy.

● Use of wood wherever practical would greatly extend the supply of bauxite, iron ore, coal, petroleum, and natural gas.

● Among the major raw material resources, only wood is biodegradable.

● Wood insulates 6 times better than brick, 15 times better than concrete, and 1,770 times better than aluminum.

Review Questions

1. Name the substance that holds the cells of a tree together.
2. How can you determine the age of a tree?
3. What are two ways to classify wood?
4. What forms the figure in wood?
5. Define *shock absorption*.
6. What are the three major air pollutants?

Facts about Wood

John Chapman: Pioneer Conservationist

The pioneers who settled many parts of what is now the United States were faced with the task of clearing forests. Society was then primarily agricultural. The pioneers were more self-sufficient than we now are. Farming was essential to survival on the frontier. In many areas, farming could not begin until a field had been cleared of trees. The pioneers cut down trees, but many also planted trees—fruit trees, primarily. Today, one of those pioneers who planted fruit trees is still remembered as "Johnny Appleseed." You may have thought "Johnny Appleseed" to be a fictional character. He was, though, a real person. His name was John Chapman.

Chapman was born in Massachusetts in 1774. Around 1800, he began to collect seeds from apple cider presses in western Pennsylvania. Some of these seeds he gave to pioneers heading west. Around this time, Chapman began a series of journeys that took him first into Ohio and later into Indiana. As he traveled, he sold and gave away appleseeds and saplings from the many forest nurseries that he established. On his journeys, he revisited these nurseries, pruning the trees. He was cheerful and knowledgeable about the wilderness. He lived in harmony with the Native Americans. To many frontier pioneers, he was a well-known figure.

That John Chapman is still remembered is due to his generous giving of appleseeds, as well as his picturesque appearance. He is said to have dressed unusually and in a ragged fashion. Drawings of Johnny Appleseed highlight that aspect of his character. One story has him wearing a coffee sack as a shirt, holes being cut in the bag for his arms. Usually, he is shown as being barefoot, his trousers ragged, and his hair long. Though John Chapman gave the appearance of being a carefree wanderer, he was a professional nurseryman. He sought to make a profit on the saplings and seeds he sold. His generous nature, though, prevented him from withholding seeds from those he thought needed them.

After his death, many stories about him began to circulate. Some were true, others were exaggerated. One story, though, indicates his selfless patriotism. During the War of 1812, he traveled 30 miles to summon American troops to Mansfield, Ohio. The people in that settlement were under threat of attack by Native American tribes fighting for the British.

The work of John Chapman has been as enduring as his legend. Many of the orchards on the Midwest American frontier in the early 1800s sprang from seedlings provided by John Chapman. He was one of the earliest American conservationists. In March of 1845, John Chapman died of exposure near Fort Wayne, Indiana.

Chapter 67

Lumbering and Wood Products

After studying this chapter, you will be able to:
- Distinguish between the two major methods of harvesting trees.
- List the basic steps in lumber manufacturing.
- Identify the procedures being used to conserve forests.
- Describe the extent of the forest products industry in the United States.
- Identify the various layers in a sheet of plywood.
- Describe the two methods by which veneers are cut.
- Describe the main steps in the process used to manufacture particle board.

LOOK FOR THESE TERMS

air seasoning	forest conservation	peeler block
back veneer	forester	plugs
barking	forestry	plywood
bucking	green chain	reforestation
cants	hardboard	rotary lathe
clear-cutting	head faller	sawyer
cold log deck	headrig	selective cutting
core	live log deck	tree farming
crossbands	lumber core	veneer
dry kilns	paper	veneer core
face veneer	particle board	veneer slicer
felling crew	particle-board core	yarding

LUMBERING

Lumbering begins in the commercial forest. There, it is the job of a forester. The *forester* is responsible for determining the best way to harvest a given stand of timber. Foresters study *forestry*. This is the science of caring for trees.

HARVESTING

In forming a logging plan, the forester decides between two methods of harvesting: *selective cutting* and *clear-cutting*. In selective cutting, reforestation is built in. Trees of a predetermined diameter are harvested. A certain number of large trees are left behind, along with those too small to cut. These trees are left to provide seed for natural regeneration. Selective cutting is not advisable for all stands of wood.

In certain circumstances, the forester will choose clear-cutting. This is a method of cutting in which loggers remove all trees, regardless of size or age. Clear-cut areas are immediately reseeded by helicopter, replanted by hand, and naturally regenerated through stump sprouting.

In harvesting timber, the felling crew is first on the scene. Before cutting a tree, the *head faller* determines its direction of fall to make sure no standing trees will be damaged. A bulldozer then clears a soft bed of earth to cushion the fall and prevent damage to the trunk. That done, the faller makes a wedge-shaped undercut on the side facing the bed. As the backcut is made on the trunk opposite and slightly above the undercut, plastic wedges are sledgehammered into the narrow opening. These wedges start and guide the fall of the tree.

Once down, the crew removes the branches. They also saw the trunk into shorter, more manageable lengths. This last procedure is called *bucking*.

Yarding, or transporting logs to a truck landing, is done in several ways. The choice depends upon terrain, soil conditions, and method of harvesting. The *high lead*, *slack line*, and *skyline systems* all use cable rigging with a mobile yarder to move logs from the fall site to the truck landing.

When a truckload of logs arrives at the sawmill, the logs may go to the *millpond*. They might also be placed on a *live load deck*. There logs are stacked for immediate processing. If the live deck is full, the truck may unload at the *cold log deck*, where logs are stored in reserve.

LUMBER MANUFACTURING

The first step in the lumber manufacturing process is called *barking*. In some mills, a large knifelife jet of water is used. It literally peels the thick bark from the log. Barking also is done by mechanical friction drums, wedge-bladed air hammers, tractors equipped with pronged blades, or by hand.

Newly barked logs are conveyed to the *headrig* (*head saw*), a huge bandsaw. The *sawyer* uses this saw to slice the logs into large planks called *cants*. Cants are then passed through a series of saws. These saws slice, edge, and trim the lumber into various dimensions. The ways in which logs are cut are shown in Fig. 67-1. Waste material is taken to other plants to be made into lumber by-products.

Once trimmed of all uneven edges, the lumber is placed on a moving belt called a *green chain*. There it is graded according to the characteristics and quality of the wood. It is then pulled and stacked according to the size and grade.

Fork lifts carry the stack of rough lumber to an outdoor storage yard. There each piece is restacked on small cross-sticks. This al-

67-1. Route of logs through a sawmill.

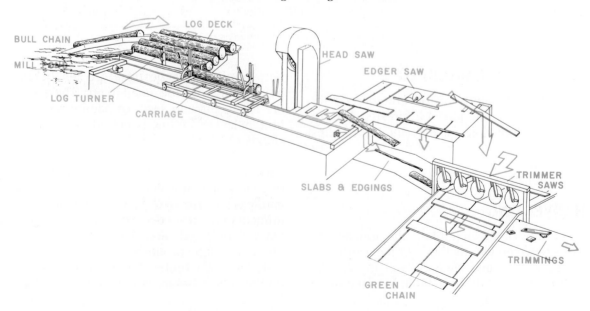

lows air to circulate between pieces. This *air seasoning* may take from six months to two years, due to the large amount of moisture found in green lumber.

Following air drying, the top grades of lumber are taken to huge ovens called *dry kilns*. Here the final removal of moisture occurs under carefully controlled conditions of temperature, humidity, and air circulation. From the dry kiln, the lumber goes to cooling sheds and on to dry sheds for storage, or to the planing mill for surfacing or remanufacture. In the planing mill, the many patterns of lumber siding, paneling, and specialty products are precision-milled. Edges and ends are trimmed. Faces are planed smooth or saw textured. There the lumber also is bundled and stored. It is then made ready for shipment.

FOREST CONSERVATION

Forest conservation is the preservation and renewal of timber. The renewal of timber resources is known as *reforestation*.

Today forest products companies do not cut and move along as they did years ago. They now grow trees as a crop. This is an economic benefit to the community. Timber is harvested on a systematic basis. New trees are planted to replace those that have been harvested.

Tree farming is another interesting development in forest conservation. The American tree farm system, promoted by the forest industries, includes thousands of certified tree farms totaling many millions of acres. In tree farming, timber is treated as a crop to be grown just like corn or wheat. Timber is harvested and regrown to produce the maximum yield year after year.

REFORESTATION METHODS

Wood is one great natural resource that can be renewed by replanting. Thus, many large lumber producers are using unusual techniques to replant the areas that have been cut.

On rough terrain, hopper-equipped helicopters seed thousands of acres of land with new trees each year. A faster and more suc-

cessful method of growing trees uses an improved seed tree program and a planting gun. The seeds are first nursery planted in cone-shaped containers filled with a mixture of fertilizer and peat moss. After about six or eight months in the nursery, the healthy seedlings, called *plugs*, are shot into the ground with a planting gun. Fig. 67-2. With this technique one person can hand-plant about 1,500 seedlings in a day. This is about 3½ times the number that could be hand-planted in the same time.

Our forests are a storehouse of wealth. There are about 5,000 specific uses for wood and wood products.

67-2. The plugs are carefully removed from their containers and planted by a gun device perfected by forest researchers. Then, sun, rain, fertilizer, and the superior seedlings combine to produce faster growing, healthier trees with more usable wood fiber.

THE DEMAND FOR WOOD

America still has about 75 percent as much forest land as it had when Columbus discovered the New World. The total area is about 758 million acres. Of that, about a third is set aside in parks, wilderness areas, watersheds, or is not suitable for growing commercial timber. This third of the American forest equals the combined total size of Norway, Sweden, Denmark, Austria, Switzerland, Holland, Belgium, and Israel. The remaining 500 million acres is the commercial forest. This land produces most of the raw material for wood products. The biggest single owner of the commercial forest is the government, both state and federal. About 28 percent of the commercial forest land is publicly held. About 4½ million private owners own almost 60 percent of the forest. The forest products industry comes in third. It controls about 12 percent of the commercial forest.

The need for wood is increasing rapidly. Many think that the need for wood is decreasing. They think that wood is being replaced by metal, plastics, and other materials. By the year 2000, the demand for saw logs will nearly have doubled. The demand for veneer logs and pulp wood will nearly have tripled. The total demand for industrial wood products will increase about 2⅓ times.

About 20 percent of the total lumber used in America comes from Canada and other parts of the world. At the same time, the United States exports an amount about equal to 11 percent of the total wood consumption in the United States. This means that our imports of lumber exceed the exports by about 9 percent. To meet the increased demands for lumber, the United States must grow more timber on both government and private lands.

FOREST PRODUCTS INDUSTRY

Forest products industries are located throughout the United States. Approximately 10,000 lumber mills, 150 plywood mills, and 16,000 logging operators employ about 574,000 people. With related operations, the industry ranks as the fifth largest employer of manufacturing labor in the United States.

The forest products industry annually processes 40 billion board feet of softwood sawtimber. This is roughly four-fifths of all wood fiber harvested each year in the United States. The balance is consumed largely by the pulp, paper, and hardwood industries. Residue from the softwood lumber and plywood industry is also used in pulp, particle board, and hardboard manufacturing.

Most hardwoods go into industrial lumber. This is used primarily for furniture making and vehicle construction, such as boats and trucks. It is used also for machinery and equipment. It is used for such manufactured products as athletic equipment and toys.

VENEERS AND PLYWOOD

Veneer is a very thin sheet of wood that is sawed, peeled, or sliced from a log.

Plywood consists of an odd number of layers of veneer and/or wood joined together by an adhesive. The grain of each layer of ply is approximately at right angles to the grain of the adjacent ply or plies. The exterior face of the plywood may be either softwood or hardwood. One surface is called the *face veneer* (the better side). The other surface is called the *back veneer*. The innermost ply is called the *core*. All other plies between the core and the face plies are called *crossbands*. Plywood is usually made with 3, 5, 7, or 9 plies, with 3 or 5 the most common. The common thicknesses are from ¼ to 1 inch in panel dimensions of 4 × 8 feet. Three common types of plywood construction are:

- *Lumber Core.* The core consists of strips of lumber bonded together.
- *Veneer Core.* The core is made of thick wood veneer. Most softwood plywoods have this type of construction.
- *Particle-Board Core.* The core is made of particle board, which is a wood composition material. This kind of plywood is commonly used for the tops of tables and cabinets.

Plywood is held together with either moisture-resistant glue or moisture-proof glue. The former is used on interior plywoods. The latter is for exterior use. Plywood has great strength and surprising lightness. In addition to the soft and hard plywoods, there are many specialty types. Included are those with special or decorative surfaces. The face of plywood may have a striated (lined) surface to give it a combed look. Another may have a brushed face to accent the grain. Another may have a sand-blasted surface. Plywoods are also available in many special grades for special purposes.

HARDBOARD AND PARTICLE BOARD

All wood products consist basically of wood fiber. Wood fibers contain cellulose and lignin. Cellulose gives wood its strength. Lignin cements the wood fibers together and makes wood solid. Fibers in wood are fairly uniform in size, shape, and properties. In lumber and plywood the fibers remain in the same position they had in the growing tree. This is not true of hardboard.

Hardboard is manufactured from wood that has been reduced to the individual basic wood fibers. Logs are cut into small wood chips. Those are reduced to fibers by steam or mechanical processes. These fibers are refined and then compressed under heat and pressure in giant presses to produce sturdy panels. Lignin holds the fibers together. Hardboard is closely related to other members of the wood products family.

Particle board is another manufactured panel material. It is made by combining wood particles with resin binders and then hot-pressing them together in panels. Particle board is different from hardboard because wood particles that are not broken down into fibers are used to make particle board. Raw material is first classified by size. The large particles are broken down mechanically, usually with a hammer mill. The small particles are then dried and mixed with a resin binder. They are formed into a mat, and pressed into a panel. Sanding may follow. The properties of particle board can be changed by using different sizes and kinds of wood particles and different binders. Particle board is made in many sizes and thicknesses. It is widely used as a core for plywood and plastic laminates.

PAPER

Each American uses an average of 560 to 575 pounds of paper every year. Almost all paper is made from wood.

Much attention is being given to the reuse of paper through recycling. This method has been promoted as one way to conserve trees and help solve the nation's waste disposal problems. Recycling is not a new idea. The paper industry gets more than 20 percent of its raw material from wastepaper. Another important source of raw material for making paper is the residue from the manufacture of other wood products such as lumber and plywood.

Review Questions

1. How many acres of forestland does America have?
2. List the three groups that own our commercial forests. Tell what percent each group owns.
3. Approximately how many people are employed in lumber and plywood mills plus logging operations?
4. List the common numbers of plies in plywood.
5. Describe the difference between veneer core and lumber core plywood.
6. What is hardboard and how is it manufactured?
7. Describe what particle board is made from.
8. Describe the two methods of harvesting trees.
9. Why is a wedge-shaped notch cut in the tree on the side towards which it is to fall?
10. What is the first step in the lumber manufacturing process?
11. What are the first large planks cut from a log called?
12. How long does it take to air-season newly cut lumber?

Facts about Wood

The Log Cabin

The log cabin was a simple shelter with several advantages. It could be built quickly from what often was the most available resource—wood. Properly chinked, it offered a fairly weathertight dwelling.

One of the great strengths of the log cabin was that it could be built using only a few tools. An axe would be needed and probably an auger. In selecting trees, the builder took some care to ensure that the logs would be roughly of the same diameter. After being felled, the trees were then cut to the needed length and trimmed of their branches. They were then notched on their ends.

Log cabins were usually simply designed, being square or rectangular. They had only a single story. Additional sleeping space would have been provided in a loft. The walls were built by stacking one log on top of another. The logs on each wall were fitted to those on the intersecting walls by means of notches. The spaces between the logs were chinked, or filled with mud or moss. Often, log cabins had no windows. If they did, they rarely held glass, which was expensive and difficult to transport without breaking. Instead, a window opening would be covered with greased paper or a dried and scraped animal hide. This would allow some light to enter the cabin, which usually had only a single room.

The roof was made of several small logs, which served as rafters, and a ridgepole, which ran the length of the cabin. For the ridgepole, a single, long, sturdy log was needed. The roof framework was covered with roughly hewn flat wooden slabs. The roof was perhaps the least weather-resistant part of the log cabin. The lyrics of many pioneer songs mention the problems of a leaking cabin roof.

The floor of the cabin usually was of packed earth. If flooring was used, it was of *puncheons*. These were logs split in half. These puncheons were then placed side by side, split side up.

The log cabin is the dwelling most associated with the American frontier. Several of our presidents were born in log cabins. Of these, the most famous is probably Abraham Lincoln, who was born in 1809 in a log cabin just outside Hodgenville, Kentucky. When he was two, the family moved to a log cabin in Knob Creek, Kentucky. Lincoln's earliest memories were of life in this cabin. Restored, this cabin is now open to the public. In his early twenties, Lincoln lived in New Salem, a small village in central Illinois. Most of its buildings were log cabins. There, he worked as a surveyor, postmaster, and storekeeper. New Salem has been restored and is open to the public.

There are several log cabins still standing, especially in the Midwest. The cabins in that region would have been built later than those in the East. A few of these cabins are still lived in. Those who have spent a winter in a well-built log cabin have found that the insulating properties of wood are remarkable. Generally, they found themselves with more firewood than they needed.

Thinking about a Career

Forester

Ann Lindbergh is a forester with a private timber company in the Northwest. She is in charge of managing and developing the timber resources of the company.

The job qualifications for foresters include a bachelor's degree with a major in forestry. Over 50 colleges and universities offer such a degree. In the course of the college program, the student may be required to spend a summer in a field forestry camp run by the school. The college forestry curriculum stresses liberal arts and communications skills.

"As well as liking to work outdoors, I also don't mind moving or living in remote places," says Ann. "The company I work for has timberland throughout the Northwest. Right now, I live in a small town of 2,000 people. This is my second move for the company in the five years I've worked for them. And, of course, there's a lot of travel during the week. I drive quite a few miles checking on the trees."

The profitability of a company's forests depends on the way in which these forests are developed. The trees must be properly cared for. They must be kept free of disease. The quality of the water in the forests must be checked. Forest fires must be prevented and fought. All of these jobs are the responsibility of the forester. It might seem that the work is all outdoors. It isn't, though. Many jobs require the completion of a written report. In this, there is a fair amount of paperwork.

"Some of my duties require that I communicate my technical knowledge to other people," says Ann. "For example, I deal frequently with loggers and owners of timberland. Some of my other duties—such as mapmaking—I perform alone. I need to make maps of forest areas. I also need to estimate the amount of standing timber. Both of these jobs require good math skills. These are very important jobs. The reports that I make serve as a basis for development of the entire forest.

"I am also responsible for protecting the wildlife in the forest. I also select and mark the trees that are to be cut. I then supervise the cutting. I plant seedlings to replace the trees that were removed. A few of my duties have been somewhat dramatic. I have, for example, fought three major forest fires. Twice, I've been involved in search-and-rescue missions for lost campers. In each of these searches, we were successful."

Foresters do not always remain foresters. They can advance to positions within the company administration. In fact, many executives in large timber companies were once foresters.

"I know that there are opportunities for advancement in my field," says Ann. "But, right now, I'm happy where I am. I earn a good salary, I enjoy my work, and I'm where I want to be—outdoors."

Developing Science, Math, and Reading Skills

Regional Air Pollution Damages Forests

One of the current concerns of scientists is to understand more fully the impact of air pollution on the growth of our forests. The burning of fossil fuels (gasoline, natural gas, and coal) damages living plants. Botanists (scientists who study plants) have found forests in Colorado, Vermont, the Carolinas, and Georgia that have been damaged by acid rain. *Acid rain* is a chemical formed when gases like sulfur dioxide or nitrogen monoxide combine with rain. Softwoods have been most affected.

Trees such as conifers, which grow at high altitudes, seem to be easily damaged. From low-lying clouds, they trap droplets that are even more acidic than the rain droplets. Acid rain also leaches (washes away) metals such as aluminum from the soil. This injures the small roots.

Chemists are able to mix up a "soup" of chemicals identical to those found in acid rain. They can then apply these chemicals to young seedlings and record the results. The experimental results prove that acid rain is a probable cause of the early death of many trees.

ACTIVITY: Investigating the Acidity of Rainfall
Materials
3 jars
Blue litmus paper (or pH paper)
Medicine dropper
Vinegar
1 aspirin
Soapy water

A. Obtain the materials listed.
B. During a rain shower, collect a sample of rain in one of the jars. Collect a sample of water from a pond, lake, river, or stream in each of the other jars. If possible, collect samples of rainwater from more than one location.
C. Litmus paper is a strip of paper that has been treated with a dye made from a plant called a lichen. Blue litmus paper is used to test a substance to see if it is an acid. Take a sample of a weak acid like vinegar. From a medicine dropper, add a few drops to the blue litmus paper. The paper should turn red, indicating that the vinegar is acid. Try the same thing with a dissolved aspirin. What happens? Repeat with a little ammonia or soapy water. These substances are what chemists call *bases*. They should not affect blue litmus, but they would turn red litmus paper blue.

Now test each of the collected water samples with litmus paper. What do the tests indicate about the chemical nature of these samples? Why do you think they tested the way they did? If a material is neither acidic or base, it is said to be *neutral*.

Note: Acidity can be measured more accurately with pH paper. If neither litmus or pH paper is available, a suitable indicator is grape juice or the water in which a few *red* cabbage leaves have been boiled. Both the grape juice and cabbage juice should turn red when an acid is added.

Activity One

Trees are woody plants growing at least 20 feet tall with a single self-supporting stem or trunk. Wood makes up most of the tree stem. Hardwoods and softwoods are the two major kinds of trees, and are classified according to their ability to resist wear. Another way of classifying trees is based on whether the wood has open or closed grain.

On pages 454-459, you are told many facts about the nature of wood, its hardness and softness, how a tree grows, and the parts of a tree.

The author tells you that trees grow rapidly in the spring when there is much moisture. It is then that springwood is formed. In the summer and fall, the tree grows more slowly. In those seasons, summerwood is formed and leaves dark summerwood rings. What else are these rings called?

Activity Two

The wood you will use in your projects was made available by a process called lumbering. This process begins in a commercial forest. There, it is the job of a forester to decide on the method of harvesting to be used—selective cutting or clear-cutting. With both methods of cutting, reforestation must take place for future generations.

Developing Reading Skills

On pages 461-465, the harvesting and manufacturing of lumber are described in detail. Read over these pages. Determine which method of harvesting lumber is used when the forester chooses to leave trees that are too small to cut, thereby providing seed for regeneration.

Activity Three

On pages 464-465, various veneers and plywoods are described. Plywood is a piece of lumber constructed with an odd number of layers joined together by adhesive. The grain of each layer of ply is at approximate right angles to the adjacent ply or plies. Most plywood comes in 4-foot by 8-foot sheets.

Read this section again. Then write an explanation of how plywood is formed. Try to include the meaning of terms such as front veneer, back veneer, core, and crossbands.

Finding the Circumference of a Circle

Refer to Fig. A, which shows a circle. The dotted line represents the circle's diameter. If you know the diameter of a circle, you can find its circumference, or the measurement of the line that forms the circle. The formula for finding the circumference is as follows:

Circumference = diameter × 3.1416

Refer to Fig. B, which shows a hickory tree. As shown, the tree is 24' tall, with a diameter of 18".

What is the circumference of the hickory tree in inches?

What is the height of the tree in metres? (To convert to metres, multiply by 0.3048.)

Developing Math Skills

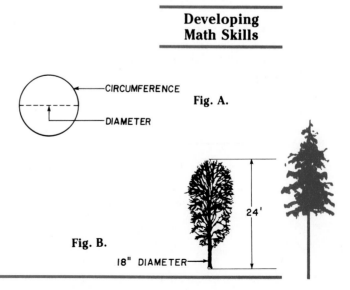

CIRCUMFERENCE

DIAMETER

Fig. A.

24'

Fig. B.

18" DIAMETER

Section VII. Industry and Technology

Chapter 68 — Upholstery

After studying this chapter, you will be able to:
- Identify the four basic kinds of upholstery work.
- List the materials commonly used in upholstery work.
- Identify common upholsterer's tools.
- List the steps in making a pad seat with a solid base and foam rubber.
- List the main steps in making a slip pad seat with webbed base and upholstery cotton.
- List the steps in making a slip pad seat with webbed base and stuffing.

LOOK FOR THESE TERMS

overstuffed seat and back	tacking tape	upholstery
pad seat	tight spring seat	upholstery tacks
rubberized hair	trimmer's shears	webbing
sinuous springs	upholsterer's hammer	webbing stretcher
stuffing regulator	upholsterer's shears	webbing tacks

Upholstery consists of adding springs, padding, textiles, or leather to provide a soft covering for a piece of furniture. There are four basic kinds of upholstery work:

- *Pad seat* (made without springs). This fits into or on the completed chair or stool. Dining room chairs usually have pad seats. Fig. 68-1.
- *Tight spring seat*. This is usually found in living room chairs. A webbing foundation supports the springs. Fig. 68-2.
- *Overstuffed seat and back*. Coil springs are used. This design is common for large chairs and sofas.
- *Sinuous (no-sag) springs*. These use foam rubber or rubberized hair. They are simpler to install and less expensive than coil springs. Sofas often use both types of springs. Fig. 68-3.

68-1. This upholstered bench can be made with a pad seat.

68-2. This cutaway shows the construction of a tight spring seat. Note that the base is webbing to which the springs are tied. Over these is a piece of burlap. Over this is fibrous padding or foam rubber. Finally, the cover is applied.

MATERIALS

Some upholstery materials must be ordered from a specialty supply house. Before starting a project, check to see if needed materials are easy to find in your community.

Upholstery tacks are flathead tacks used for holding materials in place. The larger sizes are needed for tacking webbing. The smaller sizes (6 or 8 ounce, about ½ inch long) are used for fastening the coverings. The *gimp tack* is a small roundhead used whenever the head is meant to show.

Webbing is made from jute fiber. It is used as the foundation. The 3½-inch width is usually specified.

Burlap is used as a covering over webbing, springs, and stuffing. An 8- to 10-ounce (per square foot) weight in 40-inch widths is best.

68-3. A cutaway view of the interior of a quality constructed sofa. Full coil springs are used in the seat construction. Sinuous (no-sag) springs are used to construct the back.

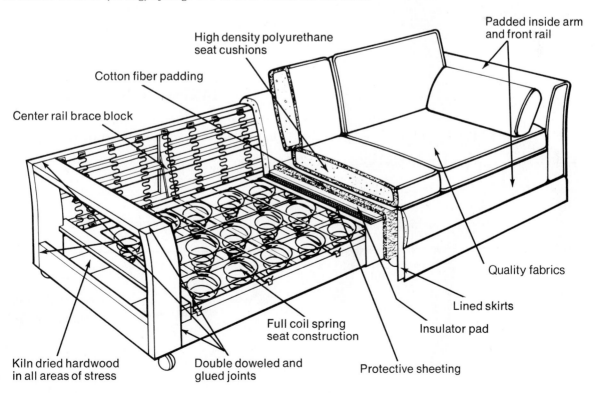

High density polyurethane seat cushions

Padded inside arm and front rail

Cotton fiber padding

Center rail brace block

Quality fabrics

Lined skirts

Insulator pad

Kiln dried hardwood in all areas of stress

Double doweled and glued joints

Full coil spring seat construction

Protective sheeting

Stuffing means a variety of materials used for filling. Among the most common are *curled animal hair*, *Spanish moss* (a plant fiber), *tow* (made from the stalks of flax plants), and *shredded foam rubber*.

Rubberized hair is a light, elastic material made from curled hair and rubber. It comes in pads of standard thickness from ¾ to 2½ inches.

Foam rubber (padding) is made from liquid latex. *Slab stock* comes in thicknesses of ½, ¾, and 1 inch. It is possible to buy *cored utility stock* that has molded cylindrical openings in it. Fully *molded cushions* in many different sizes and shapes are also available. Fig. 68-4. *Rubber cement* is used to fasten tacking tape to foam rubber.

Tacking tape is a muslin cloth tape used to fasten the foam rubber to the base.

Cotton comes in batts that are 27 inches wide and about ½ inch thick. It is purchased in a roll to use over stuffing.

68-4. This cutaway of a pad seat illustrates some of the basic materials used in upholstery.

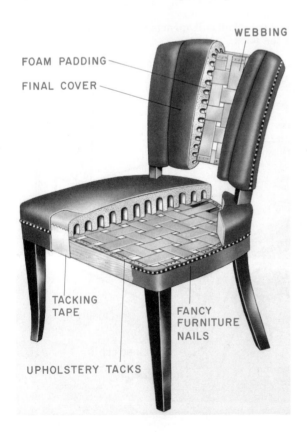

FOAM PADDING

FINAL COVER

WEBBING

TACKING TAPE

FANCY FURNITURE NAILS

UPHOLSTERY TACKS

Muslin of the unbleached type is 36 to 40 inches wide.

Fancy furniture nails come in a wide variety of head styles for places where the nails will show.

Final covers can be of fabric, plastics, or leather.

Other materials include *sinuous coil springs* and *sewing twine* for more extensive work.

COMMON TOOLS

In upholstering, the following tools are commonly needed:

● An *upholsterer's hammer* is needed for extensive work in upholstery. One head is magnetized for holding tacks. For simple jobs, a small claw hammer is satisfactory. Fig. 68-5.

● The *spring-driven stapler* or *tacker* is an ideal machine for stapling on burlap, muslin, or the finished cover. Fig. 68-6.

● A *webbing stretcher* (about 6 inches long) is needed for stretching the webbing before tacking it down. Fig. 68-7.

● *Trimmer's shears* are used for cutting foam rubber, rubberized hair, and fabrics.

● A *stuffing regulator* is a 10-inch metal pin with one sharp and one blunt end. It is used to even out irregularities under temporary coverings. An ice pick is a good substitute.

MAKING A PAD SEAT

Some of the more common ways of making a pad seat are described here.

68-5. Upholsterer's hammer.

68-6. A spring-driven stapler is much quicker than tacks and a hammer. Heavy-duty shears are needed to cut the material. When cutting foam rubber, it helps to dip the shears in water to "lubricate" them. Do not use too much water. The foam rubber can also be cut on a band saw with a 1/4-inch blade.

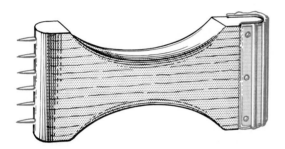

68-7. Webbing stretcher.

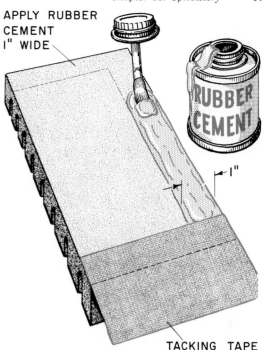

68-8. Apply rubber cement along the upper edge of the foam rubber. Then fasten the tacking tape in place.

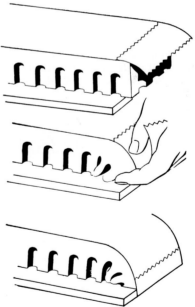

68-9. Forming a cushioned edge.

MAKING A PAD SEAT WITH A SOLID BASE AND FOAM RUBBER

1. Cut a piece of ¼- to ½-inch plywood to the required shape for the base.
2. Drill small holes evenly over the wood for air venting.
3. Select a piece of foam rubber about 1 inch thick.
4. Decide on the kind of edging you want on the seat.
   a. *For a cushioned edge.* Cut the foam rubber to shape with shears. Allow about ¼ inch extra all around, plus an extra ½ inch (12.5 mm) on the cushion edge or edges. Apply rubber cement to about half the width of the tacking tape and 1 inch along the upper edge of the foam rubber. Fig. 68-8. Cement the tape to the smooth top of the stock about 1 inch from the edge. Tuck the bottom edge of

the cushion under so that its thickness is held flat against the base. Fig. 68-9. Keep the tape taut to avoid wrinkling. Tack the tape on the underside with upholstery tacks. Fig. 68-10.

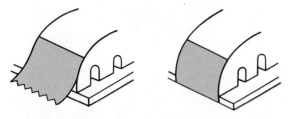

68-10. The adhesive band sticks fast to foam. Staple, stitch, or tack it down for a finished job.

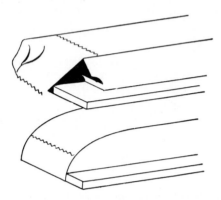

68-11. Forming a feathered edge.

68-12. Making a square edge. Note that the tacking tape has been glued to the edge of the foam rubber and then tacked to the base. Note also the holes in the foam rubber for air ventilation.

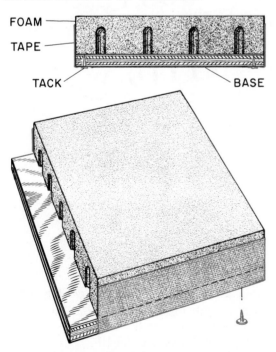

b. *For a feathered edge.* Cut the stock about ¼ inch oversize all around. Cement the tacking tape to the smooth top side about 1 inch from the edge. Bevel the lower edge as shown in Fig. 68-11. Draw the tape down so that the beveled edge is held flat against the base. Tack it in place.

c. *For a square edge.* Cut the rubber, allowing the usual ¼-inch addition all around. Cement the tape flat against the edge of the material. Tack the overhang to the base. Fig. 68-12.

5. Cover the foam rubber with a final cover.

MAKING A SLIP PAD SEAT WITH WEBBED BASE AND UPHOLSTERY COTTON

1. Make an open frame of four pieces of ¾-inch stock that will fit into the main frame of the chair or bench. The corner can be made with dowel joints, end-lap joints, or open mortise-and-tenon joints. Round the upper edge so it will not cut the upholstery fabric.

2. Apply the webbing. Fold the end of the webbing under about 1¼ inches and tack about ½ inch from the outside of the frame. Fig. 68-13. The tacks are staggered to keep the wood from splintering. Stretch

68-13. Turn the loose end of the webbing under and tack in place.

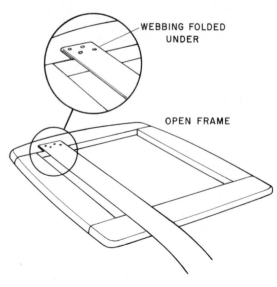

the webbing tightly over the frame as shown in Fig. 68-14. Tack it on the other side of the frame. Cut the webbing about 1¼ inches beyond the frame. Fold over, and tack down again. Place the next piece of webbing about 1½ to 2 inches away. Space the webbing so the piece will cover the opening. Then weave the other pieces through in the other direction. Fig. 68-15.

3. Tack a piece of burlap over the webbing, making sure that it is not drawn tightly. If tacked too tightly, the cloth will tear when in use.

4. Cut a piece of upholstery cotton about 2 inches smaller in all directions than the frame. Center this over the burlap.

5. Cut a piece of cotton about ½ inch larger in all directions than the frame. Center this over the first piece.

6. Apply the final covering. Cut a piece that is about 2 inches larger in all directions than the frame. Place the cover material with the good side down on the bench. Lay the seat facedown. Start tacking at the center of each side. Fig. 68-16. Work toward the corners. Tack the corners as shown in Fig. 68-17.

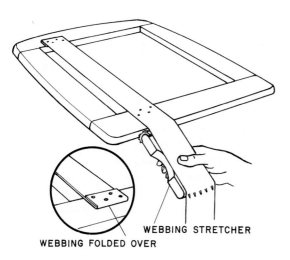

WEBBING STRETCHER

WEBBING FOLDED OVER

68-14. Stretch the webbing and tack to the other side.

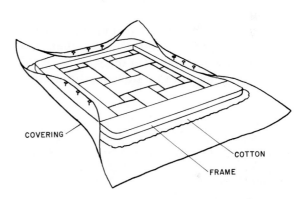

COVERING

COTTON

FRAME

68-16. Once the two layers of cotton are in place, the cover can be tacked on.

68-15. Webbing completed. Burlap must be fastened over the webbing.

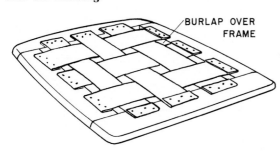

BURLAP OVER FRAME

68-17. Tack the sharp corners carefully.

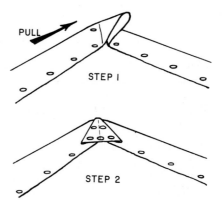

PULL

STEP I

STEP 2

MAKING A SLIP PAD SEAT WITH A WEBBED BASE AND STUFFING

1. Make an open frame and cover with webbing and burlap.
2. Place stuffing of hair or moss over the burlap. Make sure the material is well separated and free of foreign matter such as sticks. Distribute handfuls of the stuffing over the base, working it together with your fingers. Cover to a depth of about 2 inches. (A rubberized hair pad 1 inch thick, cut to size, can be used instead of the stuffing.)
3. Cut a piece of burlap or muslin about 2 inches larger in all directions than the frame. Lay the cloth over the stuffing. Hold it in place as you turn the entire unit over.
4. Start tacking at the center of each side and work toward the corners. Drive the tacks only a little way into the wood so you can remove them, if necessary, to tighten the cover. Check to see that the stuffing is distributed evenly. If not, poke a regulator through the cloth to move some of the stuffing around.
5. Place a layer of cotton over the cloth. Then apply final cover material.

Review Questions

1. Name the four basic kinds of upholstery work.
2. What kinds of materials are used for stuffing?
3. From what is foam rubber made?
4. What are the three kinds of edges that can be used on a foam-rubber pad seat?
5. Describe how to make a pad seat with a webbed base and cotton upholstery.

Chapter 69

Patternmaking and Model Making

After studying this chapter, you will be able to:
- Identify the two types of patterns.
- List the steps in making a simple pattern.
- List the steps in making a casting.
- List the steps in making a model.

LOOK FOR THESE TERMS

bottom board	gate	ramming up
casting	mock-up	riser
cope	model	scale model
draft	mold	shrinkage allowance
drag	mold cavity	shrink rule
fillet	molding board	solid pattern
fillet tool	pattern	split pattern
flask	patternmaker	sprue pin

Patternmaking and model making demand precise skills. Fig. 69-1.

PATTERNS

A *pattern* is a duplicate of something that will be cast of metal or plastic. Many machine parts start as wood patterns. *Patternmaking* is the making of these patterns.

To understand how a pattern is used, think in terms of three stages—pattern to mold to casting.

A pattern is used to make a mold. The pattern forms an impression in a substance that will hold the shape of the pattern. This is the same principle you may have used when pushing an object into modeling clay and removing it to see the result. The hollow portion formed is the *mold cavity*. The term *mold*, however, can be used to refer to just the cavity or to the cavity along with the surrounding substance.

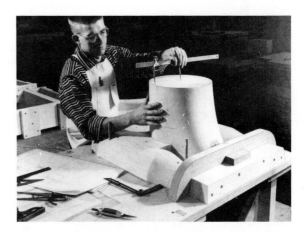

69-1. The patternmaker must be a skilled worker, because all measurements must be very precise. This pattern will be used to cast a metal part.

Two halves of a mold are placed together, with the hollow portion enclosed and an opening extending to the outside. The mold can then be used to make a *casting* by pouring molten metal into this opening. Metal that is molten has been heated enough to become liquid. The quality of the casting depends on the design and quality of the pattern.

There are two types of patterns—*solid* and *split*. A *solid pattern* has only one piece with no loose parts. It is not divided, or split. Simple patterns with at least one flat side are usually made in one piece. Several pieces of wood may be used in constructing the pattern. All are permanently fastened together before the mold is made. Fig. 69-2.

A *split pattern* is made of two or more parts. Most round or irregularly-shaped patterns are split to make casting easier. The pattern is divided for use in both halves of the mold. Fig. 69-3.

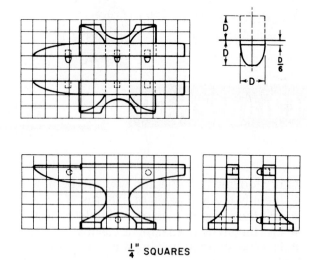

$\frac{1}{4}''$ SQUARES

69-3. A split pattern for a paperweight anvil. Note the dowels used on this split pattern.

69-2. This nutcracker can be made from several one-piece patterns. Each part is molded separately as a single piece. Once all parts have been cast, they can be assembled to make the nutcracker.

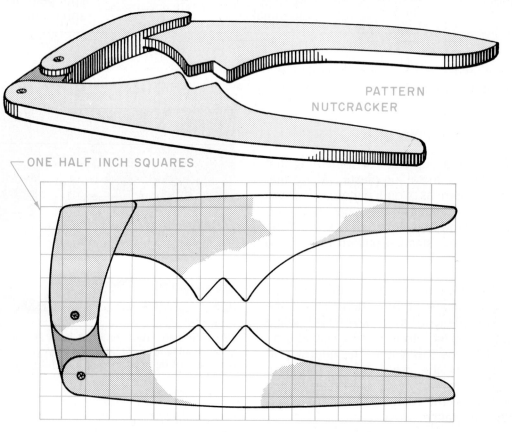

PATTERN
NUTCRACKER

ONE HALF INCH SQUARES

PATTERNMAKING PRINCIPLES

The tools and machines used in making patterns are used also in other woodworking activities.

Most patterns are made from white pine because it is less expensive, fairly easy to work, and very stable. Mahogany is excellent but more expensive.

69-4. All metals shrink, or contract on cooling, but they do not shrink the same amount. Therefore a shrink rule is needed for each different kind of metal. For example, the engine block might be made of cast iron and the pistons of aluminum. Different shrink rules would be used for making the patterns for these parts. Here, a standard rule is compared with shrink rules for iron and brass.

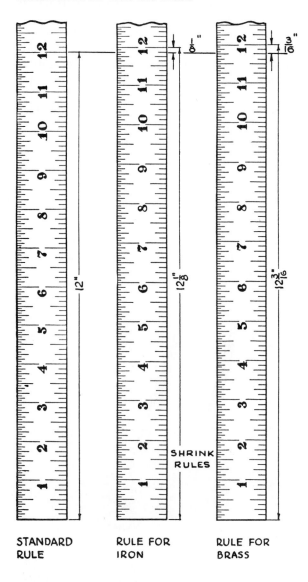

STANDARD RULE

RULE FOR IRON

RULE FOR BRASS

SHRINK RULES

Wood for patternmaking must be kiln dried and free of knots or other imperfections. For some simple (one-piece) patterns, exterior waterproof plywood can be used.

A pattern in use will absorb moisture from the damp sand used to form the mold cavity. To reduce this problem, the pattern is covered with a shellac finish. If wood parts must be glued up to make the pattern, always use a waterproof glue. Liquid hide glue can be used for simple patterns.

Metal always contracts (gets smaller) as it cools. Therefore on most patterns a *shrinkage allowance* is specified. This allowance depends on the material. These allowances are as follows: cast iron—$3/32$ to $1/8$ inch per foot; brass—$3/16$ inch per foot; bronze—$5/32$ inch per foot; and aluminum—$1/8$ to $5/32$ inch per foot.

To simplify making a pattern, a *shrink rule* is used. This is a scale on which each inch is slightly longer than the standard inch. There is a different shrink rule for each kind of metal. For example, if the pattern is cast of brass, a shrink rule that is about $3/16$ inch longer per foot is used. Fig. 69-4. Shrinkage allowances are only approximate. The exact amount depends on the size and kind of casting. For this reason, shrink rules are not used in making small patterns.

If a pattern is to be machined, some additional material must be allowed. On small castings, about $1/8$ inch is allowed for machining operations.

Two terms in patternmaking are draft and fillet. *Draft* is a slight taper on the vertical sides of a pattern. This makes it easier to draw the pattern out of the mold. The general rule is to taper each side $1/8$ inch for each foot of surface to be drawn. Fig. 69-5. The draft slopes away from the pattern face. On one-piece patterns an adequate draft can be obtained by adjusting saw cuts to an angle of 2 to 3 degrees.

A *fillet* is a concave piece of material used to round off the sharp inside corners of patterns. Fillets are usually wax, wood, or leather. The fillet lessens the danger of breakage by rounding sharp corners in the mold cavity. Fig. 69-6. It also helps prevent cracks and corner shrinkage. Fillets are installed with *fillet tools*.

Ready-made patterns of letters and numbers made of white metal are available in many sizes and designs. They are used in simple one-piece patterns to make nameplates and house numbers. *Commercial patterns*, usually of metal, are available for making all kinds of items.

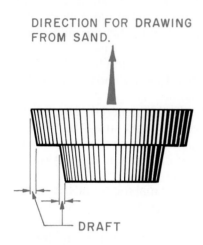

DIRECTION FOR DRAWING FROM SAND.

DRAFT

69-5. Note the direction the draft has been cut to make the pattern easier to draw (pull) from the mold.

69-6. Installing a leather fillet on a pattern with a fillet tool. This is done to round sharp corners that could break off the sand mold when the part is removed from the mold.

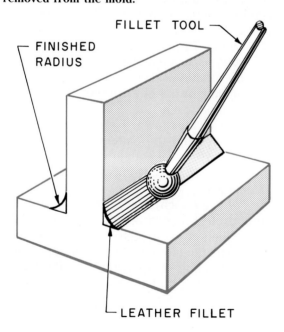

FILLET TOOL

FINISHED RADIUS

LEATHER FILLET

MAKING A SIMPLE PATTERN

A simple one-piece pattern, such as the penholder shown in Fig. 69-7 is made as follows:
1. Obtain a suitable wood, such as a piece of soft white pine about 5 × 7 inches.
2. Square up the stock.
3. Plane or cut a slight draft toward the top side on the edges and ends.
4. Sand all surfaces thoroughly.
5. Apply two or three coats of orange shellac to all wood surfaces.

The pattern is now ready for casting.

CASTING

Now that you have learned how to make a pattern, you are ready to learn how to use it to make a casting.

Sand casting is the simplest method of casting. A pattern is made of wood, metal, plastic, or wax. Wood is the most common choice. The pattern must be made slightly larger than the finished casting will be. The pattern is placed on a *molding board*. Fig. 69-8. A drag is placed around it. A *drag* is one half of an open box called a *flask*.

69-7. A penholder base that can be made with a simple pattern.

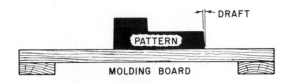

69-8. In making a casting, the pattern is first placed on the molding board with the draft side up.

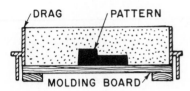

69-9. The drag side of the mold is rammed with sand and then inverted.

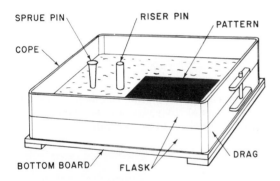

69-10. The cope side is placed over the drag and the sprue and riser pins installed.

69-11. After the cope has been rammed with sand, it is placed to one side. The pattern and pins are then removed.

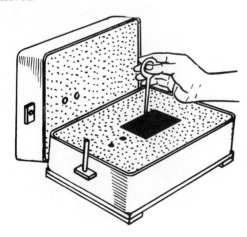

Specially prepared sand or synthetic material is then rammed (pressed) around the pattern. Fig. 69-9. This is called *ramming-up*. The mold is also vented to allow gases to escape. This is done by inserting a long needle into the sand close to but not touching the pattern. Another board, called a *bottom board*, is placed over the drag. The entire unit is then turned over, with the molding board on top and the bottom board on the bottom.

The molding board is removed. Fine parting sand is sprinkled over the surface. The *cope* (the other half of the flask) is placed over the drag. The parting sand in between prevents the two parts of the mold from sticking. Fig. 69-10. This provides the opening through which the molten metal is poured. Sometimes a *riser* (a straight pin) is placed between the sprue pin and the pattern. The riser can also be placed on the opposite side of the pattern from the sprue. The riser opening holds a column of additional metal which will feed the casting as it shrinks and hardens.

Sand is then packed in the cope until it is full and rammed firm. The sprue and riser pins are removed from the sand, leaving holes through the top half of the sand. A long metal needle is used to pierce holes in the sand to let out gas trapped in the mold. The cope is then carefully lifted off and placed to one side. Next the pattern is carefully removed. Fig. 69-11. A *gate* (channel) is cut from the mold cavity, where the pattern was, to the sprue and riser holes. This provides a track for the molten metal to follow. The cope is then replaced. Fig. 69-12.

69-12. The mold is closed.

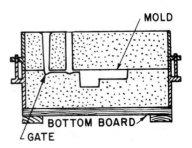

Molten metal is poured into the sprue hole to fill up the mold. Fig. 69-13. After the metal has cooled, the sand is broken up to remove the casting. Some metal will have hardened outside the casting. These unusable parts—metal from the gate, sprue, and riser holes—are cut off. The casting is then ready for finishing.

If a split pattern is used, only half of the pattern is packed in the drag. When the drag is turned over, the other pattern half is placed on the drag. Dowel pins are inserted in the holes so the pattern pieces fit together correctly. Then the sand can be packed in the cope around the second half of the pattern.

Castings can be made from cast iron, steel, aluminum, brass, bronze, copper, magnesium, and many other metals and alloys.

MODELS

Whenever a design for a new product is to be produced, the model maker must first build a scale model. A *scale model* is a small copy. The various parts compare in size in the same way that they would on the actual object. Fig. 69-14. Full-size mock-ups of vehicles are also made of wood to check the design before production begins. A *mock-up* is a full-sized model built accurately to scale. Fig. 69-15.

69-14. This wood model of the space shuttle has been covered with fiberglass. Such a model can be used for wind tunnel tests.

69-15. Sometimes a full-scale mock-up is made. This section of a jet airliner was built of wood so that all design elements could be carefully checked.

69-13. Molten metal is poured into the sprue hole to make the casting.

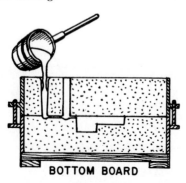

BOTTOM BOARD

MAKING A MODEL

1. Obtain a scale drawing with cross sections shown in full size. These sections are like slices of the object. They are detail drawings showing the shape of the model at different positions along its length.
2. Make a copy of the scale drawing that can be cut up.
3. Cut out the paper cross sections, leaving them somewhat oversize. Glue them to thin 1/16-inch plywood or hardboard. These will be your templates. A *template* is a pattern used to make an object.
4. Cut the templates to the correct shape. It is a good idea to leave a small straight section of the same length at the bottom of each section. This will help in aligning the templates along a center line.
5. Draw a center line on a piece of plywood or heavy wood that will be used as the work surface.
6. Place the section templates at right angles to the center line at the correct locations. Check the dimensions between each division.

7. Cut mahogany blocks of the correct size to fit between the sections. The grain of the wood should run with the longitudinal axis of the model. Make the blocks slightly oversize for working them down to size. Fig. 69-16.
8. Glue the parts together with white polyvinyl glue.
9. Now work the wood down, using the section divisions as a built-in template. Both the roughing and finishing can be done with great savings in time.
10. Apply the finish. The wood model can then be used as a master for casting metal or plastic models.

Review Questions

1. What are the two types of patterns?
2. What are the best woods for making patterns?
3. What is shrinkage? What causes it?
4. Describe draft. Why is it needed?
5. What is a fillet?
6. Name the two parts of a flask.
7. Briefly describe the casting process.
8. Describe how to build a model.
9. How does a scale model differ from a mock-up?

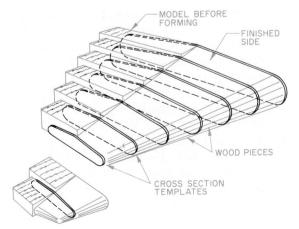

MODEL BEFORE FORMING

FINISHED SIDE

WOOD PIECES

CROSS SECTION TEMPLATES

69-16. Note how the cross-section templates have been glued in place to serve as guides in shaping the model. The blocks of wood have been formed on the right side of the model. They are ready to be formed on the left.

Chapter 70

Manufacturing

After studying this chapter, you will be able to:
- Identify the four main principles of mass production used by Henry Ford.
- List the three types of resources needed to produce goods.
- Identify the responsibilities involved in production planning.
- List the responsibilities involved in production control.
- List the responsibilities involved in quality control.
- Discuss the parts of a technological system.

LOOK FOR THESE TERMS

capital resources	jig	production control
die	manufacturing	production planning
distribution	marketing	quality control
feedback	mass production	research and development
fixture	material resources	service
gauge	output	system
human resources	personnel management	template
input	process	

The three technology groups related to wood technology include production (manufacturing and construction), communication, and transportation. This chapter will discuss manufacturing. Chapter 71 covers construction, Chapter 72 communication, and Chapter 73 transportation.

A good way to study any of these technologies is to consider it as a system. A *system* is an organized way of doing something.

TECHNOLOGICAL SYSTEMS

The "universal" model of a system is shown in Fig. 70-1. It can be used to describe any of the technological systems. Every system includes input, a process, output, and sometimes feedback.

INPUT

"Input" includes all the resources that make a system work. For most systems, there are seven basic resources: people, materials, tools and machines, information, energy, capital, and time. In order to see how such resources might be needed, let's use the example of a furniture manufacturing company.
- People. People are needed to do the work. They might include managers, clerical workers, cabinetmakers, wood finishers, and sales people.
- Materials. Lumber, fabrics, and other materials are used to make the products.
- Tools and machines. Workers need tools and machines in order to change raw materials into products.

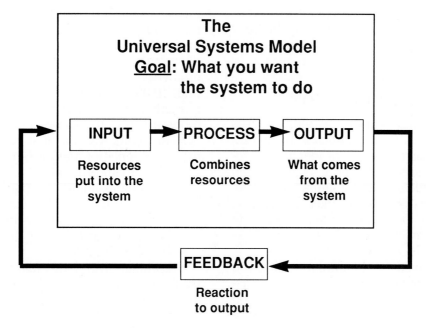

70-1. This diagram of the universal systems model can be used to describe any technological system.

- Information. This includes everything you need to know to get the job done. It could be research found in technical publications, new prices of materials, or the newest styles being shown by interior designers.
- Energy. Energy provides power for lights, heating and cooling, machine operation, drying lumber, and processing wood finishes.
- Capital. Capital is the money needed to build and operate the factory. It pays for everything from raw materials to salaries to utility bills.
- Time. Time is the measure of how long it takes to get all the jobs done. It often has an effect on capital. If a project takes too much time, capital may run out.

PROCESS

The *process* part of a system includes everything that is done to or by the resources (input). In our example of the furniture manufacturing plant, the process would use all the resources to make furniture.

OUTPUT

Output refers to the results of the system. In our example, the most obvious outputs would be the furniture and any profits gained by selling that furniture. However, many times a system creates outputs that are not as obvious but that have important impacts. Here are some possible outputs of furniture manufacturing.

- Waste from the factory in the form of pollutants and any disposal problems they create.
- Changes in people's lifestyles that new furniture designs inspire.
- Changes in a community's standard of living as a result of a factory being located there.
- Traffic problems resulting from workers going to and from the factory.
Can you think of others?

FEEDBACK

Feedback is what you learn as a result of a system's output. To a manufacturer it would include the response of customers. Are they satisfied with the product or do they have complaints? How many service calls were required to make repairs? A manufacturer would use this feedback to improve the product.

MASS PRODUCTION

The American manufacturing industry uses mass production. *Mass production* is the production of a large number of identical products. Using mass production, factories can turn out products in great numbers at relatively low costs. A study of mass production will help you to recognize and appreciate problems of large industrial plants, such as those that produce furniture.

If you have visited a furniture museum, you have seen products made by old-time craftspeople. These products were scarce. Good design and well-constructed furniture were available to only a few, usually the wealthy. Perhaps the first projects you built were made in the same manner as those made by the early furniture makers. In the past, production specialization evolved slowly among artisans and their apprentices. Up to the time of the American Revolution, it took a gunsmith several days to make a single musket. The gunsmith had to hand-fashion each piece separately and then carefully fit the pieces together. There were no duplicate parts. As the parts became worn or broken, the gunsmith had to make another part that matched.

A very farsighted man came up with an idea that dramatically improved production. Eli Whitney, the inventor of the cotton gin, developed many of the principles of mass production. These included:

● Simplification of the product.
● Standardization of each part.
● Use of specialized machines.
● Organization of workers.

Whitney was the pioneer of mass production. He reasoned that since individual parts of muskets are generally alike, they could be made exactly alike. In fact, they could be made interchangeable by using machines specially designed to make each one. The muskets could then be put together by people of limited skill. The firearms would cost less and be better quality. They could be produced in quantity. Around 1800, under a government contract, Whitney tooled up and built 10,000 muskets in a fraction of the time formerly required. This was the beginning of modern mass production.

Henry Ford was the first manufacturer to make a science of mass production by using these four main principles:

● Interchangeability of parts (developed by Eli Whitney).
● The first assembly line (first put into use by Oliver Evans in his grain elevators).
● Division of labor.
● Elimination of individual wasted motion (principle developed by Frederick W. Taylor, the original efficiency expert).

This system of making things has become the foundation of American business and industry.

To mass-produce goods, three basic resources are needed:

● *Material resources*. These include the wood, plastics, metal, ceramics, and other materials that go into the products.
● *Capital resources*. These include the factory, the machines, and the tools.
● *Human resources*. These are the people themselves and their skills and abilities.

It would be interesting for you to help plan and develop a mass-production project. Fig. 70-2. This will give you an idea of the way mass production functions. There are three basic ways the mass-production project can be handled:

● Your class may review product designs and select one to produce. With this method, just enough of the product is manufactured to allow one for each member of the class.
● An alternative is to develop a product that can be given to a local charitable organization. Often a toy or game can be produced in enough quantity to satisfy the needs of a local organization.
● Your class could manufacture an item for sale. You will need to establish a company, sell stock, elect a board of directors, do

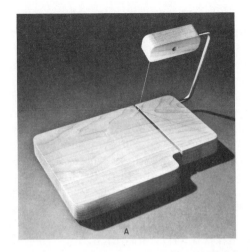

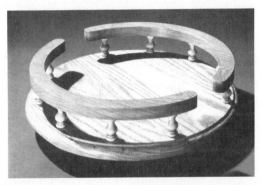

70-2. Four prize-winning mass production products. (A) The cutting board for cheese would be a good product to sell. (B) The round tray would be an attractive gift. (C) The candle holder is an accent piece that might be sold to gift shops. (D) The wood airplanes were donated to a group that provided toys for needy children.

market research, produce a product, sell it, and handle all the details of business. The class members shown in Fig. 70-3 have mass-produced clock cases and toy trains.

There are many steps that your class must take to mass-produce a project to sell. These steps are also done in industry. Fig. 70-4.

RESEARCH AND DEVELOPMENT

Before a product can be manufactured, a company must determine what the customer needs. This is known as *research*. The company must then produce a product to meet this need. This is known as *development*. Since the two activities are often closely related, they are referred to as *research and development*.

Customers' attitudes lead to the development of many new products. Video recorders and hundreds of other new products have been developed to meet consumer demands. Industry must know the buying motives, tastes, and habits of the people they serve. Producers spend millions of dollars annually to find out what the public wants and what to manufacture.

Before deciding on what to produce for sale, you need some idea of how much time can be spent on this experience. If only a few weeks are available, then a small product might be chosen. See, for example, the serving tray shown in Fig. 70-4.

Once a product has been selected, it is necessary to develop the idea into a model.

70-3. The toy trains and the clock case were mass-produced by these students.

70-4. This chart shows the steps in a manufacturing operation, from planning through selling.

To do this, the idea must first be put on paper in the form of a drawing. Then one or two of the prototypes, or pilot models, must be built. These pilot models must be accurately made so that all necessary jigs, fixtures, templates, and other items can be developed from the model. The models will also aid in deciding how to produce the product on an assembly line. All possible modifications and improvements should be made in the pilot model before production begins. To save time, your class may want to select a product already drawn, complete with a *bill of materials*, procedure sheet, and job descriptions. Such a product is shown in Fig. 70-4. The working drawings, plans, and procedures are shown in Figs. 70-5 and 70-6 and Tables 70-A, B, C, and D.

PRODUCTION PLANNING

Production planning consists of readying materials and equipment for production. Many things must be done to get ready for production. The pilot model must be analyzed to determine the operations and processes necessary for production. You must also know what standard and special equipment are needed. It will also be necessary to make jigs, fixtures, dies, templates, and gauges. A *jig* is a device made especially for

Manufacturing of a Serving Tray				
Research & Development	• Organizing • Planning • Designing • Drawing • Prototype Building			
Production Planning	• Jigs • Fixtures • Dies • Templates			
Production Control	• Production Charts • Flow Charts			
Quality Control	• Materials • Parts • Products			
Personnel Management	• Hiring • Training • Assigning • Supervising			
Manufacturing	• Cutting • Forming • Finishing • Assembling			
Marketing & Distribution (Wholesale & Retail)	• Advertising • Selling • Distributing • Servicing			

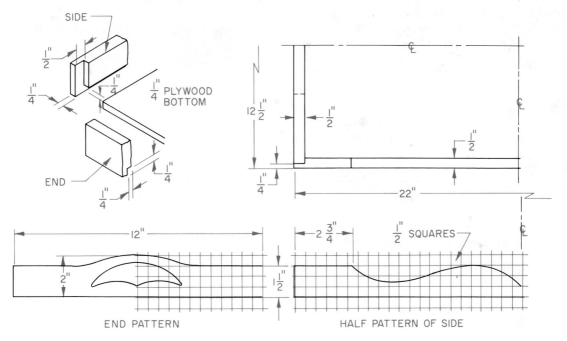

70-5. Working drawings for the tray.

70-6. Flow chart for manufacturing the serving tray.

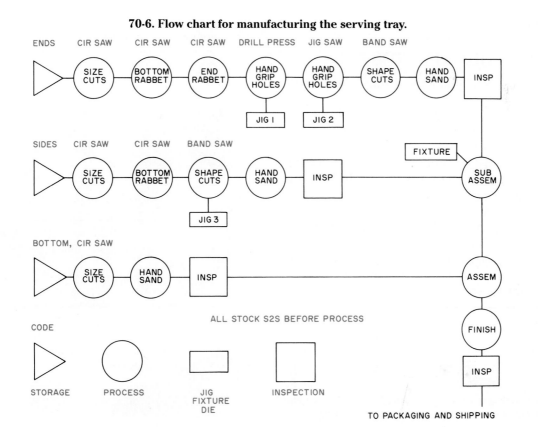

holding work and guiding the cutting tool. Fig. 70-7. A *fixture* is a device made to hold work. Fig. 70-8. Its purpose is to make it easier for the operator to locate the work accurately, support it properly, and hold it securely. A *die* is a tool for cutting or shaping parts. Dies are not commonly used in woodworking plants except for plastic or metal parts. A *template* is a metal, wood, or cardboard pattern. It is used to draw the outline of a part, locate the holes, and lay out the pieces. A *gauge* is a device used to check whether a part is the correct size. Fig. 70-9.

PRODUCTION CONTROL

Production control consists of setting up a production line so that there is a smooth flow of materials through the plant. Materials such as lumber, plywood, finishing materials, fasteners, and other materials must be ordered in adequate amounts. There must be places to store the material, keep an inventory, and handle the job assignments. Space is needed to make the plant layout, and prepare production charts, flow process charts, and schedules.

QUALITY CONTROL

All items manufactured must meet certain standards. *Quality control* consists of inspecting and testing the raw material that comes into the plant, checking the parts as they are produced, and inspecting and testing the finished product. In mass production the aim is to make a high percentage of acceptable parts, with few rejects.

In industry, many types of gauges are used to check each part as it is made and to inspect the final product. Quality control often depends on individual inspection of each part as it is made. The assembly of the product must also be checked. The finish must be checked.

Table 70-A. A Bill of Materials for the Serving Tray*

Number of Pieces	Part Name	Thickness	Width	Length	Material
2	Sides	½"	1½"	22"	Maple or birch
2	Ends	½"	2"	12"	Maple or birch
1	Bottom	¼"	12"	21½"	Birch plywood
16	No. 18 × ¾" wire brads				

*All dimensions listed above are finished size.

Table 70-B. Plan of Procedure for the Serving Tray

1. Cut sides and ends to size on circular saw.
2. Cut rabbet joints on bottom edge of side and end pieces on jointer or circular saw.
3. Cut end rabbet joints on ends of side pieces on circular saw.
4. Lay out irregular design on sides and ends, and cut out on band saw or jig saw.
5. Drill ¼-inch hole in hand grip in ends and cut out on jig saw.
6. Smooth pieces with sandpaper.
7. Assemble sides and ends with glue and wire brads, drilling nail holes slightly smaller than brads to prevent splitting the wood.
8. Cut bottom for snug fit. Sand and fasten into place with glue and wire brads.
9. Set brads, fill holes, and finish sand entire project.
10. Apply natural finish.

70-7. Using a router jig to shape parts for a grandfather clock that is being mass-produced.

Table 70-C. Production Chart for the Serving Tray

Station	Activity	Equipment	Student Distribution
Supervisor	Supervision of production	Flow charts and plans	1
1	Cut sides to width and length	Circular saw and jig	2
2	Cut ends to width and length	Circular saw and jig	2
3	Cut bottom to width and length	Circular saw and jig	2
4	Cut rabbet on bottom edges of sides and ends	Circular saw with dado head	2
5	Cut end rabbet joints on ends of side pieces	Circular saw with dado head	2
6	Drill holes in ends for hand grips	Drill press and drill with jig	2
7	Cut irregular shape of hand grips	Jig saw and jig	2
8	Cut irregular ends on sides and ends	Band saw and jig	2
9	Sand sides, ends, and bottom	Sandpaper and belt sander	3
10	Assemble sides and ends with glue and brads	Glue, brads, hammer, nailset, and fixture	2
11	Fasten base to sides and ends	Glue, brads, hammer, nailset, and fixture	
12	Finish sand complete product	Sandpaper	3
13	Apply wipe-on finish	Wipe-on finish and rags	2

Table 70-D. Materials, Equipment, Fixtures, and Jigs for Making the Serving Tray

Materials*	
1 piece, $\frac{1}{2}'' \times 1\frac{1}{2}'' \times 44\frac{1}{4}''$, for the sides	
1 piece, $\frac{1}{2}'' \times 2'' \times 24\frac{1}{4}''$, for the ends	
1 piece, $\frac{1}{4}'' \times 12'' \times 21\frac{1}{2}''$, for the bottom	
16 No. $18 \times \frac{3}{4}''$ wire brads	
2 ounces of wipe-on finish	
$\frac{1}{4}$ ounce of white glue	

Equipment	Fixtures and Jigs
Circular saw	Jig for cutting sides and ends to length
Dado head	Jig for cutting bottom to width and length
Drill press	Jig for drilling hand grips
Drills	Jig for cutting hand grips
Band saw	Jig for cutting irregular edges on sides and ends
Jig saw	Fixture for assembling the product
Belt sander	
Claw hammers	
Nail set	
Sandpaper	

*Extra lumber length has been added to allow for cutting.

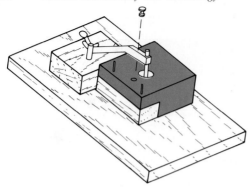

70-8. A fixture holds parts together so that they might be more easily assembled.

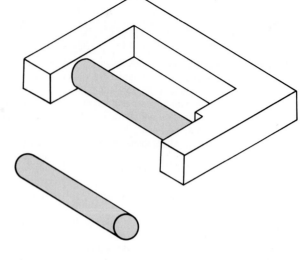

70-9. A go no-go gauge being used to check the inside dimension of a part. The gauge should fit the part. If the gauge will not go in, the part is too short. If the dimension exceeds the length of the gauge, the part is too long.

PERSONNEL MANAGEMENT

Personnel management is concerned with the use of people in mass production. To produce a product, it is necessary to select, train, and supervise the workers. Your class may want to organize committees and spend some time in preparing and training the workers.

MANUFACTURING

Once all the previous steps have been completed, your group is now ready to do the actual manufacturing of the product. *Manufacturing* consists of changing the raw material into the completed product. The value of a product depends on whether it has met quality control standards.

MARKETING AND DISTRIBUTION

Marketing and *distribution* consist of advertising, selling, distributing, and servicing the product. The finished goods must be moved from the plant to the consumers. The *consumer* is the person who uses the product. This is the business phase of mass production. If a market survey has been made, perhaps all of the products have been sold even before production is undertaken. However, it may still be necessary to package the products and deliver them to the buyers. Payments will need to be collected. The necessary records and receipts must be kept.

COMPUTERIZED MANUFACTURING

When they were first invented, computers were considered little more than complex toys. Few people believed they would become very useful or popular. Today they are everywhere. One of their most important uses is in manufacturing. They are used in designing and making products, to keep track of inventory, and in dozens of other jobs. Computers are making contributions to all of the manufacturing jobs you have read about in this chapter. Every day more and more uses are being found.

Computers have also helped introduce other new manufacturing methods. One of these is just-in-time (JIT) manufacturing. With JIT, materials are delivered to the factory as they are needed. Warehouse space is not required. Fewer workers are needed to organize and keep track of materials. Because JIT requires precise planning, every stage of the operation is linked by computer.

The most recent computer research has been in artificial intelligence. Artificial intelligence involves the use of computers to find

solutions to problems that normally require human thought. One day, artificial intelligence might be used along with CAD to find hidden flaws in product designs. It might also help production engineers solve problems that occur on assembly lines. Marketing departments could use artificial intelligence to analyze market conditions and suggest sales methods. These applications would help manufacturers become more efficient and profitable.

In Chapter 1 you read about CAD/CAM, the use of computers in design and production. Chapter 72, Communication, discusses CIM, the linking of an entire factory by means of a central (mainframe) computer.

MASS-PRODUCTION CHECKLIST

The following checklist can be used in mass-producing any product:

- Select personnel. Determine who will be responsible for each phase: engineering, production, business.
- Discuss responsibilities of all personnel.
- Select the product.
- Develop the working drawings.
- Make a bill of materials. Compute stock requirements for one product. Then multiply by the number of items to be produced.
- Construct the pilot, or prototype, models, one assembled and one "loose" so that it can be taken apart.
- Disassemble the model. Make the necessary jigs, fixtures, and templates.
- Test and time the production procedures at each stage of manufacture.
- Organize a flow chart for production.
- Establish the work stations and assign workers.

- Train the workers.
- Conduct a test run for problems.
- Make necessary adjustments or changes in the production line.
- Prepare rough stock.
- Stock each work station with necessary tools and materials.
- Begin production.
- Inspect each part and all subassemblies.
- Assemble the parts of the product.
- Apply the finish to the product.
- Make the final inspection.
- Package the product.
- Distribute the product.
- Disassemble the assembly line.
- Clean up the work stations and store jigs, fixtures, templates, and other special items.
- Evaluate the product.

Review Questions

1. Describe the four parts of every technological system.
2. Name the seven resources put into a system.
3. List the four principles of mass production developed by Eli Whitney.
4. Who was the first manufacturer to make a science of mass production and what four principles did he utilize?
5. Name the three basic resources needed for mass production.
6. Describe the three basic ways of handling a mass production project in class.
7. Describe the function of a fixture.

Facts about Wood

The Largest Wooden Building in the World

The largest wooden building in the world is in Nara, a city in Japan. The building—a Buddhist temple—houses a huge, bronze statue of the Great Buddha.

The temple, known as Todai-ji, is over 1,200 years old, having been completed in 752. It is the largest building in a temple compound that covers seven square blocks in the city of Nara. All of the buildings are excellent examples of Buddhist architecture. The oldest buildings originally had elevated floors. They were built of triangular logs joined without nails.

The temple now housing the Great Buddha is not the original temple. That building was twice destroyed by fire. The present building was completed in 1709. Between 1974 and 1980, the building was completely renovated. This renovation included the laying of a new tile roof. The 6-year renovation required the skills of over 17,000 talented craft workers.

The building is enormous, measuring 57 by 50 meters. It is 47 meters high. This is equivalent to the height of a 13-story building. The Statue of the Great Buddha in the building is made of bronze, mercury, and gold. Measuring over 16 meters in height, it is one of the largest bronze statues in the world. Its head is 3 meters wide and nearly 5 meters long.

The dimensions here have been given in metric measurements. Like most other countries in the world, Japan uses the metric system.

Chapter 71

Construction

After studying this chapter, you will be able to:
- Name the three major kinds of construction.
- List the three basic types of manufactured housing.
- List the important activities that must be completed before actual house construction is begun.
- Describe the western, or platform, method of framing.
- Identify the work that must be done to complete the inside of the house.

LOOK FOR THESE TERMS

bridging	house plans	public works construction
building permit	industrial construction	rafter
commercial construction	joist	residential construction
elevation	mobile home	sectional home
footing	modular unit	sill
foundation walls	plate	site
header	platform framing	stud

Construction is the building and/or assembly of a structure on site. The *site* is its location.

CONSTRUCTION SYSTEMS

As with the other technologies, construction can be studied as a system. Its inputs include all the resources used to create a structure, such as people, time, and materials. The process is the act of building. The primary output is the finished structure. Feedback would include people's reactions to the structure.

The four major kinds of construction include residential, commercial, industrial, and public works.

RESIDENTIAL CONSTRUCTION

Residential construction is concerned with living units for people, such as homes, apartments, condominiums, and mobile homes.

In the past, home building was part of the construction industry but many units are now factory-built.

There are three basic types of manufactured housing:

● The *mobile home*. This is a transportable structure that exceeds either 8 feet (2438 mm) in width or 32 feet (9754 mm) in length. Built on a chassis, it is designed as a dwelling, with or without a permanent foundation. Fig. 71-1.

● The *modular unit*. This is a factory-fabricated, transportable building unit designed to be used by itself or to be incorporated with similar units at a building site into a modular structure.

● The *sectional home*. This is a dwelling made of two or more modular units. It is factory-fabricated, transported to the home site, put on a foundation, and joined to make a single house. Fig. 71-2.

In the United States, nine out of ten living units (homes, apartments, and condominiums) are of wood frame construction. These units are often enclosed with wood siding, wood shingles, brick veneer, or stucco. Wood frame housing is relatively simple to construct. It is extremely sturdy, easy to maintain and repair, and relatively inexpensive. Fig. 71-3.

PREPARING TO BUILD

Locating a Lot

It is important to find a suitable lot. The shape and contour of the lot will determine, to a large degree, the size and design of the home itself. The cost of the lot should not exceed 14 percent of the total building budget.

71-1. The mobile home industry has changed remarkably.

71-2. Sectional home built in two parts. These homes are complete in every detail, including heating, plumbing, and wiring. They are moved to the site and assembled.

Developing or Selecting Plans

A house plan is a layout of the house, showing the dimensions of each room. House plans also include front, side, and rear views of the house. These views are known as *elevations*. Figure 71-4 shows a house plan, along with the rear elevation of the house shown in the plan. Complete sets of house plans are available from many sources. Many companies specialize in good stock plans. These are available from home planning services, lumber yards, and lumber suppliers. To get a good idea of what the house will cost, find out the average cost per square foot for building a home in your community. This average cost will vary with the design and detail of the house. A house with extra bathrooms and many built-ins will cost more per square foot than a simple house. A home designed by an architect usually costs 5 to 10 percent more. By adding the costs of the lot, architect's service, basic home, carpeting, furnishings, and landscaping, you can get a good idea of the total cost. As a rule, this total cost should not exceed two and one-half times the annual income of the family.

Finding a Contractor

Several contractors should be asked to bid on the cost of construction. The contractor will, in turn, hire subcontractors to do the

71-3. The abundance of wood in North America has made it one of the primary materials for home building.

electrical work, plumbing and heating installation, masonry, painting, and other jobs.

Financing

When you know the total cost of the building project, you should go to a bank or savings and loan company concerning the mortgage. Here you can get help in determining the down payment you must make and the mortgage that can be obtained. These people will also figure what your total monthly payments will be. This payment will include principal, interest, taxes, insurance, and any other fees.

Getting the Necessary Permits

Building permits must be obtained. These are issued by the local government to help ensure that buildings are built to code specifications. This must be done before you sign for a mortgage and a building contract.

Surveying and Excavation

A surveyor must set up and mark the lot lines and the building lines with stakes placed at the corners of the lot and the corners of the house. These show where the house will go. If the lot is not flat, stakes must also be placed to indicate lot contours.

At this point a bulldozer usually excavates the ground for the basement and foundation. For a plan without a basement, only a trench may be dug for the foundation. There are three common ways of providing a foundation for a house. Homes without basements are built on a concrete slab or with a crawl space under the house. Both of these require a trench to be dug for the footings that go below the frost line. For homes with a partial or full basement, mechanical equipment is brought in to excavate the basement.

BUILDING THE BASEMENT

Footings are the poured concrete bases on which the basement walls or the house is built. These must be deep enough to support the entire load of the house and at least 6 to 8 inches wider than the walls. Footings must rest on solid earth. Sometimes wood forms

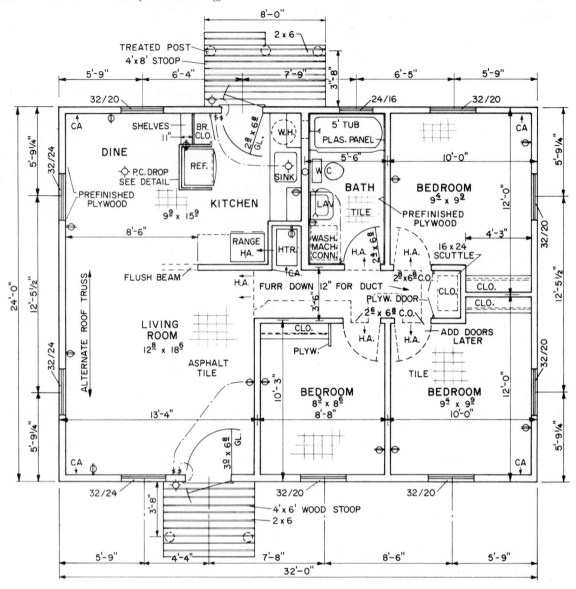

71-4. A house plan is a layout of the house. It gives the dimensions of each room.

are used for the foundations. In other cases, they are poured directly into the trench.

After footings are cured, the *foundation walls* are built of either poured concrete, concrete block, or all-weather wood materials. For a poured concrete basement, foundation forms of wood and metal are erected. The cement is brought in by truck and the basement walls poured. If concrete block is used, the mason will build the walls block by block. The permanent wood basement uses gravel footings and walls of treated wood and plywood with space for windows.

After the walls have been completed, drain tile is placed around the outside of the foundation walls to ensure a dry basement. The exterior of the walls should also be waterproofed. To keep basement walls from caving in, the earth is not replaced around the basement walls until the building has been erected. A cement foundation must also be poured for the I-beam post that holds up the floor. The top of the basement walls should be at least 6 to 8 inches above ground when the landscaping is finished.

At this stage of building, pipes for sewer, water, and gas are laid in the basement area where a meter and shut-off valves are installed for the water and gas. Temporary electric service is brought into the area for the builder's use.

BUILDING THE HOME

Most on-site builders have at least part of the home prefabricated in a manufacturing plant. It is common practice, for example, to buy lightweight, trussed rafters and floor units for installing. Fig. 71-5. Some builders also buy prefabricated wall sections. Other items may also be manufactured, such as prehung doors, kitchen cabinets, and closet interiors. As mentioned earlier, the entire house can be prefabricated in a manufacturing plant. It can then be brought to the site with all parts cut, ready for assembly. With this method, it takes only five or six days to rough-in the house.

FLOOR FRAMING

Lumber for framing the house is delivered and stacked on site. A metal beam (a horizontal, load-supporting member) spans the distance between the foundation walls and the bearing post. This beam is laid in pockets in the basement wall and fastened to the wood or metal bearing posts spaced about 7 feet apart across the basement. Holes are drilled in a sill plate to go with the anchor bolts and the foundation wall. A *plate* is a horizontal support that provides anchorage.

In some parts of the country it is important to place a metal termite shield over the foundation wall before putting the sill plate in place. A *sill* is a horizontal piece forming one of the lowest members in a framework. Sills are set back far enough from the face of the foundation to allow for sheathing, siding, or brick veneer. In installing the sill plate, mortar is first spread on the foundation wall. Then the termite shield is placed. The sill is fitted over the anchor bolts. Nuts are fastened to the anchor bolts to hold the sill firmly in place.

The most common method of framing a house is to use the western, or platform, frame. Fig. 71-6. In this, the first floor is built on top of the foundation wall as though it were a platform. The outer ends of the floor joists or trusses rest on sills. The inner ends rest on a beam. The floor joists or trusses are installed 16 to 24 inches on center. Double joists are used for all partitions. *Joists* are parallel pieces that hold up the boards of a floor. A double header is placed around the basement stairwell and around an opening for the fireplace. These joists carry the weight of the floor. They must be stiff enough not to bend or vibrate. *Bridging* is placed between the floor joists to stiffen the floor and distribute the load. Whenever regular joists must be cut to provide an opening for a stairwell or fireplace opening, extra joists called headers must be installed at right angles to the regular joists. A *header* is a beam fitted at one side of an opening to support the free ends of floor joists, studs, and rafters.

The next major step is to add the subflooring. A common practice is to use plywood. This gives a solid subfloor and is quickly installed.

71-5. In the truss-framed system of construction, the units are built in a factory. They are then delivered to the site. Each unit consists of the floor and roof trusses and the rough wall framing. Using these prefabricated units, the house can be enclosed in a day or two.

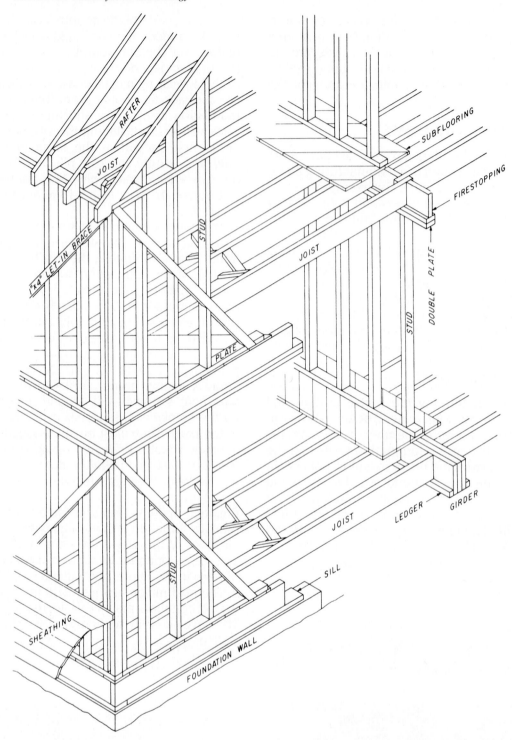

71-6. This platform framing method for a two-story house is commonly used in building.

WALL FRAMING, INCLUDING PARTITIONS AND STAIRS

Exterior wall framing, which includes the sole plate, studs, headers, top plates, and fire stops, is made of 2 × 4's or 2 × 6's. Interior walls are similar but do not include fire stops. These walls are assembled on the subfloor and then raised in place and nailed to the subfloor. These serve as a base for the exterior and interior wall covering. They also support the upper floors, ceiling, and roof. The openings for doors and windows must be adequately framed. To guard against plaster cracks, at least a double 2 × 4 should be placed over small window openings. A double 2 × 6, 2 × 8, or 2 × 10 should be placed over the wider ones.

Partitions are built for the rooms and closets according to the floor plan. The corners are reinforced by using multiple studs. A *stud* is one of the smaller uprights used in the framing of a building. Sometimes the walls are reinforced by installing let-in braces or fire stops.

Immediately after the walls are in place, sheathing is added to the exterior. This is usually fiberboard, gypsum board, or plywood. Openings for windows and doors are cut in the sheathing after it has been installed.

CEILING AND ROOF FRAMING

Ceiling joists are installed direct, as ties between the exterior wall and interior partitions. They can also serve as a basis for flooring in the attic. These ceiling joists carry no floor load except as might be used for light storage in an attic. They are usually spaced 16 inches on center. Roofs are built by installing rafters nailed to the top plate and to the ridge board. *Rafters* are parallel beams that support a roof. Fig. 71-7. They may also be built with a trussed roof.

COMPLETING THE EXTERIOR

The roof is covered with plywood similar to that used for the rough floor. The edge of the roof is completed using two boards. One board is called the fascia and the other the soffit. After the sheathing has been added, a cover of the building paper is tacked in place. At this point masons build the chimney, fireplace, and brick exterior. Exterior windows and doors are installed before the exterior brickwork is completed. The roof is finished by installing flashing (metal used for waterproofing) and shingles, usually asphalt. The siding for the exterior walls may be of various kinds.

INSTALLING UTILITIES

As the carpenters and sheet-metal workers are working on the exterior of the house, work is also progressing on the inside. After the basement floor has been poured, sheet-metal workers install the furnace and duct work for heating and air conditioning. Wires are strung and rough wiring installed in the walls. Locations are marked for outlets and switches. Plumbing is installed. Large pieces of equipment, such as the hot water heater, water softener, and bathtub, are put in place.

71-7. Rafters are used to frame the roof.

COMPLETING THE INSIDE OF THE HOUSE

Blanket insulation is now nailed or stapled in place between the walls. The inside walls are covered with gypsum board or panel, if it is dry-wall construction, or rock lath and plaster for wet-wall construction. Blanket or loose insulation can then be installed in the attic.

Rough door openings are cased in and the doors hung. The finished flooring is installed and the stairways completed. All of the trim is added around doors and windows. Kitchen cabinets and other built-ins are constructed by the carpenter or brought in ready-made and fastened in place.

Tile workers complete the ceramic tile installation. Specialists install flooring material in the kitchen, bathroom, and utility room. Countertops are added. Electrical fixtures, plumbing fixtures, and similar accessories are installed. All necessary interior and exterior painting and finishing is done. The home is then landscaped.

COMMERCIAL CONSTRUCTION

Commercial construction includes buildings whose primary purpose is business, or commerce. Banks, stores, and offices fall into this category. Fig. 71-8. The materials used include steel, concrete, brick, stone, glass, plastic, and wood. Wood is needed in every stage of construction. For example, the forms for concrete foundations and poured concrete walls are built of wood. The interiors of

these buildings also require many different kinds of wood materials for doors, trim, built-ins, and furnishings. Fig. 71-9. The church in Fig. 71-10 is being built with a skeleton frame of laminated beams.

Some high-rise buildings are constructed using the cast-in-place method. Fig. 71-11. A movable tower crane is placed in the center of the site. First, wood forms are built. Then workers insert steel rods inside to reinforce the concrete. Liquid concrete is brought to the building site by large ready-mix trucks. The concrete is placed in a bucket and then hoisted up by the crane and poured into the forms. After each floor is completed, the

71-9. The interior of this bank has built-ins and other furnishings made of wood materials. Skilled carpenters and cabinetmakers build and install such furnishings.

71-8. The skeleton of this office building is of reinforced concrete columns with wood roof trusses. Concrete blocks will be used to complete the walls.

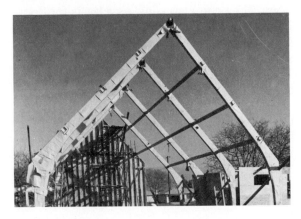

71-10. The skeleton for this church is made of laminated beams.

crane is raised and the next level is built. Skyscrapers can be built to fifty or more stories using this method. The exterior of the building is then covered with brick, stone, or panels of reinforced concrete, glass, or plastic.

INDUSTRIAL CONSTRUCTION

Industrial construction is used primarily for manufacturing facilities. Power plants and large warehouses would also fall into this category. Industrial buildings may require heavier materials. Some factory buildings are constructed of a skeleton of steel shapes, such as I-beams assembled with rivets or welded together. Fig. 71-12. The steel frame is then covered with curtain walls of glass, ceramic, plastic, or other materials.

PUBLIC WORKS CONSTRUCTION

Public works construction creates structures for public use. These include schools, libraries, parks, railroads, bridges, dams, harbors, towers, tunnels, oil drilling platforms, power plants for public utilities, and highways. Fig. 71-13. Public works buildings are made using methods similar to those used for commercial buildings.

For structures such as bridges and highways, many different methods are used. Materials include earth, gravel, sand, steel, petroleum products, concrete, glass, and plastic. Wood is needed to complete all of these structures. Some structures, such as a small bridge, may be completely of wood.

71-12. The skeleton of this factory building is of steel shapes. Note the crane in the background used to raise the heavy metal pieces to their proper location.

71-11. This parking garage was built using the cast-in-place method. One floor is created at a time. Note the reinforcing rods that project up for the next floor. These rods will be boxed in by wood forms before the concrete is poured.

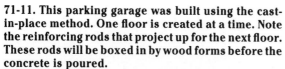

71-13. Roads, bridges, and tunnels are needed for a modern highway system.

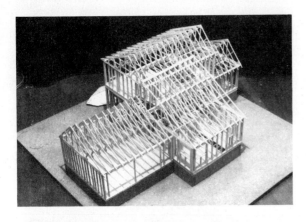

71-14. Building a model house to scale will help you understand construction techniques.

MODEL CONSTRUCTION

If you do not have an opportunity to build an actual part of a home, one of the best ways to learn construction is to build part or all of a scale-model house. Fig. 71-14. Building a scale model also gives you a chance to see house plans in three dimensions and to learn about good construction techniques. Model building will help acquaint you with the construction industry. If you are building a model by yourself, you may want to construct only a portion of the home. Here are some suggestions:

● *Scale.* The ideal scale for model building is 1½ inches equal one foot, which means that the building will be ⅛ full size. With this scale, a 2 × 4 would be ¼ × ½ inch; a 2 × 6 would be ¼ × ¾ inch; and a 2 × 10 would measure ¼ × 1½ inches. Note that these are all the nominal (name sizes) of the lumber, not the actual sizes. In building the house you can then refer to these as 2 × 4's, 2 × 6's, etc., as you would in building a full-size house.

● *Materials.* The lumber used can be scraps of basswood, redwood, yellow poplar, or pine. Often waste lumber can be obtained from lumber yards. Stock can be cut to size in quantity on a table saw, jointer, or planer. Panel stock for the interior and exterior of the house can be made from very thin hardboard. Cardboard can also be used. One-sixteenth and ¹⁄₃₂-inch veneers are also ideal. Nails should be in proportion to the scale size. For example, for framing use 19- or 20-gauge wire nails. For spiking, use ⅝-inch, No. 19, or ¾-inch, No. 18, gauge nails. One-half-inch nails can also be used for nailing the shingles.

● *Tools.* Basic woodworking tools can be used in model construction. The important ones are a good, small miter box, five-ounce tack hammer, long-nose pliers, back saw or dovetail saw, small block plane, architect's scale, and bench tool.

● *House plans.* Any standard set of house plans can be used for model building. It is best to select a one-story ranch home. This will reduce construction problems.

● *Other materials*. A wide variety of other materials can be used to build a model. For example, a piece of plywood or particle board can form the lot layout. The foundation can be made from a rigid foam plastic to which a mixture of portland cement and water has been applied. All layouts should be made using the architect's scale. The cutting, fitting, and nailing should be done in the same manner as for a small take-home project. Perhaps only part of the interior and exterior wall needs to be covered with thin veneer and hardboard. The same is true for the roof. Shingles can be made from sandpaper or from thin wedges of cedar blocks. All materials for building model homes, even windows and doors, are available commercially from many companies. For landscaping materials, flocking can be used for grass. Wire and foam rubber can be used for trees and shrubbery.

BUILDING A DOGHOUSE

Carpentry differs from making small projects. In heavy construction, large-dimension framing stock and large nails are used. The cutting is less accurately done. Some carpentry experiences can be obtained by building outdoor items. In doing this, you will be handling materials much the same as for building a home.

The doghouse, Figs. 71-15 and 71-16, can be a useful project. The materials needed are listed below.

Lumber
Base, House Frame, and Rafters: 5 pcs. 2″ × 4″ × 8′
Siding: 8 pcs. 1″ × 4″ × 10′
Roof, Sides, and Floor: 2 pcs. 4′ × 8′ × ½″ exterior plywood

Hardware and Other Materials
Frame to Frame: 8d nails as required
Plywood to Frame: 4d nails as required
Siding to Plywood Covering: 3d finishing nails as required
Asphalt Roofing Paper: 2 pcs. 3′ × 4′
Shingles: sufficient amount for 16 sq. ft. coverage
Roofing Nails: ⁷⁄₁₆″, as required

Use 2 × 4's to build the base and cottage-style frame. The rafters are 16⅞-inch long 2 × 4's beveled at 45 degrees on both ends to form a gabled roof. Exterior plywood for flooring and frame covering adds strength as well as extra protection against the weather. For the sides, front, and back install 1 × 4's over the plywood. These need only be sawn and nailed in place without overlap. Apply roofing paper over the plywood roof deck. Cover these with shingles of your choice. Stain or paint the doghouse.

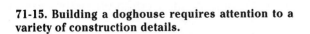
71-15. Building a doghouse requires attention to a variety of construction details.

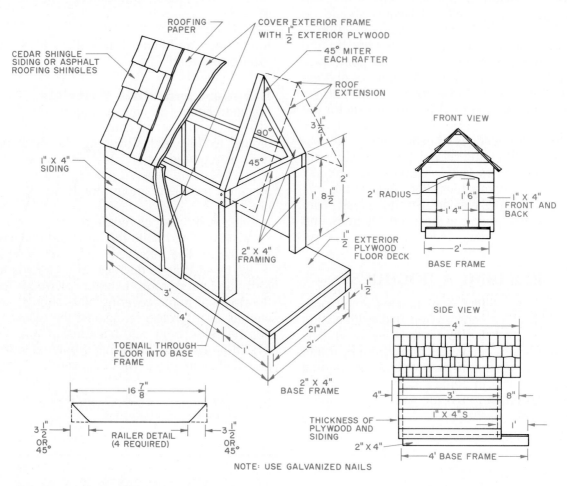

ROOFING PAPER

COVER EXTERIOR FRAME WITH ½" EXTERIOR PLYWOOD

CEDAR SHINGLE SIDING OR ASPHALT ROOFING SHINGLES

45° MITER EACH RAFTER

ROOF EXTENSION

FRONT VIEW

1" X 4" SIDING

90°

45°

3½"

2'

2' RADIUS

1' 6"

1" X 4" FRONT AND BACK

1' 8½"

1' 4"

2" X 4" FRAMING

½" EXTERIOR PLYWOOD FLOOR DECK

BASE FRAME

2'

3'

4'

1½"

SIDE VIEW

4'

TOENAIL THROUGH FLOOR INTO BASE FRAME

21"

2'

1"

4"

3'

8"

16 ⅞"

3½" OR 45°

RAILER DETAIL (4 REQUIRED)

3½" OR 45°

2" X 4" BASE FRAME

THICKNESS OF PLYWOOD AND SIDING

1" X 4" S

2" X 4"

1'

4' BASE FRAME

NOTE: USE GALVANIZED NAILS

71-16. Plans for building the doghouse shown in Fig. 71-15.

Review Questions

1. Name the four kinds of construction.
2. How does a mobile home differ from other types of manufactured housing?
3. What is the most common method of framing a home?
4. Describe the cast-in-place method of construction.
5. Tell how to build a scale model.

Chapter 72

Communication

After studying this chapter, you will be able to:
- Identify ways of communicating.
- Describe a communication system.
- Briefly describe graphic communication, technical design, computer communication, optics, and audio and video communication.
- Name several communication devices and their applications.
- Tell how communication is used in the wood technologies.
- Discuss the impacts of communication technology on wood technology.

LOOK FOR THESE TERMS

audio systems	fax machines	optics
communication	graphic communication	technical design
computer communication	modem	universal product codes (UPC)
computer-integrated manufacturing (CIM)	networks optical fiber	video systems

What do the following activities have in common?
- Reading this book.
- Making a sketch of a new product.
- Developing a new product with the aid of a computer.
- Operating a machine using numerical control.
- Selling a mass-produced product by telephone.

All these activities involve communication. Does communication have anything to do with woodworking? Of course, because basically *communication* means to send a message in which you share information, ideas, or instructions.

Most communication is done by means of language, pictures, or signs and signals. When you ask someone a question, write a letter, or read a book, you are of course using language. When you look at a photograph or read a technical drawing to learn about parts, sizes, and assembly methods, you are communicating by means of pictures. When you see a flashing red light near a railroad crossing, you stop because that signal has communicated to you that a train is coming.

People are not the only ones who communicate. Animals and machines communicate as well. Communication can also take place among the different groups. For example, communication can be person-to-person, person-to-machine, machine-to-machine, and machine-to-person. Fig. 72-1. You probably take part in this kind of crossover every day in your woods class. Your instructor tells you to make a drawing (person-to-person), and you draw it using your computer (person-to-machine). Your computer sends it to the plotter (machine-to-machine) and asks you if you want to save the drawing (machine-to-person).

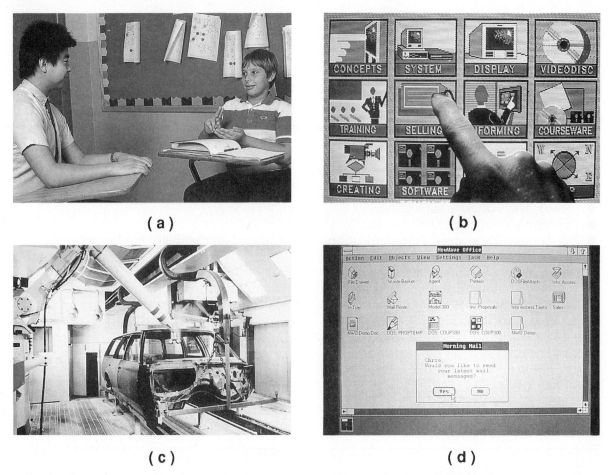

(a)   (b)

(c)   (d)

72-1. (a) Person-to-person: these people are using sign language to talk to one another. (b) Person-to-machine: a touch-screen allows people to talk to a computer. (c) Machine-to-machine: In this factory, a computer tells a robot how to spray paint a car. (d) Machine-to-person: computers talk to people when they ask for instructions.

COMMUNICATION SYSTEMS

Like the other technologies, communication is a system. It includes input, a process, output and sometimes feedback. Fig. 72-2. A good example of one kind of comunication system is the telephone. Let's say you are using the phone to order plywood. The input is what you say into the telephone—your order. The process is the way your message is carried over the phone lines. The output is heard by the person on the other end of the line. Feedback is the plywood you receive as a result of your call.

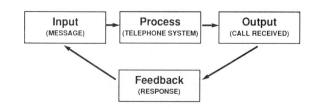

72-2. The universal systems model can be applied to communication systems, such as the telephone.

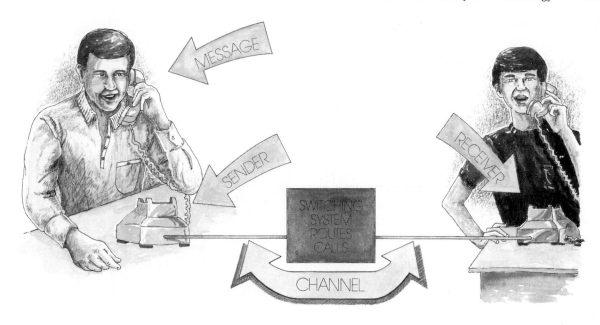

72-3. Every communication system includes a message, sender, channel, and receiver.

Another way to describe a communication system is to say it includes a message, a sender of the message, a channel through which the message travels, and a receiver. Fig. 72-3.

Five types of communication systems play an important role in wood technology. They are considered technical communication systems. They include graphic communication, technical design, computer communication, optic systems, and audio and video communication.

Keep in mind as you read that many of these communication systems overlap. For example the lenses that are part of a camera (optics) are also part of a TV camera (audio and video). Also, computers have rapidly become part of all the other communication systems.

GRAPHIC COMMUNICATION

Graphic communication is done by means of "printed" words and pictures. This book, an advertisement for wood products, and the instruction manual that comes with a new woodworking machine all fall into the category of graphic communication. Fig. 72-4.

The oldest method of graphic communication was used by the Chinese as early as A.D. 200 An image was carved into a wooden block. Ink was applied to the raised surface. Then the block was pressed against another material, such as paper, to transfer the image. This type of printing was used for centuries. Then in 1450, in Germany, Johannes Gutenberg developed movable type, and printing underwent great changes. Each of Gutenberg's metal letters was a separate unit and could be used over and over in different combinations. Printing was speeded up and books could be produced on a press in large numbers.

Until recent years, the printed word was usually composed with ink and paper. Today, printing is changing again. Copy machines, for example, use a charge of static electricity to attract a powder to an image area. The powder is then fused to the paper with heat. Fig. 72-5. Another new method, ink jet printing, uses spray guns to reproduce an image on almost any surface. The "printer" and "paper" never even touch.

TECHNICAL DESIGN

A special form of graphic communication that deserves its own category is *technical design*. The sketches, plans, and other drawings used by architects, engineers, and woodworkers are all products of technical design.

In Chapters 3 and 4 you read about many aspects of technical design, including different types of drawings and how to make them. Chapter 1 covered CAD (computer-aided drafting), the use of computers in technical design. With CAD, the drawing appears on the computer screen and then is reproduced on paper using a printer or plotter. Fig. 72-6.

COMPUTER COMMUNICATION

As discussed in Chapter 1, computers process information, and *computer communication* is done extremely quickly by means of electrical impulses. Every day, more and more uses are found for computers. CAD, for example, can be applied to design needs

72-5. Photocopies are made when static electricity is used to attract powders to an image area.

72-6. A plotter creates an image using multicolored "pens." Flatbed plotters fit on a desktop. Drum plotters, used for large drawings, stand on the floor.

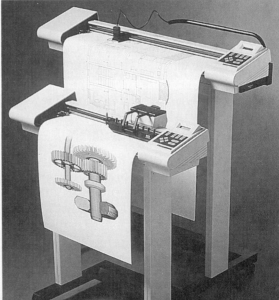

SALE!
Tomorrow only
ALL WOOD TABLE AND CHAIR SETS....50% OFF

HOMETOWN FURNITURE
Northwoods Mall

72-4. Graphic communication includes advertising. Drawings or photographs are used as well as words.

other than basic drawing. Families of items, such as types of fasteners, can be drawn and stored in the computer. When a new part must be created, the basic drawing is called up, copied, and adapted to the new design specifications. CAD can also help with stress analysis. When an architect needs to know if a structure will be strong enough, a model of the structure is created using the computer. The computer analyzes the structure in terms of the forces that will act upon it and suggests any needed changes.

Combined with non-drafting software, CAD can be used to prepare such things as bills of materials. The computer carries out calculations and helps transmit orders. With database software, CAD can keep track of large inventories of items. Types of wood materials and where they were used in a particular building can all be kept on file and called up as needed later on, such as for repairs.

Some computer attachments make it possible for information to be sent over long distances. Let's say you are a woodworker who specializes in custom-made cabinets. You have a computer and *modem*, a device that allows you to send data (information) over

telephone lines. An architect in another state with the same equipment could send you the plans for a house. The plans would then appear on your own computer, ready for your use.

Computer *networks* are groups of people who have a shared interest and who are linked together by means of computers. They can send one another messages or access electronic "bulletin boards" that contain items of general interest. Linkage is usually achieved by means of telephone hookups.

Fax machines are another device used for high-speed data communication. Fig. 72-7. Although they can work without a computer, a computer makes them easier to use and more flexible. Even photographs can be faxed almost instantly by means of electronic signals that travel over telephone lines.

72-7. Fax machines transmit copies of documents electronically over phone lines.

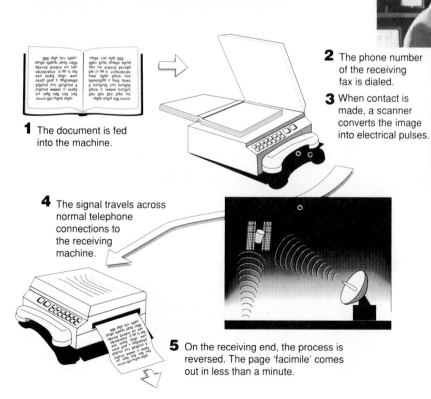

1 The document is fed into the machine.

2 The phone number of the receiving fax is dialed.

3 When contact is made, a scanner converts the image into electrical pulses.

4 The signal travels across normal telephone connections to the receiving machine.

5 On the receiving end, the process is reversed. The page 'facimile' comes out in less than a minute.

You read about CAM (computer-aided manufacturing) in Chapter 1. *Computer-integrated manufacturing (CIM)* is similar to CAM in that computers are used to operate machinery. However, with CIM every operation in the entire factory is linked. Fig. 72-8. Computers are used to order materials, keep track of inventory, monitor quality control, aid in production, and so on. Because all workstations are controlled by a central mainframe computer, the work of one department is readily available to another department. As a result, work is not duplicated, and accuracy is improved.

OPTICS

Optic communication systems use light to transmit messages. An optic system you are already familiar with is your eyes. Another is the camera. In your eyes the light passes through a lens and strikes light-sensitive cells. The cells send the message to your brain by means of the optic nerve. In a camera, light passes through a lens and records an image (the "message") on film.

In recent years, other optic systems have been developed. One is the laser, which was discussed in Chapter 1. Another is fiber optics. An *optical fiber* is a thin strand of glass, smaller in diameter than a human hair and coated with plastic. These fibers can carry light for more than 100 miles and can even make light turn corners. Telephone companies are using optical fibers to replace copper telephone wires. A single strand of fiber can carry up to 40,000 telephone conversations—as many as a wire cable several inches in diameter. Fig. 72-9.

72-9. If each fiber optic strand can carry over 40,000 calls, how many can this cable with eight strands carry altogether?

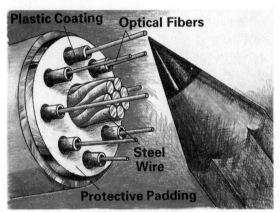

Fiber-Optic Cable

72-8. With CIM, all areas of a factory are linked by means of a large mainframe computer.

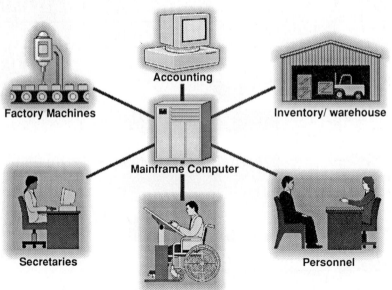

When you speak into a telephone that is part of a fiber optic system, your voice is changed into an electrical signal. This signal activates a laser which pulses on and off. The pulsing beam enters the optical fiber. The coating on the fiber keeps the beam inside until it reaches the opposite end. There, the laser light is changed back into an electrical signal and then into the sound of your voice.

Lasers and optical fibers are also used to read the *universal product codes (UPC)* found on wood items and other products. Fig. 72-10. This information is transmitted to a computer that keeps track of how many of an item are purchased and how many remain in inventory.

AUDIO AND VIDEO COMMUNICATION

Audio and video systems include the telephone, telegraph, radio, television, record player, audio tape or compact disc player, and video cassette recorder (VCR).

With both audio and video systems, the message is changed by a microphone or TV camera into electrical energy and then transmitted. Sometimes this electrical signal goes through a wire or optical fiber, as with most telephones. At other times it is combined with another, stronger signal that carries it through the atmosphere. This is typical of radio or TV transmission. These atmospheric signals are often relayed to a satellite orbiting the earth. The satellite strengthens the signal and sends it back to a satellite dish on earth. Fig. 72-11. By means of the satellite, the signal can travel much farther than it would unaided.

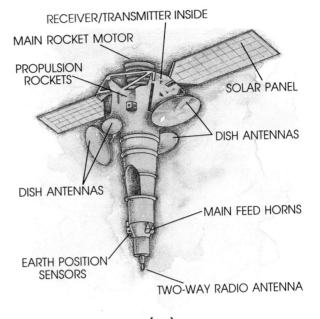

RECEIVER/TRANSMITTER INSIDE
MAIN ROCKET MOTOR
PROPULSION ROCKETS
SOLAR PANEL
DISH ANTENNAS
DISH ANTENNAS
MAIN FEED HORNS
EARTH POSITION SENSORS
TWO-WAY RADIO ANTENNA

(a)

(b)

72-11. Satellites circling the earth (a) send and receive signals from satellite dishes (b). As a result, signals can be sent much farther.

72-10. Bar codes now appear on thousands of items. They carry inventory information as well as price.

ChoiceWood
Made in the USA

RED OAK
CHÊNE
ROBLE ROJO

1X6X2
19X140X609

073291087319
Weyerhaeuser

Audio and video communication are important to wood technology. Some of their uses are familiar; others may be new to you. For example, telephones and answering machines transmit daily business, advertising, and sales messages. Telephone's link to the computer makes data transmission possible. Weather information, vital to forestry workers, comes over radio and television channels. Audio and video systems are useful for advertising as well. You may also have seen programs such as "This Old House" and "Yankee Workshop" on public broadcasting channels. Two-way radios are used by businesses that make deliveries of wood products, to summon repair or logging crews, and by guards patrolling lumber yards and other facilities.

Fig. 72-12 gives brief information about several other common communication devices.

Fig. 72-12

CAMERA

The word "photography" means to "write with light." Photographic film is coated with chemicals sensitive to light. These chemicals capture the  image. Film for so-called "instant" cameras also contains developing chemicals.

CALCULATOR

The small hand-held calculators you use every day are really simple computers. They contain a tiny microchip that acts as the central processing unit. The "keyboard" is the number pad. The calculator shown here is a special type used in construction.

CORDLESS PHONE

Cordless phones are really a combination of telephone and radio. A small radio transmitter sends a signal to the base of the phone. Inside the base, the message is changed to an electrical impulse that then travels through regular phone lines. Car, or cellular, phones work on the same principle. The "cells"  are units of distance with radii of 9-12 miles. At the center of each cell is a computerized switching station that helps transfer the radio signal from point to point.

COMPACT DISCS

The disc itself is made of plastic. The sound waves created by your favorite rock group are changed by a microphone into an electrical signal.  This signal is then changed into the same electronic code used by computers. The code is burned into the disc by means of a laser that creates tiny pits in its surface. When you put the disc into a player, these same things happen in reverse. Another laser "reads" the reflected light from the pitted surface and sends the information to a computer. There, the information is changed into an electrical signal and sent to the speakers. The speakers change it back into the sound waves you hear.

COMMUNICATION IN FURNITURE MANUFACTURING

Furniture factories depend upon many methods and devices of communication. Most large manufacturers are corporations with stockholders, boards of directors, managers, production workers, a sales force, clerical workers, and so on. For efficiency and good company morale, person-to-person communication is essential at all levels.

On a typical day a manager might dictate a memo to a secretary by first placing it on a dictating machine. The secretary types it on a typewriter, word processor, or computer. It may be sent to recipients by means of a computer network, or it may be photocopied and "hard" copies distributed. If the information is for a branch office or plant, it may be sent there using a fax machine.

When a product is first proposed, a designer makes sketches using drawing equipment or a computer. After the design is approved, final drawings are made. If the product is to be made on a computer-controlled machine, the specifications must be entered into the computer. (If the design has been made using a computer, this step may be unnecessary.)

During production, a central computer may be used to keep track of each piece of material being processed. UPCs are placed on each item. Optical scanners at each work station record the progress of the material through the plant.

Finished products are then distributed to retailers. Catalogs, telephones, computers, and other communication devices may become involved in this step. The furniture may also be advertised in newspapers and magazines and on radio or TV. When a piece of furniture is sold, the sales person may check by means of computer to see if that item is in the warehouse. The order and delivery date may then be entered into the computer. If the buyer uses a credit card, another electronic device may check to be sure the card is valid.

COMMUNICATION IN CONSTRUCTION

As in manufacturing, communication is also used in every step of the construction process.

To determine the need for a structure, a study of the community may be made using topographic maps, zoning maps, and other graphic resources. Preliminary sketches are made using drawing equipment or computers.

An architect is hired to design the structure. This person will use drafting equipment or a computer and plotter to develop plans and a set of construction prints.

As the construction company prepares to build, financing is obtained, and estimates and bills of material are prepared. Devices such as computers, telephones, typewriters, fax machines, answering machines, and photocopy machines may all be used. They will also come into play as subcontractors and other workers are hired and materials are ordered. During building of high-rises, two-way radios are often used to communicate with workers on upper stories.

When the structure is ready to sell, it is advertised in newspapers and monthly catalogs of buildings for sale. Information about the structure may also be available on computers in a realtor's office.

IMPACTS OF COMMUNICATION SYSTEMS

All technological systems have impacts, or effects, on the world around them. Some of these impacts are good; some are bad. They affect individuals, society, and the environment. A few of these impacts that affect the wood technologies are described below.

- New communication products have inspired new designs in wood. Fig. 72-13. Until a few years ago no one had heard of a computer desk or an entertainment unit made to hold TV, VCR, and audio equipment. Today, they are common in many homes. Designers are needed to create the designs, and woodworkers are needed to make the products.

● Loggers and firefighters connected to a dispatcher by CB radios can get messages faster and easier. This in turn speeds up their other operations.

● So-called "smart" houses are making changes in construction methods. Fig. 72-14. These houses are controlled by computer. The wiring consists of two main cables, one for electricity and the other for electronic services. Heating, cooling, intercom, telephone, television, security, and other systems are automatic. Owners can control lights, temperature, and appliances from many locations throughout the house.

● Photocopy machines and computers have created a demand for paper products, an important part of the wood industry.

● Radio and television advertising have helped sustain the demand for other wood products, such as furniture.

● Communication technologies have speeded up the way we do things. Information is transmitted almost instantly. This creates stress on workers at almost all kinds of jobs, including those in the wood industries.

● Communication systems have affected the environment by making people aware of ways in which our forests and other areas are managed. While some logging companies feel this threatens jobs, in the long term it may secure some of those jobs for the future.

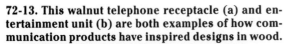

72-13. This walnut telephone receptacle (a) and entertainment unit (b) are both examples of how communication products have inspired designs in wood.

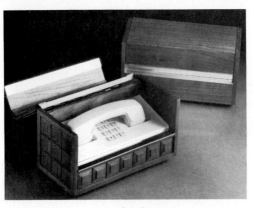

(a)

(b)

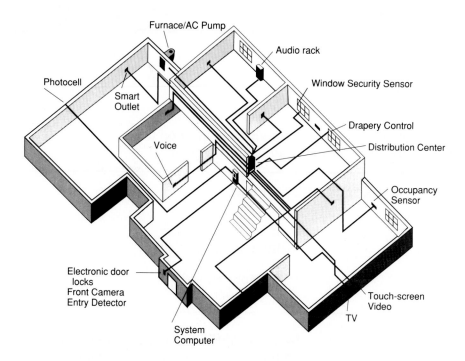

Furnace/AC Pump

Photocell

Smart Outlet

Audio rack

Window Security Sensor

Voice

Drapery Control

Distribution Center

Occupancy Sensor

Electronic door locks
Front Camera
Entry Detector

Touch-screen Video

TV

System Computer

72-14. A computer controls many of the systems in this smart house.

Review Questions

1. Define communication.
2. Describe the universal systems model.
3. Name the five types of technical communication systems.
4. Who developed movable type?
5. How do copy machines differ from "paper and ink" printers?
6. Into which type of communication system would you place drawings used by architects and woodworkers?
7. Name three ways in which computer communication might be used in wood technologies.
8. Name three optic systems.
9. Name three common communication devices that might be used in furniture manufacturing. Name three that might be used in construction.
10. On what three things do all technological systems have an impact?

Chapter 73

Transportation

After studying this chapter, you will be able to:
- Name the three types of transportation.
- Describe a typical transportation system.
- Name the industrial transportation methods commonly used in wood technology.
- Identify vehicles used in forestry, in a saw mill, and in construction.

LOOK FOR THESE TERMS

air and space transportation
bulldozer
container ships
crane
excavators
freighters

fork lift trucks
land transportation
marine transportation
ties
transportation

Transportation involves the movement of goods and people from one location to another. Transportation is an essential part of wood technology, from the planting of trees to the delivery of furniture and materials for construction.

In recent years, there has been an explosion in transportation technology. For example, the time needed to travel by plane from New York City to Moscow today is the same as the time it took to travel from New York City to Philadelphia by train in 1833. All improvements in transportation have been designed to reduce the time and/or cost of getting from one place to the other. The ideal route is a straight line between one location and another.

TRANSPORTATION SYSTEMS

Like manufacturing, construction, and communication, transportation is a system. It has inputs, a process, outputs, and feedback.

Consider the airplane as a typical transportation system. The airplane must be operated by people using materials, tools and machines, capital, energy, information, and time. Airports, control towers and hangars, ground support, food service, baggage handling, and repair crews all provide resources. Fig. 73-1. The process is the act of moving the passengers or cargo. Arrival at the destination is the main output.

Other outputs may be good or bad. An airplane provides the quickest way to get from one place to the other, which is good. The plane also adds pollutants to the air and creates excessive noise when taking off and landing. These are bad. Consider the airplane's total impact on our world. How has it changed the way people live and work?

Feedback also occurs in transportation systems. For example, passengers demand planes which are larger, faster, quieter and more comfortable.

TYPES OF TRANSPORTATION

There are three basic types of transportation: land, air and space, and marine. Many

73-1. Workers load logs on these trucks for delivery to saw mills.

73-2. The world's largest flying "boat," the *Spruce Goose*, is being drawn by a tugboat. The plane is built entirely of wood and is an example of air and space transportation. The little tugboat (marine transportation) is a steam vessel with a powerful engine. Tugs are used to move large ships in and out of harbors and for towing barges and rafts of logs. A barge is a hollow vessel with no engine and is used for cargo.

times the same people or cargo travel on more than one type of transportation before reaching the destination.

LAND TRANSPORTATION

Land transportation includes such vehicles as railroads, subways, monorails, cars, trucks, elevators, pipelines, and conveyor belts. Some, such as subways, move people. Others, such as pipelines, conveyor belts, and trucks, move materials. Fig. 73-2.

Wood is widely used in rail transportation. Trains travel on a bed of ties and steel rails. The *ties* (cross ties) are square wood beams about six feet long. They are laid 21 inches apart on a bed of gravel and crushed rock. Steel rails are laid atop the ties. The wood under the steel rails cushions the shock as the train's wheels glide over. Wood and man-

ufactured wood products are also used to line freight cars that ship finished products such as furniture and appliances.

AIR AND SPACE TRANSPORTATION

Air and space transportation is usually the fastest and most direct transportation method. Fig. 73-3. Airplanes provide air transportation for both people and goods. Airplane wings are designed so air will flow more rapidly over the top of the wing. This reduces pressure on the wing. As a result, the air underneath the wing pushes the wing

73-3. This diagram shows how the air pressure under the wings of a plane lift it when pressure above the wing is lessened.

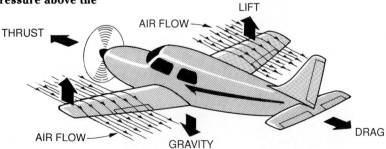

upward. The resistance created by the air as the plane moves through it is overcome by the thrust of the engine. Fig. 73-4.

Other air vehicles include hot-air balloons and dirigibles. Their use is usually limited to entertainment and advertising. One exception is the use of balloons and blimps in logging. See page 521.

Rocket power has made space exploration possible. The Space Shuttle is designed to be flown back to earth after each mission. It may someday help make a space station possible. Scientists hope that some manufacturing may take place there.

73-4. Air transportation requires resources, or inputs. The process is the flight itself, and the output is arrival at a destination. Feedback would come from customers.

MARINE TRANSPORTATION

Marine transportation occurs on the open sea and on inland waterways. Most modern ships do not carry passengers. They carry freight or serve as ice breakers and oil tankers.

TRANSPORTATION IN FORESTS AND MILLS

Many vehicles are used in forestry. Helicopters plant and fertilize trees. They are ideal for forestry because they can move slowly, remain stationary, and fly low over trees. A helicopter has a horizontal propeller called a rotor. It moves as it does by changing the pitch of the rotor. Fig. 73-5.

73-5a. This helicopter is getting ready to transport wood items.

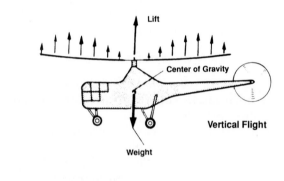

Straight Up or Hovering

Forward Flight

73-5b. A helicopter changes direction by changing its pitch, or angle. Where does the lift occur in this diagram?

73-7. This crawler tractor, called a log feller, is operated hydraulically. Its wide metal tracks make it capable of carrying heavy loads over soft or rough terrain.

73-6. Balloons are used to bring logs down steep mountainsides. (1) The balloon is pulled up the slope. The loggers have secured chokers around the logs. (2) As its towline is slackened, the balloon gains height. The balloon is drawn toward the landing area. (3) The balloon deposits its load on the landing.

Small airplanes fertilize small seedlings during their early growth and patrol the forest for fires. Tanker planes help fight forest fires with chemicals and water. A balloon is often used when logging on steep slopes. Fig. 73-6. Blimps, small non-rigid airships, are sometimes needed to carry logs out of rough terrain.

Small yellow buses called "jimmeys" transport loggers from camp to the cutting site. Heavy duty crawler tractors with huge shears, called "log fellers," snip off trees up to 18 inches in diameter. A hydraulic clamp holds the tree and the shears cut if off. Fig. 73-7. Other tractors drag logs to the loading site. Rubber-tired "skidders" move and load logs onto trucks. Cranes load and unload logs from trucks or railroad cars. Fig. 73-8. A *crane* is a movable hoist for lifting and moving

73-8a. This small tractor can drag a huge log.

73-8b. A log loader is capable of hefting big loads into trucks.

73-8c. A crane lifts logs from a railway flatcar.

heavy objects by means of a swing arm or a lifting apparatus supported by an overhead track.

Trucks and trains transport logs to the mill. The process of turning logs into lumber is described in Chapter 67. Conveyors, including the bull chain, carriage, and green chain, move the logs and lumber through the mill.

TRANSPORTATION IN MANUFACTURING

Lumber and wood products are shipped to a furniture plant by truck or train. Fig. 73-9. Green lumber is stored in the open air for air drying. Then it is placed in a dry kiln where it is dried to the correct moisture content.

73-9. Lumber is being unloaded from a boxcar.

Carts, dollies, and/or conveyors move the parts or furniture from one workstation to the next. Fig. 73-10. The finished product is shipped to retail stores by truck or train.

Freighters are commercial ships used to carry logs, lumber, and wood chips from the south and west coasts of the United States to countries in the Pacific basin and all over the world. Fig. 73-11a. There, most of these materials are converted to manufactured products such as furniture and building materials. They are then shipped back to the United States.

73-10. Furniture moves through this factory on a conveyor.

73-11a. Lumber is being loaded on this freighter for shipment overseas. The large ocean-going vessel is diesel powered.

73-11b. The containers on this ship are kept locked during the trip. This keeps the contents safe.

Container ships move finished products in containers to protect them and ensure safe delivery. They are used to move large quantities of furniture from Europe and other countries. Fig. 73-11b.

TRANSPORTATION IN CONSTRUCTION

Lumber and manufactured wood products, such as plywood and particle board, are shipped by train or truck to manufacturers of doors, windows, trim, siding, and so on. These mill items are then shipped to building-supply centers. At the building-supply center, *fork lift trucks* unload and move products from railroad cars and trucks to storage areas. Fig. 73-12a.

At the construction site, bulldozers and/or graders remove the topsoil and pile it nearby for future use. *Bulldozers* are crawler tractors with a ripper on the back that loosens the soil and a blade on the front that moves it. A grader has an angled blade between its front and rear wheels. *Excavators* are used to dig the holes for basements and trenches for utilities. Fig. 73-12b.

73-12a. Fork lift trucks usually have electric motors. They lift and carry heavy objects by means of steel "fingers" inserted under the load.

73-12b. An excavator can remove topsoil and dig the hole for a basement. It has a crane on one end fitted with a bucket that scoops the dirt. The other end is fitted with a scraper.

Trucks of all sizes and kinds haul materials to the building site. Cranes lift floor and roof trusses into place. Fig. 73-12c.

73-12c. This crane is lifting roof trusses into place.

Review Questions

1. Define transportation.
2. Name four inputs to a transportation system.
3. Name three kinds of land transportation.
4. Name three kinds of air and space transportation.
5. What type of transportation would an ocean-going freighter be?
6. Of what type of transportation is a conveyor?
7. Name two outputs of air transportation.
8. Why are helicopters widely used in forestry?
9. Name five vehicles used in construction.
10. How does marine transportation relate to woodworking?

Thinking about a Career

Architect

Paul Hartman is an architect in a medium-sized architectural firm. His primary responsibility is the design of residential housing.

Because architects are responsible for critical design features of a house, they must be licensed. This license can be obtained only after several years of education and training. A licensing exam must then be passed. Before qualifying for the licensing exam, a person must have a bachelor of architecture degree followed by 3 years of practical experience in an architect's office. A person with a master of architecture degree and 2 years of experience is also qualified for the licensing exam.

"I graduated from a state university with a bachelor of architecture degree," says Paul. "It was a 5-year program. The master of architecture degree is awarded on completion of a 6-year curriculum. Soon after graduation, I got a job at this firm. It's in my hometown. I was lucky in that, I guess. I would have been willing to move, though. I started work here as a drafter. Most of my work the first year was preparing architectural drawings. I also made models of structures.

"My college architecture program included courses in architectural theory, engineering, and design. I also took courses in English, mathematics, physics, and economics. I had some natural abilities in some of these areas. I have always been interested in the technical side of things. My strong interest in design was, I think, a big help. I had done a fair amount of freehand sketching in high school.

"I think I first thought of architecture as a possible career during the summer between my junior and senior years in high school. I tried to get a job in this very office that summer. I wasn't successful. The next summer, after my senior year, I was able to get a job with a general contractor, though. I carried brick and helped with cement work. Though I didn't actually do much building, I was on residential construction sites all summer. That helped me learn something about the way a house is constructed."

As well as designing the house, Paul also specifies the building material. He ensures that the design and specifications for the building conform to local and state building codes. The architect does not work alone. Much of his time is spent talking with other architects or with engineers or contractors.

"In a few years, I suspect I will have an opportunity to become an associate in this company," says Paul. "What I really want to do, though, is start my own business. Residential housing construction has been steady here for some years now. The best predictions are that people will continue to move into the area. This should mean a continued need for new housing."

Developing Science, Math, and Reading Skills

**Developing
Science Skills**

Scientists Seek Ways to Make Wood Products Safer

In recent years scientists have become increasingly concerned about the safety of some wood preservatives. A preservative is a chemical applied to wood to help prevent it from rotting. The EPA (Environmental Protection Agency) has been reviewing major preservatives, such as creosote and arsenics. They are trying to determine if they are serious health hazards.

It was proven experimentally that certain preservatives are carcinogenic (cancer-causing). These substances produce tumors in laboratory animals. The greatest possibility for health damage was found to exist for those workers applying the preservatives. However, some of these chemicals can be absorbed through the skin. To prevent this, the EPA suggests sealing over with varnish or shellac any treated objects—such as outdoor furniture—that might be in frequent contact with skin.

ACTIVITY: Investigating Types of Preservatives
Materials
Wrappers from a variety of foods such as white breads, cereals, dessert
  pies, and candy bars
Salt water (prepare by dissolving 2 tablespoons of salt in 1 cup of warm
  water)
Nail polish remover
Bleach
5 small pieces of wood, each approximately 4″ × 4″ × 4″

A. Obtain the materials listed.
B. Preservatives are important to daily life in many ways—in addition to their abilities to protect woods. For example, many foods have chemical preservatives added to help them retain their freshness. Potassium sorbate is one, for example. Using a variety of labels from foods, make a list of substances listed as food preservatives.
C. Carefully soak the pieces of wood in separate jars containing bleach, salt water, and nail polish remover. Soak one piece in ordinary tap water. Do nothing to the last sample. Label each sample. Leave all the pieces soaking overnight. Dry the pieces carefully. Leave them in a warm, damp place for two or three weeks, if possible. One suggested place would be a dark closet. Then observe carefully. Do any pieces show signs of mold (such as might be found on a piece of bread in a refrigerator)? Which of the substances tested would be the best preservative for wood? Why did early explorers often soak their meats in brine (salt water) before leaving on long journeys?

Activity One

Residential construction is an industry where wood is in heavy demand. In the United States nine out of ten living units (homes, apartments, and condominiums) are of wood frame construction. In the past, home building was part of the construction industry. Now, however, many units are factory-built. Examples of factory-built housing are mobile homes, modular units, and sectional homes.

Homes of wood frame construction are often enclosed with wood siding, wood shingles, brick veneer, or stucco. Wood frame housing is relatively simple to construct and is relatively inexpensive.

On pages 496-502, the author takes you through the steps involved in building a home. Why are all of these steps important?

Activity Two

The best way to learn to build a house is to take part in its construction. However, if that is not possible, the author suggests that the next best way to learn construction is to build all or part of a scale-model house. On

**Developing
Reading Skills**

pages 502-503, the author tells you that building a scale model gives you a chance to see house plans in three dimensions. It also enables you to learn good construction techniques. The scale of ½ inch to one foot is suggested. This means that the building will be one-sixteenth full size.

What kind of lumber would you select for your model construction?

Activity Three

This book gives you in-depth detail about model construction as an ideal way of learning the construction trade.

Review pages 502-503. Then close your book. Write a brief explanation of how you would construct a model house. Be sure to include the materials, tools, and plans that would be necessary. Write your plans so clearly that someone else could follow it.

Reading Working Drawings

Refer to Fig. A. The base of the workbench shown there is made of 2 × 4's. The working top is of 1½″ solid birch.

What is the width of the top in inches?

If the top overhangs the left end of the base by 1′ to accommodate a bench vise and overhangs the base by 3″ on the right side, what is the length of the top in inches?

How much does the top overhang the front of the base in inches?

**Developing
Math Skills**

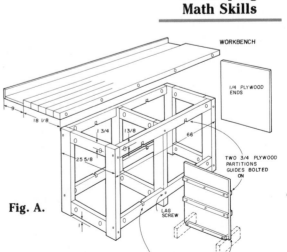

Fig. A.

Section VIII. Projects

Project 1
Cutting Board

Use router cutter on all edges, both sides, and on hole.
Use ⅜" rounding over bit.

Construction notes: Nail two boards together and cut on band saw. Glue together using alternating woods. Surface after gluing. Cut corners. Drill hole. Rout. Sand and oil, using mineral oil.

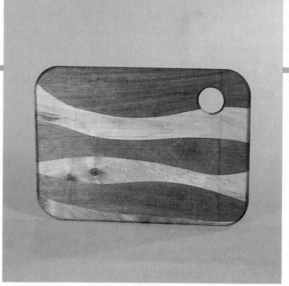

Ed Wright, Toms River High School East, Toms River, NJ

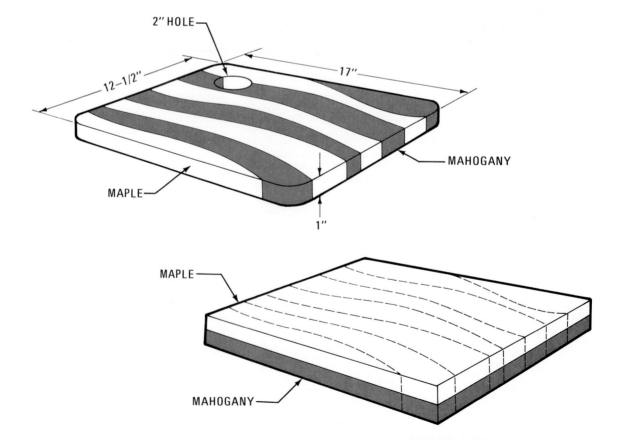

Project 2
Jewelry Box

If desired, divide the inside of
the box into compartments.
Line with felt glued in place.

½″ stock

Ed Wright, Toms River High School East, Toms River, NJ

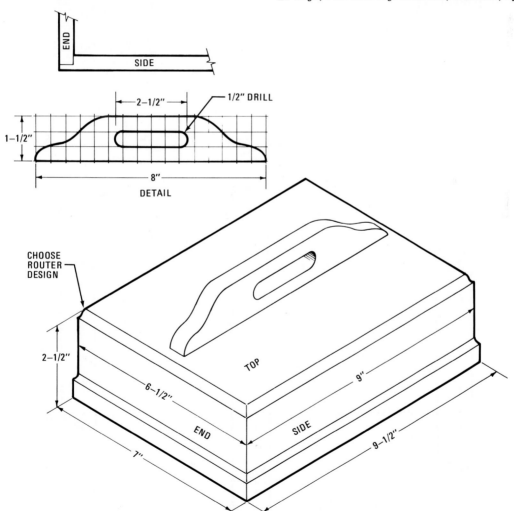

Project 3
End Table

8 legs and rails: ¾″ × 1¾″ × 13″
Top: ¾″ × 17″ × 17″

Fasten with glue and nails or 18
flathead #6 1¼″ wood screws.
Counterbore and plug.

Ed Wright, Toms River High School East, Toms River, NJ

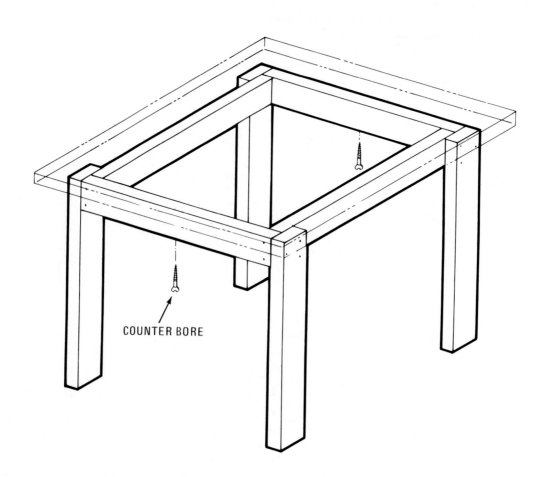

COUNTER BORE

Project 4
Corner Hutch

¾" #2 pine

6 shelves 9¼" × 9¼" × 13⅛"
2 sides ¾" × 10" × 68"
1 top piece ¾" × 14¼" × 9"
2 upper rails ¾" × 1¾" × 26"
1 midrail ¾" × 1¾" × 14¼"
2 lower rails ¾" × 1¾" × 28¾"
1 bottom piece ¾" × 2½" × 14¼"
1 door ¾" × 10¾" × 28¾"
2 hinges
1 handle
1 door catch

Fasten shelves with glue and nails.
Fasten front pieces and rails with glue and nails or ½" #8 F.H. wood screws.
Counterbore and plug.

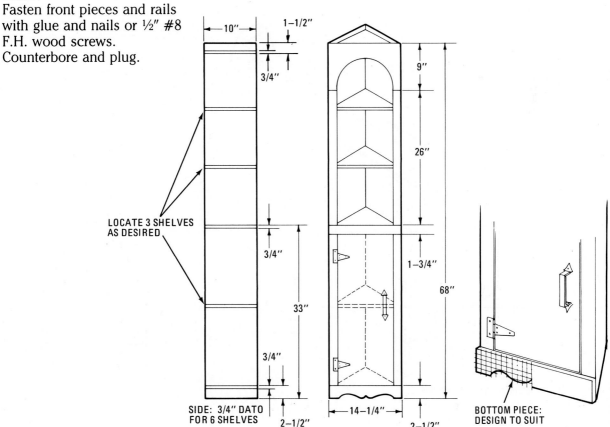

LOCATE 3 SHELVES AS DESIRED

SIDE: 3/4" DATO FOR 6 SHELVES

1–1/2"
3/4"
3/4"
3/4"
3/4"
33"
2-1/2"
10"

9"
26"
1-3/4"
68"
14-1/4"
2-1/2"

BOTTOM PIECE: DESIGN TO SUIT

Project 5

Woodworker's Toolbox

Pine, 2 ends ¾″ × 7⅛″ × 9″
Pine, 1 bottom ¾″ × 6⅝″ × 16″
Plywood, 2 sides ¼″ × 3½″ × 16¾″
1 dowel, ¾″ × 18″
1 dowel, ⅛″

Paint or stain as desired.

Ed Wright, Toms River High School East, Toms River, NJ

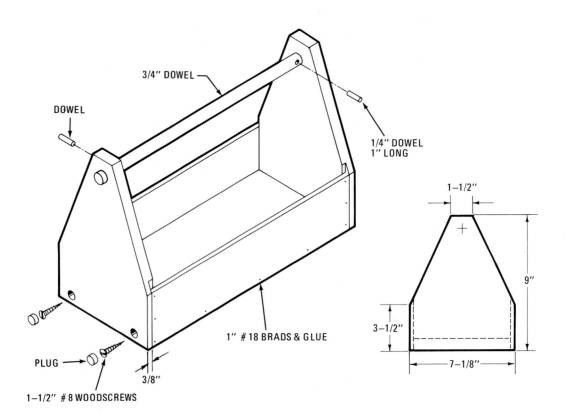

3/4″ DOWEL

DOWEL

1/4″ DOWEL
1″ LONG

1−1/2″

1″ # 18 BRADS & GLUE

9″

3−1/2″

7−1/8″

PLUG

3/8″

1−1/2″ # 8 WOODSCREWS

Project 6

Stool

White Oak Stock

1 top, ⅞″ × 13″ × 13″
4 legs, ⅞″ × 1¾″ × 23″
2 rails, ⅞″ × 1¾″ × 12″
2 rails, ⅞″ × 1¾″ × 10½″
2 base, ⅞″ × 1¾″ × 10½″
2 foot rest, ⅞″ × 1¾″ × 12″
2 foot rest, ⅞″ × 1¾″ × 10¼″

Fasten with 1½″ #8 drywall screws. Counterbore and plug.

Ed Wright, Toms River High School East, Toms River, NJ

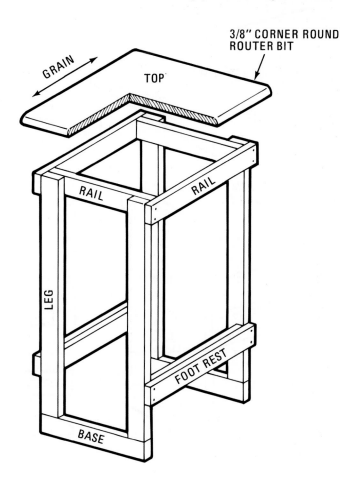

Project 7
Trestle Table

Ed Wright, Toms River High School East, Toms River, NJ

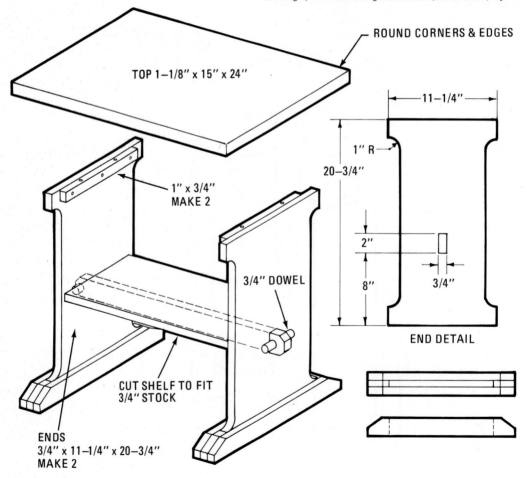

ROUND CORNERS & EDGES

TOP 1–1/8" x 15" x 24"

1" x 3/4"
MAKE 2

3/4" DOWEL

CUT SHELF TO FIT
3/4" STOCK

ENDS
3/4" x 11–1/4" x 20–3/4"
MAKE 2

11–1/4"

1" R

20–3/4"

2"

8"

3/4"

END DETAIL

Project 8
Book Rack and Drawer

Sides and shelves, ¾″ stock
Fasten with 1½″ #8 wood screws
and plug.

Drawer detail
½″ stock. Nail and glue. ¼″ plywood
bottom.
Hardware: 1 knob.

Ed Wright, Toms River High School East, Toms River, NJ

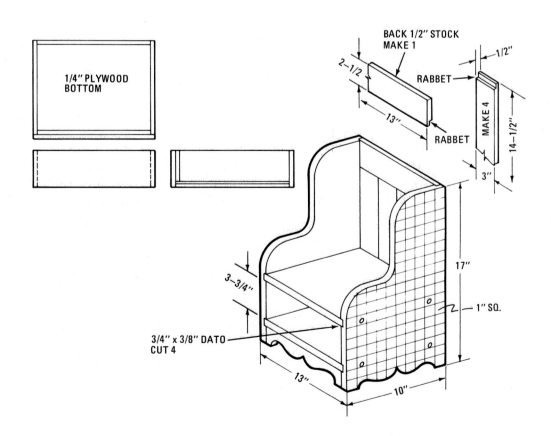

1/4″ PLYWOOD
BOTTOM

BACK 1/2″ STOCK
MAKE 1

2–1/2

RABBET

13″

RABBET

1/2″

MAKE 4

14–1/2″

3″

17″

1″ SQ.

3–3/4″

3/4″ x 3/8″ DATO
CUT 4

13″

10″

Project 9
Boat Plaque

Bill of Materials

Name _____   Date Started _____

Project ____Boat Plaque_____   Date Completed _____

No. of Pieces	Size			Part Description	Material
	T	W	L		
1	¾"	3¾"	8¾"	Rear Sail	Pine
1	¾"	2½"	7½"	Front Sail	Pine
1	½"	½"	14½"	Mast (2 parts)	Pine
2	¾"	1"	7¾"	Hull	Pine
1	⅛"	1"	7¾"	Hull	Masonite
1	⅜"	¾"	¾"	Keel	Pine
1	⅜"	12"	12"	Backboard*	Plywood A/C
1	½"	—	48"	Edging	Sisal Rope
6				1" #6 F.H. Screw	
30				1" #18 Ga. Brad	
1	½" dia.		2", or to fit	Edging Guard	Copper Tubing
1				Saw Tooth Picture Hanger	

*NOTE: Shape backboard as desired. Attach rope with brads.

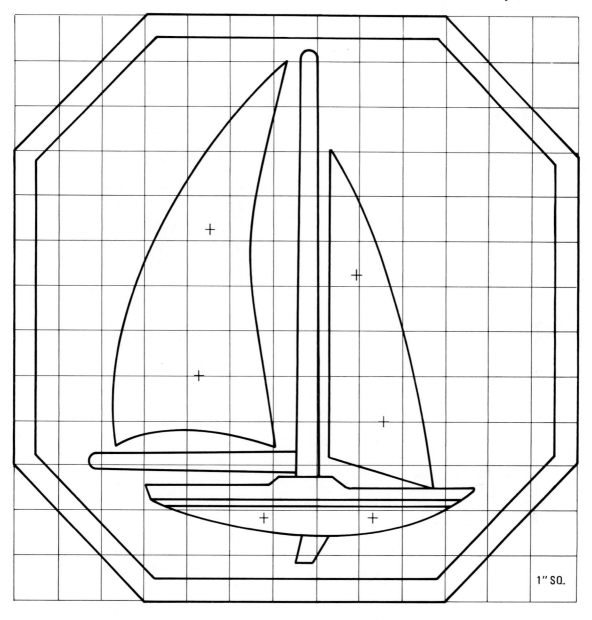

1" SQ.

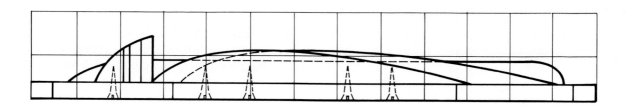

Project 10

Mirror

Industrial Arts Department, Jackson High School, Jackson, NJ

STEPS FOR MIRROR CONSTRUCTION

1. Cut stock: Back piece: ¾″ × 11¼″ × 18″
   Shelf: ¾″ × 3½″ × 8″
2. Select and trace a design on the back piece. Avoid knots.
3. Cut perimeter design and shelf. Use a band saw, jig saw, or saber saw.
4. Drill ⅜″ holes in waste areas of the internal design to allow for cutting with the band saw or jig saw. Drill three pilot holes to attach shelf.
5. Cut away excess areas. Double-cut saber saw blades work well. HINT: Attach a ¾″ × 2″ × 10″ piece of scrap pine to the back side of the back piece in the shelf position. Use the scrap piece to clamp the plaque in a vise for cutting. The scrap piece will help keep the 11″ × 18″ board from warping.
6. File all rough-cut edges and corners.
7. Rout all front edges of the plaque and the top front edge of the shelf. Use a ⅜″ diameter corner-round router bit with a ⅛″ pilot.
8. Rout the back surface of the design and ⅜″ around the outside edge so the mirror can be inserted. Rout ⁵⁄₁₆″ to ⅜″ deep using a ⅜″ diameter, 2-flute, straight, carbide bit.
9. Sand all areas and prepare for the finish material.
10. Attach the shelf: use 1¼″ #8 F.H. wood screws
11. Stain and finish.
12. Install the hanger.
13. Insert the mirror and a cardboard backing piece using glazing points.

Project 11
Gum Ball Machine

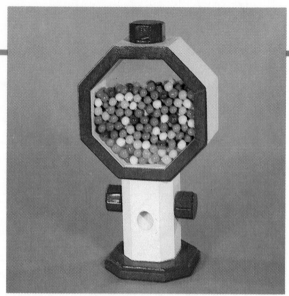

Alan Nadrowski, Jackson High School, Jackson, NJ

All wood is ¾″ unless otherwise specified. Decorate as desired.

Bill of Materials

Name _____   Date Started _____

Project ___Octagon Gum Ball Machine___   Date Completed _____

No. of Pieces	Size			Part Description	Material
	T	W	L		
1	¾″	5½″	5½″	Base	Pine
1	4″	4″	5½″	Column	Pine
8	¾″	3¼″	3¼″	Octagon Gum Ball Container	Pine
1	1″	1″	3¾″	Dowel Gum Ball Pocket	Pine
3	1″	2″	2″	2 Handles & 1 Top	Pine
1	¾″	¾″	1″	Refill Plug	Pine
2	¹⁄₁₆″	5″	5″	Windows	Plexiglas

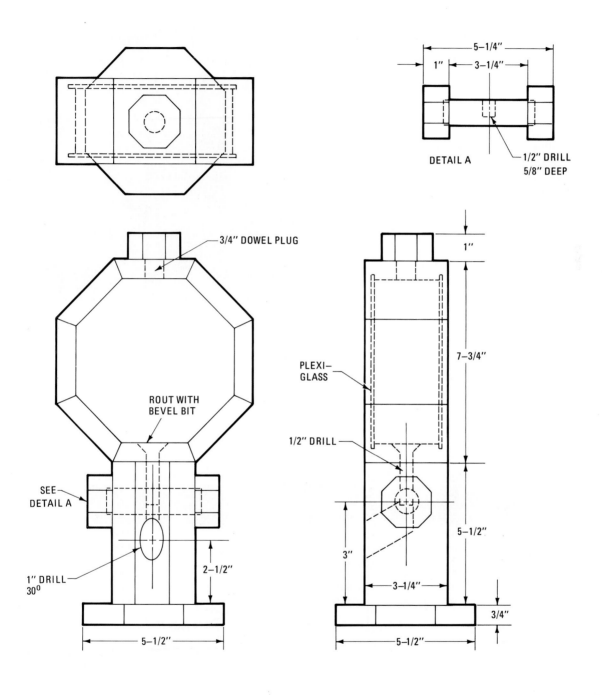

5–1/4"

1" 3–1/4"

DETAIL A

1/2" DRILL
5/8" DEEP

3/4" DOWEL PLUG

ROUT WITH
BEVEL BIT

SEE
DETAIL A

1" DRILL
30°

2–1/2"

5–1/2"

1"

PLEXI–
GLASS

7–3/4"

1/2" DRILL

5–1/2"

3"

3–1/4"

3/4"

5–1/2"

Project 12

Trash Can

Lift collar and insert a long plastic trash bag. Fold the top 1″ of the bag over the top edge of the basket. Secure by replacing the collar.

Attach bottom with finishing nails and glue.

Alan Nadrowski, Jackson High School, Jackson, NJ

Bill of Materials

Name _____   Date Started _____

Project __Trash Can_____   Date Completed _____

No. of Pieces	Size			Part Description	Material
	T	W	L		
2	¾″	10½″	27½″	Sides	Pine
2	¾″	12″	27½″	Front & Back	Pine
1	¾″	9″	10½″	Bottom	Pine
2	¾″	2½″	12¼″	Collar	Pine
2	¾″	2½″	13¾″	Collar	Pine
1	¾″	9⅞″	11⅜″	Top	Pine
1				Knob and Fastener	
16				#6 1¼″ F.H. Wood Screws	
12				4d Finishing Nails	

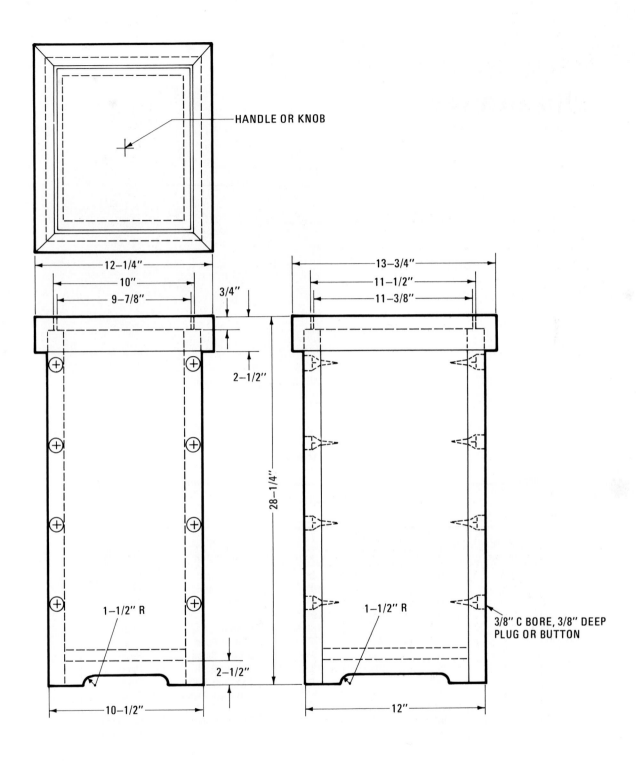

HANDLE OR KNOB

12–1/4″
10″
9–7/8″
3/4″
2–1/2″
28–1/4″
1–1/2″ R
2–1/2″
10–1/2″

13–3/4″
11–1/2″
11–3/8″
1–1/2″ R
3/8″ C BORE, 3/8″ DEEP
PLUG OR BUTTON
12″

Project 13
Miniature Cabinet with Drawer

Alan Nadrowski, Jackson High School, Jackson, NJ

Bill of Materials

Name _____   Date Started _____

Project ___Miniature Cabinet with Drawer_____   Date Completed _____

No. of Pieces	Size			Part Description	Material
	T	W	L		
2	¾″	2″	3″	Front Frame	Pine
2	¾″	2″	18″	Front Frame	Pine
2	¾″	9¼″	5″	Sides	Pine
1	¾″	10¾″	19½″	Top	Pine
1	¾″	9¼″	16½″	Bottom	Pine
1	¾″	4″	15″	Drawer Face	Pine
2	¾″	2⅞″	9¼″	Drawer Sides	Pine
1	¾″	2⅞″	12¼″	Drawer Back	Pine
2	¾″	2″	7″	Top Side Trim	Pine
1	¾″	2″	16½″	Top Back Trim	Pine
2	¾″	1⅜″	8½″	Drawer Guides	Pine
1	⅛″	12¾″	9¾″	Drawer Bottom	Masonite
1	⅛″	5½″	17″	Back	Masonite

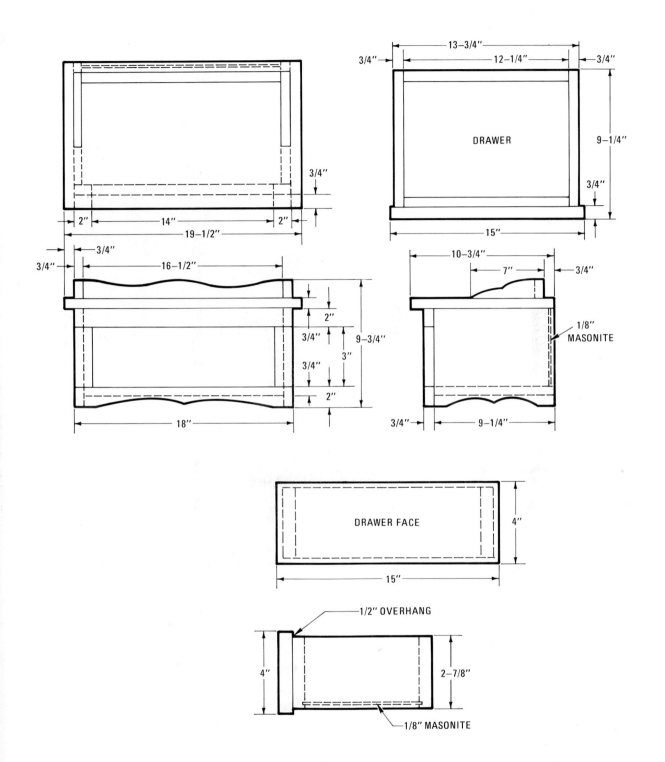

Project 14
Cheval Mirror

Interior Detail

Attach part 19, drawer brace, to the underside of the top, directly above the drawer guide.

Industrial Arts Department, Jackson High School, Jackson, NJ

Bill of Materials

Name _____   Date Started _____

Project __Cheval Mirror__   Date Completed _____

Part No.	Part Name	No. of Pieces	Thickness	Width	Length
1	Sides	2	¾″	9″	6¼″
2	Top	1	5⁄4″	10″	20″
3	Back	1	¼″	6″	17¾″
4	Front Top Frame	1	¾″	1¼″	19″
5	Front Bottom Frame	1	¾″	2″	19″
6	Front Side Frame	2	¾″	2″	3″
7	Bottom	1	¾″	8¾″	16½″
8	Turned Posts	2	1⅞″	1⅞″	14″
9	Top Molding Back	1	¾″	1¾″	15½″
10	Top Moldings Side	2	¾″	1¾″	6″
11	Drawer Front	1	¾″	3¾″	14¾″
12	Drawer Sides	2	¾″	3″	8½″
13	Drawer Back	1	¾″	2½″	12½″
14	Drawer Bottom	1	¼″	8½″	13″
15	Mirror Frame Top	1	¾″	4″	15⅜″
16	Mirror Frame Bottom	1	¾″	2″	11⅜″
17	Mirror Frame Sides	2	¾″	2″	13⅜″
18	Drawer Guides	3	¼″	¾″	8½″
19	Top Brace	1	¾″	1¼″	8½″
20	Turned Knobs	2	1¼″	1¾″	1¾″
21	Dowels	2	⅜″	⅜″	3¼″
22	Mirror	1	⅛″	12″	12″
23	Knob	1			

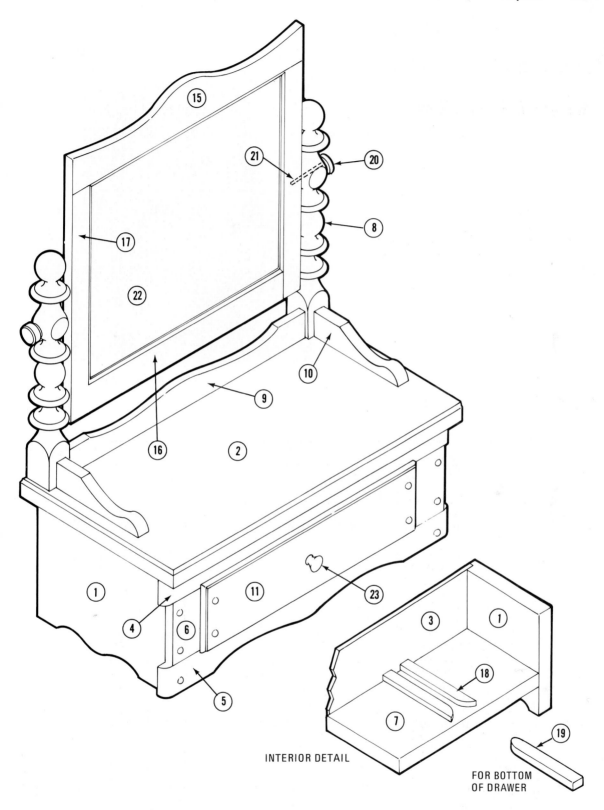

INTERIOR DETAIL

FOR BOTTOM
OF DRAWER

Project 15

Cranberry Picker Magazine Rack

Bill of Materials

Part Number	Number of Pieces	Part	Size
1	2	Ends	¾ × 5¾ × 18½
2	1	Bottom	¾ × 5¾ × 16
3	1	Lower Front	¾ × 1¾ × 16
4	1	Center Front	¾ × 4 × 16
5	1	Upper Front	¾ × 2¾ × 16
6	1	Lower Back	¾ × 4 × 14½
7	1	Center Back	¾ × 2¾ × 14½
8	1	Upper Back	¾ × 2¾ × 14½
9	2	Feet	1½ × 2 × 10½
10	1	Handle	¾ × 2½ × 14
11	14	Dowel Rods	⅜ × 9½
A	2	Flat Head Wood Screws	1½ × 10
B	4	Flat Head Wood Screws	1¼ × 10
C	30	Brads	1½ × 18

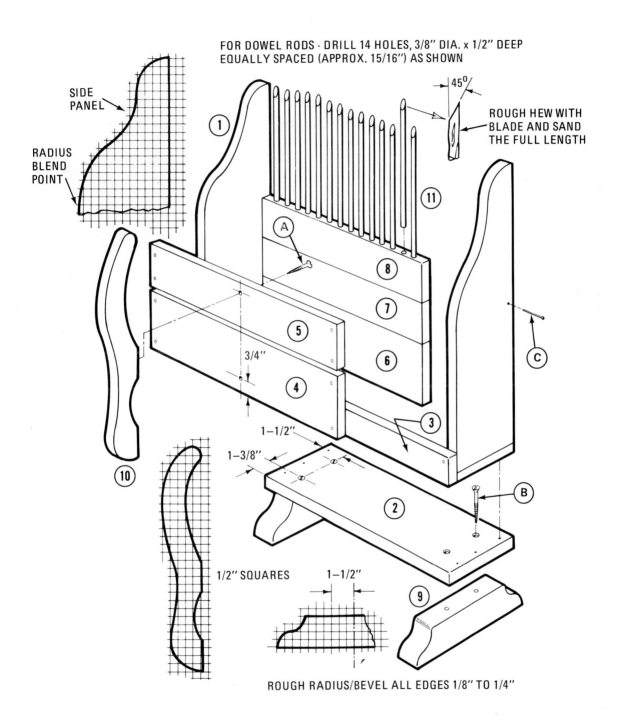

FOR DOWEL RODS - DRILL 14 HOLES, 3/8″ DIA. x 1/2″ DEEP
EQUALLY SPACED (APPROX. 15/16″) AS SHOWN

SIDE
PANEL

RADIUS
BLEND
POINT

45°

ROUGH HEW WITH
BLADE AND SAND
THE FULL LENGTH

①

⑪

Ⓐ

⑧

⑦

⑤

⑥

3/4″

④

Ⓒ

1–1/2″

1–3/8″

⑩

②

③

Ⓑ

1/2″ SQUARES

1–1/2″

⑨

ROUGH RADIUS/BEVEL ALL EDGES 1/8″ TO 1/4″

Project 16

Tall End Table

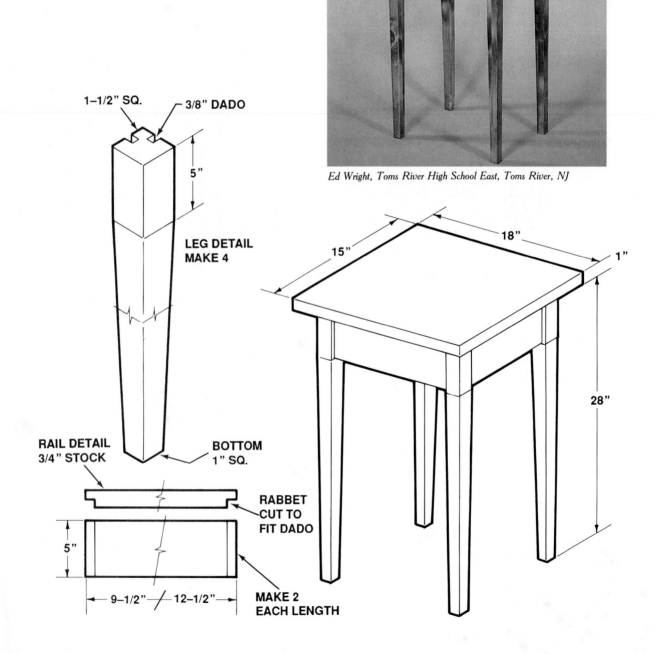

Ed Wright, Toms River High School East, Toms River, NJ

1–1/2" SQ.   3/8" DADO

5"

**LEG DETAIL
MAKE 4**

**BOTTOM
1" SQ.**

18"

15"

1"

28"

**RAIL DETAIL
3/4" STOCK**

**RABBET
CUT TO
FIT DADO**

5"

9–1/2"   12–1/2"

**MAKE 2
EACH LENGTH**

Project 17

Gavel

Walnut or another dark hardwood is recommended.

1. Turn the head first and then the handle.
2. When turning the handle, work first on the large areas. Start at one end and work all the way to the other end. Then work on the small areas.

Developed by Bill Schaaf, Jefferson County Schools, Arvada, CO

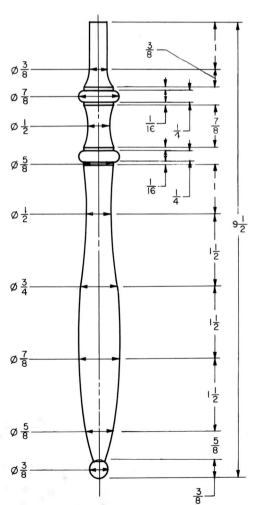

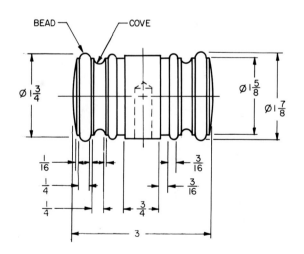

ALL DIMENSIONS ARE IN INCHES

Project 18
File Folder Cabinet

For top, bottom, and sides, use ½" fir or birch plywood. For the back use ¼" plywood.

1. Cut all pieces to size, except for the back.
2. Cut rabbet joints on the sides.
3. Cut grooves in the sides for shelves.
4. Assemble the unit.
5. Cut the back to fit.
6. Glue the unit together.
7. Using a scroll saw, cut recesses in the shelves and hand-shape them with a file.
8. Check the shelves for fit.
9. Finish the unit.

Developed by Bill Schaaf, Jefferson County Schools, Arvada, CO

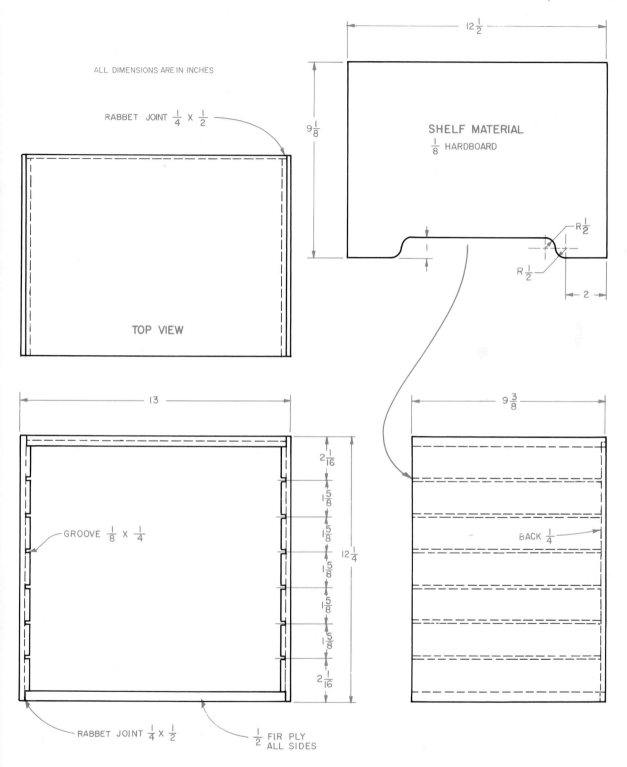

ALL DIMENSIONS ARE IN INCHES

RABBET JOINT $\frac{1}{4}$ X $\frac{1}{2}$

$9\frac{1}{8}$

$12\frac{1}{2}$

SHELF MATERIAL
$\frac{1}{8}$ HARDBOARD

R $\frac{1}{2}$

R $\frac{1}{2}$

2

TOP VIEW

13

GROOVE $\frac{1}{8}$ X $\frac{1}{4}$

$2\frac{1}{16}$

$1\frac{5}{8}$

$1\frac{5}{8}$

$1\frac{5}{8}$ $12\frac{1}{4}$

$1\frac{5}{8}$

$1\frac{5}{8}$

$1\frac{5}{8}$

$2\frac{1}{16}$

$9\frac{3}{8}$

BACK $\frac{1}{4}$

RABBET JOINT $\frac{1}{4}$ X $\frac{1}{2}$

$\frac{1}{2}$ FIR PLY
ALL SIDES

Glossary

Words set in ***bold italics*** are defined elsewhere in the Glossary.

Abrasive paper. A heavy paper covered with rough material such as flint, garnet, aluminum oxide, or silicon carbide. It is used to smooth wood surfaces before or between finish coats.

Adhesive. A sticky substance that holds materials together. Pastes, cements, and glues are all adhesives.

Air and space transportation. The use of flying vehicles, such as airplanes and the Space Shuttle, to move people and cargo.

Air-dried (AD) lumber. Lumber that is cut into logs, stacked, and dried in open air.

Annual rings. Tree rings formed by the growth of ***springwood*** and ***summerwood***. They indicate yearly growth.

Angle divider. A device used to transfer angles from one piece of wood to another.

Arbor. A shaft or spindle on which a tool is mounted.

Audio systems. Communication systems that transmit messages by means of sound and hearing.

Auger bit. An auger without a handle for use in a brace.

Awl. See ***Scratch awl***.

Back (tenon) saw. A hand saw with a metal ridge along the back of the blade.

Bar clamp. A clamp with one or two steel bars and two jaws. It is used for gluing large surfaces edge to edge.

Bench hook. A board that hooks over a workbench. A high edge on one end prevents materials from slipping.

Bench plane. One of three hand ***planes*** (jack plane, smooth plane, fore plane) that differ only in size.

Bench rule. A 12-inch rule used for simple measurements. One side is divided into eighths, the other into sixteenths.

Bevel. Any angle other than a right angle. An angular surface across an edge of a piece of stock.

Bill of materials. A list of all materials (including their cost and dimensions) needed to build a project.

Biscuit joint. A wood joint strengthened by means of a biscuit-shaped piece of wood.

Bit gauge. See ***Depth gauge***.

Bit stock drill. A bit designed to be used in a brace.

Blind hole. A hole cut only partway through a workpiece.

Block plane. A small ***plane*** with a single cutter used for planing end grain, and the ends of ***molding***, trim, and siding.

Board foot. The measurement used for purchasing solid lumber: a piece 1 inch thick, 12 inches wide, and 12 inches long or its equivalent.

Bow. A wood defect. It is a deviation flatwise from a straight line drawn from end to end of a piece.

Box nails. Flathead nails used primarily for light carpentry and for the construction of packing cases.

Brace and bit (bit brace). A boring tool composed of two parts—the bit that does the cutting, and the brace that is the handle, holder, and driver of the bit.

Brad. A thin, wire nail similar to a ***finishing nail***.

Breast drill. A boring tool similar to a ***hand drill***.

Bulldozer. A crawler tractor with a ripper on the back that loosens soil and a blade on the front that moves it; used in construction.

Butt chisel. A standard weight, short-bladed ***chisel***.

Butt hinge. A hinge that requires that a recess be cut. It is used for surface-mounted or flush doors.

Butt joint. A simple joint where the ends of two pieces butt to form a square-cut joint.

Cabinetmaker. A highly skilled woodworker.

Cabinet clamp. See *Bar clamp*.

Cabinet scraper. A blade mounted in a holder for scraping and smoothing wood.

Caliper. A measuring tool used primarily for measuring round objects.

Cambium. A layer of tissue one cell thick between the *xylem* (sapwood) and the *phloem* (inner back) of a tree. It divides repeatedly to form new wood and bark cells.

Carpenter. A person who works with wood to build houses and commercial buildings.

Carpenter's (framing) square. A flat, steel square with a 24-inch body and a 16-inch tongue. It is used for checking squareness, marking lines, and laying out rafters and squares.

Casing nail. A heavy nail with a small, conical head that can be set below the wood surface. It is used for installing doors, windows, and trim.

Caul. A metal plate used in veneering. It is heated and placed on the *veneer* to keep it in position while the glue hardens.

C-clamp. A small C-shaped clamp used mostly for irregularly shaped pieces.

Centerline. In drawings, that line that locates the center of arcs and circles, or divides the drawing into equal parts.

Centimeter. One one-hundredth (0.01) of a meter.

Chamfer. An angle cut only partway across the corner or edge of a board.

Chalk line reel. A metal case containing blue chalk and a reel for winding out and rewinding a string for marking long lines.

Check. A wood defect. It is a crack or split across the annual rings on the end of a board.

Chisel. A cutting and chipping tool with a beveled blade and a tang or socket set into a wood or plastic handle. It comes in various widths and weights.

Chuck. An adjustable holding device found on a variety of tools, including drill presses and lathes. It holds bits and blades.

Circle cutter. See *Fly cutter*.

Claw hammer. A hammer with a claw for pulling nails from wood.

Clinching. Bending over nail points pounded through two (or more) boards. It is done to secure the joint.

Combination square. A tool with a blade and a handle used for checking squareness, levelness, plumb, and miters. It is also used for measuring and marking distances. Some have a level and a scriber in the handle.

Commercial construction. The making of structures whose primary purpose is business or commerce.

Common nails. Flathead nails ranging in size from 2d to 60d. They have a larger diameter than finishing nails and are used mainly in rough carpentry.

Communication. The sending of a message in which information, ideas, or instructions are shared.

Compass saw. A 12- or 14-inch saw with a tapered blade used to cut gentle curves and internal cuts. It is larger than a keyhole saw.

Computer. An electronic machine that stores information, manipulates data, and solves problems.

Computer communication. A method of communication that is done by means of electrical impulses.

Computer-Integrated Manufacturing (CIM). A manufacturing method in which every operation in a factory is linked to a main computer.

Computer Numerical Control (CNC). The use of computers to control machine operation by means of a numerical code.

Coniferous. A class of trees that do not shed their leaves annually. Coniferous trees produce softwood.

Container ships. Large cargo vessels that move finished products in containers to protect the products and ensure safe delivery.

Coping saw. A narrow-bladed saw set in a U-shaped frame. It is used for cutting curves and for scroll work.

Corrugated fasteners. Small, rippled, rectangular pieces of steel used to reinforce joints and make repairs.

Counterbore. A bit that drills a shallow hole for recessing a screw head.

Countersink bit. A bit that cuts a tapered end to an existing hole to receive a flathead screw.

Crane. A piece of heavy equipment with a movable hoist and swing arm for lifting and moving heavy objects.

Crook. A wood defect. It is a deviation edgewise from a straight line drawn end to end.

Crossbands. The *veneer* plies between the core and the face ply in plywood.

Crosscut saw. A small handsaw designed to cut across the grain of a board.

Cup. A wood defect. It is a curve across the grain or width of a board.

Customary system. A measuring system used in the United States and formerly used in other English-speaking countries. It is based on traditional measurement units. Also called the *English*, or *Imperial*, system.

Dado. A groove cut across the grain of a board.

Dado head. A set of two blades and a few chippers used to make wide cuts.

Dado joint. A joint made by fitting the end of one board into a *dado* cut into another board.

Decay. Wood rot.

Deciduous. A class of tree with broad leaves that are shed in the fall and winter. Deciduous trees produce *hardwood*.

Decimal system. A numerical system that divides units into subunits divisible by ten.

Deft. A semigloss, clear, interior wood finish.

Depth gauge (bit gauge). A gauge that controls the depth to which a hole can be drilled. It attaches to the shank of an *auger bit*. It is adjustable to the required drilling depth. The gauge, which turns with the bit, stops the *drill* when it strikes the wood surface around the hole.

Die. A tool for cutting or shaping parts.

Dimension line. In a drawing, a line that shows the dimensions or distances between lines. It has an arrowhead at one or both ends and is broken in the center.

Dividers. A two-legged tool used for a variety of purposes including laying out an arc or circle, scribing, and stepping off measurements. On some types, one leg can be removed and replaced with a pencil. (This is sometimes called a *pencil compass*).

Double plane iron. That part of a hand *plane* that does the cutting. A *plane iron* and a plane iron cap held together with a screw.

Dovetail saw. A small, fine *backsaw* used for making smooth joint cuts.

Dowel. A small, cylindrical wood peg used to strengthen joints.

Dowel joint. A *butt joint* reinforced with *dowels*.

Doweling jig. A device used to simplify the drilling of dowel holes. It is adjustable to work on wood up to 3 inches thick.

Drawer guide. A device (usually a track) which supports a drawer and ensures smooth sliding.

Draw knife. A tool consisting of a long, narrow blade and two handles set at right angles to the blade. It is used for shaping and smoothing by pulling the blade over wood.

Dressed lumber. Lumber that has been put through a surfacer (planer).

Drill. A tool that bores holes.

Drill guide. A device that holds a drill straight for accurate drilling.

Dry lumber. Lumber with a moisture content of 19 percent or less.

Dual dimensioning. A method of drawing in which dimensions are shown in both customary and metric measurements.

Edge grain lumber. The *softwood* equivalent of *quarter-sawn lumber*.

Edge joint. A joint in which wood pieces are joined edge to edge. It is commonly used in panel construction.

Enamel. A semiopaque finish composed largely of colored *varnish* similar to paint.

End lap joint. See *Lap joint*.

Epoxy cement. A strong *adhesive* that works on a variety of materials. It comes in two parts (resin and hardener) that must be mixed.

Escutcheon nails. Small brass nails with round heads used for their decorative quality.

Excavator. A piece of heavy equipment used to dig holes for basements and trenches for utilities.

Expansion bit. A bit having its cutters arranged to allow radius adjustment so that one tool can bore holes of different diameters.

Extension line. In a drawing or sketch, a line that extends out from the outline. It provides two lines between which measurements or dimensions can be shown.

FAS. Grade of lumber. The abbreviation stands for "firsts and seconds."

Face edge (joint edge). Truest and best edge of a board. The first edge to be planed.

Faceplate turning. A method of turning on a lathe in which just one end of the stock is connected to the lathe.

Face surface. Truest and best surface or side. It is the first to be planed.

Fax machines. Communication devices that send a facsimile (copy) of a document by means of electronic signals over telephone lines.

Featherboard. A piece of wood tapered at one end. It has saw *kerfs* on the other end to provide flexibility while holding stock against the fence of a table saw.

Feedback. The information gained as a result of a technological system's output.

Fence. A machine tool part designed to limit movement and/or act as a guide, such as the fence on a circular saw.

Figure (in wood). The patterns formed by the color, *annual rings*, and *medullary rays* in wood, along with cross grain, wavy grain, and *knots*.

File. A long, narrow, tapered steel blade with ridges (teeth) for cutting, smoothing, and shaping.

Filler. Liquids and pastes used to seal the pores of wood and add beauty to a finish.

Finishing nail. The finest of all nails, used for fine cabinetmaking and finish carpentry.

Flat chisel. See *Skew*.

Flat-grained lumber. A method of cutting *softwood* so the *annual rings* form an angle of less than 45 degrees with the surface of the board.

Fly cutter (circle cutter). An adjustable tool used in a brace, *drill*, or drill press to cut out various sizes of circles. The cutter is a vertical *chisel* held in an arm by a setscrew.

Folding rule. See *Zigzag rule*.

Footings. The poured concrete bases on which basement walls or a house is built.

Fore plane. An 18-inch *plane* used on long surfaces and edges.

Forester. A person trained in the science of developing and maintaining forests.

Fork lift truck. A small truck with a hydraulic "fork" attached that slides underneath heavy loads and moves them from place to place.

Forstner bit. A bit without a lead screw. It can bore holes to any depth without breaking through the wood. It produces a flat-bottomed hole.

Framing square. See *Carpenter's square*.

Freighter. A commercial ship used to carry such things as logs, lumber, and wood chips.

Gain. A recess cut in wood to receive hardware such as hinges or handles.

Glazing. Applying a transparent color to a finished wood surface to produce a hard luster.

Glue blocks. Triangular wood blocks glued in place to reinforce corners in cabinetmaking.

Gouge. A *chisel* with a curved blade.

Graphic communication. Communication done by means of "printed" words and/or pictures.

Green lumber. Lumber sold with a moisture content of more than 19 percent.

Hacksaw. A metalworker's saw often used by woodworkers for cutting metal fasteners or hardware.

Half lap joint. A joint made by sawing away half the thickness of each piece, making the joint the same thickness as the whole stock.

Hammer. See *Claw hammer* and *Upholsterer's hammer*.

Hand drill. A tool with a three-jaw chuck that operates like an eggbeater to hold twist drills for drilling small holes.

Hardboard. A strong manufactured board formed by wood fibers highly compressed under heat and pressure.

Hardware. Metal and plastic pieces such as hinges, locks, pulls, knobs, and drawer slides.

Hardwood. Wood from *deciduous* trees such as oak and maple.

Heartwood. The dense, dry wood at the core of a tree.

Hole saw. A large, circular drill attachment that can bore holes much larger than any bit, and which cuts out a disc instead of leaving only sawdust.

Industrial construction. The making of structures whose primary purpose is manufacturing and industry.

Inlaying. See *Marquetry*.

Inner bark. See *Phloem*.

Input. The resources required by a technological system.

Inside beveled gouge. A tool used for woodcarving and turning.

Inside cut. A sawcut that cannot be made by starting at the outside of a piece.

Jack plane. A 14- or 15-inch *plane*, probably the most commonly used plane.

Jig. A device that simplifies a hand or machine tool operation by holding the tool during cutting operations or by serving as a *template*.

Jig (scroll) saw. A small power saw used primarily for internal and external irregular cutting. Wood up to 4 inches thick can be cut. The table tips for mitering and beveling.

Jointer plane. A 22- or 24-inch plane, for planing very long stock such as the edges of doors.

Jointing. Smoothing and straightening the edge of a board.

Kerf. The cut made by a saw. The width is equal to the set of the saw teeth.

Key. A small piece of wood put in a joint to hold it firmly together.

Keyhole saw. A tapered, narrow-bladed handsaw used for cutting small openings and curves. Smaller than a *compass saw*.

Kiln. A heated chamber designed for drying wood. It is pronounced *kill*.

Kiln-dried (KD) lumber. Lumber (usually *hardwood*) that is dried in *kilns* to a moisture content of about 6 to 12 percent.

Knot. A wood defect. The base of a limb forms a mass of fiber running at an angle to a board.

Lacquer. A transparent finishing material. It is usually applied with a sprayer, but it can also be brushed on.

Laminate. To build the thickness or width of material by gluing several layers together, all with the grain running in the same direction.

Land transportation. Moving people and goods on land; usually done by means of wheels and/or rails.

Lap joint. One of several types of joints in which half the thickness of each piece is cut away making the joint the same thickness as the rest of the stock.

Laser. (1) a machine that produces a very narrow and intensive beam of light that can be focused onto a very small spot. (2) A high intensity beam of light that is emitted over a narrow frequency range and that can be directed with high precision.

Level. A device used to determine whether a surface is level (horizontal) or plumb (vertical). Some levels can be used to determine the angle of a surface.

Lignin. An organic *adhesive*. It is the substance in wood that holds the individual cells of the wood together.

Lumber core plywood. A *plywood* in which the core is not *veneer*, but strips of lumber bonded together.

Machine spur bit. A power drill bit with two spurs on the tip as well as a lead screw.

Marine transportation. Moving people and goods by way of the sea or inland waterways.

Marking gauge. A wood or metal gauge consisting of a beam, head, and point. It is used to mark a line parallel to the grain of the wood.

Marquetry. A wood craft similar to mosaic in which different colored woods are set into a larger piece to create a design.

Medullary rays. Lines of cells running at right angles to the *annual rings*.

Mending (repair) plates. Flat, steel plates used to strengthen or repair joints.

Metre stick. A rule one metre long (approximately 39.27 inches). A metre is the basic SI metric unit for measuring length.

Metric system. A measuring system based on natural units of 10.

Miter box. A metal box in which a *back (tenon) saw* can be adjusted to make straight cuts or angular cuts from 30 to 90 degrees.

Miter joint. A joint made by joining two wood pieces cut at an angle (typically 45 degrees).

Modem. Device that makes it possible to send computer data over telephone lines.

Modular unit. A factory-built, transportable building unit.

Mortise and tenon joint. A strong joint made by fitting the tenon (projecting or male part) of one piece into the mortise (receiving or female part) of another piece.

Mortising chisel. A thick, heavy *chisel* used especially for cutting mortises.

Nail claw. A round or hexagonal steel bar with a curved and slotted end for pulling nails. Smaller than a *ripping bar* or crow bar.

Nail set. A small metal tool with a tapered end and a point that is highly cupped. It is used to sink the head of a nail below a surface.

Network. A group of people who are linked together by means of computer because of a shared interest.

Numerical control (N/C). A system for directing the work of machines by means of tapes or cards. These store instructions and give them to the machines at the proper time.

Object line. In a drawing, a line that represents edges or surfaces that can be seen.

Oblique drawing. A *pictorial drawing* in which one side of the object shown appears close to the viewer. The other sides are slanted away.

Oil stain. A wood stain made by mixing coloring in an oil base.

Oilstone. A rectangular whetstone used for sharpening cutting tools.

Offset screwdriver. A modified S-shaped *screwdriver* used when a screw cannot be reached by a straight-bladed screwdriver.

Optical fiber. A thin strand of glass coated with plastic and used to send messages.

Optics. Systems that have to do with light.

OSHA. The Occupational Safety and Health Administration.

Output. What results from a technological system.

Panel. Any large, rectangular wood piece.

Paring chisel. A small, lightweight *chisel*.

Particle board. A manufactured panel material. In making it, wood chips (large particles) and resin binders are compressed under heat and pressure.

Particle board core plywood. A *plywood* with a core of *particle board*.

Parting tool. A lathe tool used to cut grooves and to cut away stock during faceplate turning. Also used as a wood carving tool.

Paste filler. A thick wood *filler* made of ground silicon, linseed oil, coloring, *turpentine*, and a drier.

Pattern. A wood, metal, or plastic device consisting of one or more parts from which a sand mold is made for casting the part in metal.

Peeler block. A log suitable for cutting into *veneer*.

Pencil compass. See *Dividers*.

Penetrating finish. One of several types of oil finishes that sink into the wood instead of laying on top of it like paint.

Penny. A term used to note the size of a nail (abbreviated with a small d). A 2d nail is the smallest, and 60d the largest.

Perspective drawing. A *pictorial drawing* showing an object as it appears to the eye.

Phillips head. A term referring to screws with cross slots in their heads and compatible *screwdrivers*.

Phloem (inner bark). The cells formed between the *cambium* and the outer *bark* that transport food produced in the leaves throughout the tree.

Pictorial drawing. A type of drawing that looks like a photograph.

Pilot hole. A hole drilled to receive the body of a woodscrew.

Pith. Highly porous cells at the center of a tree (inside the *heartwood*). Sometimes, the pith rots, leaving a hollow tree.

Plain sawn lumber. The cheapest and most economical way to cut *hardwood*. The log is squared and cut lengthwise from one end to the other.

Plan of procedure. A step-by-step listing of how to build a project.

Plane. A hand-held tool with a blade for smoothing a wood surface. Many types are available, including the *jack plane*, *block plane*, *jointer plane*, and *router plane*.

Plane iron. The blade of a *plane*.

Plastic wood. Puttylike plastic that can be colored and used to plug holes in wood.

Platform (Western) framing. The most common type of house framing in which the first floor is built like a platform on top of the *footings* or foundation wall.

Plug cutter. A drill attachment that cuts round, slightly beveled plugs used to cover screw heads.

Plywood. An odd number of layers of *veneer* and/or wood joined together by an *adhesive*, each layer at right angles to the next.

Pocket chisel. A short-bladed (4½-inch) heavy *chisel*.

Porosity. A term referring to how fast moisture moves through wood. In less porous woods, moisture moves slowly.

Power bore bit. A bit that cuts a clean hole without clogging.

Process. The action that takes place within a technological system in order to produce output.

Public works construction. The making of structures for public use.

Pumice. An abrasive powder made from lava mixed with oil or water. It is used as a polish in finishing.

Push block. A wood stick used to push stock through machine cuts.

Putty knife. A flat knife for applying putty or spackle.

Quarter round. A *molding* that is one-fourth of a circle. It is used as trim.

Quarter-sawn lumber. A *hardwood* cut so the *annual rings* are perpendicular to the face of the board. It is more expensive but thought to be more beautiful than *plain-sawn lumber*. It shrinks and cups less than plain-sawn lumber.

Rabbet. An L-shaped cut along the end or edge of a board.

Rabbet and dado joint. A strong joint often used in drawer construction in which a *dado* is cut into one piece and is fitted around a *rabbet* with a tongue cut into the end of another piece.

Rabbet joint. A joint made by fitting the end of one piece into a *rabbet* cut into another piece.

Rasp. A filelike tool that has coarse, pyramid-shaped projections as cutting points across its surface.

Reciprocating saw. A portable power saw that cuts nearly any type of material with back-and-forth motion. Sometimes called a *saws-all*.

Relief cut. A way of avoiding backing out of a cut or catching the blade in a tight turn.

Resawing. Cutting through thick boards to make thinner boards.

Residential construction. The making of structures in which people live.

Ripping. Sawing wood with the grain.

Ripping bar. A strong, heavy iron bar for prying things apart and pulling nails. One end is a *nail claw*, the other is a *chisel*.

Rip saw. A handsaw designed for cutting with the grain.

Robot. A reprogrammable device designed to move materials, parts, and tools. It also refers to a specialized device used for doing a variety of tasks.

Rottenstone. An abrasive powder mixed with water or oil and used in finishing as a polish.

Rough lumber. Lumber sold at the lumberyard just as it comes from the sawmill.

Router plane. A plane used to surface the bottom of grooves or other recesses.

Saber saw (bayonet saw or hand jig saw). A portable power saw useful for cutting internal and external curves. It has a saberlike blade and an up-and-down action.

Safety glasses. Protective eyewear. Only eyewear approved by the American National Safety Institute should be worn in the lab. Safety lenses, both plastic and glass, tested and approved by ANSI will bear the manufacturer's trademark on both the lens and the temple piece. Safety glasses must be worn in the lab at all times.

Sanding block. Any device used to grip abrasive paper for smooth, level hand sanding. Usually made of rubber or wood.

Sapwood. Newer wood found between the *heartwood* and the *cambium*.

Scraper. A flat rectangular blade with a burred edge used for smoothing wood surfaces.

Scratch awl. A sharp, pointed metal tool held in a wooden handle and used for indenting lines and marking holes.

Screwdriver. A tool for driving screws. It has a handle and a blade. The blade tips vary to fit an assortment of screw types.

Screwdriver bit. Specialized brace bit for setting screws.

Scribing. Marking a line by scratching.

Scroll saw. See *Jig (scroll) saw*.

Sealer. A liquid mix applied between finish coats to prevent bleeding.

Semiporous wood. Wood that requires *filler*, but not as much as porous wood. Semiporous woods include maple, birch, and gum.

Shellac. A resinous substance produced from the secretions of lac bugs and used as a wood finish.

Shrink allowance. Making patterns for metal pieces larger than actual size to allow for the shrinkage of metal.

Shrink rule. A rule on which the units are actually bigger than regular units. It is used for figuring *shrinkage allowance*.

Site. The location of a structure.

Sketch. An undimensioned, freehand drawing.

Skew (flat chisel). A lathe tool ground on both sides to a sharp edge. Also used as a wood carving tool.

Sloyd knife. A small knife used for cutting, trimming, whittling, and layout work.

Smooth plane. A small, lightweight bench *plane* used primarily for short pieces and final planing.

Softwood. Wood from coniferous trees such as fir and pine.

Solvent. A substance that dissolves another substance.

Speed (spade) power bit. A *power bore bit* with a spade-shaped cutter.

Spline joint. A *butt joint* strengthened by cutting a groove in each member and inserting a thin wood strip (spline) in the groove to connect the two.

Split. A wood defect. It is a lengthwise crack or break in a board.

Spokeshave. A cutting and smoothing tool for irregularly shaped pieces. It looks like a scraper with two handles.

Spring clamp. A clamp that looks and works like a large clothespin.

Springwood. The more porous wood that grows in the spring when water is more abundant. It is not apparent in all woods. See *Summerwood*.

Steel tape. Flexible rule of thin steel that retracts into a protective case. It is used for measuring irregular and regular shapes.

Stock cutting list. An addition to the *bill of materials* that includes dimensions with allowances for cutting, planing, and other operations.

Stop chamfer. A *chamfer* that does not extend the whole length of a board.

Straightedge. Any tool with a straight edge used for making straight lines.

Summerwood. Less porous wood that grows in summer. See *Springwood*.

Surform® tools. A variety of tools, all with teeth set at a 45-degree angle, used for forming, shaping, and cutting away wood.

System. An organized way of doing something.

Tacking tape. A muslin cloth tape used in *upholstery*.

Tack rag. A piece of cloth moistened with thinned varnish used to wipe particles from wood before finish is to be applied.

Tang. The long, pointed end of a *chisel* or *file* that is driven into handles or inserted into a machine *chuck*.

Taper. A gradual decrease (narrowing) in size, as of a round or rectangular piece, or a hole.

T-bevel. A measuring tool for laying out angles.

Technical design. A form of graphic communication used in technology; usually involves drawings and plans.

Template. A metal, wood, or cardboard pattern used to draw the outline of a part and to locate holes within that part.

Through chamfer. A *chamfer* that extends the entire length of a board.

Ties. Square wood beams about six feet long used to cushion steel rails in railroad tracks.

Toenailing. Pounding nails in at an angle to fit the end of one board against the surface of another.

Trammel points. Two metal pointers that can be attached to a wood or metal bar such as a rule or square, and used to lay out distances between two points. They can also be used to scribe arcs or circles larger than those made with *dividers*.

Transportation. The movement of people and goods from one location to another.

Try square. A measuring tool used to lay out right angles and to test squareness.

Turpentine. A *solvent* made from pine resins: solvent for *oil stains*, *varnish*, and *enamel*.

Twist. A wood defect in which a board turns or winds at the edges.

Twist drill. Most commonly used bits. A wide variety of sizes are available for cutting wood, metal, and plastics.

Undercoat. A coating applied before the final coat of paint job.

Universal Product Code (UPC). A "bar code" attached to items that enables a computer to identify and keep track of them.

Upholster's hammer. A small hammer with a magnetic face for picking up tacks and pounding them into place.

Varnish. A clear finishing material made of gum resins and vegetable oils, plus necessary *thinners* and driers.

Varnish stain. A one-coat finish consisting of *varnish* plus color.

V-block (bevel block). A block of wood with a V-shape cut the length of the top surface. Used for holding *dowels* or other cylindrical pieces while sawing or drilling.

Veneer. A thin slice of wood used as cross plies in the manufacturing of plywood, and also used to cover unattractive surfaces.

Veneer core plywood. A *plywood* with a core of thick wood *veneer*. Most industrial plywood is this type.

Video systems. Communication systems that transmit messages by means of pictures and sight.

Vise. A tool with two jaws, one fixed and one that moves as a handle is turned. The jaws are usually wood-lined to prevent dents or scratches to the pieces being worked.

Vise Grip. Brand name for a locking-plier wrench.

Wane. A defective board that has a poor or missing portion.

Warp. Any variation from a true or plane surface. It includes *bow*, *crook*, *cup*, *twist*, or any combination of these.

Webbing. A strip of woven burlap 3½ inches or 4 inches wide used as a foundation for many types of chair seats.

Western framing. See *Platform framing*.

Wind. See *Twist*.

Working drawing. A drawing showing detailed dimensions of a project.

Xylem. The cells formed inside the *cambium* that take nutrients from the roots up through the tree.

Zigzag rule (folding wood rule). A folding rule that comes in lengths of 4, 6, or 8 feet.

Index

Photo Credits

American Plywood Association, 502
Apple Computer, Inc., 15
Aratex/Arnold & Brown Photographers, 96, 309, 311, 312
Arnold & Brown Photographers, 94, 96, 97, 165, 213, 215, 305, 309, 310, 311, 312, 313, 314, 315, 317, 319, 320, 322, 323, 326, 328, 335, 336, 348, 356, 513, 514
Audio Visual Center, Western Michigan University, Kalamazoo, MI, 118

Builder's Square/Arnold & Brown Photographers, 94, 96, 215, 335, 348, 356, 513

Calculated Industries, Inc., 514
Caterpillar Tractor Company, 504, 523
Century Furniture Company, Hickory, North Carolina, 516
City of Kalamazoo, MI, 503

Dallas/Fort Worth International Airport, 520
Delta International Machinery Corporation, 379
Demanes Interiors/Arnold & Brown Photographers, 97
Dremel, 54

Bob Gangloff, 508, 509, 512, 513
George Kock Sons, Inc., 522
Georgia-Pacific Corporation, 97, 497, 523
Peter Getz/Circle Design, 267, 332, 431, 511, 517

Hall's Furniture/Arnold & Brown Photographers, 313, 320
Houston Instruments, 510

International Business Machines Corporation, 508

Koppers Company, Inc., 503

Lamella Corporation, 216
Long Beach Tourist Bureau, 519

Manual High School/Roger B. Bean, 98
Mishima, 17, 18

Naked Furniture/Arnold & Brown Photographers, 326

Port Authority of New Jersey/New York, 523
Liz Purcell, 60

Cloyd Richards, 519, 551, 553

Roecker's Interiors/Arnold & Brown Photographers, 310, 311, 312, 317, 322, 328

Barb Spink, 92, 485, 508
Jeff Stoecker, 512

Western Electric News, 516
Western Wood Products Association, 519, 521, 522
Woodruff High School/Roger B. Bean, 508

U.S. Forest Products Laboratory, 524

Xerox Corporation, 510, 511